A Century of Sculpture in Texas, 1889–1989

PATRICIA D. HENDRICKS and BECKY DUVAL REESE

Archer M. Huntington Art Gallery
College of Fine Arts
The University of Texas at Austin

International Standard Book Number 0-93521-18-X
Library of Congress Catalog Card Number
Copyright © 1989 by The University of Texas at Austin
All rights reserved
Printed in the United States of America

First Edition, 1989

Requests for permission to reproduce material
from this work should be sent to
Archer M. Huntington Art Gallery,
The University of Texas at Austin,
Austin, Texas 78712.

Distributed by the University of Texas Press,
Box 7819, Austin, Texas 78713-7819.

Partially supported by the Texas Commission on the
Arts, a state agency and the National Endowment of
the Arts, a federal agency.

This book accompanies an exhibition titled
A Century of Sculpture in Texas, 1889–1989

Archer M. Huntington Art Gallery
College of Fine Arts
The University of Texas at Austin
June 16–August 13, 1989

Amarillo Art Center
September 2–October 22, 1989

San Angelo Museum of Fine Arts
November 9–December 23, 1989

El Paso Museum of Art
January 13–March 31, 1990

Not all works of art will be shown in all
locations.

Frontispiece: Pompeo Coppini, *Equestrian Monument to
Terry's Texas Rangers,* 1907 (*see also p. 22*)
Photograph: Tourism Division, Texas Department of
Commerce

Cover: Luis Jimenez, *Vaquero,* 1981, acrylic on
fiberglass, 16½′ × 10½′ × 5½′, Collection of Frank
Ribelin, Dallas
Photograph: George Holmes

A CENTURY OF SCULPTURE IN TEXAS   1889–1989

A CENTURY OF SCULPTURE IN TEXAS   1889–1989

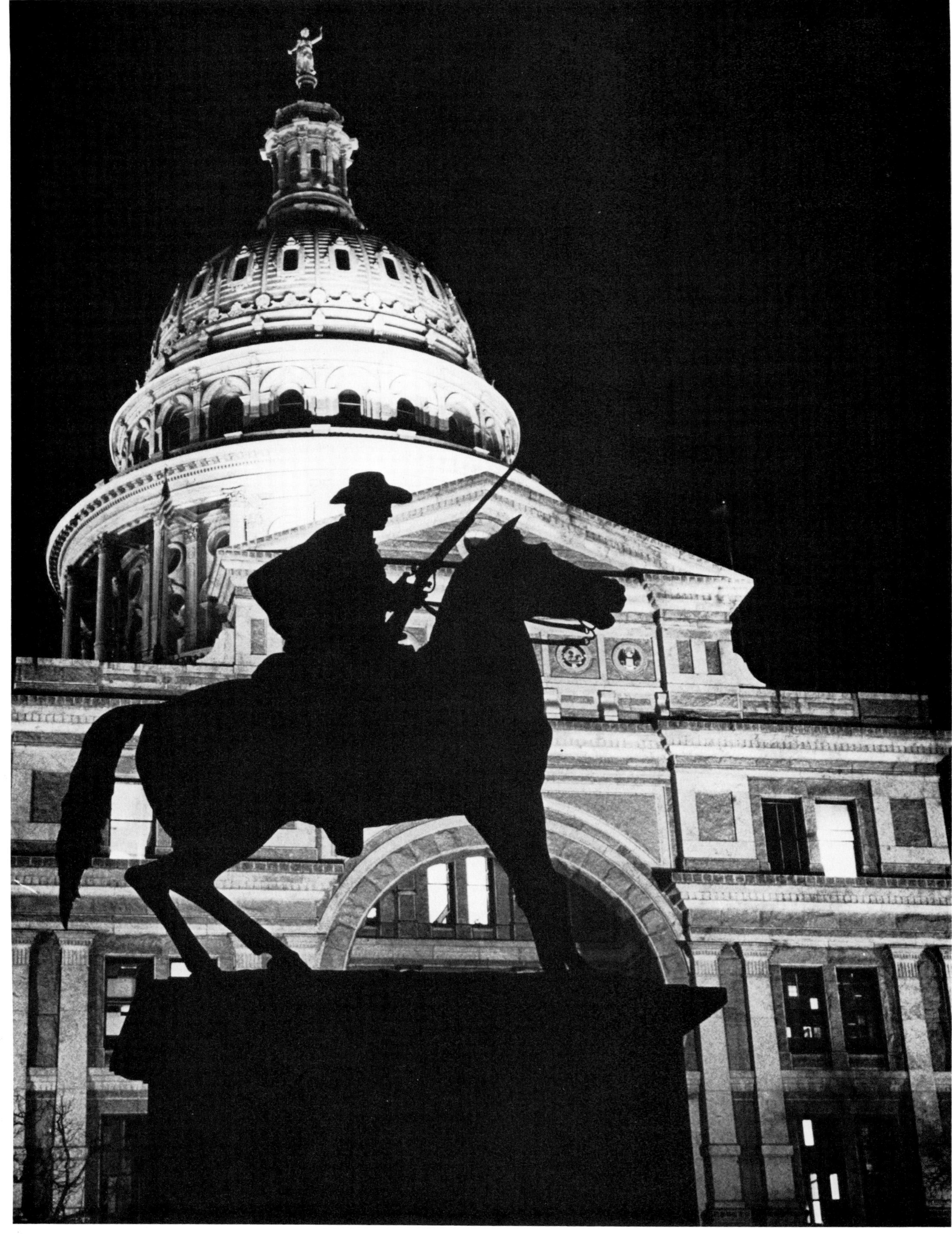

CONTENTS

FOREWORD

From the historical to the avant-garde, art in Texas has reflected not only its provincial beginnings but also the international influences of art, which now effect every aspect of the globe. *A Century of Sculpture in Texas*, like the history of Texas itself, mirrors how the state has changed from its early beginnings, what contributions have been made by its sculptors to the regional and national art worlds, and how today Texas is in the vanguard of every aspect of the creative arts.

For the past three years, both in the conceptualization and in the organization of this exhibition, Becky Duval Reese and Patricia D. Hendricks, co-curators, have wrestled with the styles and evolution of creative form made by native-born Texans and by those who have come from the outside to call Texas home. These choices have not been easy and have been tempered by a myriad of artistic factors.

I want to thank the lenders, institutions, individuals, and artists without whom this exhibition would not have occurred. The Huntington is particularly grateful to the Texas Commission on the Arts and the Archer M. Huntington Museum Fund for making this exhibition possible. The TCA's grant was absolutely essential for the exhibition, one that will be shared with three other venues in the state of Texas. Additionally, Amanda Stover, Director, Amarillo Art Center, Howard Taylor, Director, San Angelo Museum of Fine Arts, and Leonard Sipiora, Director, El Paso Museum of Art, deserve our thanks for agreeing to participate in this exhibition.

Exhibitions of this size and complexity do not miraculously appear without the support of the entire museum staff, whom I personally thank for their dedicated effort. The Huntington is known as a center for all aspects of the visual arts, not just for Central Texas but for the entire state, and we are delighted to be able to work with our colleagues in Texas to present this exhibition to a wide and diverse audience.

Eric McCready
Director
May, 1989

LENDERS TO THE EXHIBITION

AIR Gallery, Austin
Amon Carter Museum of Art, Fort Worth
Eugene C. Barker Texas History Center,
The University of Texas at Austin
Jesús Bautista Moroles
Eugene Binder Gallery, Dallas
Ronald Boling
Robert Bourdon
Julie Bozzi
Steve Brudniak
Hiram Butler Gallery, Houston
Murray W. Camp, Austin
Ms. Laura Carpenter, Dallas
Ms. Joanne Cassullo, New York City
John Christensen
J. Michael Ciszek
Thelma Coles
Conduit Gallery, Dallas
Coppini-Tauch Studio, San Antonio
Dallas Historical Society
Dallas Museum of Art
David L. Deming
Davis/McClain Gallery, Houston
Distinctive Vision, Austin
James Drake
Elisabet Ney Museum, Austin
Rowena C. Elkin
El Paso Public Library
Vernon Fisher
Fort Worth Gallery, Fort Worth
Harry Geffert
Linnea Glatt
Jeannette and Irving Goodfriend
Graham Gallery, Houston
Allan Hacklin
Al Harris
Paul Rogers Harris, Dallas
Harris Gallery, Houston
Harry Ransom Humanities Research Center,
The University of Texas at Austin

Joseph G. Havel
Teme Paul Hernandez
Hubbard abc Estate, Lubbock
Archer M. Huntington Art Gallery,
The University of Texas at Austin
Emily Jennings
Luis Jimenez
Janet Engle Kastner
Ed and Nancy Kienholz, rural Idaho
Haydn Larson
Thana Lauhakaikul
Janie C. Lee Gallery, Houston
R. S. Levy Gallery, Austin
Ken D. Little
Bert L. Long, Jr.
Meredith Long Gallery, Houston
Jesse Lott
Jim Love
Ken Luce
William Lundberg
Dr. and Mrs. Blaine McLaughlin, Fort Worth
Dalton Maroney
Cesar A. Martinez, San Antonio
Jack K. Maxwell
Octavio Medellin
The Menil Collection, Houston
The Metropolitan Museum of Art, New York
Adams-Middleton Gallery, Dallas
Modern Art Museum of Fort Worth
Mark Monroe
Moody Gallery, Houston
The Museum of Fine Arts, Houston
Mr. and Mrs. Thomas Marion O'Connor,
Victoria
Office of Cultural Affairs, The City of Dallas
Marcelle and David Orman
Willie Ray Parish
Parks and Recreation Department,
City of Austin
Gerald J. Patrick

Bogdan Perzynski
Mr. and Mrs. T. Turner Pope III, Houston
Chris Powell
Donald D. Redman
Red River Valley Museum, Vernon, Texas
Claudia Reese
Mr. Frank Ribelin, Dallas
Mary M. Rollins, Houston
Rosenberg Library, Galveston
The San Antonio Museum Association
Mr. and Mrs. H. Irving Schweppe, Houston
Marvin Seline Gallery, Houston
Mr. and Mrs. Marvin Seline, Houston
Daniel Sellers
George Smith
Oz and Paul Srere, Dallas
C. M. Stagg
State Preservation Board, Texas Capitol,
State of Texas, Austin
Read Stremmel Gallery, San Antonio
Gisela-Heidi Strunck
James Surls
David and Risa Sutton, Big Sandy
Texas Gallery, Houston
Texas Memorial Museum,
The University of Texas at Austin
Patricia Tillman
Toby Topek, Houston
Umlauf Sculpture Garden, Austin
The University of Texas at El Paso
Robert Wade
Shoshana Wayne Gallery, Santa Monica
Dorothy Austin Webberley
Weiner Collection, Fort Worth
Mr. and Mrs. Keith S. Wellin, New York City
Barry Whistler Gallery, Dallas
Mac Whitney
Ben Woitena
Nicholas W. Wood

PREFACE

The Archer M. Huntington Art Gallery at the University of Texas at Austin is the state's largest university art museum and, because we are part of a major research institution, we view original research and documentation as primary responsibilities. For ten years the Huntington has offered to our diverse campus and community audiences survey exhibitions dealing with Texas art. In 1979, *Made in Texas* examined the work ofsome sixty contemporary painters and sculptors living in the state. In 1983, in connection with the University's centennial celebration, the Gallery presented *Images of Texas,* which documented over 150 years of Texas paintings. Catalogs published in conjunction with these exhibitions have become valuable additions to the scholarship of Texas art history.

Several years ago we recognized that an examination of the history of sculpture in Texas had not been conducted. To that end, we turned our attention to the subject. *A Century of Sculpture in Texas* is the first museum exhibition ever to survey the history of sculpture in the state. Eighty-five artists are included in the exhibition with over one hundred works displayed. Borrowed from museums, private collections, and artists throughout the state, the sculpture fills the Huntington Art Building Gallery and spills over to adjacent outdoor sites. Traditional nineteenth-century neo-classical carved figures are counterpoised by a variety of contemporary pieces, offering an extraordinary opportunity to view distinctive artistic expressions of many of the state's major sculptors.

The pre-contemporary works selected for this exhibition represent a period of time beginning roughly one hundred years ago and continuing past the first half of this century. Somewhat paralleling Texas society as a whole, more than half the sculptors associated with Texas during the earliest decades were born outside the state, with a number born and trained in Europe. By the decades between the World Wars, the ratio between native-born and immigrant sculptors significantly changed in favor of the native Texan. The basic intent of all the sculptors belonging to that time and place was to copy nature in an effort to capture in their artwork the physical characteristics of the person or animal they wished to portray. Working in materials of bronze, marble, plaster, terra cotta, or wood, their interpretations of nature, though inspired by the real world, were most often filtered through idealistic conceptions of their subject matter. In the late decades of the period, a new emphasis on formalist concerns was introduced which vied with traditional goals of naturalism, resulting in both a greater degree of abstraction and the introduction of distortion for expressive purposes, as artists turned from an idealized replication of animate forms toward more subjective interpretations of such figural themes.

By the mid-twentieth century, artists broke with traditional uses of sculpture and with attendant ties to the human figure. Sculptors looked to newly created styles of art for their compositional forms. They examined new techniques and began to experiment with twentieth-century materials. Steel and the oxyacetylene torch, found objects and video, for example, replaced standard materials of clay, bronze or wood. Sculptors established new uses for their art as well. No longer bound to create monuments to great deeds or great people, sculptural forms changed as did the meanings implicit within them. Since the mid-twentieth century, Texas sculptors have reflected the major national and international trends in art. The state's sculptors have also invented totally distinctive works which could only have come from Texas. Based primarily on knowledge and training gained from university art departments, Texas sculptors are aware of the world around them. Some Texas sculptors image myths of the state in their work while other Texas sculptors look elsewhere for their inspiration. There is no one distinctive style of contemporary sculpture in Texas. To that end, the contemporary section of *A Century of Sculpture in Texas* is grouped according to technical approaches such as "assemblage" and "direct metal." Or the categories are arranged more generically like "figurative," "abstract," or "minimal." The groupings are arbitrary and offer more a means by which to comprehend a large body of work rather than a definitive placement of specific work within limiting categories. Contemporary sculpture takes myriad forms, encompasses diverse materials, and expresses manifold ideas. The objects created by Texas sculptors today are as diverse as the hands that made them.

It is indeed gratifying to research a subject as vast as one hundred years of Texas sculpture and to discover the high quality of work that has been and is currently being created. From this large survey exhibition, we anticipate that other museums and art institutions will focus on specific historical eras or particular styles of Texas sculpture. We hope this will be the case, for the artist transcends the prosaic and offers us, the viewers, glimpses of other truth and realities.

Becky Duval Reese
and Patricia D. Hendricks
May, 1989

ACKNOWLEDGMENTS

Many individuals have contributed to the preparation of this exhibition and catalogue. First of all, I would like to thank my colleague and co-curator, Becky Reese, for her faith in the project, which helped to keep it alive. Her critical eye and special insights into the development of contemporary sculpture in Texas have produced a vital and exciting representation of post-traditional sculpture in Texas. Thanks must also go to our director, Eric S. McCready, both for his support of the project and for his sympathetic reading and constructive criticism of my manuscript. I also want to thank the staff of the Huntington for their patience and moral support, offering a special thanks to those who have given of their time and expertise for the exhibition, including Lynne Adele, Pony Allen, Hank Bartell, Jonathan Bober, Cecilia Carter, Joann Goodman, Jessie Otto Hite, Clyde Holleman, George Holmes, Sue Ellen Jeffers, Bob Jones, Sara McElroy, Sue Mayer, Amy Roberts, Jill Robertson, John Sager, Jane Scroggs, Susan Sternberg, Mark van Gelder, Tanya Walker, George Weil, and David Willard.

I also wish to express appreciation for the generous support and cooperation of the lenders to the exhibition, both private and institutional, and would like to give particular thanks to Octavio Medellin and Mrs. Medellin, Charles Umlauf and Mrs. Umlauf, Electra Waggoner Biggs, and Dorothy Austin Webberley, for their assistance. The endorsement of the project by the Texas Commission for the Arts in the form of two grants has enabled the project to take form, while demonstrating once again the importance that the commission's continued support represents for the arts in Texas.

Many have provided support, often by helping me obtain photographs and archival materials, and I am indebted to each of them. Among these is a group of individuals whose thoughtful assistance was more than generous and especially important to the exhibition. Included among these are Ellen Buie, Assistant Curator, Jerry Bywaters Collection on Art of the Southwest, Southern Methodist University; Bonnie Campbell, Curator of the Capitol, Texas Preservation Board; Mary Clayton, Waco; Lise Darst, Curator, Special Collections, Rosenberg Library, Galveston; Jim Fisher, Administrator of City Museums, City of Austin; Bill Green, State Historian, Texas Preservation Board; Ann Huskinson, Director, Red River Valley Museum, Vernon; Charles J. Long, Curator, Coppini-Tauch Studio, San Antonio; Prince MacKenzie, Assistant Curator, El Paso Museum of Art; Tedd Miller, *Electra Star,* Ballinger Mills, Galveston; Peggy Riddle, Director of Research, Dallas Historical Society; Margaret Robinette, City Coordinator of Public Art, City of Dallas; and Cecilia Steinfeldt, Curator of Texas Art, Witte Museum, San Antonio Museum Association.

I also greatly appreciate the contribution and friendly cooperation of all those listed below, each of whom helped bring the catalogue and exhibition closer to completion: staff of the Eugene C. Barker Texas History Center, The University of Texas at Austin; Melinda Barton, Sam Houston Regional Library, Liberty; Jan I. Bernstein, Registrar/Assistant Curator, The Brooklyn Children's Museum; Laine Biggerstaff, Dallas Historical Society; Alice Bingert, Librarian, Washington, New Jersey, Public Library; Virginia Bols, Archivist, Southern Methodist University, Dallas; Ellen Brown, The Texas Collection, Baylor University; Gigi M. Brown, Greater Houston Convention and Visitors Bureau; Don E. Carleton, Director, Eugene C. Barker Texas History Center, The University of Texas at Austin; Anne L. Cook, Photograph Librarian, State Department of Highways and Public Transportation; Yvonne R. Cowell, Waco; Polly Cox, Wichita Falls; staff of the Dallas Museum of Art (including: Eileen Coffman, Judy Cohen, Amy Shaftner, and Liz Simon); Mrs. Price Daniel, Liberty; Ila N. Dannelley, Elgin; David B. Dearinger, Assistant Curator of Paintings and Sculpture, National Academy of Design, New York; Lynn Denton, Assistant Director, Texas Memorial Museum, The University of Texas at Austin; Grace Dinkins, Office of Rights and Reproductions, National Portrait Gallery; staff of the El Paso Public Library (Joe Brady, Head of Southwest Collection, Mary Sarber, Coordinator, Main Services and Collections, et al.); Suzanne D. Evertson, Austin; Joan Farmer, The Old Jail Museum, Albany; Eunice Glosson, Registrar's Office, National

Portrait Gallery; Jeannette and Irving Goodfriend, Austin; staff of the Harry Ransom Humanities Research Center, The University of Texas at Austin (including: Kathleen Gee, Curator, Iconography Collection, Leslie Kronz, Registrar, May E. MacNamara, Photography; Sue Murphy, Conservation; Patrick Keeley, Photography); Melanie L. Hendricks, Hattiesburg, Mississippi; Jill Hoffman, Media Relations, Department of Commerce, State of Texas; staff of The Museum of Fine Arts, Houston (including: Diane Arnold, Assistant to the Registrar; Charles Carroll, Registrar, and others of his staff; Alison de Lima Greene, Assistant Curator of Twentieth Century Art; Carrie Springer, Curatorial Assistant); Anne B. Hubbard, Lubbock; Milan R. Hughston, Associate Librarian, Amon Carter Museum; Rita Humphrey, Assistant Director, Armstrong-Browning Library, Waco; Gloria Jaster, Administrator, Winedale Historical Center, The University of Texas at Austin; Kent Keith, Director, The Texas Collection, Baylor University; Lynn and Lee Kern, Dallas; Donald Knaub, Director, The Meadows Museum, Southern Methodist University; Lisa Shippee Lambert, Head, Special Collections, Rosenberg Library, Galveston; Maurine Lasko, Library, Ryerson and Burnham Libraries, Art Institute of Chicago; Teresa and Robert Leone, Austin; Martha Long, Llano County Historical Society; Patrick McGuire, Director, Institute of Texan Cultures, The University of Texas at Austin, San Antonio; Ella McKinney, Waco; Andrea Mark, Special Collections, George Washington University; Martha Mincey, Curator, Department of Art History, University of Delaware; Jane Myers, Associate Curator, Amon Carter Museum; Rose Montgomery, Registrar, The Museum, Texas Tech University; Theodora Morgan, Editor, *National Sculpture Review,* New York; Glori Morris, Parks and Recreation Department, City of Houston; Maria Munoz-Blanco, Curator of Exhibitions, The Meadows Museum, Southern Methodist University; W. Reilly Nail, Jr., Director, The Old Jail Museum, Albany; staff of the Elisabet Ney Museum, Austin; Marcelle Orman, Dallas; Mary Anita Paddock, Public Affairs, Visitors Bureau, Houston; Nancy Paine, Curator of Collections, The Brooklyn Children's Museum; Greg Pearson, Director, Daughters of the Republic of Texas Museum, Austin; Nina Pruitt, Weiner Collection, Fort Worth; Sam Ratcliffe, Curator, Jerry Bywaters Collection on Art of the Southwest, Southern Methodist University; Janet Reed,

Texas State Cemetery, Austin; Richard Reynolds, Photojournalist, Department of Commerce, State of Texas; Frances Richard, Texas Historical Commission, Austin; Robin R. Salmon, Archivist, Brookgreen Gardens, South Carolina; staff of the San Antonio Museum Association (including: Rick Casagrande, George Anne Cormier, Kim Peel, and Gabriela Truly); Robert Schaadt, Director-Archivist, Sam Houston Regional Library, Liberty; Jerry Schefcik, Curator, Amarillo Art Center; Bette L. Siegel, The Commonwealth of Massachusetts State Library, Boston; staff of the State Archives, Texas State Library (including: Jean Carefoot, Marcia Evans, Michael Green, et al.); Bernice Strong, Archivist, Texas History Research Library at the Alamo, Daughters of the Republic of Texas, San Antonio; Elaine Brown Sullivan, Texas Memorial Museum, Austin; Scott Sullivan, Chairman, Art Department, North Texas State University; Patricia H. Svoboda, Catalog Researcher, Catalog of American Portraits, Washington, D.C.; David Thomas, Austin; Staff of the State Archives, Texas State Library, Austin; Martha Utterbach, Director, Texas History Research Library at the Alamo, Daughters of the Republic of Texas, San Antonio; Kevin Vogel, Valley House Gallery, Dallas; Dorothy Waller, Dallas; Belle Wesp, Coppini-Tauch Studio, San Antonio; Nancy Wiley, Dallas Historical Society; Anita Williams, Fort Worth; Michael E. Wilson, Houston Metropolitan Research Center, Houston Public Library; Rachel Wright, Curatorial Assistant, Fort Worth Art Museum; and Jan Wyatt, The Harris County Heritage Society, Houston.

In addition, I want to offer a special thanks to George Lenox, Designer and Associate Director, and Barbara Spielman, Managing Editor of the University of Texas Press for their professionalism and unfailing courtesy and patience while working under a less than ideal timetable. Finally, I am very pleased that three other Texas museums will host this exhibition, The Amarillo Art Center, the San Angelo Museum of Fine Arts, and the El Paso Museum of Art, and wish to extend my thanks to their directors, Amanda Stover, Howard Taylor, and Leonard Sipiora respectively, for their interest and participation.

Patricia D. Hendricks
May 1989

ACKNOWLEDGMENTS

Many fine and generous people have helped make possible both the exhibition and the catalog for A Century of Sculpture in Texas.

I thank the artists for creating the sculpture and for expanding our vision. I thank the lenders to the exhibition for their willingness to share their cherished works of art for an extended period of time. I thank the Texas Commission on the Arts for assisting with the funding of this project and ensuring a wider audience for it. I thank co-curator Pat Hendricks for her research and work on the historical period of Texas sculpture. And I thank Adele Thanheiser for the time and care she gave to the compilation of the biographies of the artists.

Numerous, too, are those who have assisted in many ways — from helping to gather research materials to editing my manuscript to providing photographic support — I am especially indebted to Bette Redman Reichman, Arthur J. Mayer, Jonathan Bober, and George Holmes. Those with whom I work on a daily basis provide positive support and make my working life a real pleasure. I thank Sue Mayer, Lynne Adele, Susan Sternberg, Fran Prudhomme, Donna Vliet, and Rachel Martin-Hinshaw.

I thank, too, the individuals at the many institutions and galleries who assisted me with innumerable details: Eugene Binder, Tamber Johnson, Barry Whistler, Barbara Davis, Robert McClain, Cynthia Cage, Dutch Phillips, Bill Graham, Karim Davezac, Betty Moody, Lisa Barkley, Fredericka Hunter, Hilary Borrow, Julia Bakke, Marla Price, Vicky Vincent, Michelle Locke, Julie Perry, Hiram Butler, Cecily Horton, Janie C. Lee, Margaret Griffin, Maria Watson, Trent Read, Jeffrey Moore, Chuck Cooper, Becky Levy, Paul Rogers Harris, Murray W. Camp, Alison de Lima Greene, Linda Wilhelm, Adair Margo, and Sherry Owens of the Texas Sculpture Association.

I thank Frank Ribelin of Dallas for making it possible for us to show in Austin Luis Jimenez's monumental *Vaquero.*

I thank Eric McCready, director of the Huntington Art Gallery, for his support of the exhibition and the catalog *A Century of Sculpture in Texas.* I also thank others on the staff who so capably discharged their duties: Sue Ellen Jeffers, Jessie Hite, Jane Scroggs, David Willard, and the members of the technical staff — Bob Jones, John Sager, Henry "Pony" Allen, Clyde Holleman, Bob Newhouse, and George Weil — who carefully handled the installation of the exhibition.

I thank George Lenox for his masterful design of the exhibition catalog and Barbara Spielman for her precise copy editing of the manuscript.

I thank museum directors Amanda Stover of the Amarillo Art Center, Howard Taylor of the San Angelo Museum of Fine Arts, and Leonard Sipiora of the El Paso Museum of Art, for bringing A Century of Sculpture in Texas to their institutions and for allowing us to share the richness and depth of sculpture in the state with an expanded audience.

Many individuals are involved with organizing an exhibition. But now I thank the viewers for looking at the sculpture, for studying their responses to it, and for taking away a greater understanding of the creative ideas and thoughts that shape contemporary Texas sculpture.

Becky Duval Reese
May 1989

PART 1

Patricia D. Hendricks

Texas Sculpture and the Figural Tradition

TEXAS SCULPTURE AND THE FIGURAL TRADITION (1860–1960)

Because of the state's stormy political history, it is likely that as the nineteenth century neared its end some citizens had lived in Texas under five separate flags: those of Spain, Mexico, the Republic of Texas, the Confederacy, and the United States.[1] Inevitably, during much of the period, Texans were preoccupied with the problems of development. As late as mid-century, the land had not been fully explored and expeditions were still trying to establish routes across the state;[2] moreover, it was not until 1881 that the last battle was joined between the Indians and the Texans.[3] In those formative years little thought could be given to sculpture, for the cultural elements that contribute to patronage and to the nurturing of the sculptor were largely absent. It should not be surprising that it would be the last of the century before sculpture would gain any measure of viability in Texas.

The Earliest Evidence

The earliest examples of sculpture and its patronage in Texas probably appeared before the nineteenth century in the Catholic missions and churches.[4] Sculpture would have taken the form of religious icons, occasionally sculpted by an adherent under the guidance and encouragement of a local priest. There would be no other systematic support for sculpture in Texas before the late years of the nineteenth century, and it would then center on earthly rather than heavenly icons, as the sculptor was called on to memorialize the illustrious deeds of past Texans. With the nineteenth century ending, public spaces and cemeteries were made ready to receive monuments dedicated to the remembrance of brave men. Death, that painful link to past lives and lost comforters, also assumed the important role of verifying heroes and defining the body politic's heritage. The resulting memorial images were, in fact, a cultural product that would satisfy the need to connect history's heroes with the promise of a moral mandate for the state's future.

Before sculpture began to collect on grassy knolls in public spaces and at grave sides, examples of sculptural activity in Texas were rare. However, despite the highly unsettled conditions that greeted any visitor to the area before the Civil War, at least one American sculptor of considerable professional reputation is known to have come to Texas. A self-taught portrait sculptor who had already achieved success with the portraits of President James Buchanan and the English author Charles Dickens, among others,[5] Henry Dexter (b. 1806 New York; d. 1876 Massachusetts) made his way to Galveston in 1859 by crossing the Gulf of Mexico from Louisiana. Dexter then traveled 135 miles by stage coach to Austin in order to "take" the likeness of Governor Sam Houston (Fig. 1), whom he admired.[6] The likeness was reportedly developed through the use of a life mask and the "model" completed "in two or three long working days."[7]

---

1. The sequence of flags over Texas is Spain, 1519–1685; France, 1685–1690; Spain, 1690–1821; Mexico, 1821–1836; Republic of Texas, 1836–1845; United States, 1845–1861; Confederate States, 1861–1865; United States, 1865 to the present. (The present flag of Texas was also the flag of the Republic of Texas.)

2. The discovery of gold at Sutter's Mill in California hastened the exploration of West Texas. As late as 1848 a group of Texas Rangers was near death after becoming lost trying to open a route to El Paso from San Antonio, but in 1849 routes to El Paso were established. Other exploration of the West Texas area followed.

3. The last battle occurred in January 1881 in the Texas Sierra Diablo initiated by the Texas Rangers against Chief Victorio's Apaches.

4. Established by the Franciscans in the El Paso area in 1680, the San Antonio de la Ysleta and Nuestra Senora de la Concepcion del Socorro were the first Spanish missions in Texas. In all, up to forty missions were established across Texas by the Spanish. See Don Graham, *The WPA Guide to Texas*, p. 142, for comments about sculpture and early missions.

5. Though he executed nearly 200 portrait busts, Dexter also did ideal works with such titles as *The Young Naturalist* and *Nymph of the Ocean*.

6. Sam Houston (b. 1793 Rockbridge County, Va.; d. 1863 Huntsville, Tex.). Lived with Cherokee Indians and was adopted under the tribal name "The Raven." In Tennessee: member of the U.S. House of Representatives and seventh governor. In Texas: helped establish the Republic, becoming its first president, instrumental in its annexation, successively United States Senator and seventh governor. Upon the secession of Texas from the Union in 1861, Houston refused to take an oath of allegiance to the Confederacy and was deposed.
   "Dexter thought Houston a great man, and such he was, – great in his place and time, – and a giant in stature" (Albee, John. *Henry Dexter, Sculptor*, p. 91).

7. Ibid.

The Houston bust was one of a group of thirty-two plaster portraits of the nation's governors Dexter completed in 1859–1860. All thirty-two appear to have been included in a brief exhibition in the Doric Hall of the Boston State House. Because of public threats over their presence after the Civil War had begun, the busts of the southern governors were removed from the Boston State House to Dexter's studio.[8]

With the outbreak of the Civil War, Dexter's original plans to translate the busts into marble were thwarted and only a few were ever copied. John Albee in his memorial to Henry Dexter,[9] noted which were copied, but Houston's bust is not among them. Though many of the busts were lost, a plaster cast of the Houston bust has survived and is presently on exhibition at the Daughters of the Republic of Texas Museum.[10] The Texas plaster, which carries an oval, stamped metal copyright plate bearing the inscription "HENRY DEXTER, FECIT/ BOSTON 1860 COPY RIGHT SECURED," is presently identified as the same cast that was included in the Boston exhibition, probably meaning the Texas plaster was cast in 1860 after Dexter returned home to his studio.[11]

The account of his Texas trip (as told by Albee) confirms the undeveloped conditions of the state at that time. Dexter, who is believed to be the first professional sculptor to have entered the state, noted that the insignia of the true Texan was a dirk in the belt and a pipe in the mouth. In Texas, Dexter found no sweet milk, no meat but pork, and northern apples at ten dollars a barrel. And yet he noted there were "herds of cattle numberless" and that "sheep whitened the wide plains [all on free and unfenced range]."[12]

Though the presence of professional sculptors was yet to be, it is likely there were at least a few naïve sculptors in the state during this period. One such carver was Johann Sladek (1803–1863 or 1868), who came to Texas from his native Czechoslovakia in 1860. At his death, he bequeathed a set of shadow boxes (Fig. 2) he had carved to each of his six children. Populated with small figures, each set represented a biblical story, and each box depicted a scene from that story. Through descent in the family one set of his carved boxes has survived, preserving the sense of personal piety and artistic expression found in Sladek's carvings.[13]

There are other isolated and usually scanty accounts of sculptors appearing in the state before the last years of the century. Active in Austin during 1873–1874, a sculptor calling himself Professor M. Caifassi operated a museum containing marble statuary and life-size wax figures at Colorado and Cypress streets, a site located in the downtown area south of the state capitol and near the Colorado River.[14] Not much is known about Professor Caifassi, but in 1873 he, too, did a bust of the highly revered Sam Houston.[15]

In the Texas State Cemetery in Austin, there is a memorial figure (Fig. 3) at the head of the grave of John Hemphill (1803–1862) carved from marble by Professor Caifassi in 1874.[16] Despite the stiffness of the form and other anatomical limitations, the sculpture is appealing. A slightly smaller than life-size figure representing grief, her left hand blots her tears as she leans against a Doric column on top of which is placed an urn bearing a lone star. Her wavy hair spills from under a long veil of mourning that she wears over her head, and a Greek chiton falls over her plump nineteenth-century proportions. Other classical references are seen both in the figure's gesture and in the regular cadence of her drapery's folds, as seen from the back view. The seven tomes stacked at her feet serve as attributes associated with the departed

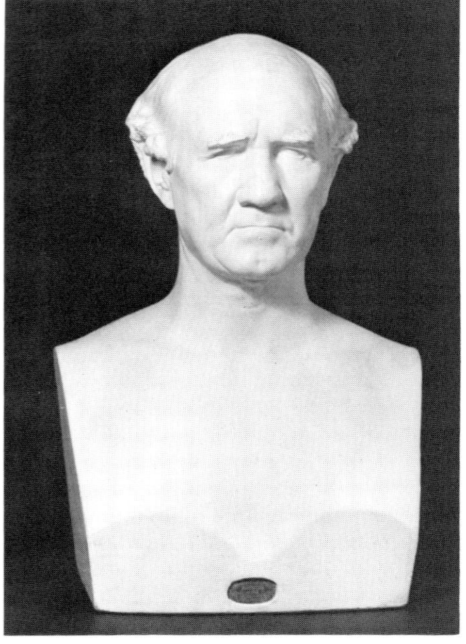

FIG. 1
HENRY DEXTER (1806–1876)
Sam Houston, *1859–60*
Plaster
22⅜ in. high × 15½ in. wide
Collection of the Texas Preservation Board, State Capitol, long-term loan to The Daughters of the Republic of Texas Museum, Austin
Photograph provided by The National Portrait Gallery, Washington, D.C.

8. Ibid., p. 96.

9. Ibid., pp. 114–115.

10. It has been on long-term loan to the Daughters of the Republic of Texas Museum from the state of Texas since ca. 1915 (Gregg Pearson, Director of the Daughters of the Republic of Texas Museum, phone conversation, April 21, 1989).

11. Its provenance between 1860 and its (undated) acquisition by the state of Texas is not clear at this point (see note n. 10 above). In 1969 a unique bronze (first and only casting) of this plaster was made by the National Portrait Gallery in Washington. As late as 1968 there existed a second plaster cast painted with a metallic paint in the Museum of History and Technology (now the Museum of American History) in Washington. It was described as a weak cast in U.S. Memorandum: Dr. Reed from M. Fabian, June 13, 1968 (from the files of the National Portrait Gallery). The present location of the MHT cast is unknown.

12. Albee, *Henry Dexter*, p. 91.

13. Cecilia Steinfeldt. *Texas Folk Art*, pp. 210–216. The boxes illustrated are from the set of six inherited by the artist's daughter Frances Sladek, and which remained in the family until 1972 when they were donated to the Winedale Historical Center near Round Top, Texas, an extension of the University of Texas at Austin. Sladek is buried in Live Oak Hill Cemetery near Ellinger, Texas.

FIG. 2
JOHANN SLADEK (1803–1868)
Untitled *(View of Shadow Boxes), ca. 1865*
Carved wood, polychromed
Each box ca. 9 × 11 × 3 in.
Collection of the Winedale Historical Center,
Fayette County, The University of Texas at Austin
Photograph provided by the Winedale Archives,
Round Top, Texas

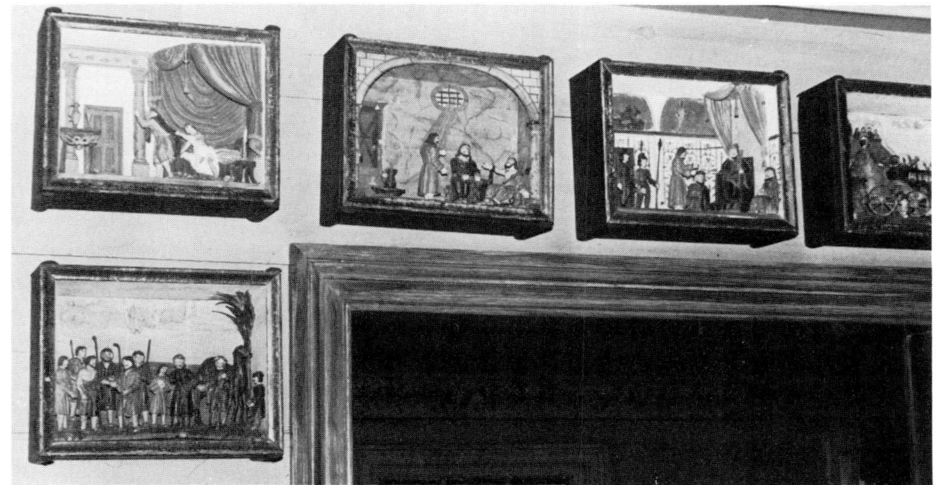

FIG. 3
M. CAIFASSI (active 1873–1874)
John Hemphill Memorial, *1874*
Signed and dated
Marble
Texas State Cemetery, Austin
Photographer: Phyllis Frede, Austin

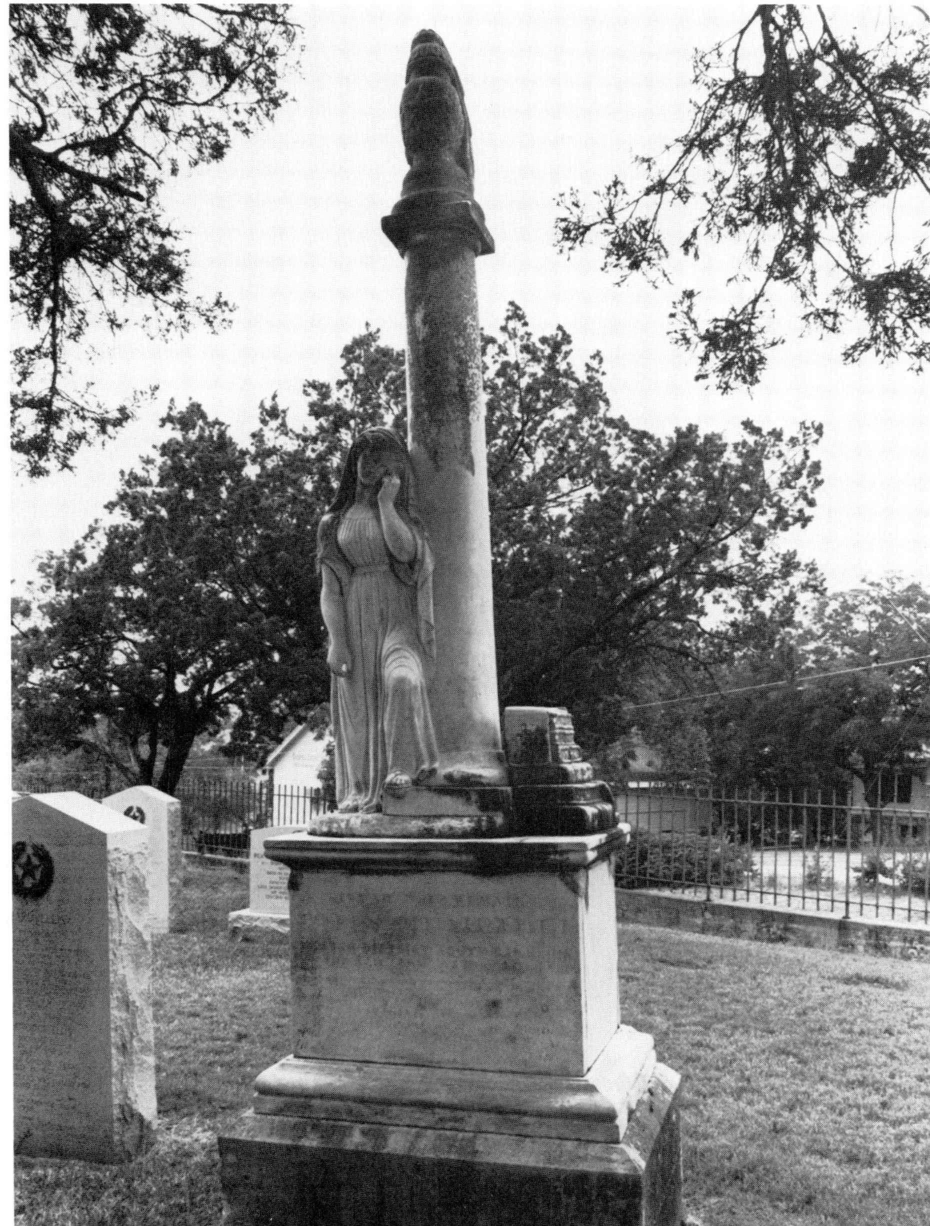

14. *Austin Daily Statesman* (undated), Archives of the
State Historian, State Preservation Board: "The
Professor has now connected with his museum a
panorama of the Franco-Prussian war, which
makes his exhibition more entertaining than ever."

15. *Austin Daily Statesman*, February 1, 1873, p. 3
(from Archives of the State Historian). The
location of the Caifassi plaster bust of Sam
Houston is unknown. The bust possibly appears in
a photograph of the office of Governor L. S. Ross
in the temporary (1883) capitol building. The
original photograph, dated 1887 or 1888, is in the
Austin History Center, Austin Public Library, L. S.
Ross Biographical File.

16. It is signed on the base in the back, "Austin, Texas
1874 Professor Caifassi made this monument."

17. John Hemphill (b. December 18, 1803, Chester
District, S. C.; d. January 3, 1862, Richmond, Va.).
Former chief justice of the Supreme Court of Texas
(1840–1857) and United States senator from Texas
(1857–1861).

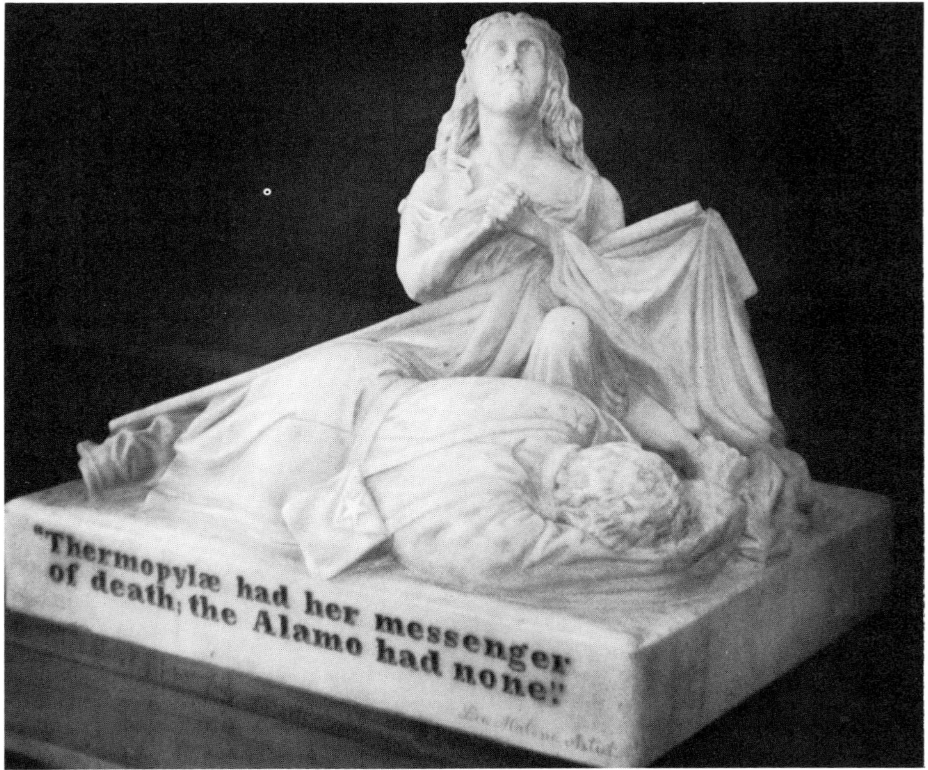

FIG. 4
CLOTILDE LEE MALONE (1860–1891)
The Fall of the Alamo, *completed ca. 1880–81*
Signed
Marble
ca. 30 × 24 in.
*Collection of the Texas Preservation Board, State
Capitol, long-term loan to The Daughters of the
Republic of Texas Museum, Austin*
*Photograph provided by the Daughters of the
Republic of Texas Museum, Austin*

and probably refer to the former Texas Supreme Court justice's study of jurisprudence.[17]

A few years later in Waco, about a hundred miles north of Austin, a young girl named Clotilde Lee Malone[18] (b. May 27, 1860, Nashville; d. August 5, 1891, Waco) completed a marble carving titled *The Fall of the Alamo* (ca. 1880–81), a naïve work (Fig. 4) that may be the first sculpture in Texas to depict a historical event.[19] On the base the sculptor carved the inscription, "Thermophylæ had her messenger of death, the Alamo had none."[20]

Self-taught, Malone worked on the sculpture for about six years, which may account for some variation in the treatment of the two figures. The majority of her school years had been spent in a remote part of Brazil (1865–1875), a revolt on her father's part against the presence of carpetbaggers in Waco following the Civil War.[21] Though Texas is not always remembered as a "southern" state, the strength of Mr. Malone's sentiment suggests the passions felt by many Texans after the Civil War. The following description of the Malone sculpture was printed in a Waco newspaper upon the exhibition in the city of the completed work.

The State of Texas is represented by a woman . . . , the Alamo by a dead soldier. The woman is bending over the soldier, with the broken staff of the Lone Star . . . across her lap. Her upturned face is intended not to express exquisite beauty of feature, but the mingling of two distinct emotions of the mind, and they are grief and vengeance. The Lone Star on the brow, . . . the dead soldier . . . are all forgotten as you gaze on that face . . . . Her grief is too great for tears or wild gesticulations. She looks heavenward, as if she would dare to inquire . . . what this means, that the last soldier of liberty in . . . Texas lies . . . his spirit fled, and not a single messenger to tell of the defeat and death . . . . you can read with equal plainness her oath of vengeance, San Jacinto is foretold in every feature . . . . her grief is bitter . . . . There is not the slightest indication of submission to tyranny.[22]

18. The artist chose her name, "Clotilde Lee," when she was about ten; before that time she had been called "Ittie." Malone is buried in the Oakwood Cemetery in Waco (Miss Mary Clayton to Patricia Hendricks, February 14, 1989).

19. Malone carved at least one other marble work, a sleeping child on a couch (unidentified Waco newspaper account, Alba Malone Scrapbook, The Mary Clayton Papers, Texas Collection, Baylor University, Waco).

20. Archives, DRT Library at the Alamo; J. Frank Dobie: "The Alamo's Immortalization of Words." pp. 402–410. Malone's quote repeats an earlier epitaph inscribed on a ten-foot-high obelisk dedicated to the heroes of the Alamo and cut from the stone ruins of the Alamo in 1841. The obelisk was purchased by the state of Texas in 1858, after having been found wrecked in a New Orleans marble yard, only to be mostly destroyed during the state Capitol fire of 1881 (General Laws of The Seventh Legislature, 1858, p. 130). The source of the Thermophylæ quote appears to be a speech written by Thomas Jefferson Green for Gen. Edward Burleson to deliver to his troups at Gonzales, after calling the then organizing Army of Texas together, making the news known to them that the Alamo had fallen. The text of the Burleson speech varies from the inscriptions on the two sculptures (Malone's and the 1841 obelisk), which substituted "death" and "doom" for Burleson's use of the word "defeat." In 1891 another memorial to the Alamo adopting Burleson's Thermophylæ quote (using the original word "defeat") was installed on the state capitol grounds. See also the use of the quote again during dedication ceremonies for Amateis's Heroes of 1836 monument in Galveston (note 74).

21. It is not known what kind of training Lee Malone had while in Brazil from 1865–1875. Her father taught in or near Sabara in Brazil at a boys' school (Clayton to Hendricks, February 14, 1989). Also see *The Elusive Eden: Frank McMullan's Confederate Colony in Brazil,* by William Clark Griggs, Austin: University of Texas Press, 1987. Although Malone was not associated with the Texas colony in Brazil that Grigg details, *Elusive Eden* does suggest in its text and bibliography the scope of the exodus to Brazil by Confederate supporters from the southern states. (I am indebted to Barbara Spielman of UT Press for leading me to this reference).

22. Alba Malone Scrapbook.

23. *Waco [?] Examiner:* A. Malone Scrapbook.

24. Ibid.

25. *Senate Journal,* March 28, 1899, pp. 577–578.

26. For a discussion of painting in Texas during this period, see Pauline A. Pinckney, *Painting in Texas.*

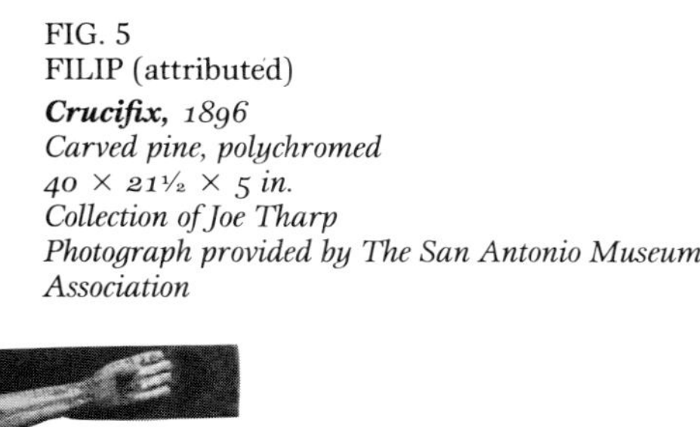

FIG. 5
FILIP (attributed)
Crucifix, *1896*
Carved pine, polychromed
40 × 21½ × 5 in.
Collection of Joe Tharp
Photograph provided by The San Antonio Museum
Association

Lee Malone's sculpture received much favorable newspaper publicity. One article commented that the sculptor hoped to sell her work to the state of Texas to be exhibited in either the Senate Chamber or the Hall of the House of Representatives.[23] Even if the sculptor had lived longer, she might not have succeeded in pursuading the State to commit money to the purchase of her work, due to the state's unsettled economy during that period. It is not even certain a majority would have been persuaded of the work's artistic merits, as suggested by the response of one independent-minded reviewer whose assessment of the sculpture included, in addition to favorable comments, words of reservation about its overall quality.[24]

After the sculptor's death, her mother offered *The Fall of the Alamo* to the state of Texas in memory of her daughter. In 1899 a resolution accepting the gift was put forth by the Texas Senate, expressing the state's appreciation as it spoke of the "historic and most dreadful massacre" at the Alamo, emphasizing "the pride with which Texans delight to recall the magnificent valor of their forefathers."[25] The extended language of the resolution and the newspaper coverage that earlier accompanied the showing of the Malone sculpture in Waco make it clear that the events of the Alamo, like the battles of the Confederacy, were very much alive in the memory of Texans. An understanding of the level of those feelings, which many worked to keep alive, is valuable in putting into perspective the deeply felt sense of patriotism that would encourage the growing number of commissions for memorial sculptures dedicated to these and other heroes for decades to come.

Heroic Monuments and Some European-Trained Sculptors

In the last decade of the nineteenth century, although the large majority of Texas artists continued to be painters, sculptural activity in the state increased noticeably.[26] Among those producing sculpture were stone cutters and the artisans who continued a wood-carving tradition. There was also a growing number of immigrant sculptors who had received academic training in Europe before coming to Texas. The sculpture produced in that decade ranged from the crucifix (Fig. 5), attributed to Filip (active in the 1890s?)[27] to the secular portraits of Texans executed by the highly trained German sculptor, Elisabet Ney.[28] Due in large part to Ney's success in convincing private and public patrons to commit resources to portrait sculpture, interest in sculpture quickened, providing the needed momentum to promote a more robust sculptural climate in Texas.

Among the various factors that contributed to an improved environment for potential sculptors and their patrons were tangible changes, such as the miles of railway that had crisscrossed most of the state by the end of the eighties, not only making travel for the individual

27. Steinfeldt, *Texas Folk Art*, p. 217. The crucifix originally belonged to Johanna Sluber, who came to Texas from Austria in 1882, settling in Ammansville, where she is believed to have had the work carved especially for the family prayer room. The crucifix remained the property of her descendents until 1977 and is attributed to Filip, a carver in Schulenburg, Texas, who made religious figures on special order. Steinfeldt points to the influence of Czech and Lithuanian folk art.

28. First trained by her stone-cutter father, Ney became the first woman accepted by the sculpture department at the Munich Academy of Art and was then admitted to the Berlin Academy of Art, which before her admittance had generally been closed to women. During Ney's academic training she studied under the sculptor Max Widnmann (b. October 16, 1812; d. March 6, 1895), the history painter Johann Baptiste Berdellé (b. March 15, 1813; d. July 19, 1876), and the sculptor Christian Daniel Rauch (b. January 2, 1777; d. December 3, 1857).

easier but also contributing to a greater social and commercial stability. Another important factor had been the evolution from the personal and collective priorities of a frontier to those belonging to a young state, a timely development as that auspicious date approached when oil would be discovered at Spindletop on January 10, 1901.

Notable even before Spindletop was a rising sense of the materialism that already had helped form the tastes of much of the rest of the country but generally had been submerged in the state during preceding decades. Materialist concerns in Texas before the twentieth century did not truly match those of the Gilded Age satirized by Mark Twain but did coincide with an age of enterprise for Texas. The merchant class, cotton, ranching, and banking industries, and other entrepreneurial activities that fed the growth of financial achievement were being invigorated, despite tumultous political and economic pitfalls experienced along the way. The emerging public philosophy was one better able to accommodate the sculptor's vision, and the development of private wealth was occasionally accompanied by notable philanthropic expressions of civic devotion, including important sculptural commissions.

Two cities, Galveston and Austin, led the way in opportunities for sculptors in the state. Although already locked in competition with Houston for the commercial prize that shipping supremacy bestowed, a competition it would in the end lose, Galveston was able to maintain its ranking throughout the nineteenth century, its busy seaport making it the most important shipping center in the Gulf outside New Orleans. It was a city of wealth and sophistication and, along with Austin, the state capital, one of the first to attract sculptors.

Appearing in the Galveston City Directory as a resident for the years 1884–1885, 1888–1889, and 1890–1891, was Thomas Willoughby, wood-carver.[29] It is probable that Willoughby carved the intriguing bas-relief *Young Galveston* (Cat. 1) during one of those periods. The purpose of this handsome relief, with its many symbolic references to the island city, is unknown. The work, which may owe something of its character to the English tradition of wood carving, depicts Young Galveston seated on her mother's lap, the two figures composed against the background of a scalloped shell. The Texas star is worn by the child around her neck and by the mother in the part of her hair. The mother holds half a wreath in her left hand,[30] the child a (Texas) rose in her right hand. At the feet of the mother are stacked three bales of cotton, the chief product shipped out of the Galveston port. On the lower bale is the inscription "Young Galveston/Texas." It is not clear why there is an inconsistency in style between the mother's face and that of her child. Despite that somewhat puzzling juxtaposition, the viewer finds an overriding harmony between the components.

In his munificent will, the self-made Galveston millionaire Henry Rosenberg (b. 1824 Bilten, Switzerland; d. 1893 Galveston)[31] left substantial funding to the city to ensure the continued support for cultural and educational activities he had begun there. He also left "$30,000 for the erection of not less than ten drinking fountains for man and beast in various portions of the city of Galveston."[32] Twelve were placed in March 1898, and five larger fountains erected in October 1898. The fountains were designed by the sculptor John Massey Rhind (b. 1860 Scotland; 1936 United States), all in a light gray granite ornamented with bronze (some in the form of a dolphin), with each fountain bearing the inscription: "Gift of Henry Rosenberg."[33] Four artist's presentation watercolors for the fountains (Cat. 2–5) are included in this exhibition.[34] Drawing "C" depicts one of the few fountains to have survived,[35] now located on the Galveston County Courthouse lawn.

29. Willoughby was listed as a wood-carver in the Galveston City Directory.

30. According to the donor, Sidney Burnham (Sidney Burnham to the Institute of Texan Cultures, September 9, 1985): The wreath is broken, probably due to the fragile nature of the short grain; the carving was stripped of its original coat of several layers of dark varnish while it was still in England. Willoughby was a paying guest in the Liverpool home of Burnham's parents where he worked in the same workshop as Burnham's father. Around 1913 Willoughby left his carvings in the care of Burnham's parents and was never heard of again. Another carving by Willoughby of a Mexican girl was retained by Burnham.

31. *Henry Rosenberg, 1824–1893*, pp. 89–96.

32. *Ibid.*, p. 94. Rosenberg's will stipulated that the "bequest, however, is upon the proviso that the city of Galveston shall obtain an abundant supply of good drinking water within five years after my death."

33. Ibid., *Rosenberg*, pls. 23a & b. Eight of the fountains are illustrated.

34. Other presentation drawings by Rhind for the fountains in the Rosenberg Library include figures dressed in the attire of the Southwest, in a serape, for example. There is no evidence that Rhind traveled to Texas for this commission.

35. That any of the fountains have survived is a testament to the citizens of the city who have through continued effort saved much of the physical evidence of a remarkable cultural heritage. One battle was lost by the Galveston Civic League in 1949, when the mayor of the city commended the street commissioner for ordering what the historical preservationists referred to as the "wanton destruction of the people's property." The street commissioner hammered one of Rhind's remaining drinking fountains to dust because, as the mayor put it, "it was a traffic hazard, a breeding place for flies, and a loafing place for men." The street commissioner's action against the fountain was taken despite the fact that the Galveston Civic League had made previous arrangements to pay for the fountain's removal to a new location (*Galveston Tribune*, November, 16, 1949, p. 1, col. 8).

36. Those who studied under John Massey Rhind's father include Alexander Milne Calder, another Scottish sculptor who would immigrate to America. (See n. 74.) The Rhinds (grandfather, father, and brothers) were active as architectural sculptors in Edinburgh.

37. Jules Dalou (1838–1902) was exiled from Paris to London because of his involvement with the Commune. Among Rhind's many works are the *Crawford W. Long Monument*, Georgia's tribute to Statuary Hall in the nation's capitol (as was Ney's figure *Stephen F. Austin*), and the *George Washington Memorial* in Newark, New Jersey. Rhind was one of the four sculptors who won the competition for the doors for Trinity Church in New York.

38. Ney was buried at Liendo.

FIG. 6
JOHN MASSEY RHIND (1868–1936)
Benjamin Franklin Stephenson Monument,
1866
Bronze and stone
Over life-size
Washington, D.C.
Photographer: Abbie Rowe, National Park Service,
U.S. Department of the Interior; photograph
courtesy Department of Art History, University
of Delaware

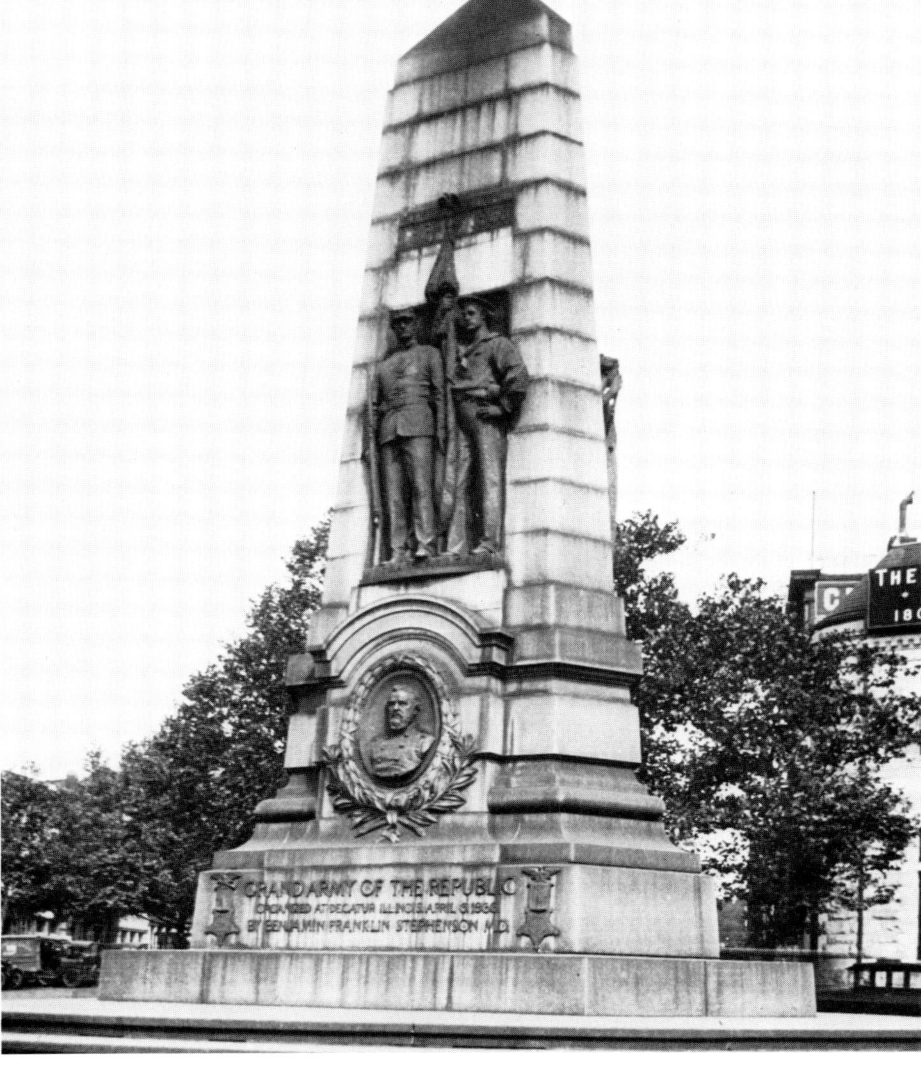

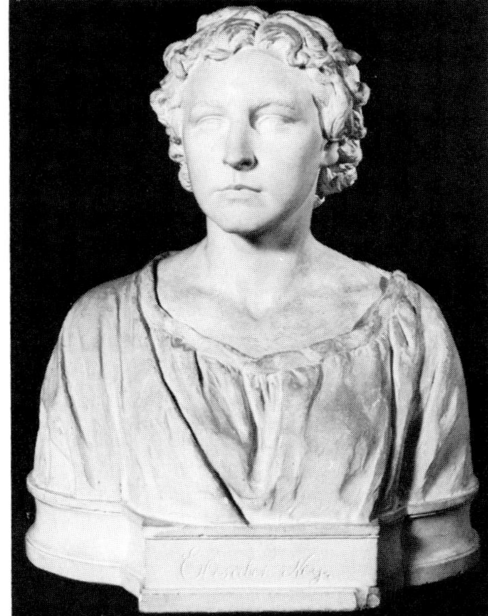

FIG. 7
ELISABET NEY (1833–1907)
Self-Portrait, *begun 1860s, completed 1903*
Signed
Plaster
20½ × 19 × 11½ in.
Harry Ransom Humanities Research Center Art
Collection, The University of Texas at Austin
Photograph provided by the Harry Ransom
Humanities Research Center, The University of
Texas at Austin

Rhind, who had had his first artistic training in Edinburgh studying under his sculptor and stone-cutter father,[36] also had studied in Paris and London with Jules Dalou, and Rhind's sculpture reflected the ideals and the confidence promoted by the École des Beaux-Arts. After marrying the daughter of an architect for whom he was working in London, Rhind and his bride departed London for the United States in 1889, arriving at a good time for decorative sculptors as American architects following the Beaux-Arts style were beginning to incorporate sculpture with their architectural projects. Rhind was a popular and prolific sculptor (Fig. 6) who maintained a studio both in New York and in New Jersey.[37]

Another European immigrant, the sculptor Elisabet Ney (b. January 26, 1833, Munster, Westphalia, Germany; d. June 29, 1907, Austin),[38] arrived in Texas in 1873, settling on a plantation named Liendo, near Hempstead. Born in a small German town, Ney (Fig. 7) would become an international figure, exhibiting her work in France, Italy, America, and Germany. In 1871, despite professional success Ney left Europe rather suddenly with her husband, Dr. Edmund Montgomery, for Thomasville, Georgia, with the hope of establishing a utopian community there. After setbacks, the Montgomerys moved to Texas, still seeking the philosophical life envisioned by men like Goethe and Rousseau.[39]

Settling in Texas, Ney took over the running of their plantation, sparing her scientist-philosopher husband in order that he might pursue his career of writing and research.[40] After nearly a decade of economic hardship, Ney began overtures toward resuming her sculpture career. In 1882 she did the portrait bust of their friend and county neighbor Governor Oran Roberts. Two years later she lost out on the award of a memorial commission in San Antonio; the winning monument was a granite obelisk, twenty feet in height. At that time the obelisk remained the preferred choice over portrait figures for most cemetery monuments in Texas.[41]

Ney continued with her efforts to reestablish her career in Texas, and arranged to have some of her works shipped to Texas from her long-closed studio in Munich. She exhibited six of these in San Antonio, but there was little response there to her sculpture. In 1887 she modeled portraits of influential friends in Galveston, the Julius Runge family.[42] Julius, Texas born and German educated, was a cotton broker and the acting German consul. The Runge portraits did not lead to other commissions.

In the 1890s Ney's luck began to change, and two decades after her arrival in this country she resumed her professional career. It was probably due both to the support and influence of her old friend former Governor Roberts and to her experience in exhibiting her sculpture at the 1867 art exhibition in Paris[43] that she was selected by The Women's World's Fair Exhibit Association of Texas (also referred to as the State Board of Lady Managers) to provide sculptures for the Texas pavilion being planned for the Chicago World's Columbian Exposition in 1893.[44] Ney's contract with the State Board of Lady Managers called for her to produce life-size plaster figures of two of Texas's most revered heroes, Sam Houston and Stephen F. Austin (Cat. 6).[45] She moved quickly to build a studio in Austin in which she could work, calling it Formosa. Due to construction and family problems during the year, Ney was only able to complete the figure of Sam Houston in time for exhibition at the Columbian Exposition.

Striving to be faithful both to the physical appearances and ideal representations of Houston and Austin, Ney gathered images of her subjects, where possible, as well as available documentation and personal testimony, combining the information with her own conception of the spirit of these courageous men. Austin's nephew Guy Bryan and other family members provided Ney with valuable information about Austin.[46] In her effort to evoke in the viewer the reality of the man and the challenges he met, Ney elected to portray him in clothes natural to his role, a choice which she later referred to with pride as quite original. A Kentucky rifle and map of the territory are prominent attributes, each suggestive of the demands placed upon the colonizer. The tree stump suggests the domestication of the wilderness, while the inactive position of the powder horn may point to the pacifist nature of Austin's mission.

Ney's figure of Stephen F. Austin is simply conceived with smooth and yet distinctive features presented in a naturalistic style. The truth-based treatment by the sculptor of Austin's hair, brows, and the details of his costume creates a decorative interplay, compatible with Ney's depiction of the slender, almost delicate figure of Austin. The result is an image that conveys to the viewer the sense of a man of some cultural refinement.

39. She and her scholar husband were well read, and Ney's readings ranged from Petrarch and Rousseau to Winkelmann and Goethe to writings on modern socialism. Their readings no doubt influenced their utopian interests in America, as well as her views on the obligation of the sculptor to society. In her possession at her death was a miniature plaster bas-relief profile portrait of Goethe, sculpted by Bosy, 1831, which Ney no doubt kept as an important possession, an homage to Goethe and his ideas rather than to the work of Bosy, as she seemingly had no real interest in collecting the work of other sculptors. She also admired Garibaldi, whom she had known, referring to him as a "Prometheus." In 1867 after her earlier observation about Garibaldi, Ney sculpted a large and powerful figure of Prometheus (Ney Museum, Austin). Emily Fourmy Cutrer has already linked the ideas of these individuals to Ney's interests and beliefs very well (*The Art of the Woman*).

40. He was also, no doubt, spared because he was tubercular.

41. The Washington Monument, the white marble obelisk chosen to honor George Washington in the nation's capitol, was completed in 1884 and opened to the public in 1888. Its presence must have exerted an influence on many, both because they found it visually and intellectually moving, and because it represented official sanction, surely reinforcing the preference of many Texans for an obelisk when selecting a memorial. The perception that added height lent added symbolism to a monument was also enhanced by the fact that the Washington Monument stood slightly over 555 ft. high.

42. Julius Runge was acting German consul in Galveston in 1872. In 1897 Ney modeled a medallion in plaster of the Runges' daughter Margaret (Mrs. Thomas Adrian Rose of Dallas), now in the collection of the Dallas Museum of Art. A bronze cast was given to the Elisabet Ney Museum by a descendent.

43. The second World's Fair in Paris.

44. The Association (Lady Managers) was organized to see to the representation of Texas at the Chicago World's Columbian Exposition in 1893, an exposition that followed the example of the Paris Exposition of 1889.

45. Stephen Fuller Austin (b. 1793 Austinville, Va.; d. December 27, 1836 Columbia, Tex.): Filled important role in achievement of Texas independence. Completed his father's dream to establish a colony in Texas, bringing the first 300 families to the territory from the United States. Died at forty-three, of pneumonia contracted in his capacity as the Republic's first secretary of state under Sam Houston, working three days and nights in unheated rooms of temporary capitol buildings in Columbia, Texas, preparing instructions for the Texas minister to take to Washington. Called "Father of Texas."

46. Ney received the greatest amount of information about Stephen F. Austin from Austin's nephew, Col. Guy Morrison Bryan. In addition to personal descriptions, Bryan provided Ney with an engraving of Austin, made after an earlier oil painting: "engraving . . . taken from an oil painting given by Austin to his sister (My Mother) . . . painted [in 1835] . . . by an artist in New Orleans" (Bryan to Ney, September 24, 1892, from *Sursum!*, by Mrs. J. W. Rutland, p. 30). The engraving became the basis for Ney's sculpture composition of Austin.

47. Bryan to Ney, October 7, 1892 (ibid., pp. 30–31).

48. Bryan to Ney, September 24, 1892 (ibid., p. 30).

49. Bryan to Ney, September 26, 1892 (ibid., p. 30).

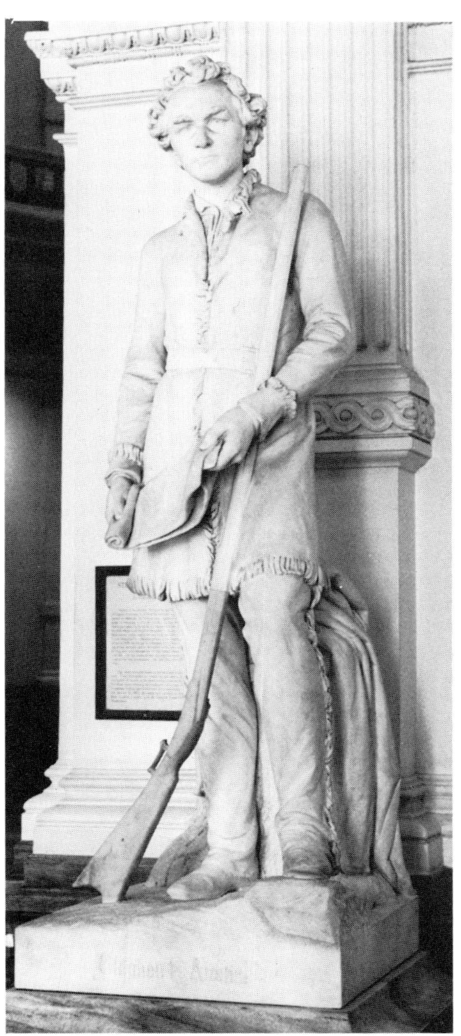

FIG. 8
ELISABET NEY (1833–1907)
Stephen F. Austin*, 1902*
Marble
76½ in. high
Collection of the Texas Preservation Board,
State Capitol
Photographer: Phyllis Frede, Austin

Austin's nephew told Ney his uncle was "an educated refined gentleman," who was "at home in Courts & polished society, as well as in camp & among pioneers." [47] He explained that Austin was a man of "graceful & easy carriage," a "graceful dancer, & of attractive manners," and a man whose eyes appeared "generally thoughtful when not in conversation." [48] Ney's aim was to incorporate those qualities of his personality as well as his physical appearance, such as his heavy brows and deep-set eyes. [49] After completing the figure of Austin, Ney expressed an admiration for Austin, the man, in a letter to a friend, writing that although Austin had "less the stamp of an aggressive warrior [than the companion figure of Sam Houston], his deeds, his courage, his sufferings, his love for others entitled him to equal recognition with those who became foremost on the battlefield of actual war." [50]

After Ney had sculpted William Jennings Bryan from sittings in her studio in 1900, [51] the members of the state legislature became more inclined to listen to and approve a proposal for an appropriation to pay for marble copies of the Austin and Houston plasters. In 1901 the Twenty-Seventh Texas Legislature voted to approve the funds needed to produce marble copies of those figures. [52] In the end, the casts of Austin and Houston were each translated twice into marble. The first pair was cut in the Berlin studio of Franz Lange during the autumn and early winter of 1902. [53] Ney participated in the refinements of the carvings and maintained a close supervision of the general carving. Upon their arrival in Texas the marbles of Houston and Austin were installed in January 1903 in a particularly well-chosen and well-lighted location in the entry hall of the Texas state capitol, in front of the massive pilasters guarding the threshhold of the rotunda, a location where they can be seen today and a location that Ney was forced to battle to win over other proposed and less desirable locations in the capitol (Fig. 8) . The translation of these figures from plaster into marble for the state capitol had been part of the original agreement between Ney and the State Board of Lady Managers, but the necessary funds to cover the expenses had remained unavailable until the legislature gave its support.

From the time of the early 1890s the citizens of Texas had been promoting the commissioning of a monument to the Texas Civil War hero General Albert Sidney Johnston (Fig. 9), second in command to Robert E. Lee. In 1902 when Ney was seventy-two, the Texas Division of the United Daughters of the Confederacy announced that the contract for the erection of a marble memorial to the general, to be placed over his grave at the State Cemetery in Austin, had been signed and awarded to Ney, and would be filed with the Department of State. [54]

Ney, working under her own conception of the great general lying in an "intense, grand repose," relied on realistic detail to reconstruct the scene. The details of his uniform are faithfully portrayed. He lies on the handmade litter that was used to carry the fallen hero from the battlefield at Shiloh. The battle flag of the Confederacy [55] serves as his blanket, draping down from his body across the edge of his bier to brush the ground, adding both formal strength and emotional resonance. His head rests on a pillow of rushes cushioned by the flag of Texas. Filling the space between the litter and the ground are swaying grasses, which respond formally to the linear details of the flags, drapery, and costume. An aura of nobility and poignancy surrounds Ney's *gisant* as it lies interred above the general's grave in a glass box, over which is built a wrought- and cast-iron Victorian gothic chapel (Fig. 10). The plaster cast of the general illustrated in the catalogue is dated 1900, a year before the agreement for funding was issued. With the carving completed in the spring of 1904, the marble version of the general was shipped from Seravezza to St. Louis,

50. Ney to Rebecca Fischer, July 18, 1900 (ibid., pp. 80–81).

51. William Jennings Bryan (1860–1925), nominated for U.S. presidency for second time in 1900.

52. C. W. Raines. *Year Book for Texas*, 2:22–28.

53. The second pair, which would be permanently installed in the national capitol, was cut in Seravezza by Antonio Bocci. Ney to Dibrell, February 1, 1904, Rutland, *Sursum!*, pp. 134–135. At that time Seravezza was "only ½ hour drive" (Ney to Taylor, February 7, 1904, ibid, pp. 135–137) from Carrara .

54. Raines, *Year Book*, 2:86.

55. There were four Confederate flags, and of these one was the official "Battle Flag" (Dunovant to Ney, January 13, 1902, from Rutland, *Sursum!*, p. 102). The flag in Ney's sculpture represents the official Confederacy flag assigned to battle.

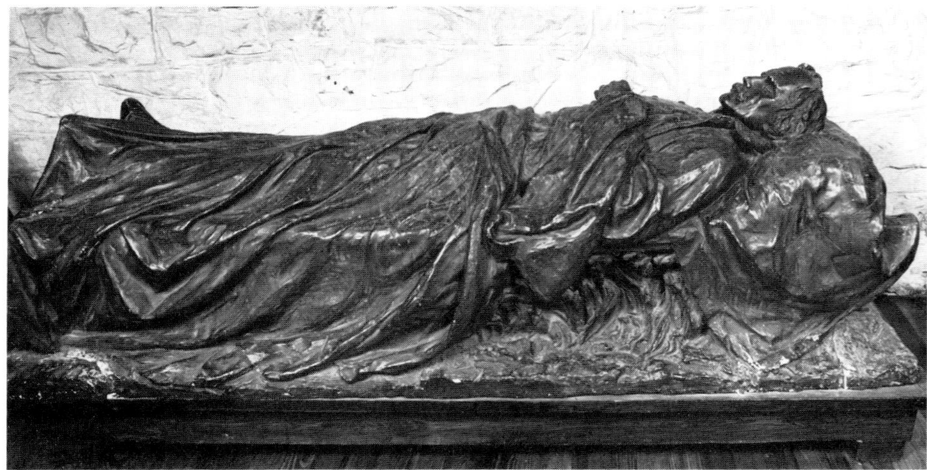

General Albert Sidney Johnston Memorial,
1900
Painted plaster
89½ × 28½ × 32½ in.
Collection of the Elisabet Ney Museum, Austin
Photographer: Phyllis Frede, Austin

Missouri, in time to be exhibited in the Texas Building at the World's Fair, where it won a bronze medal.[56]

Though Ney's reputation as a sculptor was built on her portrait busts of the leaders of Germany and Texas, modeled by the sculptor within an idealizing but naturalistic style, there were exceptions.[57] Even while Ney was still in Europe, there were isolated examples in her work of other sorts of subject matter, including allegorical and classical subjects. In this country, though her focus on portraits of distinguished figures represented an even greater percentage of her total output than had been the case in Europe, Ney did produce a few works that fell outside the portrait category. One such work is the *Cherub* (Cat. 7), which had been asked for by a "gentleman in Fredericksburg," who Ney reported had requested of her "the little cherub below the Sixtine [sic] Madonna by Raphael." The *Cherub* was carved in marble around 1905 for the Schnerr family in Fredericksburg, Texas.[58] The plaster *Cherub* in the exhibition is the cast from which the Fredericksburg marble was copied.

Despite the range of subject matter found in her previous work, the *Lady Macbeth* (Cat. 8), a psychological study of a literary figure, stands alone in Ney's oeuvre. In the tragic figure of a woman who is unable to remove the stains of her past, it is apparent that the sculptor was able to empathize with her subject's emotional dilemma, if not the character of Lady Macbeth. Ney, herself, perceived Macbeth to be a work that would "fascinate any beholder," and recalled with pleasure the German sculptor Prof. Ernst Herter's comment about the Macbeth, that she was "grandly beautiful".[59] Barefoot as she sleepwalks, the slightly oversize figure of Macbeth is tense as her upper body twists to the left away from its axis as if to reach out and escape her emotional burden. Works by Shakespeare had been a topic of interest among German/European intellectuals while Ney was still living there,[60] and it may be that the ethical situation this character represented had been a topic Ney had previously discussed with others, certainly with her husband who wrote a sonnet about the sleepwalking Lady Macbeth.[61]

It is unclear when the Lady Macbeth sculpture was first begun, but the actual modeling of the clay statue was started in 1900. The figure was finished by 1902 and shipped to Berlin for translation into marble. Ney hoped to exhibit the finished marble in St. Louis and was greatly disappointed when Franz Lange told her there was not a large enough block of marble available[62] for the figure of Lady Macbeth, forcing Ney to wait

56. The Johnston figure was exhibited in 1904 in St. Louis at the Louisiana Purchase Exposition, before being installed in the Texas State Cemetery in Austin.

57. Including the portraits of such figures as Garibaldi and Schopenhauer. Her own self-portrait (Fig. 7), begun during the 1860s, was completed in her Austin studio in 1903, so that it could be cut in marble during Ney's stay in Seravezza to supervise the execution of the Houston and Austin statues for the capitol in Washington and the Albert Sidney Johnston memorial for the Texas State Cemetery in Austin. (She left on that journey in November 1903, her second trip to Europe that year.)

58. The quoted material is from a letter by Ney to Dibrell, October 16, 1905 (Rutland, *Sursum!*, p. 171 and n.). The marble is in the Fredericksburg cemetery. The *Cherub* by Ney is based on one of Raphael's two cherubs at the bottom of Raphael's painting, the *Sistine Madonna* (1513), an image which Ney no doubt would have had stored in her visual memory from first-hand knowledge of it before coming to America.

59. Ney to Dibrell, November 18, 1902 (Rutland, *Sursum!*, pp 115–116).

60. Cutrer (*Art of the Woman*, p. 212) first commented on the possible connection between Ney's choice of subject matter and the nineteenth-century interest in the topic of Shakespeare in Europe (see Koppel S. Pinson, *Modern Germany: Its History and Civilization.*, 2d ed. [New York: Macmillan Co., 1966] pp. 9–10, 44).

FIG. 10
ELISABET NEY (1833–1907)
General Albert Sidney Johnston Memorial,
1904
Marble
89½ × 28½ × 32½ in.
Texas State Cemetery, Austin
Photographer: Phyllis Frede, Austin

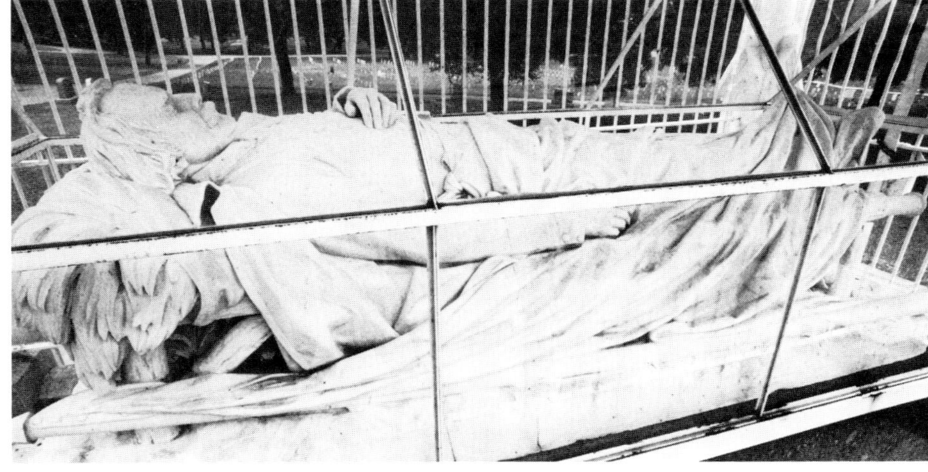

61. *Sonnet on Lady Macbeth* by Edmund Montgomery, Rutland, *Sursum!*, p. 120.

62. Ney blamed the lack of marble on a marble syndicate which had developed a marble monopoly (Ney to Taylor, March 7, 1904, ibid., p. 141).

63. Ibid., pp. 152–153. Ney to Taylor, May 21, 1904, and Ney to Taylor, May 26, 1904 (pp. 155–156); Ney to Taylor, February 7, 1904 (pp. 135–137).

64. It is possible that Cosimo Docchi cut the *Cherub* before his return to Italy.

65. Ney to Dibrell, October 16, 1905 (Rutland, *Sursum!*, p. 169).

66. Widow of William H. Huddle (1847–1892), Texas history and portrait painter who studied at the Academy of Design in New York and was one of the group who withdrew to set up the Art Students League. [W. Huddle painted the *Surrender of Santa Anna* on which Amateis' Galveston bas-relief representing the surrender of Santa Anna following the Battle of San Jacinto is based. (fig. 15)]

67. Marguerite Huddle Slaughter (b. 1892 [or earlier]; d. February 6, 1976). Another work by Huddle is the plaster bust of Baron Justus von Liebig, German chemist, dated ca. 1895, in the collection of the Austin History Center. The work is after Elisabet Ney's 1868 bust of Liebig.

until her next trip to Europe to have the figure cut into marble, thus missing the opportunity to exhibit the marble Macbeth in St. Louis.

As a contingency plan, a duplicate cast of the Macbeth had been sent to St. Louis, but Ney changed her mind and decided against showing the plaster there.[63] Of the two plaster versions of this figure, it is the cast in this exhibition that is believed to be the original from which the marble was cut. *Lady Macbeth* is the only one of Ney's marble works other than the *Cherub* to have been cut in Austin.[64] Ney brought back with her upon her return from Italy, a young Italian marble carver, Cosimo Docchi, to work on the *Lady Macbeth,* though Ney always did much of the finishing work on her marbles. This time was no different, despite her poor health and the fact that she was not strong. Docchi returned to Italy September 4, 1905.[65]

Though Ney made repeated efforts to establish an academy of sculpture in Austin, she did not offer formal classes at Formosa. She did train the assistants she needed, an important requirement for a sculptor whose first major commissions in Texas were awarded when she was in her sixties. Other than her (few) assistants, Ney is known to have had one pupil. The student was Nannie Carver Huddle (b. 1860 Alabama; d. 1951), a woman who had had considerable training as a painter and was the recent widow of a Texas artist.[66] Ney was full of sympathy for the young mother and widow, and the older sculptor offered to teach her to model as a means of helping Huddle through a difficult emotional time. The two became close friends, as well as teacher and pupil. Huddle, who studied in New York at the Art Students League and under William Merritt Chase, and who continued to paint late in life, became interested in sculpture under Ney's encouragement. Some evidence of her work under Ney's tutelage has survived, and the two works by Huddle in the exhibition are among the very few extant examples of work done by a pupil of Ney. The *Stephen F. Austin* bas-relief (Cat. 9) by Huddle was probably done after a work by Ney; the *Marguerite Huddle* bust (Cat. 10) is a portrait of Huddle's daughter.[67]

At Ney's death, Nannie Huddle tried to buy the sculpture *Lady Macbeth*, in an effort to make sure that Ney's memory and legacy were not lost. But another friend of Ney, Mrs. Ella Dancy Dibrell, joined in a competition with Huddle, ultimately succeeding in obtaining control over both the sculpture and Formosa. The results of Dibrell's victory were positive ones, as she was able to arrange for the marble of *Lady Macbeth* to be placed on exhibition at the National Museum of American Art, where it remains today in the Lincoln Gallery, and for Formosa to be held in perpetuity as a museum for Ney's works.[68]

Ney's importance as a Texas sculptor during the decade of the 1890s is indisputable, but her influence over sculpture commissions did not extend, for the most part, past the capital city to the other cities of Texas. This fact can be attributed in part to her disdain for sculpture competitions and her refusal to enter them. In 1895, despite Ney's best efforts to the contrary,[69] sculptors were invited to submit designs for a memorial to the heroes of the Texas Revolution of 1836. Henry Rosenberg's bequest to the city of Galveston had included, in addition to the Rhind drinking fountains, a $50,000 proviso for a memorial tribute to the heroes of 1836. The winning entry selected by the Rosenberg executors was one from a Washington, D.C. sculptor, Louis Amateis (b. 1855 Turin, Italy; d. 1913 Washington, D.C.).[70] By that time Amateis had been an American citizen for seventeen years and was a professor of fine arts as applied to architecture in the Corcoran Scientific School at Columbian University in Washington, D.C.[71] Before coming to this country, Amateis is reported to have studied architecture in the polytechnic school in Turin and sculpture in the Royal Academy of Turin, winning a gold medal there and a silver medal at the National Exposition in Turin in 1880.

After winning the Galveston competition, Amateis opened a studio in Rome where he worked nearly three years on the Texas Heroes monument (Fig. 11). At the request of the United States ambassador to Italy, a committee of Italian sculptors inspected Amateis's work and pronounced the figures worthy.[72] The bronzes were then shipped to Galveston, along with the architectural portion of the monument, which was carved of a light gray granite quarried in Concord, New Hampshire.[73]

When the monument arrived in Galveston, a program for its unveiling was held on San Jacinto Day, April 21, 1900, the sixty-fourth anniversary of the decisive battle in the fight for Texas' independence. The spectacular nature of the day's program reaffirms the overriding function of sculpture in Texas during this period as being one of inspiration and instruction.[74]

The monument matched the day's program in its complexity and grandeur, Amateis having more than met the expectations of the public and the executors of Rosenberg's will. As has been alluded to earlier, a memorial monument's height in Texas (as elsewhere) reflected some measure of its significance. Beckoning the viewer and pointing toward the heavens, the height of such monuments provided symbols that could be linked to moral issues. Amateis' monument, which commemorates the major events in Texas' war for independence, is seventy-four feet high. Crowning the monument is a twenty-two-foot-high figure of Victory (Fig. 12), proudly described at the time as the second-largest bronze statue in America.[75] Victory, whose rose-entwined sword signifies peace, holds a crown of laurels for the heroes of the war and wears the Texas star in her crown (Fig. 13). On the east and west sides of the monument are allegorical figures: Defiance, clad in armor, holds an unsheathed sword, while Peace holds her sword downward and raises the coat of arms of the Republic of Texas. On her head Peace wears the lone star of Texas and a crown of laurels, emblematic of success and victory. Genii (Fig. 14) on the north and the south sides hold medallions bearing the names of Sam Houston and Stephen F. Austin. Additional references to numerous other Texas heroes are inscribed on the subbase. Above those inscriptions are four bas-reliefs depicting the four most important events in the war for independence, one of

68. In ca. 1908 S. H. Holmes, curator of the National Gallery of Art, wrote to Mrs. Dibrell that he saw in the Macbeth, "a superb work, displaying genius of the highest order . . . . I trust that good fortune will so befall us that it may find its final resting place in our Gallery" (Rutland, *Sursum!*, pp. 138–139). Formosa was deeded to the city of Austin in 1941, and in 1972 Formosa became a National Historic Site, a rare extant example of a nineteenth-century American sculptor's studio, and one that has retained its original furnishings.

69. The committee in charge of the competition invited Ney to consult with them in 1896. She would not; rather she wanted them to ditch the competition and award the commission to her. They did not. See Cutrer, *Art of the Woman*, pp. 165–168; and Ney to Miller, dated after 1895 [1897?], Rutland, *Sursum!*, pp. 84–87. Judge Clarence Miller, dean of The University of Texas Law School, was "Ney's friend and legal adviser."

70. The commission for the monument was awarded in November of 1896.

71. Columbian University is now George Washington University. (*George Washington University Handbook* lists Amateis' position during his tenure as professor of fine arts as applied to architecture.) According to the *Galveston Daily News*, April 22, 1900, p. 10 ff., and Allen Johnson, ed., *Dictionary of American Biography*, 1928, pp. 239–240, Amateis' previous American commissions had included portrait busts of distinguished figures (President Chester Arthur, for example). He had also received commissions for architectural sculpture, largely for McKim, Mead & White. For the facade of St. Cecilia's Church in New York, Amateis produced what was described in 1900 as the largest terracotta sculpture in America, a figure of St. Cecilia (in situ today). By that date he had also made several "parlor" sculptures, including a marble statue of Youth, portrayed as a nude girl of fifteen years spinning along on roller skates and holding a garland of flowers. Amateis produced other works for Texas commissions, including a *Seated Portrait of Henry Rosenberg* (1906) for Galveston, as well as another Texas monument in Corsicana, Texas. He was represented at the Louisiana Purchase Exposition in 1904 and the Pan-American Exposition at Buffalo in 1901.

72. *Galveston Daily News*, April 22, 1900, pp. 10 ff.: G. [Giulio?, 1837–1917] Monteverde; E. [Emilio?, b. 1846] Gallori; and G. Ferrari.

73. Ibid. Sculpture arrived on the steamship *Middleham Castle*. The bronzes of Victory, Defiance, and Peace were cast in Rome by Bruno; the two groups of genii and the four bas-reliefs were cast there by Nelli.

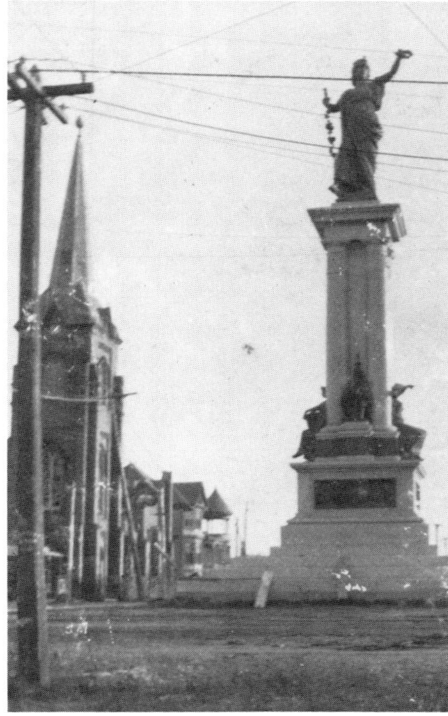

FIG. 11
LOUIS AMATEIS (1855–1913)
***Tribute to the Heroes of the Texas Revolution
of 1836*** *(reversed image showing effects of
hurricane on near-by church)*, *1900*
Bronze and gray granite
74 ft. high
Broadway and Rosenberg avenues, Galveston
*Photograph provided by the Rosenberg Library,
Galveston*

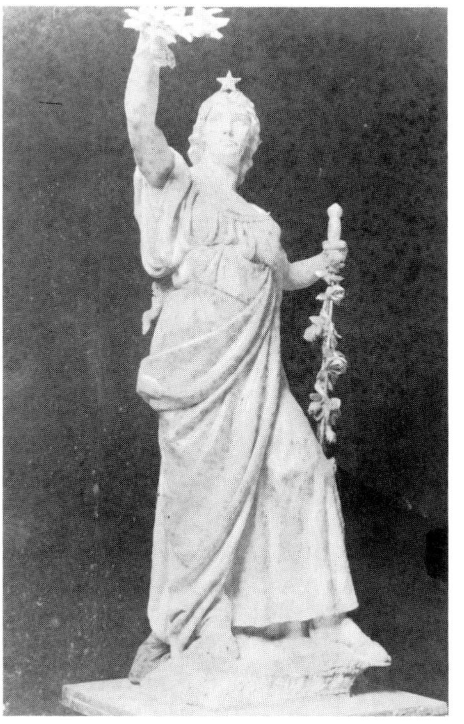

FIG. 12
LOUIS AMATEIS (1855–1913)
***Victory (detail from Tribute to the Heroes of
the Texas Revolution of 1836)***, *ca. 1899*
Plaster
22 ft. high
*Photograph provided by the Rosenberg Library,
Galveston*

74. Ibid. The unveiling ceremony was accompanied by
a flower parade, which seemingly represented all
aspects of Galveston life from pony carts and
bicycle floats to the Knights of the Ancient Essenic
Order and the Italian Mutual-Benevolent Society
to, as the local newspaper described it, "200 Red
Men," dressed in war paint and "in all the
implements of aboriginal warfare," marching
before a float of the Daughters of Pocahontas.
Garlands of flowers and mottos, such as "I am
willing to die for my country," were everywhere.
The celebrities included the governor of the state
and other political officials, along with descendents
of the honored heroes. The sculptor himself was
on the speakers' platform, and amid long speeches
and poems Amateis was introduced in order that
he might take a bow and sit back down, suggesting
the hierarchical position assigned the sculptor.
Organized groups of children sang songs like the
popular adaptation of *Dixie*, "Away Down South
in Texas," to the approximately 10,000 viewers.
For the occasion, Judge M. E. Kleberg's speech
included a paraphrase of the by now familiar
quote: "Thermophylæ had its messenger of defeat
the Alamo had none" (see n. 20; also see Cornelia
Branch Stone, R. Waverly Smith, and Ballinger
Mills, *Monuments of Galveston*, p. 4, Rosenberg
Library Archives). The photograph of the
sculpture (Fig. 12) was taken shortly after the
great hurricane that hit a scant four months
after its dedication, killing six-thousand. The
photograph shows a church that had not been
totally destroyed, but which was tilted. The
monument was undamaged.

75. The largest was reported to be the 37-foot-high
William Penn statue in Philadelphia by Alexander
Milne Calder (b. 1846 Aberdeen, Scotland;
d. 1932), dated ca. 1889, and installed on top of
the Philadelphia City Hall, which was completed
in 1901.

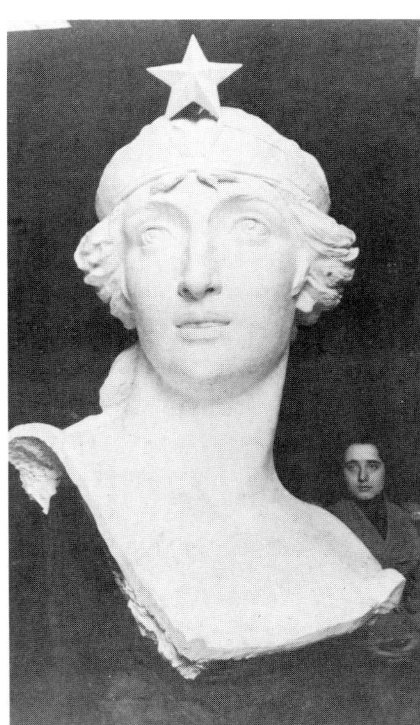

FIG. 13
LOUIS AMATEIS (1855–1913)
***Head of Victory (first version, shown with
model)***, *ca. 1899*
Plaster
*Photograph provided by the Rosenberg Library,
Galveston*

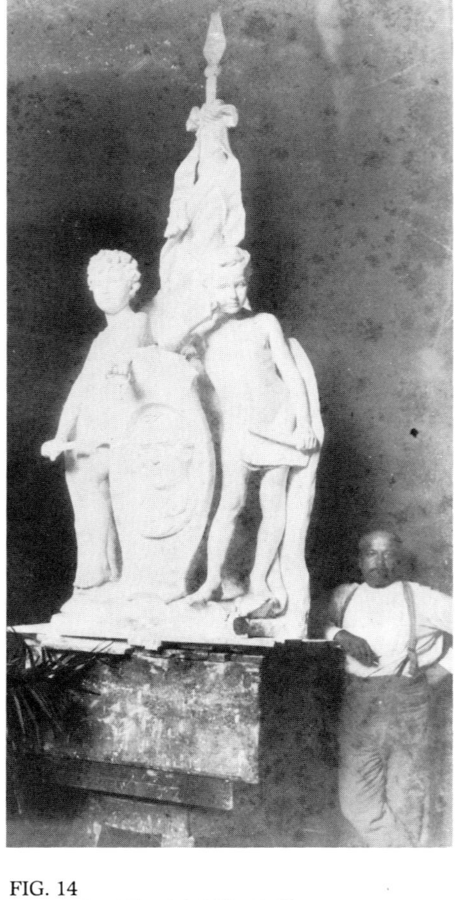

FIG. 14
LOUIS AMATEIS (1855–1913)
Louis Amateis in Rome Studio Standing by Genii (detail from Tribute to the Heroes of the Texas Revolution of 1836), *ca. 1899*
Photograph provided by the Rosenberg Library, Galveston

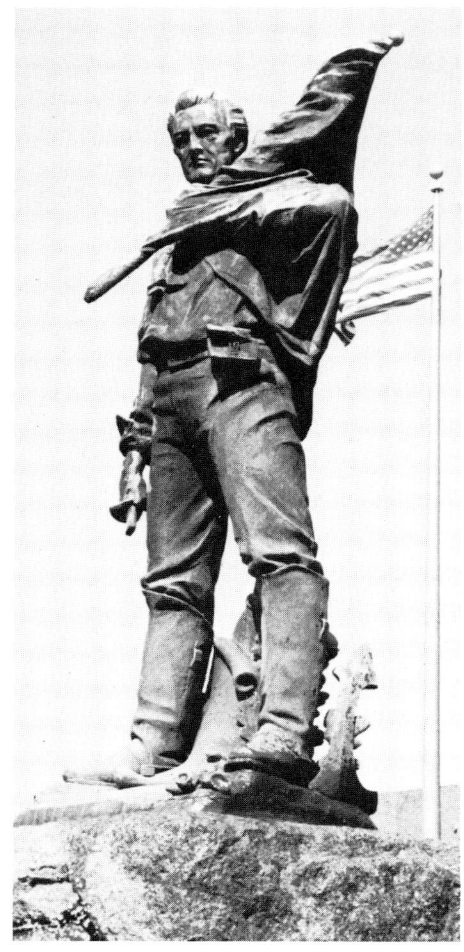

FIG. 16
LOUIS AMATEIS (1855–1913)
Confederate Monument, *1894–1912*
Bronze
Figure, ca. 9 ft. high
County Courthouse, Central Park, Galveston
Photographer: Lise Darst, Galveston

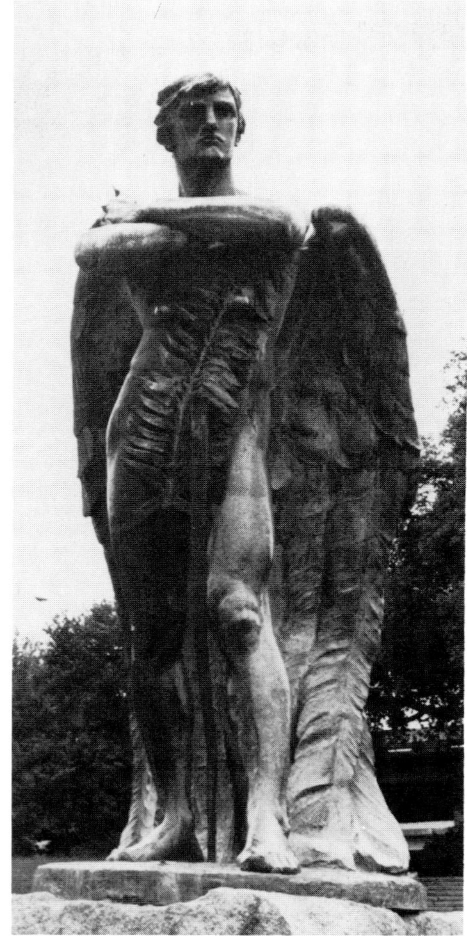

FIG. 17
LOUIS AMATEIS (1855–1913)
The Spirit of the Confederacy Monument, *1907*
Bronze
Over life-size
Sam Houston Park, Houston
Photograph provided by P.H.

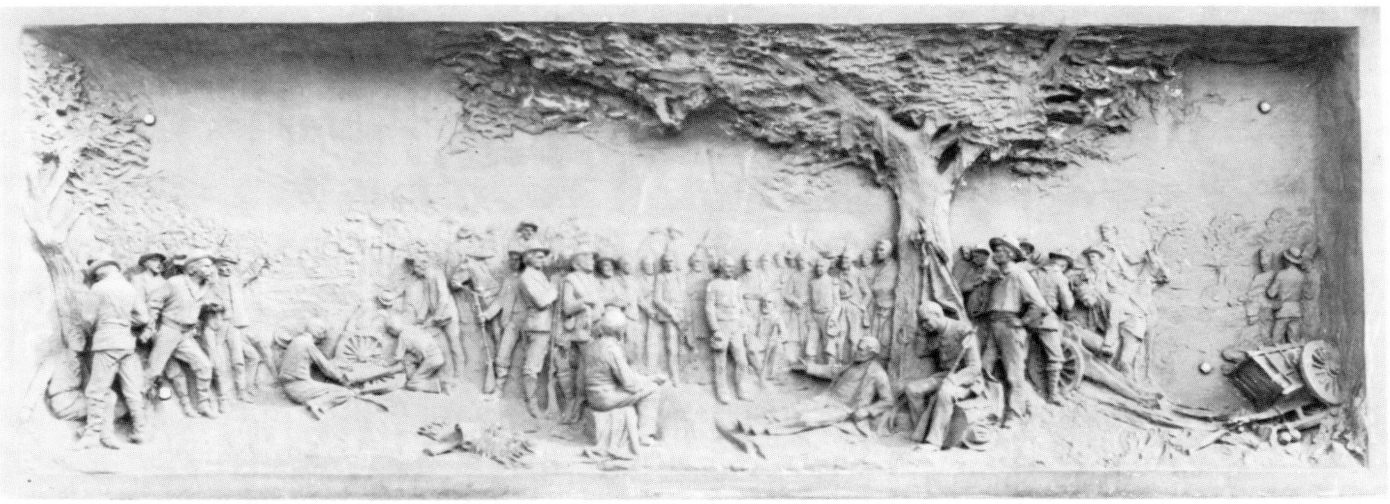

FIG. 15
LOUIS AMATEIS (1855–1913)

Surrender of Santa Anna, The Battle of San Jacinto (detail from Tribute to the Heroes of the Texas Revolution of 1836), *ca. 1899*
Plaster
Photograph provided by the Rosenberg Library, Galveston

76. The battle of San Jacinto was fought at the junction of Buffalo Bayou and the San Jacinto River. (Huddle was the husband of Nannie C. Huddle.) Prints of his paintings may have been available to Amateis (see n. 65).

77. *Galveston Daily News*, April 22, 1900; *Rosenberg*, p. 10 ff; S. J. Wheeler, "Memorials to Heroes," Rosenberg Library Archives.

78. The statue arrived in Galveston in 1911 but was not scheduled for unveiling until June 3, 1912. The interpretation portrays the soldier pressing the flag to his heart, his sword broken and gun dismantled, with his head held high. "Dignified Resignation" is inscribed on the base (*Galveston Daily News*, June 4, 1912).

79. Funded by the United Daughters of the Confederacy, Chapter 186, *The Spirit of the Confederacy* belongs to the City of Houston and is located in Sam Houston Park. The work was signed in Washington, D.C., by L. Amateis and cast in New York by the Roman Bronze Works. On January 20, 1908, it, too, was accompanied by a long dedication attended by close to five-thousand people, but in this case there was also a runaway horse and carriage that ran amok through the crowd breaking bones and injuring six individuals (*Houston Daily Post*, January 20, 1908, p. 4.; *Houston Chronicle and Herald*, January 20, 1908, p. 5).

80. Though representing a romantic ideal, the work may have been inspired by Amateis' first child, born while the sculptor was in Rome working on the Galveston Texas heroes monument. His son, Edmond Romulus Amateis (b. February 7, 1897), became a successful sculptor and past president of the National Sculpture Society, a member of the National Academy of Design and the National Institute of Arts and Letters.

which, representing the surrender of Santa Anna following the Battle of San Jacinto (Fig. 15), is based on the 1886 painting in the state capitol, *The Surrender of Santa Anna*, by William H. Huddle.[76] Finally, inscribed above the four granite columns are the words Patriotism, Honor, Devotion, and Courage, which according to the contemporary press signified for Texans the four qualities of character that produced Texas Independence, words no doubt invoked that afternoon by the speaker, whose topic was "Significance of the Monument to the Youth of Texas."[77]

Shortly after the sculpture competition for the *Tribute to the Heroes of the Texas Revolution of 1836*, Amateis won another sculpture competition in Galveston. In 1899 his design for the *Confederate Monument* was accepted by the Galveston chapter of the United Daughters of the Confederacy. His contest submission for the monument, a hand-colored photograph of his clay maquette, has survived (Cat. 11). Although his was the winning submission, the maquette seen in the photograph differs from the finished sculpture (Fig. 16).[78]

Other works by Amateis in Texas include *The Spirit of the Confederacy Monument* (Fig. 17) located in Sam Houston Park in Houston and dedicated January 20, 1908. With wings folded, the twelve-foot-high Spirit of the antebellum South rests its arms on a down-turned sword, one hand clasping the palm of peace and the other holding laurels earned on the field of battle. The sculpture stands on a naturally composed base of rocks in a small picturesque park, preserved much as it was on the date of dedication.[79]

Amateis left behind in Galveston an undated and unsigned plaster bas-relief which bears the inscription "Mother's Love" (Cat. 12), and which features a mother and her young child. Through the sculptor's tight cropping, an intimate moment between the two figures is sensitively brought into focus for the viewer. The mother's delicately described blouse and hair could easily belong to the dress and hair styles of the earliest part of this century and thus be contemporary with the time the sculptor spent in the Galveston area. It is even possible that these are the portraits of specific individuals, but the idealized and Italianate treatment of the faces of the mother and child suggests they represent instead a romantic ideal.[80]

Also trained in Italy, Enrico Filberto Cerracchio (b. 1880[?] Italy; d. March 20, 1956, New York),[81] who came to

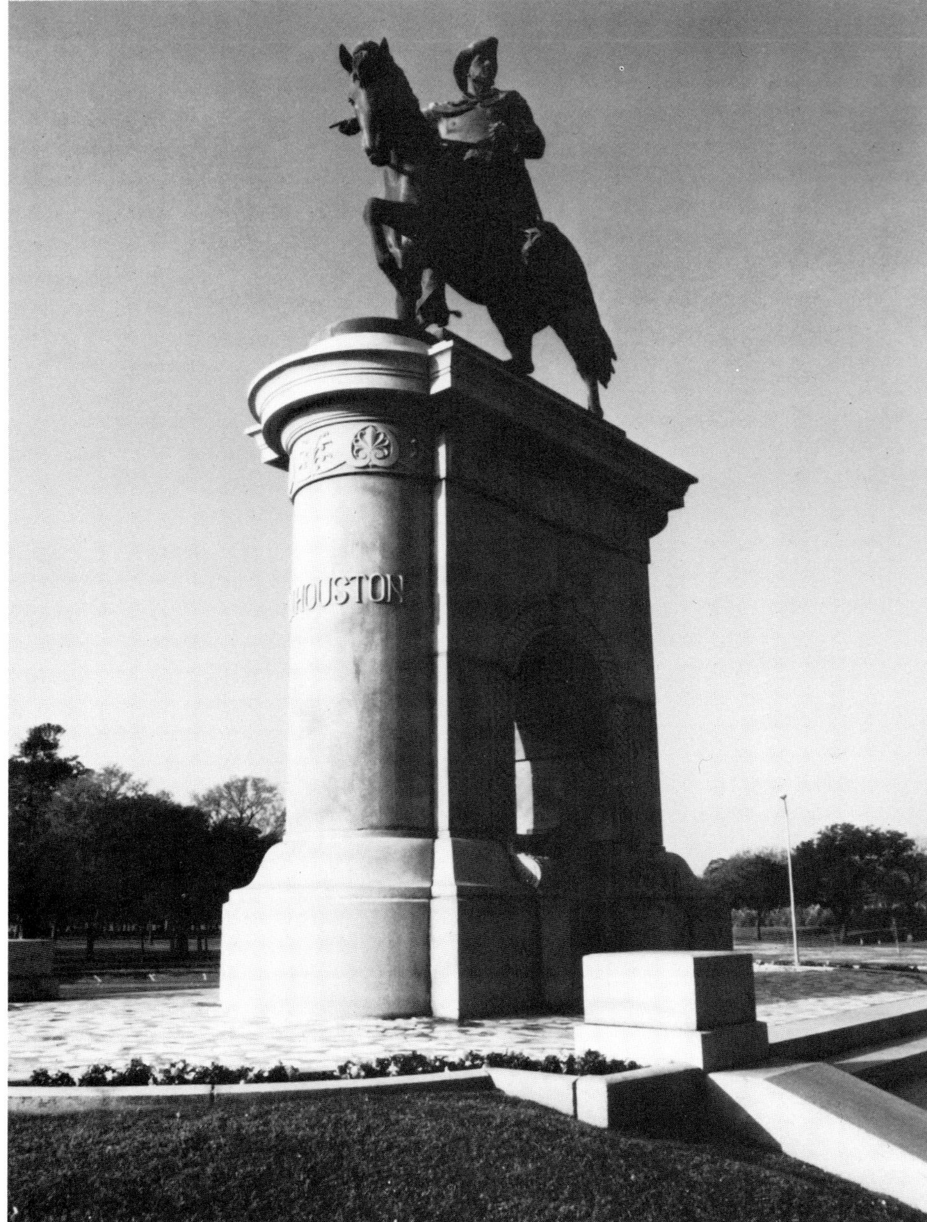

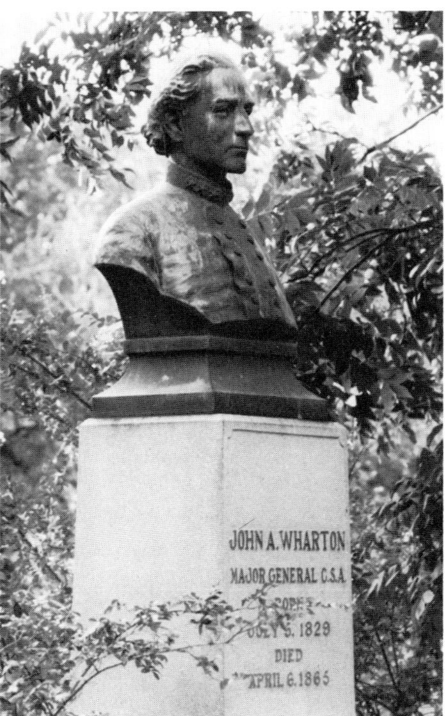

FIG. 18
ENRICO FILBERTO CERRACCHIO
(1880[?]–1956)
Equestrian Statue of General Sam Houston,
1925
Bronze
Heroic size
Hermann Park, Houston
Photograph provided by the Greater Houston
Convention and Visitors Bureau

FIG. 19
ENRICO FILBERTO CERRACCHIO
(1880[?]–1956)
Memorial Bust of John A. Wharton,
Date undetermined
Signed, l.l. above base, "E. Cerracchio, Sc."
Bronze
Over life-size
Texas State Cemetery, Austin
Photographer: Phyllis Frede, Austin

America in 1900, had graduated from the Institute Avellina in Italy, where after receiving a diploma in 1898, he worked under the sculptor Raffaele Belliazzi. Becoming an American citizen in 1905, Cerracchio settled in Houston where he spent forty years, maintaining during the latter part of this period a studio in both Houston and New York. He was identified as living in New York at the time of his death. After World War I, Cerracchio won some fame for two American Doughboy monuments; one executed for the Italian government and one presented to General John Joseph Pershing by the city of Houston. Cerracchio's fine bronze equestrian statue of *General Sam Houston* of 1924 (Fig. 18), is placed at the entrance to Hermann Park in Houston where it rests above a broad expanse of parkland, high on a stonework arch produced by Teich's Monument Works in Llano.[82] (See information on Frank Teich below.)

81. The accuracy of the 1880 birthdate may depend on whether Enrico Filberto Cerracchio is also Benezit's Eugenio-Filiberto Cerracchio, born Castel Vetro Val Eurtore, 1880 (Benezit, 1976). Also see Fielding, *Dictionary of American Painters, Sculptors and Engravers*, p. 141, which lists Enrico Cerracchio as born in 1880.

82. A massive equestrian statue, *General Sam Houston* was unveiled August 12, 1924, despite the fact that the son of the hero sought to prevent the unveiling ceremonies on the grounds that the statue did not resemble his father (Graham, *The WPA Guide to Texas*, pp. 304–305). The figure of Houston points toward the site of the Battle of San Jacinto. The statue was donated in 1925 by The Women's City Club of Houston to commemorate their newly acquired voting rights (City of Houston Arts Inventory, provided by the Department of Parks and Recreation).

83. M. A. Ferguson was elected governor of Texas on November 9, 1924, succeeding her husband, who had been impeached. On that same date Nellie Taloe Ross was elected governor of Wyoming, succeeding her husband who had died. Because Ross was sworn in on January 5, 1925, and Ferguson sworn in on January 20, 1925, Governor Ross became the first woman governor in the United States. For the farmer and against the Ku Klux Klan, Ma Ferguson was called a rural demagogue by her enemies. Some note was taken of her administration outside the state, e.g., see "American Civil Liberties Union Congratulates Governor Ferguson on Her Action." *New York Times*, (August 22) 21:6.

84. Wharton (b. July 5, 1829; d. April 6, 1865) who came to Texas from Tennessee, was a delegate to the Texas Secession Convention in 1861. He joined the Confederate Army as a Captain in Terry's Texas Rangers, and was made a Major General in 1863. See also *Austin Statesman*, October, 20, 1963.

85. According to the artist, he was given private drawing lessons as a child and trained at the art school in Nuremburg, later studying in Dresden under the sculptor Johannes Schilling (b. June 23, 1828; d. March 21, 1910), and also assisting Schilling with the national monument, *The Watch on the Rhine*, erected near Coblenz. Sometime during those studies Teich worked a year under the Franciscan Brothers at Deddelbach on the Main, where he was trained in the design of sacred figures and mausoleums.

86. It bears the names of many firemen who lost their life in the line of duty, with names having been added since its dedication. The first name is that of Eugene T. Deats, who lost his life in a fire at the Blind Institute in Austin in 1877. The present bronze figure of the fireman is a replacement and its inscription reads, "MFD by W. H. Mullins, Salem, Ohio, J. Segesman, Sculptor (Bill Green, State Historian)." The events surrounding the replacement of the first bronze with a second figure are not known.

87. Elisabet Ney had believed the commission for the Confederate monument would be hers. See Ney to Gen. Hardeman, August 3, 1893 (Rutland, *Sursum!*, p. 33). The four military branches of the Confederacy were the Navy, Cavalry, Artillery, and Infantry.

Included in the exhibition is Cerracchio's 1926 marble bust of Governor Miriam A. Ferguson (Cat. 13), a governor known by the public throughout her term of office almost exclusively as "Ma" Ferguson, a sobriquet derived from her initials by the press.[83] One might have assumed that Cerracchio, attracted to the grand image of monumental sculpture, would find the life-size and therefore more intimate portrait less inspiring. One could also argue that the unyielding realism of this bust reflects a minimum of empathy on the artist's part for his subject (a woman in a man's job). In truth, though employing a life-size format, his treatment has lent a monumental quality to the subject, addressing both the honor of the office and the dignity of the sitter, seen in the erectly held head and resolute but attentive countenance. He produced other portrait busts, including those of Albert Einstein, Vice-President John Nance Garner, Houston financier Jesse Jones, and Texas Confederate hero John A. Wharton (Fig. 19). The bust of Wharton was moved to the Texas State Cemetery in 1963.[84]

Active in Texas during this period were many stone cutters and carvers associated with the marble and granite yards in the state, who represented a different kind of training and aesthetic than did sculptors like Amateis and Cerracchio. Among these, Frank Teich (b. September 22, 1856, Lobenstein, Thüeringen, Germany; d. January 27, 1939, Llano, Tex.), who had received his training in Germany,[85] was probably the most successful in obtaining sculpture commissions.

Teich emigrated to the United States in 1878, and in 1879 went to Chicago where he was placed in charge of the stone carving for the Cook County Courthouse. Moving to Texas around 1883, Teich secured employment with the contractor for the new Texas State Capitol building in Austin. While working as superintendent of the granite cutters during the construction of the State Capitol, his skill with stone could be observed, no doubt helping Teich obtain later sculpture contracts throughout the state.

When Teich worked on a sculpture monument the amount of his involvement varied. In some cases Teich's stone company was responsible for the architectural base, probably carved primarily by Teich, while another person would be employed to actually carve the figures from stone or model the figures before they were cast in bronze. The correct sculptor credit for some of the works associated with his name is thus not clear. The 1896 *Firemen's Monument* on the grounds of the state capitol is generally credited to Teich although the wording inscribed on the gray granite base, "built by F. Teich/San Antonio, Texas" (east face, n.e. corner) and "Jaeggli and Martin Contractors, Brenham, Texas" (north face, n.w. corner), does not provide definitive information about the degree of his involvement. The monument is dedicated to the Texas firemen who have died in the line of duty between 1877 and 1932.[86]

In 1899 upon receiving a contract for a Confederate memorial, also to be placed on the capitol grounds, Teich sent an inquiry to the Roman Bronze Works in New York seeking a sculptor who would come to San Antonio and work for him, in order to model a large figure of President Jefferson Davis. In addition to the figure of Davis, the design called for four appendant figures to be carved of granite, representing the four military branches of the Confederacy.[87] Pompeo Coppini, who was employed by the Roman Bronze Works doing wax finishing work at the time, accepted Teich's offer. When the state review committee came to San Antonio to inspect Coppini's clay figure of Davis and the Confederate servicemen of granite, they were impressed enough with Coppini's work to reject as inferior the granite figures that had been carved.

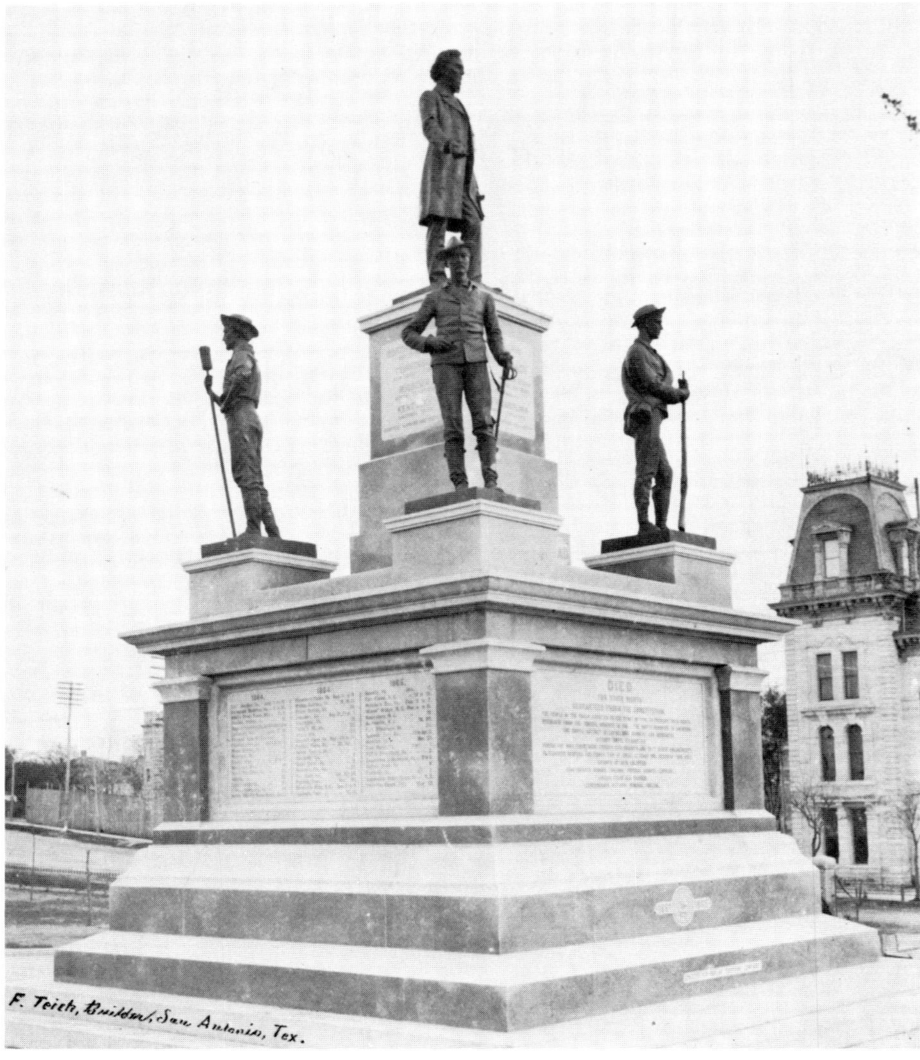

FIG. 20
POMPEO COPPINI (1870–1957)
Confederate Memorial, *1901–1903*
Bronze and granite
Upper figure 7 ft. 9 in. high, other figures 7 ft. high
Texas State Capitol Grounds
Photograph provided by the Texas State Archives

The rejected figures apparently had been carved by Charles Shambauch, Teich's other sculpture assistant. Refusing the stone figures, the committee asked that Coppini model the four Confederate servicemen for the monument (Fig. 20).[88] When the unveiling took place in 1903, the grand program of events was in the tradition of those held in Galveston in 1900 for the Texas Heroes monument of 1836.[89]

Teich became primarily a sculptor of the South. In the manner of other portrait sculptors of the time, when Teich came to Texas he steeped himself in the history of the Civil War in anticipation of possible sculpture commissions.[90] Teich's research left him well prepared to respond when the newly organized Texas branch of the United Daughters of the Confederacy (UDC) began in the late 1890s to support commissions for Confederate monuments. Springing up not unlike the campaniles of the Italian city-states in their reflection of civic pride and their concern with height, Confederate monuments began to dot the state as UDC chapters grew in number from 7 chapters with fewer than 500 members in 1896, to 110 chapters with 5985 members in 1902.[91] The affectionate remembrance by Teich's daughter of her father's "regiment of Texas Confederate soldiers" was a recognition of the success he enjoyed as a sculptor of Confederate monuments.[92] The larger number of his

88. Raines, *Year Book,* 2:81–82; and Pompeo Coppini, *From Dawn to Sunset,* pp. 70, 72–75, 79–84, 89, 91. These accounts differ in certain details such as the use of a model for the Jefferson Davis figure (Coppini tells of using one; the Raines account believes there was no model).

89. Raines, *Year Book,* 2:82–86.

90. Coppini, *Dawn to Sunset,* pp. 86, 90. Interview of Teich by Hazel Oatman Bowman, February 13, 1932, archives of the Llano County Historical Society. Ney also considered the study of Texas history a requisite to her role as sculptor.

91. Raines, *Year Book,* 2:86.

92. Unidentified newspaper article, Llano County Historical Society archives.

93. Coppini. pp. 81.

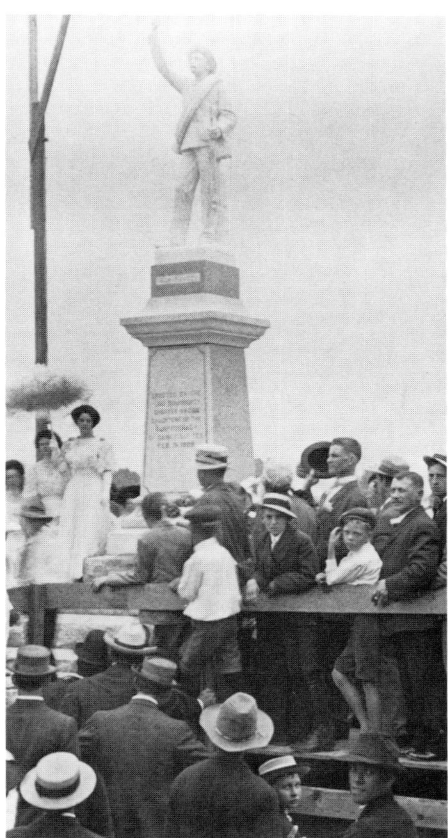

FIG. 21
FRANK TEICH (1856–1939)
***Dedication of Confederate Monument,
Gainesville,*** *1909[?]*
Photograph provided by the Texas State Archives

FIG. 22
FRANK TEICH (1856–1939)
Confederate Monument, *1896–1897*
Marble with granite base
Figures 9 ft. high, 60 ft. high overall
Pioneer Park, Dallas, CD.1896.1
*Photograph by Lee Clockman; photograph provided
by Office of Cultural Affairs, City of Dallas.*

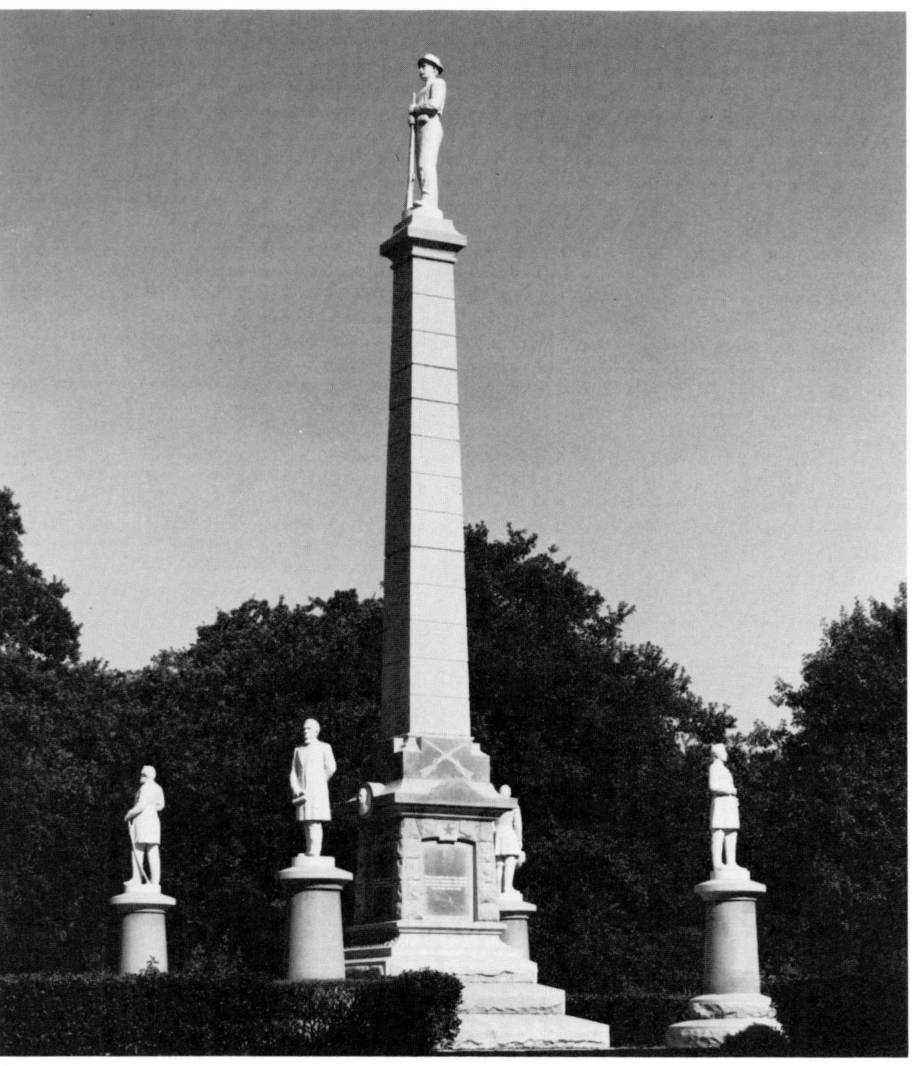

"regiment" are in Texas, but they appear throughout the South. As each Confederate figure was completed (Fig. 21–22), Teich's reputation as a sculptor for the Confederacy was enhanced, giving him preference over competitors seeking sculpture contracts with the UDC, and in 1896 Teich was made an honorary member of the Dallas Chapter of the Daughters of the Confederacy. According to Coppini, Teich and other stone cutters shared with the members of the UDC their belief that the gray granite of his quarries was a better choice than bronze to represent the gray army of the Confederacy.[93]

In the decades before World War I, most commissions for figure sculpture in Texas were designed as memorials to heroes, sanctioned and supported by the state or an organization such as the UDC, the Daughters of the Republic of Texas, or the State Firemen's Association of Texas. There were isolated exceptions. One of the earliest is Teich's full-length portrait figure of the colorful Abel Head (Shanghai) Pierce located near Blessing, Texas. Pierce is credited with the following statement, "I was a private in the Confederate army. I want you to build me a statue higher than that of any general . . . . But I won't pay you a damned cent unless it is a fair likeness." The statue in gray marble stands on a ten-foot-high base in the Deming's Bridge Cemetery (now Hawley Cemetery) near Blessing, where Pierce ranched with his

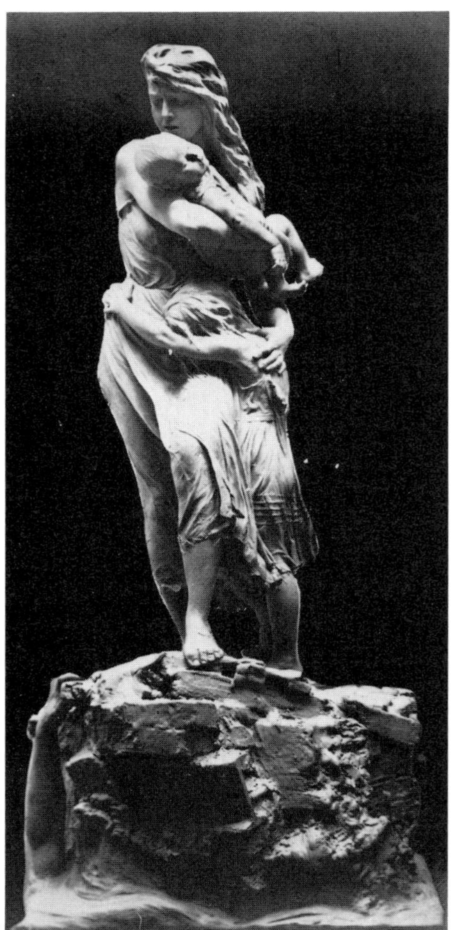

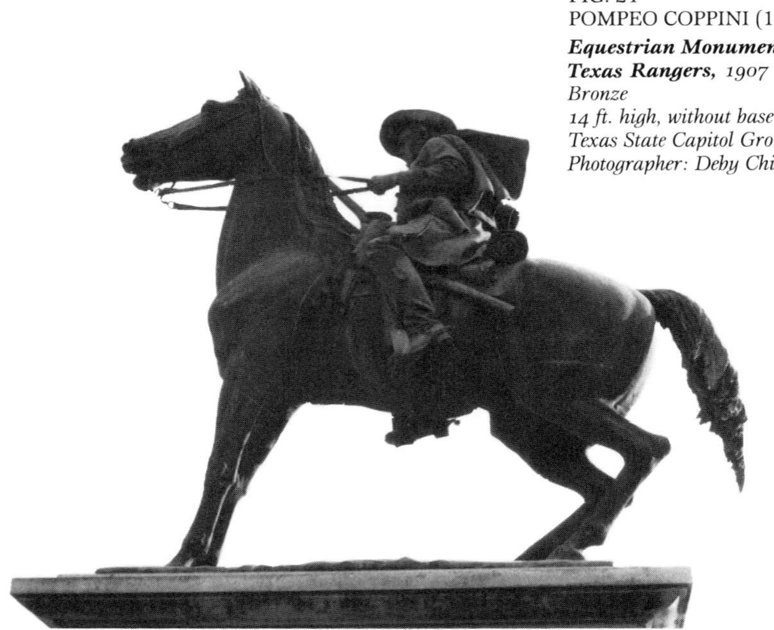

FIG. 24
POMPEO COPPINI (1870–1957)
***Equestrian Monument to Terry's
Texas Rangers,*** *1907*
Bronze
14 ft. high, without base
Texas State Capitol Grounds
Photographer: Deby Childress, Austin

FIG. 23
POMPEO COPPINI (1870–1957)
Victims of the Galveston Flood, *1904*
Plaster
ca. 9 ft. high
Location unknown
*Photograph provided by the Coppini-Tauch Studio,
San Antonio*

brother Jonathan in the 1880s on a million acres near Matagorda Bay. The statue of Pierce was completed and accepted in 1895.[94] Teich executed many other works, although care must be taken in identifying them as some misattributions have been found, no doubt due to confusion over the extent of his participation in the execution of certain monuments.

Pompeo Coppini (b. May 19, 1870, Moglia, Italy; d. 1957, San Antonio), the sculptor who had moved to San Antonio to work for Frank Teich, came to the United States in 1896, after having studied sculpture at the Academy of Fine Arts in Florence, the city of his youth.[95] When Coppini came to Texas in 1901 to work on the Confederate monument for the grounds of the state capitol, he was ignoring warnings he had received regarding the wild lawlessness[96] of San Antonio. Coppini found, however, that San Antonio reminded him of Italy and after the Teich commission was completed, Coppini opened his own studio in the city.

The year before his arrival in San Antonio, Coppini participated in a New York benefit held in September of 1900 in response to the devastation of the Galveston hurricane.[97] For that event Coppini modelled a small group representing the victims of the Galveston flood. A little over three years later, Coppini redid that work in his San Antonio studio, resulting in a changed composition from the original New York sketch. In preparation for exhibition at the St. Louis World's Fair in 1904, Coppini cast the new full-size version of the *Victims of the Galveston Flood* (Fig. 23) in plaster. The shipment

94. Llano County Historical Archives; phone conversation with the Blessing United States Post Office, Spring, 1989; Walter Prescott Webb, ed. *The Handbook of Texas*, 2:376. Blessing was originally named "Thank God, Texas."

95. On his own initiative, while growing up in Florence, Coppini read about the Florentian sculptors of the Renaissance: Michelangelo, Donatello, Della Robbia, Benvenuto Cellini, Gian Bologna (Coppini's spelling) and others (Coppini, p. 10). He also became involved in Free Masonry, which no doubt influenced his way of thinking for the rest of his life (ibid., p. 35 and passim).

96. Ibid., p. 70. For his account of his first observations regarding the San Antonio of the time, see pp. 75–78.

97. In New York Coppini's small sculpture group representing the victims of the Galveston flood was auctioned for five hundred dollars in the ballroom of the Waldorf-Astoria (ibid., p. 58). The hurricane struck the city of Galveston on September 8–9, 1900.

98. Ibid., pp. 99–100, 103–104. In 1914 the 1904 *Victims of the Galveston Flood* was given to the University of Texas in Austin, along with other works. By 1935 the location of *Victims* was not known (ibid., pp. 209–211).

99. Ibid., pp. 120–122,124–127,130–131. Coppini explained that for the Terry's Texas Rangers monument, he was $3000 short having enough to give the bronze contract to the Roman Bronze Works, as he would have preferred, because the contract for the monument specified the die be in one piece. The county would not permit such a huge block to be hauled over the Colorado River bridge, making it necessary to roll it over the riverbed wrapped with logs and chains, in order to get it to the capitol grounds, for it weighed over 22,000 pounds.

100. Troutman's white silk flag had a single blue star centered on an open field, and was inscribed "Liberty or Death" (Webb, 2:804).

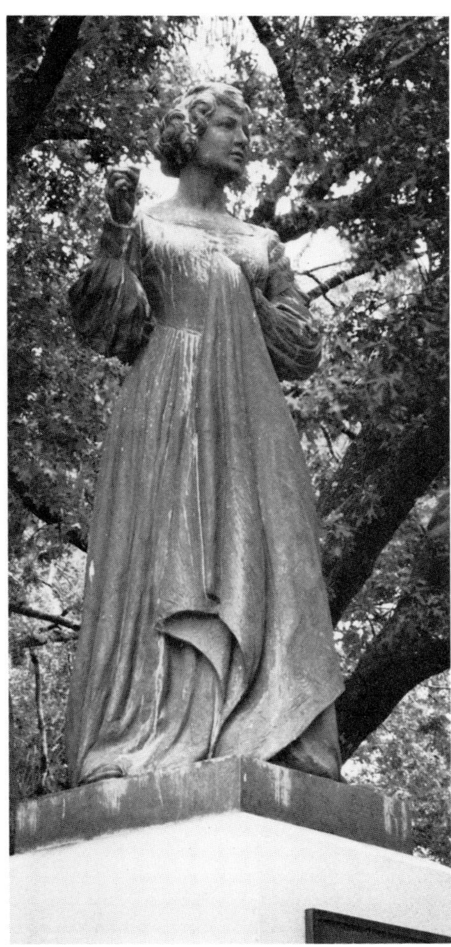

FIG. 25
POMPEO COPPINI (1870–1957)
Joanna Troutman Memorial, *1914–1915*
Bronze
Life-size
Texas State Cemetery, Austin
Photographer: Phyllis Frede, Austin

FIG. 26
POMPEO COPPINI (1870–1957)
Littlefield Fountain, *completed 1928*
Bronze
Heroic size
21st and Whitis Streets, The University of Texas at Austin
Photographer: Deby Childress, Austin

101. Coppini, *Dawn to Sunset*, pp. 250–251.

102. Admiral George Dewey's Arch of Triumph, erected at the southwest end between 23rd and 24th Streets where Fifth Avenue meets Broadway. The arch, erected in 1899, in honor of the admiral's visit to New York, was not permanent and was eventually torn down. Coppini was working as an assistant to Karl Bitter (b. 1867 Vienna, Austria; d. 1915 New York), making enlargements in plaster under Bitter for the Arch. Coppini learned direct carving on plaster techniques and a direct-on-plaster enlarging scheme using stilt-like pantographs, from Bitter (ibid., p. 61). Bitter had been assigned the "Combat" group. Thomas Craven, *Sculpture in America*, p. 469.

did not reach the Fine Arts Building in St. Louis by the designated cut-off date of March 15. As a result, *Victims of the Galveston Flood* was exhibited instead in the Texas State Building at the Fair, over which Coppini retained some resentment.[98]

Following his initial success in Texas with the Confederate monument (Fig. 20) at the state capitol, Coppini received a number of commissions across the state for other Confederate monuments. He also won the competition for another Confederate memorial to be erected on the grounds of the capitol. The commission was for the 1907 equestrian monument to Terry's Texas Rangers, heroes of the Eighth Texas Cavalry (Fig. 24).[99]

With Texas Governor Oscar B. Colquitt in office Coppini gained a patron, and in 1914 Colquitt asked Coppini to model the figure of Joanna Troutman (b. 1818 Georgia; d. 1880 Georgia) (Fig. 25). In that year the governor had Troutman's remains disinterred from her grave in Georgia and placed in the Texas State Cemetery. Although other flags had been designed during the Texas rebellion, Troutman was credited with having designed the first Texas flag, and it was her flag that flew over the battle at Goliad.[100] Coppini's figure of the eighteen-year-old Troutman, flag and needle in hand, stands today above her grave.

In 1919 Coppini was contacted by Major George W. Littlefield of Austin, an Austin philanthropist, regarding a commission for a large architectural monument to be located at the University of Texas in Austin.[101] Having had the experience of working on the Dewey Arch in New York,[102] Coppini was firmly opposed to the arch that Littlefield proposed, because he was convinced the large and elaborate arch would cost twice the amount Littlefield was willing to commit and because he felt the architectural problems it posed were great. Coppini's alternate proposal of a fountain was eventually made agreeable to Littlefield. The sculptor's fountain plan, which called for an allegorical fountain group, plus six full-length figures and flanking pylons, was itself altered, much to Coppini's displeasure. So that the fountain might better complement the main building and the vista between, the pylons and their statuary were eliminated at the recommendation of the University architect, Herbert M. Greene. The eliminated portrait statues were integrated into the landscaping program developed by Paul Cret, who had been employed as architect by the University after discussions of the project had already begun. Seen today (Fig. 26), the fountain shares with Cret's completed architectural program a complementary function, and despite Coppini's wish to sue the university

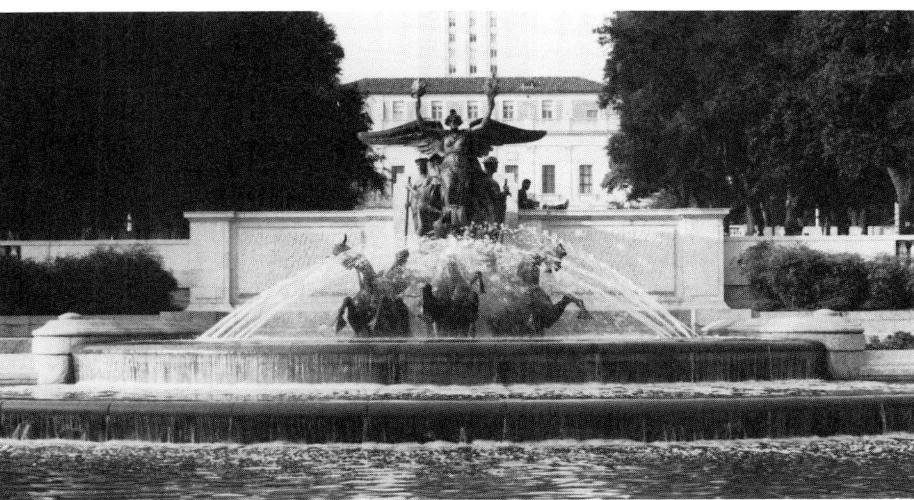

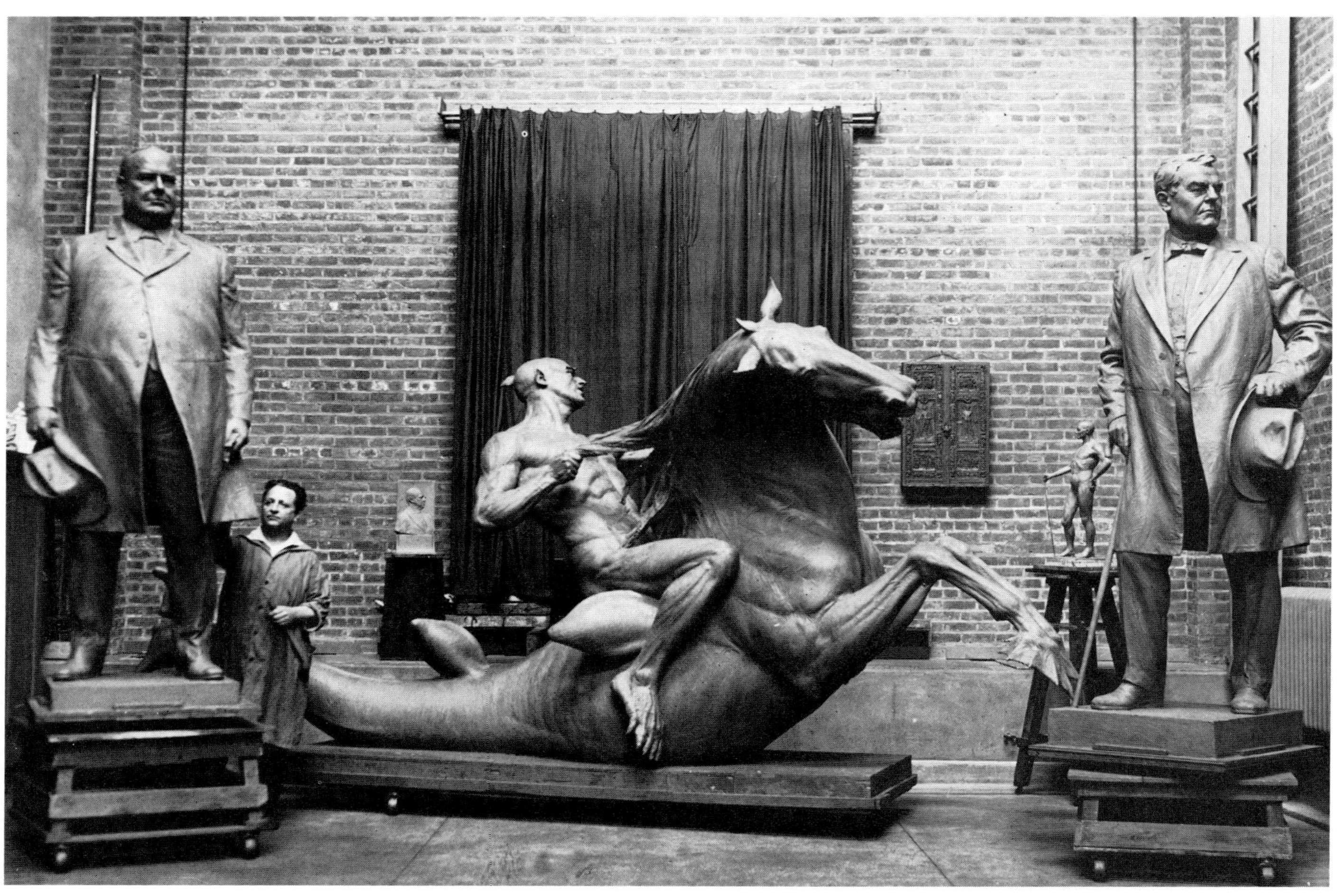

FIG. 27
POMPEO COPPINI (1870–1957)
Coppini in New York Studio with Sea Horse and Figures Associated with Littlefield Memorial Entrance Gate Project, *ca. 1926*
Photograph provided by the Coppini-Tauch Studio, San Antonio

over the results, in retrospect the existing fountain is probably a better solution than would have been Coppini's planned incorporation of the [static] pylons.[103]

In 1919 after having moved his sculpture studio to Chicago three years earlier for financial reasons, Coppini moved his studio again, this time to New York because of the cost of shipping the Littlefield Fountain models from Chicago to the Roman Bronze Works Foundry in Brooklyn. Two factors caused him to change his sculpture technique while working on the fountain. The first of these occurred earlier when the clay froze and cracked on two in-progress commissions in his studio. He vowed never again to rely on clay and to instead use plastelene, a non-hardening clay imported from Italy. The second factor was that Coppini did not like to use enlarging machines, even for the oversized Littlefield Fountain figures (Fig. 27). As a result, Coppini and his frequent assistant, Waldine Tauch, modeled directly the final full-size figures for the Littlefield Fountain. Since the cost of clay was $25 per ton and Italian plastelene $700 per ton, Coppini, in order to save money, built an armature that closely approximated the final sculptured form. This enabled the sculptor to coat his armature with a thinner layer of plastelene, thus cutting his cost for the large figures.[104]

On April 29, 1933, the Littlefield Fountain was dedicated to the honor of the men who had died in France during the First World War. Led by three sea horses (Fig. 28) symbolizing the sea power of the United States, the figure of Columbia (Fig. 29) brings for the first time her

103. Coppini, *Dawn to Sunset*, p. 250 and passim.

104. "Plastelene" is spelled differently in each artist's account. The spelling here is taken from Ralph Mayer's *The Artist's Handbook*, p. 604. Mayer comments that the original Italian plastelene was said to be composed of tallow, sulphur, and a special clay. Coppini, *Dawn to Sunset*, pp. 284–285.

FIG. 28
POMPEO COPPINI (1870–1957)
Sea Horses, (detail, Littlefield Fountain),
1920s
Bronze
21st and Whitis streets, The University of Texas at Austin
Photographer: Deby Childress, Austin

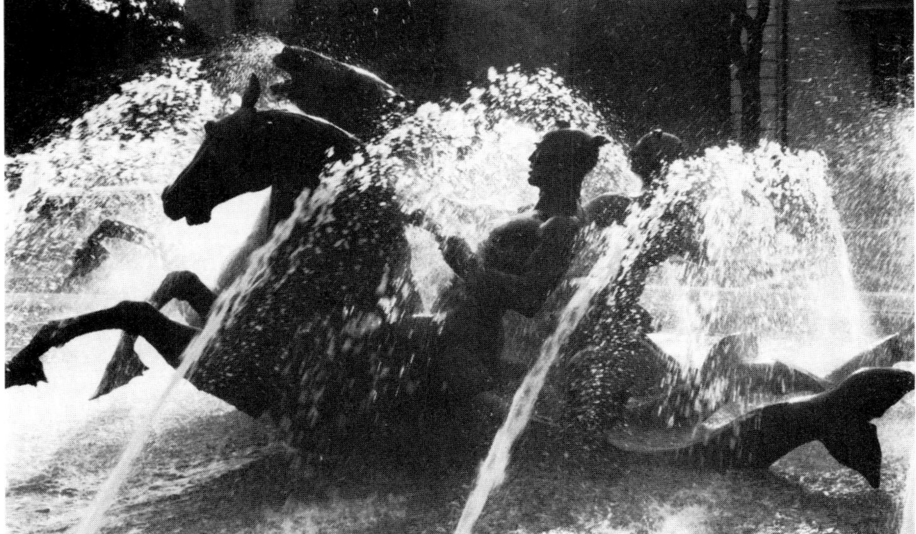

FIG. 29
POMPEO COPPINI (1870–1957)
Columbia Flanked by Her Army (detail, Littlefield Fountain), *1920s*
Bronze
21st and Whitis streets, The University of Texas at Austin
Photographer: Deby Childress, Austin

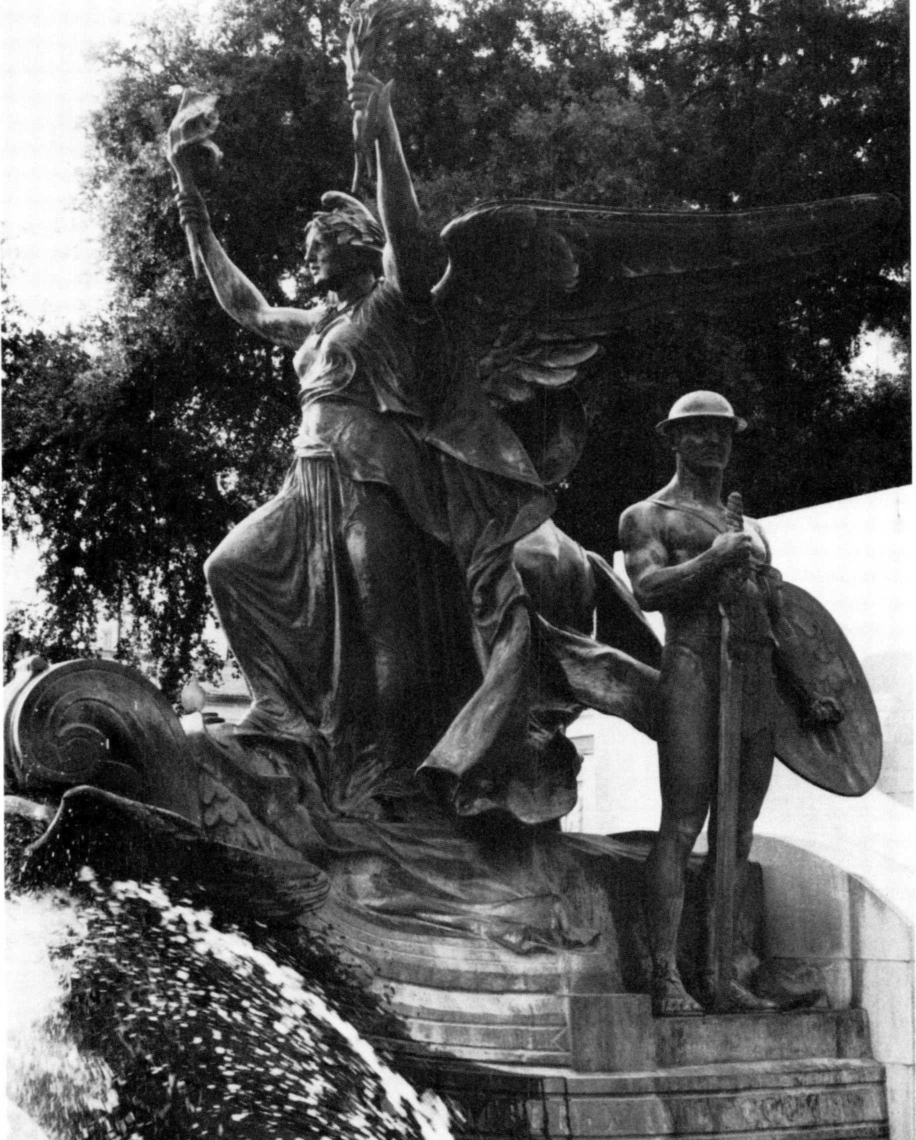

Army and Navy across the sea in defense of world democracy. Though the center sea horse portrays the wild force of Mob Hysteria, Hysteria is kept in check by the disciplined manpower of the Navy and the Army.[105]

Coppini's strongly stated belief was that "art must build character" and "unless art is inspired by religion, history, or patriotism, . . . leading to the progress and advancement of civilization, . . . it is without an uplifting mission . . . and is not really fine art but simple commercial decoration." When these aims are not met, it "is caused by criminal indifference and a greedy passion for money." In spite of his beliefs, during the depression years of 1931–1935, Coppini tried his luck at "commercializing," as he called it, producing small bronze works. While these works were offered by galleries, they did not sell well, with the exception of a small horse called *Freedom*. During this period, Coppini also did some work for the Gorham Company, including *The First Catch* (Cat. 14 and Fig. 30).[106] From the first of his stay in New York, Coppini veered from his philosophical guidelines and created such works as *Love Awakening* (Cat. 15) with its Bouguereau-like subject.[107]

Coppini, as had Ney, long entertained visions of the establishment of an art school, first in San Antonio and later openly proposing that he be made head of a fine arts department at the University of Texas. Finally, during the war years, in 1943, with an honorary doctorate from Baylor University Coppini was appointed head of the art department at Trinity University in San Antonio, a post he held for two years.

During her childhood Waldine Amanda Tauch (b. January 28, 1892, Schulenburg, Tex.; d. 1986 San Antonio), Coppini's long-time assistant and colleague, had formed three-dimensional images using household materials. Noticing Tauch's talent, the Brady Tuesday Club, of Brady, Texas, offered to raise funds for Tauch's art education and contacted Coppini in San Antonio to ask if he would accept Tauch as a pupil. Coppini agreed and Tauch arrived in San Antonio on June 10, 1910, becoming so much a part of the household that when she reached adulthood Coppini tried to obtain permission from her family to adopt her, although he was unsuccessful. Coppini became quite dependent upon Tauch as his sculpture assistant and she helped him produce a number of his works, although she also produced memorial commissions of her own. Tauch was working in her own studio in San Antonio, when Coppini arrived in New York to work on the Littlefield Fountain commission, but in the summer of 1923 Coppini called to ask Tauch to nurse Mrs. Coppini, who had fallen. Once in New York she was enlisted to work with Coppini on the Littlefield Fountain.

In New York, Tauch began to produce small genre figures, which she sold to the Gorham Company. It may be that this marketplace was the catalyst that led her to further explore a more personal vision than that associated with the very sober and highly realistic monuments so basic to the oeuvres of Coppini and Tauch. For these smaller figures, as with most of her sculpture, she employed models, using both amateurs and professionals. Among her works were *The Boy and the Eel*, cast in bronze by the Gorham Company in 1924, and the whimsical young nude balancing on her surfboard (Cat. 16). Though the figure is innocent of the true body movement of a surfer and self-conscious in its pose, there is a sculptural strength in the compact solidity of Tauch's smoothly modeled surfer. The symbolic and ideal *Gulf Breeze* (Cat. 17) of 1929 recalls through its subject the allegorical references found in Clyde Chandler's fountain of 1916, which is discussed later; although Tauch's *Gulf Breeze* with its swirling hair is far more romantized than is Chandler's sedate and generally more classical representation of ideal beauty.

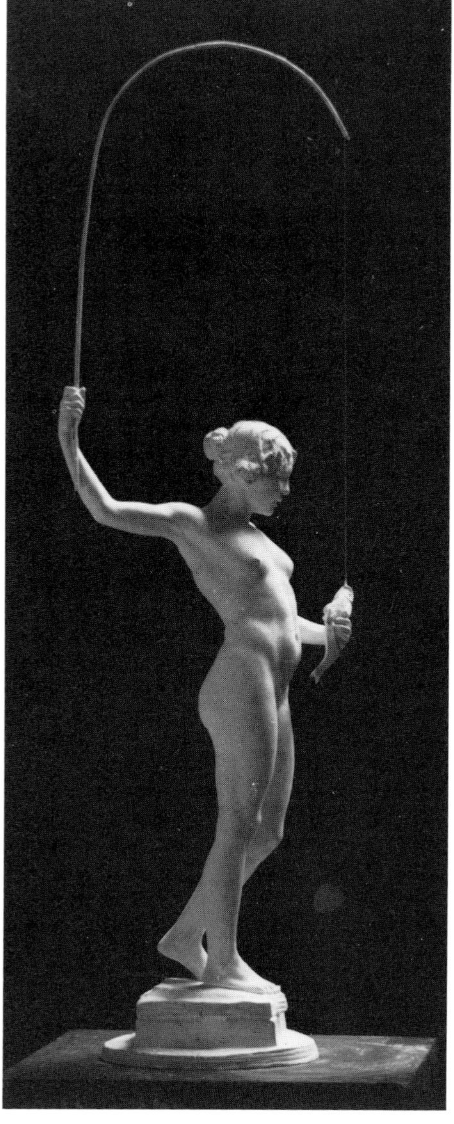

FIG. 30
POMPEO COPPINI (1870–1957)
The First Catch, ca. 1933
Plaster
32 in. high
Coppini-Tauch Studio, San Antonio
Photograph provided by Coppini-Tauch Studio,
San Antonio

105. Ibid., pp. 314–315, 344.

106. Ibid., pp. 322–323. The right arm of the plaster version of *The First Catch* was broken at the time the bronze cast was made. This accounts for the difference in the gesture of the right arm between the plaster and bronze versions.

107. The skillful French academy painter William-Adolphe Bouguereau (1825–1905) is remembered for romantic subjects manifesting a combination of coquettish innocence and desire.

FIG. 31
WALDINE TAUCH (1892–1986)
Clinging to Youth, 1945
Magnesite
24 in. high
Collection of the Coppini-Tauch Studio,
San Antonio
Photograph provided by Coppini-Tauch Studio,
San Antonio

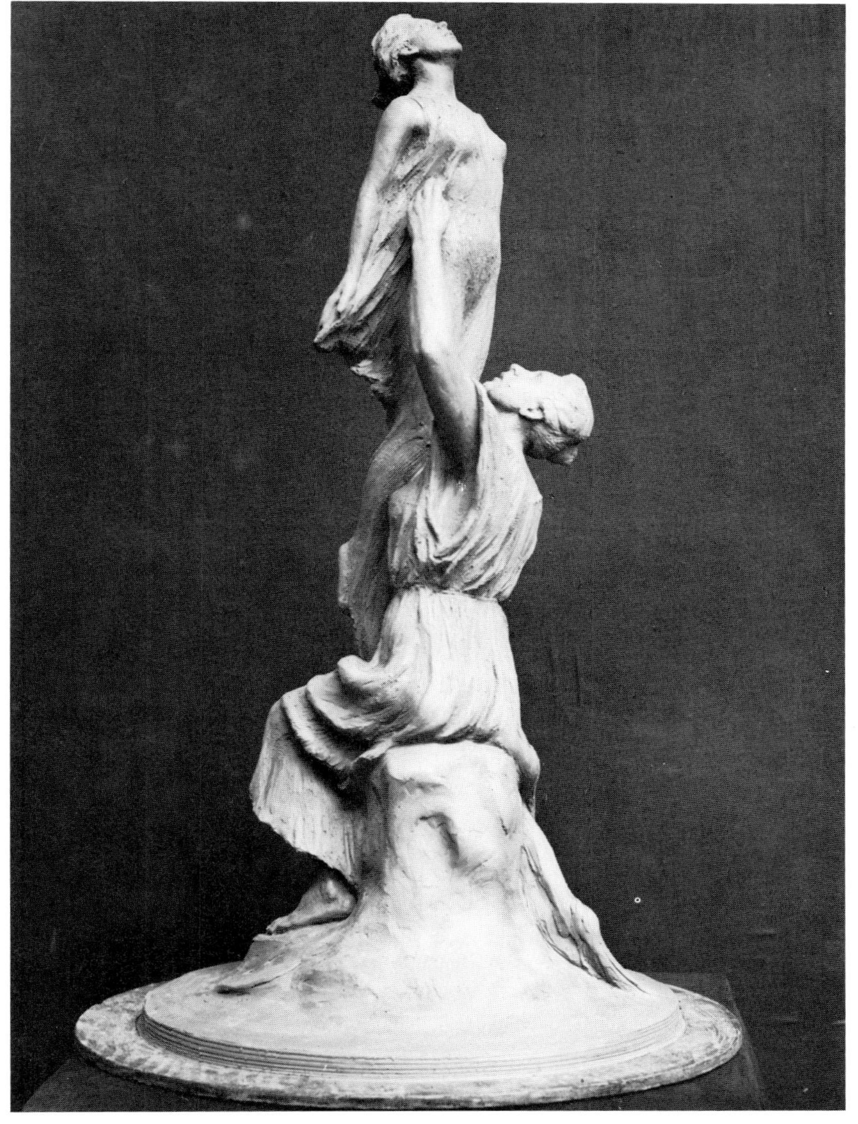

108. Bessie Potter Onahotema Vonnoh (b. August 7,
 1872, St. Louis, Mo.; d. March 8, 1955); Loie Fuller
 (1862–1928), American dancer who developed a
 serpentine dance for which she was known in
 Paris.

109. e.g.; Raoul Larche, French (1860–1912): *Loie
 Fuller*, ca. 1900; *Loie Fuller Dancing*, ca. 1900;
 Agathon Leonard, French, (1841–1923): *The
 Swirling Scarf*, 1900. The Art Nouveau style was
 one of the attractions at the Paris Exhibition
 of 1900.

In 1945 Tauch modeled *Clinging to
Youth* (Fig. 31), a sculptural expression far removed from the detailed and often
imposing realism of the monuments which she and Coppini had often produced.
The statuette brings to mind in its pictorial aspect the work of the American
sculptor Bessie Potter Vonnoh, and recalls somewhat in the directional fluidity
of its draperies and the [if somewhat rigid] lift of its gesture the Loie Fuller,[108] or
fin de siècle, decorative figures of the art nouveau period.[109] The slightly smaller
than life-size *After the Bath* (Cat. 18) of 1946 captures the quintessential private
moment, recalling in its conception and style the work of earlier American sculptors. Tauch continued to produce memorial sculpture and in her seventies completed two heroic figures, one of General Douglas MacArthur (dedicated in
1969). The eclectic character of her oeuvre and of Coppini's before her is a result
of the conflicts between the preset parameters of style and content assigned the
didactic public monument, on the one hand, and the sculptor's own natural in-
clinations, on the other hand.

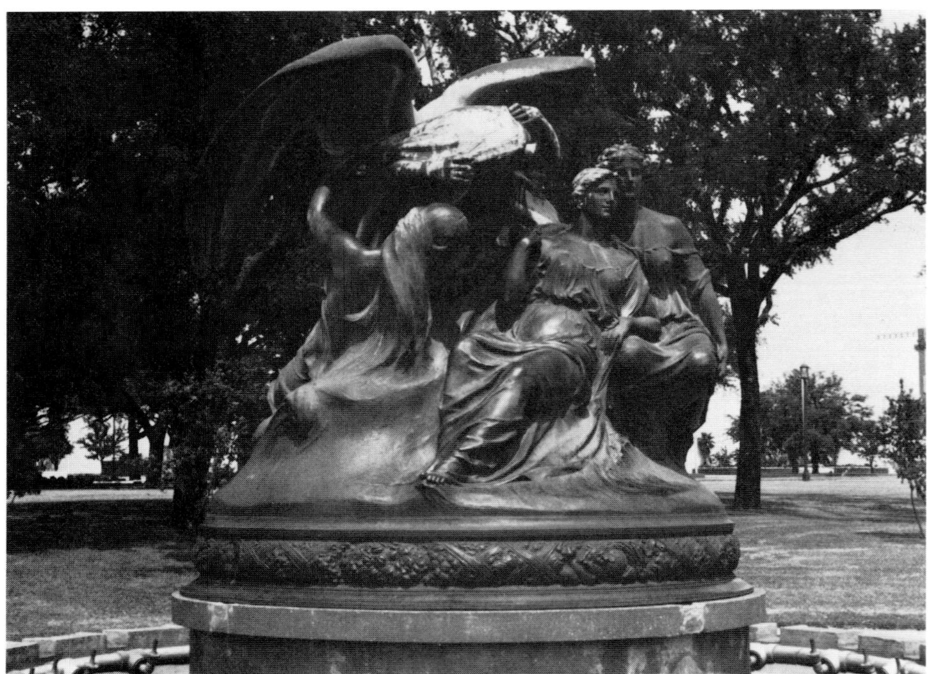

FIG. 32
CLYDE GILTNER CHANDLER (b. 1879)
The Gulf Cloud (Captain Sydney Smith Memorial Fountain), *1916*
Bronze with granite fountain basin
Sculpture: 13½ ft. high × 10 ft. diameter; basin:
36 in. high × 30 ft. diameter
Fair Park, Dallas
City of Dallas, CD.1916.1
Photograph provided by P.H.

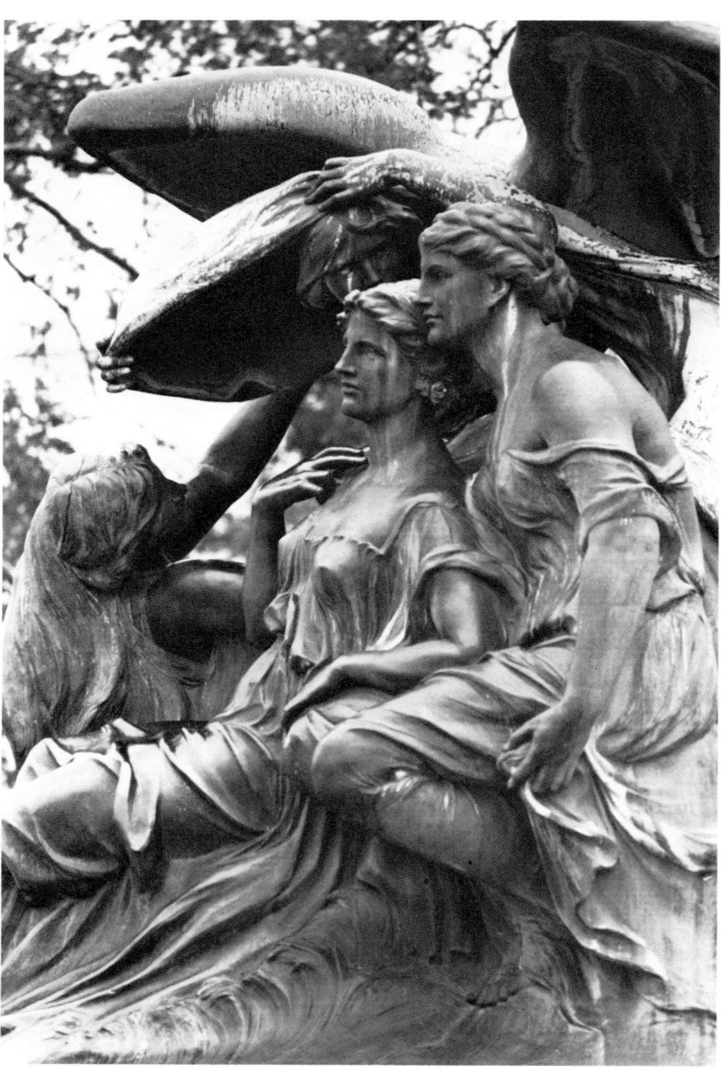

FIG. 33
CYLDE GILTNER CHANDLER (b. 1879)
The Gulf Cloud: detail (Captain Sydney Smith Memorial Fountain), *1916*
Bronze with granite fountain basin
Sculpture: 13½ ft. high × 10 ft. diameter; basin:
36 in. high × 30 ft. diameter
Fair Park, Dallas
City of Dallas, CD.1916.1
Photograph provided by the Dallas Historical Society

In 1941 Tauch was granted an Honorary Doctorate of Fine Arts degree by Howard Payne College in Brownwood, Texas, only a few months after Coppini received the same degree from Baylor University in Waco, enabling her once again to assist Coppini, this time as his faculty member at Trinity University in San Antonio. In 1945, when Coppini and Tauch resigned from Trinity, they founded the Academy of Fine Arts in San Antonio, later named the Coppini Academy of Fine Arts. Today the Coppini-Tauch Studio in San Antonio serves as a museum for their works.

As the twentieth century had moved forward, figurative sculpture in Texas had continued to be presented in a naturalistic manner. Nineteenth-century heroes, though, were invoked less often as martial memories faded and the didactic and philosophical meanings of sculpture were given less emphasis. New sculpture themes appeared which were associated with a kind of ideal innocence; often expressing the embodiment of youth or a pride of place not self-conscious enough to be termed chauvinistic, but which found pleasure in the uniqueness of the state's lands and people.

The first major bronze sculpture commission in Dallas, *The Gulf Cloud (Captain Sydney Smith Memorial Fountain)* (Fig. 32–33), was awarded to Clyde Giltner Chandler, (b. June 18, 1879, Evansville, Indiana; d. after 1930[?]).[110] Although the work is named for the first secretary and manager-general of the State Fair of Texas, the allegorical subject matter of Chandler's fountain does not relate to the honoree but rather offers a poetic tribute to the special physical characteristics of the state. Unveiled at the opening of the Texas State Fair in 1916, it is a massive composition with a granite basin and bronze figures. At its unveiling Chandler explained the allegorical meaning behind the work, later identifying as her inspiration for the fountain's composition the lines "From my wings are shaken the dews that waken / The sweet buds everyone," by the nineteenth-century English poet Percy Blysshe Shelley (1792–1822).[111] The four figures, a mother and her three daughters, symbolize the beneficial interaction among four of Texas' natural attributes. The first sister typifies the prairies of Texas, another the mountains, and the third sister is Gulf Cloud. Their mother, the Gulf, reclines at the feet of her daughters, the fluid lines of her drapery and figure expressing the rhythmic movement of the ocean's waves.

The taller figure of Mountain is clothed in drapery representing the mists and clouds, which from time to time encircle her form. Prairie is identified by the jasmine flowers in her hair and the few flowers and grains growing at her feet. The winged figure of Gulf Cloud momentarily hovers above the others before fulfilling her mission, providing the lands with rain.[112] From the basin below a fine spray is sent above the figures, cloaking the sculpture in a mist, which as it clings to the wings of Gulf Cloud, gently falls on the figures below. On the ornamental band around the base of the sculpture is a garland representing flora produced in Texas. Bolls of cotton anchor the overlapping ribbons.

Working on the project in her Chicago studio, she began by making two models in clay. The first, one foot high, was executed without detail, indicating mass and line. The second, three feet high, was an exact counterpart of the completed fountain, accurate in its detail. In addition to the maquettes mentioned above, the Dallas Museum of Art has in its collection a highly detailed plaster cast slightly over one foot high.[113]

Chandler's family settled in Dallas while she was still a baby, and her early art study was there with the Texas painter Robert Onderdonk. Later Chandler became a student at the Massachu-

---

110. Her last known address was 633 Tenth Street, Santa Monica, in the decade of the 1920s.

111. From the poem *The Cloud*, 1820.

112. Pursuing an ideal naturalism, Chandler obtained sea gulls from the Field Museum of Chicago as models for the wings of Gulf Cloud. *Dallas Morning News*, October 8, 1933.

113. Dallas Museum of Art, 1943.22, plaster, 14½ × 15 × 11 in., gift of Florence Rogers.

setts Normal Arts School in Boston for two years. In 1903 she was awarded a scholarship from the Dallas Art Association for study with the noted sculptor Lorado Taft. Her studies with Taft at the Art Institute of Chicago lasted three years; she also worked two years as one of his assistants. Sometime during the period of her studies or immediately after, Chandler spent a year of study and travel in England and southern Italy.

With her studies completed, Chandler returned to Chicago and opened a sculpture studio in the Fine Arts Building in Chicago, receiving only two small commissions the first year, a bronze fountain in Bay City, Michigan, and a memorial tablet for South Bend, Indiana. Chandler also participated in at least two of the annual Exhibition of Works by Chicago Artists, exhibiting *Blindman's Bluff*, *Hunting for the Fairies*, *Winter*, *Autumn*, and *Scherzo* in 1908, and *Kathleen* in 1909.

It was soon after moving to a new studio building Taft had erected, taking space adjoining Taft's own studio, that Chandler received her first large commission, the Sydney Smith Memorial for Fair Park at Dallas. The influence of Lorado Taft on Chandler's work can be seen both in the sculpture's form and its subject matter. Gulf Stream as she peers out from under her cloak and wings, relates both in her gesture and sculptural form to that of Taft's *Daughter of Pyrra*, a figure of romantic symbolist conception that was planned as part of the monumental *Fountain of Time* group Taft first conceived in 1909 (which was also inspired by a poetry quotation).[114] In addition, the treatment of mass and the flowing harmonious forms of Chandler's fountain sculpture follow the formal tenets taught by her teacher.[115]

Chandler revealed a lively personality critical of the existing quality of Dallas sculpture in a letter written to Elisabet Ney on June 14, 1900. Indicating a high regard for Ney, Chandler's letter began by expressing her happiness over a letter she had received from the Austin sculptor, who had encouraged Chandler about her work. Despairing over the available sculpture in Dallas, Chandler wrote of "the frights that *decorate* the City Park" and of the "atrocious creature with a crooked face, glaring eyes and misshapen limbs." Longing "for iconoclasts" among the Texans, Chandler asserted she "would gladly knock off a stone head or two." She went on to assure Ney that "nothing would have pleased me more than the opportunity to study with you or to just look at your wonderful work again. It is the only sculpture that I have seen for five years and I am 'art hungry.'"[116]

The theme of Chandler's allegorical composition points to a shifting focus in Texas that was moving from an active patriotic fervor fixed on heroes and heroic events toward a "nationalistic" pride in the land and the collective personality of the people of the state, often expressed in terms of the cowboy and the horse. Belonging to that category is the work of John Gutzon de la Mothe Borglum (b. March 25, 1867, Bear Lake in Idaho Territory; d. March 6, 1941, Chicago). Borglum's parents encouraged him to study art, and after some earlier training he traveled to Paris in about 1887. In Paris, Borglum enrolled at the École des Beaux-Arts and the Académie Julian, returning to the United States in 1893. Despite the academic training Borglum received in Paris, the most important French influence on Borglum's work was the sculpture of Auguste Rodin (1840–1917), apparent in the two works by Borglum included in the exhibition.

After the Chicago Exposition, Borglum traveled to London because at the time it was known to be most receptive to American western art. He had his first successful public exhibition there and received many orders for portraits and two commissions for a series of mural

FIG. 34
GUTZON BORGLUM (1867–1941)
Mares of Diomedes, *1903*
Bronze
62 in. high × 103 in. long
Collection of The Metropolitan Museum of Art,
Gift of James Stillman, 1906
Photograph provided by The Metropolitan Museum
of Art

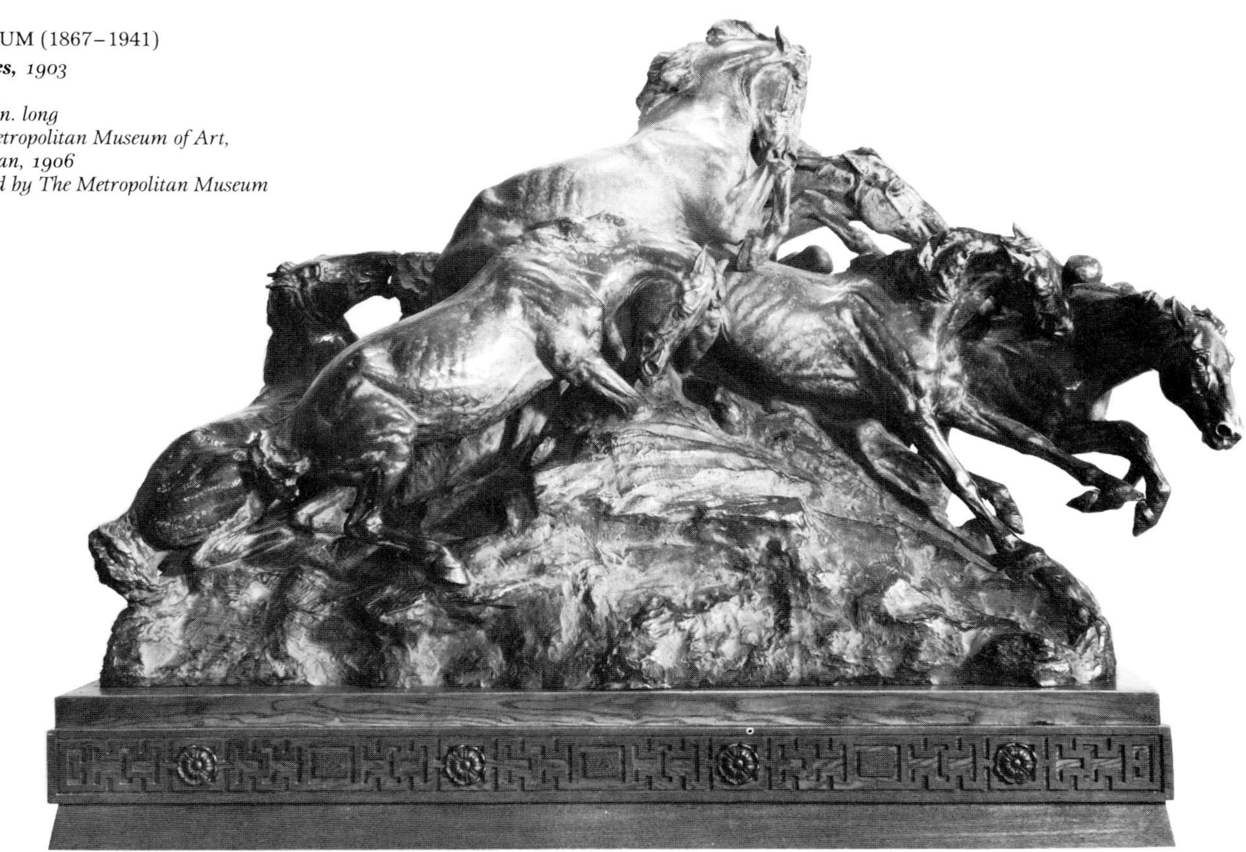

decorations. His early *Indians Pursue* (Cat. 19), or (*Apaches Pursued by U.S. Troups*), that was exhibited at the 1901 Exhibition of Fine Arts in Paris, may have been modeled during his stay in England. It was not until after his death in 1941 that his widow made arrangements on behalf of the Witte Museum in San Antonio for it to be cast in New York by the Roman Bronze Works.[117]

Returning to the United States in 1902, Borglum began to work in one of the many New York studios of the time that had been remodeled from a stable. Here in the following year he created his first great sculptural success, the *Mares of Diomedes* (Fig. 34). Borglum exhibited this group of six galloping horses and other works at the Louisiana Purchase Exposition in St. Louis in 1904 where he won a gold medal. The *Mares of Diomedes* became the first piece of sculpture purchased by the Metropolitan Museum of Art for its permanent collection.

After World War I, Borglum began what was to become the largest Civil War monument of all, *The South's Lost Cause.* To be carved into an 800 × 2,000-foot area on Stone Mountain, near Atlanta, the project was not completed because of disagreement between Borglum and the Stone Mountain Confederate Memorial Association.[118] Borglum became best known, however, for a second mountain sculpture on Mount Rushmore in the Black Hills of South Dakota. Here with his son Lincoln he began *The Shrine of Democracy*, carving into the 1,300-foot-high mountain the heads of four United States presidents. Borglum stated in an August 25, 1935, newspaper article, that he would be carving an even greater project for Texas than the Georgia or South Dakota works, a full-relief with mammoth figures to be carved on the walls of the Hueco Tanks, large natural cisterns near El Paso.[119]

114. Beatrice Gilman Proske, *Brookgreen Gardens Sculpture*, pp. 42–44; M. A. Rolfe, "Our western sculptor — Lorado Taft," *The Western Architect*, 33:42–46, April 1924. The Victorian poet Austin Dobson's (1840–1921) lines from *The Paradox of Time: A Variation on Ronsard:* "Time goes, you say? Ah no! / Alas, Time stays, *we* go."

115. Proske, *Brookgreen*, p. 43; Rolfe, " — Lorado Taft," p. 44.

116. Rutland, *Sursum!*, pp. 78–79.

117. The Witte Memorial Museum (today the Witte Museum, San Antonio Museum Association) paid the expense of the casting, and the artist's widow gave the work to the Witte.

118. Borglum refused to include the figure of a Ku Klux Klansman, eventually stopping work and destroying his models. He was taken to court but was found within his rights to destroy his work.

119. *San Antonio Express*, August 25, 1935. The article stated that Borglum had selected a "magnificent upthrust 160 feet high upon which he will carve four or five walking figures, each approximately 120 feet high." The project was never started.

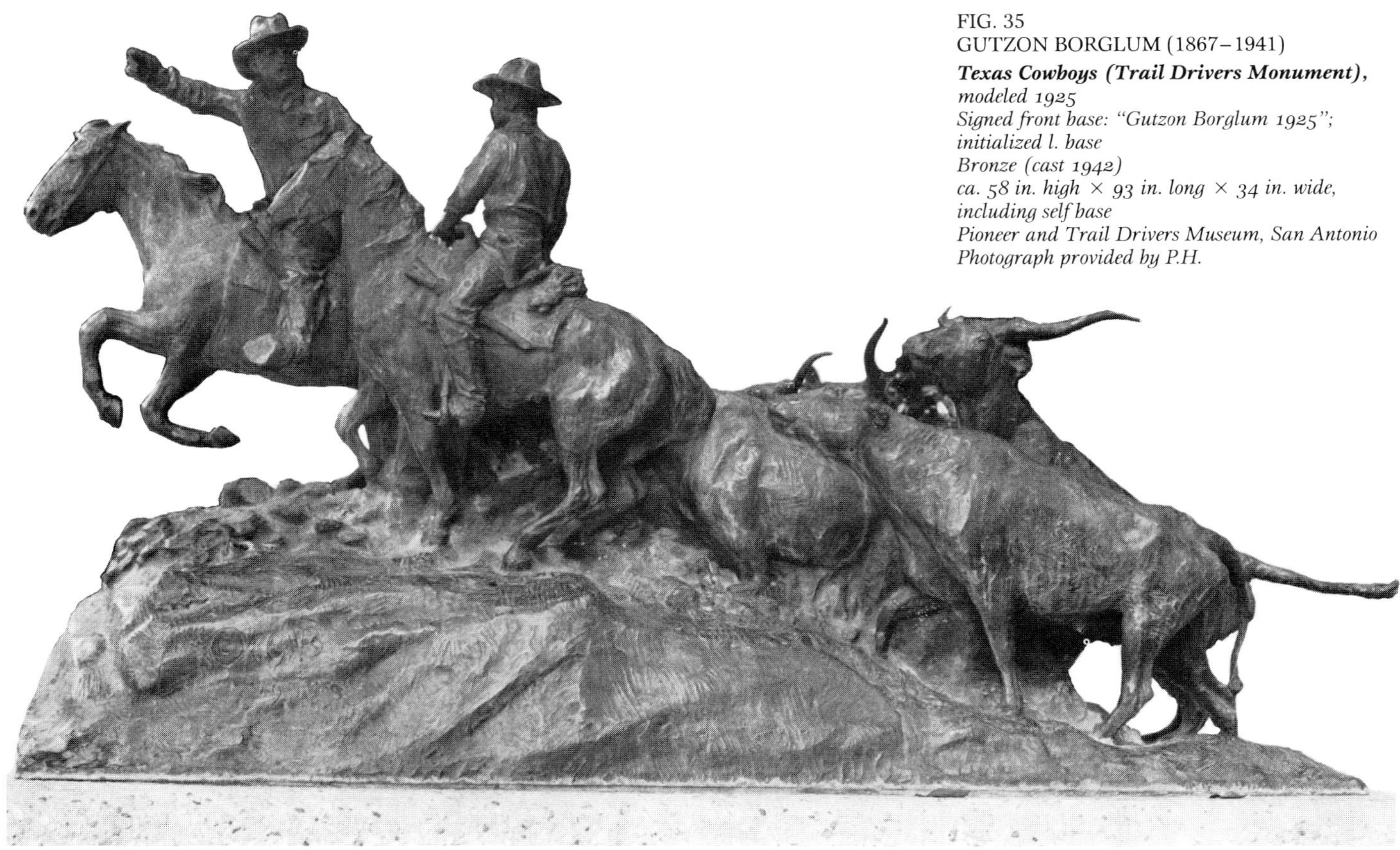

FIG. 35
GUTZON BORGLUM (1867–1941)
Texas Cowboys (Trail Drivers Monument),
modeled 1925
Signed front base: "Gutzon Borglum 1925";
initialized l. base
Bronze (cast 1942)
ca. 58 in. high × 93 in. long × 34 in. wide,
including self base
Pioneer and Trail Drivers Museum, San Antonio
Photograph provided by P.H.

Before the colossal portraits of Mount Rushmore totally consumed his interest, Borglum had primarily been an artist of western themes, and when the Old Time Texas Trail Drivers' Association proposed to Borglum that he create a monument to be placed in San Antonio commemorating cattle drives along the Chisholm Trail from San Antonio to the railroad centers of Kansas, he agreed, moving to San Antonio in 1924. For his studio he selected the lower pump house in Brackenridge Park behind the Witte Museum. The fund raising for the monument included a barbecue in Brackenridge Park in 1926, where Will Rogers gave $1,000 toward the cause. In the end, partly because of lack of funds, the original plans were altered. It was a sketch-working model for the Trail Driver's monument, placed on exhibition in the Witte Museum by 1926, that was finally cast in bronze and titled *Texas Cowboys* (Fig. 35).[120] That bronze is composed of two cowboys on horseback driving a group of Longhorns, a much reduced version of the original, larger-scale group which would have been composed of many more figures. The painted plaster figure, *Cowhand* (Cat. 20), was done by Borglum in preparation for the larger-scale unrealized version of the Trail Drivers Monument. It was 1942 before the finished bronze of Texas Cowboys was placed next to the Witte Museum in front of the Pioneer, Trail Drivers, and the Texas Rangers Memorial Building in San Antonio.

Between 1924 and 1937, Borglum spent much of his time in the Brackenridge studio, later known as the Mill Race Studio, modeling the Mount Rushmore heads as well as other commissions received from throughout the United States. In 1937, explaining that he had decided to move to California, Borglum took the studio key to the Witte's director and offered the studio as a gift to the museum.[121]

A second outstanding sculptor of horses who produced important work in Texas was Alexander Phimister Proctor (b. 1862 Bosanquit, Ontario, Canada; d. 1950 Palo Alto, Calif.). In late 1871 Proctor moved with his family to a homesite near Denver, Colorado, where as a youth he collected specimens of wild animals, studying and sketching them; he would later blend his professional life as a successful sculptor with the rugged life, remaining close to nature and its wildlife.

After what was already a long and distinguished career,[122] Proctor received a letter from the Southern Women's Memorial Association regarding an equestrian statue of Robert E. Lee (Fig. 36) for Dallas. The association wanted two mounted figures, Lee and a young Confederate soldier who would be seen looking to Lee for guidance. Picturing Lee as a leader fighting against fate and insurmountable difficulties, Proctor's first model showed the general and the young man in a storm, their hat brims bending, their capes whipped by the wind, the heads of their horses[123] lowered against the storm, tails and manes blown by the gale. But when Dallas representatives visited

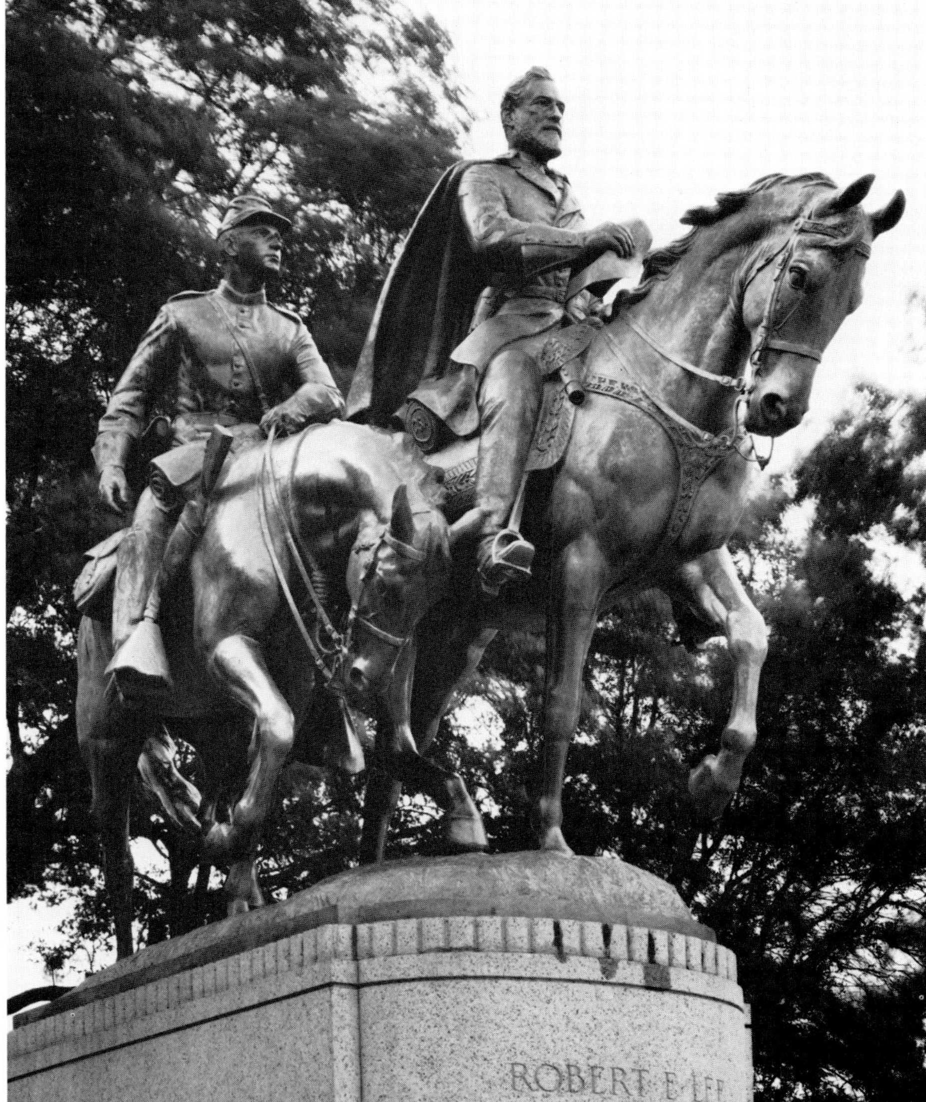

FIG. 36
ALEXANDER PHIMISTER PROCTOR
(1862–1950)
Robert E. Lee and the Confederate Soldier,
1935–36
Signed and dated
Bronze
Heroic size
Lee Park, Dallas
City of Dallas, CD.1936.1
Photographer: Lee Clockman; photograph provided by Office of Cultural Affairs, City of Dallas

120. An illustration of the sketch-working model on exhibition in the Witte appears in Woolford and Quillan, *The Story of the Witte Memorial Museum*, p. 48. Geo. W. Saunders, pres. and organizer of the Old Trail Drivers Assoc., posed for the lead cowboy.

121. *Ibid.*, p. 121.

122. Proctor, who had received many commissions and much honor, first studied at the National Academy of Design (later an academician) and the Art Students League and then in Paris (in part as a co-recipient under the first Rinehart Scholarship), working at the Académie Julian and the Académie Colarossi. He received awards at the St. Louis exposition of 1904 and the Panama Pacific Exposition in San Francisco in 1915 and from the Architectural League in New York in 1911.

123. Lee is portrayed astride his horse Traveller.

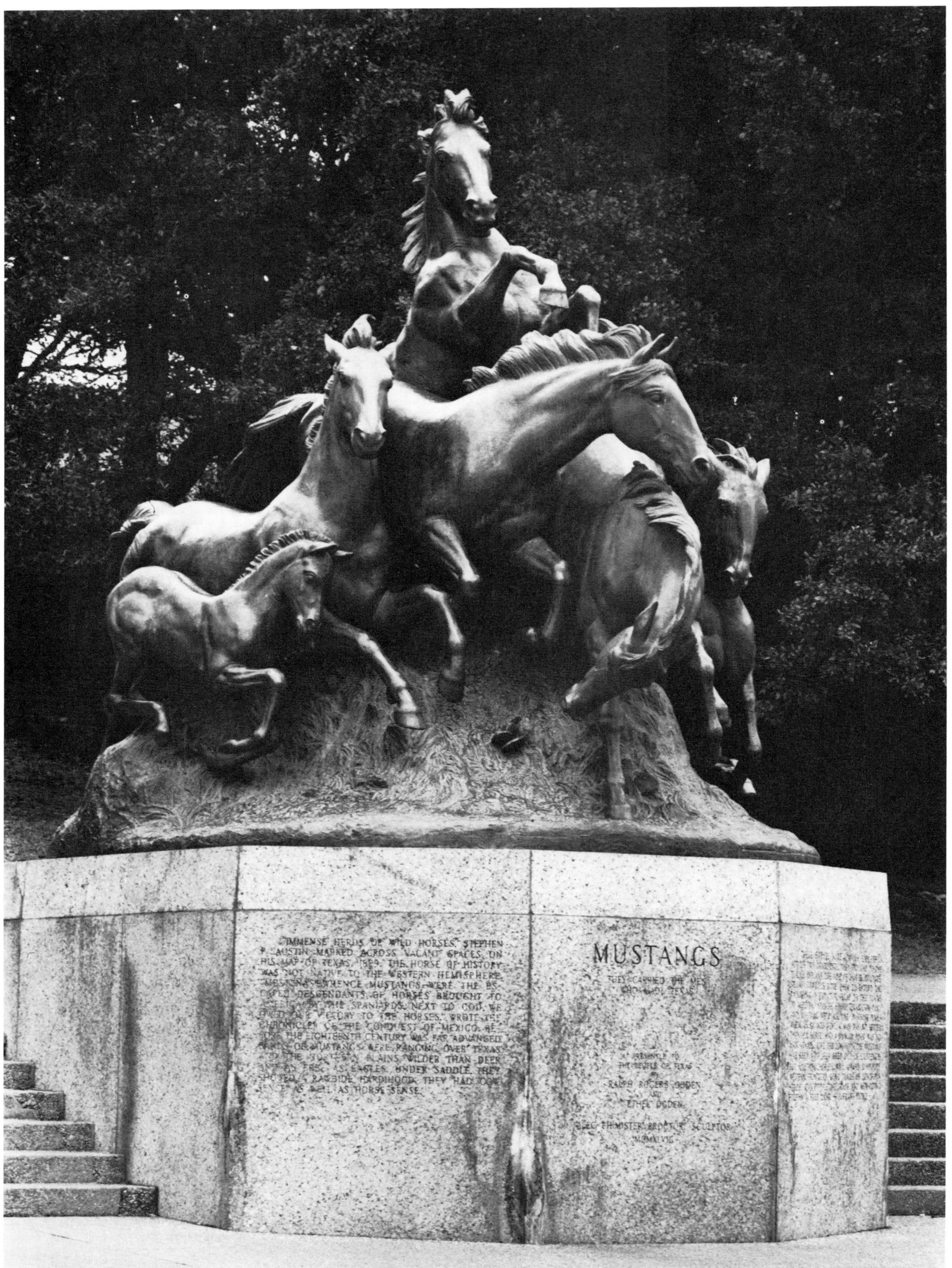

FIG. 37
ALEXANDER PHIMISTER PROCTOR
(1862–1950)
Mustangs, *1939–40, dedicated 1948*
Bronze
15 ft. high from plinth to top of mustang's head
21st and San Jacinto streets, The University of
Texas at Austin
Photographer: George Holmes, Huntington Art
Gallery, The University of Texas at Austin

Proctor's Connecticut studio, the composition did not agree with their image of Lee. Proctor came to accept the southern view that Lee, himself, had not been defeated. Proctor's second model reflected the sculptor's changed concept, with Lee marching forward. His small working model was accepted, but Proctor decided to decline the commission because of the terms of the contract. In August 1933, Proctor stopped in Dallas and while there made another sketch. The model was accepted and a new contract was signed.

When the composition was fairly well established in New York, Proctor shipped the plastelene model to his Connecticut studio so he could work on the horses outdoors. When preparing to enlarge the work, Proctor engaged Gozo Kawamura, who would later work on the sculpture project for the Texas Centennial Exposition in Dallas, to enlarge the working model to full size using the pointing machine process. Perhaps responding to the cost, Proctor decided to do away with modeling the group in plastelene and go directly into plaster for the enlargement, although for the heads of Lee and the young soldier he used the softer material of plastelene because it is better suited to the description of small details. Building and finishing the large model consumed another full year, plus the efforts of several assistants including those of Proctor's son Gifford.[124] The Lee Monument was dedicated in 1936.[125]

Two years later, while Proctor was living in Seattle, he received a letter from J. Frank Dobie, the Texas historian, stating that a friend of his, Ralph Ogden, wanted to donate a sculptured group of mustangs (Cat. 21; Fig. 37) to the University of Texas in Austin. Proctor immediately started a small model, about 15 inches high, of six mustangs in a compact group. As soon as it was completed, Proctor packed the plaster model in his car and left for Texas. While showing the model to the Ogdens and the Dobies, and after agreeing that a colt should be added to the group, a contract was drawn. Dobie wanted the group to represent real mustangs and above all not to be "modernistic caricatures." In this Dobie found in Proctor, the realist, a kindred spirit.

Dobie made arrangements for Proctor to use any of the horses he wanted on the million-acre King Ranch in South Texas. The mustangs were released into a 900-acre pasture on the Rancho Los Palos where the Proctors lived during the time the sculptor was modeling the horses. As none had ever been handled, the mustangs were authentic models, actually threatening Proctor's safety if he came too close. The resulting sculpture group was composed of one colt, one stallion, and five mares, representing a family of mustangs in the wild.

Proctor's working model was three and one-half feet high, making each horse about twenty-two inches high at the withers. He chose to place the stallion at the top, dominating the composition, and to show each animal of the group as much as possible by placing the group on a mound, a solution which had been used by Gutzon Borglum for his *Mares of Diomedes* (Fig. 34). Not wishing for any part of any horse to be less complete than another, Proctor modeled each horse on all sides as though it were to stand alone, while building a harmonious whole. He also made measurements of the horses because he wanted his mustangs to look like mustangs, not just generic horses.[126]

Where Coppini and other sculptors had experienced difficulty with the cold, for Proctor it was the heat, dust, and cold. On the ranch the thermometer in their cabin sometimes registered as high as 114° and in his studio it was occasionally 119°. Proctor had to sprinkle his plastelene model with ice water to prevent it from melting. By hanging two layers of burlap on all sides of the cabin and then soaking the burlap with water, a

124. Gozo Kawamura (b. 1886 Japan; returned to Japan 1939). According to Proctor's own account, the bronze figures weigh seven tons. Hester Elizabeth Proctor, *Alexander Phimister Proctor*, p. 196.

125. President Roosevelt, while seated in his limousine, pulled the cord for the unveiling at the dedication of the Lee monument (Ibid., p. 197).

126. Proctor. pp. 198–199.

"Texas cooler" was made. Some days the model had to be covered because of dust storms. During the winter, northers blew into the studio. When the model was finished, Kawamura was asked to enlarge the group with the pointing machine. Proctor had paid for ten tons of bronze and reserved it for casting, but the government would not release critical metals during this period. For several war years the mustangs remained in the Gorham Bronze Foundry at Providence, Rhode Island.[127] Finally, in 1948, the mustangs were cast and installed at the University of Texas. Dobie's words are engraved on the base of the statue:

These horses bore Spanish explorers across two continents. They brought to the Plains Indians the age of horse culture. Texas cowboys rode them to extend the ranching occupation clear to the plains of Alberta. Spanish horse, Texas cow pony and mustang were all one in those times when, as sayings went, a man was no better than his horse and a man on foot was no man at all. Like the Longhorn, the mustang has been virtually bred out of existence. But mustang horses will always symbolize western frontiers, long trails of Longhorn herds, seas of pristine grass, and men riding free in a free land.

— J. Frank Dobie.

At the dedication of the monument in May 1948, Dobie added these words: "As I behold these glorious plunging creatures that Phimister Proctor has arrested in enduring bronze, they inspire in me a kind of release and elation. I am free with them and with the wind, in spaces without confines, and in times beyond contagion from 'the world's slow stain.'"[128]

Traditional Careers Begun after World War I

The sculpture of Bonnie McLeary (b. 1890, 604 Soledad Street, San Antonio; d. 1971)[129] offers another example of the changing emphasis in sculpture at this time, both in content and in patronage. McLeary, who lived in San Antonio, had her first art lessons in the Chase School of Art in New York. Later she traveled with her grandparents to Italy and France, studying painting for a short time at the Académie Julian in Paris with William-Adolphe Bouguereau.[130] In 1912 McLeary began to study sculpture with James Earle Fraser at the Art Students League.[131]

It was 1921, however, before her career as a sculptor was begun. That year was filled with important firsts for McLeary. Having opened her first studio in New York on McDougal Alley, McLeary also exhibited her work for the first time, showing her supple bronze figure *Aspiration* at the National Academy of Design. In that same year *Aspiration* (Cat. 22) was acquired by the Metropolitan Museum of Art through donation, becoming the first sculpture by a Texan to be accessioned by the Metropolitan. That acquisition, so early in her career, no doubt significantly enhanced her reputation as a sculptor and effected the degree of success she experienced.

Described by McLeary as her favorite sculpture, *The Blessed Damozel* (Cat. 23) of 1926 is at once neoclassical, romantic, and visionary. This work was suggested to McLeary by the lines of the English Pre-Raphaelite poet and artist, Dante Gabriel Rossetti, "The blessed damozel leaned out / From the gold bar of Heaven; / Her eyes were deeper than the depth / Of waters stilled at even; / She had three lilies in her hand, / And the stars in her hair were seven."[132] Its languid gesture and the cool and smooth surface of the white marble are well suited to the dead Rossetti heroine awaiting

127. Ibid. pp. 199–200.

128. J. Frank Dobie, *The Seven Mustangs*, p. 11. From an address made May 31, 1948, at the dedication of the monument. Provided by the Texas Memorial Museum, The University of Texas at Austin.

129. McLeary may have spelled her name at different times as both McLeary and MacLeary. She signed both *The Blessed Damozel* and *Aspiration*, however, "McLeary." The biographical sheet at the National Academy of Design, for which she likely provided the information, lists her name as MacLeary and the interview she gave a New Jersey newspaper in 1963 lists her name as MacLeary. There are other instances of exchanged spellings of her name. She was first married to Ernest W. Kramer, and later to James McGahan.

130. Esse Forrester O'Brien. *Art and Artists of Texas*, p. 258.

131. Carnegie Library Autobiographical Files, San Antonio, June 1, 1924, San Antonio Public Library. James Earle Fraser (b. 1876, Winona, Minn.; d. 1953).

132. Daniel Gabriel Rossetti (1828–1882). *The Blessed Damozel*, first published in 1850, had "the greatest influence of any Pre-Raphaelite literary production" (Reuben Post Halleck, *Halleck's New English Literature*, [New York: American Book Co., 1913], p. 464). Rossetti's own painting of *The Blessed Damozel*, 1875–1878, is in the Fogg Museum's collection, Cambridge, Mass.

133. Janet Scudder (b. October 27, 1873, Terre Haute, Ind.; d. June 9, 1940, Rockport, Mass.). Edith Barretto Parsons, née Stevens (b. July 4, 1878, Houston, Va.; d. September 26, 1956, New Canaan, Conn.).

134. McLeary's fountain piece, *Ouch!* (dated before 1925), was in the Brooklyn Children's Museum by 1929 (Carnegie Library Autobiographical Sketch, San Antonio; Annie Laurie Williams Crain, "Texas Sculptor Wins New Laurels"). There are surviving photographs showing McLeary's sculpture at the Brooklyn Children's Museum taken before the fountain was apparently removed from the grounds in anticipation of the razing of the original buildings in the late 1960s (Jan I. Bernstein to Patricia Hendricks, April 10, 1989).

135. Mildred Burgess, "A Sculptor Demonstrates the Unity of Man," *Independent Woman*, p. 18, from the vertical files of the New York Public Library, quoted in Broder, *Bronzes of the American West*, p. 230.

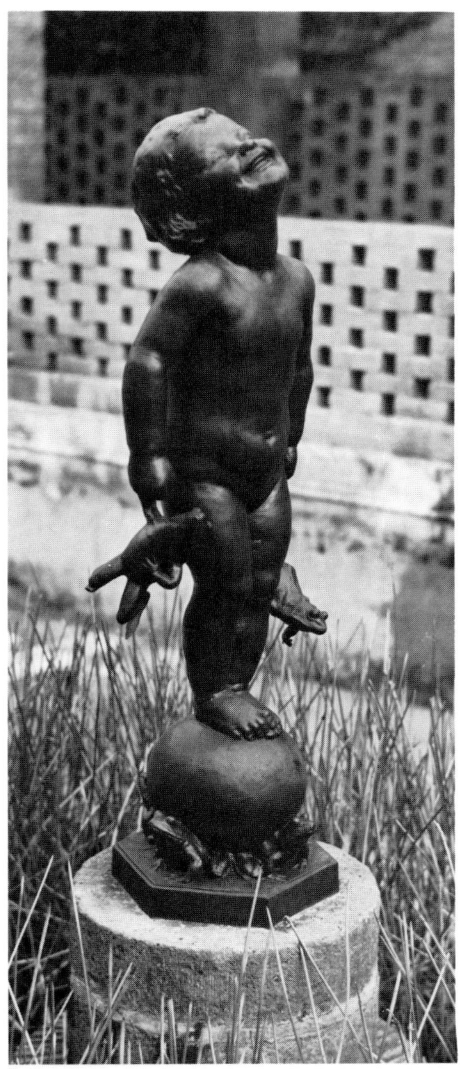

FIG. 38
EDITH BARRETTO PARSONS (1878–1956)
Frog Baby, *ca. 1917*
Bronze
39½ in. high
Collection of the Brookgreen Sculpture Gardens,
South Carolina
Photograph provided by Brookgreen Sculpture
Gardens, South Carolina

her beloved. The treatment of the hands may reflect the influence of McLeary's teacher Bouguereau.

When speaking of her sculpture, McLeary adopted a more pragmatic attitude about sculpture than most previous Texas sculptors. She spoke freely of how she could make sculpture profitable, thus offsetting the cost of importing the several hundred pounds of plastic clay from Italy required for one life-size figure. This was to be done not only through contract work but also by selling small replicas of each statue through jewelers and novelty shops. A practice that, though Coppini attempted to pursue, he (and other sculptors) felt obliged to condemn. McLeary did not seem to be ruled by the grand concepts that had inspired the previous generation and, when quoted as saying she felt her fountains and garden pieces should always be joyous because a garden is joyous, she was, in fact, marketing her work for a changing patron. Her frequent portrayals of children may also have been influenced by the many portraits of children produced by her sculpture instructor James Earle Fraser. Other sculptors of the time whose work fell within the same genre include Janet Scudder and Edith Barretto Parsons (Fig. 38).[133]

The titles of McLeary's works, when compared to the often ponderous titles of patriotic monuments, underscore the changing audience to which her work was directed. Among her garden pieces was *Squawkie Birds*, a fountain piece shown in the Spring Exhibition at the National Academy of Design in 1928 and taken to Philadelphia for the Outdoor Sculpture Exhibition of the Art Alliance. Other titles included *Ouch!*, *Goosie Goosie*, *Aurora*, *Ariadne*, *Gossip,* and *Inspiration.*[134]

McLeary did produce some dedicatory sculpture, verifying that the pull of heroic commissions occasionally continued to be a factor at this time, even for artists like McLeary. In Puerto Rico there are two works by the sculptor, a memorial still standing on the campus of the University of Puerto Rico dedicated to the Puerto Rican patriot Don Luis Múñoz Rivera, the George Washington of Puerto Rico, and a World War I memorial, *Victory,* unveiled on Armistice Day 1928 at San Juan.

During the time of her activities in New York, McLeary continued to spend time in Texas, referring to Texas as her true home. In 1935 she attended two separate dedications of her work in Waco. The first work, a bust of Dr. A. Joseph Armstrong, the Elizabeth Barrett and Robert Browning scholar, was presented to the Armstrong Browning Library; the second was the Rotan Memorial, which was presented to the Antoinette Memorial Home.

In addition to the attention paid during this period by Texas sculptors to regional themes and to the poetic ideal (Borglum, Proctor; McLeary, Chandler), there was a growing interest in the portrait bust. A factor that prompted artists to look more closely at the individual, or at humanity as expressed through the individual, was introduced in June of 1933 when the Field Museum of Chicago opened a permanent exhibition space called The Hall of Man. More than 100 life-size figures were installed there, representing the races of the world. Combining art and anthropology, they were by the American sculptor Malvina Hoffman, who had traveled world-wide to create *Races of the World.* There was favorable response to the project and to Hoffman's 1936 book, *Heads and Tales,* which described it. Mildred Burgess wrote, ". . . all are portraits of distinct personalities, vibrant with life, unique as individuals . . . through them we are made to see that the brotherhood of man is a fact and not just a pious phrase."[135] Hoffman's work and the supportive responses to it were influential on other artists, including some Texas sculptors.

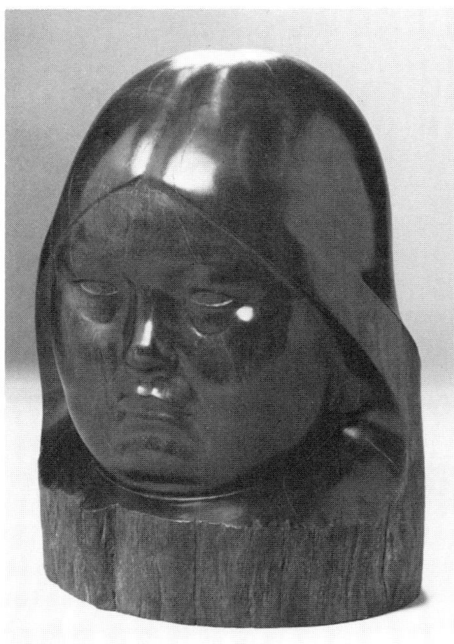

FIG. 39
URBICI SOLER (1890–1953)
Untitled *(Head of Young Girl), 1947*
Date carved on underside
Wood
13 × 10 × 8 in.
Collection of the El Paso Public Library
Photographer: Darst-Ireland Photography, El Paso

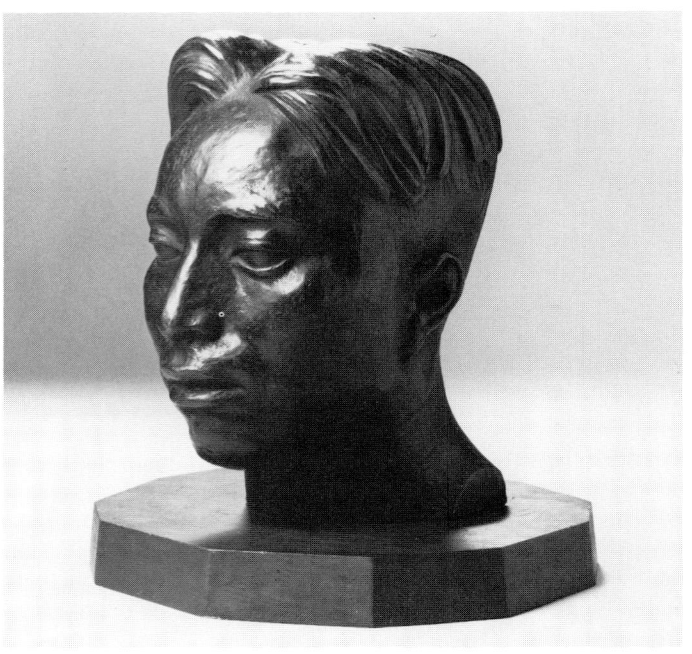

FIG. 40
URBICI SOLER (1890–1953)
Untitled *(Head of Young Man, Oaxaca), 1935*
Initialed and dated, site noted
Bronze
11½ × 10 × 7½ in., base 2 in. high
Collection of the El Paso Museum of Art, gift of
Mr. and Mrs. Clifton K. Hillegass
Photographer: Darst-Ireland Photography, El Paso

Of the many artists who may have been influenced by the project, none was closer to Hoffman's result in terms of the wedding of art and anthropology than was Urbici José Francesco y Manonelles Soler (b. June 21, 1890, Farran, Lérida, Spain; d. January 15, 1953, El Paso). After training in Barcelona, Soler traveled to Munich in order to study the methods and teachings of the German classicist Adolf von Hildebrand.[136] While in Munich, Soler opened a school of sculpture, the Soler Schule, and before returning to Spain spent time in 1920 in the Paris workshops of the French sculptor, Émile Antoine Bourdelle (1861–1929), who earlier had been Rodin's chief assistant. Though his career in Spain was underway, Soler left for Argentina in 1925 after receiving an invitation from Jorge Bunge, Argentine architect and former student in Soler's school in Munich, to travel to Buenos Aires to carve statues for government buildings.[137]

During his stay in Argentina, Soler received a commission from the Spanish government to produce a collection of busts of the outstanding native types of Latin America. In 1930, beginning in Chile,[138] and continuing his project in Peru, Ecuador, and Panama, he modeled portrait busts of the indigenous peoples, and in late 1931 his collection of portrait busts was exhibited at the California Palace of the Legion of Honor in San Francisco. After the exhibition, Soler stayed in San Francisco, serving as director of the School of Modern Art for eighteen months, until he was forced to depart due to immigration laws. After settling in Mexico City for a period, Soler left and traveled to Oaxaca (Cat. 24) and other areas to study the Mixtecas, Zapatecas, Tarascans, and other Indian groups, returning to his subject matter as late as 1947 while he was living in El Paso (Fig. 39–40).[139]

In 1937 Soler returned to the United States to create the forty-foot high cruciform figure *Cristo Rey* (Fig. 41), which stands on the mountain peak Sierra de Cristo Rey, overlooking El Paso, at a point of confluence for two countries, two states, and two cities. The emphasis of Soler's sculpture of Christ the King is on outline and frontality, a silhouette on which a harmonious arrangement of lines provides definition and decoration. His highly linear interpretation echoes in concept as well as style the *Christ of the Andes* in Argentina, and the figure of *Christ* sited on the peak known as Corcovado in Brazil. Of stone gathered by Soler in the Austin area, the figure also can be related stylistically to some of the work seen at the 1936 Texas Centennial Central Exposition, such as the large cast stone figures by Lawrence Tenney Stevens.[140] The figure Cristo Rey was dedicated on October 17, 1940.

Following the completion of *Cristo Rey*, Soler taught briefly at Tulane University and then traveled to New York where he opened the School of Sculpture and Applied Arts. Unhappy because of the spreading influence of modern art and after a trip to South America, Soler returned to El Paso, where he began teaching sculpture at the El Paso College of Mines, now the University of Texas at El Paso. There his portraits of the Indians

FIG. 41
URBICI SOLER (1890–1953)
Cristo Rey, *1937–1940*
Stone
40 ft. high
Sierra de Cristo Rey, overlooking El Paso
Photograph provided by the El Paso Public Library

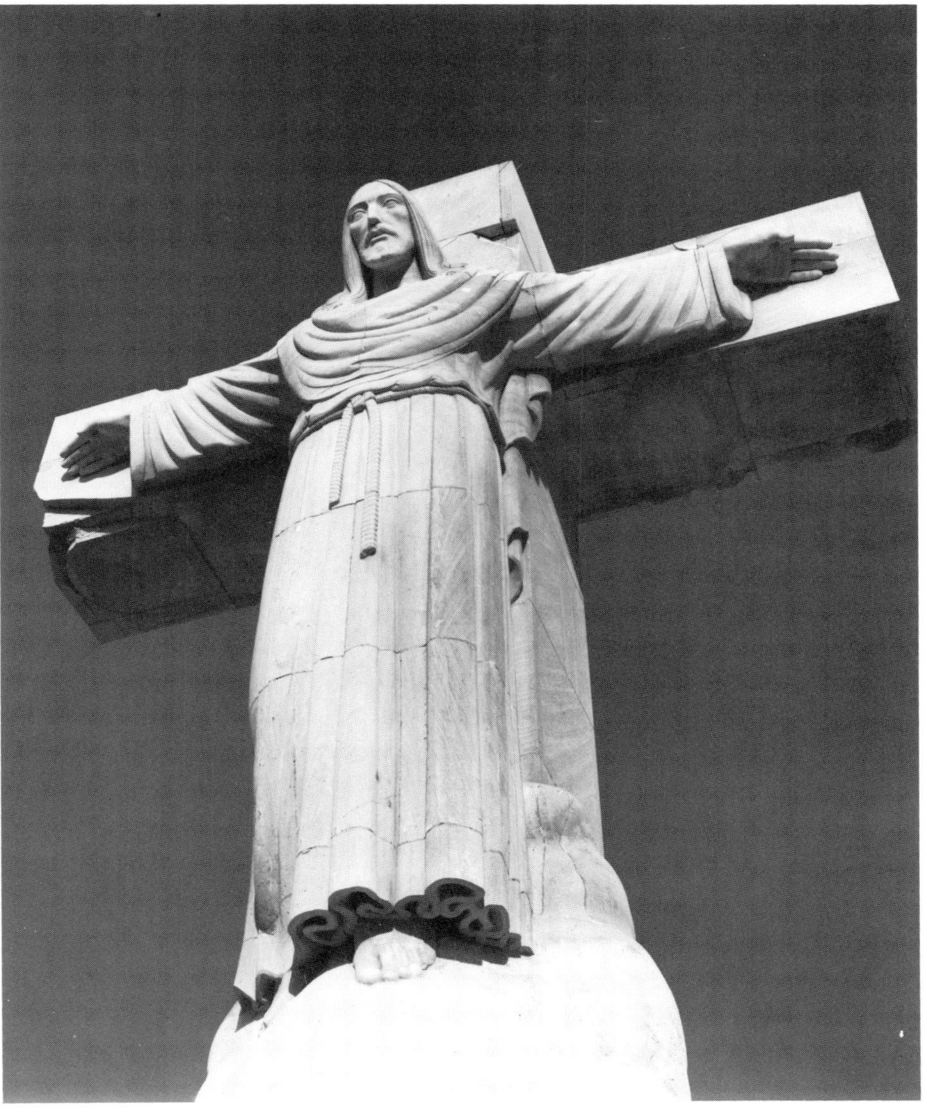

136. Adolf von Hildebrand (1847–1921), wrote *Das Problem der Form* (1893). With strong ideas about the form sculpture should take (e.g., preserving the mark of the sculptor's tool on the sculpture), Hildebrand's writings and teachings were of importance to the revitalization of sculpture. His influence was not as great as that of the (French) sculptor, Auguste Rodin (1840–1917), but was of significance for the development of sculpture in the twentieth century.

137. El Paso Public Library archives.

138. Starting in Chile, Soler went to the reservation of the Araucanian Indians, where he created the first examples of the collection. Traveling from there, he went to Peru, Equador, and Panama, before settling in San Francisco for a period. El Paso Public Library Archives.

139. The inscription on the l. back of the Young Girl with Braids (Cat. 24), "Ysla D Yunuen Patzcuaro," indicates it was modeled on the island of Yunuen in Patzcuaro where Tarascan Indians live. The location and people group which inspired Soler's sculpture of the wooden head (Fig 38) done in 1947 is unknown, although Soler made trips into Mexico during this period to observe the methods used in pottery production, which the sculptor was attempting to establish in El Paso.

140. The titles of the Stevens works are *Texas* (Fig. 46), *Confederacy*, and *Spain*.

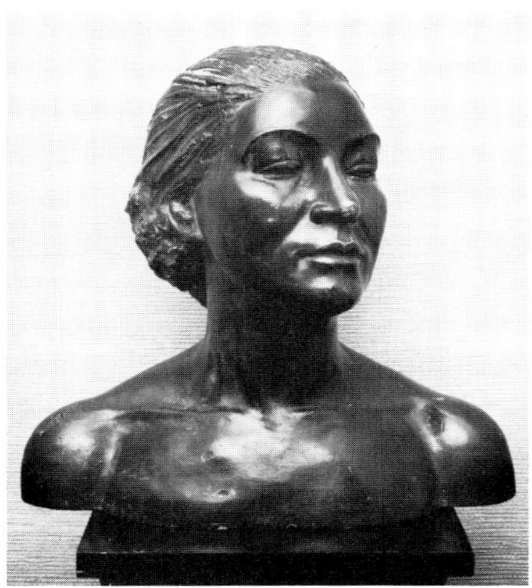

FIG. 42
ELECTRA WAGGONER BIGGS (b.1912)
Enigma, *1937*
Painted plaster
15 in. high
Collection of the Red River Valley Museum, Vernon
Photograph provided by Red River Valley Museum,
Vernon

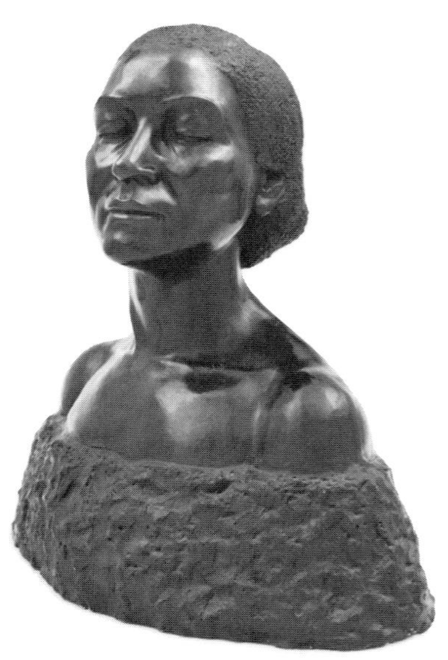

FIG. 43
ELECTRA WAGGONER BIGGS (b. 1912)
Enigma, *original marble carved 1937*
Painted plaster
ca. 23 in. high
Collection of the Amarillo Art Museum
Photographer: Scott Hyde, Amarillo

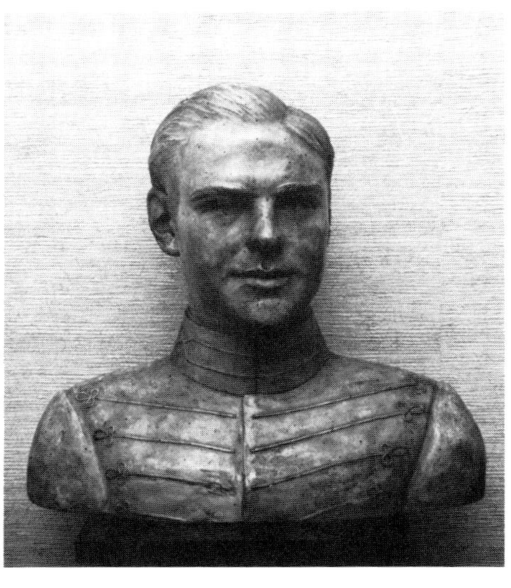

FIG. 44
ELECTRA WAGGONER BIGGS (b. 1912)
Portrait Bust of Amon Carter, Jr. (in Culver
Military Academy uniform), *1938*
Plaster, antique finish
15¼ in. high
Collection of the Red River Valley Museum, Vernon
Photograph provided by Red River Valley Museum

of Latin America, through both exhibition and classroom example, exerted an influence on his pupils. Soler died in his home at the foot of Sierra de Cristo Rey, and a special marker has been placed above his grave by the state of Texas.[141]

Also represented in the exhibition, Electra Waggoner Biggs (b. November 8, 1912, Fort Worth) is another sculptor whose primary body of work has been the portrait bust. While in New York to attend a private school for girls, she had the opportunity to study sculpture for a brief period in Greenwich Village. Her studies there and contact with others who were studying to be or who already were sculptors encouraged Waggoner to pursue her interest in sculpture. She traveled to Paris, where she spent some time studying marble carving and worked in a bronze foundry. Despite these experiences most of her learning was through observation, and she remains basically self-taught, describing the art of making sculpture as essentially a process of line drawing.

During the time she was in Paris, Waggoner carved a head from black Belgian marble that she titled *Enigma*.[142] In an ouevre dedicated to realism where most works are portrait busts, generally identified by the sitter's name, *Enigma*'s title is an exception. After exhibiting the work in the Paris Salon d'Automne in 1937, where it won a third prize, Waggoner returned to New York to exhibit *Enigma* at the Jacques Seligmann Galleries in the spring of 1938, along with thirty other life-size portrait busts, fanciful figures, statuettes, and bas-reliefs, including her *Self-Portrait* (Cat. 25) of 1936.[143]

For exhibition at the National Museum of Women in the Arts, Washington, D.C., a bronze copy of *Enigma* was cast in 1988 from the plaster in the Red River Valley Museum in Vernon (Fig. 42). For the 1988 cast, the artist chose black bronze to more nearly approximate the 1937 black marble version. It is that bronze which is in the exhibition (Cat. 26). There is another plaster cast of *Enigma* (Fig. 43) in the permanent collection of the

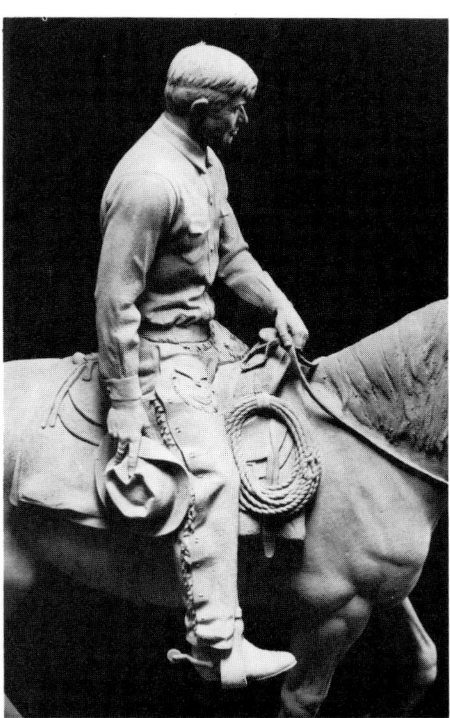

FIG. 45
ELECTRA WAGGONER BIGGS (b. 1912)
Riding Into the Sunset: detail (Will Rogers
on "Soapsuds"), *1937–1941[?]*
Plaster (Bronze 9 ft. 5 in. high, Will Rogers
Memorial Coliseum, Fort Worth)
Photograph provided by the artist

Amarillo Art Museum, a gift from the artist. The Amarillo work is not identical to the Vernon plaster. The difference lies in the rough-textured drape around the shoulders and in the hair style. It was the Vernon plaster that was first cast from the clay, carried to Paris by the artist, and served as the model for the marble. The Amarillo plaster was actually cast from the marble bust, and shows the changes made in the hair and the base of the shoulders for the marble version. The artist has explained that the difference in treatment was her response to the difference in the mediums in which she was working. The difference in hair styles of the two may also reflect an effort on the artist's part to respond to the dual Amerindian and Afro-American heritage of the sitter.

Though primarily a sculptor of portrait busts (Fig. 44), Waggoner accepted a commission from Amon Carter, Sr.[144] to create a life-size equestrian statue of Will Rogers. For the commission Waggoner traveled to Santa Monica and drove daily to the ranch of Will Rogers' son, where a cowboy whose build was similar to that of Rogers posed on Rogers' horse, Soapsuds. Having completed a small clay study about one and one-half feet high, Waggoner carried the model to New York where a craftsman with a pointing machine enlarged it in plastelene to a height of about four feet. Working on the plastelene, Waggoner developed the final model. Confident over the result, she sought and received the unanimous approval of Rogers' friends and family. After the model again was enlarged in plastelene, this time to life-size, Waggoner could see the legs of the horse were anatomically incorrect. She tore down the finished piece completely, along with two years of work, and started over. This time she arranged to use a New York police horse physically similar to Soapsuds, and another man similar in physical build to Will Rogers was posed on a barrel in her New York studio, while a veterinarian brought in to observe the work in progress was available to correct the sculptor if necessary. The equestrian figure (Fig. 45) took five years to complete (1937–1941[?]). The original bronze stands in front of the Will Rogers Memorial Coliseum in Fort Worth. A second bronze is in the collection of the Will Rogers Memorial Museum in Claremont, Oklahoma, and a third is at Texas Tech University, Lubbock.[145] Waggoner continues to work as a portrait sculptor in her studio outside Vernon.

The Introduction of Modernism
and the Texas Centennial of 1936

When Governor James V. Allred succeeded Ma Ferguson in 1934 and signed the legislation that created the Texas Centennial celebration, it was hoped the Centennial would generate money in a time of widespread economic depression. The exact degree of financial benefit it brought the state has been debated, but its impact on the the arts was of lasting importance. The year 1936 was important for Texas sculptors, with many sculptors, both American and European, working on the Fair Grounds in Dallas in preparation for the Centennial Exposition, and with younger Texas sculptors like Michael Owen working there as sculptural assistants. In addition to the stimulation found in a community of sculptors working toward the same goal, and the increased opportunity for sculpture commissions, an exhibition of sculpture was organized for the new Dallas Museum of Fine Arts for the Centennial celebration, which presented the work of nationally and internationally known sculptors. Also included in that exhibition were the Texas sculptors Octavio Medellin, Mike Owen, Allie Tennant, and Evaline Sellors, along with other selected local sculptors.[146]

---

141. Placed there by the Texas Historical Commission State Marker Program.

142. Waggoner modeled in clay and cast in plaster the head of *Enigma* while she was still in New York. She took the cast to Paris with her in 1937, carving the marble herself in the marble shop where she was studying.

143. *Art Digest,* May 1, 1938. The *Self-Portrait* was carved in New York in 1936.

144. Waggoner modeled a portrait bust of Amon Carter, Jr., as a student at Culver Military Academy, dated 1938 (Fig. 44), and a portrait bust of Amon Carter, Sr., (Fort Worth philanthropist), dated 1943.

145. The original bronze was dedicated in 1947.

146. Exhibition catalogue. Dallas Museum of Fine Arts, June 6 – November 29, 1936.

In order to obtain approval for official Centennial memorials for their districts, almost all counties, cities, and towns in Texas sent representatives to a June 1935 meeting held in the Capitol Senate Chamber. The meeting led to a list of approved statue subjects for the Centennial and decisions regarding their location. The distribution of the commissions and the direction of the giant project came under the aegis of the Centennial Commission of the State Board of Control. The competition for the commissions was intense. Sixty-seven sculptors entered one competition alone. Waldine Tauch told of going to the capitol in Austin where her sculpture offerings were set on pedestals in the basement alongside many other entries so they could be judged by the Board of Control representatives. Out of that experience Tauch received the commission for *The First Shot Fired for Texas Independence* and the statues of *Moses Austin* and *Isaac Van Zandt*.[147] Bonnie McLeary traveled from New York to enter the competitions, winning the commission for the Milam memorial, honoring Ben Milam, a hero of the Texas revolution, which was erected in San Antonio.[148]

Centennial commissions granted to the old-guard Texas sculptors were for the most part not associated with the Texas Centennial Central Exposition located on the site of the Dallas State Fair at Fair Park but were for local memorials scattered across the state, like those awarded Tauch and McLeary. An exception was the commission Pompeo Coppini received for six bronze statues to be placed in the Hall of State on the fair grounds in Dallas. Coppini's six Texas heroes that today greet the visitor entering the great semi-circular Hall of Heroes include the figure *Colonel James Walker Fannin* (Cat. 27). For the figure of Fannin, Coppini incorporated romanticized dramatic gestures not present in his portrayal of the other five figures. Illustrating two of the captured hero's legendary last requests, Fannin pulls back his shirt with his left hand, indicating a wish to be shot in the heart, and with his right holds out his watch so that it might be given to his wife.[149] Coppini, who had moved from San Antonio to a New York studio to work on the commission, was visited by representatives of the Centennial committee who came there to oversee his progress. Among these was an expert on historical costumes, whose only recommendation was that Fannin's coat be lengthened from jacket to tunic length, repeating the attention to realistic detail demanded for patriotic monuments by Texas sculptors and patrons from the time of Elisabet Ney.[150] Though Coppini's figures stand apart from the general modernistic style of the buildings and sculpture of the Dallas Centennial Exposition, they seem unexpectedly appropriate in the entry hall of that splendid Art Déco building, dedicated to the history of Texas.[151]

After George L. Dahl had been appointed supervising architect for the Dallas Centennial complex, he brought Lawrence Tenney Stevens (b. 1896 Boston; d. 1972) to Dallas to work on the Centennial project. Stevens' contribution to the Centennial grounds in Dallas was a significant one and it is his work, in conjunction with Raoul Josset (b. 1898 Burgundy, France; d. 1957 United States), in particular, that signals the leitmotiv for the esplanade of the Texas Centennial Exposition.[152] Working in harmony with the overall program of the Centennial architecture, each produced colossal figures which in their decorative modernism demonstrated the continuing influence of the late Art Déco style (see *Spirit of the Centennial* and *Texas*; Figs. 46–47).[153]

One of the assistants for the Fair Park sculpture projects was Michael G. Owen, Jr. (b. May 2, 1915; d. 1976), whose art training had begun in Dallas with the painter Jerry Bywaters.[154] Early in his sculpture career Owen began to sculpt animals. One of those works is the recum-

147. *First Shot Fired for Texas Independence*, life-size bronze bas-relief, 1935, unveiled 1936, dedicated 1937, at Gonzales, near the site of the original battlefield. *Moses Austin*, a 10-ft.-high bronze figure, 1937–38, unveiled 1939 on City Hall Square, San Antonio.

148. The heroic bronze figure faces the grave of Ben Milam who was killed during the siege on Bexar in December, 1835. It is located on the west edge of Milam Square, between W. Commerce, W. Houston, and N. San Saba streets, and Santa Rosa Avenue.

149. The requests are perhaps apocyrphal, perhaps true. In any event his requests were not honored by his captors. The legend of his last three requests also included a request that his men be allowed to disperse since they had surrendered in good faith. None were spared. James Walker Fannin led the Texans in the Battle of Concepcion, and commanded the regiment that was killed at Goliad. Jessamine Younger and Peggy Riddle, eds., *A Gathering of Symbols*, 1986, p. 67.

150. Herbert Gambrell, director of Historical Exhibits at the Dallas Centennial Exposition (Coppini, *Dawn to Sunset*, pp. 364).

151. Although other architects were also associated with the project, it was Houston architect Donald Barthelme who designed the Hall of State. The spelling of his name is approximated through the initials of the names of the Texas heroes inscribed on the entablature of the building.

152. Stevens: Dahl had met Stevens in Rome where Stevens was studying at the American Academy (1922–1925) after having won the Prix de Rome. Earlier Stevens studied with Charles Grafly (b. 1862 Philadelphia; d. 1929) and Bela L. Pratt (b. 1867 Norwich, Conn.; d. 1917) in Boston, and also took several courses in anatomy at Tufts University Medical School. Dahl put Stevens in charge of the coordination of the sculpture program for the Centennial at Fair Park in Dallas. There Stevens executed three colossal statues, symbolizing Spain, the Confederacy, and Texas. His works have been exhibited at the Pennsylvania Academy of Fine Arts, the Architectural League in New York, the National Academy of Design, and the Boston Museum of Fine Arts. Josset: Trained in the Beaux-Arts tradition in Paris (returning to his studies after WW I) and had studied under Emile-Antoine Bourdelle (b. October 30, 1861; d. 1929). Executed war memorials outside Paris, and in 1927 immigrated to the United States, settling in Chicago. In 1935 Josset became a naturalized citizen. José Martin (b. 1891 France; d. 1984 Dallas) was the sculptor builder for Josset's *Spirit of the Centennial*. Martin and Josset had been friends in France and they immigrated to the United States together in 1927. In March of 1936 Martin came to Dallas to assist the Centennial sculptors with their maquettes, armatures, etc., and during one period went three days without sleep in an effort to have the Centennial open on time. Martin stayed in Dallas and his works there include the *Allegorical Figure of the State Fair of Texas* (1938) located in Fair Park; he also did architectural decorations for a number of buildings in the city, including Baylor Hospital. Information from the Archives of the Dallas Historical Society.

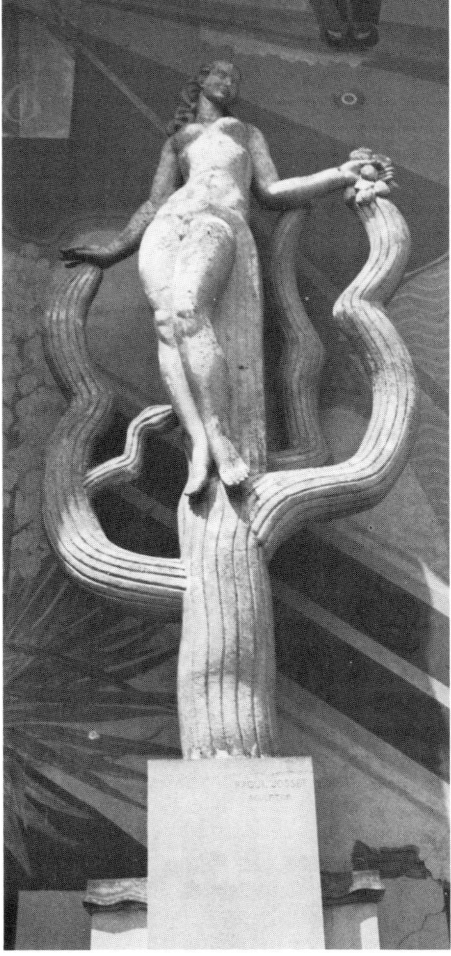

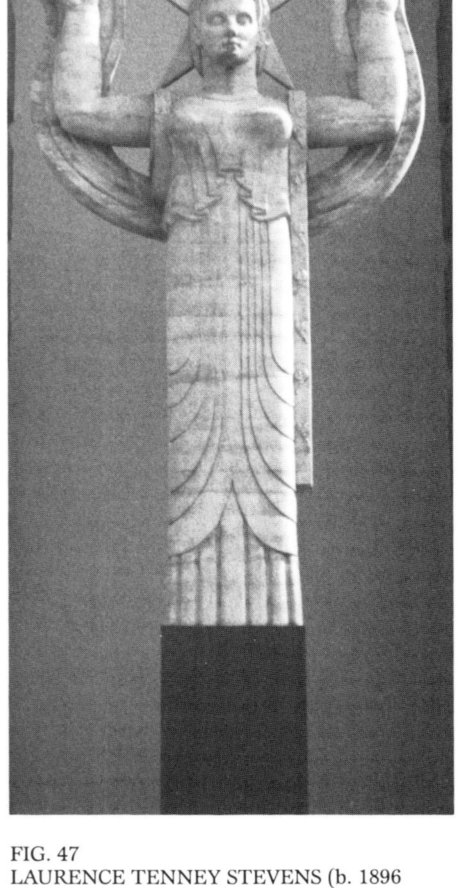

FIG. 46
RAOUL JOSSET (b. 1898 Burgundy, France;
d. 1957 United States), sculptor designer
JOSE MARTIN (b. 1891 France; d. 1984
Dallas), sculptor builder

Spirit of the Centennial, *1936*
Signed, "RAOUL JOSSET/SCULPTOR"
Concrete with plaster and gesso over armature
coated with silver-color metal paint(?)
20 ft. high
Maintenance Building, Fair Park, Dallas
City of Dallas, CD.1936.2
Photograph provided by Dallas Historical Society

FIG. 47
LAURENCE TENNEY STEVENS (b. 1896
Boston; d. 1972)

Texas, *1936*
Cast stone
20 ft. high, base 12 ft. high
Centennial Building, Fair Park, Dallas
City of Dallas, CD.1936.12
Photograph provided by the Dallas Historical
Society

153. The figure of the *Spirit of the Centennial* (Fig. 43) was inspired by the singer Georgia Carroll (information provided by the Dallas Historical Society).

154. Jerry Bywaters (b. 1906 Paris, Tex.; d. 1989 Dallas), was in Rick Stewart's words "one of the most important figures in the history of Texas art" (*Lone Star Regionalism*, p. 160). Bywaters had studied at the Art Students League in New York and with John Sloan. A "champion of regional art," he was named director of the Dallas Museum of Fine Arts in 1942, serving there until his retirement. His writings and teachings were extremely influential for artists of the Dallas area, as well as for other artists in the state.

155. In 1946 Owen was working in Washington, D. C., as a commercial artist, first for the Commerce Department and then for the Navy. He commented that during this period he had been "winning a few prizes in Washington for painting and sculpture" (Owen to Bywaters, 21 June 1946), Bywaters Archives, Southern Methodist University.

bent figure *Peruna,* 1937, the mustang mascot of the Southern Methodist University (SMU) athletic teams. The stylized horse (Fig. 48) with its masterful design lies above the grave of the first Peruna on the SMU campus near the athletic building. The location of other animals sculpted by Owen and exhibited during this period is not known.[155]

Before Owen's career was shortened by a disabling disease, he carved the compelling and distinguished portrait bust of the folksinger Huddie "Leadbelly" Ledbetter (b. 1885 near Mooringsport, La.; d. December 6, 1949, New York, N.Y.). Leadbelly had lived in Dallas' Deep Ellum district many years before, but in 1943 was living in the New York apartment

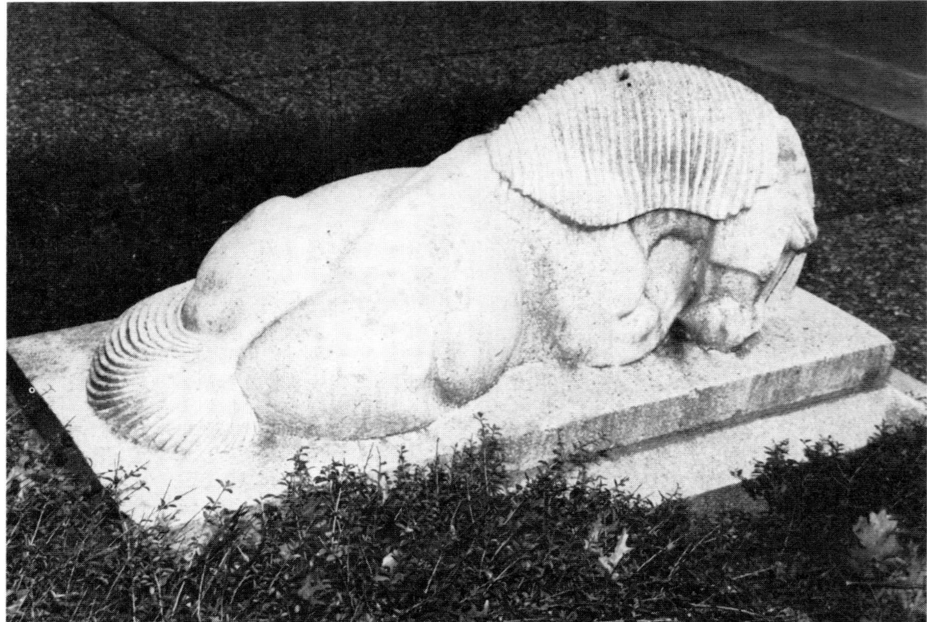

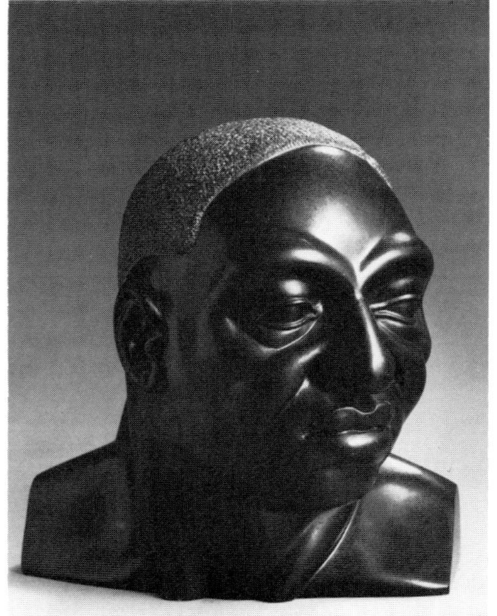

FIG. 49
MICHAEL G. OWEN, JR. (1915–1976)
Leadbelly, 1943
Black serpentine
12 × 11½ × 9½ in.
Collection of the Dallas Museum of Art, Mr. and Mrs. Tom Gooch Fund Purchase Prize, Twelfth Annual Texas Painting and Sculpture, 1950–1951
Photograph provided by the Dallas Museum of Art

where he sat for Owen (Fig. 49). In a 1950 letter to the Dallas Museum of Fine Arts, Owen wrote the following regarding the sculpture and its subject.

I noticed in the newspaper article that the stone was called black Belgian marble. Actually it isn't anything so exotic. It was quarried not far from Charlottesville, Virginia, and is called Black Serpentine. It was the first time I had ever heard of the stuff being black. If you'll notice it seems quite a bit more crystalline than marble.

The way I happened to do the head went like this. A young fellow I had known in Dallas by the name of Ralph Knight had gone to New York a year or so after I went to Washington. He was interested in folk music and became acquainted with Leadbelly. It was at Ralph's instigation that I did the head — he got me the stone, sent pictures (I first roughed out the head in clay at home in Greenbelt) and then arranged the sitting at his apartment in New York. Leadbelly sat for me one afternoon and I finished the clay model at that time. From that I worked out the stone cutting, only being able to work on it in my spare time. All in all it was about a full month's work, I guess. During the time he was "sitting" for me (playing his guitar and singing) he played "Goodnight Irene," but at that time the folk music devotees did not consider the tune "true folk music." Still it pleased me when it became a popular song. It's too bad Leadbelly couldn't have lived to see himself gain such popularity. [156]

During the time of the Centennial celebration in Dallas, the sculptors in the area received a good deal of critical attention, in both the local and national media. In an entry titled "Progressive Texas" for the 1936 special Centennial number of the *Art Digest,* the regionalist painter Alexandre Hogue noted the virility of certain sculptors in Texas who are included in this exhibition:

A few years ago art in America was all cluttered up with "lady" artists. Many sections still tolerate them, but in Texas and particularly in Ft. Worth, Denton and Dallas, woman is no longer inhibited by the "pretty" complex. Instead she has become so virile that almost all our sculptors are women. Such women as Allie Tennant and Dorothy Austin of Dallas, Evaline Sellers of Fort Worth, and Ione Franklin of Commerce are sculptors worthy of the art. But why have not the he-men of Texas gone in for sculpture? This I cannot answer but perhaps it is because many years ago our first real sculptor, Elizabeth [sic] Ney, was a woman or perhaps we may find a vague answer in the familiar gag of a few years ago, "out in Texas where men are men and women are governors." [157]

156. Owen to the Dallas Museum of Fine Arts, 11 April 1950, Owen file, Dallas Museum of Art Library. First quoted in Stewart, *Lone Star Regionalism,* p. 102.

157. *Art Digest,* June 1936, p. 18

158. The figure is nine-ft. high, the overall height for the sculpture is eleven ft.

159. Proske, *Brookgreen,* p. 481. Also letter from Tennant to Proske, June 7, 1989.

160. American sculptor Paul Manship (1885–1966). The theme of the archer already had been reintroduced and given validity as a theme in modern art by the French sculptor Bourdelle. There is no evidence suggesting Bourdelle's, *Heracles the Archer,* (enlarged version ca. 1914), had a direct influence on Tennant's choice of subject matter, although the work was generally known to sculptors.

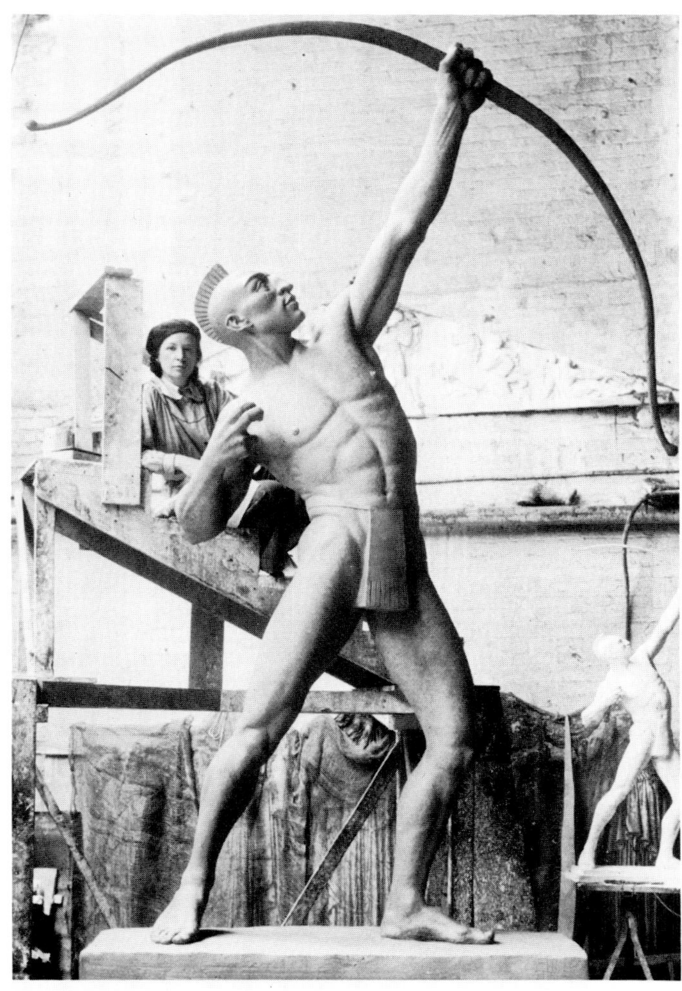

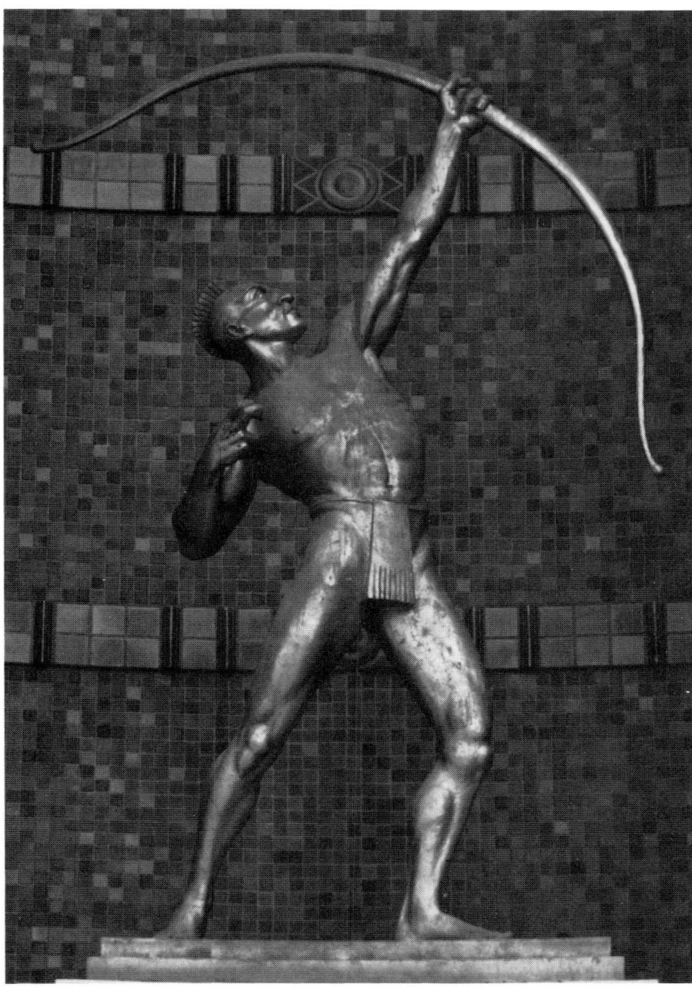

FIG. 50
ALLIE VICTORIA TENNANT (1898–1971)
Allie Tennant in New York Studio with Tejas Warrior, *1935*
Photographer: DeWitt Ward, NYC; photograph provided by The Jerry Bywaters Collection on Art of the Southwest, Southern Methodist University, Dallas

FIG. 51
ALLIE VICTORIA TENNANT (1898–1971)
Tejas Warrior, *1936*
Gold-leaf on bronze
11 ft. × 3½ × 2 ft. (figure ca. 9 ft. high), base 4 × 48 × 32 in.
Hall of State (The State of Texas Building), Fair Park, Dallas
City of Dallas, CD.1936.26
Photograph provided by the Dallas Historical Society

Despite the humorous tone of the material, the compliment was a serious assessment of the talents of Tennant, Austin, Sellors, and Franklin.

Allie Victoria Tennant's (b. 1898 St. Louis; d. 1971) notable contribution to the Centennial is the gilt bronze, nine-foot[158] Indian warrior above the entry to the Texas Centennial Hall of State. Named in tribute to the friendly Indian tribe for which Texas was named, the *Tejas Warrior* (Fig. 50–51) was commissioned by the Centennial committee. A smaller version (Fig. 52) of this work, cast from the working model, was subsequently purchased by Archer M. Huntington for Brookgreen Sculpture Gardens in South Carolina, with special permission of the State of Texas.[159] Tennant's warrior, who reaches upward as he stretches his bow, shares a kinship with the smoothly abstracted action figures of Paul Manship and as such represents a turning away from the Beaux-Arts and Renaissance models of such artists as Coppini and even from the influence of Rodin as seen in the work of Borglum.[160]

Tennant was brought to Texas while a small child and spent her youth in Dallas. A student in 1927 and 1928 at the Art Students League in New York, she studied anatomy with George Bridgman and sculpture with Edward McCartan. Speaking of the Art Students League, Tennant told the *Dallas Morning News* in 1928 that because the league was a cooperative "run by students for students" it was unique. She said further, "New ideas, which find difficulty of expression in other types of organizations, are here given

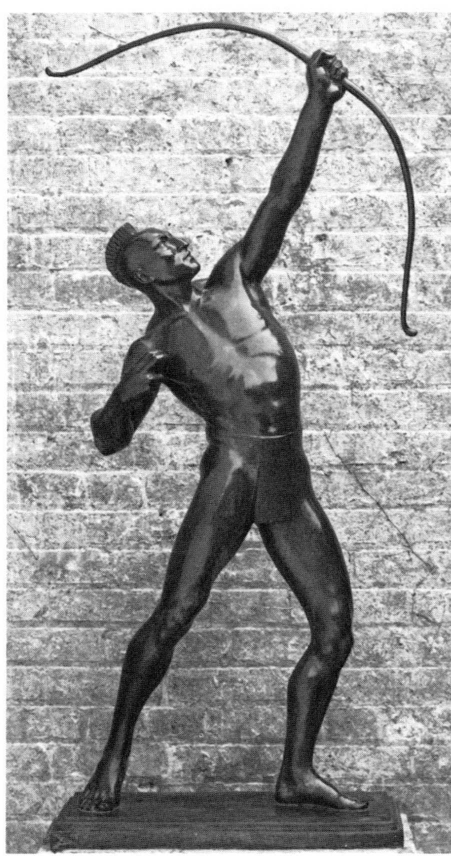

FIG. 52
ALLIE VICTORIA TENNANT (1898–1971)
Tejas Warrior, *1936*
Signed and dated
Bronze
53 in. high
Collection of the Brookgreen Sculpture Gardens,
South Carolina
Photograph provided by Brookgreen Sculpture
Gardens, South Carolina

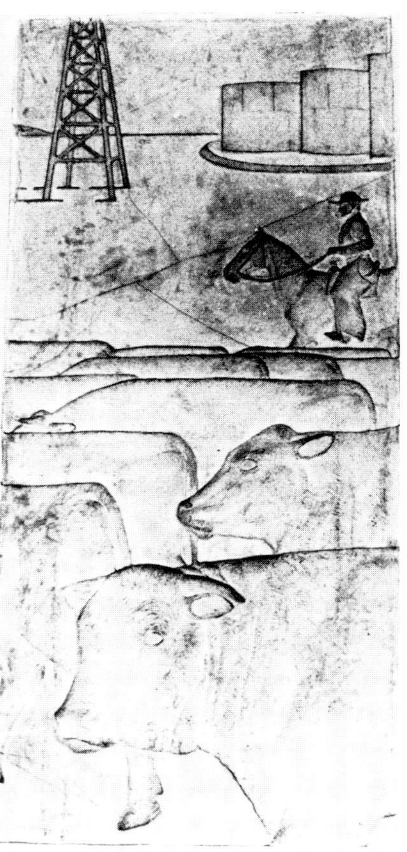

the opportunity to develop." Tennant's public endorsement of the Art Students
League no doubt influenced other young Texas sculptors to study there.

Having achieved recognition as a por-
trait sculptor with such works as the bronze head of *Mrs. George K. Meyer* (Cat.
28), in 1934 Tennant was elected to membership in the National Society of Sculptors. The following year her *Negro Head (Negro)* (Cat. 29) won the Kiest Memorial Fund Prize in the Seventh Annual Dallas Allied Arts Exhibition.[161]
Though the image remains a highly vital one, the abstract qualities of the sculpture are also emphasized through a sympathetic interaction between the symmetry of the features' pure shapes and the hard reflective stone.

Tennant created reliefs for the Dallas
Aquarium at Fair Park, as part of the Centennial program, and under the Federal
Works Agency a 1940 relief depicting *Cattle, Oil,* and *Wheat,* for the United States
Post Office in Electra, Texas (Fig. 53). In this same period, she also produced at
least one garden sculpture, *The Darling April (April),* 1932 (Fig. 54).[162]

For the Dallas Centennial project, Do-
rothy Austin (b. January 3, 1911, Dallas) carved a life-size cowboy in white pine.
Located in the wing of the Hall of State that is dedicated to the range life of West
Texas, Austin's 1936 *Cowboy* (Cat. 30) is a forceful icon with an almost primitivistic presence. Resting on a four-foot high wooden base bearing the Texas star, it
towers above the visitor in a room decorated with fabled working brands under-
scoring the vastness of the cowboy's territory, including the brand of Electra
Waggoner Bigg's enormous "spread," its acreage just under the size of the State
of Rhode Island. Austin also received a commission to design six panels depicting

161. Mrs. Myers was President of the Dallas Art
Association. *Negro Head* is a direct carving.

162. *The Darling April (April)* received the Garden Club
Prize at the Southern States Art League exhibition
in 1932 (Bywaters Archives, Southern Methodist
University, Dallas).

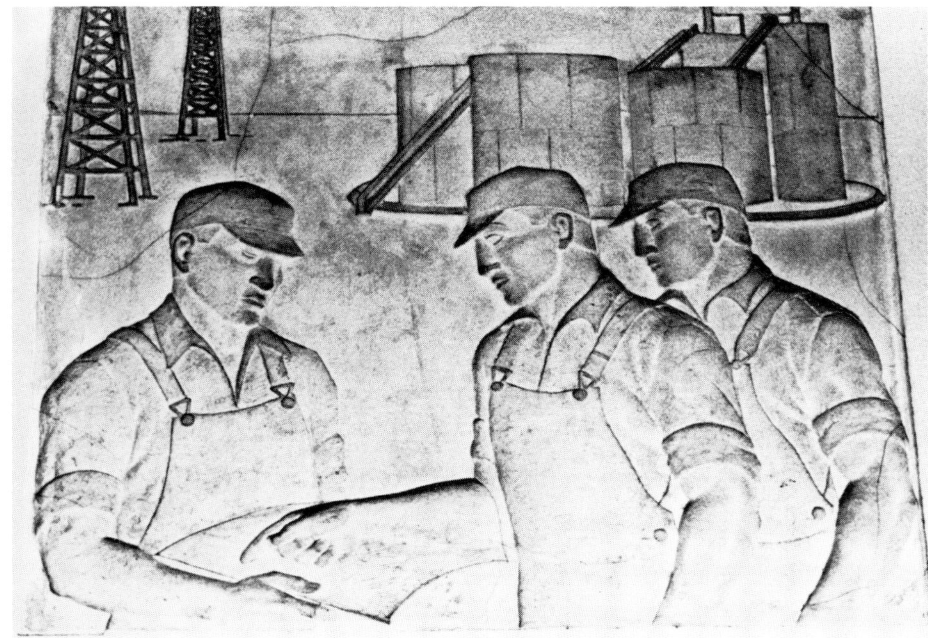

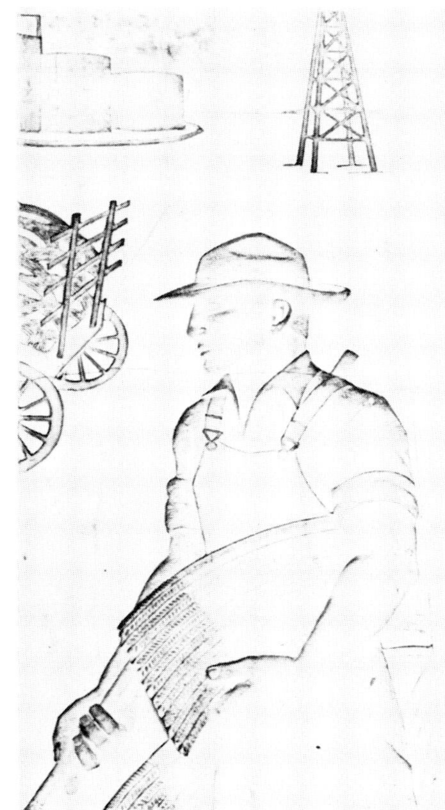

FIG. 53
ALLIE VICTORIA TENNANT (1898–1971)
Cattle, Oil, and Wheat, *1940*
Maximum measurement, ca. 48 in.
Electra Texas Post Office
Photographer: Teddie Miller, Electra

163. The plaster cast of the *Negro Head* was destroyed, leaving the bronze in the exhibition (cast by Gorham) the only existing cast. "At that time, it was difficult to find suitable wood in larger blocks. The [Male] Torso is composed of a number of pieces — glued and doweled together to make a unit from which the sculpture was carved" (Austin to Patricia Hendricks, March 29, 1989).

164. Rick Stewart, *Lone Star Regionalism*, p. 153. Reed who was a supporter of the artists of Mexico, had given José Clemente Orozco his first exhibition in New York City.

165. *New York Times*, March 7, 1937.

166. Also an etcher and blockprinter, Karl (Mrs. Smith) studied with the sculptor Leo Lentelli (b. 1879, Bologna, It.; d. 1961 U.S.) who came to the U.S. in 1903; the etcher Joseph Pennel (b. 1857 Philadelphia; d. 1926); George Bridgeman, who taught anatomy at the Art Students League (b. 1864 Bing, Canada), and the Scottish sculptor Archibald Dawson (d. 1938 in Scotland). She was a member of the Art Students League and the American Federation of Arts, and active in the 1930s. She maintained addresses in both California and Houston, Texas, during the 1930s and may have been most active in San Diego, where she also exhibited her sculpture.

plant forms for the three sets of bronze doors at the north entrance to the new Dallas Museum of Fine Arts, which was part of the Centennial building program in Fair Park. By that time the work of Austin, who had studied sculpture with Arthur Lee and William Zorach at the Arts Students League, had been exhibited at the Museum of Modern Art in New York and the Pennsylvania Academy of the Fine Arts in Philadelphia. In addition to *Cowboy*, Austin produced a variety of directly carved, vigorous works in both stone and wood during the 1930s, and in 1932 exhibited two works in the Fifth Annual Dallas Allied Arts Exhibition. The first was a sensitively modelled bronze bust, *Negro Head*, (Cat. 31) which was awarded first prize in sculpture; the second a head sculpted in white pine and reminiscent of the giant heads of the Olmecs, titled *Noggin (Mexican Head)* (Fig. 55), which was purchased by the Dallas Art Association and acquired by the Dallas Museum of Fine Arts. The following year, Austin carved a series of muscular torsos, including the black walnut *Male Torso* (Cat. 32).[163]

While in Dallas in 1936 to visit the Centennial, the director of the New York Delphic Studios, Alma Reed, had the opportunity to look at the work of the Dallas artists.[164] As a result, Reed gave Austin her first one-woman show. Austin's *Two Figures* of 1937 (Fig. 56), along with other works from the Delphic show, received favorable comment in the New York press.[165]

Outside of the Dallas-Fort Worth area other artists also used direct carving methods during the 1930s, to produce simplified figures, often restrained in movement. If working with wood, they might, as had Mabel Fairfax Karl (b. June 27, 1901, Glendale, Ore.),[166] incorporate the

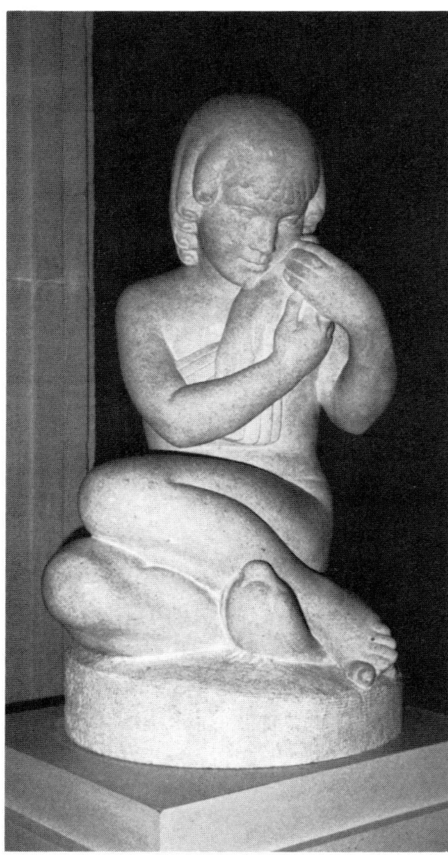

FIG. 54
ALLIE VICTORIA TENNANT (1898–1971)
The Darling April (April), *1932*
Pink Tennessee marble
31 in. high
Private Collection
Photographer: Dorothy Waller, Dallas

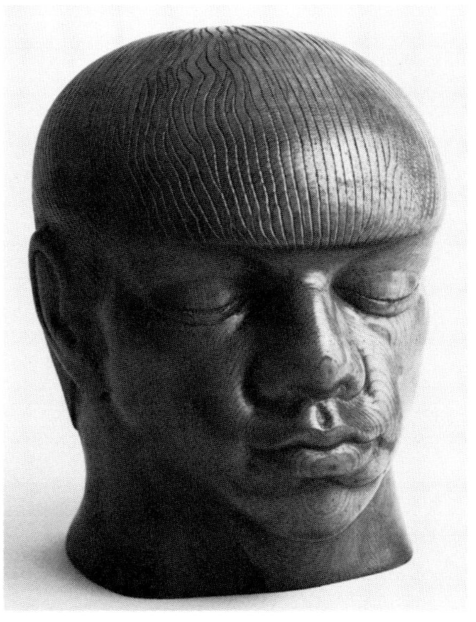

FIG. 55
DOROTHY AUSTIN (b. 1911)
Noggin (Mexican Head), *1932*
White pine
13 × 8 × 10¾ in.
Collection of the Dallas Museum of Art, gift of
Anonymous Friend, 1933.22
Photographer: David Wharton, Dallas;
photograph provided by the Dallas Museum
of Art

patterning of the grain or include stylized attributes, seen in the plant forms at the feet of *Eurydice.*

Orpheus and *Eurydice* (Cat. 33–34) were exhibited in 1934 in the 10th Annual Houston Artists Exhibition of Houston Artists where they were awarded a purchase prize. In Greek legend, Orpheus was said to have played the lyre so beautifully that he charmed all nature. When his wife, the nymph Eurydice, died he was permitted to bring her back to earth from Hades provided he not look back at her. Disobeying, he lost her forever. The classical subject matter chosen by Karl is unusual among the works by Texas sculptors of this period.

Ione Ruth Franklin (b. ca. 1893, San Antonio; d. 1976, San Antonio)[167] had studied at the Art Students League with both William Zorach and Robert Laurent, sculptors who were the leading advocates of direct carving in this country. That she and other Texas sculptors came under the influence of their teachings is not surprising.[168] Direct carving of stone or wood was a way of reacting against the complicated processes required for the heroic bronzes and marbles of the earlier sculptors who, though they might stay with their pieces to the end, nonetheless needed the help of technicians to complete their works. One of the results was that it was not always clear how large a role the assistant played in the sculptor's final result. It was a desire on the part of the modern sculptor for a closer relationship with the process of creation, coupled with the impact of primitive art, that had turned sculptors toward direct carving. In Paris as early as 1907, Brancusi[169] had used direct stone carving, employing it in a modern idiom, but in this country it was not until after Robert

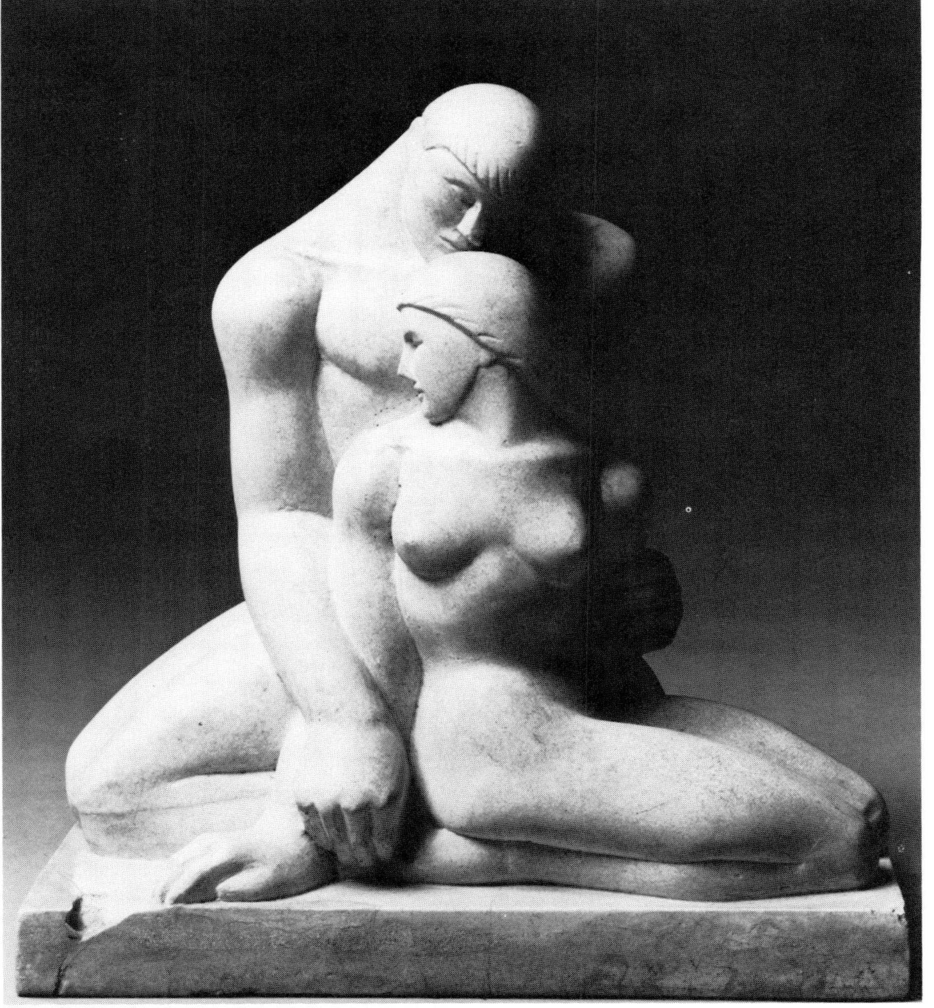

FIG. 56
DOROTHY AUSTIN (b. 1911)
Two Figures, *1937*
Limestone
12½ × 11¾ × 6½ in.
University Art Collection, 1975.24, Gift of Karl Hoblitzelle, Southern Methodist University, Dallas
Photograph provided by The Meadows Museum, Southern Methodist University, Dallas

Laurent and William Zorach began to produce figurative work in stone in the 1920s that American sculptors embraced direct carving in a kind of truth-to-materials ethic, sensing a newfound integrity in the experience. Franklin's *Young Mother,* (Cat. 35) carved in 1944, shares similar composition and stylistic concerns with William Zorach's 1926 *Child with Cat*.[170]

Bess Bigham Hubbard (b. February 18, 1896, Fort Worth; d. 1977, Lubbock), whose work also reflects the influence of the work of William Zorach,[171] had spent her early years as an artist working in two-dimensional media. In the 1940s Hubbard began to work as a sculptor, producing small stone figures using the direct carving method favored by so many Texas sculptors of the period. By the mid-forties, Hubbard was using Taos, New Mexico, Indians as models for her work, and in 1947 carved the *Crusita of Taos* (Fig. 57) from Indiana limestone. Crusita won honorable mention at the premiere showing of the Texas Sculptors' Group at the Witte Memorial Museum in San Antonio. It later was shown in Abilene, Houston, and Fort Worth.

In 1948 Hubbard carved a small figure titled *Green Goddess (Thinking Woman)* (Cat. 36) which was exhibited in New York with the American Allied Artists 37th Annual Exhibition in November 12–28, 1950, in the National Academy of Design. Along with its finish of pol-

167. Franklin taught studio art at East Texas State [Teachers] College (now East Texas State University) from 1928 to 1955, serving as chairman of the Art Department from 1936 until her retirement in 1955.

168. Both Laurent (b. 1890 France; d. 1970 U.S.) and Zorach (b. 1887 Lithuania; d. 1966 U.S.) were brought to live in the U.S. while still children. Laurent had used direct carving techniques in wood as early as 1913, applying that technique to stone in 1921. Two years later, in 1923, Zorach began to carve directly in stone.

169. Constantin Brancusi (b. 1876 Roumania; d. 1957), active Paris.

170. *Child with Cat*, 1926, Tennessee marble, 18 in. high, Museum of Modern Art, N.Y., Gift of Mr. and Mrs. Sam A. Lewisohn.

171. An influence that clearly was in the air in Texas at the time and no doubt reinforced for Hubbard when her work was critiqued by Zorach.

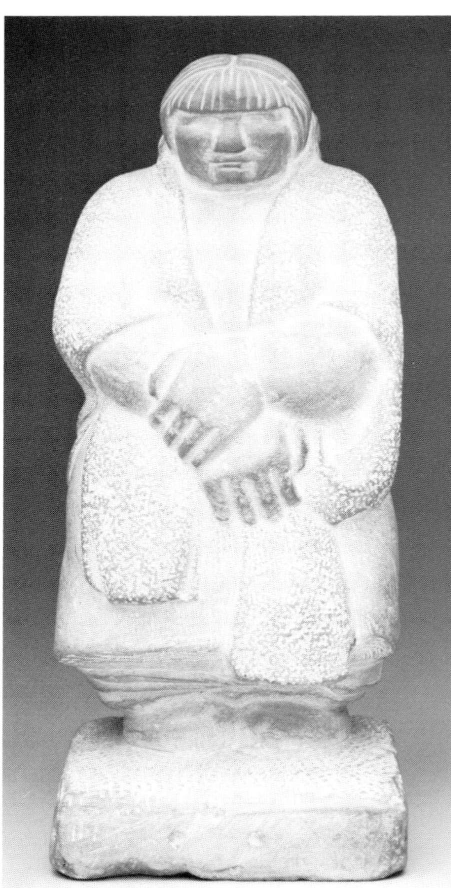

Crusita of Taos, *1947*
Indiana limestone
14 × 6 × 6 in.
Collection of the Dallas Museum of Art, Dallas Art
Association Purchase, 1947.36
Photograph provided by the Dallas Museum of Art

ished and smooth surfaces, the dark marble of the figure suggests once more the influence of Zorach.[172] The *Goddess* was later exhibited April 1 – May 1, 1957, at the Fort Worth Art Center Sculptors of Texas Exhibition. Also included in that exhibition were works by Octavio Medellin, Charles Umlauf, Charles Williams, and Evaline Sellors (*Praying Mantis*, Cat. 38). By 1949, possibly under the influence of Medellin,[173] Hubbard produced the sculpture titled *Grief*, carved from limestone. During the late sixties and seventies she became interested in the casting process, producing at that time a number of small pieces of bronze and chrome.

The animal sculpture that appears in the work of another of Hogue's "virile" sculptors, Evaline C. Sellors (b. 1907, Fort Worth), is quite unlike the works created by the American and French animal sculptors (Borglum and Proctor; Antoine Louis Bárye, 1795–1875). Their goals had been to breathe the appearance of life and spirit into bronze replicas of their animal subjects. In that respect, Sellors' concern was more with conveying the general character of a species, while at the same time focusing on the formal elements of the work. Produced through direct carving, the compact and simplified form of *Winter (Sleeping Fawn)* (Cat. 37), 1947, readily recalls once again the work of Zorach, although Sellors points to her wartime work for North American Aviation as a major influence on the simplification of form in her work. She has explained that the beauty of the industrial forms were a direct influence on her work, contributing to a further turning away on her part from the academic images of her earliest sculpture.[174]

172. Zorach also used dark stone and combined rough with polished surfaces. An example that would have been known to his students and followers was his *Head of Christ*, 1940, Black granite, Museum of Modern Art, N.Y., Abby Aldrich Rockefeller Fund.

173. Whose work she knew, and who also had critiqued her work.

174. Telephone interview with the artist, Spring, 1989.

175. David Smith (b. 1906; d. 1965), American sculptor whose early work was influenced by surrealist subject matter. Roberto Matta Echaurrian (b. 1912, Chile): surrealist painter working and living in Paris. Sellors spent two formative years in Paris, ca. 1929–1930.

176. In her more naturalistic sculpture of *Eve*, ca. 1950 (Fig. 57), Sellors also produced an elongation of the face and nose. The sculptor has said, however, there was no influence on her work by Amadeo Modigliani, and that when creating a sculpture it was the material, itself, that suggested to her the development of the form. (Modigliani (1884–1920), Italian painter and sculptor who settled in Paris in 1906, becoming a leader in modernism in art. Modigliani concentrated on portraits of young women, characteristically portrayed with attenuated bodies and elongated noses.)

177. Evaline Sellors was joined by Blanche McVeigh and Wade Jolly in forming the Fort Worth School of Art (Sam Cantey III: photocopy of a typed, undated manuscript on the arts in Fort Worth, ca. 1971).

178. *Octavio Medellin, Sculptor*. Privately printed, ca. 1985, provided by the artist. Medellin began his art studies in San Antonio in 1921, studying painting with José Arpa and life drawing with Xavier Gonzales. In 1928 Medellin studied at the Art Institute in Chicago, taking night classes.

179. Ibid. Carlos Mérida (b. 1893, Guatemala; 1984, Mexico), though born in Guatemala, Mérida is often considered a Mexican painter because by 1919 he was living and working in Mexico City. He began to incorporate surrealism into his work around 1930. Mérida and Medellin were in Denton, Tex., teaching art at the same time in the 1940s.

180. Spring, 1989, conversations with the artist.

181. *Octavio Medellin, Sculptor*.

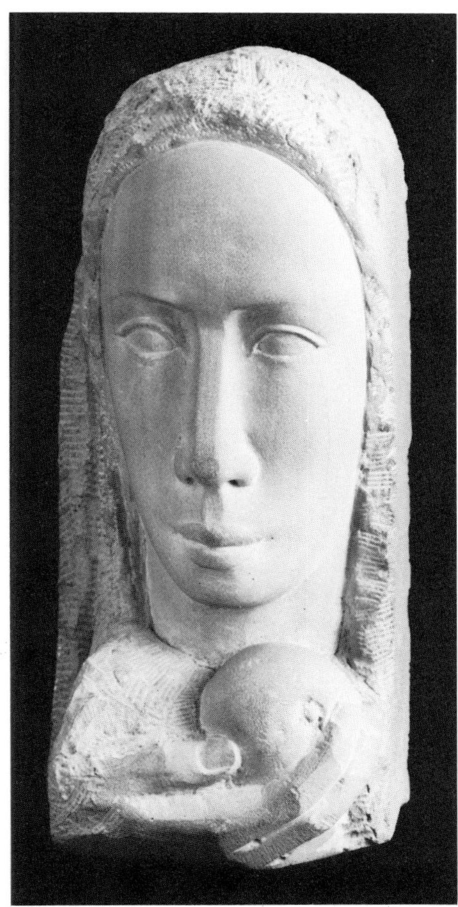

FIG. 58
EVALINE SELLORS (b. 1905)
Eve, *ca. 1950*
Red sandstone
18 × 8 × 6 in.
*Collection of the Modern Art Museum of Fort
Worth, Museum Purchase*
*Photograph provided by the Modern Art Museum
of Fort Worth*

The erect and enlarged metallized form of the *Praying Mantis* (Cat. 38) of 1954 is not so quickly linked to the work of others, although it does bring to mind in its implied but contained threat the potentially threatening faunas created by sculptors who had responded to the ideas generated by the surrealists, such as the predatory birds of David Smith, as well as the interest of the surrealists in the insect as subject matter (Matta).[175]

In her terra-cotta *Ode to a Cotton Picker* (Cat. 39) of 1953, as with her animal studies, Sellors also sought to portray the character of her subject. Unrealistic by earlier standards, the *Cotton Picker* gives credence and great character to the human image. When the earlier traditional portrait sculpture of realists like Soler and Waggoner are contrasted with Sellors' terra-cotta head, the recognition of a turning point in Texas sculpture is again made. In its exaggeration of form for expressive purposes, seen in the enlarged eyes and elongated face, the viewer finds the use of devices characteristic of modern art's independence from nature. Even in her earlier bust of *Eve,* ca. 1950 (Fig. 58), Sellors seemed to be departing from a strict observance of nature.[176]

Sellors, along with other Fort Worth artists, founded the Fort Worth School of Art in 1931, where she taught sculpture, and where as part of a strong exhibition program the faculty brought to Fort Worth its first exhibition of the works of the School of Paris artists Derain, Braque, Matisse, Picasso, and others.[177] Sellors had studied art at the Pennsylvania Academy of Fine Arts, and had been awarded scholarships for European study in 1929 and 1930.

A sculptor who has been an influence on other Texas sculptors, both through his work and his teaching, Octavio Medellin (b. 1907, Matehuala, San Luis Potosi, Mexico) had come with his family to live in San Antonio from Mexico in 1920. After having studied art in San Antonio and in Chicago at the Art Institute,[178] Medellin traveled to Mexico, taking an extended tour of the Gulf coast area, traveling as far as Veracruz. Responding to the expressive art forms of his own heritage, he was particularly moved by the art of the Indians of the Yucatán, whose use of art was tied to their daily lives. He also met and became life-long friends with the Mexican artist, Carlos Mérida.[179] The visual and emotional experiences of his trip to Mexico were to exert a lasting influence on Medellin.

Upon returning to San Antonio, in 1931, Medellin associated himself with a group of San Antonio artists and founded La Villita Art Gallery, teaching sculpture there and at the Witte Museum for several years during the depression. During this period, responding to his memories and to a personal heritage that had been reaffirmed during his time in Mexico, Medellin carved *The Spirit of the Revolution* (Cat. 40–41), through which the sculptor speaks of the realities of revolution and the need for peace in the lives of the people. In this sculpture of complex and personal symbolism, the woman holds up her hands as symbols of the cross, reflecting the heirarchy of the Church; the kneeling figure with the gun represents the Revolution; and close between them is the serpent Quetzalcoatl, representing the Indian peoples of Mexico and symbolizing their God of Fertility. Around the base, on a predellalike arrangement, are carvings that depict images of peace and struggle.[180]

In 1938, after another formative trip to Yucatán to research Maya-Toltec art, Medellin and his family moved to Denton, where he became sculptor-in-residence at North Texas State Teachers College, now North Texas State University, from 1938 to 1942.[181] Just before moving to Denton he carved *The Struggle* (Cat. 42), which Medellin has characterized as being symbolic of the struggle of life for the family unit, a struggle that properly results in an uplifting human experience.[182] The combat between the two figures is primarily an internal one, and its portrayal is realized in the arrested movement of the figures. The power of these figures is reinforced by the artist's activation of the grain and texture of the very hard rose sandstone.

In 1942 Medellin was given a one-man exhibition at the Dallas Museum of Fine Arts. Seven of his pieces were sent on a national tour and were represented in the 1942 exhibition The Americans showing at the Museum of Modern Art in New York. One of his most expressive works from the period is *El Ahorcado (The Hanged One)* (Fig. 59). A remembered image from his early years, it is currently on tour with the exhibition The Latin American Spirit: Art and Artists in the United States, 1920–1970, organized by the Bronx Museum of the Arts. Also carved in this period is the 1949 *History of Mexico* (Fig. 60), which tells the story of Mexico's history from the earliest Indians up to the time of Medellin's creation of the work.

Another example of Medellin's sensitive treatment of wood is found in the figure of *Moses* (Cat. 43) of 1955. Moses' prophetic role is defined in the expressive nature of the figure's gesture. Medellin has identified the role of Moses to also be that of an "uplifting" symbol, imbued with a spirit that reflects that which is good in and for humanity. As with other works directly carved by the artists in this exhibition, the works by Medellin that are discussed here were all carved from materials native to Texas, with the exception of *The History of Mexico.*

Because of the general growth in the appreciation and practice of the arts in Texas, by the 1930s and 1940s increasing numbers found opportunities to study sculpture in Texas, rather than having to travel outside the state for their training. The trend was probably given impetus by the federal art assistance programs during the Depression years and by the general restrictions of the war years that followed. One of those teacher-sculptors was Medellin, who taught for many years. After spending five years teaching at North Texas State College in Denton, Medellin was pursuaded by the painter and critic and then assistant museum director Jerry Bywaters to move to Dallas, where Medellin became a member of the staff of the Dallas Museum of Fine Arts, teaching sculpture there for twenty-one years. He also taught at Southern Methodist University, Dallas, in 1946–1947 and 1962–1966 and taught at the Cooke County Junior College in Gainesville during the period of 1964–1966. Founding the Medellin School of Sculpture in Dallas in 1966, he served as director and teacher until 1980.

Though there are figurative sculptors like Medellin, whose sculpted figures transcend the question of nude or clothed, the nude has continued to represent an important part of the figurative tradition. The naturalistic full-length nude is interpreted in the exhibition by Coppini, Tauch, and McLeary. Stripped of clothing, or the artifices of daily existence, the nude has for centuries been reverently portrayed by the sculptor for the very nature of its human form and, by extension, special expression of humanity. With the advent of modern art, the nude figure frequently became the partial figure, as forecast by Rodin's *Walking Man,* 1877–78 (and *Torso of Walking Man* of the same date). In itself an acknowledgment of the sculpture fragment reclaimed from antiquity, *Walking Man* was conceived as a whole and altered later as its arms were torn away by Rodin. Although Rodin did not pursue this experiment, the partial figure would become an expression of modern art in and of itself, the torso found to be just as expressive of the total as the head. Of the two partial figures discussed in this essay, the earlier torso by Austin is the more traditional in that it is basically naturalistic and retains a reference to the An-

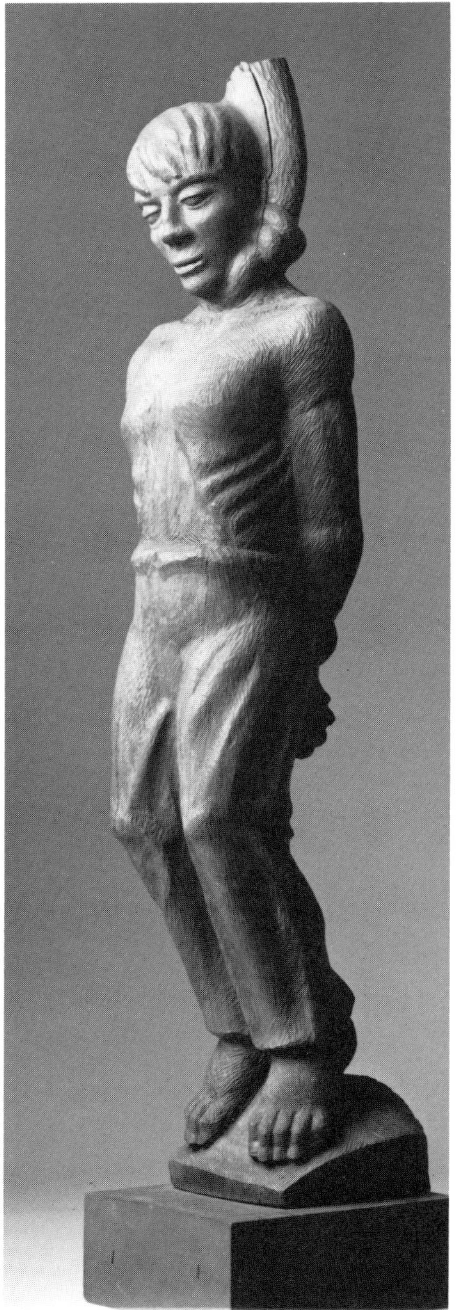

FIG. 59
OCTAVIO MEDELLIN (b. 1907)
El Ahorcado (The Hanged One), *ca. 1942*
Black walnut
42 × 10½ × 10 in.
Collection of the Dallas Museum of Art, Kiest Memorial Purchase Prize, Fourteenth Annual Dallas Allied Arts Exhibition, 1943
Photograph provided by the Dallas Museum of Art

182. The third figure represents parenthood. Spring, 1989, conversations with the artist.

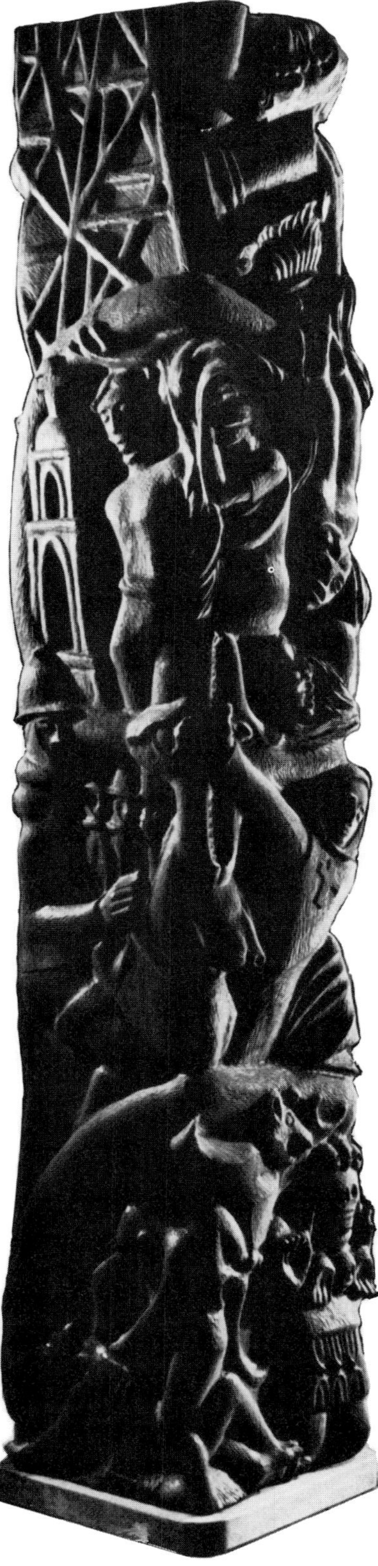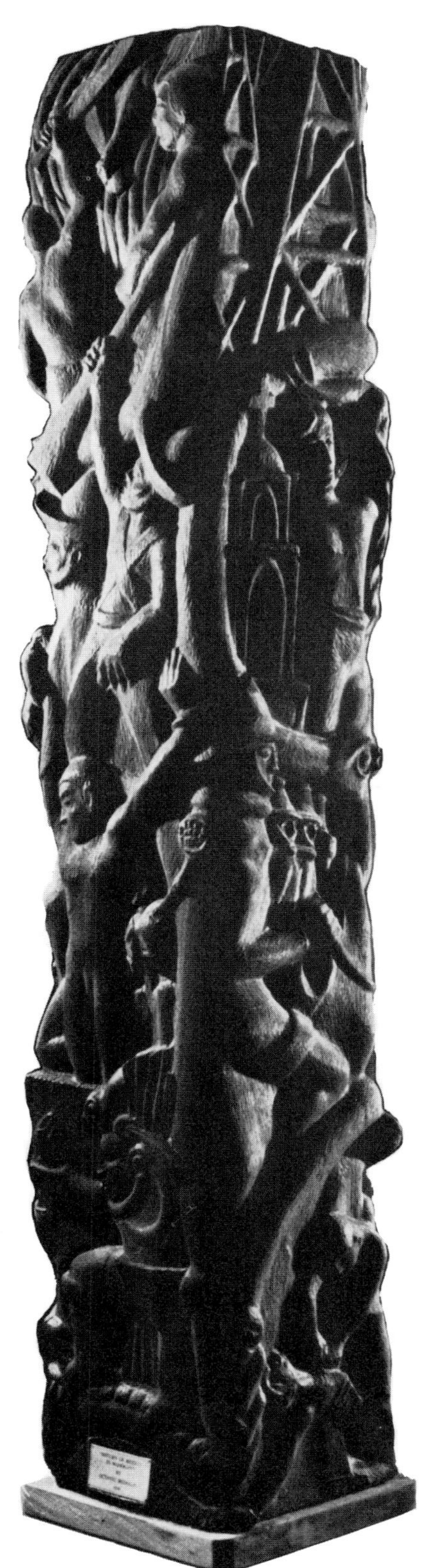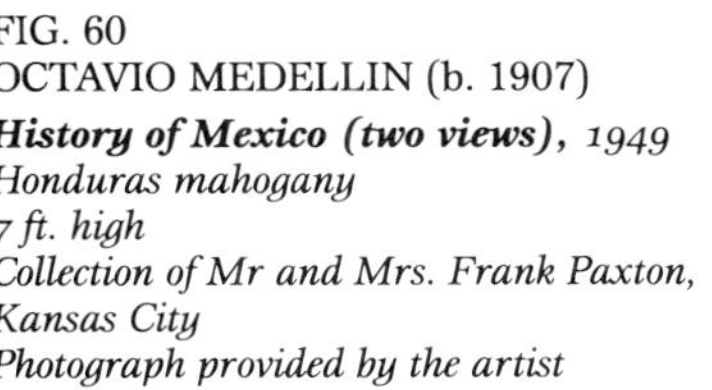

FIG. 60
OCTAVIO MEDELLIN (b. 1907)
History of Mexico (two views), *1949*
Honduras mahogany
7 ft. high
Collection of Mr and Mrs. Frank Paxton,
Kansas City
Photograph provided by the artist

tique. In contrast, the later *Torso* (Cat. 44) by Charles Truett Williams (b. March 24, 1918, Weatherford, Tex.; d. March 30, 1966, Fort Worth), is a nonnaturalistic and post-Cubist rendering of the female form.

Retaining both the head and a sense of gesture, absent or reduced in the Austin torso, Williams' work in its stylized and abstracted interpretation of the human figure relies on exaggeration of the body's gesture and distortion of its form for expressive purposes, and to emphasize the design of the component parts. The resulting image offers an energetic and moving evocation of the splendor of the human form. Williams, who also worked with metals, both in the more traditional medium of cast bronze and in welded forms, was one of the first sculptors in the state to work with found objects. He also completed commissions for monumental sculptures and fountains suited to public spaces.

Ishmael Soto (b. February 25, 1932, Austin) and Williams are the two sculptors represented in the essay to have received their art training through a college degree program[183] and, as such, represent the changing demands and environment for the sculptor student and teacher that occurred in Texas and elsewhere following World War II. Training in college art departments would become a near mandatory route for the student of sculpture, as colleges tended to replace art institutes and academies, with the G.I. bill providing enrollment incentives.

Soto, who has been working primarily as a ceramist for close to two decades, teaching in San Antonio and at the University of Texas at Austin, and at his own pottery design studio in Blue, Texas, was for a short period around 1960, intensely involved in the production of sculpture. Much of that work was iron welded, nonfigurative sculpture, but he also was involved in sculpting the human figure. The figure that is in the exhibition was Soto's first figurative sculpture of the period and was directly modeled in wax (Cat. 45).[184] Although its surface and form suggest the eroded, existentialist figures of Germaine Richier and Alberto Giacometti, Soto, moved by the tactile character of his medium, was more attracted to the expressive quality of the surface and the resulting moving (if not existentialist) interpretation of the human figure, than to the philosophies of the Europeans.[185] Though they were done in the same year, the figure (Fig. 61) in the collection of the Dallas Museum with its broad curving planes and simplified geometric shapes presents a different aesthetic from that of the Houston figure, recalling the work of Giacomo Manzù, in whose work Soto observed a serenity and strength that Soto has acknowledged as an inspiration for the Dallas work.[186]

Charles Umlauf (b. Karl Julius Umlauf, July 17, 1911, South Haven, Michigan)[187], who taught sculpture at the University of Texas at Austin from 1941 to 1981, retiring as Professor Emeritus, came to Austin from Chicago where he had studied at the Art Institute under Albin Polasek and others.[188] Just before moving to Austin he worked in the Fine Arts Project Studios in Chicago creating fountain sculpture. Once in Austin, Umlauf quickly established a successful and busy career, receiving much attention for his work. Two of the works in the exhibition that represent Umlauf are from that first decade. The first of these is the *Pietà* (Cat. 46) of 1944–1945. One of the leading sculptors of religious art in the country, Umlauf's other portrayals of religious subjects, though remarkable, have never surpassed the 1944–1945 *Pietà* in its synthesis of expressive form and content. Its formal complexities are meant to be viewed in the round, the composition evolving as the viewer circles the three figures composing the work.[189]

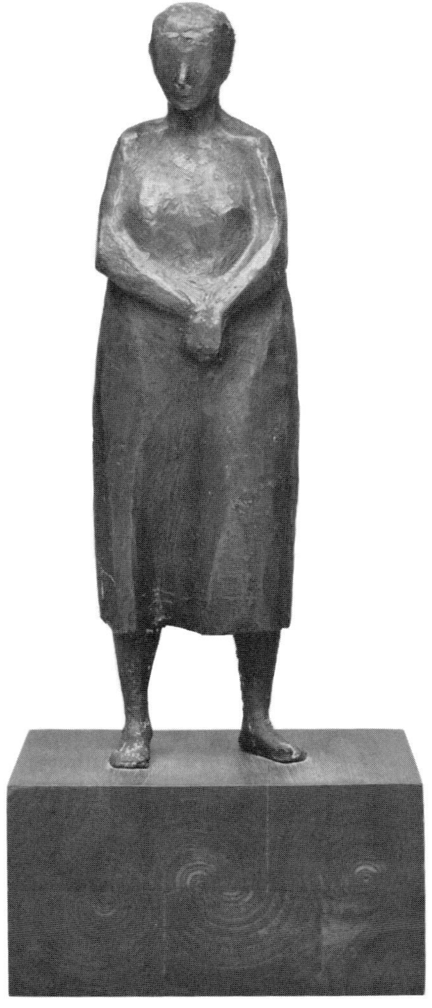

FIG. 61
ISHMAEL H. SOTO (b. 1932)
Standing Figure, *1960*
Bronze
13¾ × 3¾ × 2¾ in.
Collection of the Dallas Museum of Art, Sears, Roebuck & Company Purchase Prize,
22nd Annual Texas Painting and Sculpture, 1960
Photograph provided by the Dallas Museum of Art

FIG. 62
CHARLES UMLAUF (b. 1911)
African Woman, *1948–1988*
Brazilian rosewood
14 in. high × 21 in. long, with base
Collection of the Umlauf Sculpture Garden, Austin
Photographer: Dewey Mears, Austin; photograph
provided by of the artist

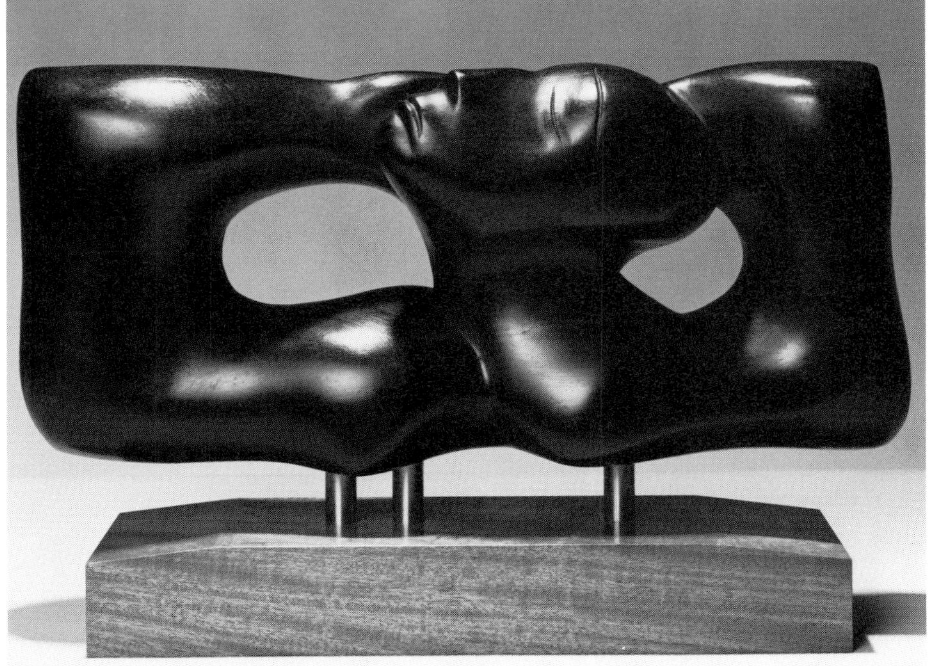

183. Ishmael Soto: B.F.A., The University of Texas at Austin; M.F.A., Cranbrook Academy of Art, Bloomfield Hills, Michigan. Charles Williams: B.F.A. and M.F. A., Texas Christian University, Fort Worth.

184. Cat. 45 was exhibited at HemisFair in 1968, San Antonio, April-October, *The Sphere of Art in Texas,* and in 1971–1972 in *Texas Painting and Sculpture* (Dallas, San Antonio, Austin, Fort Worth, Lubbock).

185. Germaine Richier, French (1904–1959), pupil of Rodin and Bourdelle, influenced by Giacometti; Alberto Giacometti, Swiss (1901–1966), surrealist, pupil of Bourdelle; Giacomo Manzu, Italian (b. 1908).

186. Soto used a model for the Dallas figure, but did not for the Houston figure. Having recently returned to sculpture, Soto currently is sculpting three-to four-foot-high nonrepresentational works cut from trees growing on his own land, his material including post oak and blackjack, and occasionally hickory. For these hardwood sculptures Soto uses a chain-saw and direct carving, sanding the wood until there is a smoothness that allows the colors of the wood to be seen, but which nevertheless reveals the tool marks of the sculptor.

187. Family names changed in 1917.

188. Albin Polasek (b. 1879 Moravia; d. 1965, U.S.).

189. The third figure is the Mary Magdalene.

190. Houston; Pasadena, Calif.; Austin; Dallas; Lubbock; Lake Charles, La.; Peoria.

191. Paul Gauguin (1848–1903) began to introduce primitive references into his work after viewing tribal art at the Paris World's Fair in 1889, and while in the islands of the South Pacific. He first went to Martinique in 1887, then to Tahiti 1891–1893, and finally to the Marquesas in 1895.

192. Gibson A. Danes in *The Sculpture and Drawing of Charles Umlauf,* p. 12. British sculptor Jacob Epstein (1880–1959), French sculptor Henri Gaudier-Brzeska (1891–1915), Russian-French sculptor Ossip Zadkine (b. 1890 Smolensk, Russ.; d. 1967), German sculptors Ernst Barlach (1870–1938), Kathe Kollwitz (1867–1945), and Wilhelm Lehmbruck (1881–1919)

193. The facial expression, which was also retained, is characteristically an important source of meaning in Umlauf's work.

A subject of great pathos in Christian iconography, Umlauf's *Pietà*, with its highly expressionistic treatment is closer to the northern gothic prototype than to any of the tender Pietàs produced by Michelangelo and can be seen to postdate the German expressionist movement in this century. With its anguished surfaces and angular composition, the sculpture was a response on the artist's part to the suffering inflicted by the war. While still in plaster the *Pietà* was exhibited in a one-man show at the Museum of Fine Arts, Houston, in 1947. In that same year the Museum of Fine Arts commissioned a bronze cast of the work from the Roman Bronze Works in Corona, New York. Currently there are seven casts.[190]

Umlauf's carved wood *Standing Figure* (Cat. 47) of 1943 points to the influence of primitive art forms which had first appeared in the work of Gaugain[191] and which offered the modern artist a new avenue through which to discover the human spirit. Umlauf had first recognized the power of primitive art when in Chicago as a student at the Institute. He was also moved by the transformations of the figure in the work of Epstein, Gaudier-Brzeska, and Zadkine, and has expressed his admiration for the expressionist tradition of northern Europe seen in the work of Barlach, Kollwitz, and Lehmbruck, and for the work of many other sculptors including Rodin, Bourdelle, and Brancusi.[192] Despite his reverence for the figure, Umlauf has produced some nonrepresentational work; and has also taken the figure to a highly abstracted state, though retaining a sense of animation through the use of gesture (*African Woman*, Fig. 62).[193]

During the 1950s and 1960s, along with other subject matter, Umlauf produced a number of animal sculptures, employing both bronze and stoneware. These include the muscular terra-cotta *Standing Horse* of ca. 1960 (Cat. 48), which, in its translation of the work of the artists of the T'ang Dynasty, points again to the artist's interest in the art of non-Western cultures.

Summary

Sculpture in Texas had its beginnings in the late nineteenth century when cultural development overtook the frontier and when the call to memorialize past heroes and events in stone and bronze introduced a lasting dialogue between the sculptor and the patron. In this period of monuments to leaders of the past and the battles they had fought, the role of sculpture was one of edification and much effort and money was expended for that purpose. Memorials, and the unveiling ceremonies that launched them, offered the Texas collective consciousness a catharsis against the persistent memories of past struggles, won and lost, and at the same time a social and political affirmation of the past, present, and future.

The early monuments were executed by sculptors who had emigrated to Texas from Germany and Italy. They applied to their sculpture the academic ideals absorbed through their European training, executed within the usually detailed guidelines supplied by those who commissioned the monuments.

With the effects of World War I, the events of the Alamo and the Civil War were to a degree shuffled to a background position for a new generation of Texans. When the war was over, monuments to the doughboy and General Pershing were erected in the state, and at least one monumental fountain was dedicated to the heroes of that war. Though there was a devotion to the memory of these heroes, fewer monuments were erected on their behalf than had been erected previously, perhaps because the war had been fought far away on foreign ground by forces not drawn exclusively from among fellow Texans.

As the number of commissions for historic monuments in Texas was reduced, the purpose of monuments in Texas, which increasingly included fountains surmounted by sculpture groups, was redirected from war and its heroes, often toward a pride in place. Programs for public commissions, still the primary support of the sculptor, praised the characteristics of the land and culture. Some of the sculptors receiving these commissions, though native born, had studied in Paris, others received their training outside Texas at sculpture centers like the Art Institute of Chicago, and the work they produced tended to reflect the influence of the French Beaux-Arts school.

With the 1920s Texas sculptors increasingly turned toward the patronage of the private collector, who welcomed subjects reflecting an ideal innocence. The sculptors offered their new patrons genre subjects; table top statuettes, and small garden fountains, often populated by cherubic and happy children. In addition to widespread changing social and economic factors, the new subject matter may have at times been a result of the artist's greater sense of self-determination, often due to either a short-term or a long-term absence from the lingering regionalist viewpoint in Texas that helped in varying degrees to shape the form and content of past sculpture.

By the 1930s increased attention was paid to the portrait bust, influenced in some part by an interest in "the distinct personality" [194] generated by the work commissioned for The Hall of Man in the Natural History Museum in Chicago. Even during the most venturesome times, prior to the 1930s, figurative sculpture in Texas more often than not represented a conservative viewpoint on the part of the sculptor and the patron. By that decade an interest in both the formalist and the thematic concerns of modern sculpture had appeared in Texas, when sculptors returning from study outside the state brought home an enthusiasm for direct carving and native materials

194. Burgess, "A Sculptor Demonstrates the Unity of Man," p. 18. (See n. 135.)

along with an appreciation for Cubist and primitivistic art concepts. The excitement generated by the sculptural styles displayed at the 1936 Texas Centennial Central Exposition in Dallas, as well as the increased attention given sculpture during that period, reinforced and stimulated further the interest in modernistic art trends that had been introduced to Texas.

A catalyst that prompted a "modern eye" among Texas sculptors was the concern for a truth-to-materials approach, a concern which was carried over into the 1940s and 1950s. At the same time there was an ever-broadening attraction to the formal developments that were shaping modern sculpture. Many Texas sculptors pursued a variety of figurative interpretations that stopped short of nonrepresentational art, but which offered a new way to look at nature. By the 1950s the long uninterrupted dominance of the figure in Texas sculpture was being challenged, as sculptors increasingly turned to new ideas and new materials.

Catalog

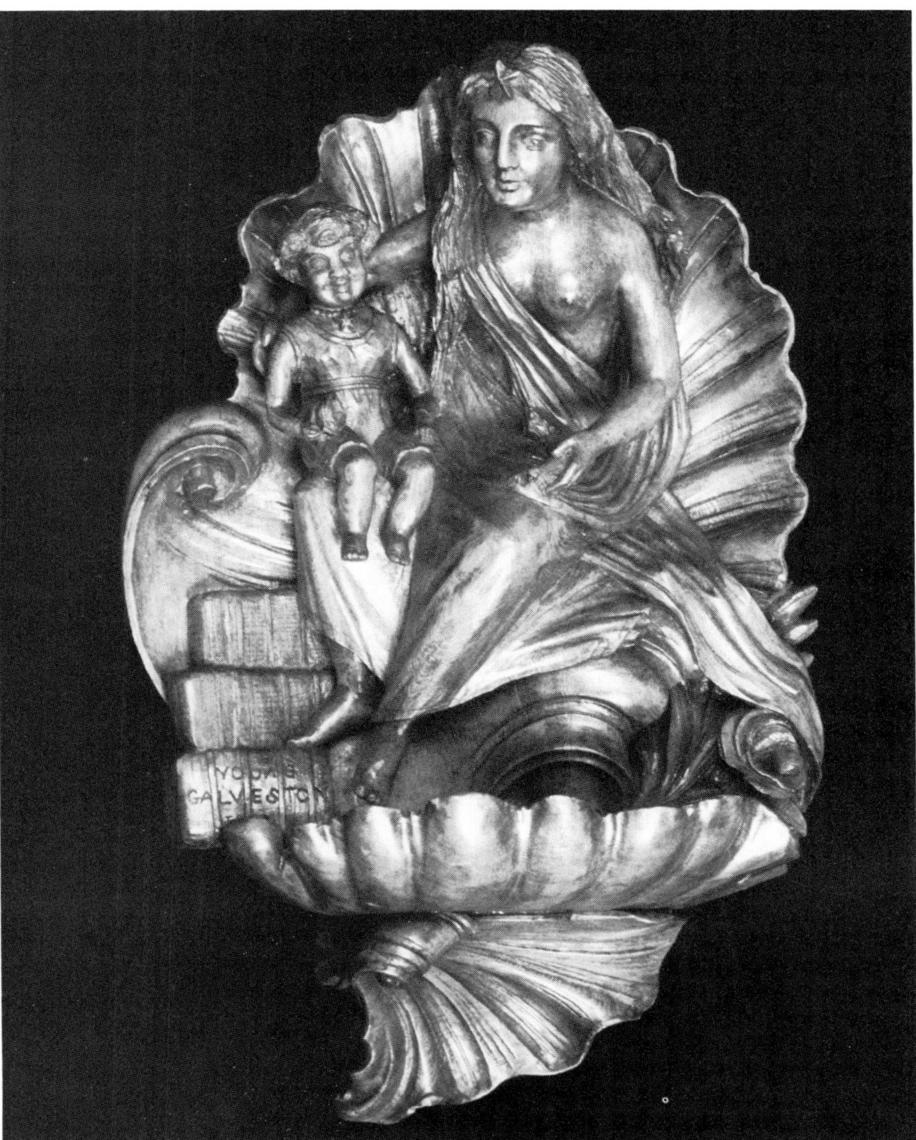

CAT. 1. THOMAS WILLOUGHBY
(active Galveston 1884–1885, 1888–1891)
Young Galveston *(between 1884 and 1891)*
Pine bas-relief
23 × 14 × 7 in.
Collection of the Rosenberg Library, Galveston
Photograph provided by Rosenberg Library,
Galveston

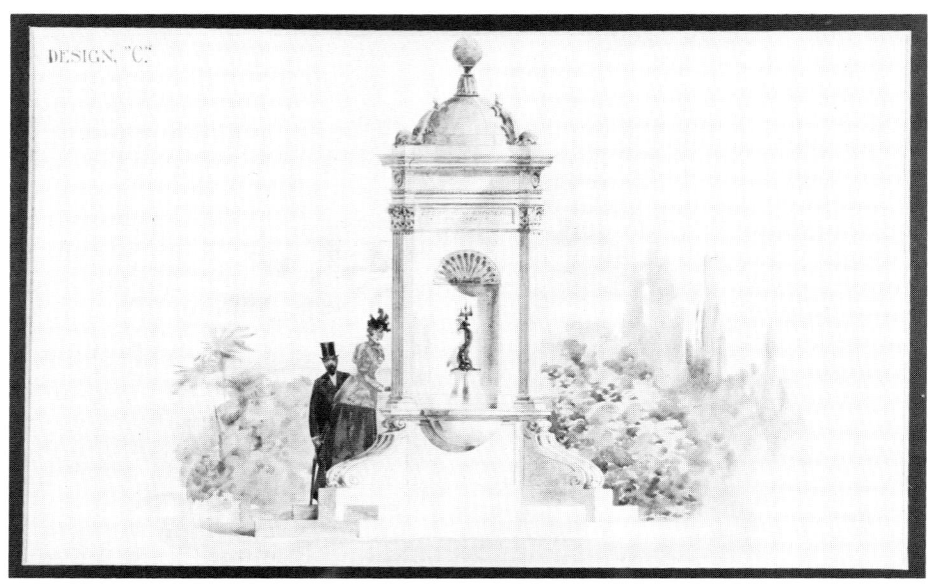

CAT. 2. JOHN MASSEY RHIND (1860–1936)
***Presentation Drawing "C" for Galveston
Fountain,*** *1897*
Watercolor on paper
12½ × 20 in., sight; 20 × 27 in., framed
*Collection of the Rosenberg Library, Galveston,
RL 84.020*
*Photograph provided by Rosenberg Library,
Galveston*

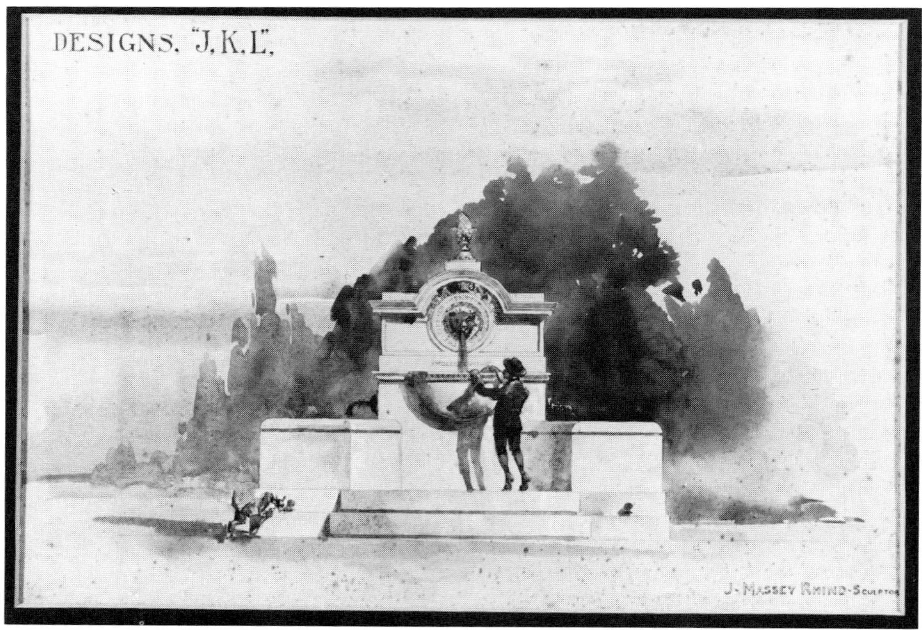

CAT. 4. JOHN MASSEY RHIND (1860–1936)
***Presentation Drawing "JKL" for Galveston
Fountain,*** *1897*
Watercolor on paper
9½ × 13¾ in., sight; 20 × 27 in., framed
*Collection of the Rosenberg Library, Galveston,
RL 84.020*
*Photograph provided by Rosenberg Library,
Galveston*

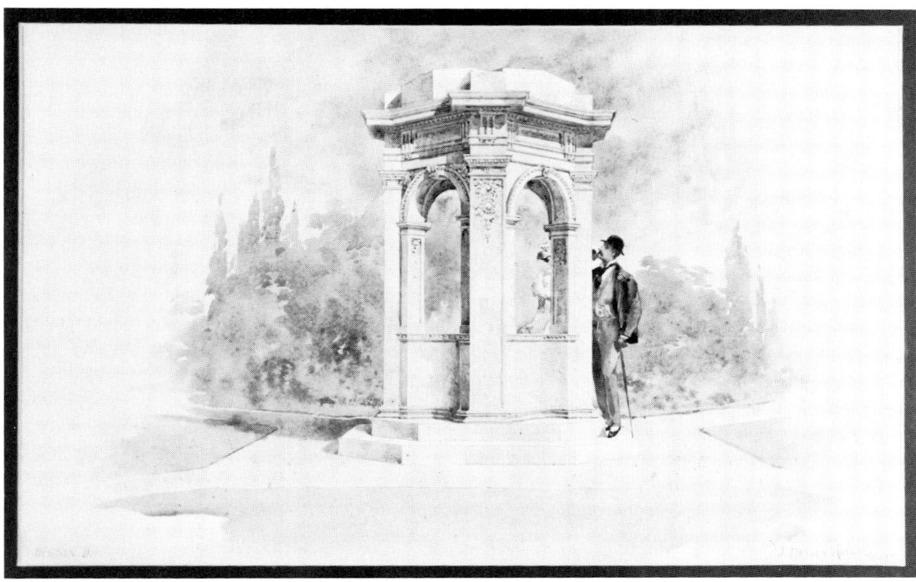

CAT. 3. JOHN MASSEY RHIND (1860–1936)
Presentation Drawing "D" for Galveston Fountain, *1897*
Watercolor on paper
12½ × 20 in. sight; 20 × 27 in., framed
Collection of the Rosenberg Library, Galveston,
RL 84.020
Photograph provided by Rosenberg Library,
Galveston

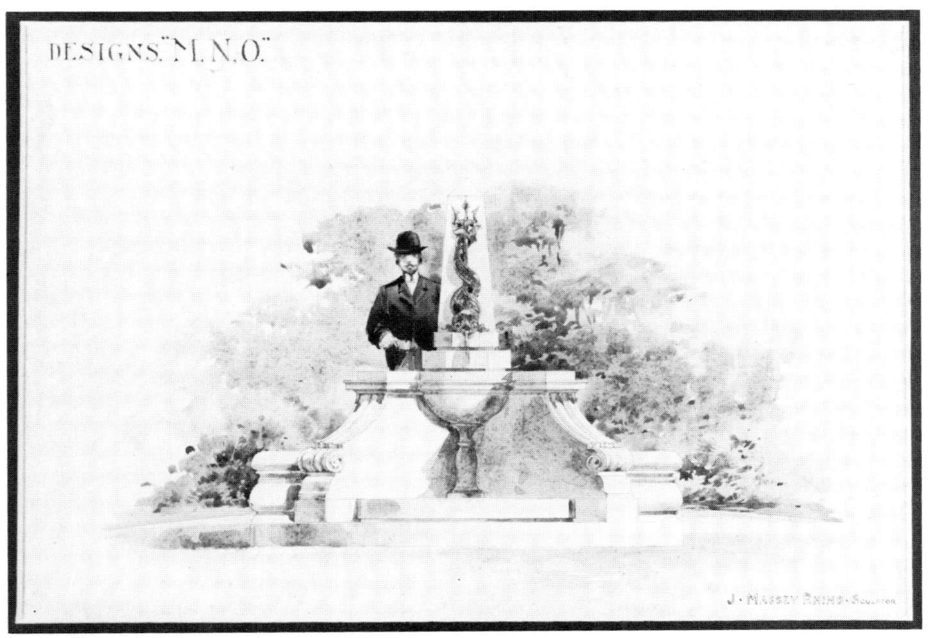

CAT. 5. JOHN MASSEY RHIND (1860–1936)
Presentation Drawing "MNO" for Galveston Fountain, *1897*
Watercolor on paper
9½ × 13¾ in., sight; 20 × 27 in., framed
Collection of the Rosenberg Library, Galveston,
RL 84.020
Photograph provided by Rosenberg Library,
Galveston

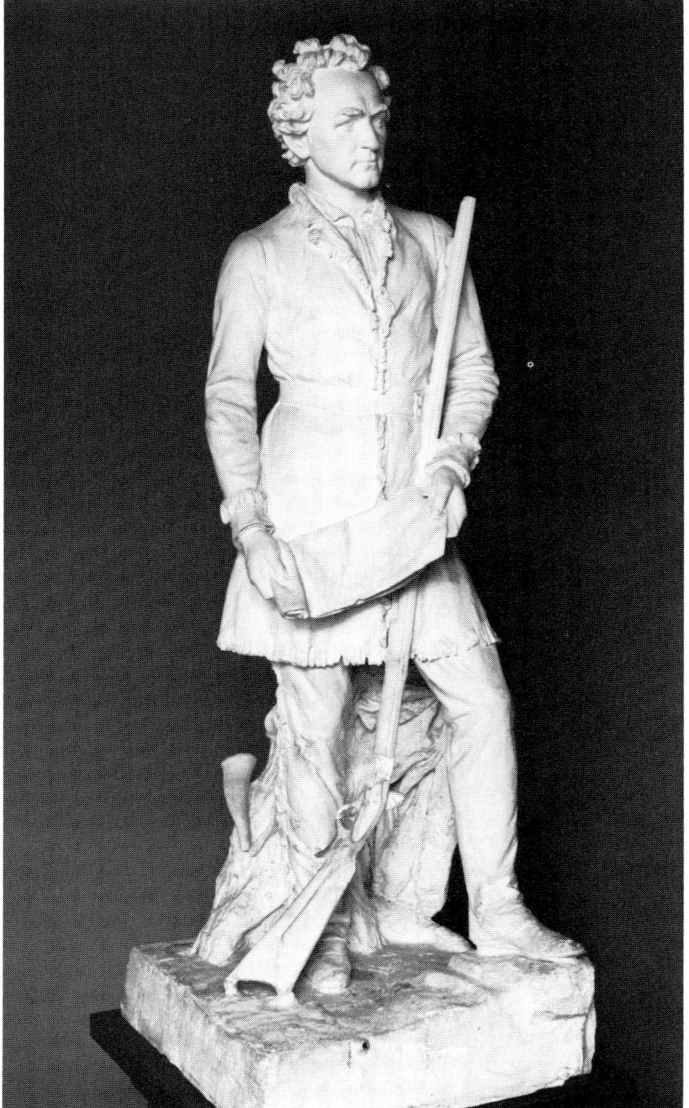

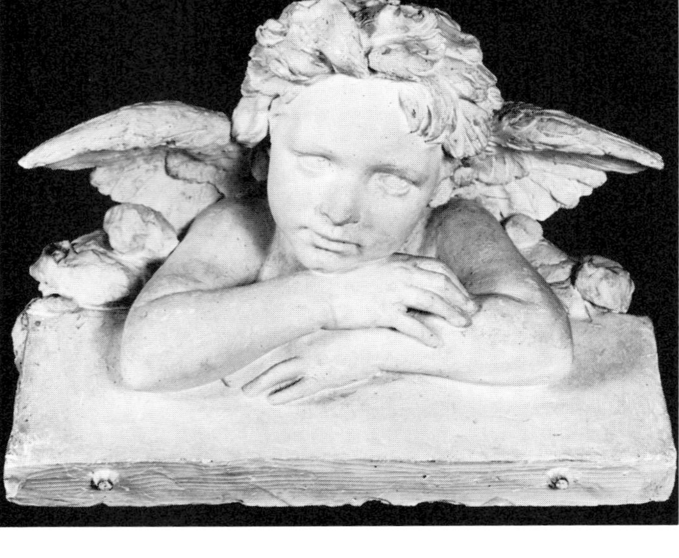

CAT. 6. ELISABET NEY (1833–1907)
Stephen F. Austin, *1893*
Plaster
Signed on base, r.: "Elisabet Ney, fec., 1893,
Austin, Tex."
76½ × 27 × 29 in. high, with base
Collection of the Eugene C. Barker Texas History
Center, The University of Texas at Austin
*Photographer: Phyllis Frede, Austin**

**Photograph shows duplicate cast in collection of the*
Elisabet Ney Museum, City of Austin

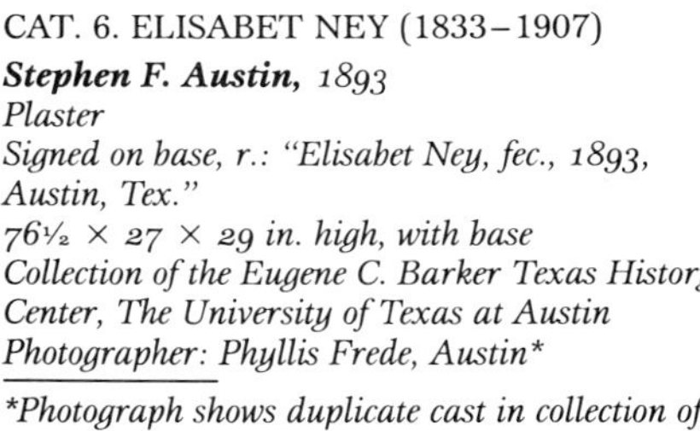

CAT. 8. ELISABET NEY (1833–1907)
Lady Macbeth, *1903*
Plaster
73¾ × 25¾ × 29½ in.
Elisabet Ney Collection, Harry Ransom
Humanities Research Center, The University of
Texas at Austin 67.78.23
Photographer: Phyllis Frede, Austin

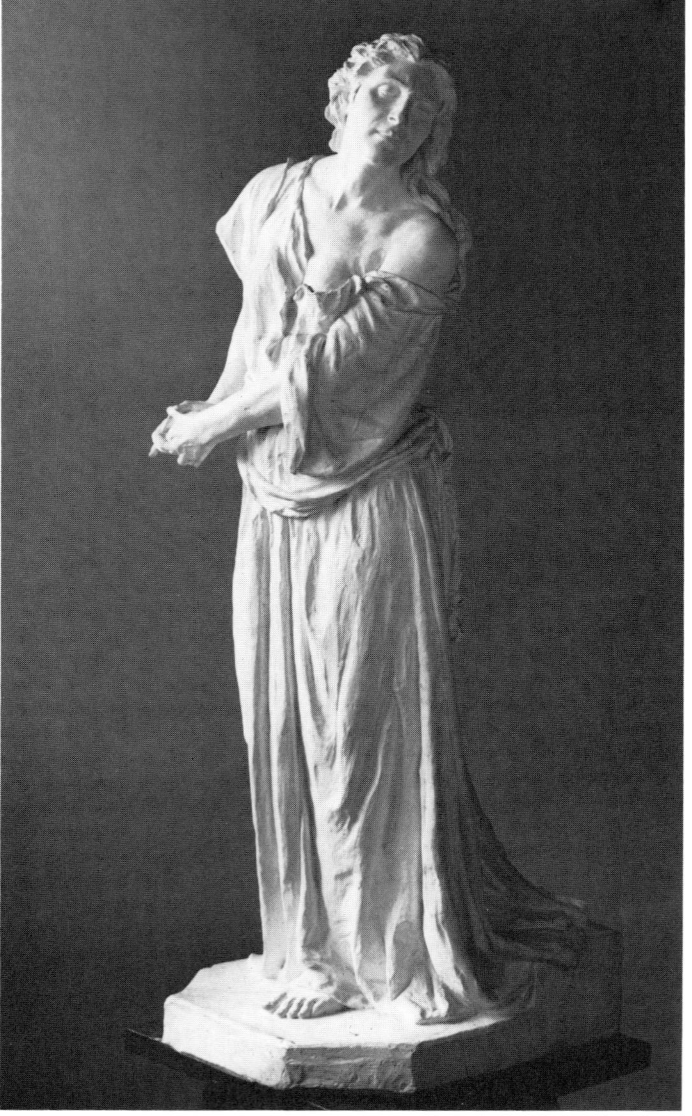

CAT. 7. ELISABET NEY (1833–1907)
Cherub, *1905*
Plaster
15 × 17 × 19 in.
Elisabet Ney Collection, Harry Ransom
Humanities Research Center, The University of
Texas at Austin 83.3
Photograph provided by Harry Ransom
Humanities Research Center, The University of
Texas at Austin

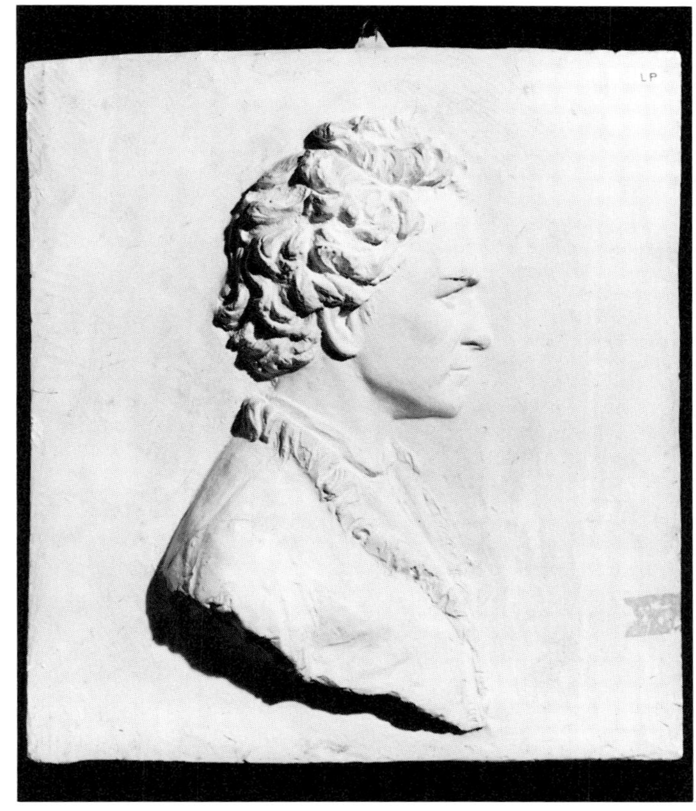

CAT. 9. NANNIE HUDDLE (1860–1951)
Stephen F. Austin, *after 1893*
Plaster bas-relief
15⅘ × 15⅗ in.
Elisabet Ney Collection, Harry Ransom
Humanities Research Center, The University of
Texas at Austin, 67.78.19
Photograph provided by Harry Ransom
Humanities Research Center, The University of
Texas at Austin

CAT. 10. NANNIE HUDDLE (1860–1951)
Marguerite Huddle, *August, 1903*
Signed and dated
Plaster shoulder bust
18½ × 14⅖ × 8⅖ in., including self base
Elisabet Ney Collection, Harry Ransom
Humanities Research Center, The University of
Texas at Austin, 67.78.18
Photograph provided by Harry Ransom
Humanities Research Center, The University of
Texas at Austin

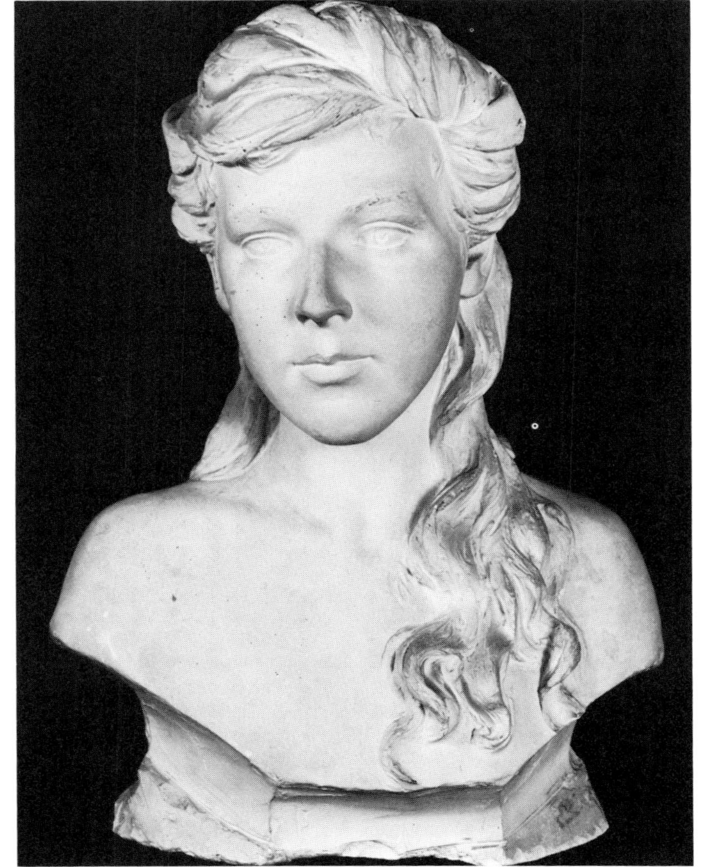

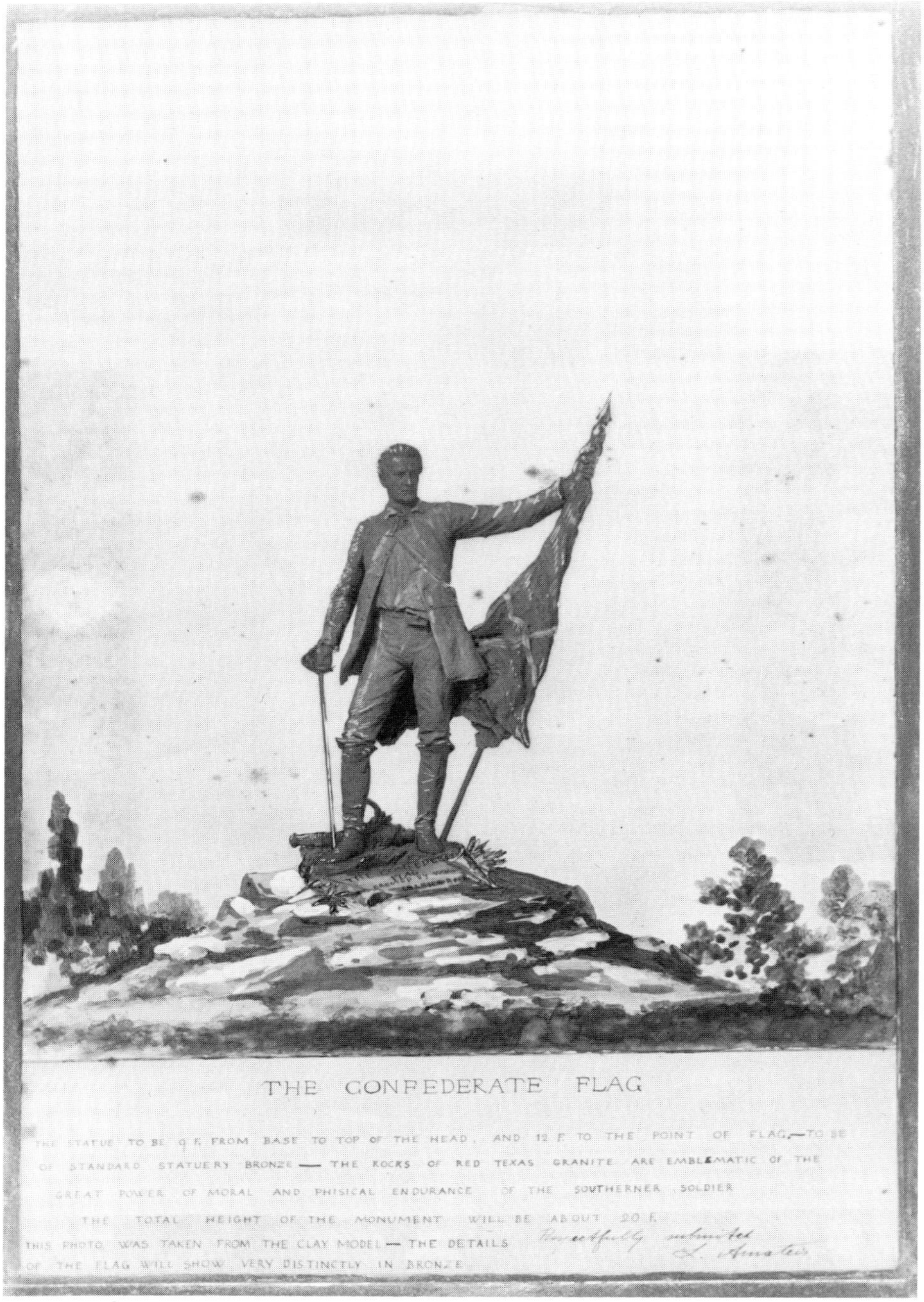

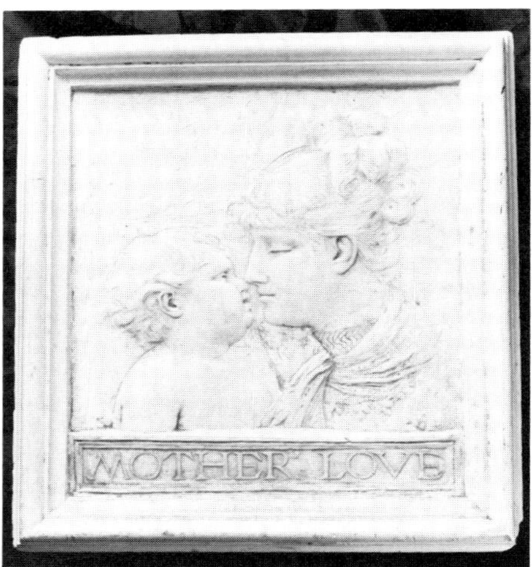

CAT. 12. LOUIS AMATEIS (1855–1913)
Mother's Love, *1907*
Plaster bas-relief
17¼ × 11⁹⁄₁₆ in.
*Collection of the Rosenberg Library, Galveston,
RL 89.001*
*Photograph provided by Rosenberg Library,
Galveston*

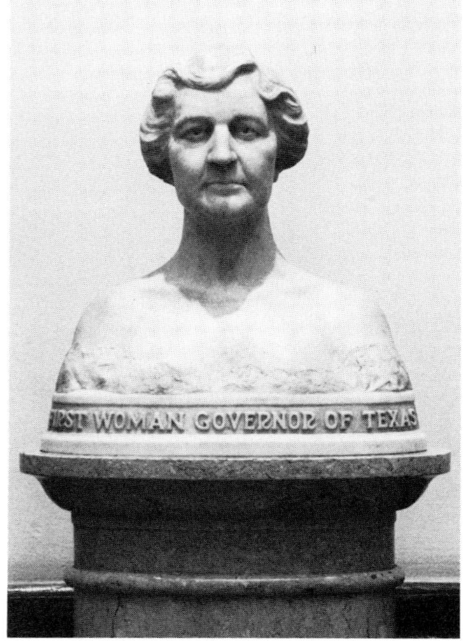

CAT. 11. LOUIS AMATEIS (1855–1913)
***The Confederate Flag (Artist's Contest
Submission for Confederate Heroes
Monument),*** *ca. 1899*
Hand-colored photograph
*14 × 20 in. sheet, including photograph and
legend*
*Collection of the Rosenberg Library, Galveston,
RL 71.041*
*Photograph provided by Rosenberg Library,
Galveston*

CAT. 13. ENRICO FILBERTO CERRACCHIO
(1880[?]–1956)
***First Woman Governor of Texas (Miriam A.
Ferguson),*** *1926*
White marble shoulder bust
21 × 20 × 10 in., marble base 48 × 24 × 15 in.
*Collection of the State Preservation Board,
Texas Capitol*
*Photographer: George Holmes, Huntington Art
Gallery, The University of Texas at Austin*

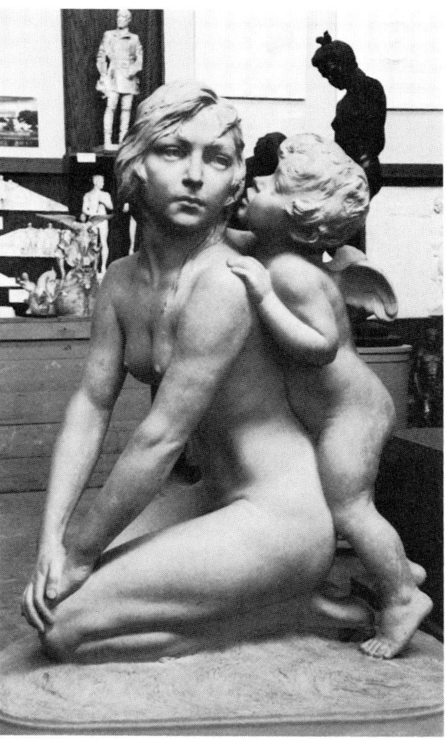

CAT. 15. POMPEO COPPINI (1870–1957)
Love Awakening, *1927–1935*
Plaster, flesh color paint
48 × 40 × 22 in. wide, including 1 in. high base
Collection of the Coppini-Tauch Studio,
San Antonio
Photograph provided by Walter J. Long,
San Antonio

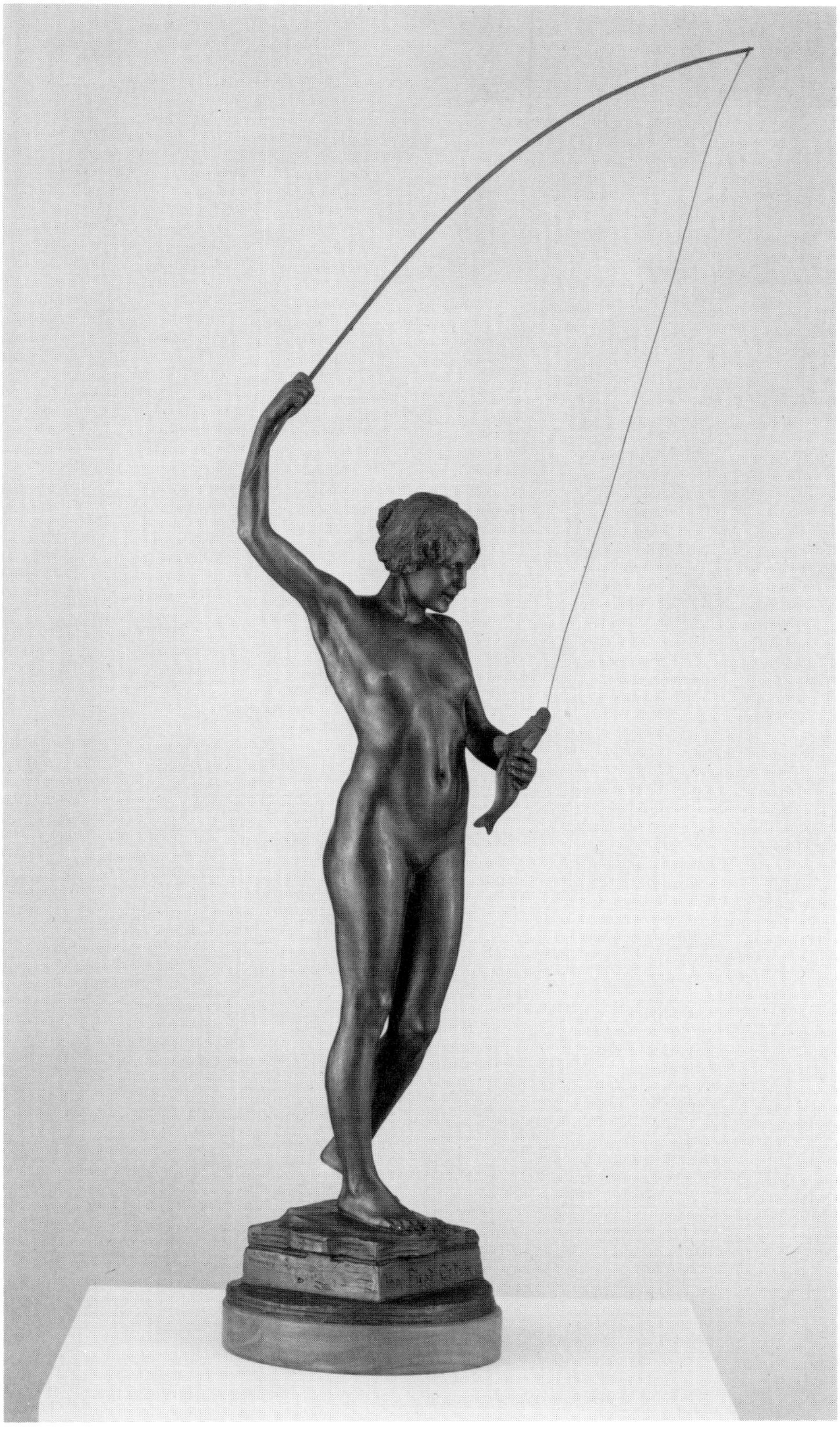

CAT. 14. POMPEO COPPINI (1870–1957)
The First Catch, *ca. 1933*
Bronze
32 in. high
Collection of the Coppini-Tauch Studio,
San Antonio
Photographer: George Holmes, Huntington Art
Gallery, The University of Texas at Austin

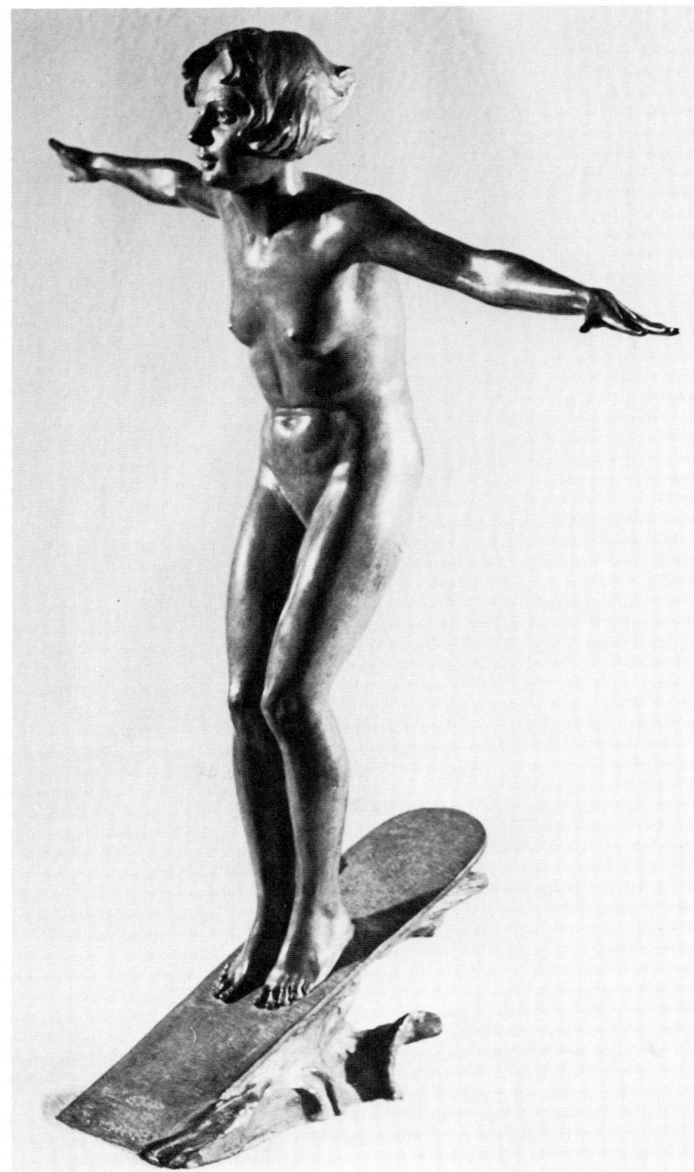

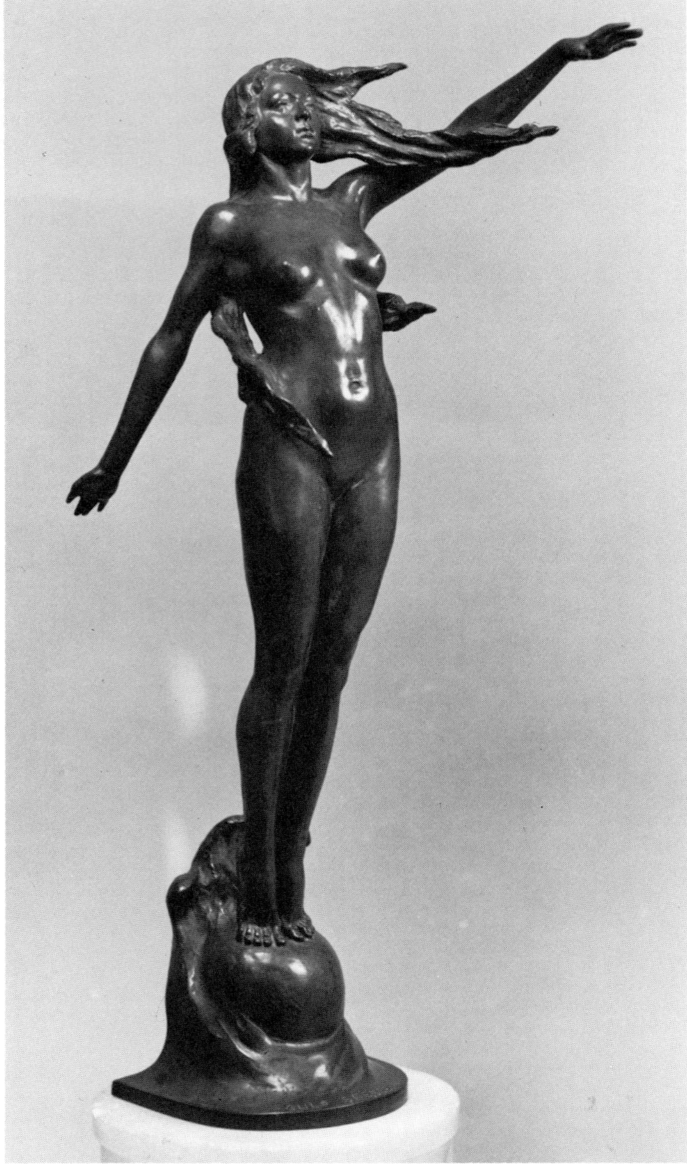

CAT. 16. WALDINE TAUCH (1892–1986)
Surfboard, *ca. 1924*
Bronze with green patina
28 in. high
Collection of the Coppini-Tauch Studio,
San Antonio
Photograph provided by Coppini-Tauch Studio,
San Antonio

CAT. 17. WALDINE TAUCH (1892–1986)
Gulf Breeze, *1929*
Signed, r. side of base, "W. A. Tauch-Sc."
Bronze with dark patina
18 × 4 × 4 in., marble base 1 × 5 × 4½ in.
Collection of The San Antonio Museum Association,
44.15.311G
Photograph provided by The San Antonio Museum
Association

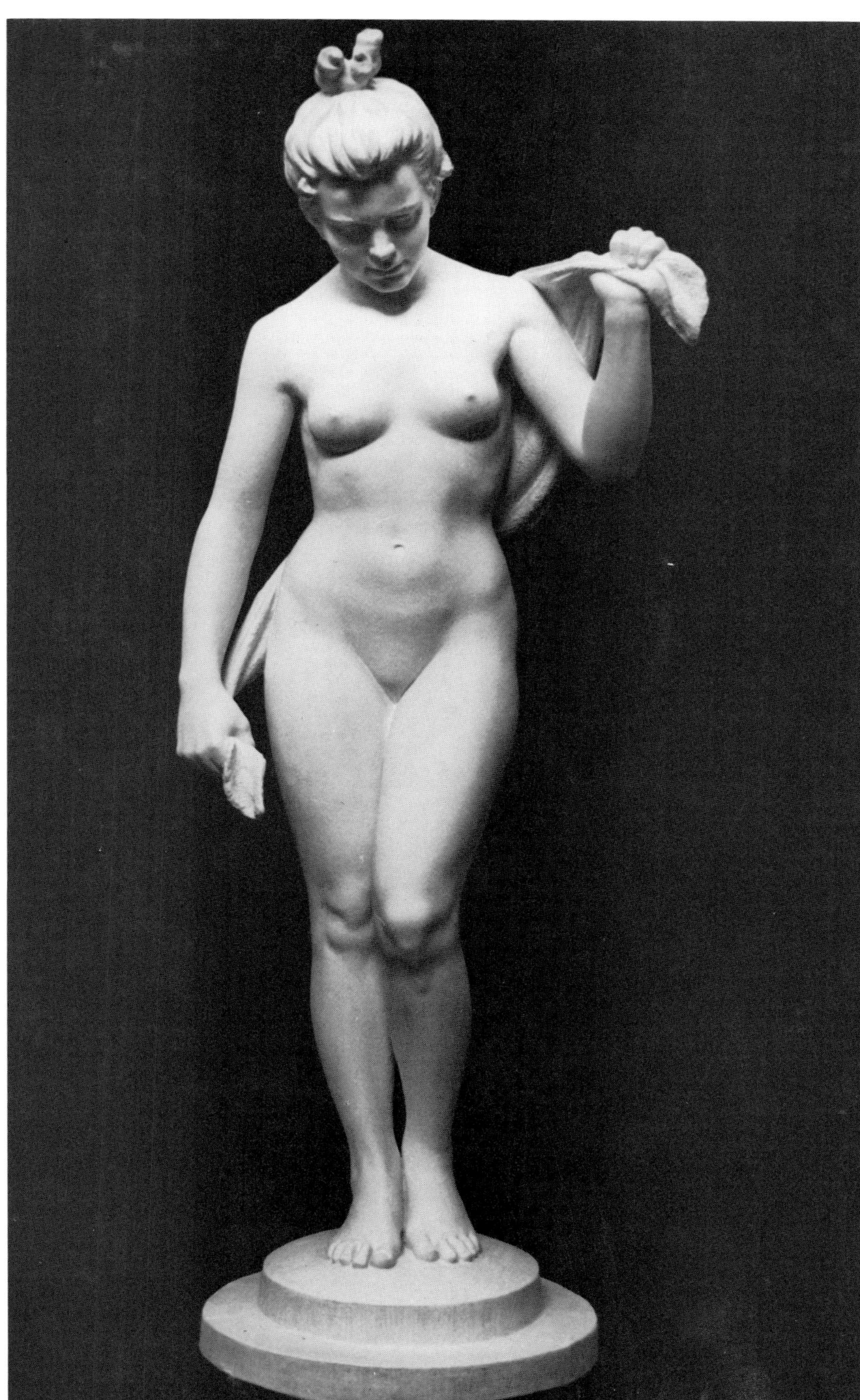

CAT. 18. WALDINE TAUCH (1892–1986)
After the Bath, *1946*
*Plaster**
53 in. high
Collection of the Coppini-Tauch Academy,
San Antonio
Photograph provided by Coppini-Tauch Studio,
San Antonio

*****After the Bath*** *is represented in the exhibition by*
a bronze cast.

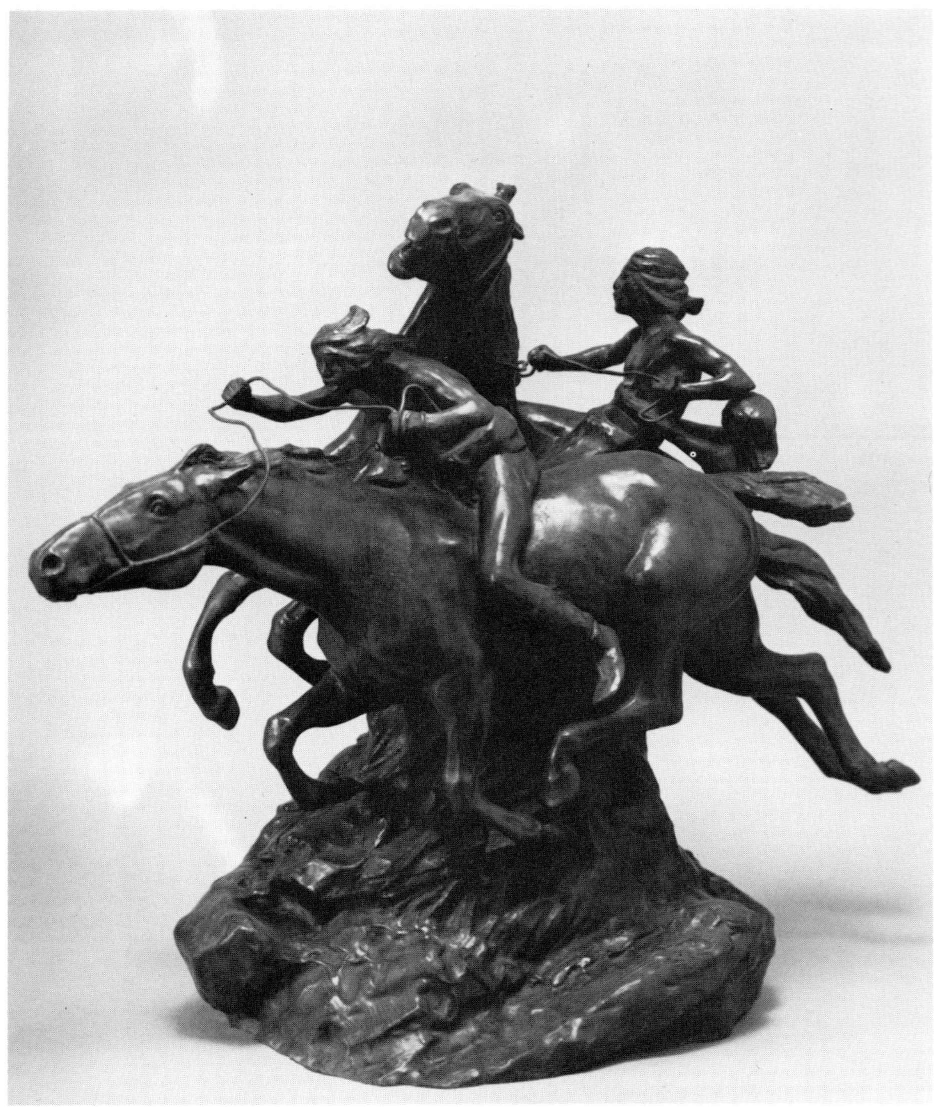

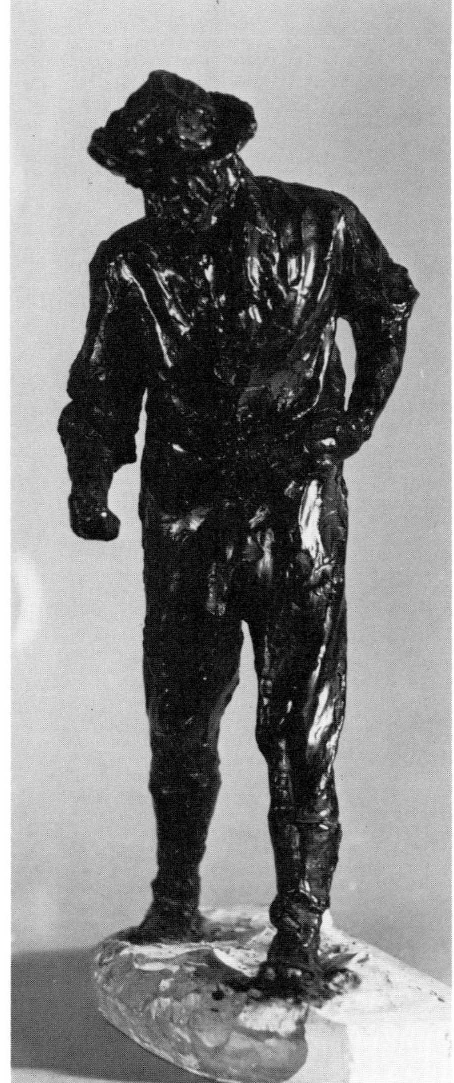

CAT. 19. GUTZON BORGLUM (1867/
70–1941)
**Indians Pursue (Apaches Pursued by U.S.
Troops),** *ca. 1901*
Signed l.l., "Gutzon Borglum"
*Bronze with dark patina (cast by Roman Bronze
Works, 1946)*
17 × 9 × 23 in.
*Collection of The San Antonio Museum Association,
46.111.163P*
*Photograph provided by The San Antonio Museum
Association*

CAT. 20. GUTZON BORGLUM (1867–1941)
**Cowhand, (model for larger figure in
uncompleted Trail Drivers Monument),**
ca. 1926
*Initialed, top of base at r., "GB" within
a circle*
Plaster, painted
16 × 6 × 10 in.
*Collection of The San Antonio Museum Association,
gift of Mrs. Gutzon Borglum, 49-17-325G*
*Photograph provided by The San Antonio Museum
Association*

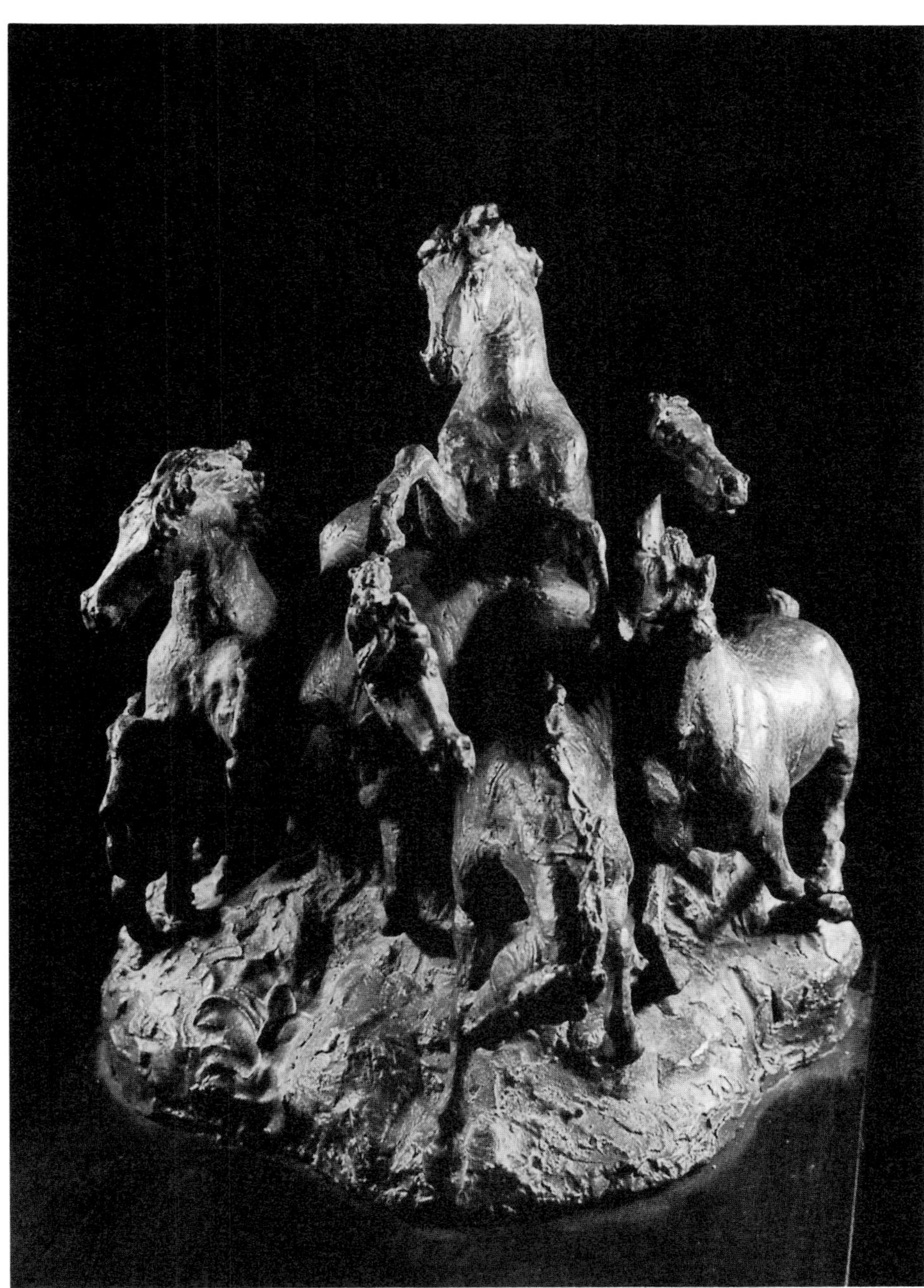

CAT. 21. ALEXANDER PHIMISTER
PROCTOR (1862–1950)
***Seven Mustangs Maquette for Mustangs
Monument,*** *1939–1940*
Bronze
13 × 9 × 11 in.
*Collection of the Texas Memorial Museum, Austin,
gift of Ralph R. and Ethel Ogden, 1948
Photograph provided by the Texas Memorial
Museum, Austin*

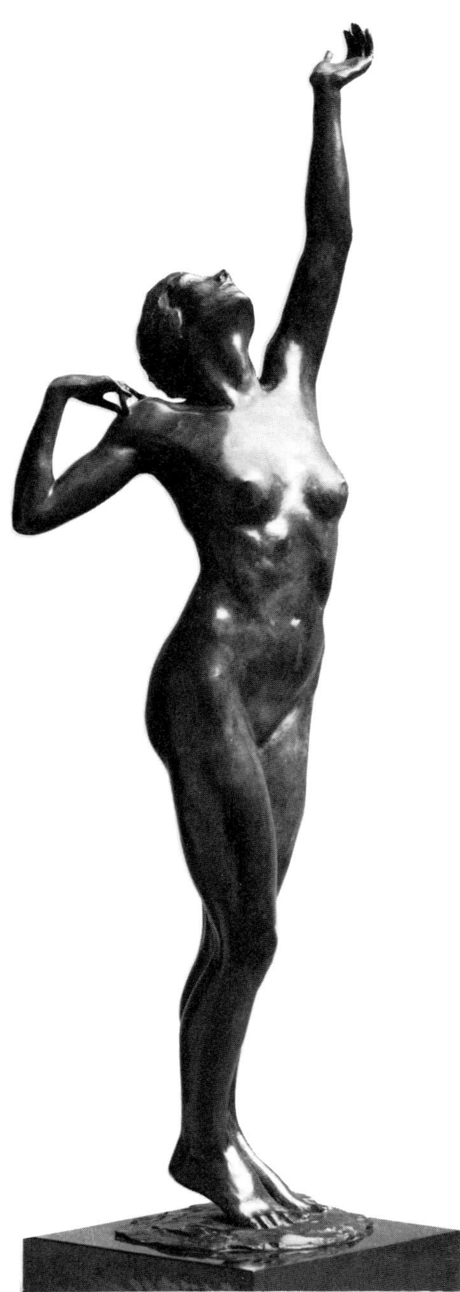

CAT. 22. BONNIE MCLEARY (b. 1890–1971)
Aspiration, *1921*
Bronze
30⅛ in. high
*Collection of The Metropolitan Museum of Art, gift
of Jamie Nadal, 1924, 24.96*
*Photograph provided by The Metropolitan Museum
of Art*

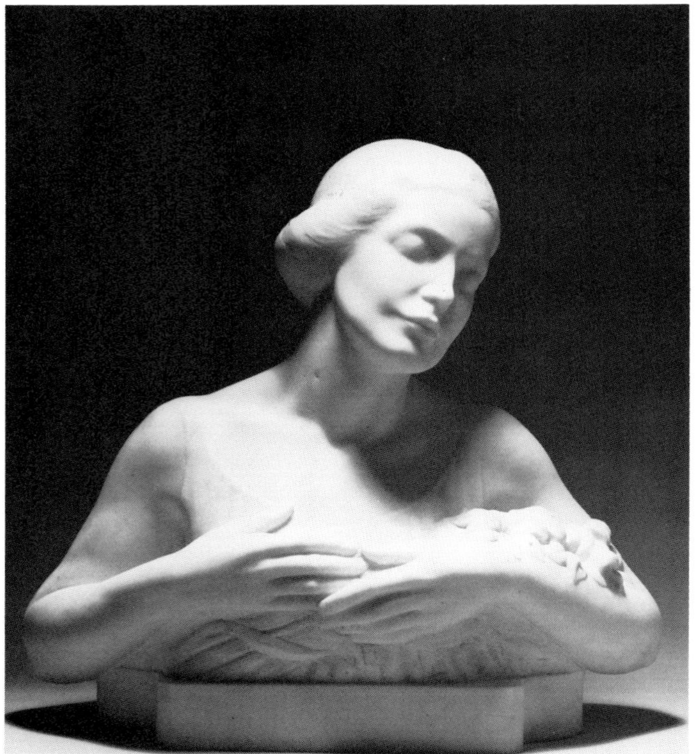

CAT. 23. BONNIE MCLEARY (b. 1890–1971)
The Blessed Damozel, *1926*
Signed on base, below l. arm, "Bonnie McLeary"
White marble shoulder bust
22 × 23 × 8 in.
*Collection of The San Antonio Museum Association,
purchased from the artist, 43.4.191.P*
*Photograph provided by The San Antonio Museum
Association*

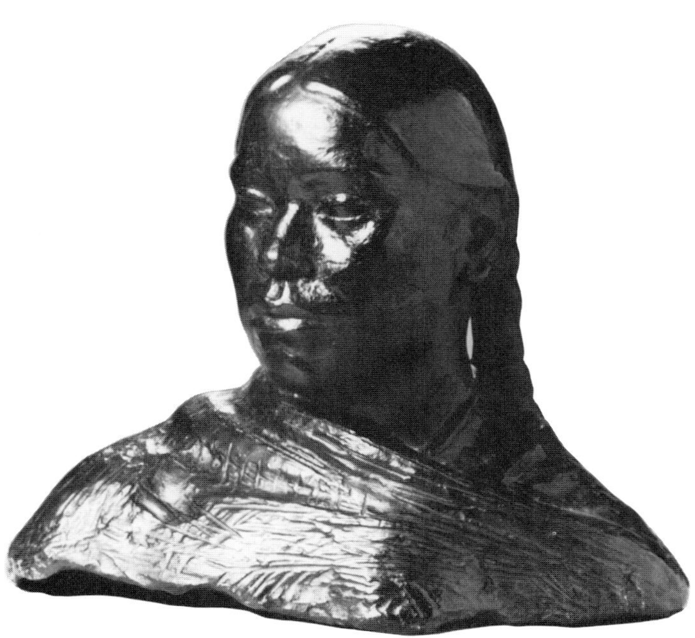

CAT. 24. URBICI SOLER (1890–1953)
Untitled (Young Girl with Braids), *1933*
*Initialed and dated; inscribed, "YSLA D
YUNUEN PATZCUARO"*
Bronze shoulder bust
14¾ × 17 × 8 in.
Collection of the El Paso Public Library
Photographer: Darst-Ireland Photography, El Paso

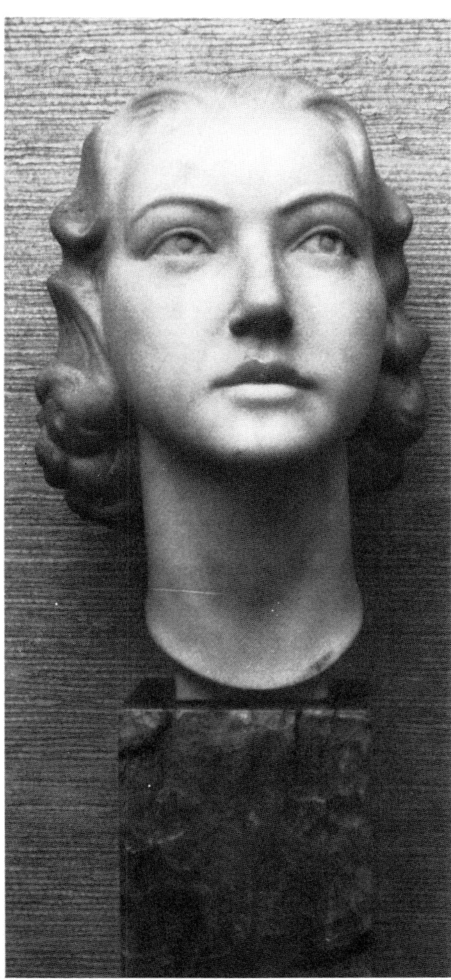

CAT. 25. ELECTRA WAGGONER BIGGS (b.
1912)
Self-Portrait, *1936*
Signed and dated, r. of self-base
Carrara marble with amethyst quartz base
21 in. high, base 5 × 7 in.
*Collection of the Red River Valley Museum,
Vernon, 76.2*
*Photograph provided by Red River Valley Museum,
Vernon*

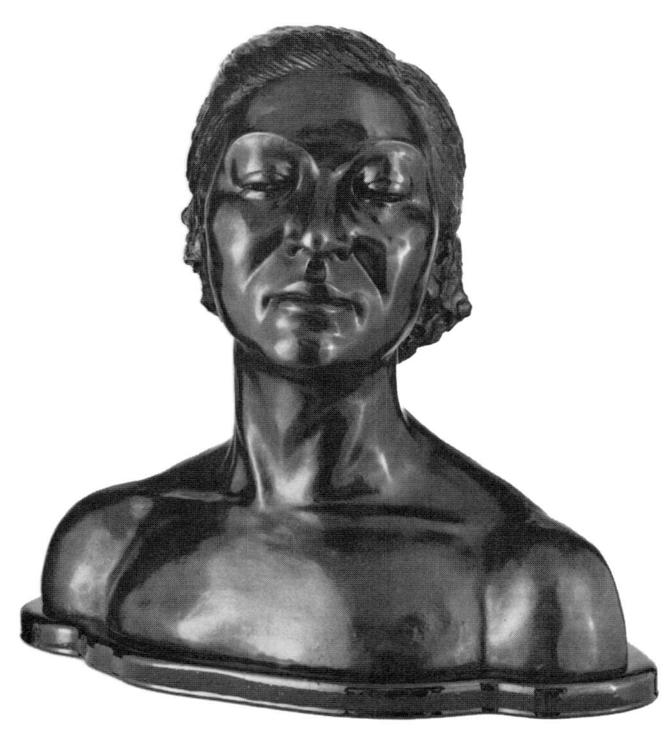

CAT. 26. ELECTRA WAGGONER BIGGS (b.
1912)
Enigma, *date of original plaster, 1937*
Signed and dated, back, l.l. shoulder
Bronze, cast 1988
15 in. high
Collection of the Red River Valley Museum, Vernon
*Photographer: George Holmes, Huntington Art
Gallery, The University of Texas at Austin*

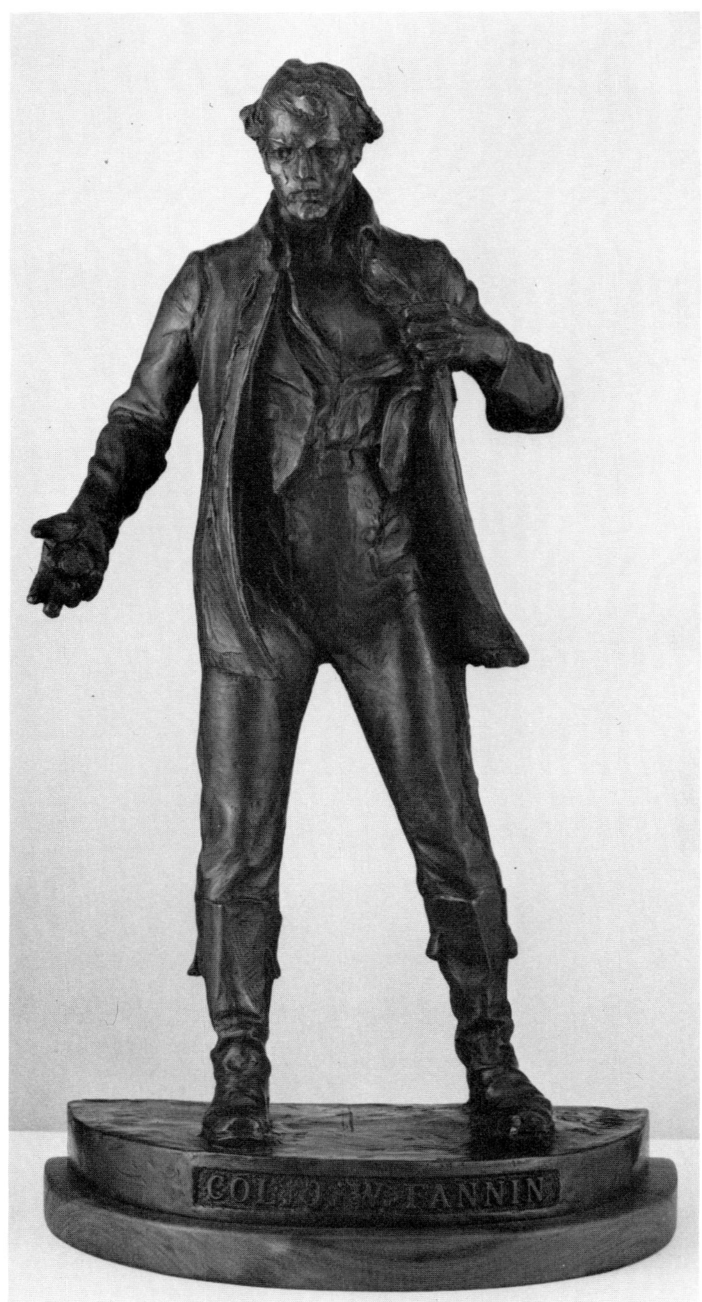

CAT. 27. POMPEO COPPINI (1870–1957)
**Colonel James Walker Fannin, (model for 7
ft. figure),** *1936*
Signed l. base, "Pompeo Coppini"
Bronze
ca. 18 in. high, with self base ca. 1 in. high
*Collection of the Coppini-Tauch Studio, San
Antonio*
*Photographer: George Holmes, Huntington Art
Gallery, The University of Texas at Austin*

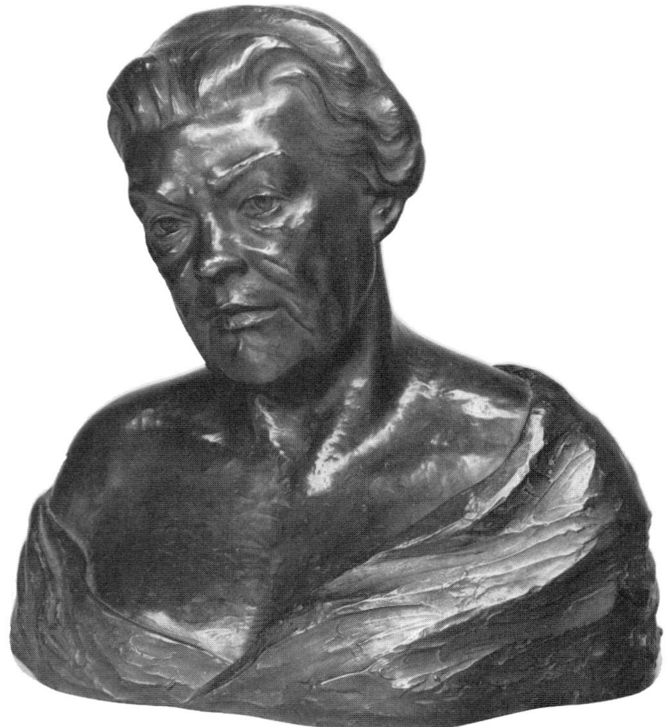

CAT. 28. ALLIE VICTORIA TENNANT
(1898–1971)
Mrs. George K. Meyer, *ca. 1933*
Bronze shoulder bust
18½ × 17¾ × 13 in.
*Collection of the Dallas Museum of Art,
Meyer Memorial Fund, 1933.23*
Photograph provided by Dallas Museum of Art

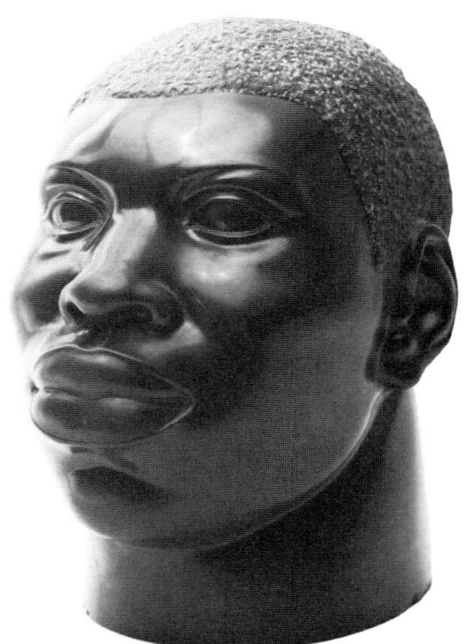

CAT. 29. ALLIE VICTORIA TENNANT
(1898–1971)
Negro Head (Negro), *1935*
Black Belgian marble
12 × 8 × 10 in.
*Collection of the Dallas Museum of Art, Kiest
Memorial Fund Purchase Prize, Seventh Annual
Dallas Allied Arts Exhibition, 1935, 1935.57*
Photograph provided by Dallas Museum of Art

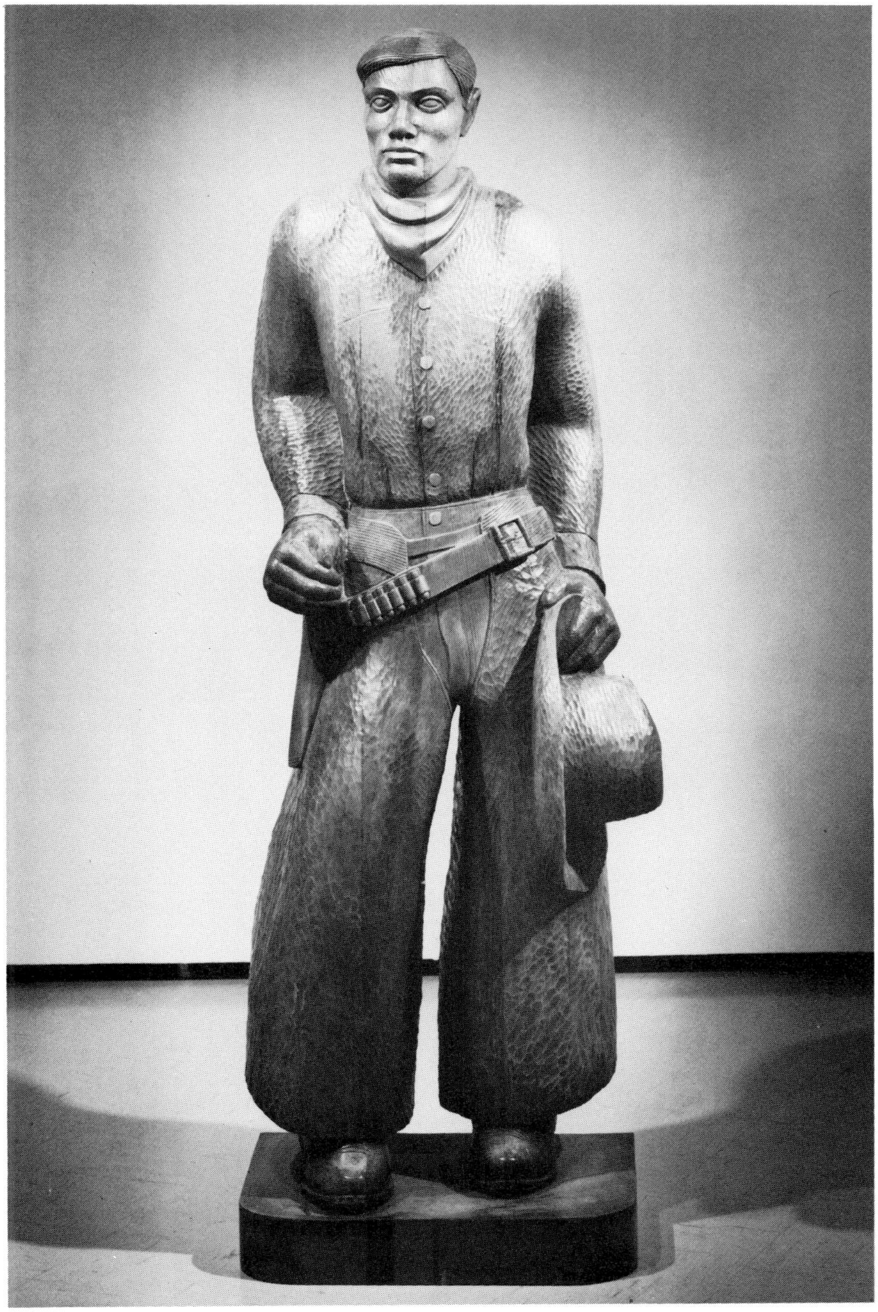

CAT. 30. DOROTHY AUSTIN (b. 1911)
Cowboy, *1936*
White pine
71 × 24 × 17 in.
Collection of the City of Dallas Park and
Recreation Department and the Dallas Historical
Society, CD.1936.38
Photograph provided by the Dallas Historical
Society

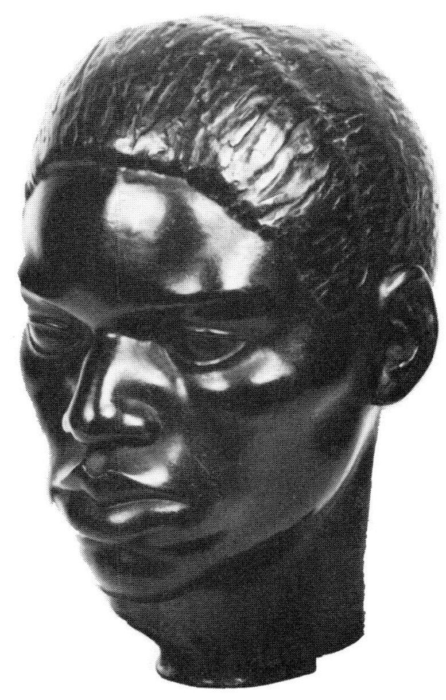

CAT. 31. DOROTHY AUSTIN (b. 1911)
Negro Head, *1932*
Bronze
17½ in. high with base
Collection of the artist
Photograph provided by the artist

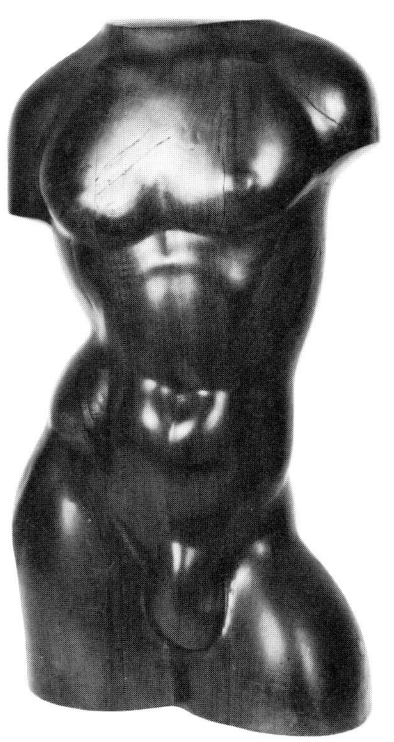

CAT. 32. DOROTHY AUSTIN (b. 1911)
Male Torso, *1934*
Black walnut
23 in. high
Collection of the artist
Photograph provided by the artist

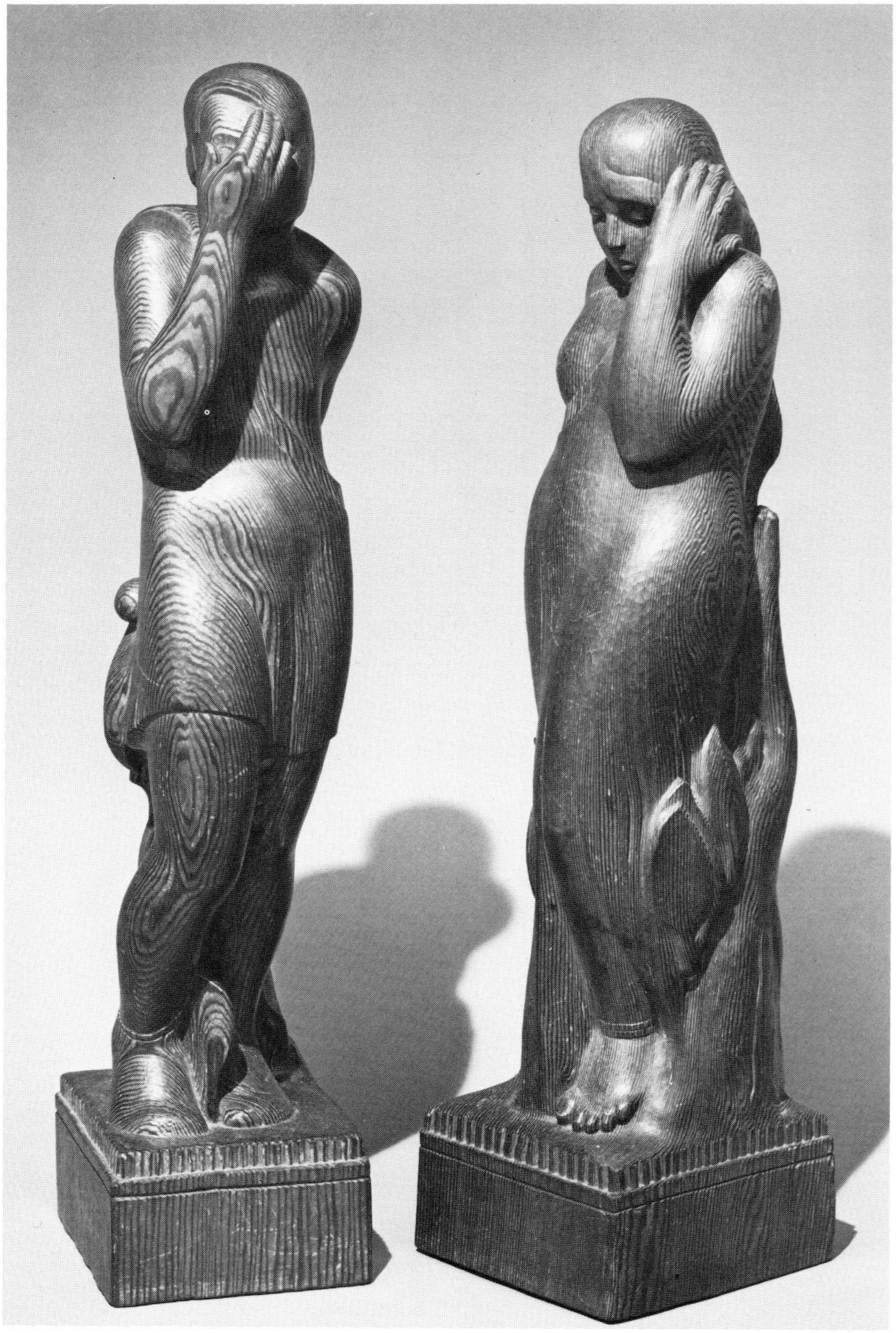

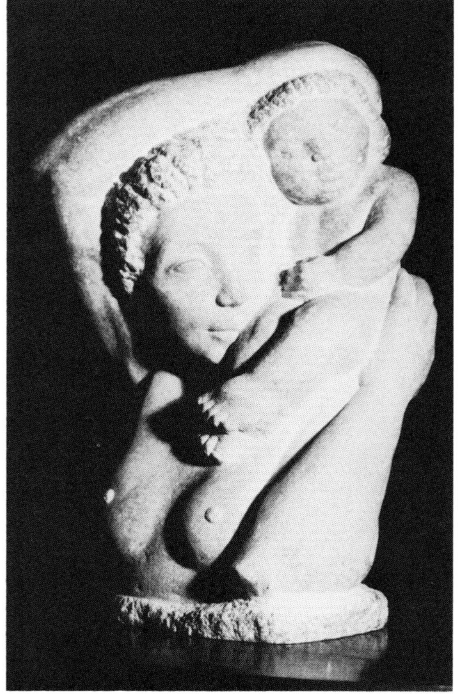

CAT. 35. IONE RUTH FRANKLIN
(1893–1976)

Young Mother, *1944*
Marble
23 × 15½ × 13 in.
Collection of Marcelle and David Orman
Photograph provided by The Jerry Bywaters
Collection of Art of the Southwest, Southern
Methodist University, Dallas

CAT. 33. MABEL FAIRFAX KARL (b. 1901)

Orpheus, *ca. 1934*
Signed l.r. rear, "KARL"
Wood
20⅛ × 4⅝ in., base 8 × 8 × 8 in.
Collection of The Museum of Fine Arts, Houston,
Purchase Prize, 10th Annual Houston Artists
Exhibition, 34.1
Photograph provided by Museum of Fine Arts,
Houston

CAT. 34. MABEL FAIRFAX KARL (b. 1901)

Eurydice, *ca. 1934*
Signed l.l. rear, "KARL"
Wood
19½ × 4⅝ × 5⅛ in., base 8 × 8 × 8 in.
Collection of The Museum of Fine Arts, Houston,
Purchase Prize, 10th Annual Houston Artists
Exhibition, 34.2
Photograph provided by Museum of Fine Arts,
Houston

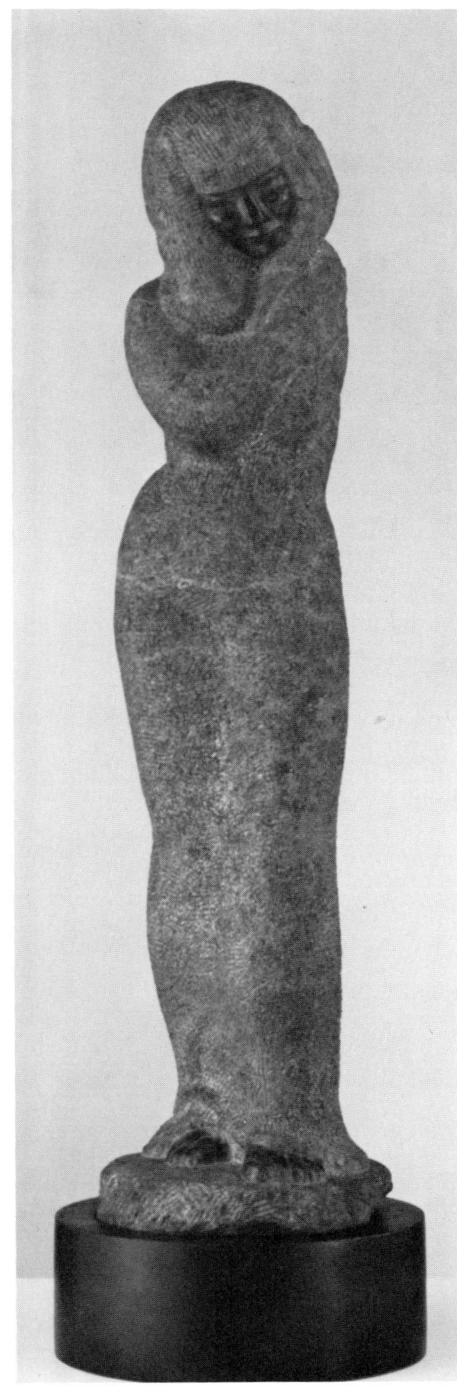

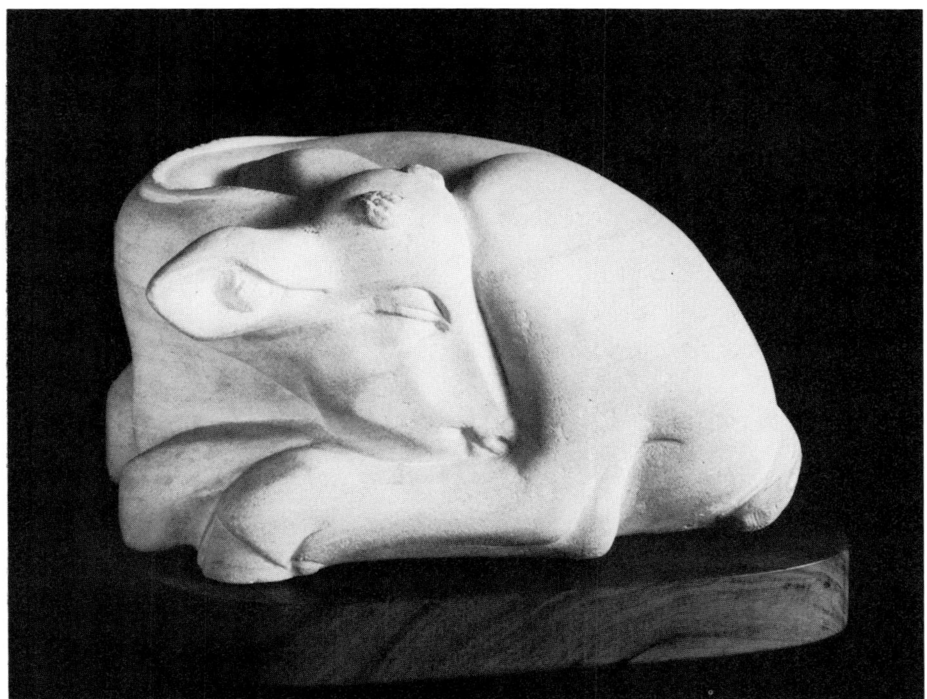

CAT. 37. EVALINE C. SELLORS (b. 1907)
Winter (Sleeping Fawn), *1947*
Limestone
6½ × 9½ × 7 in.
*Collection of the Modern Art Museum of Fort
Worth, Museum Purchase*
*Photograph provided by Modern Art Museum of
Fort Worth*

CAT. 36. BESS BIGHAM HUBBARD
(1896–1977)
Green Goddess (Thinking Woman),
1948–1949
Green marble
24 × 4½ × 5 in., base 3 × 7 in.
Collection of the Hubbard abc Estate, Lubbock
*Photographer: George Holmes, Huntington Art
Gallery, The University of Texas at Austin*

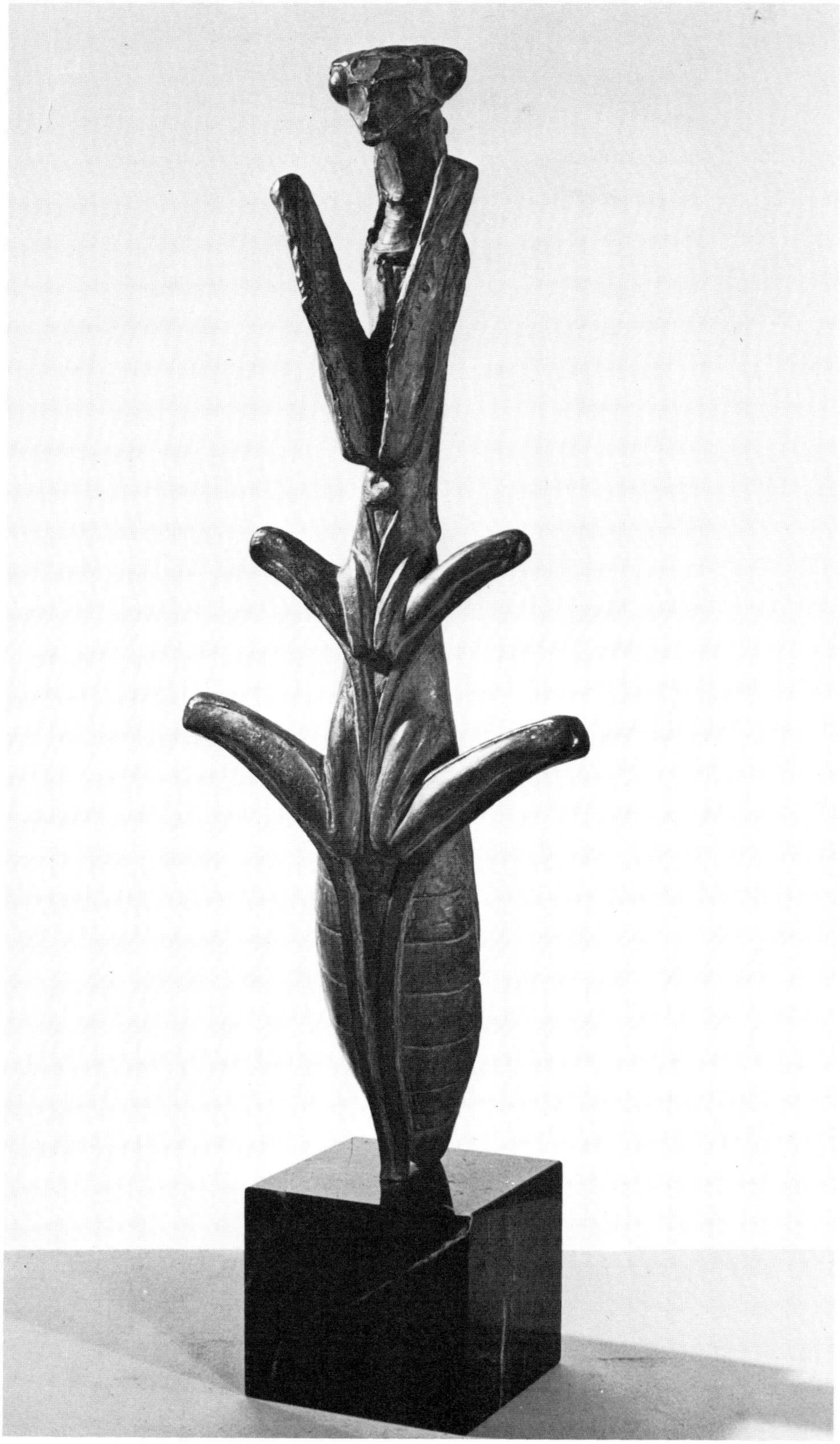

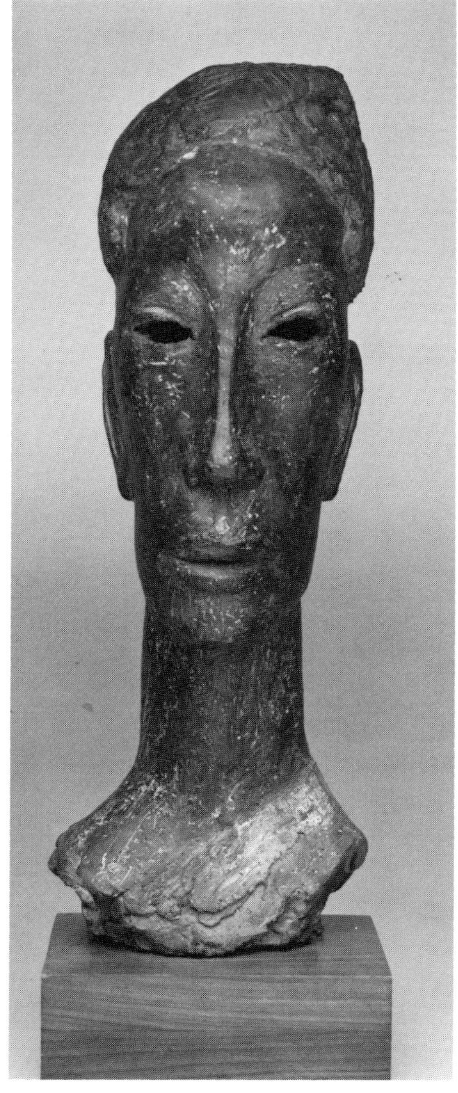

CAT. 39. EVALINE C. SELLORS (b. 1907)
Ode to a Cotton Picker, *1953*
Terra-cotta bust
20¼ × 7½ × 8½ in.
Collection of the Dallas Museum of Art, gift of the
Craft Guild of Dallas, 1953.3
Photograph provided by Dallas Museum of Art

CAT. 38. EVALINE C. SELLORS (b. 1907)
Praying Mantis, *1954*
Bronze
27 in. high, Vermont marble base 11 in. high
Weiner Collection, Fort Worth
Photograph provided by Weiner Collection,
Fort Worth

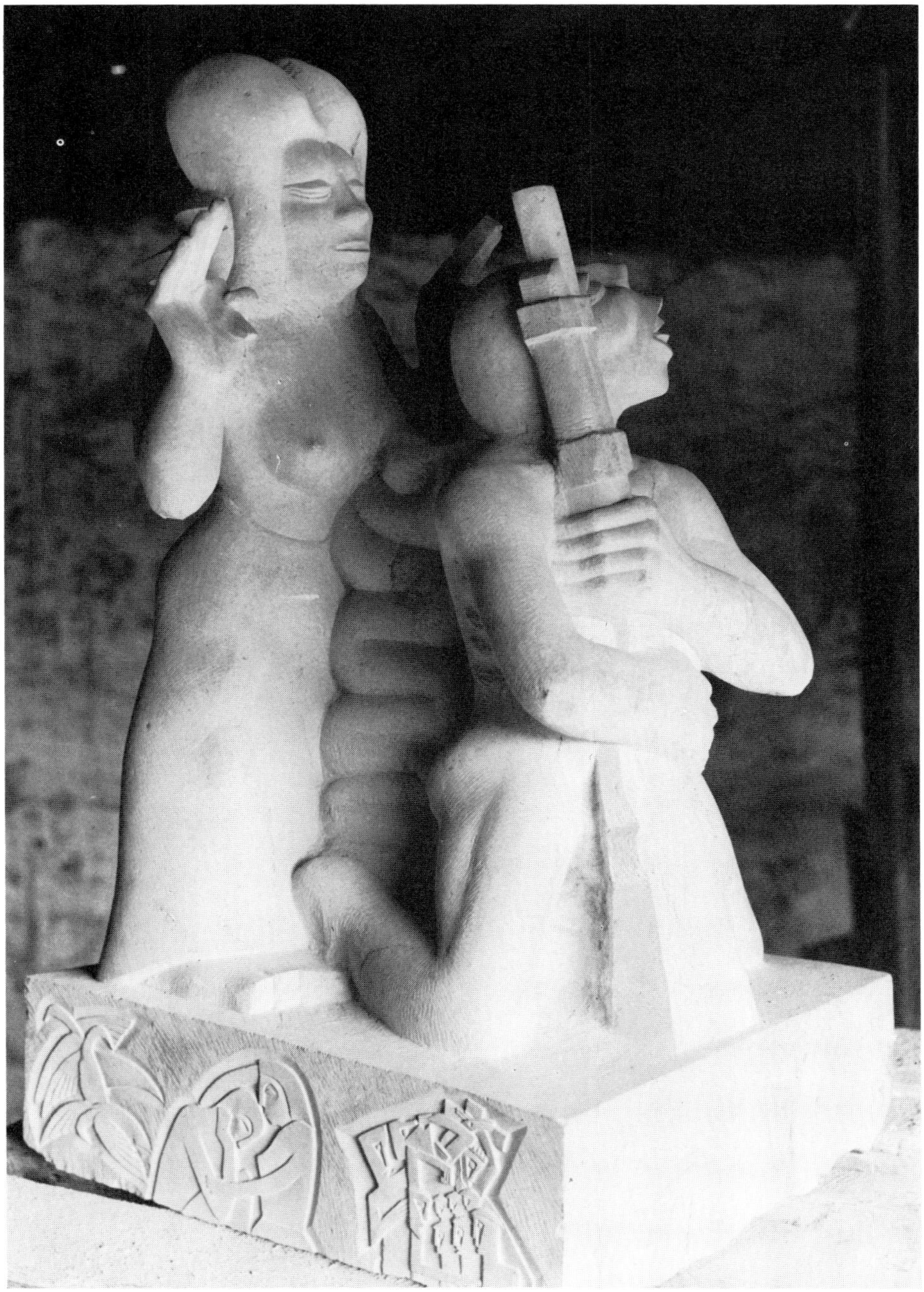

CAT. 40. OCTAVIO MEDELLIN (b. 1907)
The Spirit of the Revolution, *1932*
Texas limestone
32 × 16 × 20 in.
Collection of the artist
Photographer: Jay Simmons; photograph courtesy
of the artist

CAT. 41. OCTAVIO MEDELLIN (b. 1907)
The Spirit of the Revolution (detail), *1932*
Texas limestone
32 × 16 × 20 in.
Collection of the artist
Photographer: Jay Simmons; photograph courtesy
of the artist

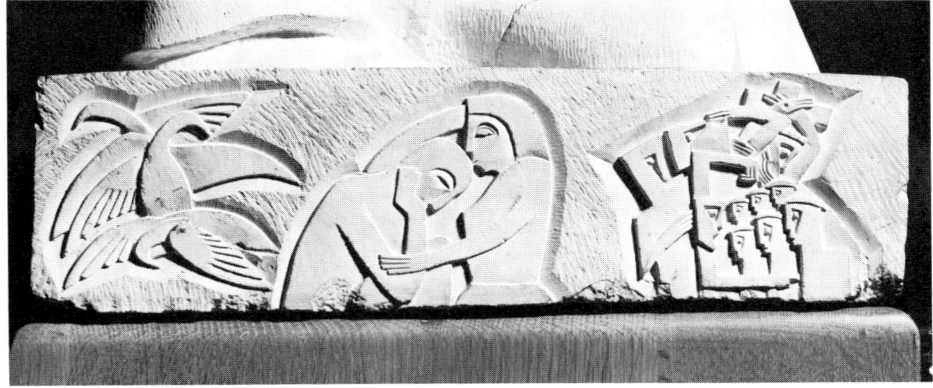

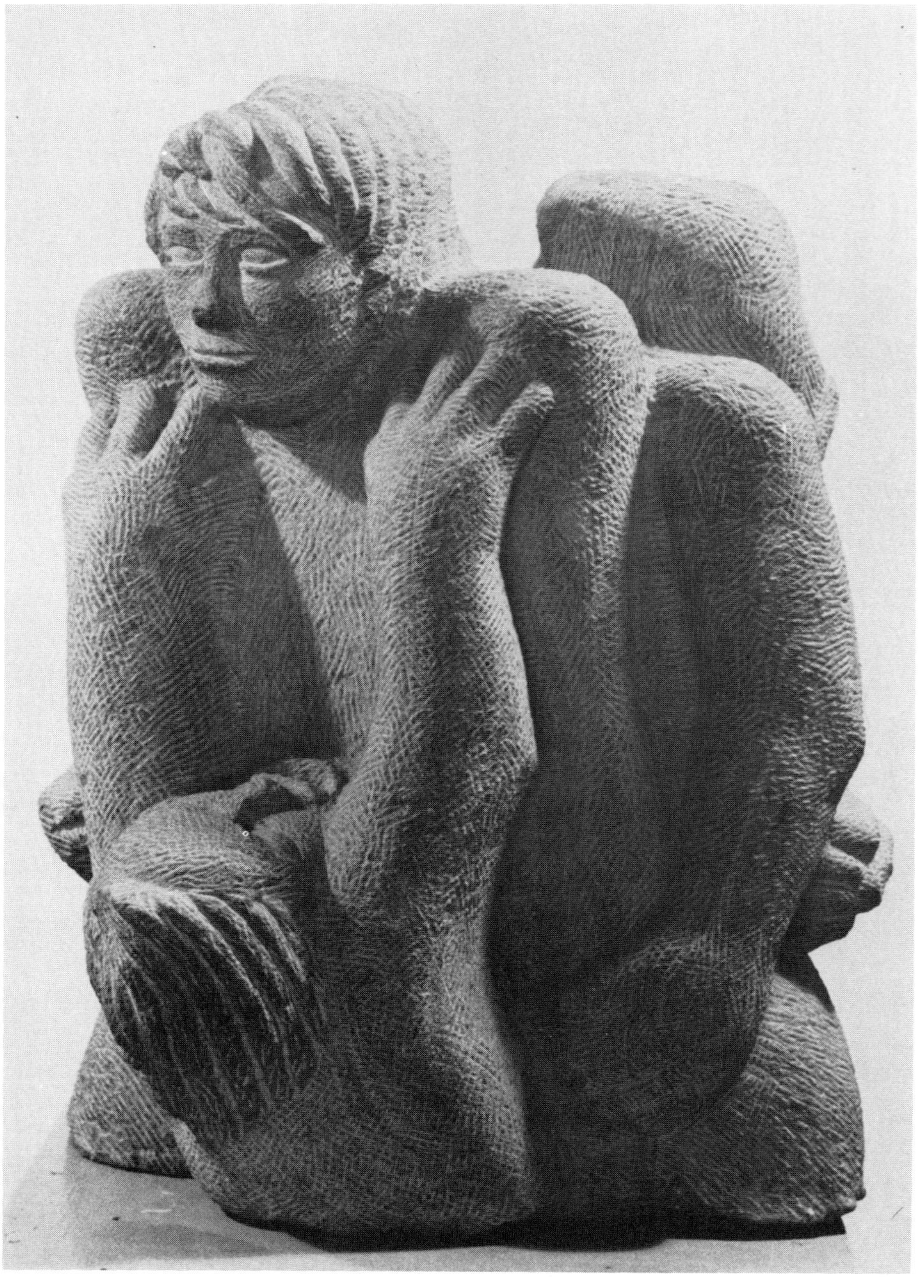

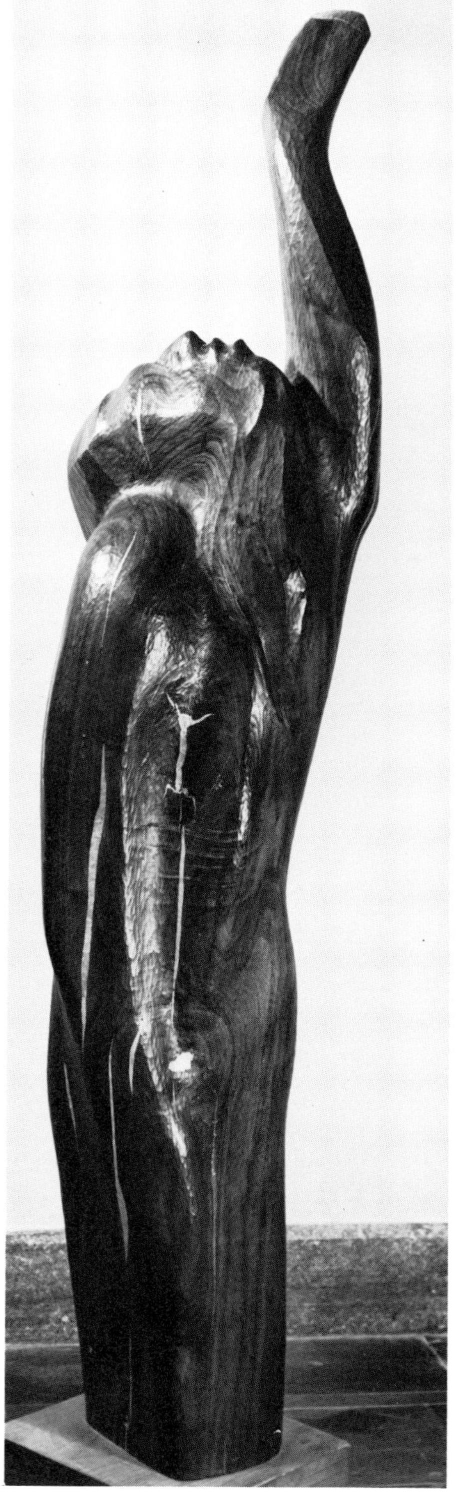

CAT. 42. OCTAVIO MEDELLIN (b. 1907)
The Struggle, *1938*
Texas rose sandstone
28 × 12 × 13 in.
Collection of the artist
Photograph provided by the artist

CAT. 43. OCTAVIO MEDELLIN (b. 1907)
Moses, *1955*
Black walnut
64 × 12 × 12 in.
Collection of the artist
Photographer: Jay Simmons; photograph courtesy
of the artist

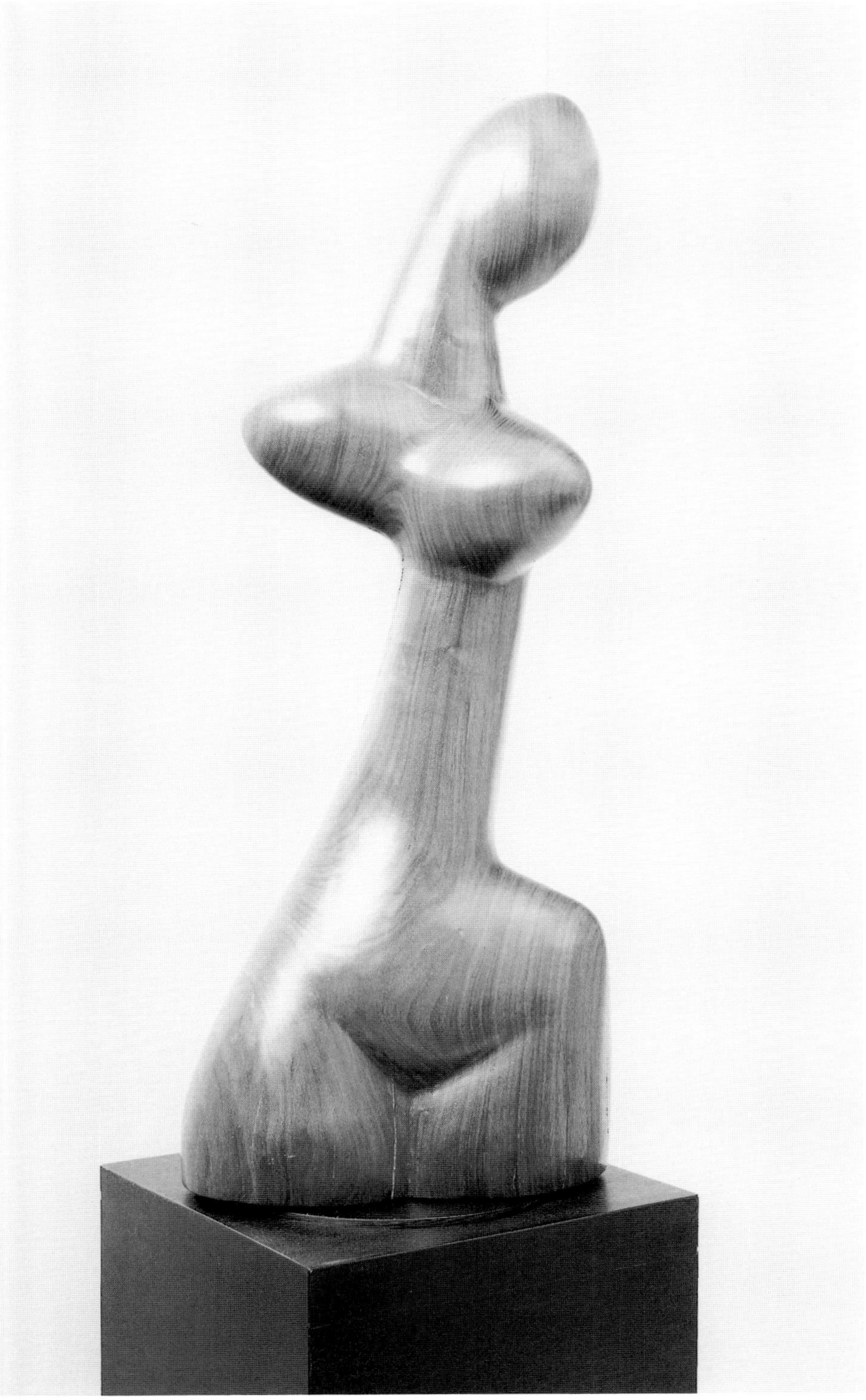

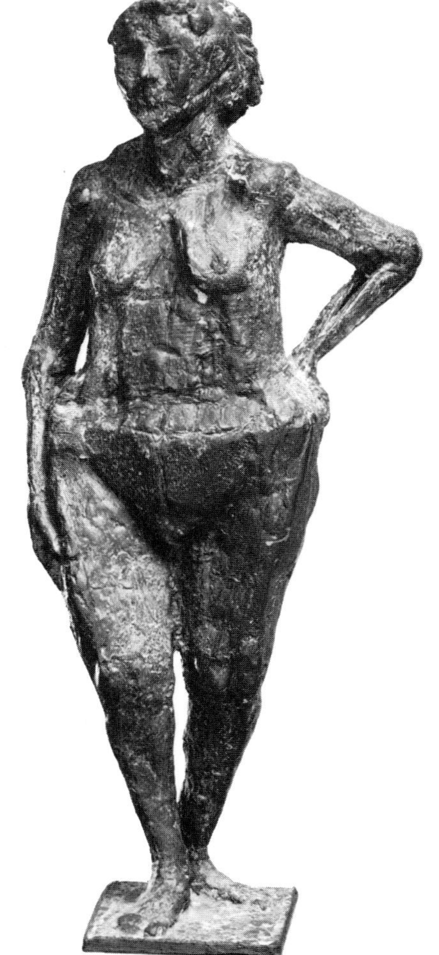

CAT. 44. CHARLES TRUET WILLIAMS
(1918–1966)
Torso, *1949*
Walnut
30 in. high
Collection of Anita Williams
Photographer: Wharton Photography, Fort Worth;
photograph courtesy of The Old Jail Art Center,
Albany

CAT. 45. ISHAMEL SOTO (b. 1932)
Standing Figure, *1960*
Bronze
22 × 9 in., base 7¼ × 6½ in.
Collection of The Museum of Fine Arts, Houston,
Purchase Prize, 23rd Annual Texas Painting and
Sculpture Exhibition, 62.14
Photograph provided by Museum of Fine Arts,
Houston

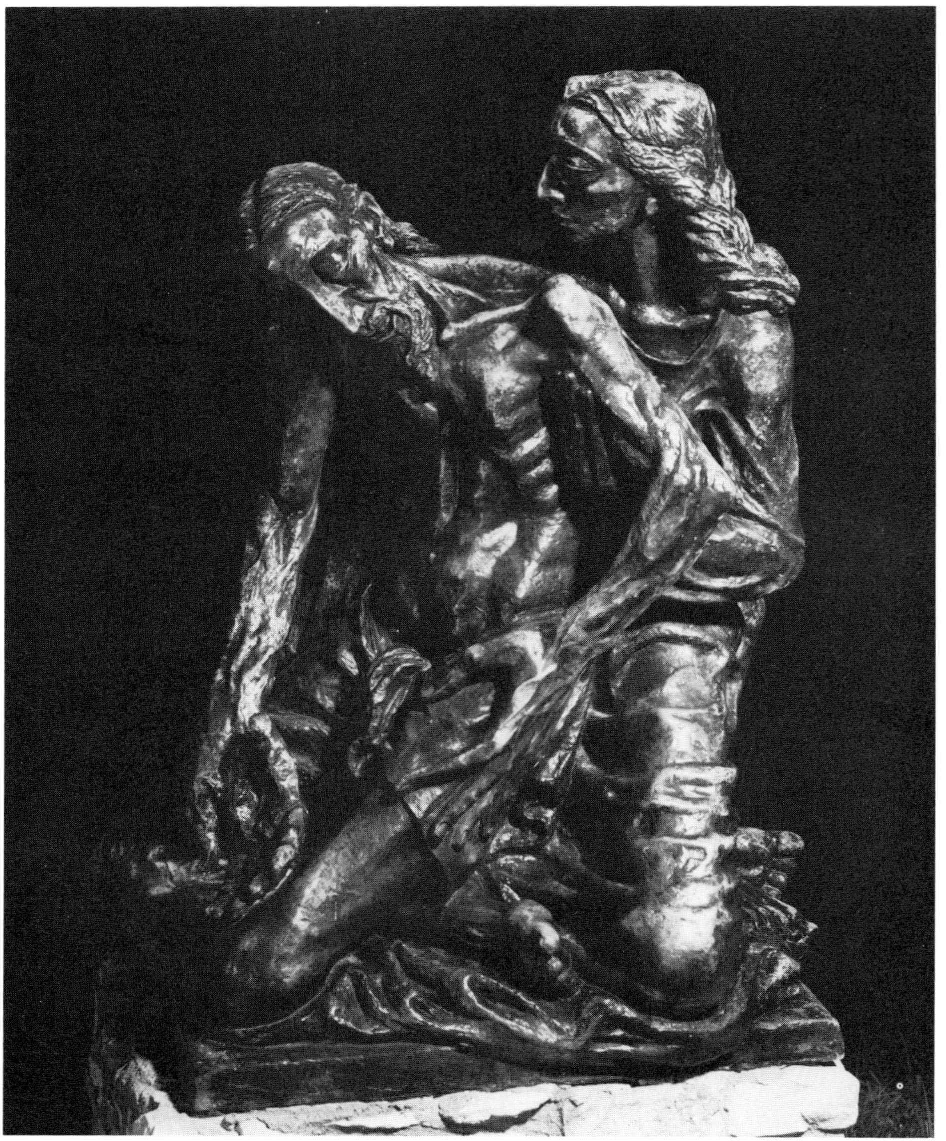

CAT. 46. CHARLES UMLAUF (b. 1911)
Pietà, *1944–1945*
Bronze (cast by Roman Bronze Works, 1947)
47 × 37 × 34 in.
Collection of the Umlauf Sculpture Garden, Austin
Photographer: Mears Photography, Austin;
photograph provided by the artist

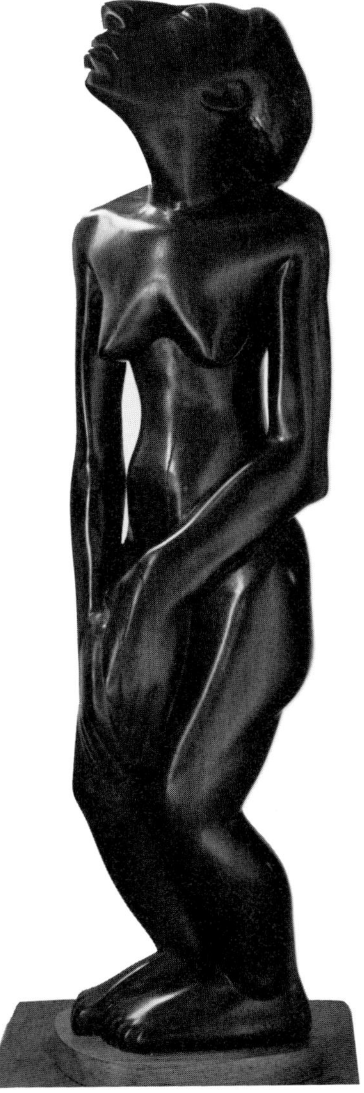

CAT. 47. CHARLES UMLAUF (b. 1911)
Standing Figure, *1943*
Rosewood
ca. 32 in. high
Collection of Jeannette and Irving Goodfriend
Photographer: George Holmes, Huntington Art
Gallery, The University of Texas at Austin

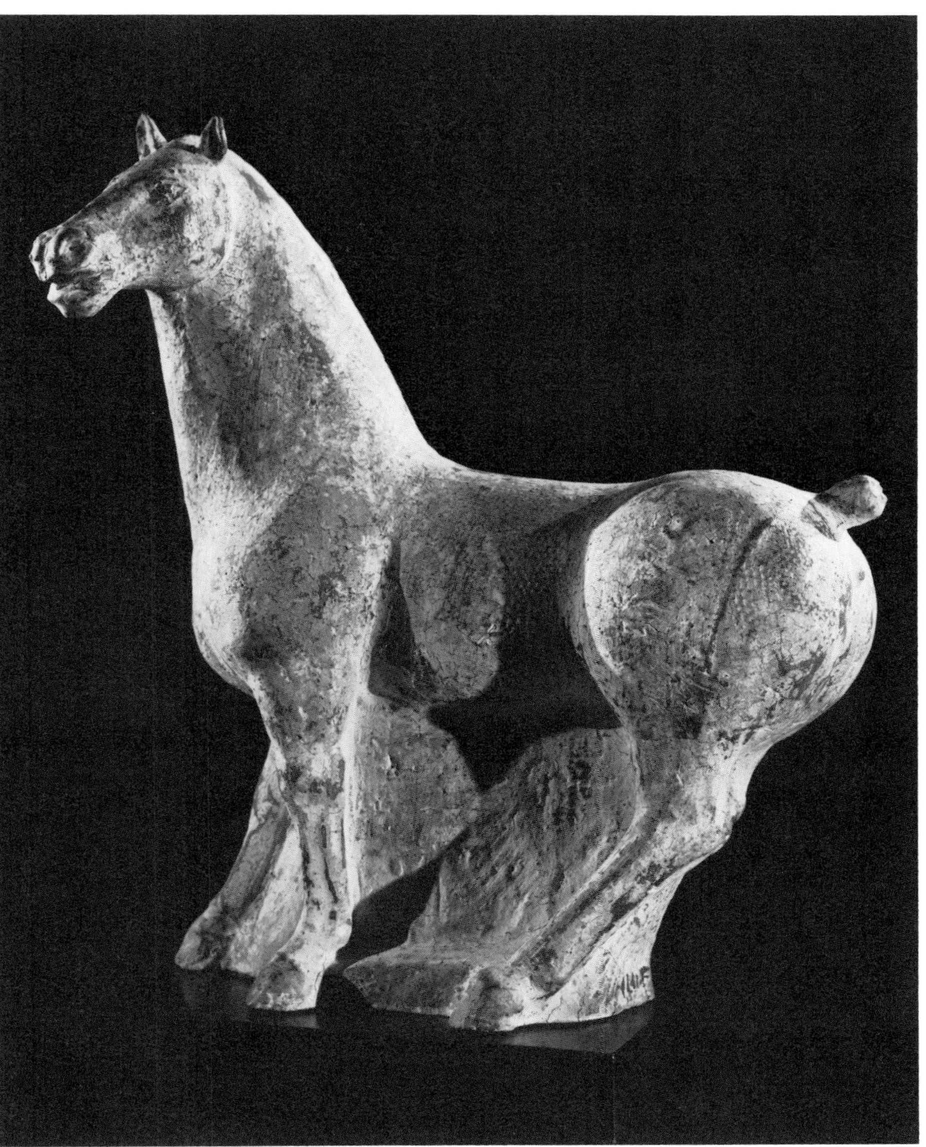

CAT. 48. CHARLES UMLAUF (b. 1911)
Standing Horse, *ca. 1960*
Signed
Terra-cotta with white mat slip glaze
20⅜ in. high, including base (7 × 11 × 17⅛ in.)
Collection of the Amon Carter Museum of Art, gift
of Edward R. Hudson, Fort Worth
Photograph provided by Amon Carter Museum of
Art, Fort Worth

BIBLIOGRAPHY

Acheson, Sam. "Texas Irresistibly Attracted Borglum, and He Exhibited Intense Interest in Its Art." *Dallas Morning News,* March 7, 1941.

"Alamo Monument." *Texas Historical Association Quarterly.* Archives of the Texas History Research Library at the Alamo, Daughters of the Republic of Texas, San Antonio.

Albee, John. *Henry Dexter, Sculptor: A Memorial.* Boston: Privately Printed, 1898. Photocopy provided by the Commonwealth of Massachusetts State Library, Boston (George Fingold Library).

"Art Bequest of Elisabet Ney, Provision for Art School as Adjunct to University." *Austin Daily Statesman,* July 2, 1907.

The Art Digest, Texas Centennial Special Number, June 1, 1936. Cover photograph is of *Confederate* by Laurence Tenney Stevens, one of the sculptor's six heroic-sized figures for the Esplanade of State at the Texas Centennial Exposition, Dallas, including the figure of *Texas* (See Fig. 44).

Art in the United States Capitol. Prepared by the Architect of the Capitol under the Direction of the Joint Committee on the Library. Washington, D.C.: United States Government Printing Office, 1976. Illustrations of Ney's *S. F. Austin,* p. 229, *Sam Houston,* p. 246.

Austin History Center, Austin Public Library. L. S. Ross Biographical File. Original photograph of Governor's office in temporary capitol with Caifassi's[?] bust of Sam Houston.

Austin Daily Statesman, February 1, 1873. Archives of the State Historian, State Preservation Board, State of Texas, Austin. Regarding "Senor" Caifassi.

"Baby as Bacchante — Work Inspired by the Age of Innocence." *New York Telegram,* January 27, 1929[?]. Barker Texas History Center, University of Texas at Austin.

Baldwin, Jean Houston Collection, Sam Houston Regional Library and Research Center, Liberty, Tex. Box 2, File #5. (Illustration of Dexter bust of *S. Houston* from undetermined newspaper source.)

Ballinger, W. P. "Disputed Authorship: Thermophylæ Had Its Messengers of Defeat; the Alamo Had None." Undated [Galveston?] newspaper. Archives of the Texas History Research Library at the Alamo, Daughters of the Republic of Texas, San Antonio.

Barkley, Mary Starr. *History of Travis County and Austin, 1839–1899.* 2d ed. Austin: Steck Co., 1967.

Bateman, Audray. "Coppini Monuments Grace Capitol Grounds." *Austin American-Statesman,* June 27, 1986.

— — —. "Elisabet Ney Carved a Special Spot in the Art, Literary Life of Old Austin." *Austin American-Statesman,* October 23, 1981.

Battle, W. J. "Art in Texas: An Outline." *Southwest Review* 14 (Oct 1928–July 29, 1929): 51–59.

— — —. "Elisabet Ney Gave First Great Impulse to Art in Texas." A book review on Bride N. Taylor, *Elisabet Ney, Sculptor, 1834–1907.* R. Niles Graham-Pease Collection, Barker Texas History Center, University of Texas at Austin.

Besozzi, Maria. "Elisabet Ney Museum Reborn." *Texas Association of Museums Quarterly* 7, no. 7 (Fall 1982): 14.

Biography of Octavio Medellin, N.d. Pamphlet provided by Medellin, and conversations with the artist, Spring 1988 and Spring 1989.

"Borglum Dies, Son to Finish Masterpiece: Heads Completed on Mountainside Rushmore Memorial." Unidentified newspaper clipping, Chicago, Ill. March 6, 1941. Barker Texas History Center, University of Texas at Austin.

"Borglum in S. A. to Begin Texas Works." *San Antonio Express,* August 25, 1935.

Branda, Eldon Stephen, ed. *The Handbook of Texas: A Supplement.* Vol. III. Austin: Texas State Historical Association, 1976.

Broder, Patricia Janis. *Bronzes of the American West.* New York: Harry N. Abrams, 1973. Illustrations of Texas works by Proctor, p. 389; Borglum, p. 380; Waggoner, p. 236.

Brooks, Elizabeth. *Prominent Women of Texas.* Akron, Ohio: Werner Company, 1896, pp. 76–78. Regarding Ney.

Burnham, Sidney, to Institute of Texas Cultures, University of Texas at Austin, San Antonio, September 9, 1985. Rosenberg Library Archives, Galveston. Regarding Willoughby.

Bywaters, Jerry. "Against Narrowness." *Art Digest.* June 1, 1936. Regarding Austin, Medellin, Owen, Sellors, and Tennant.

— — —. *Southwestern Art: A Sampling of Contemporary Painting and Sculpture,* Dallas Museum of Fine Arts exhibition catalog, April 10–May 22, 1960. Illustration of Medellin's *Moses;* also regarding Umlauf and Williams.

Caffin, Charles H. *American Masters of Sculpture.* Garden City and New York. Doubleday, Page & Company, 1913. See opposite p. 192, for illustration of *Recumbent Figure, Tomb of Father Brown,* Church of Saint Mary-the-Virgin, New York (still in situ), for one of Rhind's most eloquent works.

"Campus Closeups." *Mustang* [ca. 1960/ 1961], p. 18. Regarding Owen's *Peruna* sculpture. Photocopy from Office of University Archives, Southern Methodist University, Dallas.

Carnegie Library Autobiographical Sketches. Prepared by the San Antonio, Texas, Public Library. Some of this material also appears in the Barker History Center and the Witte Museum files. Regarding McLeary, et al.

Cerracchio, Enrico Filberto. Obituary Notice. *New York Times,* 1956. Mr. 22, 35:2.

Charles Umlauf, Sculptor. Foreword by Gibson A. Danes, Introduction by Donald B. Goodall. Austin: University of Texas Press, 1967.

"Civic League Levels Charges at City: Destruction of Property Cited by Group." *Galveston Tribune,* November 16, 1949. Regarding Rhind.

Clayton, Miss Mary, to Patricia Hendricks, February 15, 1989. Regarding Malone.

The Collection of Mr. and Mrs. Ted Weiner: An Exhibition of Sculpture and Painting. Introduction by Donald B. Goodall, University Art Museum, University of Texas at Austin, 1966 exhibition catalogue. Regarding Sellors.

"Commerce Artist Wins Honors in Exhibit Here." *Dallas Times Herald,* September 22, 1944. Jerry Bywaters Collection on Art of the Southwest, Southern Methodist University. Regarding Franklin.

"Confederate Monument Hoisted into Place." *Galveston Daily News,* January 20, 1912. Regarding Amateis.

"Confederate Monument Will be Unveiled Today." *Galveston Daily News,* June 3, 1912. Regarding Amateis.

Contemporary American Sculpture. Issued for the exhibition held by the National Sculpture Society in Cooperation with the Trustees of the California Palace of the Legion of Honor, San Francisco, April–October, 1929. Regarding Coppini, McLeary, Rhind, Stevens, and Tauch.

Coppini, Pompeo. *From Dawn to Sunset.* San Antonio: Naylor Co., 1949. In his autobiography, Coppini writes of Ney, Borglum, McLeary, and Tauch.

Cordts, Nelda. "Sculptress Lives, Works in Her Own Art Colony." *San Antonio Express,* February 7, 1965. Regarding Tauch.

Crain, Annie Laurie Williams. "Texas Sculptor Wins New Laurels." *Hollands,* January 1929. Regarding McLeary, with illustrations of her Puerto Rico works and *The Blessed Damozel.*

Craven, Wayne. *Sculpture in America.* New York: Thomas Y. Crowell Co., 1968. Illustration of Dewey Arch, p. 504; also regarding Dexter, Rhind, et al.

Cutrer, Emily Fourmy. *The Art of the Woman: The Life and Work of Elisabet Ney.* Lincoln: University of Nebraska Press, 1988.

— — —. "The Hardy, Stalwart Son of Texas': Art and Mythology at the Capitol." *Southwestern Historical Quarterly* 92, no. 2 (October 1988): 288–322. Illustrations of work by Ney, Coppini, et al.

Dallas, Catalogue data on works in the Art Collection of the City of Dallas. Provided by the Division of Cultural Affairs, Dallas Park and Recreation Department.

"Dallas Galleries to Open Four New Shows This Week." Undated Dallas newspaper. Barker Texas History Center Archives, University of Texas at Austin. Illustration of work by Austin.

Dallas Museum of Fine Arts. Annual exhibition catalogs beginning in 1940. Titles vary, e.g., 1949–1950: *Annual Texas Exhibition of Painting and Sculpture;* 1950–1951: *Annual Texas Painting and Sculpture. Annual Exhibition of Texas Painting and Sculpture.*

Daniggelis, Paul Dean. "Artist of Genius." *Southwestern Art,* 4, no. 3, pp 39–46; and Daniggelis' typed manuscript bibliography. Reproduced from the files of the Texas Historical Commission State Marker Program. Regarding Soler.

Dexter, Henry. National Portrait Gallery Archives, Catalog of American Portraits, Index Artist Sheet, Felix G. W. through Deyoung Studio (Att), 12/22/88; M. Fabian to Dr. Reed, Museum of History and Technology, June 13, 1968; Condition Report, n.d.; Charles Nagel, NPG, to Mr. Winfrey, Director and Librarian Texas State Library, January 15, 1969; Winfrey to Freshour, January 8, 1969; Corkran, Texas State Library to Girard, NPG, June 26, 1968; Schiavo, Roman Bronze Works, Inc., to Mr. Freshour, Washington, January 14, 1969; Nelson, Huntington Block, to Freshour, January 15, 1970; Covey, Austin, to Stanek, January 13, 1970; Librarian of Congress from Roberts, October 15, 1924; Corkran to Stewart, Curator, NPG, 9 May 1968.

Dobie, J. Frank. "The Alamo's Immortalization of Words." *Southwest Review,* 27, no. 4 (Summer 1942): 408–409.

— — —. "Dobie Traces Origin of Noble Epitaph to Heroes." Undated, unidentified newspaper clipping. Texas History Research Library at the Alamo, Daughters of the Republic of Texas, San Antonio.

— — —, to T. D. Affleck, Galveston, June 11, 1942. Texas History Research Library at the Alamo, Daughters of the Republic of Texas, San Antonio. Regarding Thermophylæ quote.

"Dorothy Austin Work in New York." *Dallas Morning News,* December 7, 1933.

"Electra Waggoner Debut as Sculptor at Jacques Seligmann Galleries." *Art Digest* 12, no. 21 (1938).

"Electra Waggoner Exhibition, Jacques Seligmann." *Art News* 36, no. 15 (1938).

Elsen, Albert Edward. *Origins of Modern Sculpture: Pioneers and Premises.* New York: George Braziller, 1974. The original text, here enlarged and altered, formed the introduction to the Arts Council of Great Britain exhibition catalogue *Pioneers of Modern Sculpture,* Hayward Gallery, London, 1973.

— — —. *The Partial Figure in Modern Sculpture: From Rodin to 1969.* Baltimore Museum of Art Exhibition Catalog, 1970.

Exhibition of Paintings, Sculpture, & Graphic Arts. Texas Centennial Exposition, Dallas Museum of Fine Arts. An exhibition catalog, June 6–November 29, 1936, Dallas. Includes Medellin, Owen, Sellors, and Tennant.

Exhibition of Works by Chicago Artists, February 4–March 1, 1908. Art Institute of Chicago. Information provided by the Art Institute of Chicago Library. Regarding Chandler.

Exhibition of Works by Chicago Artists, February 2–28, 1909. Art Institute of Chicago. Information provided by the Art Institute of Chicago Library. Regarding Chandler.

Falk, Peter H., ed. *Who Was Who in American Art.* Compiled from the original thirty-four volumes of *American Art Annual: Who's Who in Art: Biographies of American Artists Active from 1898–1947.* Mansfield, Conn.: Sound View Press, 1985. Regarding Chandler, Amateis, Hubbard, Austin, Franklin, and Tennant.

Fisk, Frances Battaile. *A History of Texas Artists and Sculptors.* Abilene, Tex., 1928. Regarding Amateis, Borglum, Chandler, Coppini, Karl, McLeary, Ney, Sellors, Tauch.

Fiske, Frances. "Waldine Amanda Tauch, Sculptress, Is Resident of Pelham Manor." *New Rochelle Standard Star,* August 19, 1932.

Fortune, Jan and Jean Burton. *Elisabet Ney.* New York: Alfred A. Knopf, 1943.

Freed, Eleanor Kempner. "Requiem for a Sculptor." *Houston Post,* April 10, 1966. Regarding Williams.

Freudenheim, Susan. "Monumental Studio." *Texas Homes,* February 1987, pp. 68–71. Regarding Ney: illustration of *Lady Macbeth, Self-Portrait,* and other works, along with interior and exterior views of Formosa.

Gammel, Hans Peter Nielson, comp. *The Laws of Texas, 1822–1897.* Introduction by C. W. Raines. 10 vols. Austin: Gammel Book Company, 1898.

Gardner, Albert Ten Eyck. *American Sculpture: A Catalogue of the Collection of The Metropolitan Museum of Art.* New York: Metropolitan Museum of Art, 1965. Borglum's *Mares of Diomedes,* p. 100; McLeary's *Aspiration,* p. 163.

The George Washington University Bulletin, 1890s. Special collections, George Washington University Library. Regarding Amateis.

"Gift to the Library: Handsome Bas-Relief in Plaster Presented by Mrs. F. M. Burton." *Galveston Tribune,* February 13, 1924. Regarding Amateis.

Glueck, Grace. "The Many Accents of Latino Art," *The New York Times* (Arts & Leisure), September 25, 1988. Illustration of Medellin's *El Ahorcado.*

Goldwater, Robert J. *Primitivism in Modern Art.* Rev. ed. New York: Vintage Books, 1967.

Graham, Don, *The WPA Guide to Texas with a New Introduction by Don Graham: The Federal Writers' Project Guide to Texas.* 1986. Originally, *Texas: A Guide to the Lone Star State,* compiled by Workers of the Writers' Program of the Work Projects Administration in the State of Texas, American Guide Series. New York: Hastings House, 1940.

"Group of Art Institute Faculty Members." *Dallas Morning News,* September 17, 1933. Photo of Tennant, et al.

Haacke, Lorraine. "Mexican Heritage Inspires Sculptor's Creations," *Dallas Times Herald,* November 20, 1977. Illustration of Medellin's *The Spirit of the Revolution.*

Hamilton, Eloise. "Ione Franklin's Sculpture Takes Top Prize at Museum." Unidentified Dallas newspaper, September 22, 1944. Jerry Bywaters Collection on Art of the Southwest, Southern Methodist University, Dallas. Illustration of Franklin with *Young Mother.*

Hart, Katherine. "Landmarks Association to Honor Milam's Memory: Statue by Bonnie McLeary Proposed as Memorial." *San Antonio Express,* January 12, 1930.

Henry Rosenberg, 1824–1893: Commemorating His Gifts to Galveston. Galveston: Rosenberg Library, 1918.

"Heroic Bronze Memorial to Sydney Smith: Served 25 Years as Secretary of Texas State Fair: Artist Took Inspiration for Group from Elements Typical of State." *Dallas Morning News,* October 8, 1933. Jerry Bywaters Archive on Art of the Southwest, Southern Methodist University, Dallas.

Hoffman, Malvina. *Heads and Tales.* New York: Charles Scribner's Sons, 1936, Garden City, N.J.: Garden City Publishing Co., 1943.

Hogue, Alexandre. "Progressive Texas." *Art Digest* (Texas Centennial Special Number). 10,17–18 (June 1936). Regarding Austin, Franklin, Ney, Sellors, and Tennant.

"Houston Artists Exhibit to Mark 10th Birthday for Fine Arts Museum." *Houston Post,* January 7, 1934. Regarding Karl.

Hubbard, Bess Bigham. Family files, including undated newspaper clippings and exhibition pamphlets.

– – –. Photocopies of Hubbard exhibition clippings, and other information, The Museum, Texas Tech University.

"Hubbard-Edwards Show: Sculptures to Be on Exhibit Today." *Lubbock Avalanche-Journal,* May 1, 1966.

Hutson, Alice. *From Chalk to Bronze: A Biography of Waldine Tauch.* Austin: Shoal Creek Publishers, 1978. See also for Coppini.

"Imposing Ceremony to Mark Unveiling." *Galveston Daily News,* June 4, 1912. Archives, Rosenberg Library, Galveston. Regarding Amateis.

Johnson, William. "Texas Breaks the Spell of the Bluebonnet," *Life* (Special International Edition), November 29, 1954. Regarding Umlauf.

Keeling, W. A. (State Attorney General, Dec. 1921–Jan. 1925). "Origin of Famous Alamo Inscription Traced at Austin." Austin newspaper clipping, not dated, from the Archives of the Texas History Research Library at the Alamo, Daughters of the Republic of Texas, San Antonio.

Kutner, Janet. "Library Gets Williams Works." *Dallas Morning News,* June 30, 1973.

Linz, Joe. "Dorothy Austin, Sculptor." *Southwestern Arts* (August 1932):2.

Loggins, Vernon. *Two Romantics and Their Ideal Life.* New York: Odyssey Press, 1946.

"Lubbock Sculptor Will Be Represented in Exhibition: Mrs. Chester A. Hubbard Will Be Represented at the Allied Artists of America 37th Annual Exhibition in New York in November." *Lubbock Avalanche-Journal,* October 22, 1950. Illustration of Hubbard's *Thinking Woman,* now titled *Green Goddess.*

MacAgy, Douglas. *one i at a time.* Pollock Galleries, Meadows School of the Arts, Southern Methodist University, Dallas, exhibition catalog, March 20–April 25, 1971. Regarding Williams.

M'Clain, John. "Texas Heiress Prefers to Work: Electra Waggoner's Art to Be Shown at Exhibit." *San Antonio Light,* April 17, 1940.

McCullough, L. E. "The Legacy of Leadbelly: Seminal Blues Great Remembered." *Duende: The Journal of Advocacy and Criticism for the Arts in Austin.* May 1988, pp. 25–26.

McGahey, Fred. "A Tale of Two Borglums." *San Antonio Express Magazine,* September 21, 1952.

MacLeary, Bonnie, Biographical Data Sheet. National Academy of Design Files, New York.

Malone, Clotilde. Information includes: Oakwood Cemetery records; deposition dated 1901; "Bills and Resolutions," *Senate Journal,* March 28, 1899, pp. 577–578; ten separate, undated [Waco?] newspaper articles; Malone Family, statement of lineage, 7 pp., dated both 1869 and 1892, tracing back to 1736. Alba Malone Scrapbook, Mary Clayton papers, Texas Collection, Baylor University, Waco.

Mayer, Ralph. *The Artist's Handbook of Materials and Techniques.* 3d ed. New York: Viking Press, 1973.

"Miss McLeary Is Guest in Austin Home." *Austin American-Statesman,* November 3, 1935.

"Mistress of Her Art: Elisabet Ney of Texas, Long Famous as Sculptor." *Washington Post,* May 22, 1904.

Montgomery, Edmund. Statement of Donation of works of Elisabet Ney by her husband, Edmund Montgomery, to The University of Texas at Austin, 15 July 1909, notarized 10 January 1910. Barker Texas History Center, University of Texas at Austin.

"Monument to the Texas Heroes of 1836." *Galveston Daily News,* April 22, 1900. Facsimile provided by Ballinger Mills, Galveston. Regarding Amateis, p. 10.

Murdock, Myrtle Cheney. *National Statuary Hall in the Nation's Capitol.* Washington, D.C.: Monumental Press, 1955. Ney illustrations; pp. 76–77.

"Musket Premier Empire Builder, Statuary of Texas Heroes Indicate." *Austin American-Statesman,* October 18, 1925. Archives of the State Preservation Board, State of Texas, Austin.

Neukom, Lisetta, and Mabel Sellers, "Satin Cloth Reveals New York Sun Editorial of 1850 Backing Sam Houston for Presidency." *Houston Post-Dispatch,* June 17, 1928 (with illustration of Dexter bust of Houston). Liberty, Texas: Jean Houston Baldwin Collection, Sam Houston Regional Library and Research Center, Box 2, File 5, Liberty, Texas.

O'Brien, Esse Forrester. *Art and Artists of Texas.* Dallas: Tardy Publishing Co., 1935. Regarding Amateis, Austin, Chandler, Coppini, Karl, Ney, Proctor, Tauch, Teich, and Tennant.

The Old Jail Art Center, Albany, Tex. *Beyond Regionalism: The Fort Worth School (1945–1955)*. Essays by Sallie M. Gillespie and Reilly Nail. A Texas Sesquicentennial Exhibition, April–July 1986. Illustration of Sellors' *Praying Mantis;* also included in exhibition, *Winter* and *Ode to a Cotton Picker;* illustration, Williams' *Torso.*

Opitz, Glenn B., ed. *Dictionary of American Sculptors, 18th Century to the Present.* Poughkeepsie, N.Y.: Apollo, 1984. Regarding Amateis; Borglum; Cerrachio, Chandler, Coppini, Franklin, Hubbard, Karl, Ney, Owen, Proctor, Rhind, Tauch, and Umlauf.

Owen, Michael G., Jr., to Jerry Bywaters, June 21, 1946. Jerry Bywaters Collection on Art of the Southwest, Southern Methodist University, Dallas.

"Paintings and Sculpture Will Show at Museum." *Wichita Daily Times,* February, 1952. Regarding Waggoner.

Pinckney, Pauline A. *Painting in Texas: The Nineteenth Century.* Introduction by Jerry Bywaters. Austin. University of Texas Press for Amon Carter Museum of Western Art, Fort Worth, 1967. Illustration of Wm. Huddle's *The Surrender of Santa Anna.*

Pingeot, Anne. "The Second Empire: Affirmation of the Republican Idea." In *Sculpture: The Adventure of Modern Sculpture in the Nineteenth and Twentieth Centuries.* New York: Rizzoli International Publications, 1986. Regarding fin-de-siècle statuettes, p. 96.

Porter, Bob. "Williams Dies at Age 48." *Dallas Times Herald,* April 1, 1966.

Proctor, Hester Elizabeth, ed. *Alexander Phimister Proctor, Sculptor in Buckskin: An Autobiography.* Introduction by Vivian A. Paladin. Norman: University of Oklahoma Press, 1971.

"Prof. Louis Amaties [sic] Here, Arrives with His Contractor to Complete the Texas Heroes Monument, the Bronze Work Expected Daily: Three Years a Very Short Time in Which to Do the Work, Says the Sculptor." *Galveston Daily News,* March 20, 1900.

Proske, Beatrice Gilman. *Brookgreen Gardens Sculpture.* New ed. Brookgreen Gardens, S.C.: Printed by order of the Trustees, 1968. Regarding Parsons pp. 144 and 146, illustration; Tennant, pp. 479–481.

Prouty, Dorothy. "Texas History in Bronze and Stone: One Man's Tribute to His Adopted State." *Texas Highways,* February 1982, pp. 28–33. Regarding Coppini; good illustrations, including a view of the Coppini-Tauch Studio.

"Purchase Prize." *Houston Post,* February 14, 1934. Illustration of Karl's *Orpheus* and *Eurydice.*

Quirarte, Jacinto. *Mexican American Artists.* Austin: University of Texas Press, 1973. Regarding Medellin, p. xxv and passim.

— — —. "Mexican and Mexican American Artists in the United States: 1920–1970," In *The Latin American Spirit: Art and Artists in the United States, 1920–1970.* Introduction by Luis R. Cancel. New York: The Bronx Museum of the Arts in association with Harry N. Abrams, 1988. Regarding Medellin, pp. 47–48, illustration of *The Hanged.*

Raines, Cadwell Walton. *Analytical Index to the Laws of Texas, 1823–1905.* Austin: Von Boeckmann-Jones Co., 1906. Littleton, Col.: Fred B. Rothman and Co., 1987.

— — —. *Year Book for Texas.* 2 vols. Austin: Gammel-Statesman Publishing Co., 1901–1903. Regarding Coppini, Huddle, Ney, et al.

Read, Herbert. *A Concise History of Modern Sculpture.* New York: Frederick A. Praeger, 1968.

Regan, Leila M. "Memorial to Tidal Wave Victims." *Woodmen of the World Magazine,* ca. 1966. Rosenberg Library Archives, Galveston.

"Regents . . . Accept Ney Collection . . . Valuable Statuary, Left by Late Sculptor to Be Property of the University." *Austin Daily Statesman,* June 15, 1910. Typed copy of newspaper article in Barker Texas History Center, University of Texas at Austin.

Remick, Dorothy. "Past and Present Mingle Democratically in Capitol Art Gallery." *San Antonio Express,* ca. 1923. State Preservation Board Archives, State of Texas, Austin.

Richardson, Rupert N. *Texas: The Lone Star State.* Englewood Cliffs, N.J.: Prentice-Hall, 1958.

Ripley, Josephine. "The Challenge of Clay." *Christian Science Monitor,* September 8, 1945. Regarding Waggoner.

Rogers, John William. "Imposing Statue of Tejas Indian by Dallas Artist." *Dallas Times Herald,* March 11, 1936. Illustration of Tennant's *Tejas Warrior.* Brookgreen Gardens Archives, Murrells Inlet, S.C.

Rutland, Mrs. J. W. (Willie B.), ed. *Sursum! Elisabet Ney in Texas,* Introduction by May Diane Harris. Austin: Printed by Hart Graphics & Office Centers, Austin, 1977. The correspondence recorded in Rutland has largely been dispersed from the Elisabet Ney Museum, Austin, and is now housed in the collections of the Barker Texas History Center, University of Texas at Austin; the Austin History Center, Austin Public Library; and the Harry Ransom Humanities Research Center Manuscript Collection, University of Texas at Austin, including some correspondence not contained in Rutland.

Samuels, Peggy and Harold. *The Illustrated Biographical Encyclopedia of the American West.* Garden City, N.Y.: Doubleday and Co., 1976. Regarding Borglum, Ney, Procter, and Rhind.

"Sculptor Addresses Docents." *National Museum of Women in the Arts* 5, no. 4 (Winter 1988): 3. Illustration of Waggoner.

"Sculptor Will Give Lecture." *Dallas Times Herald,* January 3, 1933. Regarding Tennant.

"Sculptor's Latest Work." *Dallas Times Herald,* August 2, 1936. Brookgreen Gardens Archives, Murrells Inlet, S.C. Regarding Tennant.

"Sculptors Named for Monuments." *San Antonio Express,* March 31, 1937. Regarding Centennial; Coppini, McLeary, and Tauch.

Sculptors of Texas. Fort Worth Art Center exhibition catalog, 1957. Regarding Hubbard (illustration of *Green Goddess*), Medellin, Sellors (*Praying Mantis,* no. 34); Charles Williams, and Charles Umlauf.

The Sculpture and Drawing of Charles Umlauf. Essay by Gibson A. Danes. Austin: University of Texas Press, 1980.

The Sculpture of Charles Umlauf. Introduction by Gibson A. Danes. Valley House Gallery, Dallas, exhibition catalog, Spring, 1959. Four views of the *Pietà,* 1944.

The Sculpture of Charles Williams, Fort Worth Art Center exhibition catalog, 1957.

The Sculpture Collection of Mr. and Mrs. Ted Weiner. Fort Worth Art Center exhibition catalog, October 5–October 25, 1959. Regarding Sellors.

"Sculpture Shows." Lubbock Avalanche-Journal, November 2, 1969. Hubbard work, *Head of Christ,* in 56th Annual Exhibition, National Academy of Design Galleries, New York.

"Six People Hurt at City Park," and "Runaway Accident Results in Broken Arms and Many Bruises," and "Unveiling of the Monument to Spirit of the Confederacy." *Houston Chronicle and Herald,* January 20, 1908. Regarding Amateis.

The Sixth Texas General Exhibition. Dallas Museum of Fine Arts, exhibition catalog, 1944–1945. Cover illustration: *Young Mother* by Franklin; also includes Hubbard, Medellin, and Umlauf.

Smith, Goldie Capers. "Texas Sculptors and Painters." In *The Creative Arts in Texas: A Handbook of Biography.* Dallas: Cokesbury Press, 1926. Regarding Cerracchio, Chandler, Coppini, McLeary, Tauch, and Tennant.

Soler, Urbici. Biographical data. El Paso Museum of Art.

— — —. Periodical clippings and biographical data. Southwest Collection, El Paso Public Library.

— — —. Text for Texas official grave marker. Texas Historical Commission State Marker Program, Austin.

Soto, Ishmael. Telephone interviews with the artist, Spring, 1989.

Southwestern Art: A Sampling of Contemporary Painting and Sculpture (Arizona, Arkansas, Colorado, Louisiana, New Mexico, Oklahoma, and Texas). Foreword by Jerry Bywaters. Dallas Museum of Fine Arts exhibition catalog, April 10–May 22, 1960. Regarding Medellin (illustration of *Moses*); Umlauf, and Williams.

Steinfeldt, Cecilia. *Texas Folk Art: One Hundred Fifty Years of the Southwestern Tradition.* Austin, Texas Monthly Press. 1981. Regarding Filip and Sladek.

Stewart, Rick. *Lone Star Regionalism: The Dallas Nine and Their Circle, 1928–1945.* Austin: Texas Monthly Press, 1985. Excellent, regarding Austin, Tennant, Medellin, Owen, and Tennant.

"Sydney Smith Memorial Fountain, in New Setting, to Delight Centennial Visitors: 'Gulf Cloud' Unveiled in 1916: Famous Piece of Heroic Sculpture." *The Dallas Morning News, Souvenir Centennial Edition,* 1936. Bywaters Collection on Art of the Southwest, Southern Methodist University, Dallas. Regarding Chandler.

Taft, Lorado. *The History of American Sculpture.* New York: Arno Press, 1969. Regarding Ney, pp. 214–215: for comments on *Johnston* and *Macbeth* sculptures; also find Chandler, Borglum, Dexter, Proctor, and Rhind.

Taylor, Bride Neill. *Elisabet Ney, Sculptor, 1834–1907.* New York: Devin-Adair Co., 1916. Reprint Austin: Thomas F. Taylor, 1938. Ney's close friend who functioned as a public relations voice for Ney, Taylor had studied journalism at the University of Texas.

Teich, Frank. Newspaper clippings, including illustrations, bibliography, and biographical manuscript. Llano County Historical Society, Llano.

Tennant, Allie, to Mrs. Beatrice Gilman Proske, June 7, 1966. Brookgreen Gardens Archives, Murrells Inlet, S.C. Regarding *Tejas Warrior.*

"Texan at Corcoran Gallery of Art." *Today in Texas,* October 1945. Regarding Waggoner.

Texas Legislative Council, ed. *The Texas Capitol: Symbol of Accomplishment.* 4th ed. Austin: State of Texas, 1986. Illustrations of Coppini, Tauch, Ney, and Cerracchio, et al.

Texas State Preservation Board. Archival information provided by the Capitol Curator and the State Historian, including: General Laws of The Seventh Legislature, The State of Texas, 1858; General Laws of The State of Texas, The Session of the Fourteenth Legislature, 1874; General Laws of The State of Texas, Eleventh Legislature, 1866.

"The Texas Academy of the Liberal Arts —
Active Steps toward an Endorsement."
Austin Daily Statesman, April 15, 1894.
Regarding Ney.

Texas Painting and Sculpture: 20th Century.
Dallas Museum of Fine Arts, et al. Essays
by Jerry Bywaters, James Chillman, Jr.,
Martha Utterback, Sam Cantey III, and
Loren Mozley. Dallas, 1971. Exhibition
catalog.

"Texas Sculptress Making Statue of President
Truman." *Today in Texas,* September
1945. Regarding Waggoner.

Thieme, Ulrich and Felix Becker, eds.
Allgemeines Lexicon der Bildenden Kunstler.
Vol. IX. Leipzig: E. A. Seeman, 1913.
Dexter, p. 197.

This New Man. National Portrait Gallery,
Smithsonian Institution Press, 1968.
Exhibition catalogue; for Dexter see p. 36.

"Tiny Commerce Artist Holds Own with
Stone." Dallas Times Herald, March 28,
1954. Jerry Bywaters Collection on Art of
the Southwest, Southern Methodist
University, Dallas. Regarding Franklin.

University of Texas at Austin. *Art Faculty:
32nd Annual Exhibition,* September 13–
October 18, 1970. University Art
Museum, College of Fine Arts, exhibition
catalog. Regarding Soto and Umlauf.

— — —. *33rd Annual Art Faculty Exhibition.*
1971. University Art Museum, College of
Fine Arts, exhibition catalog.

Umlauf Sculpture Garden, Austin. Published
and manuscript material on Charles
Umlauf.

"Unveiling of Spirit of Confederacy: Ten
Long Years . . . R. E. Lee Chapter
Consecrates a Monument to the Heroes of
the South . . ." *Houston Daily Post,* January
20, 1908. Regarding Amateis.

Waggoner Biggs, Electra. Audio recording of
artist discussing her sculpture techniques
and the making of the Will Rogers
equestrian figure. Courtesy Red River
Valley Museum, Vernon.

— — —. Interview with the artist, Fall, 1988.

— — —. Newspaper and other clippings,
including photograph of Waggoner and of
the sculpture *Riding into the Sunset.* Will
Rogers Memorial Museum Archives,
Claremore, Okla.

"Washington Woman Noted." *Washington,
New Jersey, Star.* September 19, 1963.
Provided by the National Academy of
Design, New York. Regarding McLeary.

Wasserman, Jeanne L. *Metamorphoses in
Nineteenth Century Sculpture.* Boston: Fogg
Art Museum, Harvard University Press,
1975.

Waters, Clara Erskine Clement & Laurence
Huttons. *Artists of the Nineteenth Century
and Their Works.* 7th rev. ed. Boston:
Houghton, Mifflin and Co., 1894. Reprint
(2 vols. in 1). New York: Aro Press, 1969.
Regarding Dexter, p. 204.

Webb, Walter Prescott and H. Bailey Carroll,
eds. *The Handbook of Texas.* 2 vols.
Austin: Texas State Historical
Association, 1952.

Wheeler, S. J. "Memorials to Heroes,
Galveston — City of Monuments."
Galveston Tribune [?], dated after 1938.
Rosenberg Library Archives, Galveston.

Wilbanks, Elsie Montgomery. *Art on the
Texas Plains.* Lubbock: South Plains Art
Guild, 1959. Regarding Hubbard and
Waggoner.

Williams, Anita. Material on Charles
Williams, including biographical data and
exhibition catalogues.

Williams, Charles. Archival material. Valley
House Gallery Files, Dallas.

"Williams' Sculptures for Library." *Dallas
Times Herald,* July 12, 1973.

Wilson, James Grant, and John Fiske, eds.
*Appletons' Cyclopaedia of American
Biography.* Vol. II. New York: D. Appleton
and Co., 1888. Reprint Detroit: Gale
Research Co., 1968. Regarding Dexter,
p. 161.

Witte Museum, San Antonio Museum
Association. Files on Texas artists.

Wood, Sarah Lee Norman. "The Heroic
Image: Three Sculptures by Elisabet
Ney." Master's thesis, University of Texas
at Austin, August 1978.

Woolford, Bess Carroll, and Ellen Schulz
Quillin. *The Story of the Witte Memorial
Museum: 1922–1960.* San Antonio
Museum Association, 1966. Regarding
Borglum, with illustration, p. 48, of his
Texas Cowboys, and illustration, p. 143, of
Tauch's *Gulf Breeze,* in plaster.

Wyse, Ellen B. "Bonnie MacLeary, Formerly
of Texas, Successful New York Sculptor:
With Her 'Laughing Frog,' Prize Winner
at Women Painters' and Sculptors'
Exhibition, New York." *Gossip,* February
25, 1930.

Younger, Jessamine, and Peggy Riddle, eds.
*A Gathering of Symbols: Texas History in
the Hall of State.* A Texas Sesquicentennial
Project. Dallas: Dallas Historical Society
Hall of State, 1986. Regarding Coppini,
illustration of the six figures in the Hall of
State.

PART 2

Becky Duval Reese

Experiment and Idea in Contemporary Texas Sculpture

EXPERIMENT AND IDEA
IN CONTEMPORARY TEXAS SCULPTURE

Sculpture has been described as the most difficult of all arts to understand because it demands of the viewer the ability to respond to form in three dimensions. Most of us learn to distinguish two-dimensional flat shapes early in our physical development. Often, however, we neither challenge ourselves nor make the intellectual and emotional effort that looking at sculpture demands.

In order to think of form as an entity with three dimensions, the sculptor must visualize the volume, the mass, the solidity, the weight of a work. The object must be seen in the sculptor's mind from above and below, from each side, from the front, and from the back. The sculptor must conceive the gestalt of the piece — the whole — before actual construction can begin.

Historically, sculpture has referred to the human figure in styles as dissimilar as abstracted Venus figures dating from 15,000 B.C. or works that span the ages from the Greeks and Polykleitos to Michelangelo and Rodin. The earliest uses of sculpture were for magic or ritualistic purposes. The Venus figures of 15,000 B.C. were used as fertility symbols or as magical tokens explaining the mysteries of birth. Civilizations with highly developed religious systems, like that of Egypt, used sculpture as symbols of omnipotent power or as surrogates for the afterlife. Markers for immortality, like Roman portrait busts, found their way to mausoleums or to family altars. Monuments to human achievement or to military conquest also relied on three-dimensional form to transcribe a deed into enduring significance.

Only in the twentieth century did sculpture sever its traditional tie to the human figure. Sculptors looked to the newly created style of Cubism with its fragmented and broken planes, overlapping shapes, and skewed perspectives. They also looked to the new style of Constructivism with its building up, layering over, or collaging on top of geometric abstracted shapes. Sculptors began to experiment with twentieth-century materials. For some, steel replaced clay, the welding torch replaced the chisel, and cranes removed the constraints of human size.

Sculptors of the twentieth century created a powerful art form that defied historical tradition by denying the necessity of representing the human figure. Sculptors were freed to imagine. They were at liberty to consider new possibilities in materials. Sculptors began using concave and convex shapes. They opened up holes within solid masses of materials. They relied on rough and smooth planes, geometric shapes, and abstracted images and constructed and assembled objects in achieving their new goals.

If the human figure was no longer identifiable, however, ideas based on humanistic concerns could be discerned. Subtly, twentieth-century sculptors assimilated the human presence in a variety of ways. They manipulated industrial materials and thereby demonstrated physical control over their own technology. Anthropomorphic associations were implicit in some works while in others the artist's feelings toward nature or the environment were expressed.

$H$and in hand with these innovations in twentieth-century sculpture was the idea of the new uses of sculpture. No longer tied to the necessity of manifesting religious concepts of immortality, or as paeans to war or conquest, or as rationale for superstition, the use of sculpture—the place of sculpture—changed radically. This new sculpture, based on theories of twentieth-century art and dependent on twentieth-century materials, demanded a new purpose.

Sculpture was created for public places. Not the public places of the Renaissance with its overtones of ruling families within tightly controlled city-states, but public places for the city-based masses living within a democratic society. Large-scale works, frequently of geometric shape and welded form, stood on corporate plazas and walkways serving as silent reminders of the individuals confined within the glass-boxed architecture that served as a backdrop to the sculpture. To some, sculpture in public places became heroic statements, a homage to individuals caught up in a faceless, nameless, isolated urban environment. To others, the new public sculpture became arbitrary infringements placed with little regard for individual sentiment.[1]

Whatever the form, whatever the meaning, wherever the placement, twentieth-century sculpture is successful when it engages the viewer, when it elicits a response, when it encourages questions and causes comments, and when it extends the proscribed boundaries of our everyday thought.

A mystique is attached to Texas art and artists. When James Michener was in the Lone Star State researching *Texas*, he was fascinated to discover that Texans truly believed their myths. The mythology surrounding Texas—ideas of the biggest, the best, the most unique, the most individual—makes Texas artists intriguing to themselves and to others throughout the nation and the world. Of course, not all Texas artists identify with regionalist concerns. The mystique is more complicated than that.

Texas is a big place. If the state could be folded upward with its northernmost line as a hinge, Brownsville would be 120 miles from Canada; if Texas were folded eastward, El Paso would be 40 miles off the Florida coast; if the state were folded westward, Orange would be 215 miles in the Pacific Ocean.[2] Two hundred and fifty-four counties are carved out of 267,339 square miles of land. The state is as large as all of New England, New York, Pennsylvania, Ohio, and Illinois combined. The longest north-south, straight-line distance is 801 miles. The greatest east-west distance is 773 miles. Texas is vast. It is so immense the whole can only be comprehended by its parts. The principal physical regions of the state are usually listed as the Gulf Coastal Plains, the North Central Plains, the Great Plains or Llano Estacado, and the Trans-Pecos. But these geological strata are not how the people of the state view themselves. Texans see themselves as living in East, West, or South Texas; in the Hill Country; along the Coast, or in the Valley. The ethnic diversity of Texas is as far-flung as the land mass itself and incorporates, among others, Spanish, French, Mexican, German, African, English, Swedish, Polish, and Czech. Regional patterns of culture developed through the confluence of geography and the many different nationalities that shaped the state's history.

1. My thanks to Lynn Barnett of the Abilene Cultural Affairs Council for permission to reprint excerpts from my preface to *Abilene Fourth Annual Outdoor Sculpture Exhibition*, 1985.

2. *The WPA Guide to Texas*, reprint of the 1940 *Texas: A Guide to the Lone Star State*, (Austin: Texas Monthly Press, 1986), p. 3.

3. D. W. Meinig, *Imperial Texas: An Interpretive Essay in Cultural Geography*, (Austin: University of Texas Press, 1969), p. 7.

But Texas does not exist as separated pockets of subcultures. Binding the state together is the idea of "empire," a word that aptly describes the immense scale of the geography yet goes beyond metaphor to define "a history of conquest, expansion, and dominion over a varied realm . . . the thrust of a self-confident aggressive people driven by a strong sense of superiority and destiny. . . ."[3] A band of frontiersmen had severed Texas from Mexico and the very existence of the Republic of Texas gave to the area and its people a unique identity based both on self-reliance and on self-consciousness. There is, indeed, a factual basis to the mythology.

Texas is also in transition. It is a state changing from a rural- to an urban-dominated economy. Long-held values connected to southern and western ideas of self-reliance, individual responsibility, personal integrity, and quick justice confront new standards, which oppose the chauvinistic, ethnocentric, and provincial attitudes equally at home on the "old" range. For the first time in the state's history, there is a generation that has absolutely no ties to the land. Residents today are more comfortable with the sounds of the freeways than with katydids and more at ease at the mall than outdoors. Currently, Texas is the third most populous of the United States and is expected to surpass New York in the next census. By the middle of the twenty-first century, Texas easily could be the most populous state in the country. With such an influx of population, what will become of the Texas myth?

Texas artists believe that the dominance of the New York art world is slipping, and they see Texas as a good place to live and to work. The many artists in the state live in extraordinarily varied ways. Of course more artists live in urban areas because there they can find studio space and jobs. Recently, however, artists began moving to smaller communities outside the larger cities where land is less expensive and where they have access to the city but without the attendant stress. On the one hand, the less frenetic daily pace provides a quality of life that is conducive to artistic production but, on the other, work is often completed in isolation. Texas artists frequently confront the harshness of an often violent climate — or the apathy of a generally suspicious public — but in spite of all, they continue to make their art, work at their day jobs to support their art, and find ways of meeting with each other over the state's long distances.

Artists find cultural enrichment through the state's museums, operas, ballet companies, and symphonies — and know its home-grown music and literature. Since the 1960s almost every town with a population exceeding 75,000 has built an art museum or an art center, which typically has supported the work of Texas artists. Indeed, between 1964 and 1981 thirty new museums a year were opened in Texas. Museum attendance currently exceeds 15 million annually. The Tyler Museum of Art, Amarillo Art Center, Waco Art Center, Art Museum of South Texas in Corpus Christi, and Laguna Gloria Art Museum in Austin now have exhibition histories of more than twenty years. Many of these institutions presented the first one-person shows for Texas artists who now receive national and, in some cases, international recognition. The newer museums — like the San Angelo Museum of Fine Arts, and the Art Museum of Southeast Texas, Beaumont — have joined the ranks of regional museums that document and exhibit the work of Texas artists for their local audiences.

Texas artists, like artists in other parts of the country, are influenced by and connected to the artistic and cultural aesthetics of the nation at large. Certainly since the end of World War II — with the centering of world art in New York City, with the rapid development of art departments at universities across the country, with the extraordinary growth of museums and arts centers, and with the increase of national arts publications — the exchange of information and ideas has proliferated at an incredibly rapid rate. Artists in these decades share a global aesthetic. When the work of Texas artists is shown in Dusseldorf galleries, when exchange exhibitions are organized between Houston artists and artists in Norway, and when Texas artists are shown in Berlin and the Netherlands, then we begin to recognize global connectedness. Texas artists are linked to the rest of the world; yet effects of the concerns, the influences, the history, the characteristic idiosyncrasies of their particular regions are unavoidable. Texas artists create in unique and individual styles. Yes, there is a mystique to Texas art. But is there a distinctive Texas style?

The debate over "regionalism" — the catchword for a distinctive Texas style — has been argued since the early 1970s when the work of Texas contemporary artists began to attract national attention. It is true that at that time some artists dealt with stereotypical images of Texas; they adopted the myths but presented them in new ways. Often the work was painted with irony or cast in satire. There was overall a light-hearted sensibility at work — a playfully irreverent examination of Texas history. For some, by embracing the "regionalist" concept they garnered widespread public and media attention. But other artists in Texas found the "regionalist" label too confining, too limiting; in fact, they believed it had absolutely nothing to do with the art they created because it arbitrarily classified Texas art as one shared aesthetic that drew upon Texas myths. They also realized that inherent within the "regionalist" categorization was the underlying assumption that such art was viewed as provincial, circumscribed by and contained within the geographical boundaries of the state. Thus, two camps formed within contemporary Texas art circles.

The contemporary use of the term, it should be noted, is in opposition to John Dewey's mode of Regionalism as postulated in his 1934 book *Art as Experience*. Dewey felt culture, not politics or economics, would most influence the growth of America. He urged American artists to rediscover the localities of America and use them as the basis for their art. Dewey believed that only by discovering the regional could the artist find the universal. Regionalism took on a nationalistic veneer during the Depression and later became the accepted mode of representation for Federal Arts Projects.[4] From the perspective of the 1970s, one group of Texas artists viewed Dewey-style Regionalism as a restrictive form of art — an art bound to realist imagery, violently opposed to "modernism," and unaccepting of any other mode of representation. The other group found the label beneficial in helping the public better understand what their art was about.

In 1983 and 1985 two Houston museums examined ideas of contemporary "regionalism" in major exhibitions: Southern Fictions, at the Contemporary Arts Museum; and Fresh Paint: The Houston School, at the Museum of Fine Arts, Houston. Southern Fictions postulated that, in Texas and southern art, work is emotionally based and less cerebral, there is no interest in strictly formalist concerns, narrative and figurative art predominates nonobjective work, autobiography and attachments to the land dominate, and an expressive romanticism that enhances the imagination vies with characteristics of Surrealism with references to the irrational and the subconscious.[5]

While Southern Fictions dealt with generalized aspects of the South, Barbara Rose set out to prove there was a dis-

4. Rick Stewart, *Lone Star Regionalism*, catalog for exhibition, Dallas Museum of Art, 1985, p. 22.

5. William A. Fagaly, "Southern Fictions," essay for exhibition catalog *Southern Fictions*, Contemporary Arts Museum, Houston, 1983, p. 13.

6. Barbara Rose, "Fresh Paint: Painting Is Dead, Long Live Painting in Houston," essay for the exhibition catalog *Fresh Paint: The Houston School*, Museum of Fine Arts, Houston, (Austin: Texas Monthly Press, 1985), pp. 65–93.

7. Dominique de Menil, in *Jim Love Up to Now*, catalog for exhibition at Institute for the Arts, Rice University, Houston, 1980, p. 14.

tinct and specific Houston school of art in the exhibition Fresh Paint. Rose observed that the artists in Houston shared the sensibility of a common environment, an interest in humanism and figuration, an interest in tactile surfaces, positive rather than negative imagery based on energy rather than entropy, a lack of cynicism, and an interest in the landscape.[6]

Something can be said for the definitions and distinctions posited by these two museum shows. All of the categories — from romanticism to expressionism to surrealism — can be illustrated with specific works of art. But problems arise when such generic descriptions attempt to define such an enormous group of artists. Not all Texas artists have a penchant for storytelling; not all employ exaggeration or emotionally charged imagery. Not all Texas artists fit these rather narrow definitions. Texas artists must be seen within the context of the state itself. Their concerns are as vast, immense, and gigantic as Texas. Texas artists cover an incredible territory and their art must be seen as relational to all the concerns that strike their lives. Their responses are not limited by the state's boundaries but embrace the world. It is of vital importance that Texas artists not be placed within limited, restrictive categories.

How then to comprehend the magnitude of the art of Texas? Rather than say that all Texas artists display a romantic sensibility, categorize those who do; rather than say that all Texas art is emotionally charged rather than cerebral, isloate the one from the other. Texas contemporary art can embrace the mythology of Texas. Texas contemporary art can ignore it. While plurality and diversity of style in art are widely accepted standards of categorization at the national and international levels, this has not been the case in Texas. It is time to bring this concept home and to accept that plurality and diversity of style exist in Texas contemporary art.

This essay addresses the work of sixty-five sculptors who are living and working in the state today or who at one time lived in the state and contributed to the growth of the visual arts in Texas. Some artists are discussed at greater length than others due to the contributions to contemporary art they have made nationally and internationally. The body of their work is consistently strong and merits a deeper look. Some artists are comparatively new to the state and some artists are relatively young and just beginning their artistic production. In total, the sixty-five artists herein have originated singular and distinctive works of art. All of them continue creating work that demonstrates the development and maturation of the Texas art scene from the late 1950s to the late 1980s.

In the mid 1950s three artists — Jim Love, Roy Fridge, and David McManaway — digested the prevalent ideas of art in the country and devised their own responses. The friendship of Love, Fridge, and McManaway dates from their shared experiences in Dallas in the late 1950s. Even though Jim Love had settled in Houston in 1953, it was through the combined influences of Paul Baker, innovative director of Baylor Theatre in Waco and later founder of the Dallas Theater Center; Douglas MacAgy, director of the Dallas Museum of Contemporary Arts (1959–1963); and Jermayne MacAgy, director of the Contemporary Arts Association, Houston (1955–1959) that the various stages for contemporary art were set in Dallas and Houston.

Jim Love attended Baylor University in Waco where he studied business administration until taking what he refers to as one of his many "sideways" steps.[7] He had followed his girlfriend to a drama class taught by Paul Baker, and he soon realized he wanted to drop business and

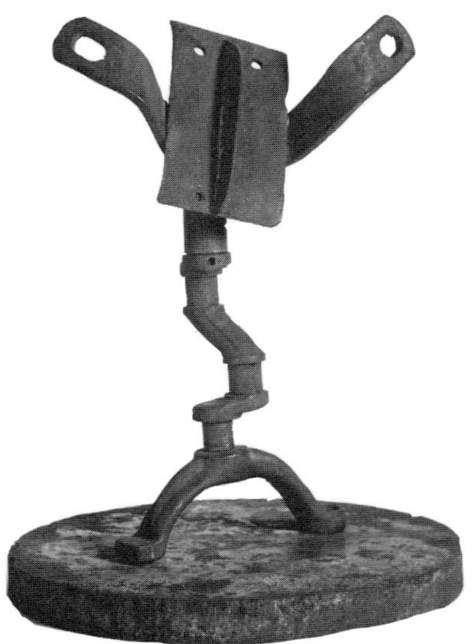

JIM LOVE, Houston

The Pedestrian
1960
steel and cast iron
13¼ in. × 10¾ in. × 10¾ in.
The Menil Collection, Houston

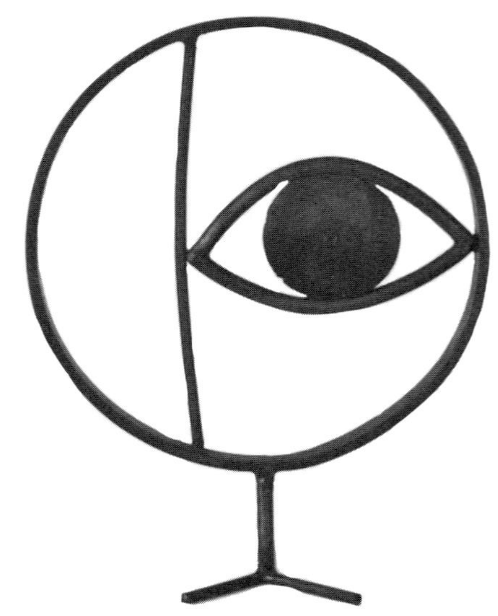

JIM LOVE, Houston

The Honeymoon
ca. 1957
12⅝ in. × 10 in. × 4⅝ in.
The Menil Collection, Houston

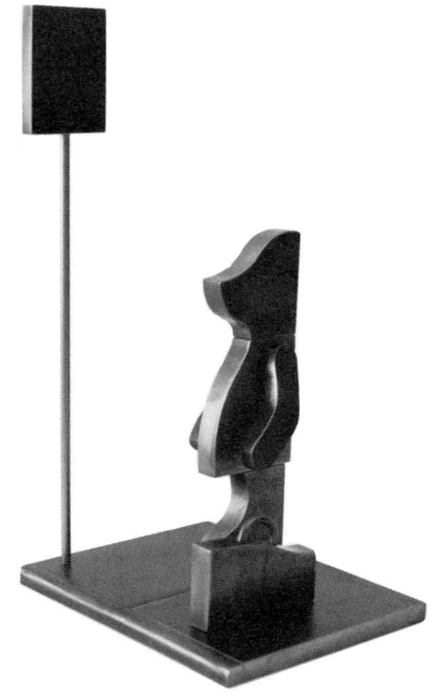

JIM LOVE, Houston

The Portable New You
1984
welded steel
11 in. × 4¾ in. × 6 in.
Courtesy of the artist and Janie C. Lee
Gallery, Houston

continue with the theater. After graduation and through Baker's introduction, he settled in Houston where he worked for Theater Inc., followed by a stint at the Alley Theatre where he began to construct sets for plays as varied as *Waiting for Godot* and *The Glass Menagerie*. Jermayne MacAgy discovered Love through his theater work, and Love began doing installations for the Contemporary Arts Association. In addition to working with MacAgy creating the extraordinary installations for which the CAA is still known[8] — such as two 1958 exhibitions: The Trojan Horse: The Art of the Machine and Totems Not Taboo: An Exhibition of Primitive Art — Love began to weld steel sculpture. He collected scraps from Waco and Fort Worth junkyards from which he constructed hybrid birds and phantasmic figures. Donald Barthelme wrote of him, "Love, an urban archeologist, makes his discoveries in the detritus of an industrial society; one bucket of odd parts from a Fort Worth junkyard yielded . . . thirty objects. The prior history of these things blesses them with a special poignancy; their previous existence endures in the life of the new object."[9] The additive process of making this found sculpture combines with visual puns to produce a sense of disjunction on the part of the viewer. We recognize the various metal parts as having had a prior industrial use; yet, through their combination they offer the semblance of a human figure. One recognizes the influences of both David Smith and Richard Stankiewicz in *The Pedestrian*, a welded sculpture composed of bits of scrap metal and old plumbing fixtures. Love toys with erotic content and visual puns with his welded steel work, *The Honeymoon*. An eye is enclosed within a circle; the eyeball itself can be interpreted as either an eye or a breast. Love creates a surreal object yet imbues it with warmth and wit.

        In the early 1970s, Love appropriated the bear as his leitmotif. Perhaps inspired by Claes Oldenburg's mice, Love has used the small metal bear in poignantly comic forms. We encounter the bear as a Trojan horse, a target, a floor mat, or Everyman.[10] In *The Portable New You* the

8. Cheryl A. Brutvan with Marti Mayo and Linda L. Cathcart, *In Our Time: Houston's Contemporary Arts Museum 1948–1982*, catalog for exhibition at Contemporary Arts Museum, Houston, 1982, p. 25.

9. Donald Barthelme, Introduction to *Jim Love Up to Now*, p. 11.

10. Ibid., p. 12.

11. Douglas MacAgy, *one i at a time*, catalog for exhibition at Pollock Galleries, Meadows School of the Arts, Southern Methodist University, Dallas, 1971, p. 25.

12. Susan Freudenheim, in "Essay/Roy Fridge: Living Fiction," in catalog for exhibition Roy Fridge, Art Museum of South Texas, Corpus Christi, 1985, unpaginated.

13. Ibid.

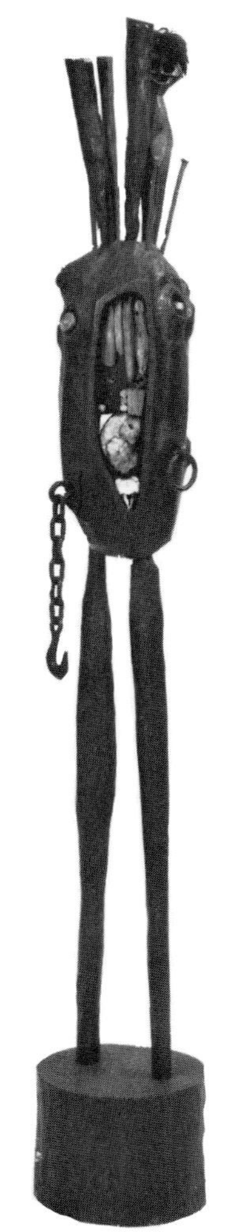

ROY FRIDGE, Port Aransas

Figure
1959
mixed media
10 in. × 10 in. × 72 in.
Collection of Paul Rogers Harris, Dallas

bear seems to wait passively by a road sign, briefcase at his feet, hands at his side, for permission to move. Douglas MacAgy referred to Love's work as embracing "the ridiculous pathos in the commonplace,"[11] a statement especially relevant to Love's bears, who become surrogates depicting the human condition.

We see in Jim Love's art reflections of Assemblage in his welded metal, found-object sculptures; we recognize ruminations of Pop Art in his steel replications of bow-ties, extension cords, nails, or jacks. And we understand that he has assimilated the ideas of modern art within the body of his unique work. But basically when we look at the sculpture of Jim Love, we see an artist coming to terms with the art of his time in the creation of distinct objects, which speak to us in a wry, soft-edged existentialist vocabulary.

Roy Fridge also was affected by Paul Baker at Baylor. In 1948, following two years in the U.S. Navy, Fridge went to Baylor University where he became involved with the theater. After graduation, he lived and worked in Dallas for ten years, earning his living making both commercial and art films and occasionally constructing sculpture which he showed from time to time.[12] Like Love, he spent time designing and constructing stage sets, and through Paul Baker, Love and Fridge met and became friends. They also shared interests in found-object assemblages. Fridge, too, scavenged parts from Dallas junkyards. Around this time, 1959 to 1960, he began making trips to Port Aransas where he collected driftwood and bones found on the beaches along the Gulf of Mexico. Finding city life no longer satisfying, Fridge retreated to Port Aransas in 1961. There, on the beaches, he began a period of isolation and his quest for the "amateur hermit," as he called himself. With only a four-year (1969–1973) break from the coast during which he established a film program at the University of Oklahoma, Fridge has continued to live in Port Aransas.[13]

Fridge's sculpture speaks the language of pagan religions and embodies a folk art derived from undefined spirits and personal belief systems. There are powerful presences in the work that evoke

ROY FRIDGE, Port Aransas

Divine Sun Ship: Burial of the Dwarf Queen
1975–76
mixed media
33¾ in. × 5¾ in. × 16½ in.
Collection of Mr. and Mrs. Thomas Marion O'Connor, Victoria

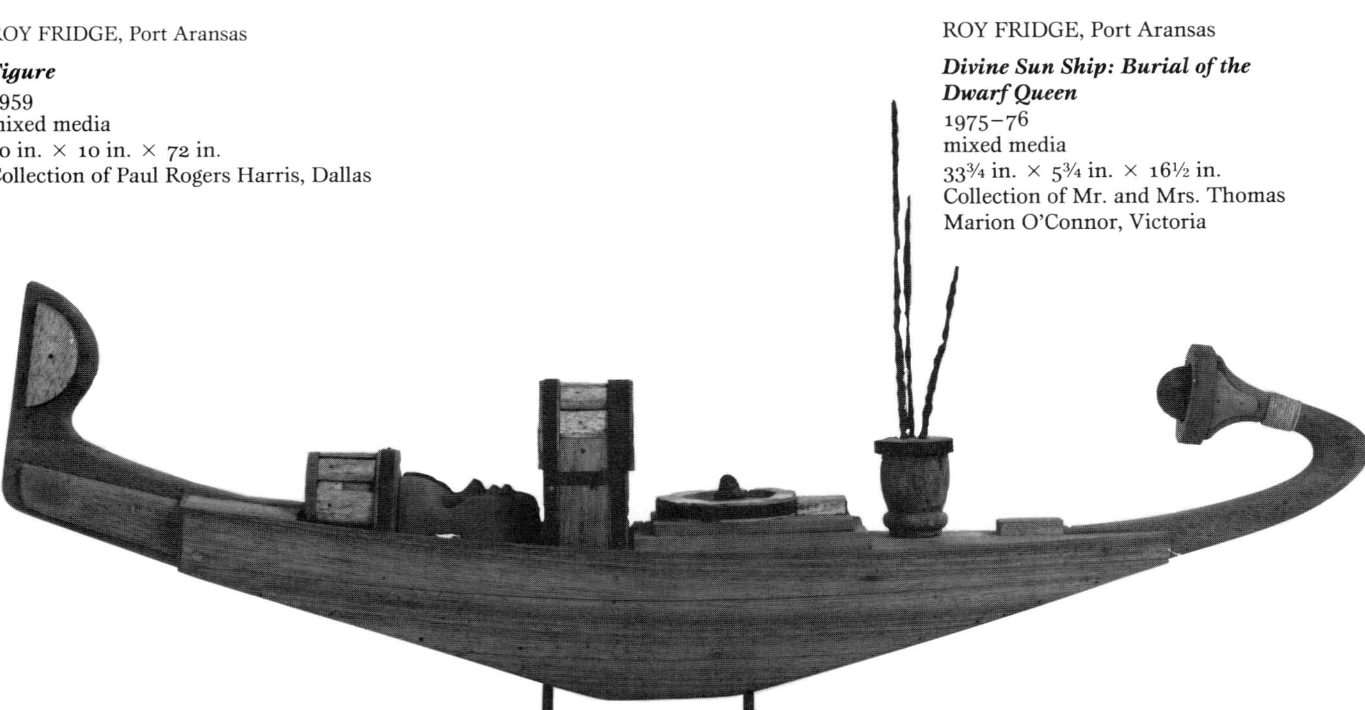

personal dreams. They conjure the unknown in their romantic and theatrical presentations.[14] Ned Rifkin has also observed that "Fridge's medium is the inherent ritual and theater of one's own life, oneself [viewed] as high priest or principal actor."[15]

Totems as autonomous objects imbued with magical powers occupied many artists throughout the forties and the fifties,[16] including Roy Fridge. In his 1959 work *Figure*, for example, bits of wood, bone, and chain form a totem, which becomes an emotionally charged, abstracted surrogate for the human body — yet at the pinnacle of Fridge's totem is a tiny smiling head, which defuses the otherwise threatening object. "These totems and reliquaries of the imagination, even though personal, have a universal appeal and identification."[17]

Throughout the seventies Fridge initially built boats for utilitarian purposes. He sailed and fished from them. Later the boats became resources for fantasy voyages to exotic places. The boats he built were both life-size and scaled-down models. In *Divine Sun Ship: Burial of the Dwarf Queen*, Fridge conjoins mythic content with wood, a doll's head, and other found materials to present a surreal passage from one world to another.

The mystical voyages that Fridge sailed in his numerous boats from the 1970s are, by the 1980s, beached to become land-based shrines. Confounded by the impossibility of finding isolation along the Port Aransas beaches, Fridge (on a part-time basis) retired to the South Texas woods where he began building shrines, examining Jungian ideas of the collective unconscious, and developing a "personal pseudo-primitive shamanic imagery."[18] *The Voyage of Initiation* is a lyrical example of Fridge's concern with myth and magic. The tall totem/shrine created of highly polished wood is topped off by two carved birds. The suggestion of a figure beckons the viewer with its outstretched arms while its horned animal skull appears to invite us even closer. The idea of figure is complete when the viewer realizes that "the biological form and the hand-crafted shape of the boat have been fused."[19]

Incorporating surrealism, folk art, and Assemblage, the work of Roy Fridge, the shaman and amateur hermit, shares with the viewer a personal and poetic vision based on his ongoing journeys.

David McManaway moved in 1959 from the University of Arkansas to Dallas where, at the Dallas Museum of Contemporary Arts (DMCA) he met Douglas MacAgy, Jim Love, and Roy Fridge. Like many artists in the area at the time, McManaway donated his labor to the DMCA. He assisted in installations, took part in discussions with other artists centered at the museum, and became a member of the energized Dallas modern art scene.[20]

Douglas MacAgy brought modern art to Dallas. It was at the DMCA that the art of René Magritte was given its first museum showing in the United States. MacAgy presented an early Pop Art exhibition and, in 1962, MacAgy included David McManaway and Jim Love in the DMCA showing of the Museum of Modern Art's exhibition The Art of Assemblage.[21] Claes Oldenburg came at MacAgy's request to the DMCA where he installed his famous *Store*. Oldenburg stayed on for several weeks and the museum presented its first Happening — MacAgy claims *Injun* was "the first Happening anywhere on museum commission."[22] Those were heady days in Dallas, and Love, Fridge, and McManaway were right in the middle of it all. David McManaway is in many ways as much an amateur hermit as is Roy Fridge; though not living in literal isolation, McManaway very much keeps his own company and rarely travels beyond Dallas.

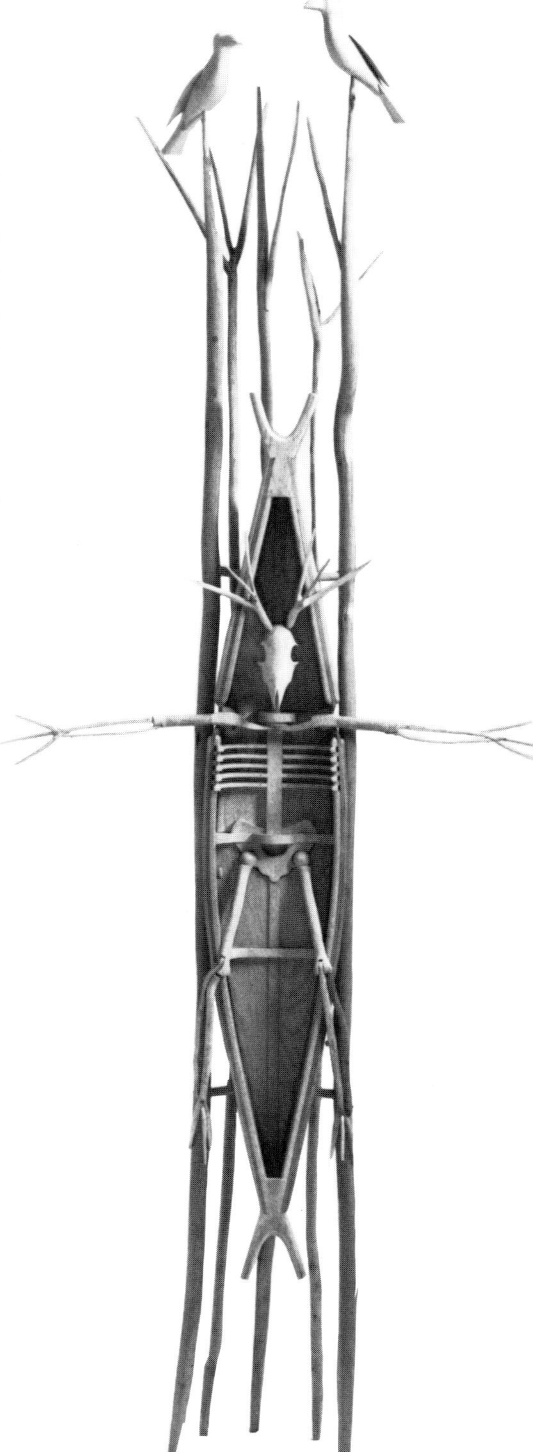

ROY FRIDGE, Port Aransas

The Voyage of Initiation
1984
mixed media
43 in. × 10 in. × 118 in.
Collection of Mr. and Mrs. H. Irving
Schweppe, Houston

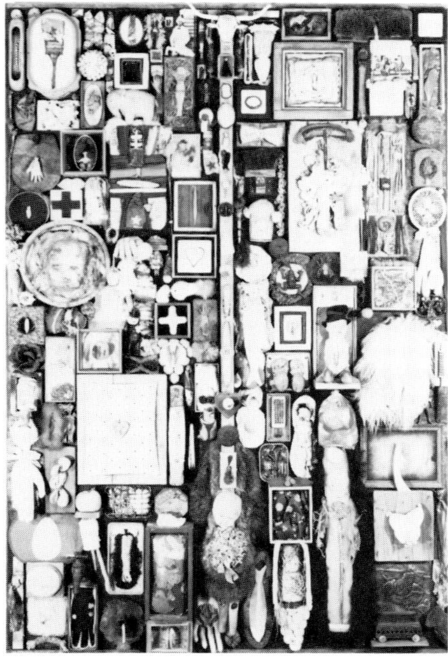

DAVID McMANAWAY, Dallas
Jomo Board No. 6
1973–1975
mixed media
48¼ in. × 73 in.
Collection of Oz and Paul Srere, Dallas

The "jomo" intrigues David McManaway. The movie *Juke Girl* influenced McManaway as a child. In the film, one character was a Jomo man whose business was selling jomos — "small bags or pouches hung from a board."[23] The movie *Juke Girl* and the idea of jomo magic followed McManaway throughout childhood to college and finally into his art. McManaway believes "jomo" derived from "an inversion of 'mojo,' which in southern black cultures could be either a voodoo charm or a euphemism for morphine."[24] As he pointed out, the phrase "I've got my mojo working" could refer to either being high on drugs or carrying a lucky piece. McManaway's use of jomo has always been based on the concept of jomo as white (good) magic, unlike the more ominous mojo black magic. McManaway's assembled jomo boards consist of diverse objects, which often become "domestic elegies" or "poetic elegies of the past."[25] Affected by Pop Art, by the surrealism of Magritte, and by other assemblagist artists' works, McManaway's art consistently refers back to himself and to his friends.[26]

McManaway, like Love and Fridge, was interested in found objects. Through the artist's hand the objects were transformed; without the alterations the objects were devoid of their magic. In the seminal *Private Joko* of 1967, McManaway reuses an old Coca-Cola bottle box and charges each space with tension. Evocative dolls' heads, a rose, and mysteriously filled pouches complete the free-standing piece. It seems the dolls are observing, judging — possibly even condemning the viewer.

By 1975, *Private Joko* has evolved into the fully realized work *Jomo Board No. 6*. McManaway's mystical objects acquire meaning through their combination. The viewer is presented dolls' heads, heart shapes, and hands; crosses (or plus symbols), paint brushes, cow skulls, and fish; fuzzy things and smooth things. There are phallic and vaginal shapes, stars, and a bow tie. The artist seems to be telling us about life and death, love and sex. But McManaway also advises that it is a mistake to try to interpret the objects as separate symbols. Only through the gestalt of the work can understanding be found.[27]

14. Fagaly, *Southern Fictions*, p. 13.

15. Ned Rifkin, *Response*, catalog for exhibition, Tyler Museum of Art, 1980, p. 11.

16. Lisa Phillips, *The Third Dimension: Sculpture of the New York School*, catalog for exhibition, Whitney Museum of American Art, New York, 1984, p. 20.

17. Fagaly, *Southern Fictions*, p. 13.

18. Freudenheim, "Essay/Roy Fridge: Living Fiction."

19. Howard Smagula, *Texas Currents*, catalog for exhibition, San Antonio Art Institute, 1985, p. 25.

20. MacAgy, *one i at a time*, p. 7.

21. Ibid., p. 8.

22. Ibid., p. 13.

23. David McManaway quoted in *David McManaway/ Works/Twenty Years* catalog by Anne Livet for exhibition, University Gallery, Meadows School of the Arts, Southern Methodist University, Dallas, 1979, unpaginated.

24. Ibid.

25. Ibid.

26. Jim Edwards, *The Poetic Object*, catalog for exhibition, San Antonio Museum of Art, 1988

27. David McManaway quoted in *David McManaway/ Works/Twenty Years*.

Dadaist humor is a common element shared in the work of Love, Fridge, and McManaway; but it is a warm wit these artists employ. No meanness is intended; no darkly ironic or cynical statement is implied. No doubt humor binds their friendship as it unites their art. They have created abstract portraits of each other and of themselves that evoke the tenderness of shared personal experiences. Each artist uses wry pun and language in his works; they all seek juxtapositions of found objects, which form narratives; and often their titles express the self-deprecating form of humor so familiar to Texans. J. Frank Dobie called it "bragging about the worst," but these three artists would see it as the best way to greet the modern world.

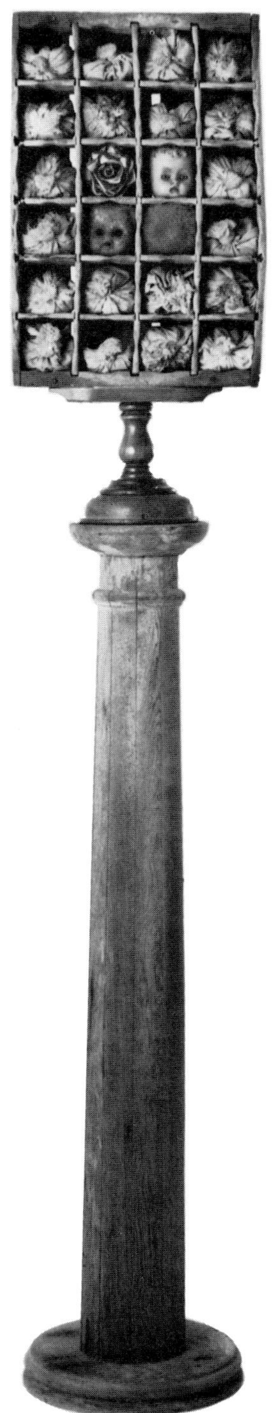

DAVID MCMANAWAY, Dallas

Private Joko
1967
mixed media
25⅜ in. × 12⅜ in. × 14 in.; base 43 in. high
Collection of Paul Rogers Harris, Dallas

By the 1960s university art departments were integral parts of higher education, and students turned to them in great numbers for their training. Indeed, the common denominator of Texas contemporary artists since the sixties is the college degree. The students learned from faculties of artists both from within and without the Lone Star State. They studied the prevailing styles of art; they visited New York City on school-sponsored trips; they read art magazines; and they met visiting artists and critics brought to the campuses for special lectures.

Luis Jimenez, James Surls, Michael Tracy, and Bob Wade share the training of university education. They also began in the decade of the sixties to forge national artistic reputations. They each have created a consistently powerful body of work that reflects knowledge and understanding of the history of art, and their work is based on a strongly formed sense of self and of place. Each has found his unique voice in Texas.

After graduating from college, Luis Jimenez went to New York City where he worked with the sculptor Seymour Lipton.[28] During this time, his work was shown at Graham Gallery and O K Harris Works of Art.[29] His sculpture confronted viewers with such outrageous images as *The American Dream,* which depicted a voluptuous woman making love with a Volkswagen, or *Bar Fly: Statue of Liberty*, which overtly satirized sacred American symbols (a radical act in the late 1960s). Few found the work polite, but none denied its power. After six years in New York, Jimenez returned to his native El Paso, where his art took a more personal turn. He incorporated into his work beliefs based on personally experienced events or emotions, and the work began to reflect a distinctive geographic and cultural place. Jimenez said:

I've always found artists who responded to a regional situation fascinating, whether it's Arthur Miller or James Baldwin or William Faulkner; these writers have been important to me in developing concepts about what I want to do. Every one of them focused on a very particular isolated situtation that they knew well, and in so doing spoke also to broader issues.[30]

Jimenez, a second-generation Hispanic American, saw life from two points of view. He was part of the Chicano culture, a culture fully accepted by neither the Mexicans nor the Americans. Straddling these traditions compelled him to operate within subcultures. His understanding of the "other" or the "outsider" became an integral force in his art. In the early 1970s he embraced the plight of the American Indian in oversized sculptures ranging from his interpretation of the frequently reproduced James Earl Fraser 1915 masterpiece, *End of the Trail* to his *Progress Series* to drawings depicting the ignoble postwar death of World War II hero, Native American Ira Hayes. In these works he redressed a skewed American history, a process he continued in his

LUIS JIMENEZ, Hondo, New Mexico

Vaquero *(see cover)*
1981
acrylic on fiberglass
16½ ft. × 10½ ft. × 5½ ft.
Collection of Mr. Frank Ribelin, Dallas

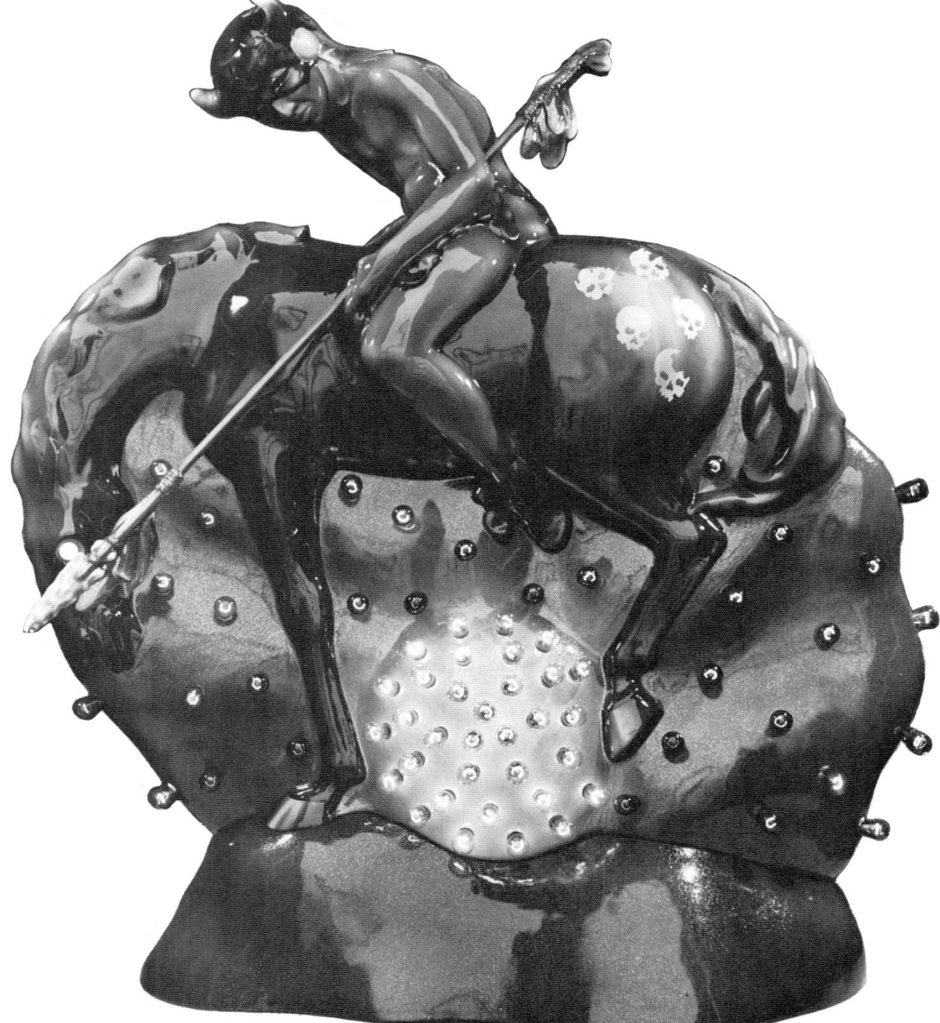

LUIS JIMENEZ, Hondo, New Mexico

End of the Trail (with Electric Sunset)
1972–80
acrylic on fiberglass, with light bulbs
84 in. × 58 in. × 39 in.
Collection of The University of Texas at El
Paso: gift of the Frederick Weisman
Company

28. Frank Gettings, *Different Drummers*, catalog for
    exhibition, Hirshhorn Museum and Sculpture
    Garden, Washington, D.C., 1988, p. 123.

29. Annette DiMeo Carlozzi, *Luis Jimenez*, catalog for
    exhibition, Laguna Gloria Art Museum, Austin,
    1983, p. 14.

30. Amy Baker Sandback, "Signs: A Conversation with
    Luis Jimenez," *ArtForum*, September 1984, p. 84.

31. Ibid.

32. Carlozzi, *Luis Jimenez*, p. 20.

monumental sculpture *Vaquero* where we learn that the first cowboys were from
Mexico and were not the Anglo heroes movies and magazines first showed us.
Jimenez forces us to remember that

It wasn't John Wayne who was the original cowboy. That's the myth. This contribution
that the Mexican community made to Texas and the image of the United States has been
totally overlooked.[31]

Jimenez's art also depicts ordinary peo-
ple, as in his multifigured, free-standing, life-size tableau *Honky Tonk,* or in his
print *Rodeo Queen*, or in the fiberglass sculpture, *Old Woman with Cat*. Illustrative
of his always charging his art with deeply held convictions, the old woman in
this sculpture represents Jimenez's grandmother. Its meaning references his feelings about the treatment or mistreatment of the elderly. In this work, the shape
of the old woman conforms to the shape of the chair in which she sits. Human
form and object meld into one. He prods our consciousness when he suggests
that our society treats the elderly like a piece of furniture — placed in a corner of
a room and out of the way. Painted in muted green colors, *Old Woman with Cat*
prompts us to remember our humanity. Jimenez's coyote in the sculpture *Howl*
not only derives from what he observed in the desert as a boy but also, as Annette
Carlozzi suggests, represents an anthropomorphic self-portrait.[32]

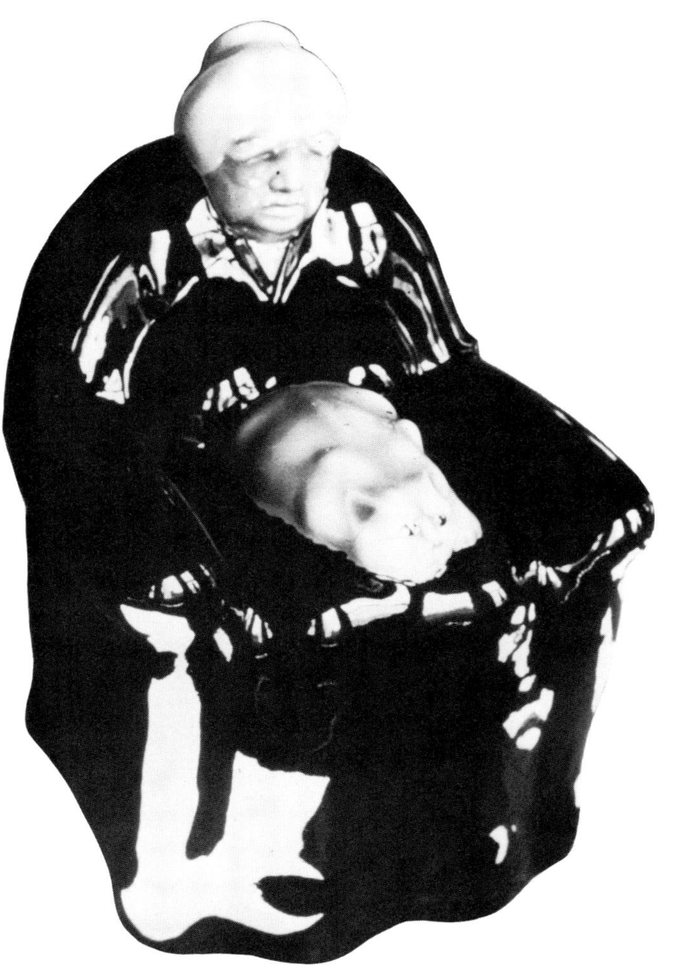

LUIS JIMENEZ, Hondo, New Mexico

Old Woman with Cat
1969
acrylic on fiberglass
40 in. × 24 in. × 25 in.
Collection of Mr. and Mrs. T. Turner Pope III,
Houston

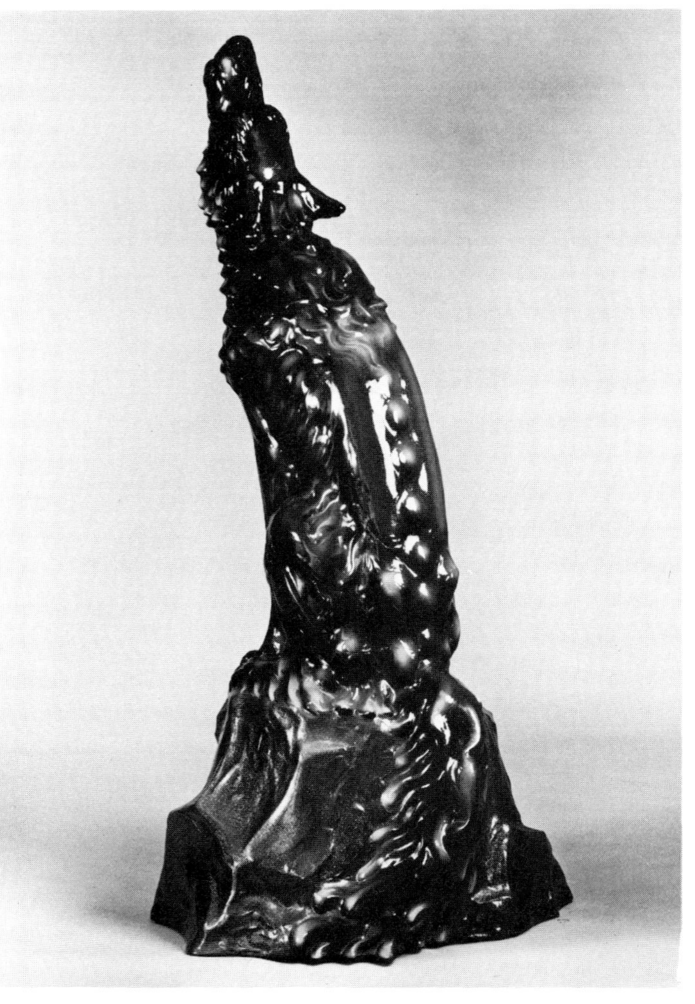

LUIS JIMENEZ, Hondo, New Mexico

Howl
1986
acrylic on fiberglass
6o in. × 3o in. × 3o in.
Courtesy of the artist and Moody Gallery,
Houston

As a young boy, Luis had learned to weld, to wire, and to work with large forms in his father's neon sign shop in El Paso. The first large-scale objects he built were hot rods. His teen-age fascination with cars, fiberglass, and bright colors carried over to his art and helped form his visual vocabulary. The sculptures are cast in fiberglass from multiple molds and then painted hot colors. Perhaps as a homage to his father—or because of his own fascination with neon—electric lights frequently appear in his work as well. In *End of the Trail (with Electric Sunset)*, the lights are devices which shock and surprise the viewer—but as they recall the lights of an outdoor movie marquee, they also satirize an American history learned from the movie screen. Fully embracing his past, his bicultural identity, and his knowledge of art, Luis Jimenez's creations make strong personal statements that transcend the artist and the Southwest to become testaments of the human condition.

33. Annette Carlozzi, Gay Block, Laurel Jones, *50 Texas Artists* (San Francisco: Chronicle Books, 1986), statement by James Surls, p. 94.

34. Don Graham, *Texas: A Literary Portrait* (San Antonio: Corona Publishing Company, 1985), p. 46.

35. Ibid., p. 55.

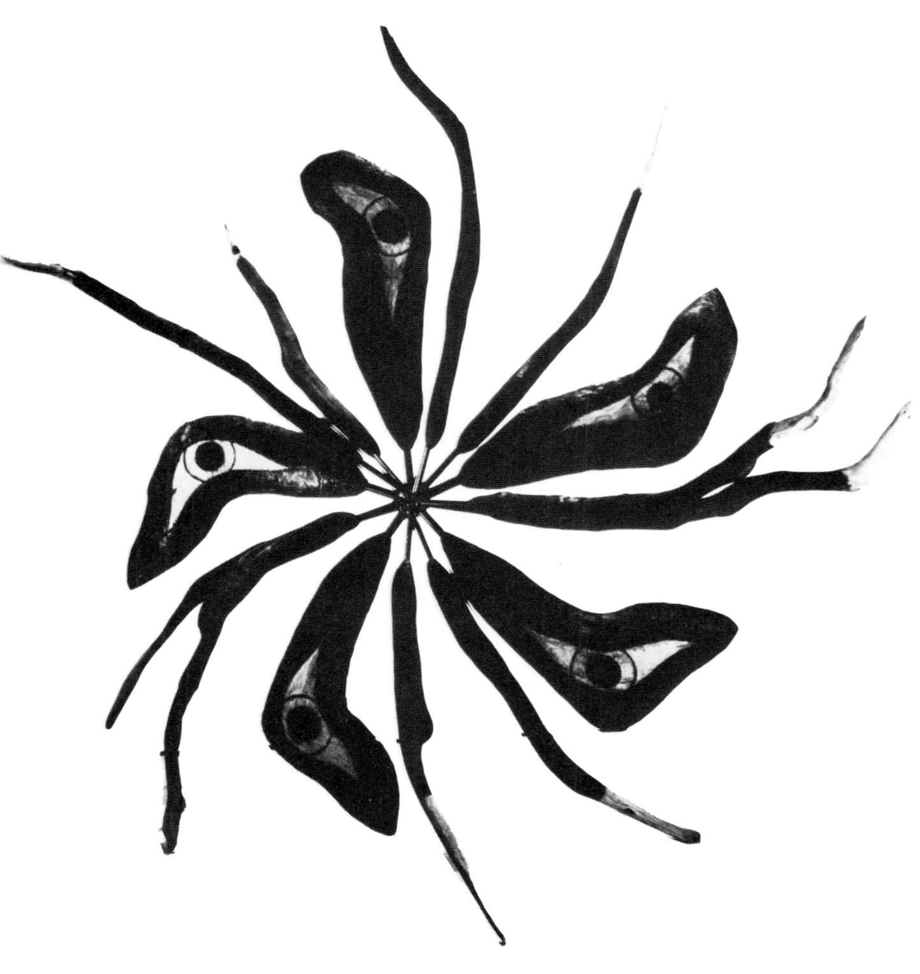

*James Surls, **Walk in See,** 1987,
pine, oak, steel, 92 in. × 60 in. × 60 in.
Courtesy of the artist and Hiram Butler
Gallery, Houston**

*It's the puff I'm after. The hocus-pocus the
Merlin types used to produce. I love it that they could wave a wand and from a flash
of light and a puff of smoke would appear an object. I make objects. It takes so long. It
would take me a lifetime to build just what I can dream in one day. I want a hundred
lifetimes and one day. I do my best.*[33]

The rhythm of James Surls' voice is that
of East Texas. He speaks in short, direct sentences, then embellishes his
thoughts with poetic vision. Surls, like many linked to this section of Texas, finds
comfort in tradition, home, and family. East Texans have a pride of place. For
the country people Surls knew growing up, there was

. . . a kind of civility that prevailed . . . at all levels of society. Those country people, for
the most part, had beautiful if not polished manners; they had an easy sense of dignity
that the world always needs and always has too little of; above all they were such decent,
modest, and generous people. . . .[34]

The writing that comes from East
Texas reflects Old South attitudes. In novels as different as George Sessions
Perry's *Hold Autumn in Your Hand* or William Humphrey's *Home from the Hill*,
the South is a place where divine powers control nature and human destiny.[35]
Giving over to nature such dire power creates a romantic sensitivity, which is
felt by Surls and by many Texans with southern sensibilities. The rhetoric of
southern writing has fundamentalist preaching at its roots. It is a writing domi-

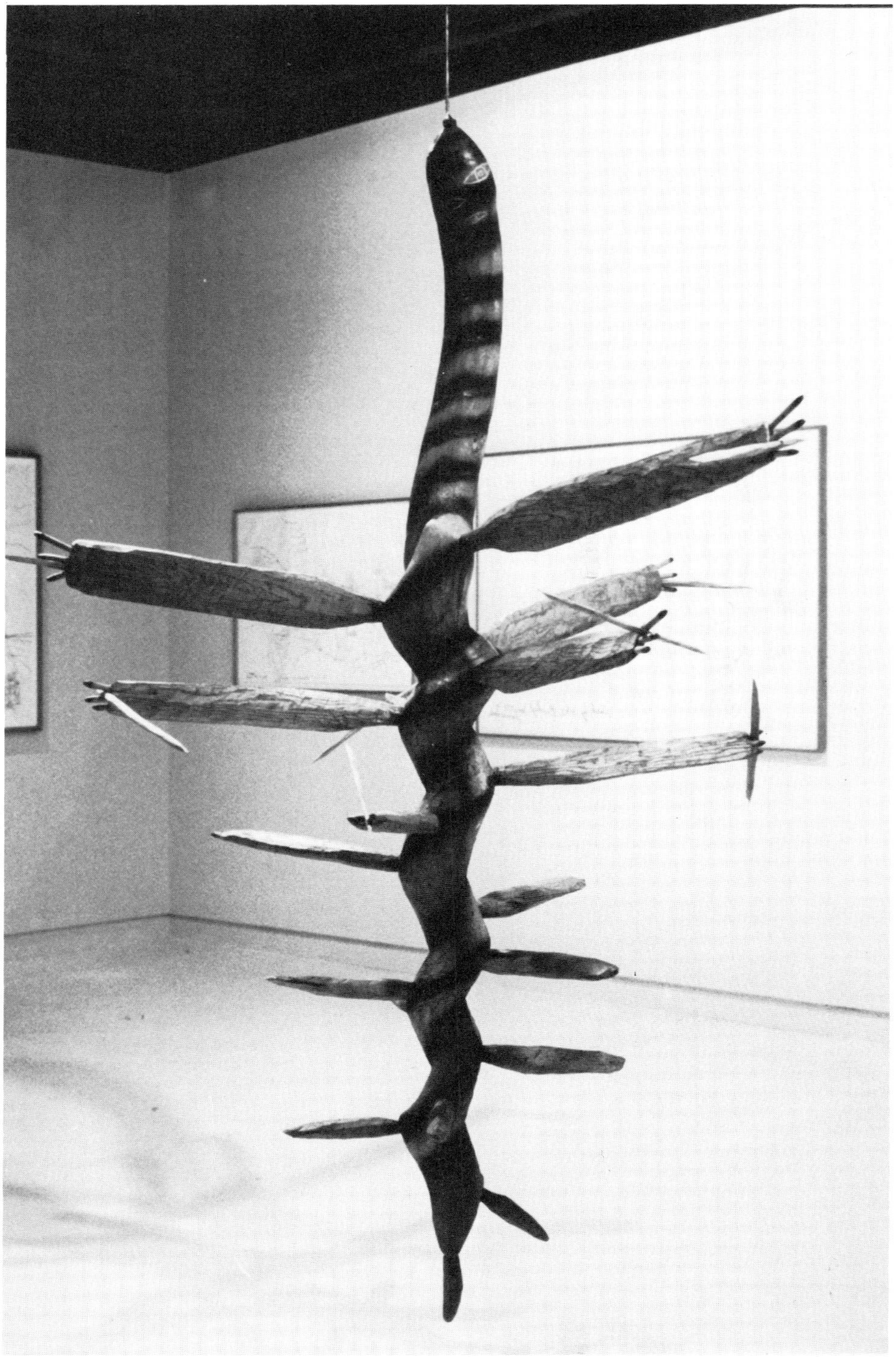

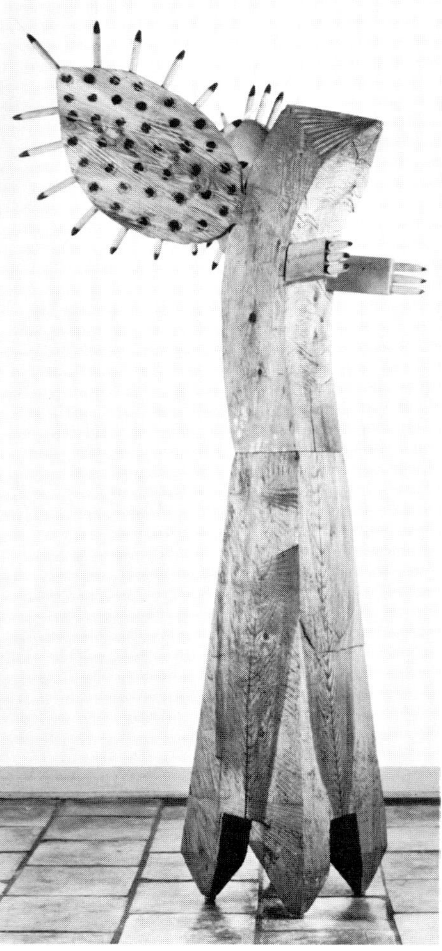

JAMES SURLS, Splendora

Dancing Man
1977
oak, pine
96 in. × 60 in. × 60 in.
Courtesy of the artist and Hiram Butler
Gallery, Houston

JAMES SURLS, Splendora

She Brings Gifts to Me
1977
bois d'arc, elm, walnut, pecan, wool
46¾ in. × 27½ in. × 26½ in.
Collection of Mr. and Mrs. T. Turner Pope III,
Houston

nated by history and the imagination; and there is an abiding interest in a social order, in the land, and in the family. Texans enjoy a good story. James Surls brings to his art the poet's heart and the storyteller's ear.

Since moving to Splendora, Texas, in 1977, for the first time in his adult life Surls feels a sense of stability.[36] This stability is important to his art, for much of the subject matter with which he deals derives from home and family. He lives on forty-two acres in the East Texas Piney Woods, where he feels he has found his "earthly home." Both the inspiration and the materials for his art come from this site.

Growing up on a farm, cutting wood with his brother, playing with his father's carpentry tools — axes, planes, draw knives, and big handsaws — and building many of his own toys conditioned Surls' art.[37] His early sculptures were rough hewn from fallen trees he found on his land, the natural shapes of the wood dictating the finished product.

But Surls eventually turned away from this process because he wanted to be in control of the sculpture from the outset. As he consciously approaches the wood with a specific idea in mind, the sculptures now derive from three categories: flowers, birds, and the human figure. In *Walk in See* the flower form assumes anthropomorphic shape with the petals having eyes and standing on three spindly legs. Surls uses the eye as his primary motif — an oblique symbol both figurative and mystical at the same time. The sculpture carved from burned pine and oak and bound with a central core of steel appears able to walk across the floor. Despite its large scale, *Walk in See* has a whimsical playful quality. In 1986 Surls said that "by 1971, I dedicated myself to 'play-liking.'" This self-granted permission to pretend — which goes back to pleasures of his childhood[38] — and to enjoy creating art gave him the confidence to develop a philosophy of life and art that was independent of outside sources.

Surls' primary resource is himself, and his pleasure in the creative process of the imagination permeates the entire body of his work. In the 1977 *Dancing Man*, we see a spiraling figure, freed from Earth, floating and gyrating from its ceiling anchor. In works like this — sculptures that move in space — the idea of union is implied:

the union of two human bodies spiraled together, the movement of individuals who are joined emotionally but not physically and, on a deeper level, the union of man with some greater being, of earth with heaven.[39]

There is a static quality to many of the sculptures from the early 1970s just as there is an overriding content of sexuality. In the 1977 *She Brings Gifts to Me*, Surls incorporates an abstracted phallus shape as but part of the total meaning. In this large sculpture, a totemic angel-figure stands slightly bent by the weight of his wings; his arms are outstretched as if accepting an offering. Surls increasingly combined male and female attributes in work from this period. The art he made in the mid to late 1970s is undeniably powerful in form and content. "Surls portrays himself more conventionally as the artist/builder or the artist/progenitor, a man wielding an ax or manifesting his sexuality."[40]

Writers and critics often refer to James Surls' art as having been inspired and influenced by African art and by Mexican and New Mexican folk art. Whatever peripheral influences may have touched him, his work expresses an originality based on a powerful and definite sense of place. The artistic sustenance he receives from his East Texas land feeds his sculpture so that it becomes the embodiment of his dreams and his visions. James Surls' sculpture tells stories from East Texas that garner universal appeal.

36. Sue Graze, *Visions: James Surls, 1974–1984*, catalog for exhibition, Dallas Museum of Art, Dallas, 1984, p. 27.

37. Ibid., p. 11.

38. Susan M. Mayer, "Art Is Serious Play: An Interview with James Surls," *Trends*, the Journal of the Texas Art Education Association, Fall 1986, p. 32.

39. Graze, *Visions: James Surls, 1974–1984*, p. 29.

40. Janet Kutner, *ArtNews*, March 1985, p. 109.

Michael Tracy's art is based on ritual and sacred mystery, sacrifice, and martyrdom. It has consistently expressed a powerful personal emotion.[41] "Nothing in Tracy's lurid, absolutely sincere art has been touched by hipness, Manhattan-style. . . . Tracy makes no such calculations. He does religious art."[42]

Michael Tracy studied for sixteen years in Roman Catholic schools. He was an altar boy by the age of eight. Religion is an important part of his life. It is also an important part of his art. Tracy is a difficult artist to capture in words because his life and his art are so completely and honestly and powerfully intertwined. Religious imagery has influenced him, as has the ritual of the sacred rites inherent in the Catholic faith. Stories of the martyrs and the saints and the lives of the artists who have interpreted them also inform Michael Tracy's art. His work examines all aspects of religion: its powers, its uses, its abuses, and its consolations.

In 1969, as part of the requirement for completion of the Master of Fine Arts degree at the University of Texas at Austin, Tracy exhibited ten large, abstract, gold paintings. The paintings' gold color evolved from Tracy's respect for late Byzantine and early Renaissance panel paintings. Tracy arranged four of the huge panels in respect to the other six works and had the four represent his father, mother, himself, and a friend. Tracy viewed the exhibition as a rite — as a ritual to be performed that would move him from one realm to another.[43] Following completion of his graduate studies, Tracy felt he had accomplished all he needed in life. He decided to retrace the sources of the western tradition in art and ultimately to kill himself. He traveled throughout Europe before his peregrinations took him to Cairo and the pyramids. He had decided that Egypt should be the place of his self-sacrifice.

By the Mycerinus pyramid he found a space without tourists and guides, took off his clothes, and danced. The heat of the Egyptian sun and the loneliness of the desert wastes attended his dance of death, of renunciation of a worldly self, of a dedication of oneself to the communal and archetypal. He had intended to walk off into the desert and be gone. It no longer seemed necessary. Through the mediation of rite, death had become a part of life.[44]

Tracy embraced at that moment, as he said, "the token fetish of the religious ritual of living."[45] In the desert of Giza, his ritual acceptance of death and of life freed him to accept fully his own life and to comprehend that his art and his life were one. Ultimately, Tracy returned to Texas, living in Galveston from 1973 to 1978. He withdrew from painting the large-scale gold abstract works, which he began to see as "backgrounds which appropriately celebrated what occurred before them."[46] He turned his energies to *Sacrifice I, 9.13.74: The Sugar,* which for the first time combined both performance and the concept of sacrifice. What came to be called the "Sugar Sacrifice" involved all that had touched Tracy previously. The mounds of sugar he saw in warehouses along the Galveston docks reminded him of the pyramids; the sugar he viewed as a source of food, and food as a tool of power. Tracy wrote:

If you believe that there are more people in this world who do not have enough to eat than there are people who do, the basic idea of sacrifice in the presence of vast amounts of food would seem natural. . . . How we eat decides justice.[47]

Tracy, with a small group of friends and supporters, completed the sacrifice in the sugar warehouse, which involved the ritual stabbing of Tracy's works of art. His art was sacrificed to food, which represented the reality of life, and in a

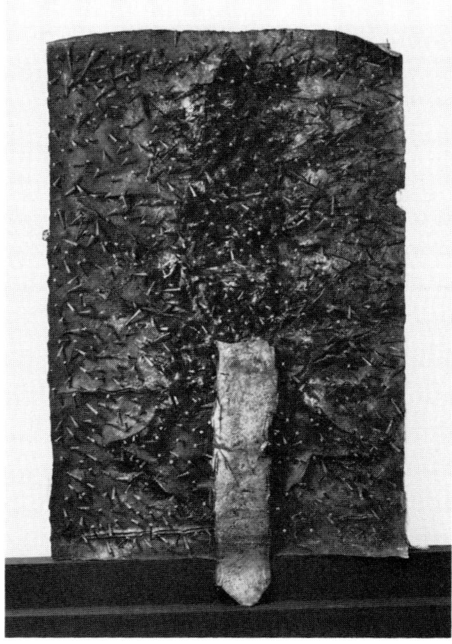

*Michael Tracy, **Momento Mori (Agony)**, 1973–1979, acrylic on canvas with hair, metal spikes, and oil paint on wooden support, 142 in. × 85 in. × 26½ in. Collection The Museum of Fine Arts, Houston, gift of anonymous donor.*

41. Susan Platt, *ArtForum*, October, 1979, p. 18.

42. Carter Ratcliff, *Art in America*, March 1981, p. 128.

43. Thomas McEvilley, "Your Flowers As My Hair: The Art of Michael Tracy," essay for catalog of exhibition Terminal Privileges, Michael Tracy, P.S.1, The Institute for Art and Urban Resources, Inc., Long Island City, New York, 1987, p. 34.

44. Ibid.

45. Ibid., p. 37.

46. Edward Leffingwell, "On the Border: An Introduction," catalog for exhibition Terminal Privileges, Michael Tracy, p. 9.

47. Ibid., p. 43.

48. Alison de Lima Greene, *Bulletin, The Museum of Fine Arts, Houston,* 11, no. 3, (Summer 1988): 63.

49. Alison de Lima Greene "One State — Eight Artists: Contemporary Visions from Texas," essay for catalog for exhibition Texas, Contemporary Art from Texas, Groninger Museum, Groningen, the Netherlands, 1988, p. 20.

50. Carlozzi, Block, and Jones, *50 Texas Artists,* statement by Bob Wade, p. 104.

complicated way Tracy's art and life became united through the performance. Sacrifice and justice, performance and personal emotion, informed the "Sugar Sacrifice" and much of the work that followed. Sacrifice, performance, rite, ritual, passion, and justice are aspects of the work of Michael Tracy. He seeks out these ideas in all that he touches.

Michael Tracy continues to examine the processes by which one culture conquers another. Europe conquered Mexico through religion when the Spanish imposed Christianity on the Mexicans. The European God perforce became the Mexican God; the ancient rites and rituals of Mexico were incorporated into New World Christianity rather than being obliterated by it. Christianity's sacrifice of the Lamb, the transubstantiation of the body and blood of Christ in communion, were joined in Mexico with Aztec rituals of blood sacrifice. The ideas of injustice, of colonialism, and of the powerlessness of the innocents inhabit the body of Tracy's art.

In 1978 Michael Tracy moved to San Ygnacio, a small community on the Texas side of the border with Mexico. In San Ygnacio, Tracy continues his search for justice in the searing sun, which is vital to his work and to his method of working outdoors. In works such as *Momento Mori (Agony)*, Tracy presents the viewer with a monumental altar constructed of acrylic paint on canvas with hair, metal spikes, and oil paint, which is placed on a wooden support covered with rebozos. A contemporary presentation of the Passion is displayed. The surface of the work is pierced and made dramatic by both its form and its inherent meaning. Tracy dedicates the sculpture to martyrs of Third World conflict. As he reminds us of redemption (through the Passion), Tracy's work stops short of that offering; it is contingent upon each viewer's personally responding and taking responsibility for the actions of the world.[48]

Tracy's deeply felt religious beliefs are reflected in works such as *Cruz de la Paz Sagrada IV (Cross of the Sacred Peace)* and in *Via Crucis;* the objects' purposes go beyond passive contemplation since they reflect also the political realities of innocents trapped between governments. Tracy intended *Via Crucis* and the *Cruz de la Paz Sagrada* as a requiem for the "forgotten ones," those who have vanished in the civil strife in Latin American countries.[49] Michael Tracy makes religious art like the altar sculpture *Epiphany* to go beyond the sacred to include the secular agonies experienced by the men, women, and children of Latin America. His art is both religious and political.

But to understand Michael Tracy's art is to understand the man. His art operates as his life. It is complicated; it functions on many levels at one time; it urges the viewer to action; its overpowering presence makes one mute before it. Michael Tracy's art is beautiful, violent, reflective, potent. It is of this world, yet suggests another. Michael Tracy gave meaning to his life before the pyramids; his art now offers that meaning to us.

If appropriation with its inside humor and self-mockery became a concern of artists of the current postmodern era, Bob Wade anticipated the idea by a decade. Wade "appropriated" the whole myth of Texas and turned it into the subject of his art.

As a young buckaroo, I used to sit on the lap of my second cousin Roy Rogers. He was making rodeo appearances in Texas towns where I grew up the son of a hotel manager.[50]

Wade lived the Texas myth because he, more than most, had direct access to it. He lived in Marfa during the filming of the movie *Giant*, and the movie stars and the sets left a deep impression. His

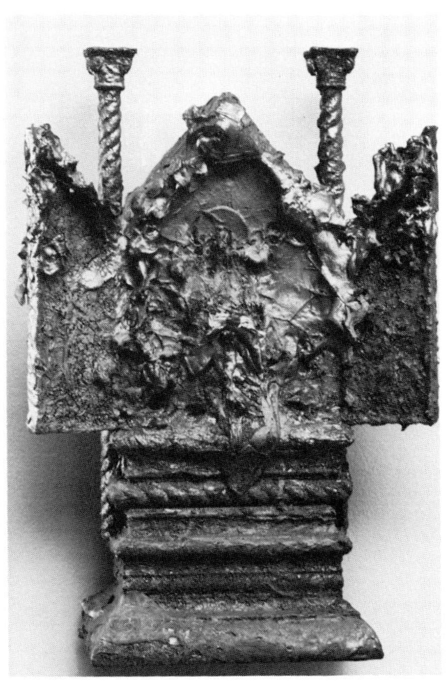

MICHAEL TRACY, San Ygnacio

Epiphany
1982
acrylic on wood
34⅛ in. × 20¼ in. × 9 in.
Collection The Museum of Fine Arts Houston, Museum purchase with funds provided by Mr. and Mrs. Fayez Sarofim, Mr. and Mrs. J. H. Kempner III, Joan Fleming, and Ron Blakenship

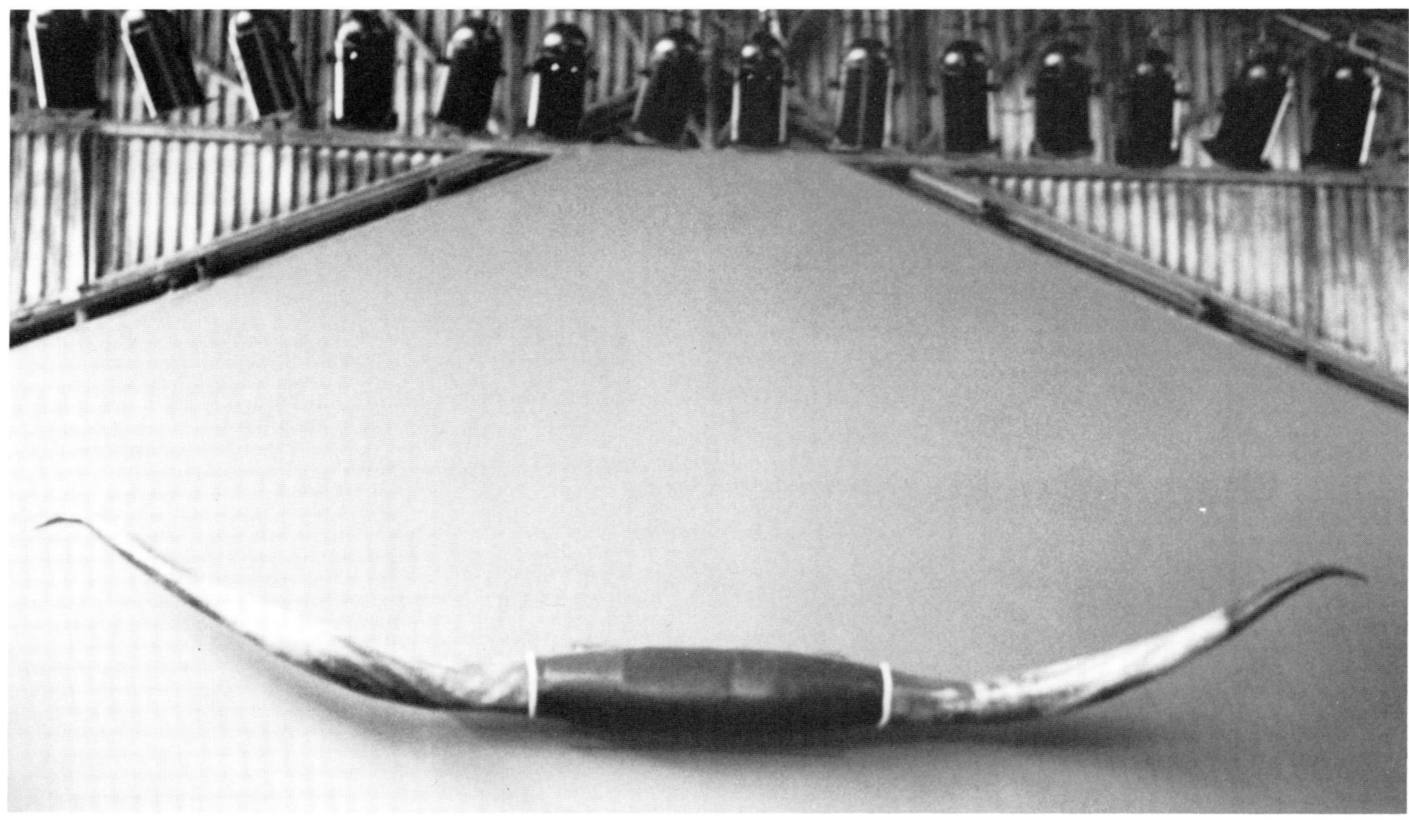

ROBERT WADE, Santa Fe/Dallas

World's Longest Longhorns
1987
plaster on steel frame
276 in. long
Courtesy of the artist and Marvin Seline
Gallery, Houston

father once managed the "tallest" hotel in Texas, and this direct connection to Texas exaggeration also impressed young Wade.[51] Throughout Wade's art, there is a show business sensibility. And from the time he left college he realized there was an audience seeking the mythic in Texas contemporary art. Texas writer and former football star Peter Gent, paraphrasing Andy Warhol, said: "Everybody was a Texan for fifteen minutes in 1980."[52]

        Peter Gent could have been discussing Bob Wade, for Wade's art attracts attention. He builds things big, then puts them on public display. He once constructed a forty-foot-tall pair of realistic cowboy boots, which now are in the parking lot of a San Antonio shopping mall. Another creation is a giant iguana forty feet long and twelve feet high, which for a time sat atop New York City's Lone Star Cafe. His six ten-foot-tall frogs, originally constructed for a Dallas nightculb, now grace a truck stop along IH-35 between Waco and Dallas. He has constructed room-sized floor pieces, such as his *Map of Texas* which he filled with kitsch from around the state. He started — but was unable to finish because of funding problems — the *Bicentennial Map*, a football-field-sized earth work, which would have presented the United States in tableau form; inspired by Robert Smithson's earth works, Wade's idea was to be a large-scale replica of the United States that accentuated such geographic features as Route 66 and the Mississippi River. And in 1977 he took Texas to Paris for the 10th Paris Biennale at France's National Museum of Modern Art. What he took were artifacts like a stuffed bucking bronco and a stuffed two-headed calf. He had his own museum on wheels, a twenty-five-foot trailer. The horse and much of the trailer's contents were stolen, and the trailer yet remains parked in a Paris suburb.

Wade, who left college at the height of the Pop Art movement, has said of his works:

They are influenced by Oldenburg's large-scale works and the Pop Art movement. My work deals with popular culture, whether it's erstwhile or sociological nonsense. It also has to do with surrealism and irony. It is sort of Texas Pop Art.[53]

His work took on its decidely Texas flavor by the late 1960s when he, along with artists George Green, Jack Mims, Jim Roche, and Mac Whitney gained national attention. The brand of art these artists created was labeled "Texas funk" — further defined as surreal, organic, and humorous.[54] By 1975, Ken Harrison's film *Jackelope*, documenting the work and working methods of Wade, George Green, and James Surls, had a wide following in the state — and helped spread the idea of "Texas funk." While Green, Surls, and Whitney left Texas funk behind years ago, Wade continues to embrace it. Wade doesn't mind that viewers might laugh at his work because of its unexpected scale.

That's fine with me because one aspect of Texans' sensibility is their concept of humor. The 'Texas Condition' — that is, that you can't tell if they're joking or not, or laughing or crying.[55]

Wade's twenty-three-foot-wide plaster *World's Longest Longhorns* continues his tradition of exaggeration of mythic Texas symbols. Longhorn cattle were important to the Texas ranching industry in the nineteenth century, and the Longhorn remains the symbol of the University of Texas at Austin, Wade's alma mater. In this piece, Wade once again presents a commonplace Texas symbol, elevates it through scale, and presents the viewer an ironic statement on the state's history and on its use of the past. Ultimately Wade challenges the viewer to decipher what is myth and what is reality.

Donald Judd is an internationally known sculptor whose works and writings in the mid-1960s defined the category of Minimalism. His art is about a system of arrangements of primary structures or geometric shapes and the gestalt they present. He stated: "The thing as a whole, its quality as a whole, is what is interesting."[56] Judd is after neutrality; he has retained a commitment to geometric simplicity in his work, which emphasizes planar surfaces, scale, sequence, and interval.[57] He uses industrial materials for his sculpture and is consistently nonreferential. The cube is Judd's basic form. While Minimalist sculpture can be a passive and therefore even tiresome art form, the continually changing perceptions of the viewer keep the work alive and provide the opportunity to discover its beauty. In *Untitled, 1967*, vertically stacked cubic forms manufactured from stainless steel and Plexiglas handsomely demonstrate Judd's consummate art form.

In 1971, after looking for permanent exhibition space for his own and his artist friends' works, Donald Judd bought land in Marfa. Since the mid-1970s he has maintained legal residence in Texas while keeping studio space in New York City and in Europe.

Judd continues to install his work on 350 acres in and around Marfa's historic Fort D. A. Russell; the restoration of buildings continues for the exhibition of Judd's friends' work. Prints by Barnett Newman, Josef Albers, and San Antonio artist Bob Tiemann and sculptures by John Chamberlain, Dan Flavin, Carl Andre, and Richard Long are on display.

It may be too soon to evaluate the effect of Judd's presence in Texas. Few artists have traveled to the remote and isolated Marfa. Yet, with the establishment of public viewing hours in 1987, more

51. Candace Ord Manroe, "After the Frogs," *Dallas-Fort Worth Home & Garden,* November 1984, p. 20.

52. Texas Literary Symposium, The University of Texas at Austin, 1983.

53. Manroe, "After the Frogs," p. 24.

54. Janet Kutner, *Bob Wade: Introduction,* catalog for exhibition Bob Wade Projects and Photoworks, Cultural Activities Center, Temple, Texas, 1984, p.3.

55. Lisa Sherman, "Bob Wade," *ArtSpace,* Spring 1983, p. 43.

56. Deborah Martin, *El Paso Herald-Post,* October 9, 1976.

57. Robert Goldwater, *What Is Modern Sculpture?,* Museum of Modern Art, New York City, 1969, p. 102.

artists, members of the arts communities, and the general public have access to Judd's Marfa land. Donald Judd's presence in Marfa adds to the notion of the eccentricities of Texas living. The fact that the authority on Minimalist art presides over the barren Marfa landscape is comparable to discovering the Cadillac Ranch in Amarillo. Buried Cadillacs and Minimalist art shock the casual visitor yet at the same time add to Texans' delight in the bizarre and the fantastic.

In Marfa, Donald Judd offers the viewer the opportunity to observe the geometric elegance of his art in a permanent space where one can count on constantly changing perceptions and a landscape conducive to the view.

When twentieth-century sculptors are grouped, typically it is according to the technical approaches they employ, such as "cast," "assemblage," "constructed," or "direct metal." Or the categories become stylistically descriptive, like "figurative," "abstract expressionist," "minimalist," "constructivist," or "architectonic." For the remainder of this essay, the artists have been grouped within similar types of categories. The groupings are somewhat arbitrary and offer more a means by which to comprehend a large body of work rather than a definitive placement of work within limited categories. Contemporary sculpture takes myriad forms, encompasses divers materials, and expresses manifold ideas. The objects created by sculptors today are as diverse as the hands that made them. While some of the sculptures could be placed in more than one category, these groupings offer a means by which the works of art can be understood.

Five artists — John Christensen, David L. Deming, George Smith, Mac Whitney, and Ben Woitena — create expressive and powerful large-scale abstract sculpture. Each artist brings to his work the contradictions of heavy metal and graceful line, massive weight and surging lift. All five artists enjoy the fabrication of their art, which becomes important in their view of themselves as builder-sculptor. They all weld, bend, hoist, and haul the heavy metals with which they work.

These five artists share an aesthetic derived from post-World War II abstraction. David Smith is the American sculptor nonpareil who created an original response to early-twentieth-century European movements, and he is the signpost by whom subsequent sculptors have guided themselves. Smith's use of the oxyacetylene torch and direct welding to assemble industrial materials in an additive process touched all artists who followed him. Later, the abstract gestures of Mark di Suvero's I-beams and Robert Bladen's geometric-shaped plates welded in monumental forms also became potent sources for younger artists.

John Christensen is the youngest sculptor in this group. His folded, graceful form in *Cuba 10, Pterodactyl* recalls the apparent motion inherent in the work of Italian Futurist sculptors like Umberto Boccioni, yet he employs his own lyrical sensibility to coloration and to texture on the work's surface. Interested in the historical event of the sinking of the *Maine* in Havana harbor on February 15, 1898, Christensen initiated a series of sculptures that recall battleships. Aware, too, of David Smith's *Cubi* series, Christensen believes he could have made an association at a subconscious level. Influences notwithstanding, John Christensen's sculpture stands on its own as a sensuous work of art.

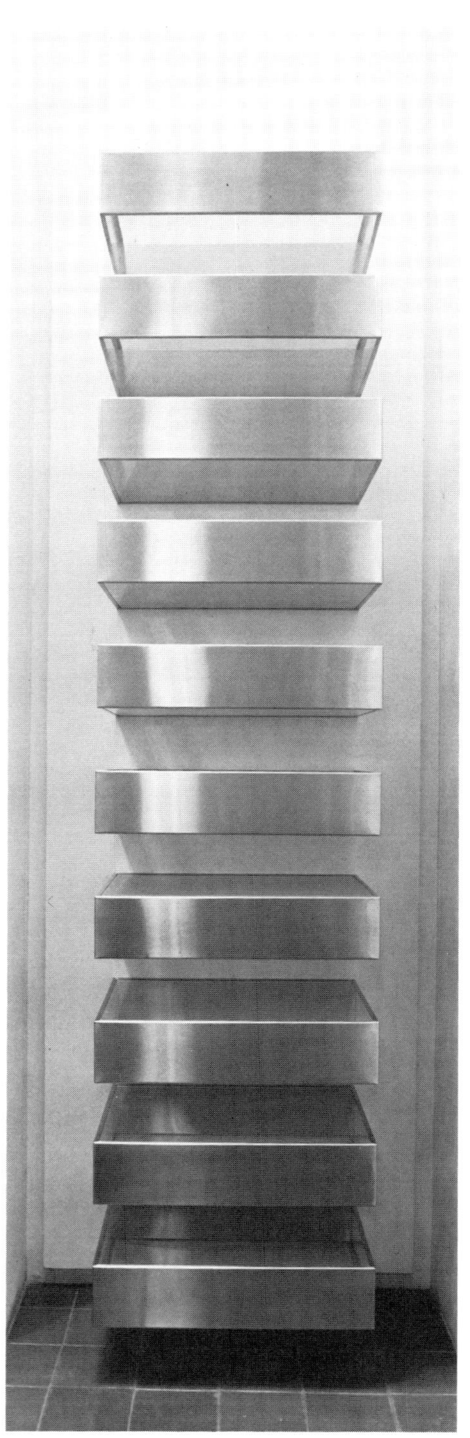

DONALD JUDD, Marfa
Untitled
1967
stainless steel and Plexiglas
10 units, each measuring 9 in. × 40 in. × 31 in.
Collection of Modern Art Museum of Fort Worth, Museum Purchase and Commission, the Benjamin J. Tillar Memorial Trust

JOHN CHRISTENSEN, Austin
Cuba 10, Pterodactyl
1986
folded steel
17 in. × 73 in. × 11 in.
Courtesy of the artist and R. S. Levy
Gallery, Austin

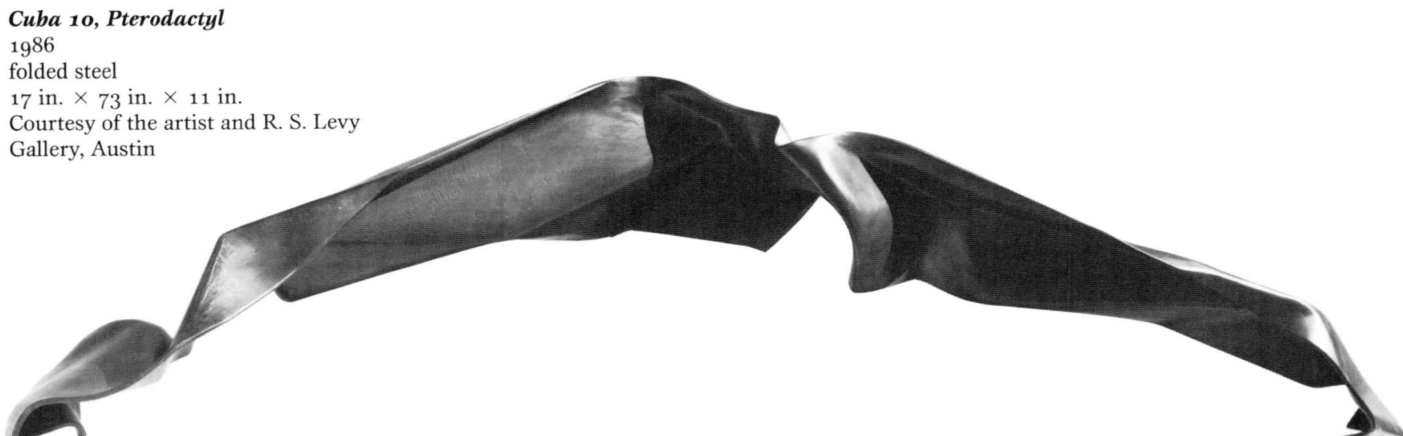

DAVID L. DEMING, Austin
Pivotal Concorde
1981
painted steel
180 in. × 540 in. × 180 in.
Courtesy of the artist and Adams Middleton
Gallery, Dallas

David L. Deming confronts the viewer with the mass and volume of monumentality derived from hollow-form construction yet implies within the abstract form a reference to technological powers. In *Pivotal Concorde*, Deming's sculpture rises dramatically from its grounded bilateral base and ascends toward the sky. Within the body of Deming's work, *Pivotal Concorde* can be understood as a powerful transition piece from his previous tripod sculptures. Painted a deep black, the sculpture challenges the viewer through its forebodingly mechanistic physicality.

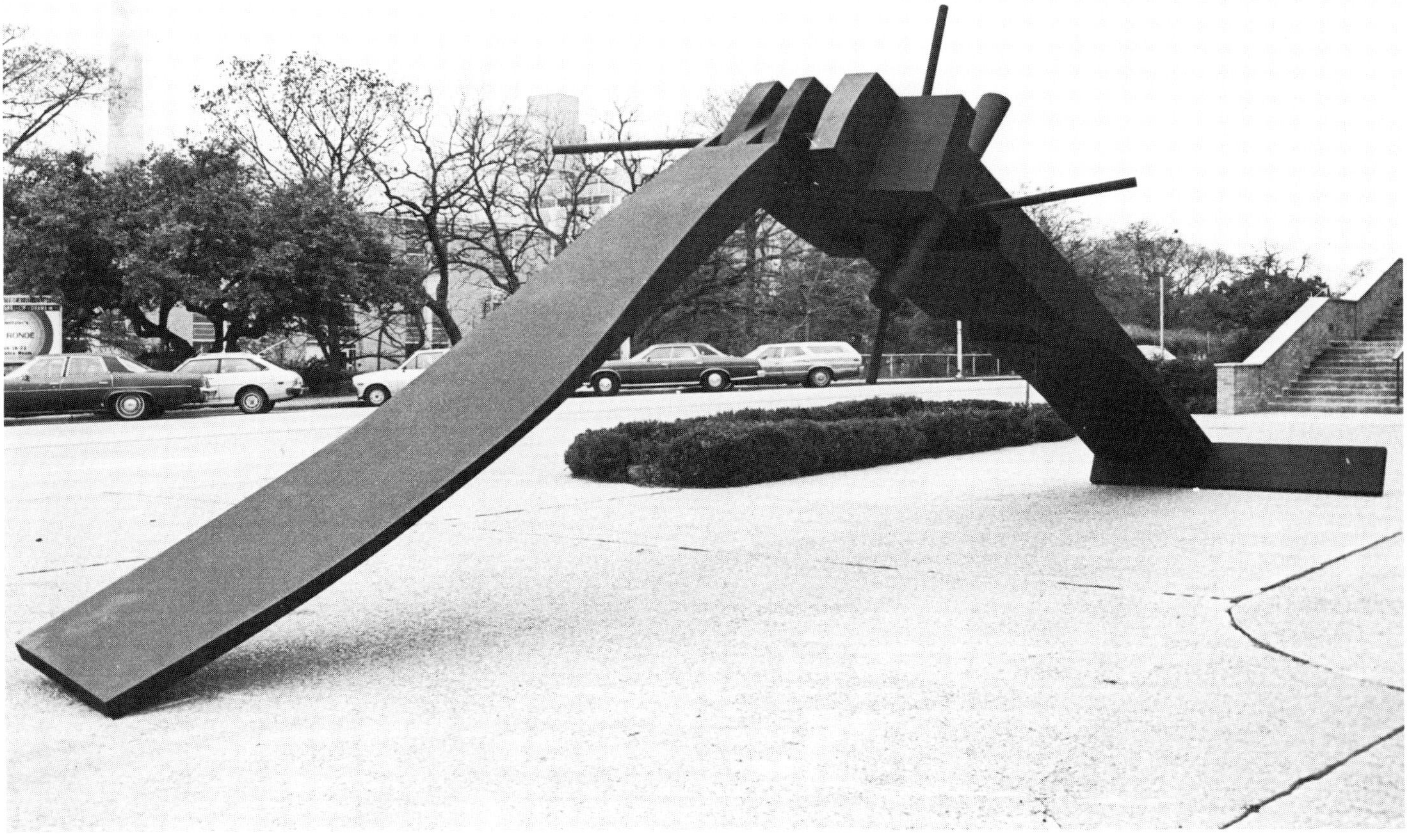

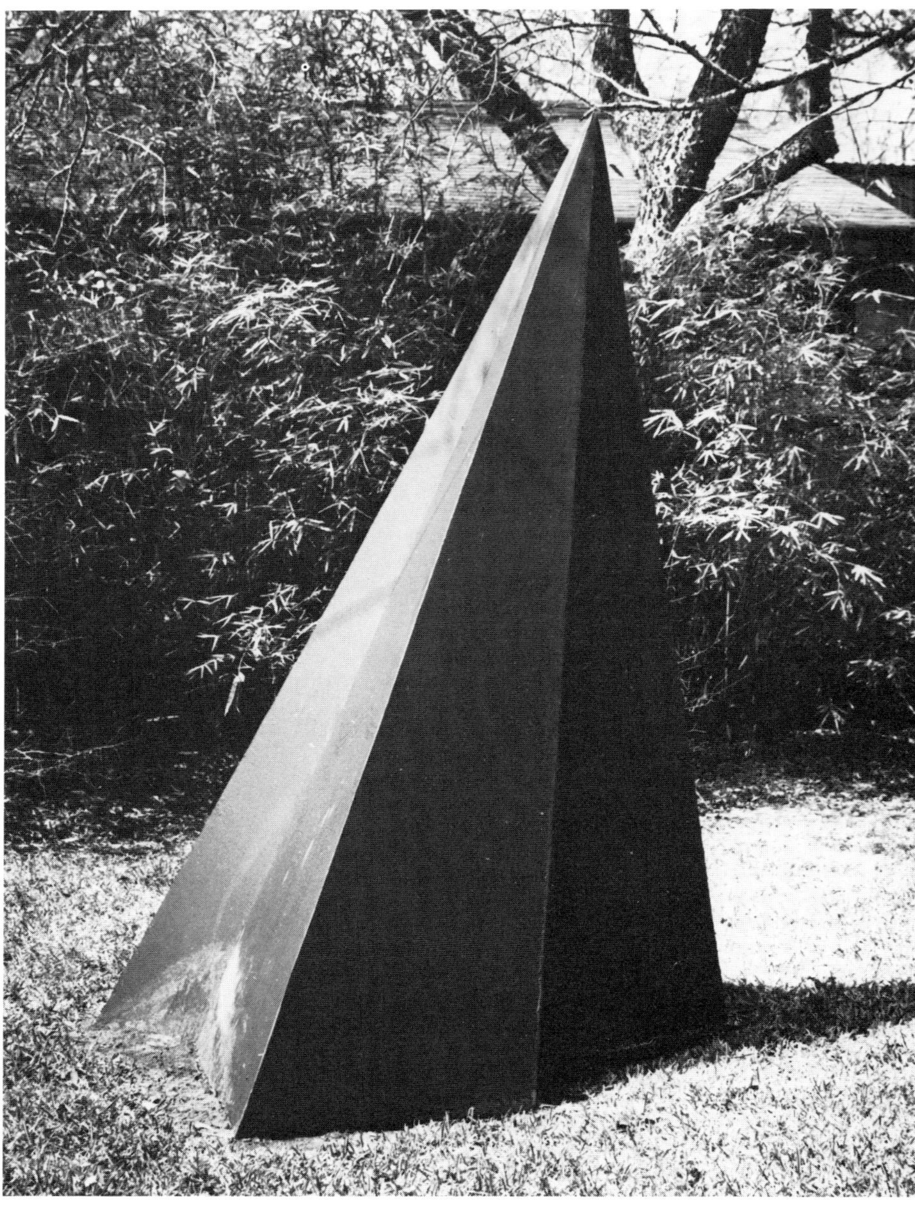

GEORGE SMITH, Houston
Buguturu
1983
steel
87 in. × 64 in. × 51 in.
Courtesy of the artist and Graham
Gallery, Houston

George Smith's welded plates of sheet metal intersect to form elegant black pyramids in *Buguturu*, his homage to Africa. Having studied with sculptor Tony Smith, George Smith embraced minimalist concepts of primary shape and structure, yet he withdrew from the minimalist tenet of content-free sculpture. Beyond the titles he gives his work, George Smith's sculpture refers to African art and Africa in many ways. Often the abstracted works refer to African architectural shapes like dogons. He incorporates African motifs on the surface of some of his works as he allows the rough welds of the metal's surface to stand for scarification patterns or for other kinds of African decoration. The geometric shapes he uses evoke hidden presences. One is aware of an inherent motion in the sweep and lilt of the modular forms. Working with opposing principles of stasis and motion, George Smith's oversized black sculptures emphasize the forms of minimalist art as they harmonize references to things African and of Africa.

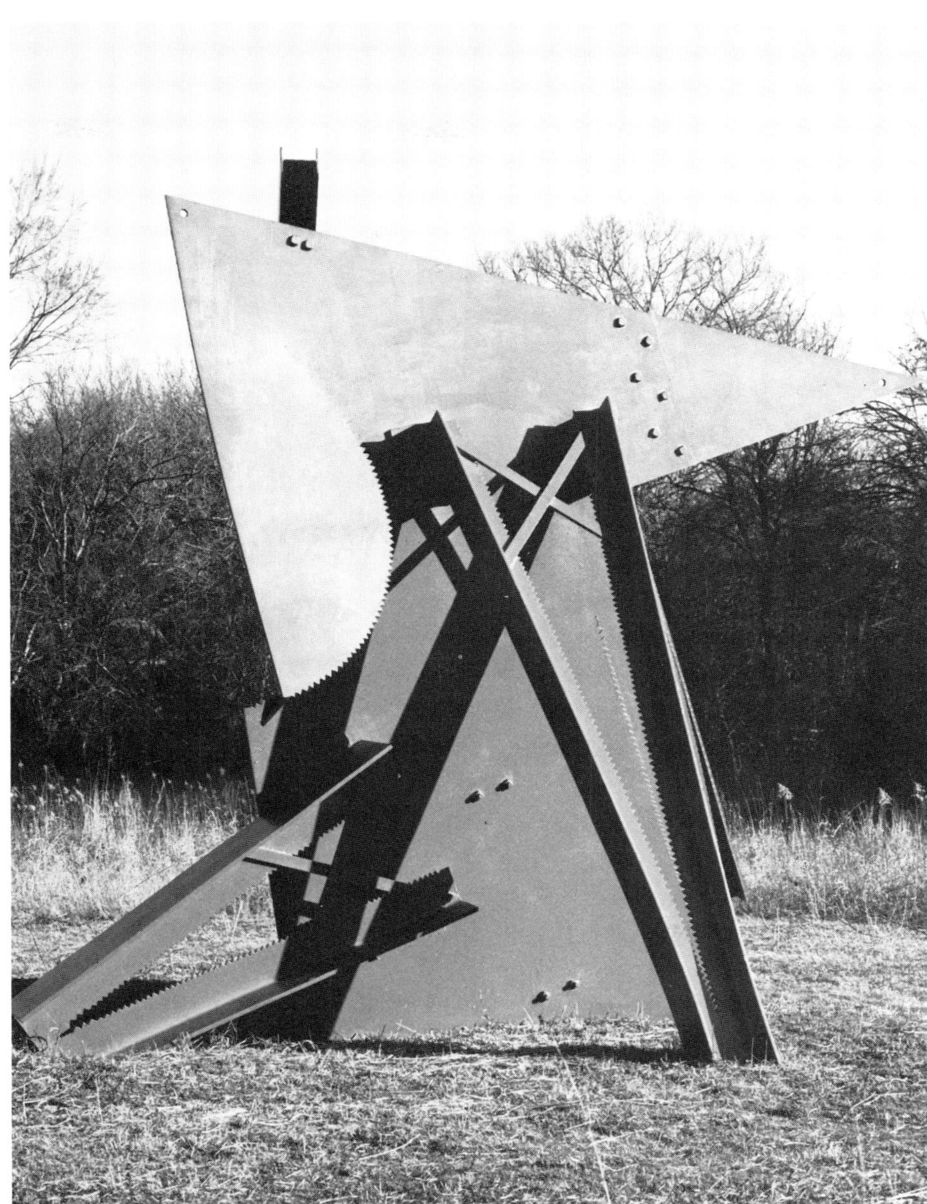

MAC WHITNEY, Midlothian

Cotulla
1979
welded steel
150 in. × 120 in. × 168 in.
Courtesy of the artist and Eugene Binder
Gallery, Dallas

Mac Whitney brings the viewer's references back to Texas in works like *Cotulla* where smooth plates of steel form graceful lines to fool the eye into believing the steel has been cut by scissors rather than by the torches and metal shears necessary to the monumental task of cutting and bending plate metal. Whitney typically names his sculptures after Texas towns. Cotulla is located in South Texas midway between San Antonio and the border. And, as he has done for some time, Whitney paints his sculptures red — "so people will notice them." Whitney is also interested in working with line. "A wavy line . . . has become a convention of mine. . . . It is like having somebody slam your brand on a steer, it's yours. I also draw in it's face . . . a drawing defining space within a framed space." [58] Mac Whitney has put his mark on his outdoor sculptures. They aren't easily mistaken — they are big, red, and linear.

58. Mac Whitney quoted in *What's Up In Texas: New Lyricism,* exhibition and catalog organized by Sally Boothe, San Antonio Museum Association, Witte Museum, 1979, p. 32.

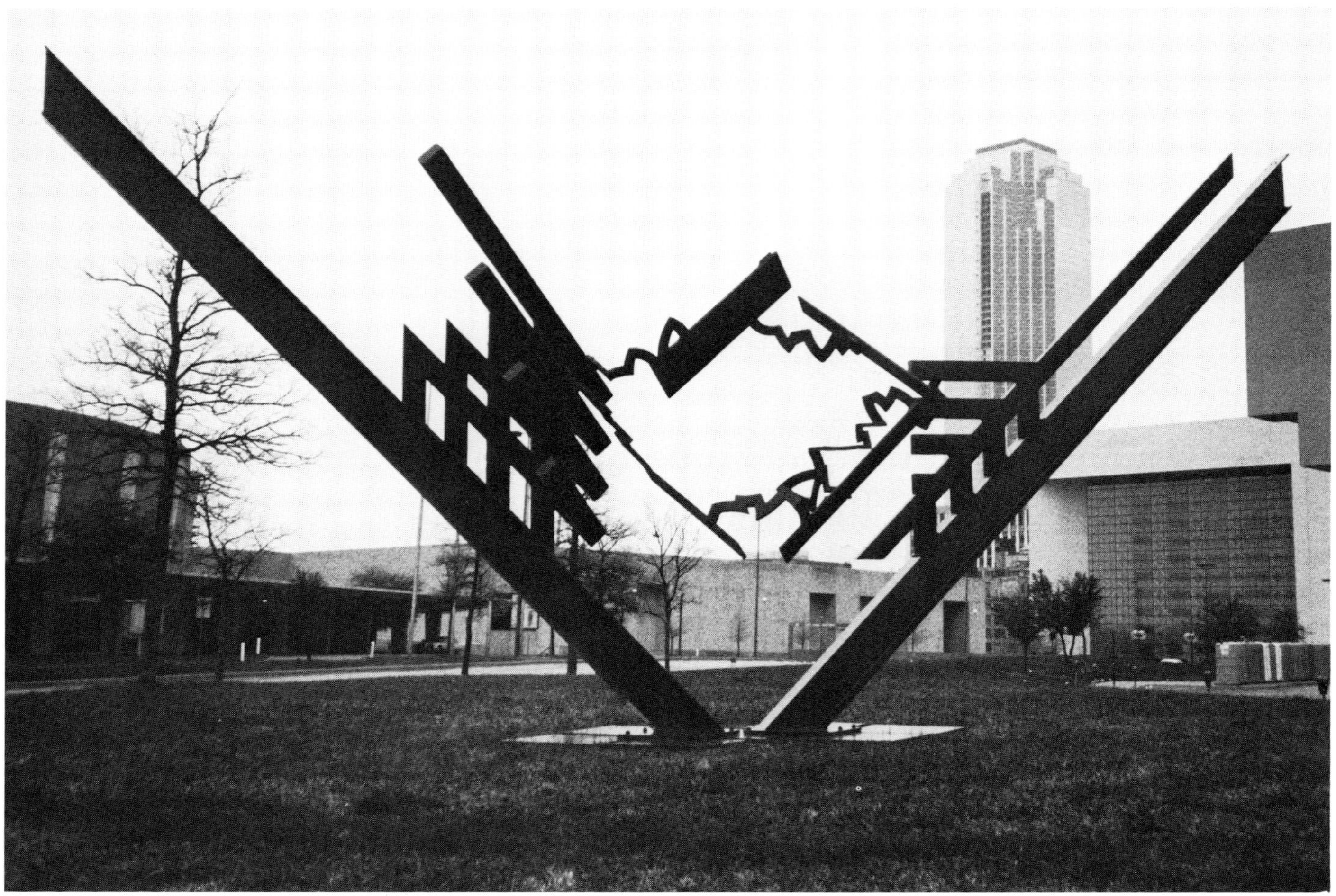

BEN WOITENA, Houston
Night Sea Passage
1985
welded/painted steel
120 in. × 240 in. × 72 in.
Courtesy of the artist

Ben Woitena's *Night Sea Passage* brackets industrial I-beams with zig-zagged lattices of steel to produce an elegant, lyrical paean to Abstract Expressionist sculpture. In Woitena's work, as in most Abstract Expressionist sculptors' work, the spaces outlined and enclosed by the solid steel contours are as important as the metal itself. Woitena is interested in leaving his own "signature" on each work and to that end he typically works with geometric shapes, albeit often with evocative filigree forms or with shapes up-ended or set on point. Woitena, like John Chamberlain and George Sugarman, also uses polychromy — here black and red — to clarify relationships between forms. Ben Woitena's welded sculptures change I-beams from cold metal to form new realities. In the process, he offers the viewer thoughtful insights into the nature of transformation.

Assemblage Art grew out of the ready-made of Marcel Duchamp and the dreamworld of the Surrealists. By combining and assembling objects removed from their original context and placed in new juxtapositions, artists created feelings of disjunction on the viewer's part. These sculptures were designed to shock and to amuse. American sculptors as unique to each other as Joseph Cornell and Louise Nevelson serve as sources for many artists working with found objects. We have seen that Texas' first generation of contemporary artists — Love, Fridge, and McManaway — fully embraced this artistic style. Subsequent Texas artists also continue to be intrigued with the ideas of Assemblage Art.

Ronald Boling's *Crow Hunter's Trophy Case* incorporates found and ready-made objects to express a specific point of view. Stacked within a nine-foot column of Plexiglas are crow decoys, trophies, plastic shotguns, medals, targets, and other objects of the hunt placed on rolling plateaus of Astro-turf. Boling's constructed and assembled sculpture speaks in a witty voice, but underneath the tongue-in-cheek references one discerns Boling's disdain of "great hunters" who kill merely for the sake of killing.

Steve Brudniak's found-object sculptures invest throw-aways of the past with new meanings. Enamored with the Tesla coil that was invented in the 1890s, his assemblage *The Imogene Icon* indirectly pays homage to its inventor, Nikola Tesla.[59] Composed of fluorescent tubes, camera lenses, electric car-window buttons, and a telephone push button, the piece plays with classical associations by its inclusion of a figure of a golden

59. Susan Chadwick, "Critic's Choice," *Houston Post*, August 29, 1986, p. 3E.

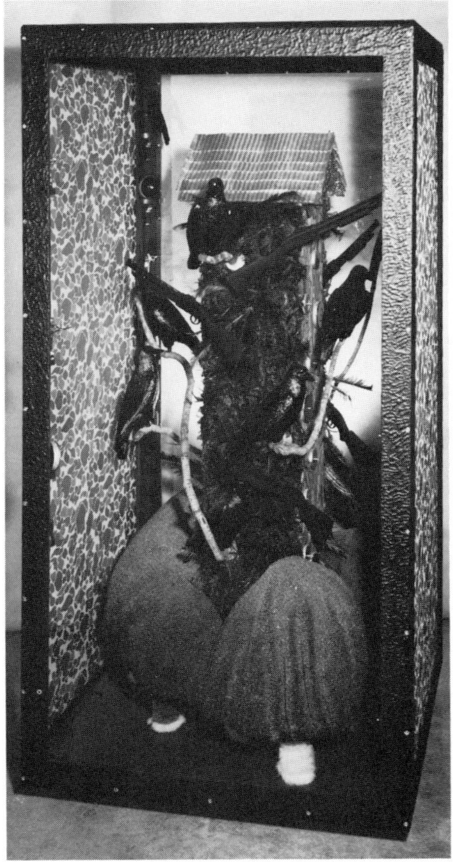

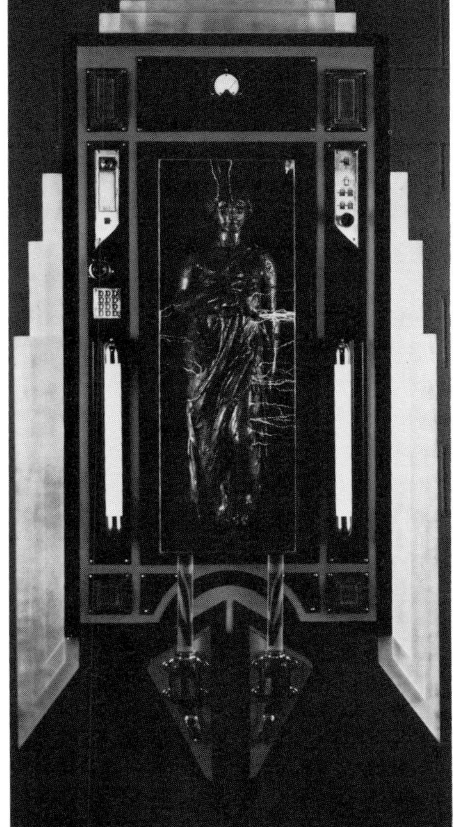

RONALD BOLING, New Braunfels
Crow Hunter's Trophy Case
1988–89
mixed media
10 in. × 48 in. × 48 in.
Courtesy of the artist and Read Stremmel Gallery, San Antonio

STEVE BRUDNIAK, Austin
The Imogene Icon
1986
mixed media with electrical lightning
88 in. × 44 in. × 24 in.
Courtesy of the artist

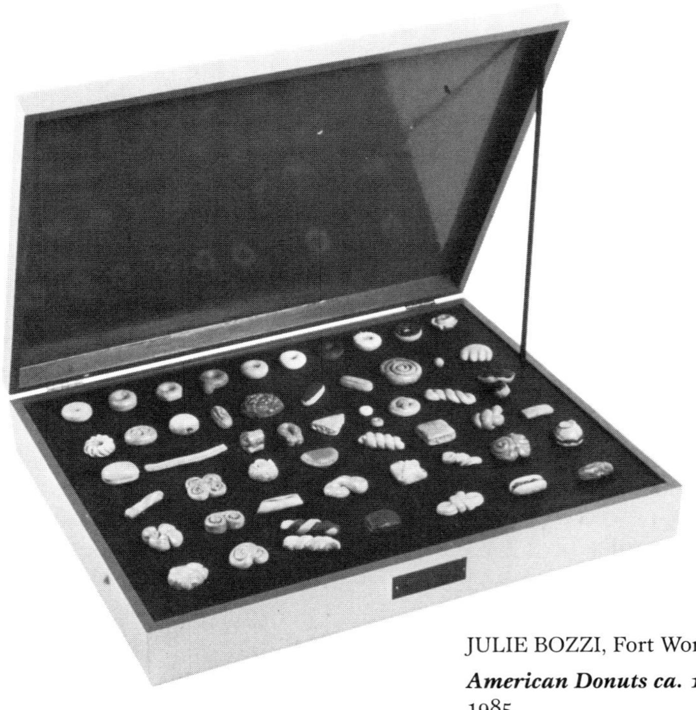

JULIE BOZZI, Fort Worth

American Donuts ca. 1980
1985
mixed media
3⅝ in. × 17 in. × 21 in.
Courtesy of the artist and Texas Gallery,
Houston

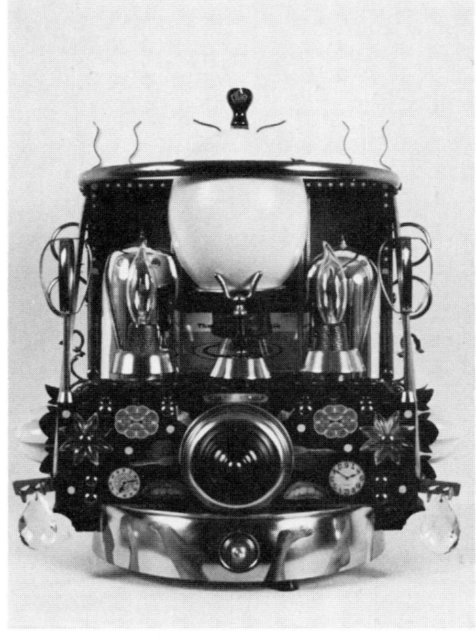

J. MICHAEL CISZEK, Houston

Homage to the Egg:
The One That Got Away
1988
found-object assemblage
17½ in. × 16 in. × 13 in.
Courtesy of the artist and Harris
Gallery, Houston, and Eugene Binder
Gallery, Dallas

goddess. Its symmetrical, well-ordered format similarly underscores archaic connections. *The Imogene Icon* flashes lightning with the touch of a key, enabling the viewer to become an active if not omnipotent participant. Brudniak's use of cast-off laboratory equipment imbues his sculptures with true pseudoscientific status.

Julie Bozzi's *American Donuts* repackages an assortment of real donuts and presents them to the viewer as analytically as a botanist would a selection of similar plants. Bozzi's lacquer box belies its handcrafted origins and looks as if it, too, were the product of manufacturers.[60] Bozzi typically "collects" objects, landscapes, or portraits. She orders and arranges the objects she collects in her boxes: the landscapes and portraits she captures in her miniature paintings. Bozzi's sculpture is humorous simply because of what she offers for observation. The format, however, maintains its quasi-scientific seriousness. While Brudniak and Bozzi incorporate ideas of science in their assemblages, each work offers a totally different point of view: Brudniak's science seems to be the stuff of old 1940s horror movie labs; Bozzi's comes directly from General Foods.

J. Michael Ciszek's assemblages recall David McManaway's work. They, too, could be called "domestic elegies." Ciszek turns up discarded small appliances like Mixmasters or toasters and reassembles them. He unites egg beaters, Aunt Jemima syrup bottles, doll arms and legs with plastic beads and other shiny things. He transforms the found objects by removing them from their understood use and in so doing challenges the viewer's expectations. In *Homage to the Egg: The One That Got Away,* bits and pieces of found and saved scraps form a resplendent minialtar to kitsch.

60. Ned Rifkin, *New Work: New York/Outside New York*, The New Museum of Contemporary Art, exhibition catalog, 1984, p. 38.

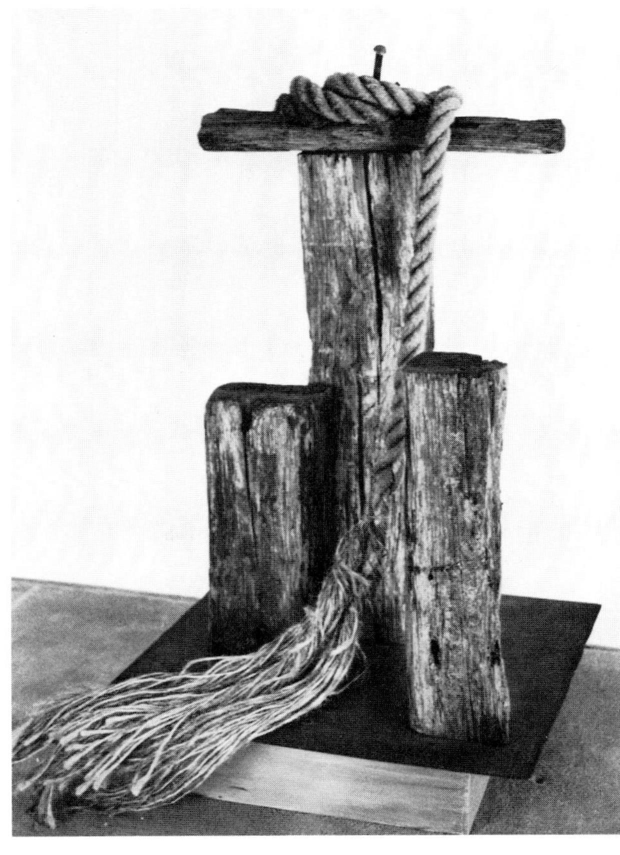

ROWENA C. ELKIN, Dallas
Ancient
1977
wood, rope, steel
50½ in. × 35 in. × 33 in.
Courtesy of the artist

Rowena C. Elkin's *Ancient* derives its meaning from her years of living in New Mexico. In that dry environment she observed the weathering process on wood posts and adobe. The sun-dried materials she observed took on enduring aspects. Elkin's combination of the rope and wood she found in the New Mexico desert evokes thoughts of durability, longevity, and survivability. The iconic form of the work — with its structure subtly reflective of a cruciform — subconsciously elicits ideas of a spiritual presence. Incorporating surrealistic characteristics of found-object construction with organic materials, Rowena Elkin brings to the viewer persistent memories of an enduring distant past.

Ken Luce's *DBPB* wall relief departs from assemblage as a reconstituted precious object; here pieces of crude wood stripped of surface finish are fused and a feeling of mystery prevails. The semblance of the totem is in this work. In fact, Luce views the sculpture as a mask. Typically, he scavenges the Houston ship channels and finds discarded wooden signs, which often are left with only partial wording intact as in *DBPB*. Luce does not tamper with the wood's surface; he neither paints nor alters that which he finds. Rather he reconforms the wood and through juxtaposition transforms original meanings. Like many of the Dadaists, Luce presents enigmatic word messages which puzzle the viewer with their covert meanings. And like many of the Surrealists, he gives his sculpture a primitive presence. Luce's work takes that which is wearing away and bestows it with second life and new meaning.

Mark Monroe's sculpture *Endless Appliance Column* recalls Marcel Duchamp's ready-mades as it borrows its title from Constantin Brancusi's *Endless Column*. Monroe's stack of metal folding chairs with electric light requires the viewer to examine notions about contemporary life. Monroe views the chair tower as a kind of archaeology. The chairs had been scavenged from a land fill, used for twelve years, and then thrown away again. Monroe dragged them out of the land fill a second time, punched holes in each chair seat to form the outline of an appliance, and made of them an art object reflective of their time. Antiquated appliances, electric lights, and throw-away metal chairs each have their own history and importance yet are transformed through the order of their arrangement.[61] Mark Monroe's sculpture reflects aspects of nostalgia. The sculptor's hand transforms the detritus of modern life and imbues it with a new significance. Absurdity, confusion, and paradox permeate the work. Mark Monroe's castoffs of yesterday are reconformed to offer the viewer another opportunity to observe and understand them within a different context.

61. Artist's statement, March 1989.

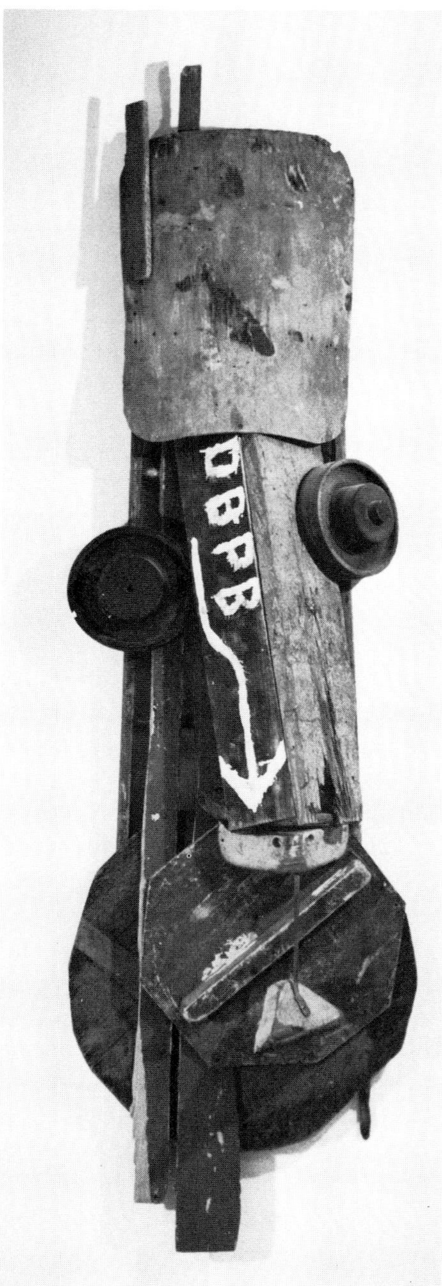

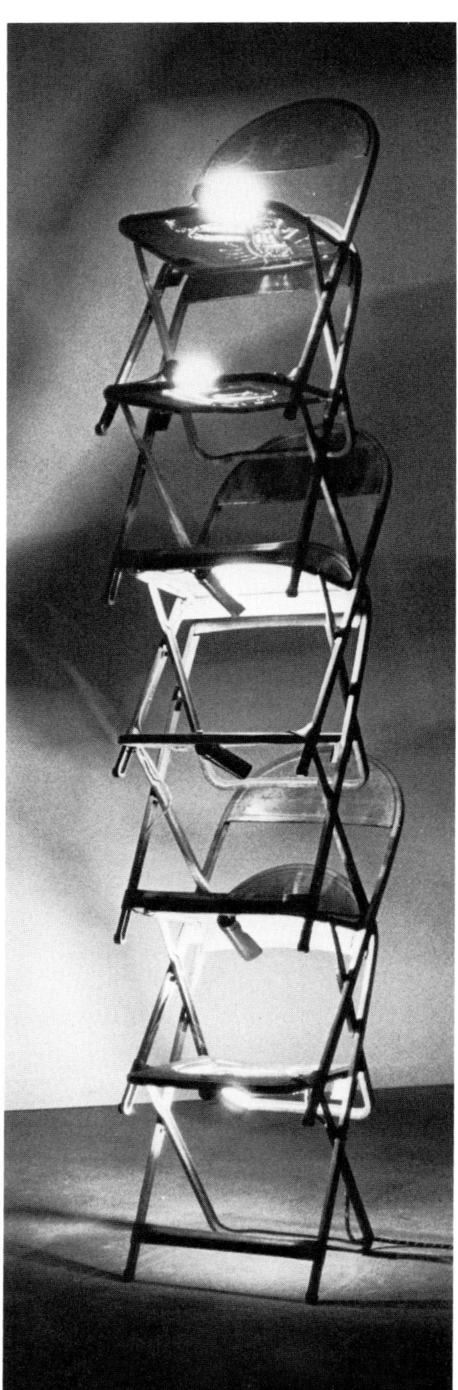

KEN LUCE, Houston

DBPB
1986
found-wood construction
114 in. × 38 in. × 16 in.
Courtesy of the artist and Davis/McClain Gallery, Houston, and Eugene Binder Gallery, Dallas

MARK MONROE, Splendora

Endless Appliance Column
1988
mixed media (stacked metal folding chairs, lights)
120 in. × 16½ in. × 26 in.
Courtesy of the artist

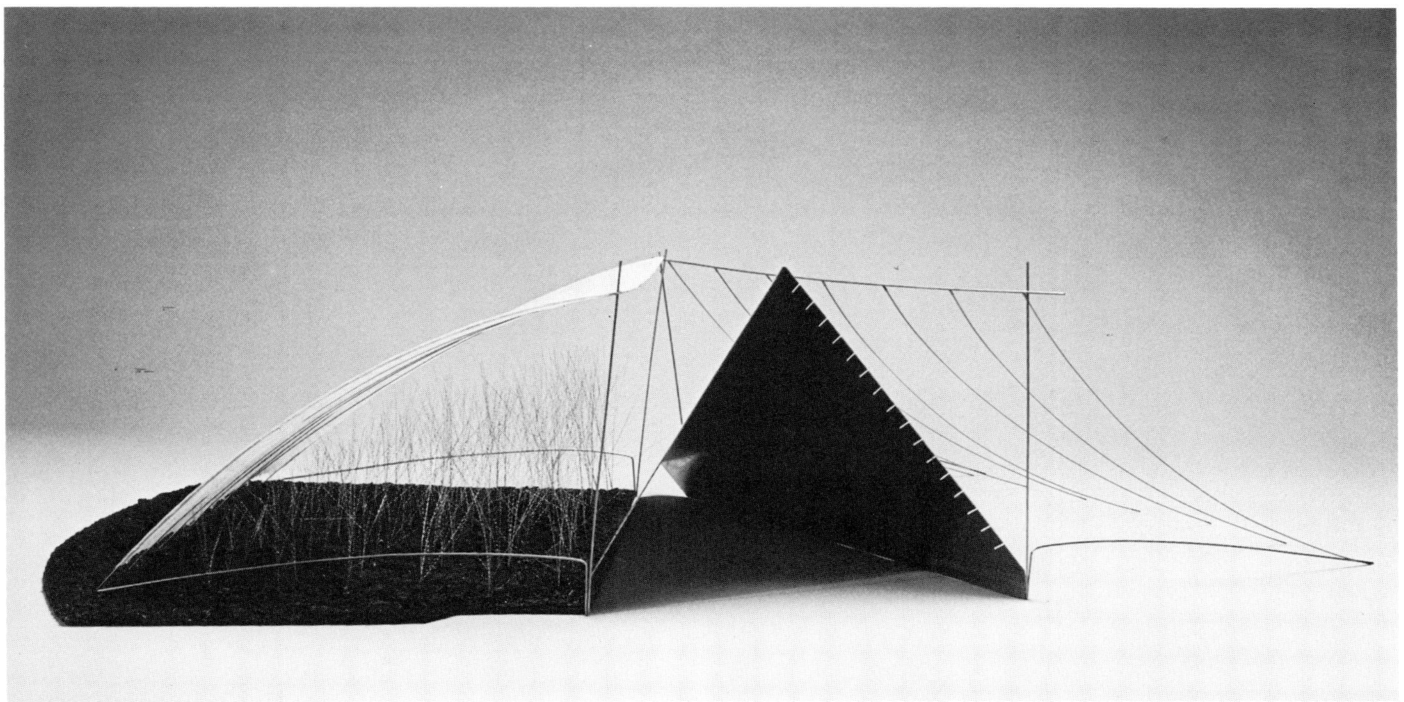

THELMA COLES, Austin

Provisional Subsistence
1984
mixed media
14½ in. × 34 in. × 59 in.
Courtesy of the artist and R. S. Levy
Gallery, Austin

Architectural themes inform the work of some Texas contemporary artists. These artists think of the forms as shelters, retreats, or asylums. Some investigate the psychic meaning inherent in the word "house," while others examine the psychological implications of sharing one. Several of the artists construct boats or vessels, which carry them either literally from one place to another or metaphorically from one spiritual realm to another. Several artists use architectural forms to replicate and interpret the world around them. Some look at life. Others examine death.

Thelma Coles' *Provisional Subsistence* examines the idea of shelter. Combining copper, stainless steel, rice paper, masonite, dirt, and resin, she creates an abstract tent form and invites the viewer in to ponder further the meanings and feelings associated with the idea. Her work embraces the concept of dualities: shared dwellings as potential sources of conflict or as blissful asylums; shelters as comforting refuges or as entrapping prisons. The refinement Coles brings to her sculpture derives from her training as a jeweler. The elegant form she presents in *Provisional Subsistence* goes beyond the idea of the conditional to anchor definitively the viewer's response.

James Drake's earliest sculptures were about replication — the virtuosic duplication in steel of objects within his immediate surroundings. Drake, for example, welded spools of yarn, work tables, and trompe l'oeil boxes complete with postage stamps — all objects he saw every day at his El Paso import rug and yarn shop. The next phase of his work concerned the construction of eight-by-twelve-foot environments: spaces like *The Trophy Room*, in which he created a monochromatic welded steel lodge loaded with realistic objects depicting the hunt. A mounted boar's head, a sailfish, bows and arrows, and guns and knives fill the darkened spaces and produce powerful sensations.

Currently, Drake's work combines welded steel with oversize charcoal drawings that replicate famous works of art — but that also carry personal meaning. Living on the border between El Paso

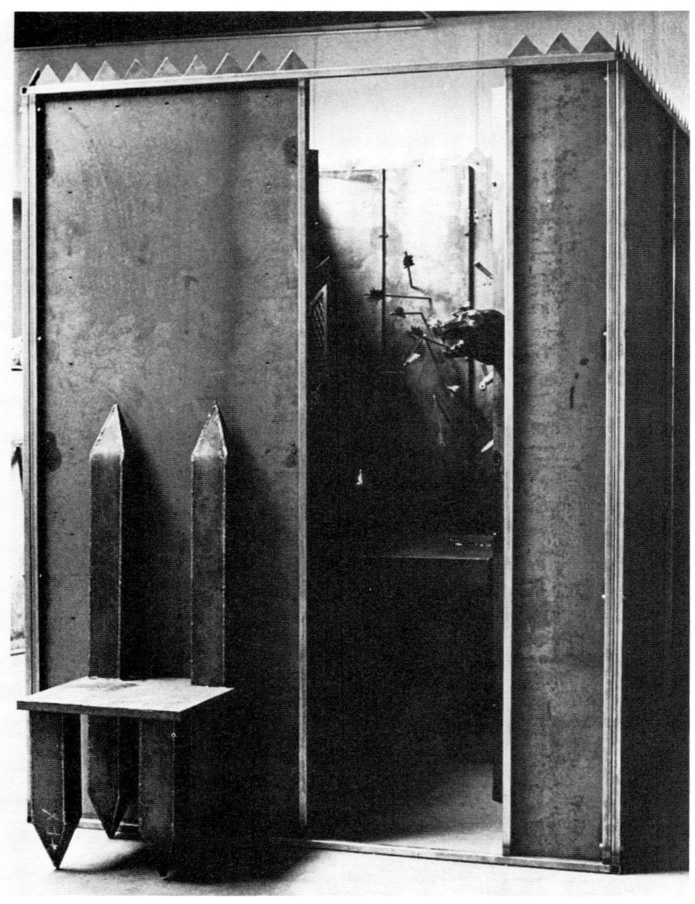

James Drake, **Trophy Room,** *1983,*
steel, 96 in. × 96 in. × 96 in.
Courtesy of the artist and Texas Gallery, Houston

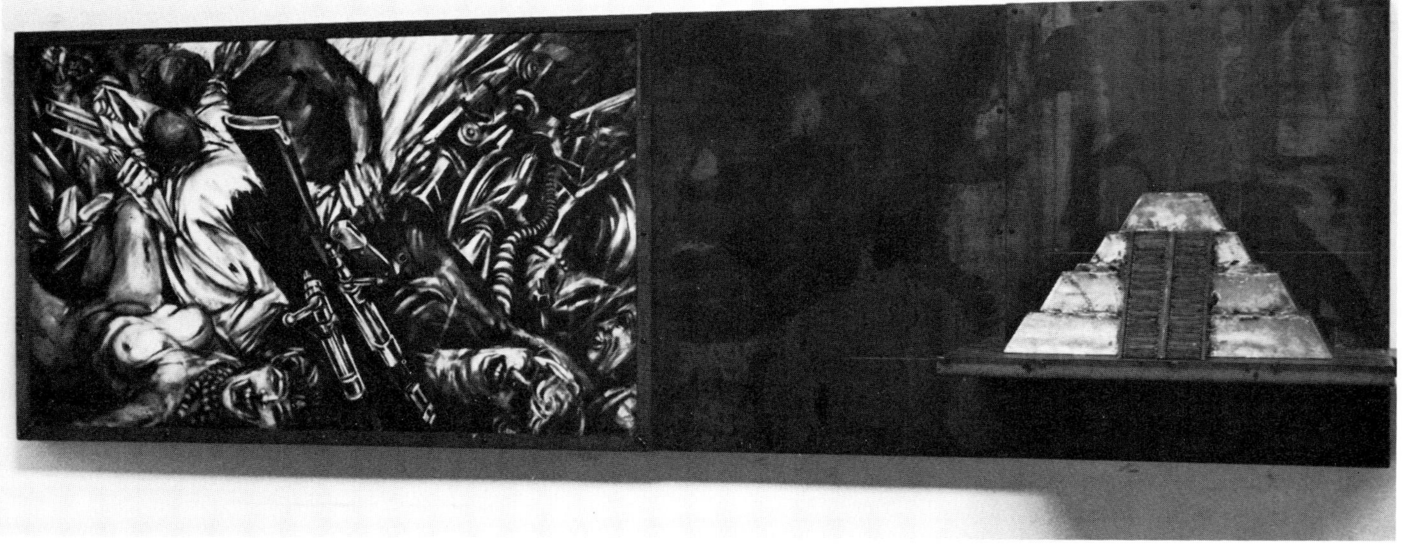

JAMES DRAKE, El Paso

The Revolution (Orozco)
1988
steel, charcoal on paper
55 in. × 186 in. × 18 in.
Courtesy of the artist, Texas Gallery,
Houston

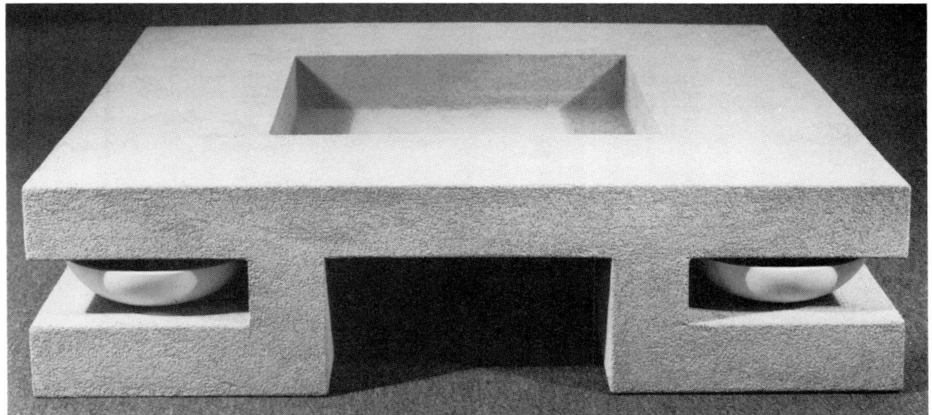

LINNEA GLATT, Dallas
Forum for a Family
1985
reinforced cement on polystyrene
16 in. × 60 in. × 60 in.
Courtesy of the artist

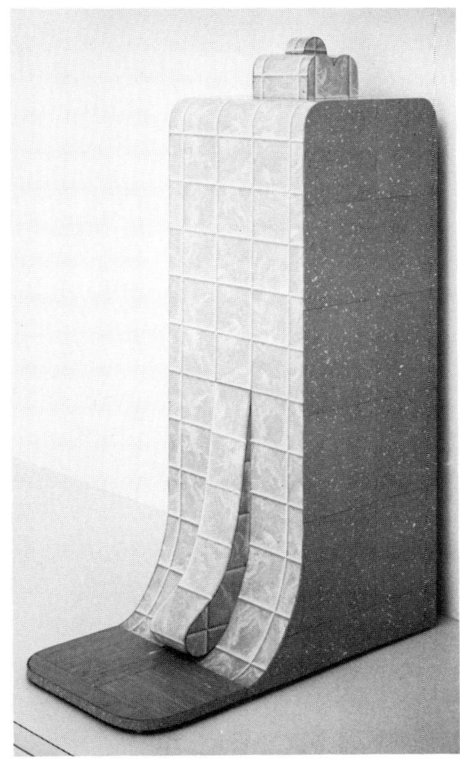

GEORGE GREEN, Long Island, New York
Fountain
1979
linoleum tiles on wood
54 in. × 17 in. × 35 in.
Collection of Laura Carpenter, Dallas

62. Marilyn A. Zeitlin, *James Drake: The Border/La Frontera*, exhibition catalog, Contemporary Arts Museum, Houston, 1988, unpaginated.

63. Linnea Glatt, personal statement in exhibition catalog *Third Coast Review: A Look at Art in Texas*, Aspen Art Museum, 1987, p. 20.

and Juarez has affected Drake's art. After he was deeply touched by a recent incident when young Mexican nationals attempting to seek work in the United States were locked in a boxcar on the Texas side of the border and died horribly while trying to escape the confines of the railroad car and the suffocating heat, Drake's work takes on political meaning. In *The Revolution (Orozco)*, Drake presents a diptych: from one panel of dark steel a welded three-dimensional pyramid (representing the Pyramid of the Sun at Teotihuacan) projects from the background while the second panel encloses and frames his drawing based on José Clemente Orozco's 1934 mural *Katharsis*. Orozco's mural deals with the battle of man against technology.[62] Drake's work is about Mexico: the Mexico before Columbus and the Mexico of twentieth-century revolution. It is about violence and power. It is about powerlessness. While Drake's early work displays the technical proficiency of a young sculptor, the later work demonstrates a compassionate understanding of the historical and cultural weight dominating the Mexican people, his neighbors across the border. James Drake's sculpture *The Revolution (Orozco)* depicts the economic exploitation of Mexico but holds out hope for humanity.

Linnea Glatt's *Forum for a Family* conjures images of a picnic table designed for a Bergman movie: all is cold, white, and devoid of gesture or movement. So complete is its neutrality that the sculpture, with its hard edges, repeating geometric shapes, and stasis, demands that the viewer's perceptions activate it. It is Linnea Glatt's idea that the viewer's perceptions not only activate but complete the work as well. In *Forum for A Family*, Glatt, a recent mother, incorporates bowl shapes within the piece. She observes that "the bowl forms have been a recent preoccupation derived from early mound forms, now inverted. The implication that the bowls are recognizable vessels for use intrigues me . . . [because of] the added symbolic significance of nurturing, sharing, and caring."[63]

George Green's *Fountain* recalls his days of "Texas funk" when outrageous objects and organic humor prevailed among several of the state's artists. Green's use of 1950s materials and his reference to Duchamp in his title unite in this stripped-down and suggestive sculpture. At first glance, the work could be placed with other Minimalist monuments, so empty is it of detail and so completely does it present itself as geometric shape. But the viewer quickly realizes that this is no sculpture a Robert Smithson or a Robert Morris could have created in the early 1960s. The entire surface of the piece is covered in green linoleum tile — the kind found in bathrooms all over the country a decade or two earlier. George Green's use of geometric shape and totally unexpected materials blatantly announces the work's connections with other sensibilities. Minimalist primary structure meets Texas funk.

Joseph G. Havel uses found objects as "seedlings" from which his objects grow. For *Marriage Is a Boat*, Havel found an ironing board — one of the kinds with circular holes in the bottom. He used the ironing board as the bottom of the boat and as the top of the house in his architecturally inspired sculpture. Adjacent to the boat/house shape is a smudge pot — like the old ones used in highway construction. In subliminal ways, Havel realized that a circle motif informed the entire work. He discovered circles in the ironing board, in the smudge pot with its circular handle, and in some of the wood, which came from a cholla cactus. The circle works as a repeated pattern within the entire sculpture and compositionally binds it together. Intending various interpretations of the idea of marriage, Havel says the sculpture could refer to a union of forms or to a marriage of opposites. The smudge pot could serve as a torch or as an altar light, or it could represent an anchor.[64] At first glance, Havel's dark form seems foreboding, but in searching for its meaning, the viewer delights in the multiple paradoxes found.

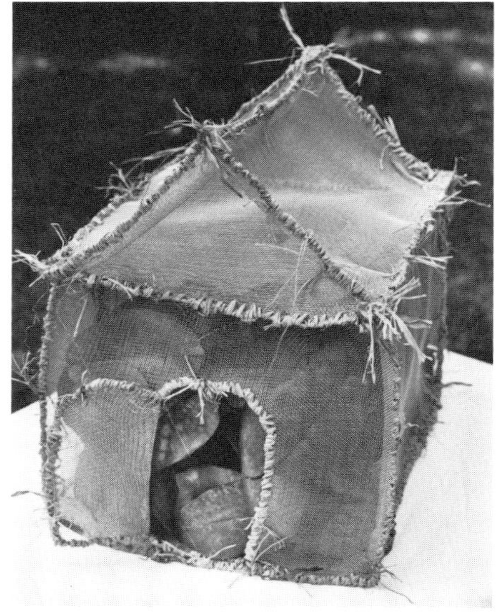

Houston artist Toby Topek's small constructions from the late 1970s and early 1980s rely on architectural themes. **Recording Time,** *1981, aluminium, wire, raffia, thread, magnolia leaves, 14 in. × 12¼ in. × 15 in.*

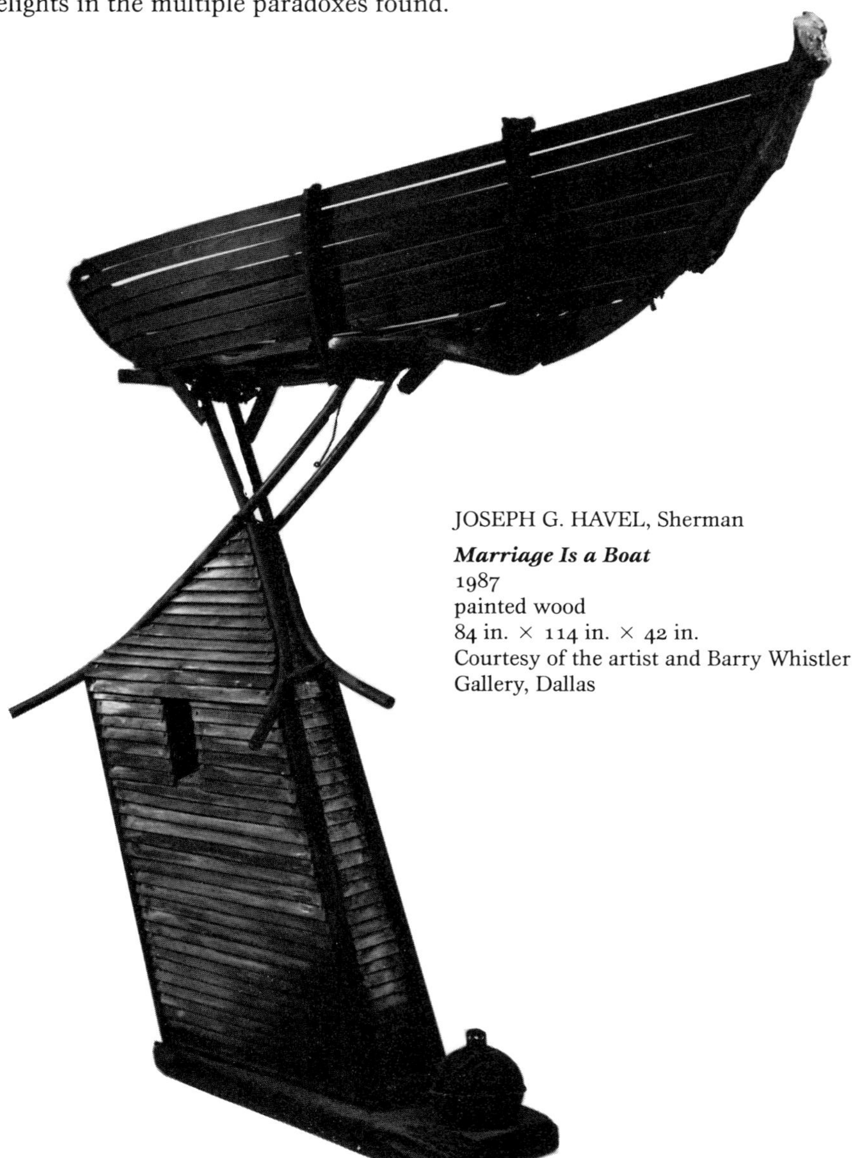

JOSEPH G. HAVEL, Sherman

Marriage Is a Boat
1987
painted wood
84 in. × 114 in. × 42 in.
Courtesy of the artist and Barry Whistler
Gallery, Dallas

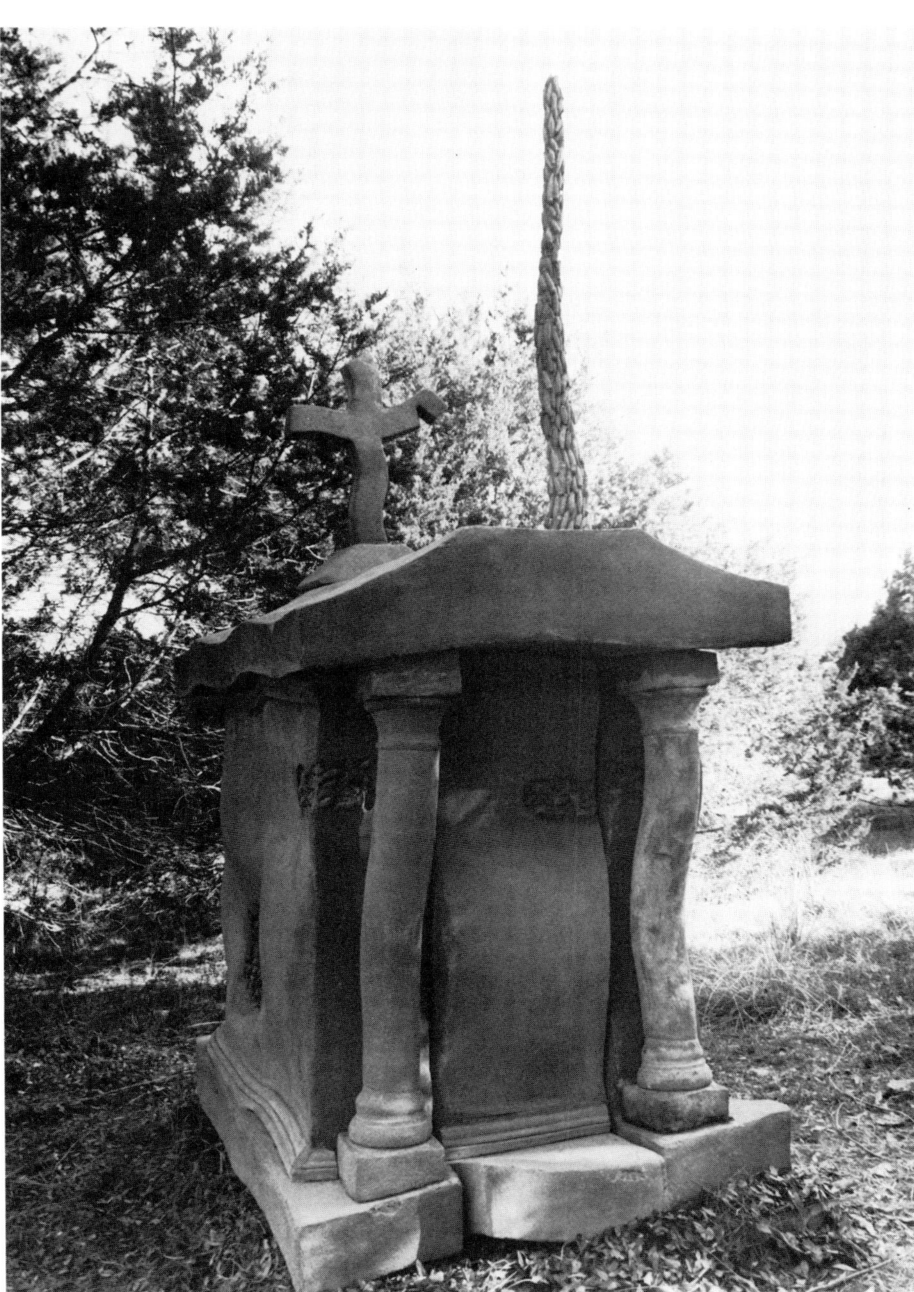

TEME PAUL HERNANDEZ, Austin

Spiritual Okra
1987
concrete
108 in. × 36 in. × 48 in.
Courtesy of the artist and AIR Gallery,
Austin

Teme Paul Hernandez derives his sources from his roots in southern Louisiana. Hernandez says that *Spiritual Okra* reflects shanties, voodoo, the classical revival in architecture, cemeteries, and the sexual power accorded okra in the south. His cement sculpture immediately recalls the aboveground cemeteries in Louisiana. Hernandez's use of the architectural past is evident in his mausoleum, which commingles a wobbly temple front, a bowed pediment, two indented Doric columns, and a Christian cross. Hernandez has taken the beauty and elegance of Greek temple architecture, which is based on balance and symmetry, and skewed it from every angle. The sculpture becomes at once temple/shanty, mausoleum/church. Hernandez's *Spiritual Okra* communicates the overlapping uses of architecture as one culture prevails over another. Yet, because the work leans so, because it operates at such an incline, one is prompted to enjoy more its whimsy and capriciousness.[65]

64. Conversation with the artist, March 1989.

65. Artists' Statement, April 1989.

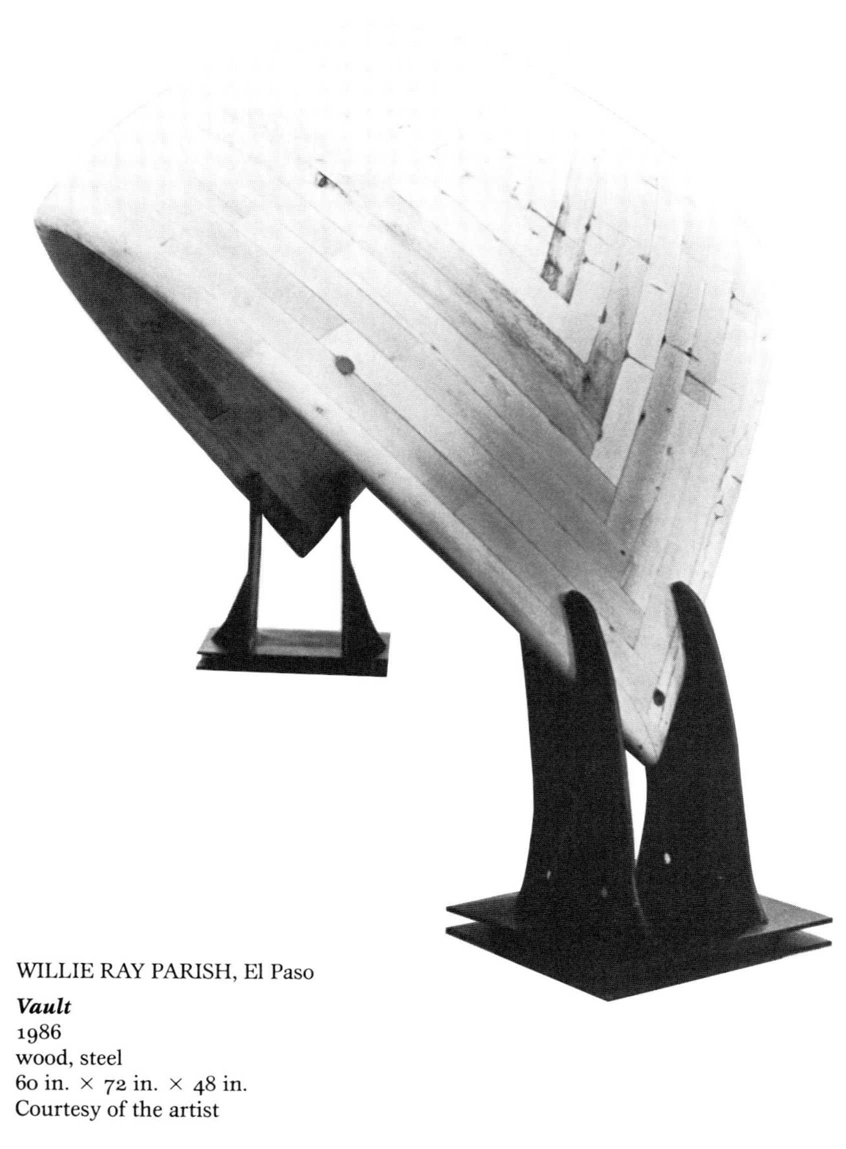

WILLIE RAY PARISH, El Paso

Vault
1986
wood, steel
60 in. × 72 in. × 48 in.
Courtesy of the artist

DALTON MARONEY, Arlington

Crecca
1987
wood/acrylic
69 in. × 22 in. × 10 in.
Courtesy of the artist and Graham Gallery, Houston

      Willie Ray Parish's *Vault* is a found wooden arch which has been inverted, reformed, and perched on fabricated steel "feet." The sculpture's laminated finish produces shimmering effects of light and color, which dissolve the solidity of the surface into impressionist bands. The idea of shelter is conveyed both in the solidity of the piece's mass and in the elegant arching of its transposed form.

      Dalton Maroney's architecture involves boat building. Maroney attended college during the mid-1960s when Minimalism was a prevailing mode of thought in the art world and he adopted this way of thinking despite feelings of discomfort.[66] Ultimately, he found a uniquely self-expressive style of art. He realized that he liked to build sculpture and that he liked boats and fishing. He blended each of these characteristics into a singular vision. In *Crecca*, Maroney's investigation into the nature and variety of boats is

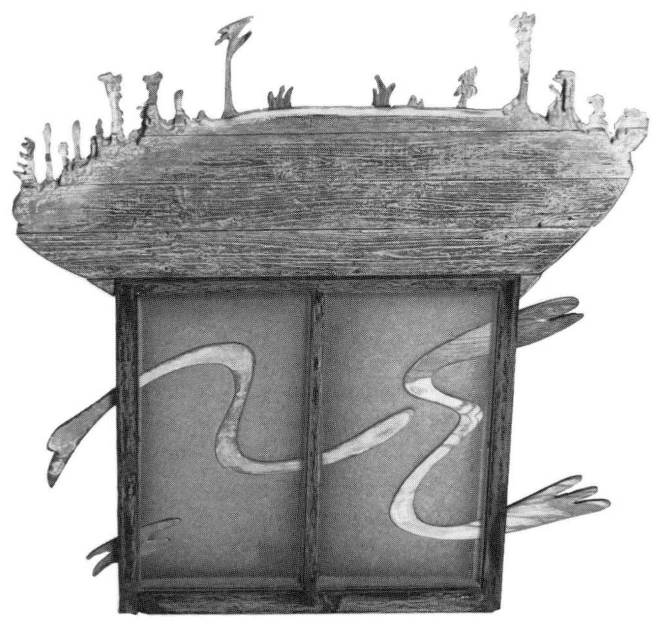

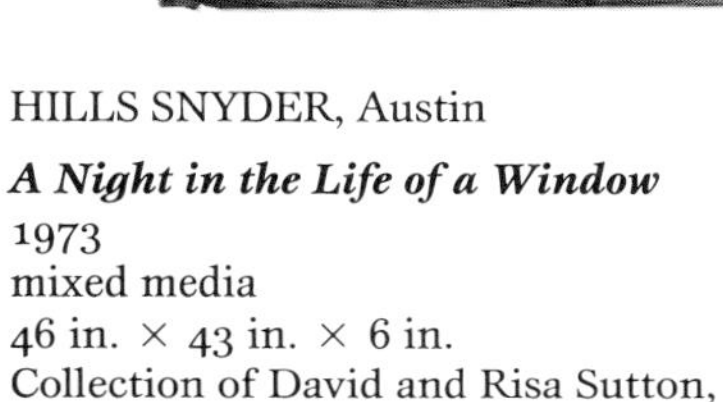

HILLS SNYDER, Austin

A Night in the Life of a Window
1973
mixed media
46 in. × 43 in. × 6 in.
Collection of David and Risa Sutton,
Big Sandy

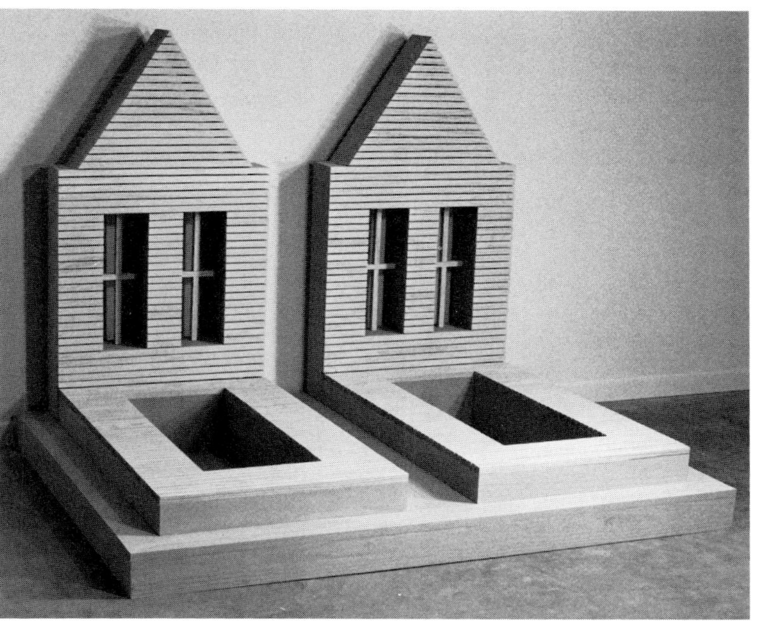

PATRICIA TILLMAN, Waco

Untitled (facades and crypts)
1983
wood/latex paint
48½ in. × 62⅝ in. × 47⅛ in.
Courtesy of the artist and Fort Worth
Gallery, Fort Worth

revealed in his painted abstracted catamaran. Ideas of craftsmanship and easily comprehended images are of concern to Maroney now that he has abandoned the Minimalist approach to art.

A Night in the Life of a Window weds artist Hills Snyder's interest in formalist art theory with found-object assemblage. Constructed in the mid-1970s, the piece represents a transition from painting to sculpture in relief format. Implying a continuity beyond the edges, Snyder's relief parallels Frank Stella's shaped canvases; yet, Snyder wants the content of the sculpture to overpower its formal aspects.[67] The idea of the window as metaphor for a mysterious, living entity infuses the work with great presence.

Patricia Tillman's architectural sculptures have gone beyond references to shelter to become spiritual surrogates for the human figure. Tillman's sculptures are conceptual, cerebral, and characteristically devoid of emotional content. Typically, the works are arranged in pairs, side by side, close to one another yet separate. Often the sculpture recalls church fronts with windows reflecting coexistent ideas of cross and sash. The works, which Tillman says stand for domestic issues like marriage, are also about dualities: she confronts issues of life and death, of oneness and separateness. In *Untitled (facades and crypts)* Tillman's miniature dwelling elicits a cool, intellectual response in its form and content as it evokes the marriage union in both life and death. A quiet, comforting presence is apparent in her architecturally-derived sculpture. Patricia Tillman's sculpture seems simultaneously to offer life and redemption.

66. Susan Freudenheim, "Making Art Against the Current," *Texas Homes*, April 1984, pp. 27–28.

67. Conversation with the artist, February 1989.

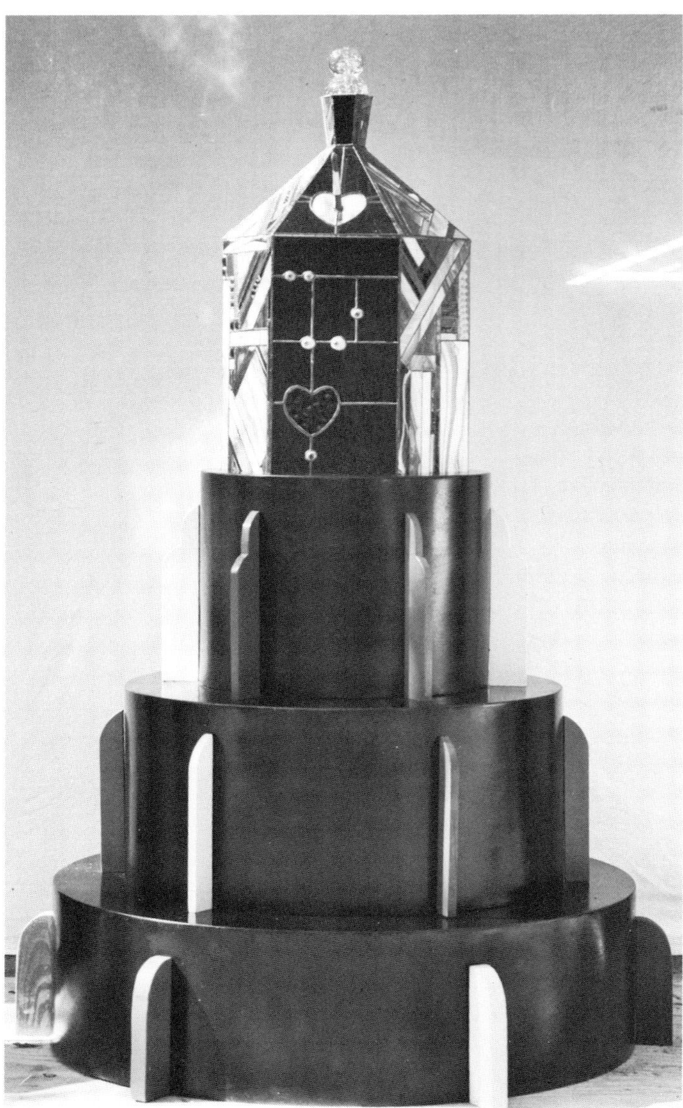

BERT L. LONG, JR., Houston

Glass House
1983
mixed media with strobe light and recording
(6 minutes)
20¾ in. × 17¼ in. × 34 in.; base 81 in.
× 48 in.
Courtesy of the artist and Hiram Butler
Gallery, Houston

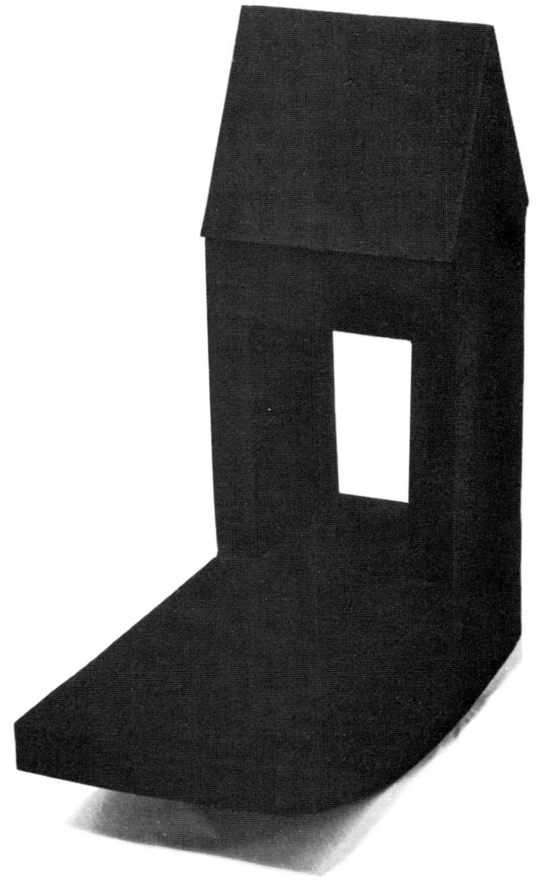

AL HARRIS, El Paso

Untitled
1987
steel/paint
25¼ in. × 21 in. × 9 in.
Courtesy of the artist and Graham Gallery,
Houston and Fort Worth Gallery, Fort Worth

 Bert Long's sculpture *Glass House* is a self-portrait that also recalls the *Mad House* of H. C. Westerman. Brightly patterned planes of color meld with personally selected symbols like the heart, the eye, and the paintbrush. Sitting atop three darkly painted circular bases, the piece is about the artist's vulnerability and the idea of living in a transparent shell, but the sculpture also is about the strength required to recognize and overcome weakness.[68]

 Al Harris' *Untitled* also recalls the idea of shelter in his abstract, welded, metal sculpture. Influenced by such Minimalist artists as Donald Judd and Joel Shapiro, Harris presents a small-scale object, constructed of flat planes — which nevertheless rocks on its curved base. Ideas of protection and comfort are especially apparent in this work, which, regardless of its cold, black color, integrates images of home and harbor.

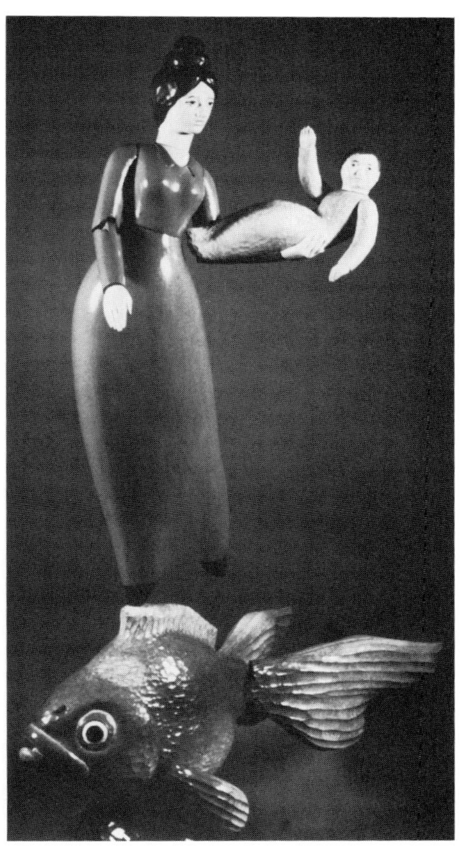

DAVID EVERETT, Austin

Oranda Madonna
painted mahogany
57 in. × 35 in. × 18 in.
Collection of Mr. and Mrs. Marvin Seline,
Houston

Rᴇalist sculpture created in the 1970s and 1980s, as with much of the art created in those two decades, bears the stamp of the individual's hand. Shapes and colors became eccentric and quirky. The artist turned away from systems and from modernism, with its emphasis on an intellectual solution to formalist problems, and embraced instead those ideas that emphasized personal expression and documentation.[69] The artists grouped within this broad realist category employ dissimilar techniques and materials. The content and meaning of their work are frequently at variance. The one characteristic that does unify the group is the artists' examination and incorporation of the figure into their sculpture.

In David Everett's *Oranda Madonna* — which recalls the early-twentieth-century work of Elie Nadelman — there is a whimsy and sense of play inherent in the articulated, polychromed mahogany sculpture. In this work the Madonna figure is smoothly carved with no chisel marks apparent on the wood. In contradistinction, the goldfish upon which the Madonna stands is roughly etched with notches and grooves of the artist's mark made visible. In the Madonna's hand she holds an infant who, like the goldfish, is worked with a rough texture. In the sculpture, the infant and the fish share ovoid shapes. The placement of the child's form both balances that of the fish and replicates its rough textures. Within this juxtaposition, Everett evokes a sense of play. Coupled with formal aspects of handsome craftsmanship and caprice, there is also a quietness about the piece that encourages the viewer to search for the work's meaning at further levels.

Emily Jennings' *Blind Man's Bluff* continues her incorporation of childhood toys and games into the form and meaning of her art. This outdoor piece includes five large heads inspired by the kids' game "Go to the Head of Your Class." In Jennings' present game, however, the artist uses the symbol of the game board to examine the effects of a highly technological society upon the environment. Jennings sees atrophy as a by-product of a technology gone bad. Viewed from the front and the back, Jennings' tokens present two different aspects. From the front the fresh-faced heads question: "Can you breathe?" From the back, gruesome computer-imaged faces ask: "Where is my nose?" Yet another of the five heads asks: "Can you think?" to be answered on the reverse with: "Where is my brain?" Through Jennings' exaggeration of the innocent games of childhood, she prods the viewer to realize that what the future holds for the environment is neither innocent nor a game.

Harry Geffert's *Gardens of Invisible Snakes and God's Little Buzzards* is an elaborate allegory in bronze. Geffert's work is cast at his studio-foundry. A master of the bronze casting process, he is able to control the surface colors of individual pieces through the use of chemicals. There is no paint applied to his sculptures. By using chemicals like ferric or copper nitrate, by applying the chemicals to hot or cold or dry or wet surfaces, Geffert controls the work and makes it respond to his wishes. In this sculpture, Geffert has produced brown, yellow, black, and green patinas on the work's surfaces. The inherent allegory in each Geffert sculpture takes on aspects of his personal life, which then transcend the personal to make more universal statements. In this work are references to Grant Wood's famous painting *American Gothic*. Male and female figures are enclosed by a picture frame. There is a life-size portrait of the artist in his foundry attire — pouring ring in hand. References are made to ancient Greece and Rome as well as to twentieth-century America.

68. Michael Samuels and James Surls, *Art — A Healing Force*, catalog for exhibition, Lawndale Annex, University of Houston, Houston, 1983, p. 45.

69. I. Michael Danoff, "Introduction" to catalog for HHK Foundation for Contemporary Art, Inc., 1980, unpaginated.

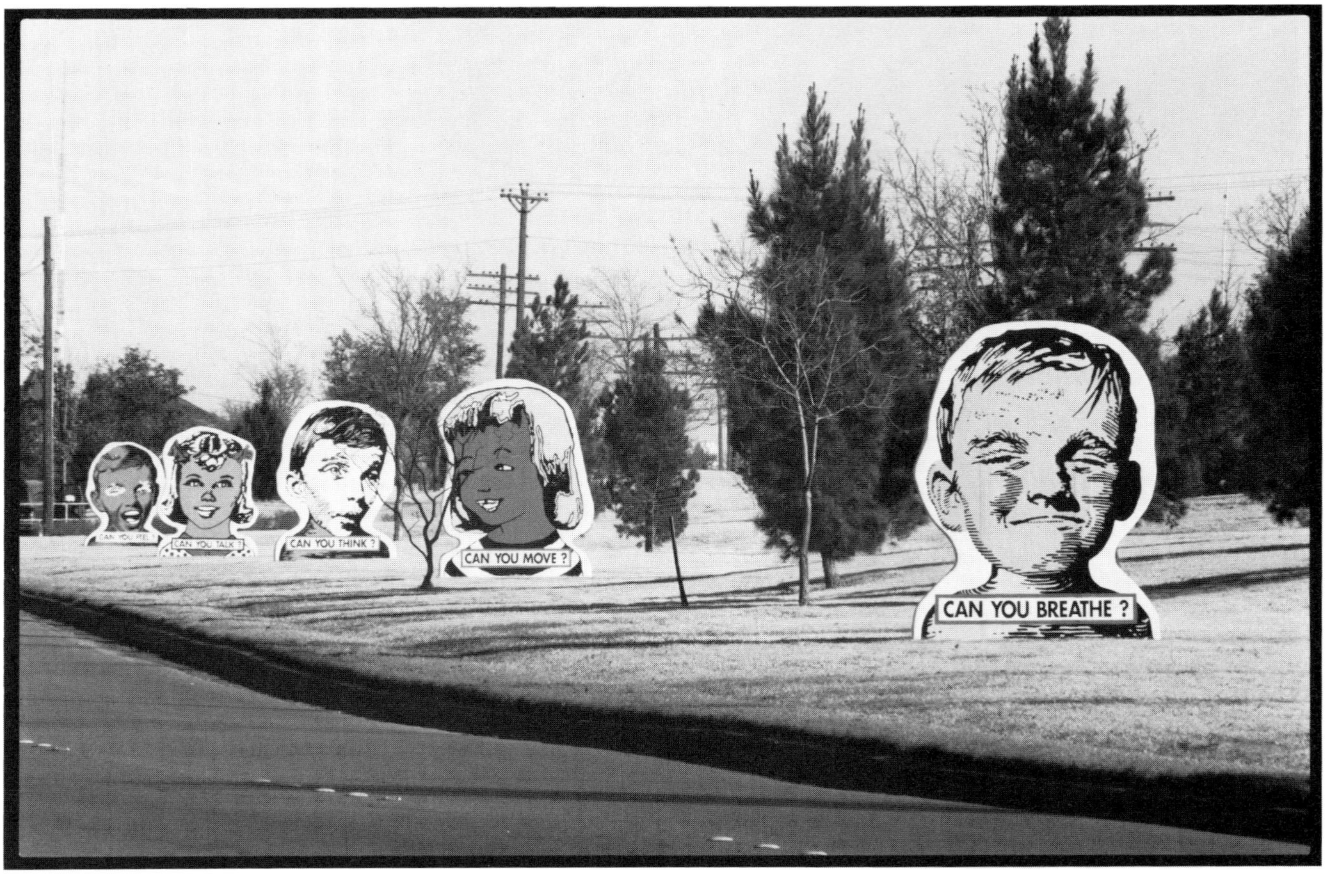

CAN YOU FEEL ?
CAN YOU TALK ?
CAN YOU THINK ?
CAN YOU MOVE ?
CAN YOU BREATHE ?

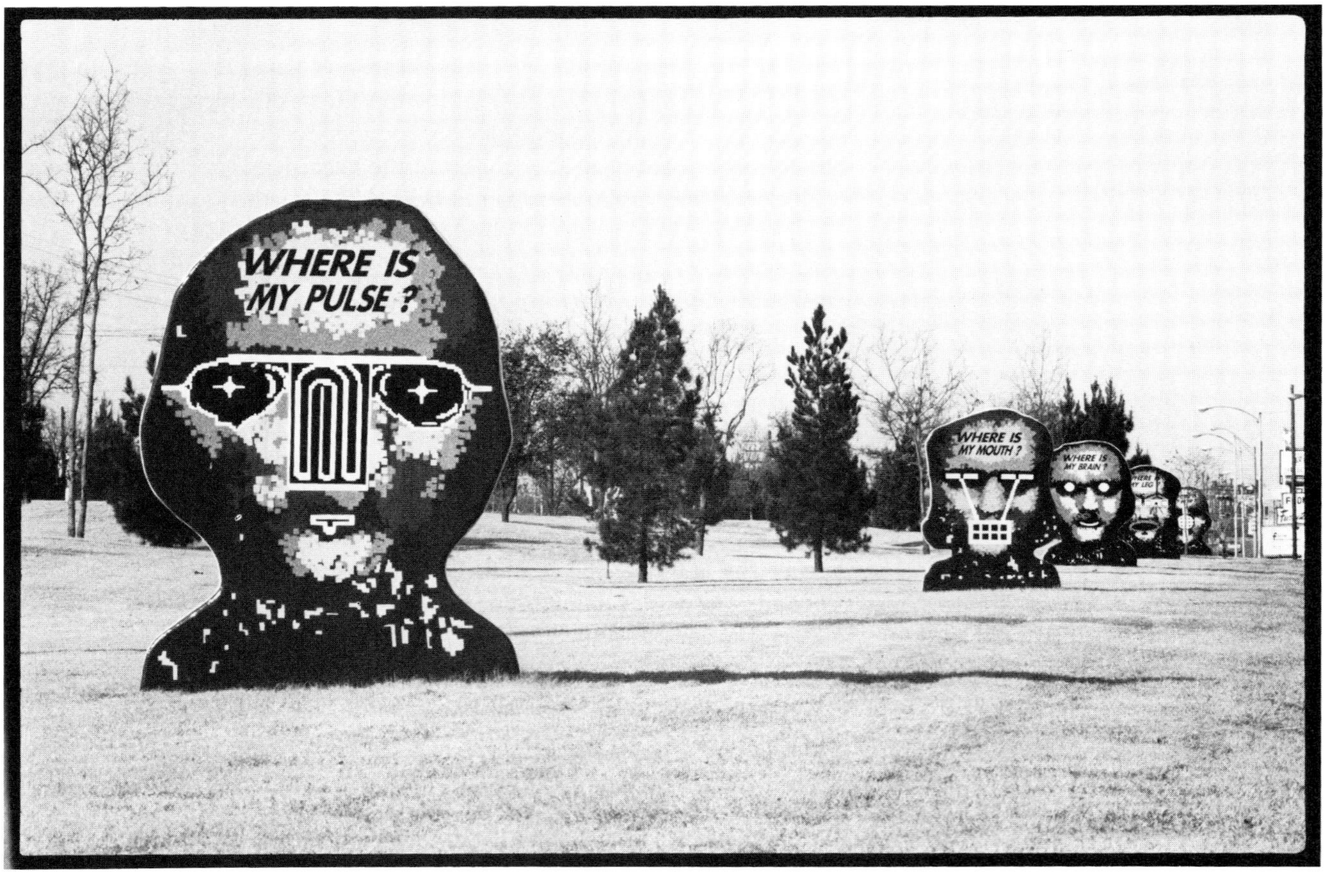

WHERE IS
MY PULSE ?
WHERE IS
MY MOUTH ?
WHERE IS
MY BRAIN ?

HARRY GEFFERT, Fort Worth

Gardens of Invisible Snakes and God's Little Buzzards
1987–88
bronze
288 in. × 288 in. × 84 in. (reduced for exhibition)
Courtesy of the artist and Fort Worth Gallery, Fort Worth

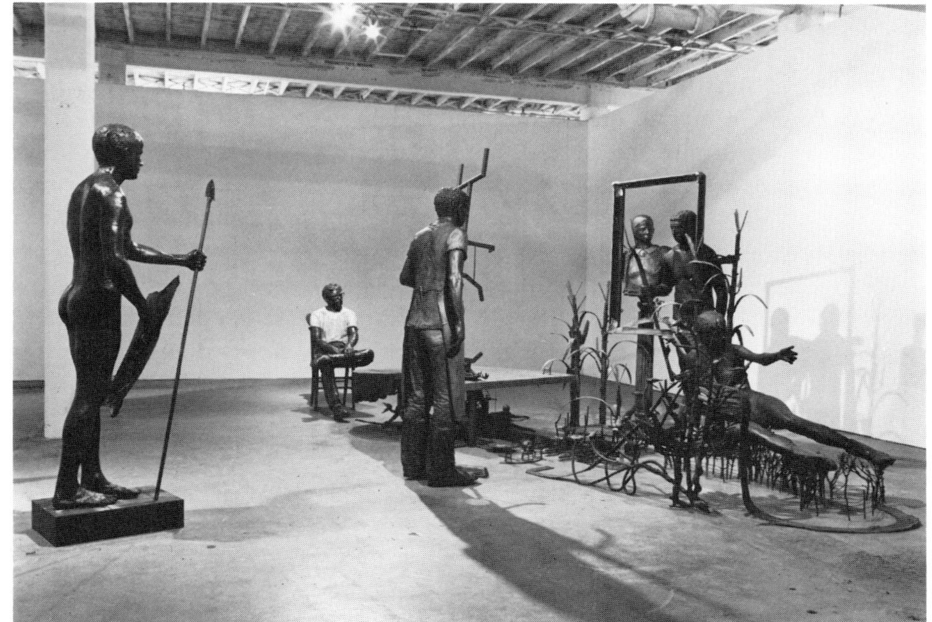

(opposite page)

EMILY JENNINGS, Abilene

Blindman's Bluff
1988
fiberglass/paint
5 pieces each 72 in. × 96 in.
Courtesy of the artist and Distinctive Vision, Austin

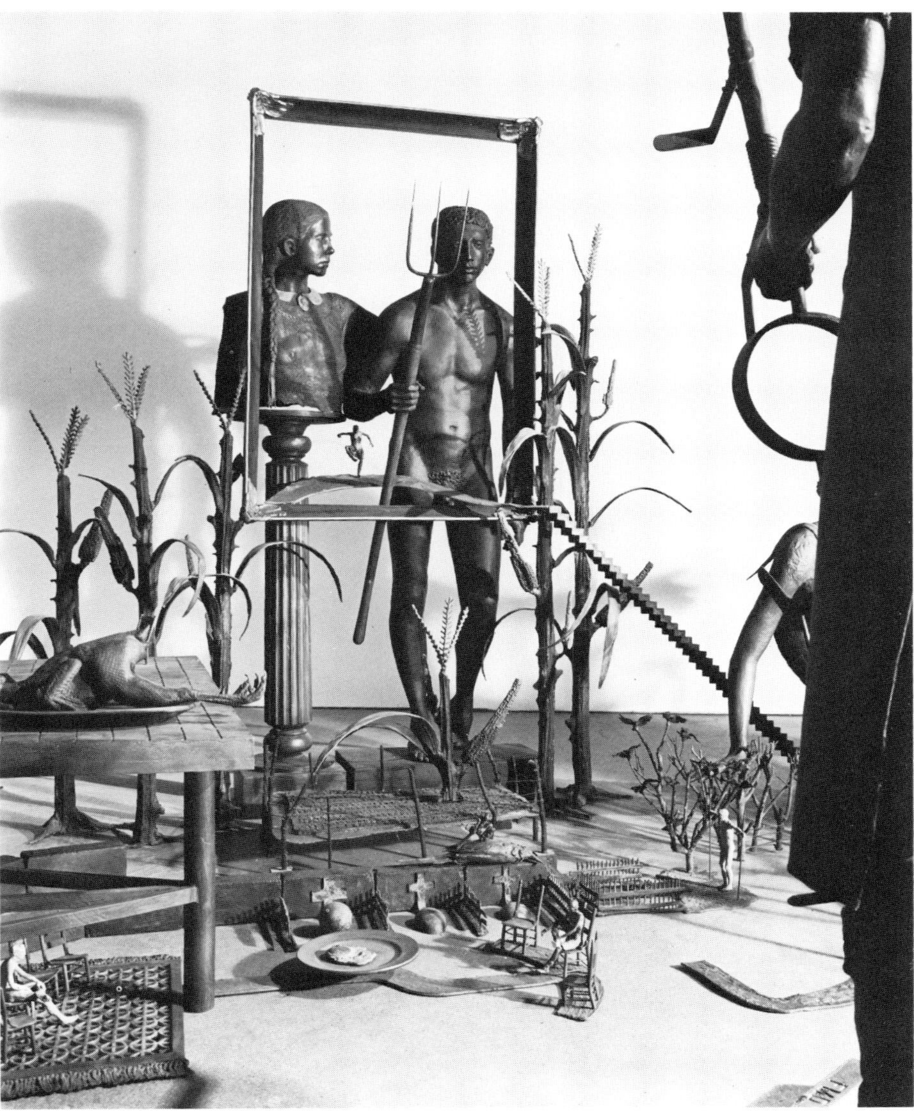

Bronze stalks of corn, fences, a small dancing figure in cowgirl boots, and other bits of bronze reality comprise the tableau. Geffert's bronze stories typically are composed of numerous pieces, which can engross the viewer for hours. The work fills the eye with myriad details that move Geffert's narrative. Harry Geffert's sculpture demonstrates the master's hand in its craft while the meanings inherent in the work operate at multiple levels.

Sharon Kopriva's sculpture evokes primordial feelings and visceral responses. Her skeletal figures frequently are parched and recall primitive fetishes. In *Woman Marred by Tumors*, Kopriva offers an image of despair and loss: the crouching figure is open and exposed; where one would expect to find life, there are skulls. Kopriva employed references to the uterus and the coffin in this work, and the pessimism it evokes is unsparing.[70]

Ken D. Little's skilled and sensitive craftsmanship is apparent in his work *Burn*. In 1980 he began to build his sculptures from discarded objects of wearing apparel he found. Little takes leather boots and shoes and from them constructs animal forms. Working with manufactured objects constructed of animal hides adds a symbolic presence to the work.

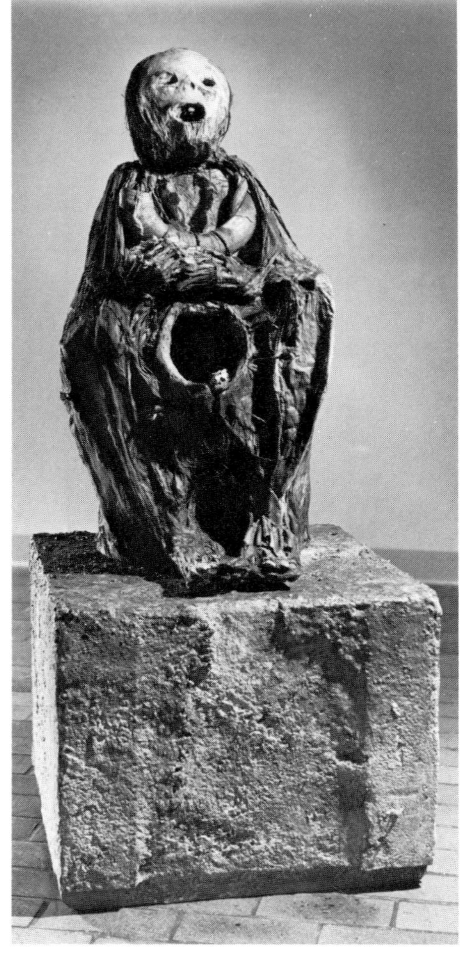

SHARON KOPRIVA, Houston

Woman Marred by Tumors
1988
papier-mâché, bone, cloth
51 in. × 24 in. × 22 in.
Collection of Ed and Nancy Kienholz

KEN D. LITTLE, San Antonio

Burn
1985
leather, paint, shoes (mixed media)
72 in. × 26 in. × 48 in.
Courtesy of the artist

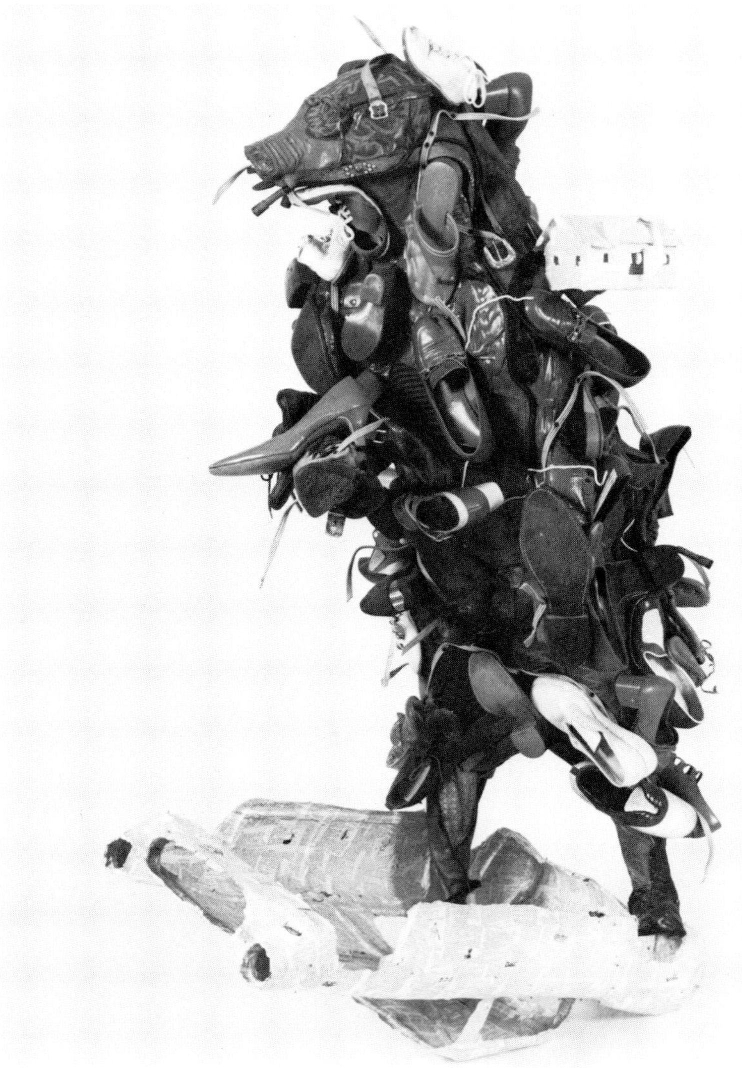

70. Elizabeth McBride, *Sharon Kopriva: Sculpture and Paintings*, W. A. Graham Gallery, Houston, 1989, unpaginated.

71. Dave Hickey, "Bestiary of Damaged Goods," essay for catalog of exhibition Ken Dawson Little: Selected Sculpture, 1982–1985, Blanden Memorial Art Museum, Fort Dodge, Iowa, 1985, p. 6.

72. Janet Kutner, "Artists Bare Their Souls," *Dallas Morning News*, March 14, 1987, p. 2C.

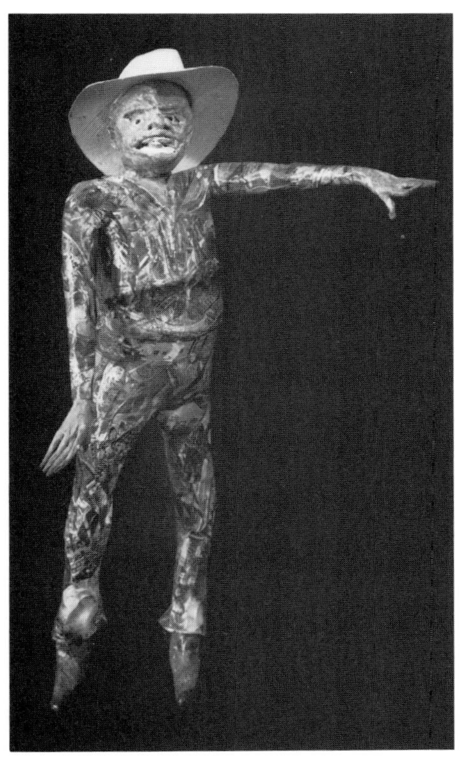

JESSE LOTT, Houston

Cowboy
1986
mixed media
26 in. × 13 in. × 8 in.
Courtesy of the artist, Hiram Butler Gallery,
Houston, and Barry Whistler Gallery, Dallas

There is a formal elegance to the sculptures; the textures are rich and warm. Implicit in the work are ideas of recycling and the larger issue of the continuity of life and death. Additionally, Little's sculpture evokes all the stories apparent in the scuffs, the marks, of the old shoes and boots: ". . . it was not only the beast he was restoring but the whole vortex of lost shapes, functions, feelings and shattered virtues redolent in the materials themselves."[71] *Burn* with its attached, papier-mâché house and car expands Little's interests beyond reconstructed animal form.

Jesse Lott's papier-mâché figures follow from his found-object assemblages. They elicit the feeling of folk art yet are by the hand of an artist who attended art school. Lott has been making the paper figures since the early 1980s. Each figure is unique and has a distinct personality; in fact, each figure represents either someone Lott knows or a person he has observed. In this figure, Lott appears to represent the stereotypical Texas cowboy. The figure dressed in hat and boots throws its head back in a broad smile. The figures stand, arms outstretched, hands open, fingers splayed. Lott once said that he believes "gesturing with the arms loosens the soul."[72]

Claudia Reese's clay figures often bring to mind the mythology of past cultures or she presents combined human and animal shapes that possess an emotionally rich environment. Her figurative sculpture is constructed by using the coil-and-pinch technique, then is glazed and fired with multiple and elaborate surface textures. In *Journey*, a type of passage is in process, recalling Greek mythology and the journey of the soul in a boat over the river Styx. Reese's figure passively and quietly travels from this world to the next.

CLAUDIA REESE, Austin

Journey
1984
ceramic
15 in. × 65 in. × 22 in.
Courtesy of the artist and R. S. Levy
Gallery, Austin

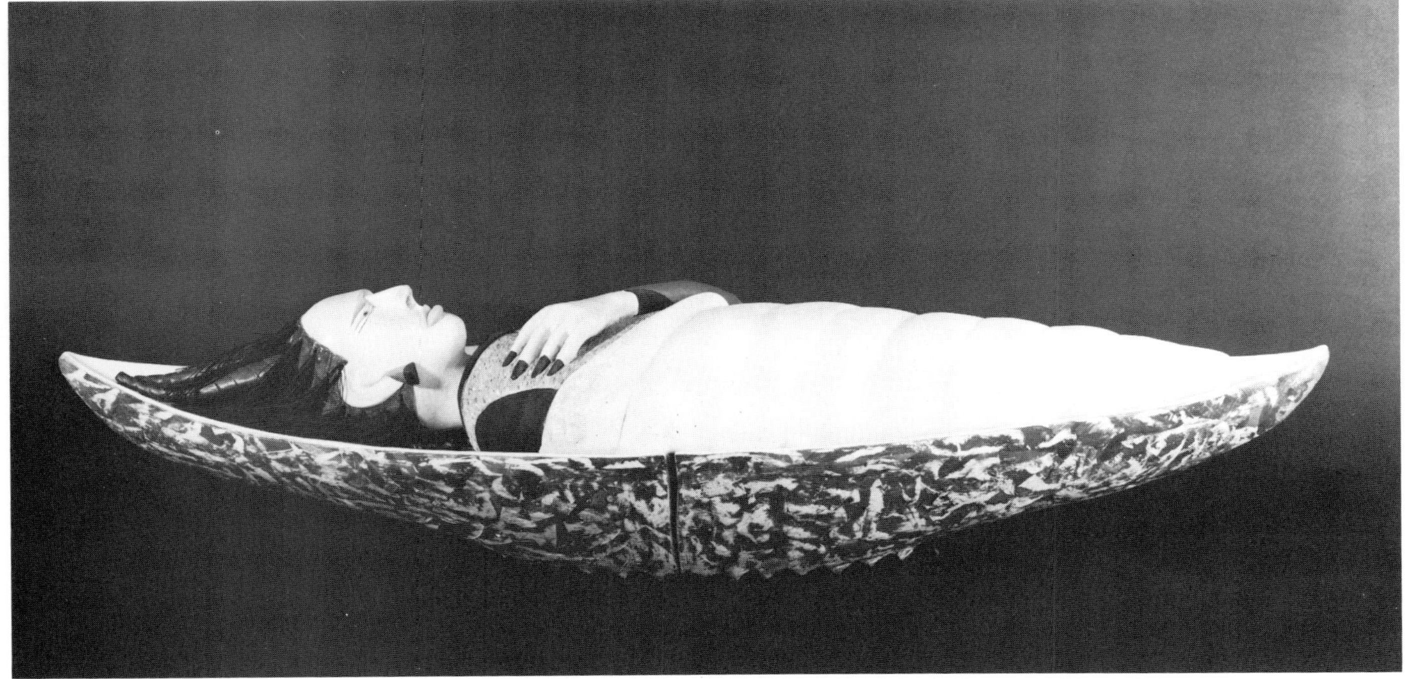

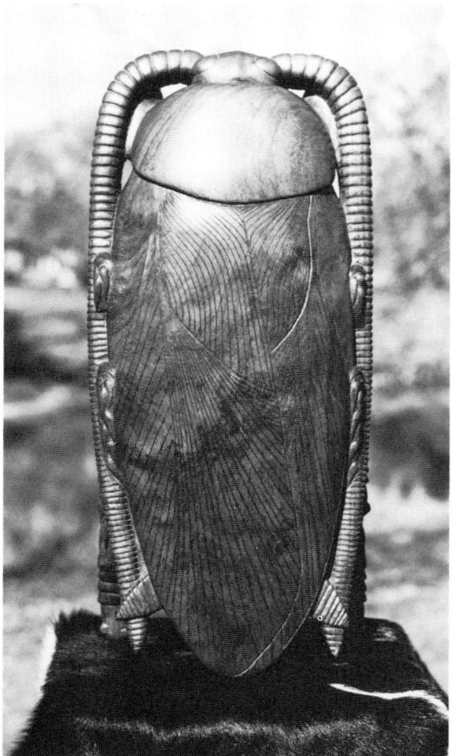

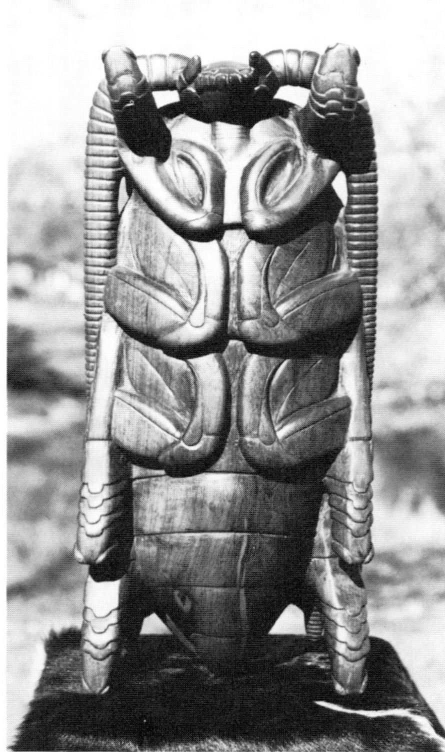

JOSE LUIS RIVERA, San Antonio
El Cucaracho
1981
mesquite
24 in. × 10½ in. × 5½ in.
Collection of Cesar A. Martinez, San Antonio

Jose Luis Rivera demonstrates a keen sensibility to wood in his realistically carved works, which elicit strong emotion. Influenced by the expressionism of such artists as José Clemente Orozco and David Alfaro Siqueiros, Jose Rivera's work encompasses historical Aztec and Indian cultural references when he seriously examines the many artistic contributions of Mexico. But Rivera also has a light-hearted side. In *El Cucaracho*, the viewer confronts an oversized cockroach, which is masterfully chiseled. The eye is completely fooled by the formal elegance of the wood carving. Only after the viewer stops and considers the subject of the piece does the artist's sense of play and fancy become apparent.

Stephen Daly, Janet Kastner, Charmaine Locke, John Hernandez, and Daniel Sellers integrate divergent ideas of figuration in their abstract sculptures.

Stephen J. Daly's *Looking* incorporates ideas of the human figure in two-dimensional format. The work could be viewed as a paper doll made large. The figure, propped up in the back by a wooden strut, is comprised of several individual parts, each drawn with colored pencils, framed separately, and then recombined to form a kneeling figure who holds a mirror. The figure looks into the mirror, which displays on its surface cryptic hieroglyphs. Daly characteristically utilizes the mirror in much of his sculpture. Stephen Daly asks the viewer to join his *Looking* figure in deciphering both message and meaning.

Janet Engle Kastner's clay sculptures are surrogates for the human figure; they stand for sentinels, guardians, or, in the present case, an "Enchantress." Kastner's black totem conveys an alluring,

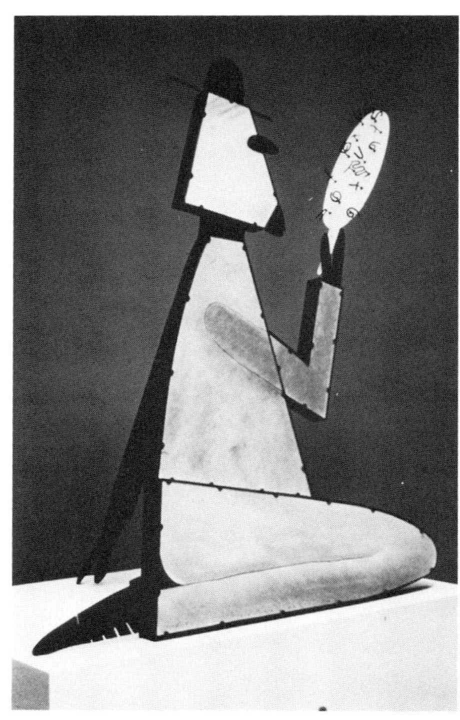

STEPHEN J. DALY, Austin
Looking
1983
pastel on paper/lacquer on steel
41 in. × 34 in. × 20 in.
Collection of Ms. Joanne Cassullo,
New York City

albeit Delphian, charm; its component parts embody a formidable whole. Interested in unexpected shifts of mood, Kastner employs disparate forms and surface textures, which generate unanticipated feelings.[73] Kastner creates tension through juxtaposition and in the process elicits enigmatic content.

Charmaine Locke's *The Natural World* derives from earlier sculptures that were somber, wrapped, and mummy-like; they bestowed powerful psychological presences. In this work, the attitude is lighter. While still dealing with the human figure, Locke offers the warmth of an inlaid wood with a surface richly enhanced by pastoral paintings of butterflies, insects, and birds whose placement represents the eyes of the figure. Beneath an expansive tree are two figures — male and female reaching out to the inhabitants of *The Natural World*. A sense of optimism and regeneration is offered in this bucolic view of The Garden before the fall.

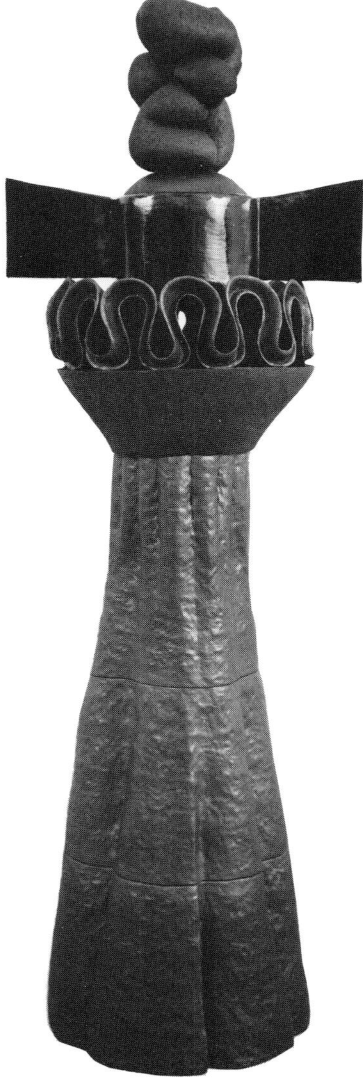

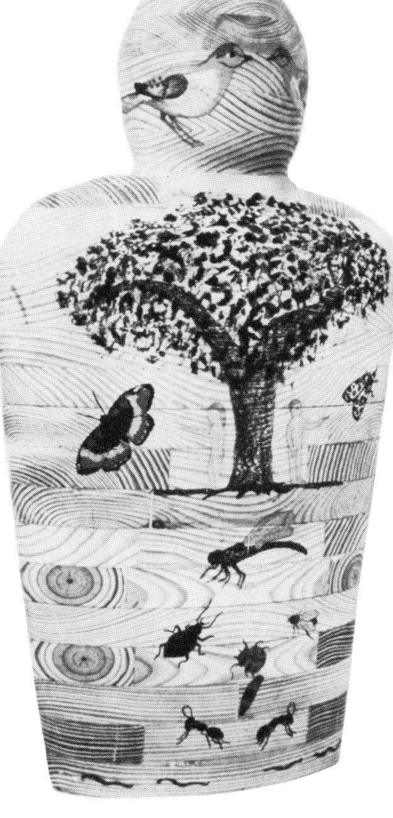

JANET ENGLE KASTNER, Austin

Enchantress
1987
clay
75 in. × 26 in. × 20 in.
Courtesy of the artist and R. S. Levy Gallery, Austin

CHARMAINE LOCKE, Splendora

The Natural World
1983
mixed media
32 in. × 13 in. × 7 in.
Collection of Toby Topek, Houston

73. Janet Engle Kastner, personal statement, in exhibition catalog *Third Coast Review: A Look at Art in Texas*, Aspen Art Museum, 1987, p. 30.

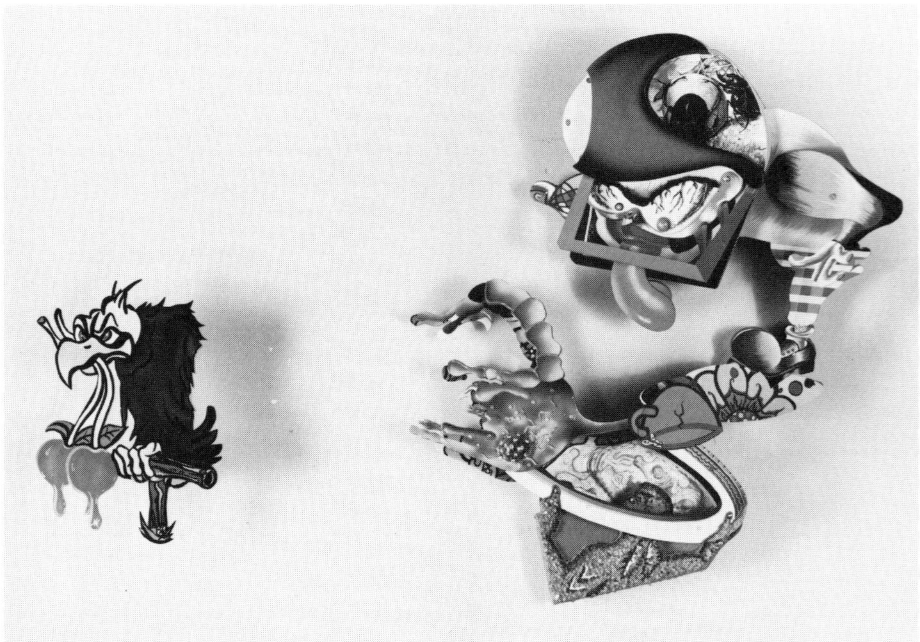

JOHN HERNANDEZ, Dallas
Breakfast Special
1987
mixed media
18 in. × 12 in. × 3 in.
Collection of Murray W. Camp, Austin

John Hernandez's wall sculptures are full of color, confusion, and contradiction. His art appears as an organic response to cartoons, *Mad* magazine, Peter Saul's painting, and all kinds of viscera. Characteristically Hernandez's work is composed of separate components arranged on a wall and interconnected through their combined meaning. In *Breakfast Special,* a high-colored bulging-eyed, gaping-tongued creature appears to be eyeing its next meal—itself an especially unappealing vulture, which has seemingly digested two smaller creatures as it holds their hearts on strings. Hernandez's work evokes feelings of both humor and disgust as it comments on vulnerability and the food chain.

Daniel Sellers' lyrical welded steel sculptures present abstracted images dealing with ideas of figuration. In *Quixote,* we recognize the artist's reference to Cervantes' novel in the stylized interpretation of the figure with lance—symbols of the adventurous Spanish nobleman, Don Quixote. In Sellers' sculpture he employs curvilinear forms and makes the sculpture appear as if drawn with steel; he works the metal as one would work with paper and scissors. Having worked the pipelines, Sellers is comfortable with torches and welding. Bringing a light touch to the heavy metal he works, he is also aware of the irony and parody that is the basis of Cervantes' novel. In Daniel Sellers' sculpture, qualities of irony and romance become inherent to his quest.

J ust as some artists of the 1970s and 1980s employed the figure in their sculptures others worked with non-objective abstraction. This use of abstraction derived from the traditional modernist tenets of Constructivism, which incorporated space as the essential basis of sculpture; space was used to interact with and penetrate the mass of sculptural form. Dense forms were displaced, and the invisible became visible through the juxtaposition of positive and negative space. Time also became an element in Constructivist sculpture as lines and shapes formed three-dimensional paths as the eye traced

DANIEL SELLERS, Fort Worth
Quixote V
1987
welded steel
68 in. × 18 in. × 20 in.
Courtesy of the artist and Fort Worth Gallery, Fort Worth

74. Goldwater, *What Is Modern Sculpture?*, pp. 64–65.

the movement of their outlines; volume was conveyed through the space the lines contained. Expressionist Constructivism visually shaped space through symbolic expressions of human emotion. There are references to nature and to organic forms. The interaction of spaces creates a fluid, open form that expresses the gestures and feelings of the artist.[74] Artists Allan Hacklin, Heather Marcus, Chris Powell, C. M. Stagg, Gisela-Heidi Strunck, and Nicholas Wood find meaning in abstract construction in their art.

Allan Hacklin's sculpture depends on Constructivist geometries for its form. His work relies on line to define the positive and negative spaces. Volume is suggested as Hacklin endeavors to make the invisible visible. His work can also be viewed as lyrical expressions that refer to nature by incorporating organic materials in the work. In *Dervish*, Hacklin takes slender slats of wood that seem to have been whittled from larger tree limbs. He stacks the wood slats in pyramid form but their presence also recalls the shape of a pyre. Around the wood, Hacklin attaches brightly painted rings. The rings appear to have been randomly thrown on the wood, somewhat like a game of horseshoes. But the elegance of the piece belies any accidental construction.

Heather Marcus' aluminum and steel abstractions also stem from modernist ideas of Cubism and Constructivism. She, like Ben Woitena, uses polychromy to define the planes of her sculpture and to describe the relationship of foreground to background. Her sculptures acquire

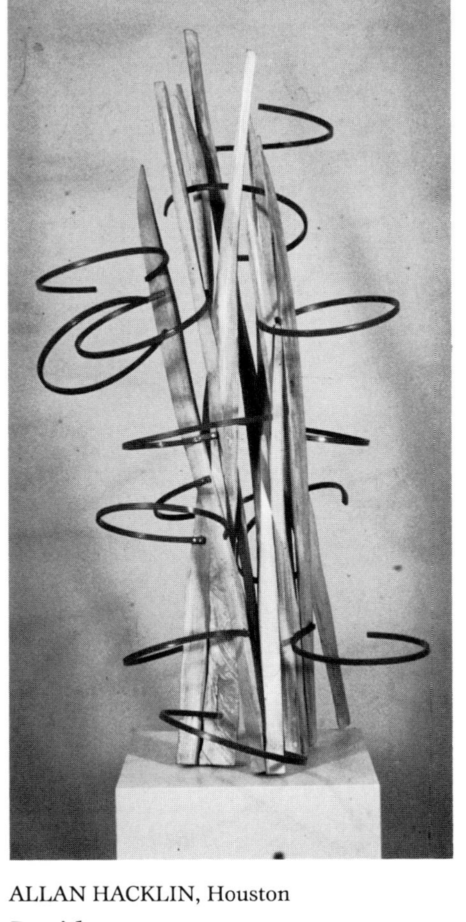

ALLAN HACKLIN, Houston

Dervish
1983
painted wood
60 in. × 30 in. × 30 in.
Courtesy of the artist and Meredith Long
Gallery, Houston

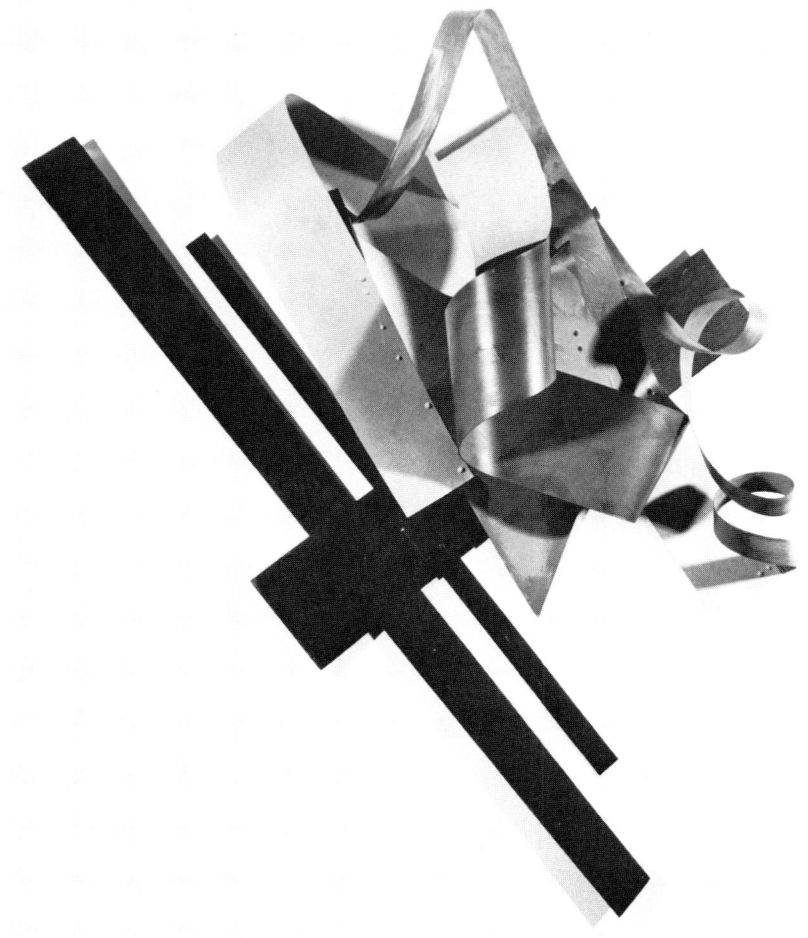

HEATHER MARCUS, Dallas

Tok
1988
oil/aluminum
57½ in. × 54½ in. × 15½ in.
Collection of Mr. and Mrs. Keith S. Wellin,
New York City

emotional intensity through the combination of their overlapping planes and through their highly charged color. In *Tok*, stylistic elements of Cubism are apparent in the juxtapostion of hard to soft shapes and curved to straight lines. Marcus similarly expresses her emotional involvement with the piece in the fluidity and gesture of the line she employs and in the work's aggressive colors.

Chris Powell's stoneware monoliths stand as abstracted monuments to some unknown entity. Recalling the Celtic Plains, the Druids, and Stonehenge, Powell's sculpture invokes a mystic past. Organically realized, the work projects a potent form as the monoliths are placed in juxtaposition. Powell intuitively invented the shapes of his sculptures, which are reminiscent of columns, vessels, or human forms. The work projects an archetypal presence that one realizes is as powerful a force in West Texas as it must have been in ancient England.

C. M. Stagg's coiled structures, like Chris Powell's, derive from organic sources. Whereas Powell uses clay, Stagg strips pine branches of their bark, then varnishes and cuts them to size. From

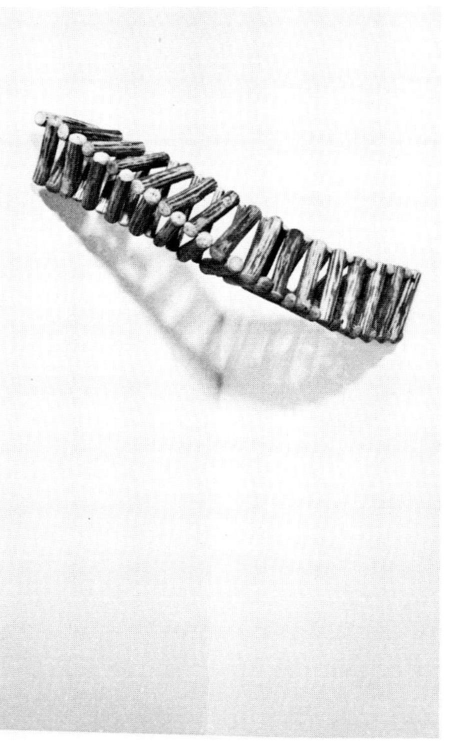

C. M. STAGG, Houston

Untitled Number 11
1988
wood
36 in. × 8 in. × 8 in.
Courtesy of the artist and Graham Gallery, Houston

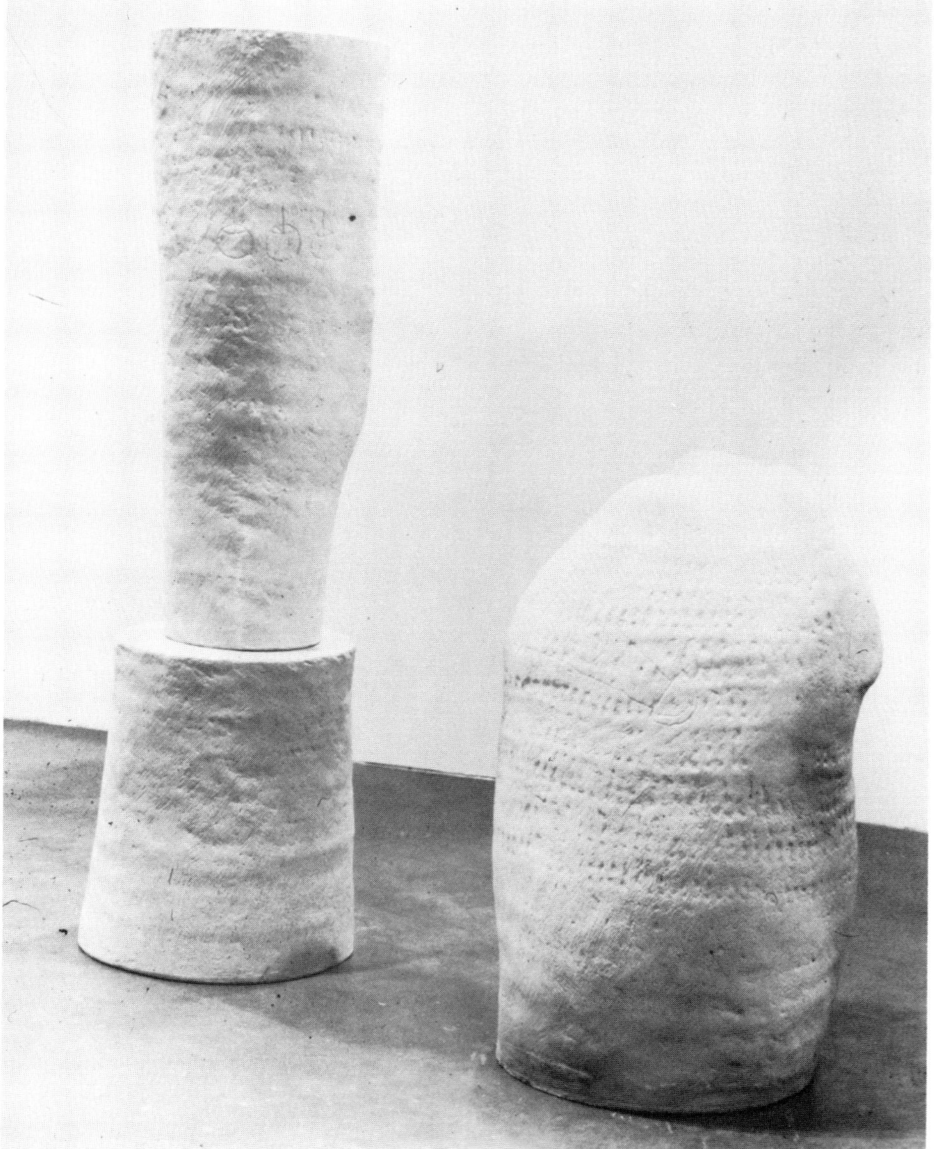

CHRIS POWELL, Fort Worth

Until I Come to Meet with You
1988
stoneware
2 objects: 65 in. h, and 39 in. h
Courtesy of the artist and Fort Worth Gallery, Fort Worth

these wooden units Stagg fashions abstracted flowers, towers, or ladders, which evoke feelings both of nature and of industry.[75] The surface of Stagg's work is handsome in its varnished luminosity. Light plays across it and creates delicate and unexpected vibrations of color. In *Untitled Number 11,* Stagg constructs his sculpture and then places it across the angle of a corner. The work seems to come to life as it appears to crawl across the wall. It evokes simultaneously both plant and animal form.

Gisela-Heidi Strunck's sculptures recall influences of Constructivism and Cubism in their formal arrangements. Strunck incorporates geometric form as the underlying structure of her sculpture but she appears to be more at home with aspects of Cubism that are representative of African art. Strunck deftly colors her sculpture, and she combines materials in such a way that one recognizes the presence of the skilled craftsman. In *Summer Dream Stairs*, Strunck's formal aesthetic unites with Surrealist content and presents the viewer a handsomely crafted object with ties to another world.

GISELA-HEIDI STRUNCK, Grapevine

Summer Dream Stairs
1986
red cedar, maple, clay, cast paper, acrylic, sisal rope, brass wire
77 in. × 42 in. × 17 in.
Courtesy of the artist and Conduit Gallery, Dallas

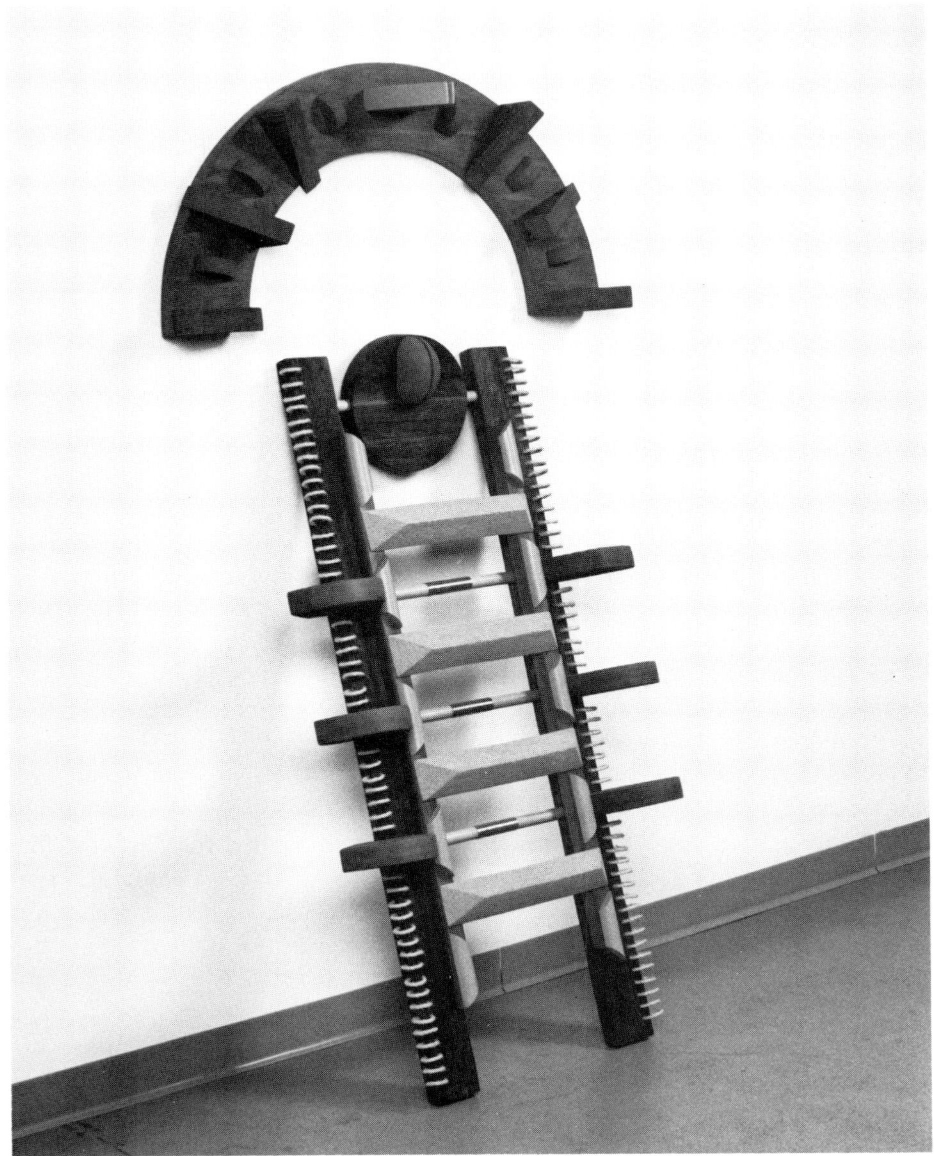

75. Patricia C. Johnson, art review, *Houston Chronicle,* July 16, 1988, p. 6.

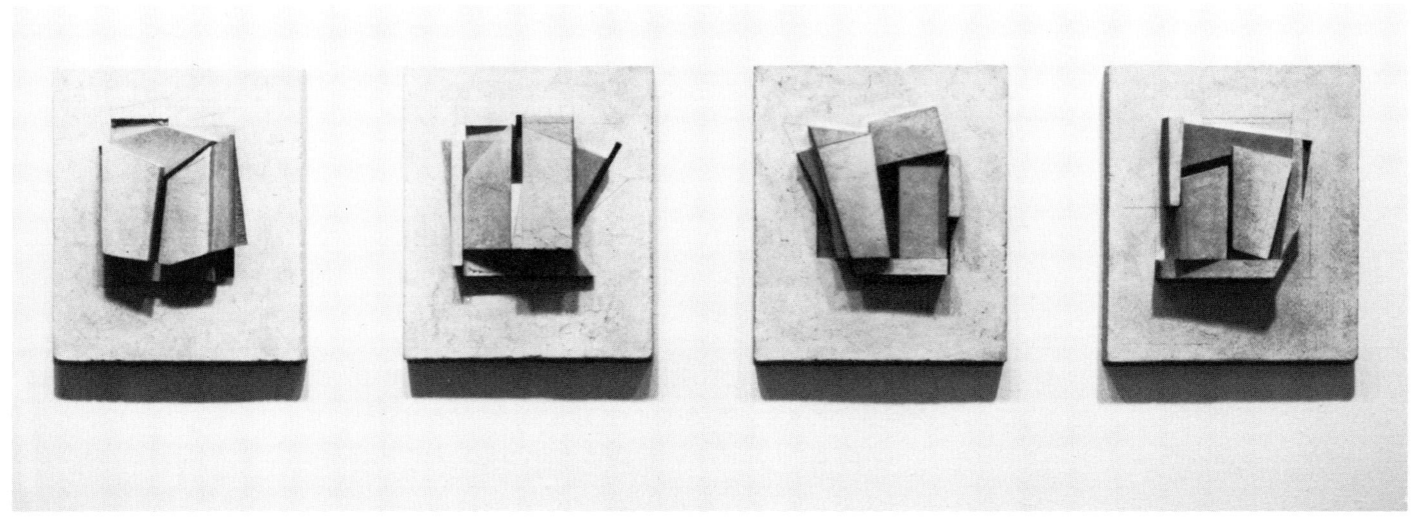

Nicholas W. Wood, **Facades II**, *1988,
terra-cotta with slips, glaze,
18 in. × 90 in. × 5 in.
Private collection*

Nicholas Wood's elegantly constructed *Facades II* is a complex of terra-cotta wall reliefs that recall Cubist painting. Wood's reliefs are built of overlapping areas of clay layered one on top of the other. Subtle changes occur as the eye travels from one to another. Shadows become an important component of these works; because the planes of the reliefs are built up, cast light takes on evocative associations. Wood uses shadow as he would another element of color and in the process provides refined abstracted icons.

Artists Jesús Bautista Moroles, Damian Priour, and Jill Sablosky work with organic references in their carved abstracted works of art.

Jesús Bautista Moroles knew that granite was his medium the first time he worked with it in college. The hardness of the material's surface coupled with the time and difficulty it took in carving impressed Moroles, who felt that the granite was in control of him. The material presented the sculptor a challenge other materials could not offer. Characteristically, Moroles' sculptures present contrasts of rough and smooth surfaces or organic forms and geometric shapes. Often the work refers to shrines, totems, or temples. It fuses the meaning of architecture with a technically sophisticated formal process, which results in potent form. Moroles generally uses Georgia gray granite or Texas pink granite in his work. In *Bas Relief*, Moroles' beheomoth slab of Georgia gray granite stands against a wall. At its top, it leans slightly away from the wall, which anthropomorphizes the piece. It is carved in eleven bands ranging from rough to smooth, which give detail to its surface. Overall the work reminds one of geological strata — layers of rock that have combined and compressed at different ages. The meaning to be found in *Bas Relief* circles back on itself. It is a slab of granite whose carving represents its origins from within the earth. *Bas Relief* overwhelms with its physical presence. One comprehends the work's solidity and weight yet delights in its sensual surfaces.

Damian Priour's *Stoneliths* juxtapose fossilized limestone with highly fused industrial glass. Priour likens them to "artifacts caught somewhere between the ritualistically carved liths of the past and the harnessed light of the future." [76] In this series of work, Priour places the blue-

76. Damian Priour, personal statement, *Third Coast Review: A Look at Art in Texas*, p. 45.

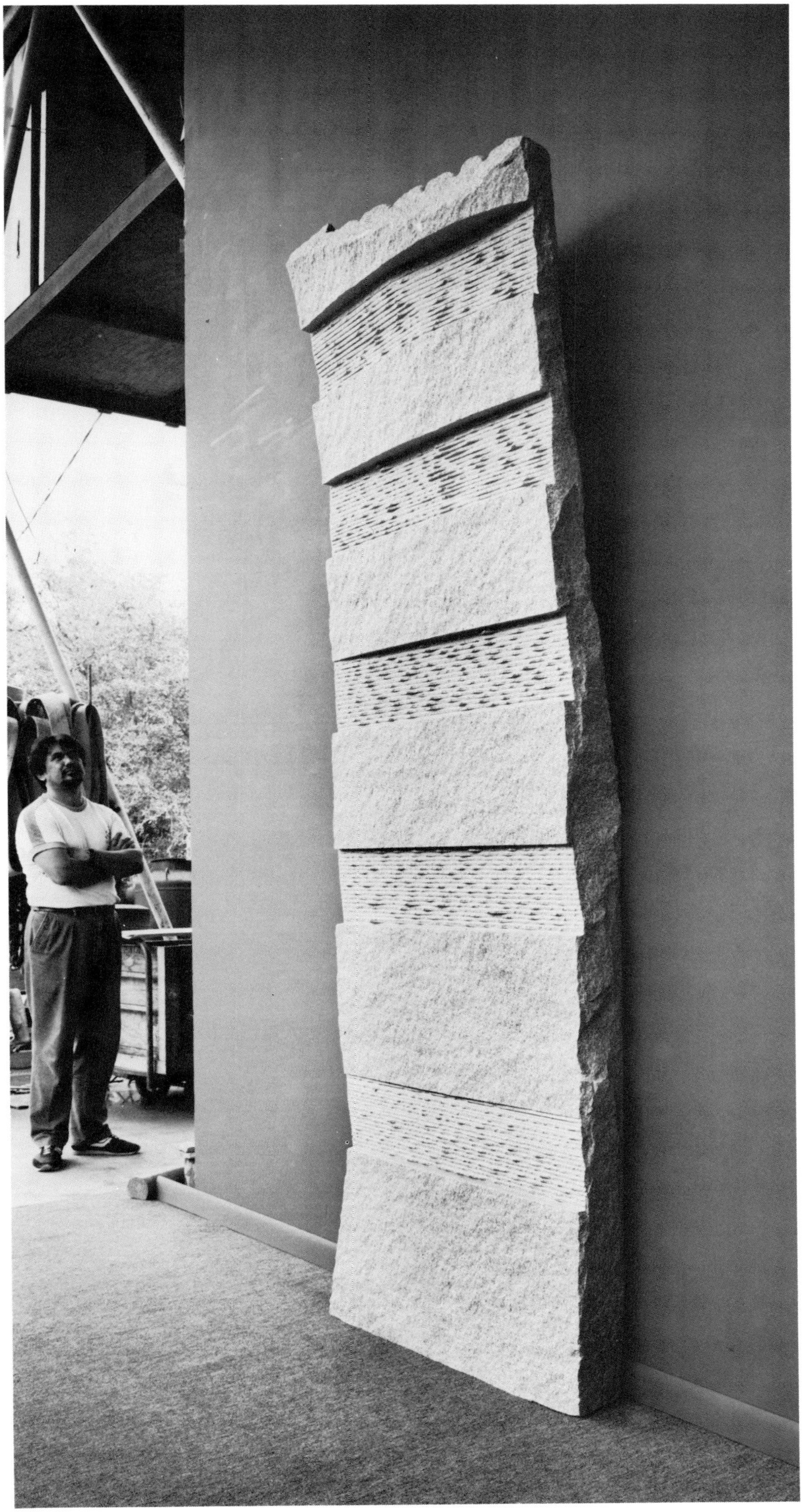

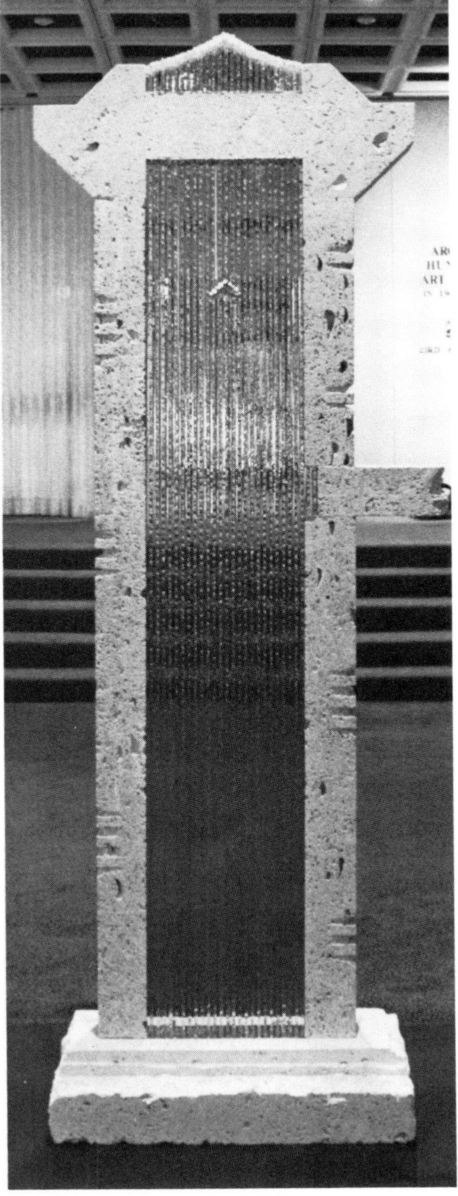

DAMIAN PRIOUR, Austin

Stonelith #136
1987
Texas limestone/plate glass
79½ in. × 25 in. × 12½ in.
Collection of Mary M. Rollins, Houston, on
long-term loan to the Archer M. Huntington
Art Gallery, The University of Texas at Austin

JESÚS BAUTISTA MOROLES, Rockport

Bas Relief
1988
Georgia gray granite
114½ in. × 37 in. × 14½ in.
Courtesy of the artist and Davis/McClain
Gallery, Houston

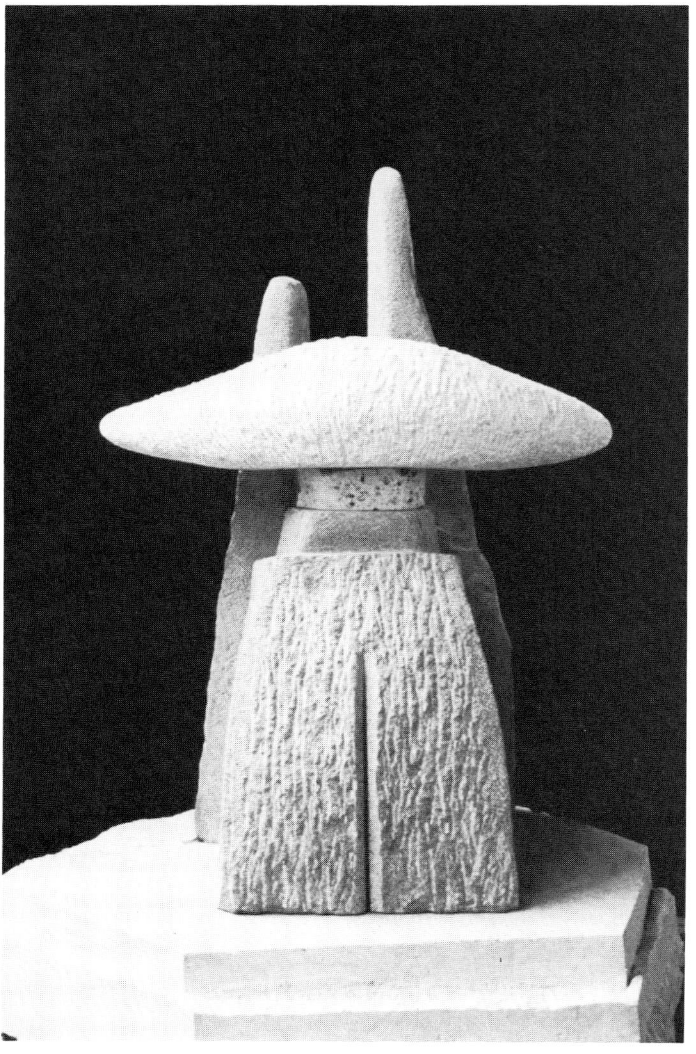

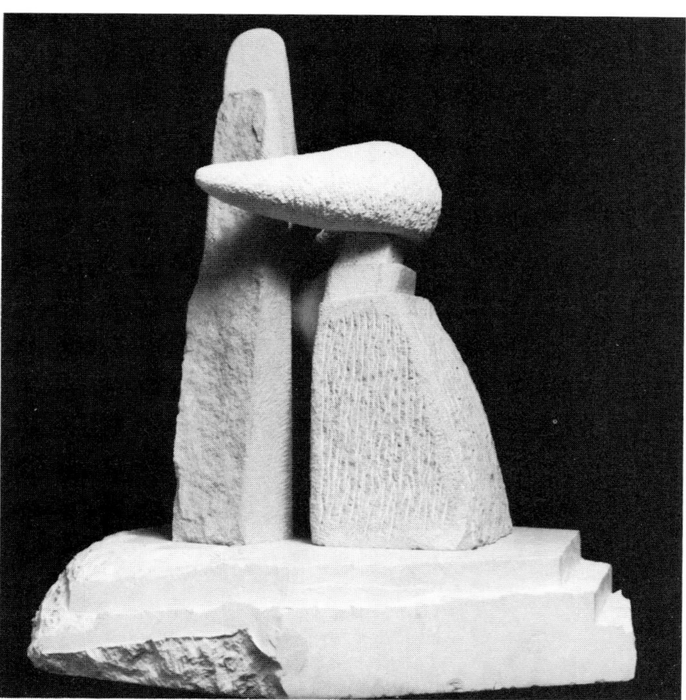

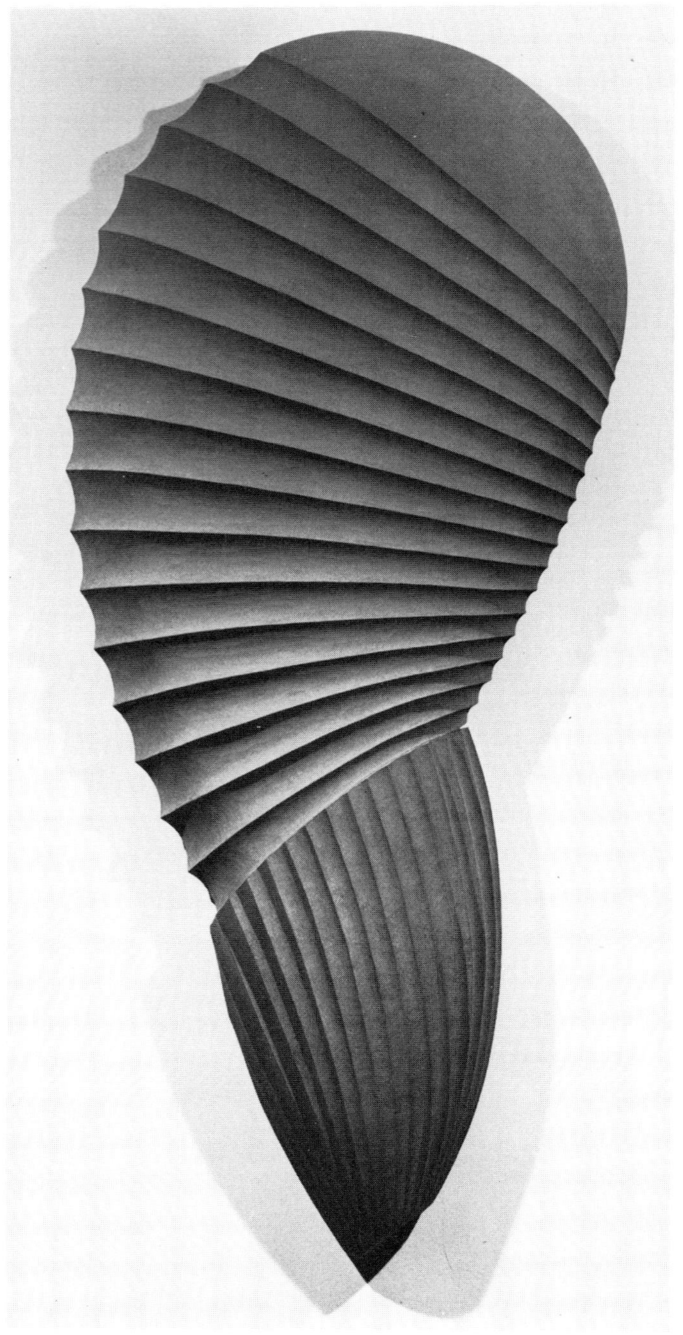

ROBERT BOURDON, Houston

Blue Velvet
1987
polychrome lindenwood
73 in. × 31 in. × 5 in.
Courtesy of the artist, Moody Gallery, Houston,
and Shoshana Wayne Gallery, Santa Monica

JILL SABLOSKY, Fort Worth

Guardian *(two views)*
1988
stone
34 in. × 28 in. × 26 in.
Collection of Dr. and Mrs. Blaine
McLaughlin, Fort Worth

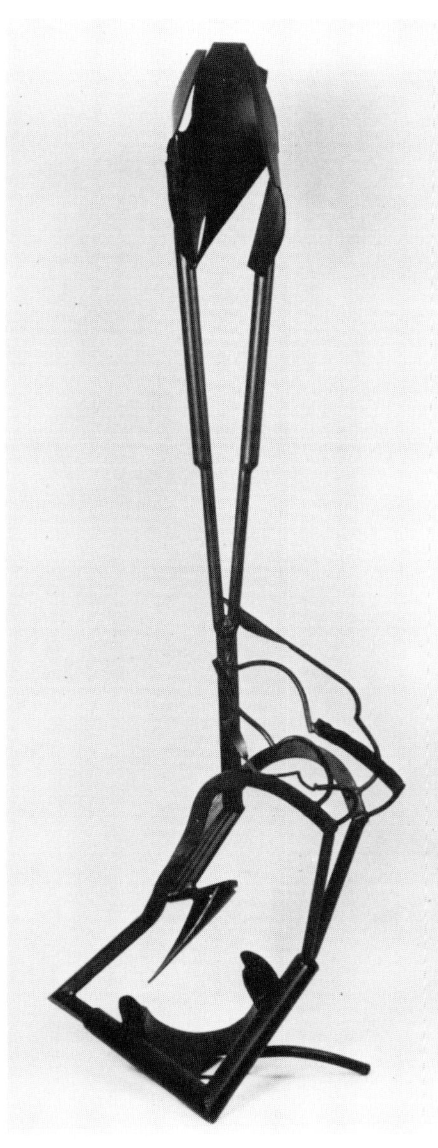

HAYDN LARSON, Houston

Family Tree
1989
steel
91 in. high
Courtesy of the artist, Read Stremmel
Gallery, San Antonio and Sally K. Reynolds
Fine Arts, Houston

green shades of the plate glass he uses in contradistinction to the white and embellished limestone with its indentations and recordings of a previous sea life. Having grown up in Corpus Christi and being comfortable with the sea and sand, Priour views the glass in his sculptures "as water frozen in time."[77] In *Stonelith Number 136,* Priour's monolithic sculpture appears to be sliced from the architecture of some ancient civilization. The silhouette of the column's post-and-lintel structure is made apparent in the cut of the limestone; the translucence of the piece glows with the interior or negative space filled with the fused plate glass. Priour has left a jagged hole in the glass, which casts shadows and changes the luminious perspective of the glass itself. Priour's stonelith columns imply strength and support as they also define grace and elegance.

Jill Sablosky's carved stone sculpture, like Damian Priour's, conjures the presence of ancient civilizations. Her works also incorporate post-and-lintel systems of construction, but, unlike Priour, Sablosky typically offers the viewer blocky, irregular, disproportionate forms that stack and sit one atop the other. There is a visceral, organic sensibility to the work, which also speaks to the architectonic. Potent images of mausoleums, monuments, and shelters are evoked in the work, which is couched in a contemporary abstract visual vocabulary. Both completely of her time and yet equally at home with the past, Sablosky captures the essence of the monolith. In *Guardian,* Sablosky presents an anthropomorphized stone figure under whose shield one could expect to find protection. Strictly abstract, the roughly carved limestone sculpture is meant to be seen from the front. It exudes the organic with several of its shapes seeming to have oozed from the hard stone. Sablosky's textures are varied; the carving of the stone evokes a refinement of technique, of sensibility, of meaning. Jill Sablosky, like Jesús Bautista Moroles, spent time in Italy carving from the stone quarries. She worked in Pietrasanta while Moroles worked in Carrara. Jill Sablosky's rough-hewn stone sculptures offer the viewer a monumentality of form imbued with classical sensibilities.

Artists Robert Bourdon, Haydn Larson, Jack Maxwell, Gerald Patrick, and Don Redman incorporate ideas of weaponry, tools, or machinery into their art. Each artist's response to these ideas is highly individualized with each using different materials and taking his ideas in different directions.

Robert Bourdon's imagery has ranged from trompe l'oeil reproductions of car doors to abstracted weapons and tools or the more organic as represented in *Blue Velvet.* While Bourdon's imagery has encompassed diverse subject matter, the form of his work remains constant. He works with carved wood, which sometimes is highly colored and polished; at other times the colors are muted or become completely monochromatic. Bourdon invests his contemporary shapes with ancient or "primitive" meanings as he refers to "a pre art-conscious."[78] In *Blue Velvet,* the surface reference is phallic, but below the surface the wall sculpture could as easily symbolize tools or weaponry. Bourdon's handsome form recalls the sculpture of contemporary artists Martin Puryear or Robert Therrien.

Haydn Larson's sculpture begins as a discarded bit of scrap metal or as a tool no longer of use and through the artist's hand becomes transformed and imbued with mysterious power. As a child, Larson spent summers on his grandparents' farm in Edinburg in the valley of South Texas. It was there that he became interested in farm tools and machinery. In 1970, following graduation from the University of Texas at Austin, Larson trav-

77. Sarah Wimer, "Glass: The Playground of Light," *Duende* 1, no. 2 (April 1988): p. 32.

78. Susan Chadwick, *Houston Post,* July 20, 1986, p. 4F.

eled to India to study an ancient art form, and there he embraced a new faith, Krishna Consciousness. Larson became a Hare Krishna monk and returned to the United States in 1974. In 1984 he moved to Houston, where he maintains his Hare Krishna faith and independently creates his art.[79] Larson's work harmoniously blends his religious faith with his early interest in the farm tools found on his grandparents' land. In *Family Tree*, Larson works with found-object materials and organic shapes to produce lyrical evocations of plant life. One can see reflections of a David Smith sculptural landscape where the steel twists and bends and outlines the negative space. *Family Tree* shows the viewer more readily the transformative process from tool to sculpture. Larson's sculptures fuse elegant surfaces with their abstracted forms. He usually welds, grinds, and paints the surfaces, which in turn reflect subtle, potent textures. Invested with a deeply felt religious sensibility, Haydn Larson's sculptures present the viewer objects of supreme authority and sovereignty.

Jack K. Maxwell's sculpture *Untitled* depicts an abstracted creaturelike object whose form derives from handsomely colored fabric, brightly polished brass plates, polished woods, and nuts and bolts held together with diaphanous, almost invisible string. He says the sculptures from the early 1980s derive from his examination of the stingray. The dichotomy of beauty combined with danger appeals to Maxwell. In the work there is an elegant use of wood; fabric takes on a skin-like appearance, stretched taut over a skeletal support. The wood and the brass form parts of the object's body and tail or antenna. The creature itself sits atop an aluminum base, which at once is separate from and a part of the whole. Some have observed an association of Maxwell's machines with Leonardo da Vinci's mechanical inventions; Maxwell says medieval weaponry, a fascination with animal and human anatomy, an interest in bilateral symmetry, and skeletal structures also intrigue him.[80] His work demonstrates his interpretations of mechanical and natural forms. Jack Maxwell's handsomely crafted sculpture allows the eye to follow paths of elegance and the mind to question its mysterious presence.

Gerald J. Patrick's coldly authoritative steel sculptures evoke various responses in viewers. Some retreat from the implied danger inherent in their form; others are drawn to it. In *Slasher*, these two contradictory attitudes are at work. On the one hand, the piece presents six fan-shaped blades of sharpened steel attached to an equal number of steel rods. The blades appear static and stationary from one point of view while they seem to rotate and move from another. The piece with its uniform steel blue color offers no warmth or consolation. On the other hand, the sculpture entices the viewer to flirt with its surface danger. It asks you to come closer. It dares you to seek the beauty in its chilly presence, to discover the subtle layers of power inherent in its concept. Patrick's sculpture is precise, machine-tooled, and industrialized; yet the refinement and sophistication of its forms project meanings of ceremony and ritual.

The kinetic art of Donald D. Redman responds to the air around it, and from this response its form is established. *Black Rogue* hangs from the ceiling and is counterbalanced at the bottom with a weight. Made of Dacron and attached to stainless steel struts, the piece evinces ideas of sailing or of floating as its movements define its formal characteristics of volume and space. Redman's father was a boatbuilder and Redman credits his father's influence on his art[81] — along with that of Luis Jimenez and James Surls, with whom he served internships. Redman's sculptures, like Haydn Larson's, are also about transformation. While Larson invests his work with spiritual value, Redman addresses laws of nature. His work, he says, is about ". . . gravity, centrifu-

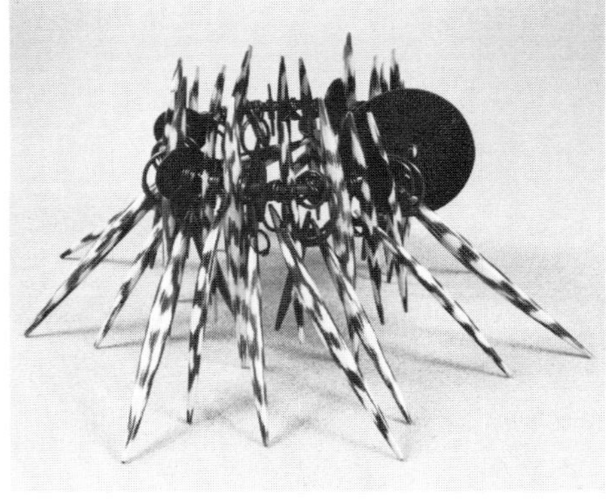

The spikey jewelry of El Paso artist Rachelle Thiewes elicits associations with tools and weapons. **Bengel II,** *1986, bracelet, 9 in. diameter (when laid flat), silver, carved slate, chemical and heat coloring.*

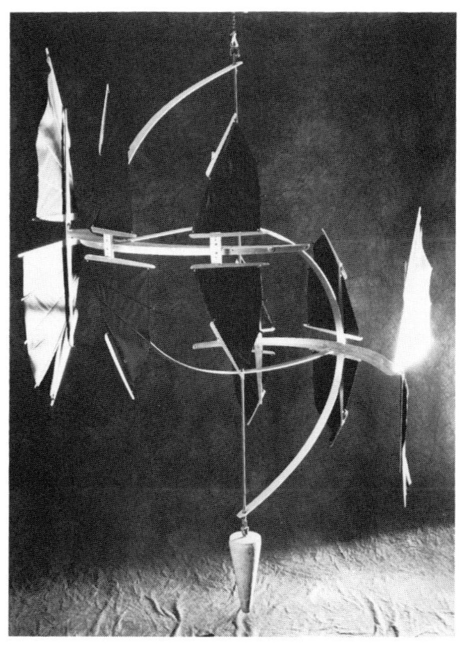

DONALD D. REDMAN, Houston

Black Rogue
1987
stainless steel, aluminum, Dacron
132 in. × 84 in. × 84 in.
Courtesy of the artist

79. Norris J. Fergeson, *Haydn Larson: Transformations,* exhibition catalog, Marion Koogler McNay Art Museum, San Antonio, Texas, 1988, unpaginated.

80. Artist's statement, 1981.

81. Susan Chadwick, *Houston Post,* May 17, 1987, p. 4f.

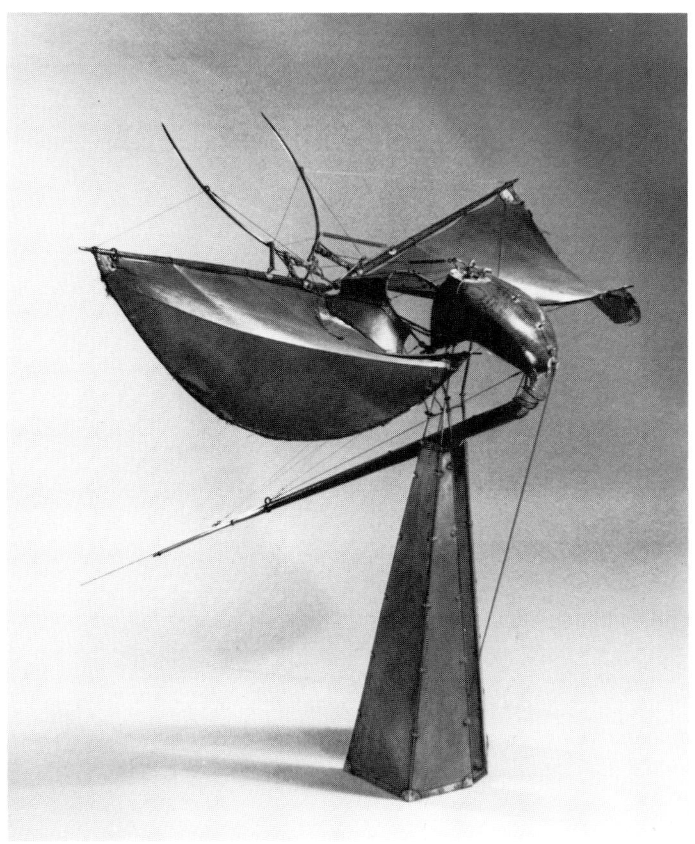

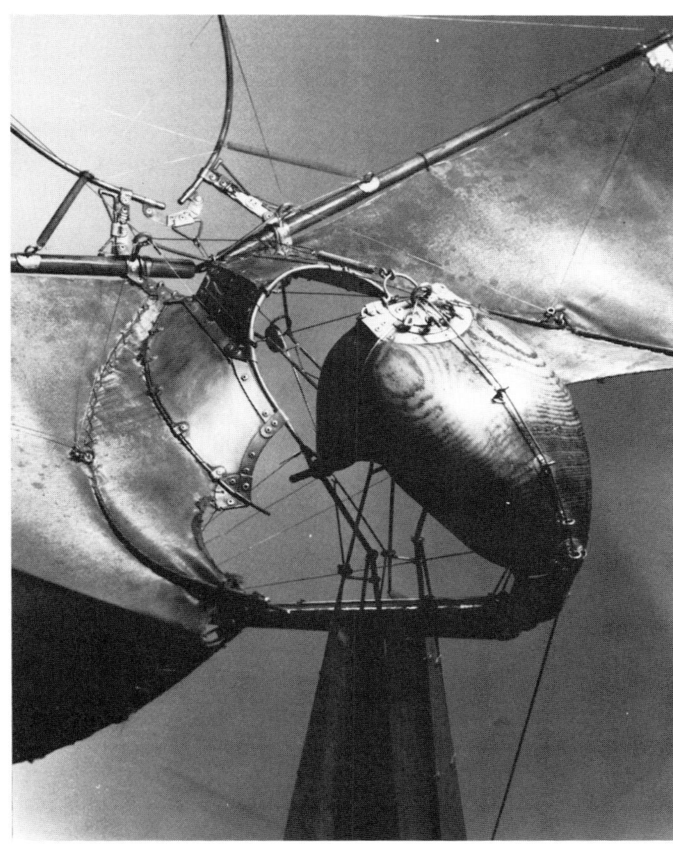

JACK K. MAXWELL, Abilene

Untitled
1981
brass, aluminum, paint, ash, stainless steel,
fabric
40 in. × 50 in. × 50 in.
Courtesy of the artist

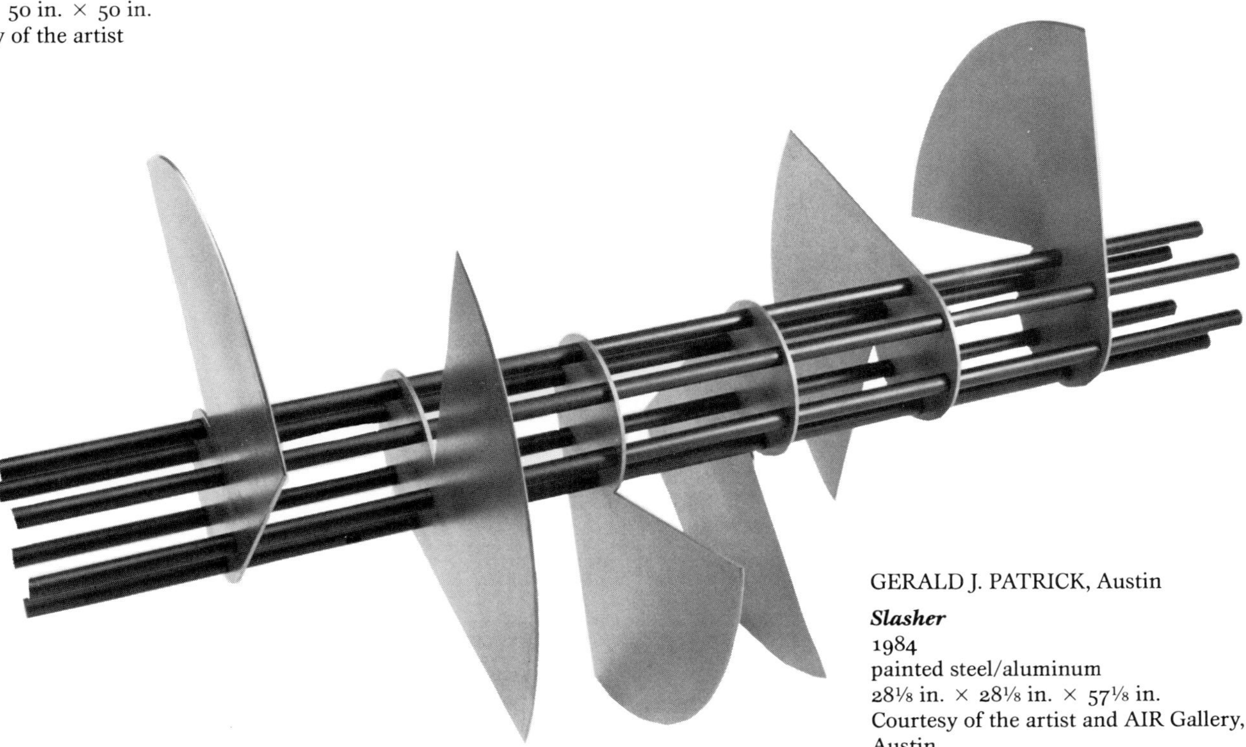

GERALD J. PATRICK, Austin

Slasher
1984
painted steel/aluminum
28⅛ in. × 28⅛ in. × 57⅛ in.
Courtesy of the artist and AIR Gallery,
Austin

gal force and balance, inspired by wind, water, growth, and decay. When you see my work in motion, it carries an entirely different personality depending on the seasons, the location, the environment."[82] Redman offers the viewer poetic, beautifully balanced "wind catchers," which rely on scientific technology for their form yet depend upon things of the earth for their interpretation.

Amarillo can boast of several important earthworks. The place is perfect for them. The land is flat, arid, accessible. And Stanley Marsh 3 owns land and lives there and supports the projects. In 1973 artist Robert Smithson with his artist wife, Nancy Holt, went to the Panhandle and staked out an earthwork, which came to be known as *Amarillo Ramp*. Marsh backed Smithson's plan to construct an earthwork in Lake Tecovas on his ranch. Smithson hired a plane to assist with aerial photography of the lake. Then he and Holt waded into the lake and staked out the piece. Dissatisfied with the original plan, however, Smithson again flew over the area in order to rechart the earthwork. The plane stalled, then crashed to the ground, killing all on board. After her husband's funeral and with the help of artist-friend Richard Serra and artist-dealer Tony Shafrazi, Holt returned to Amarillo and, following the plans Smithson laid out, completed the *Amarillo Ramp* within three weeks.[83] *Amarillo Ramp* is a spiral form built in the dry bed of Lake Tecovas. It is gradually elevated and one is unaware of the incline until midway up it. *Amarillo Ramp* provides a 360-degree vista of the landscape. In walking the ramp, one feels and recognizes relationships with nature; it makes one realize that "even if you think you know the pattern of the world, you still have to move through it to experience life."[84]

82. Don Redman, "Kinetic Rhyme," *eleven × fourteen*, l, no. 3, (summer 1988): 27.

83. John Coplans, "Robert Smithson, the Amarillo Ramp," exhibition catalog, *Robert Smithson: Sculpture*, Robert Hobbs, Herbert F. Johnson Museum of Art, Cornell University, Ithaca, New York, 1981, pp. 51–52.

84. Ibid., p. 54.

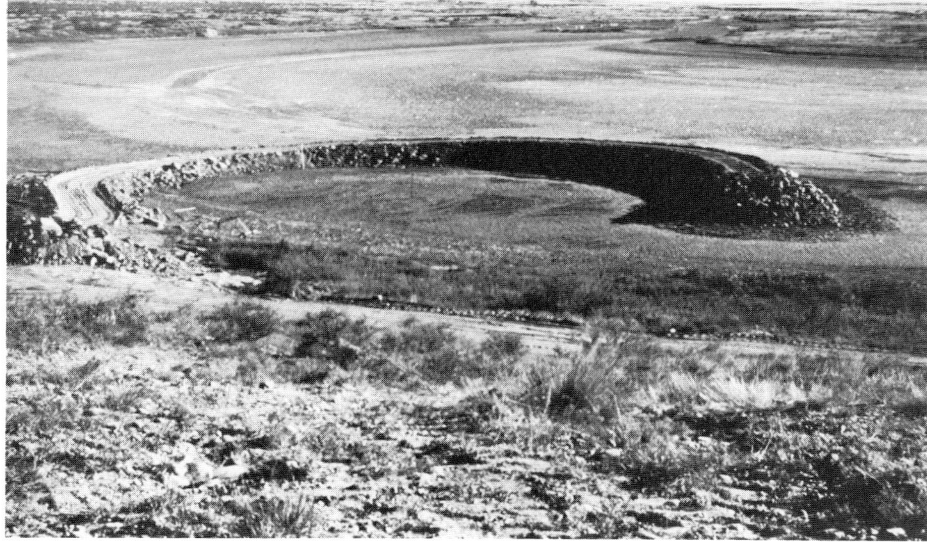

*Construction of Robert Smithson's **Amarillo Ramp**, 1973, Don Reynolds, Collection of the Amarillo Art Center.*

*Photograph of **Amarillo Ramp** by Robert Smithson, 1981, Wyatt McSpadden, Collection of the Amarillo Art Center.*

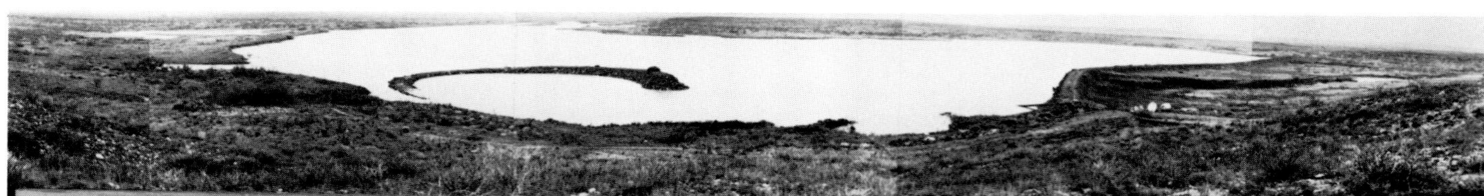

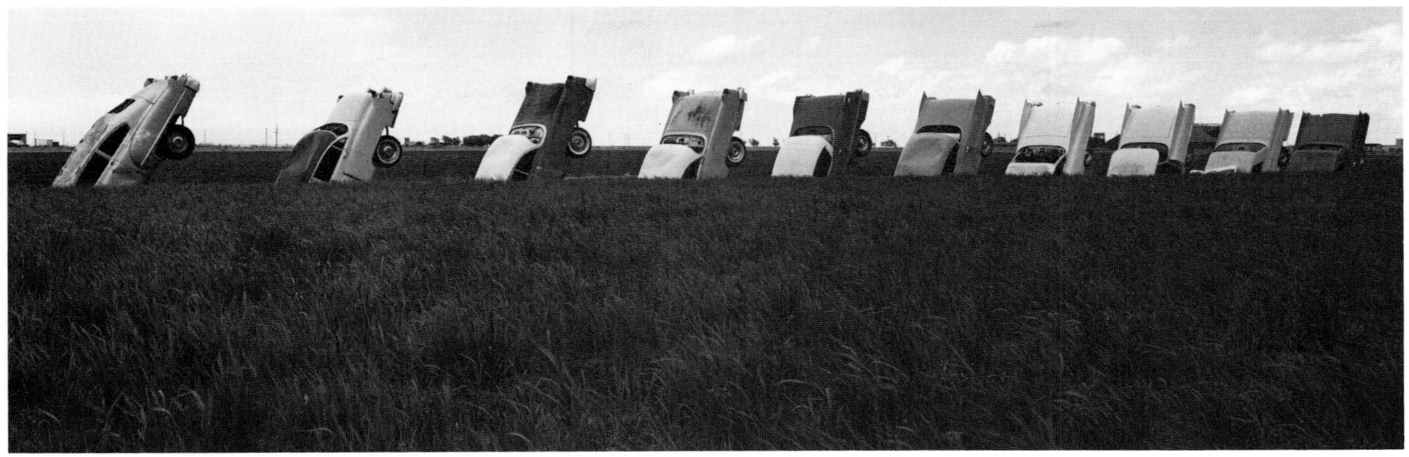

*Photograph of **Cadillac Ranch** by Ant Farm, 1981, Wyatt McSpadden, Collection of the Amarillo Art Center.*

Stanley Marsh is also responsible for *Cadillac Ranch,* a 1977 work constructed by the collaborative group, the Ant Farm. The sculpture consists of ten vintage Cadillacs buried in a maize field on the edge of old Route 66. *Cadillac Ranch*, according to Marsh, is a gift for the casual traveler. It is intended to add excitement and mystery for the automobile travelers covering the mind-numbing distances of the Panhandle. *Cadillac Ranch* certainly fulfills its intent. The piece is successful beyond its initial shock and surprise. When one gets out of the car, walks over, and looks at the work, ideas of death, decay, and destruction join first reactions of surprise and wonder. Stanley Marsh is also responsible for the earthwork entitled *Floating Mesa*, constructed by artist Edward Leicester. A horizontal band of aluminum is placed below the peak of a mesa. From a distance, the aluminum appears to cut and displace the land so that it appears to float. Stanley Marsh 3 has contributed a great deal to earthworks in the state. While some declare the works eccentric, they individually excite great interest and stand firmly as powerful works of art.

Other outstanding permanent earthworks or site-specific works in Texas include Nancy Holt's *Time Span*, commissioned in 1981 by the Laguna Gloria Art Museum in Austin. Constructed of concrete, stucco, and wrought iron, on the edge of the museum grounds near a lagoon of Lake Austin, the sculpture deals with ideas of change and the passage of time.

*Photograph of **Floating Mesa** by Andrew Leicester, 1981, Wyatt McSpadden, Collection of the Amarillo Art Center.*

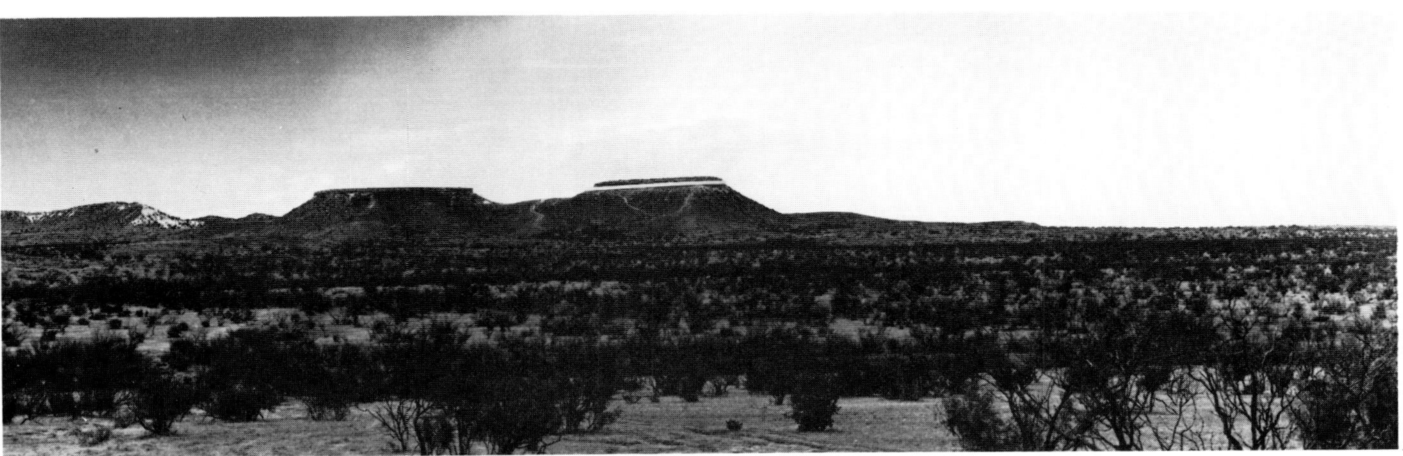

The city of Abilene commissioned artist Larry Bell to create an outdoor piece for Nelson Park Lake in 1982. Bell's glass sculpture deals with refracted and reflected light. In *Wind Wedge* triangular glass prisms cast aerial colors on the water as it provides a contemplative oasis in an arid part of Texas.

Some artists in the state are concerned with environmental sculpture. Herb Rogalla has been interested in this type of art form for over twenty years. Frances Bagley, too, continues her interest in creating a work of art that directly relates to its site.

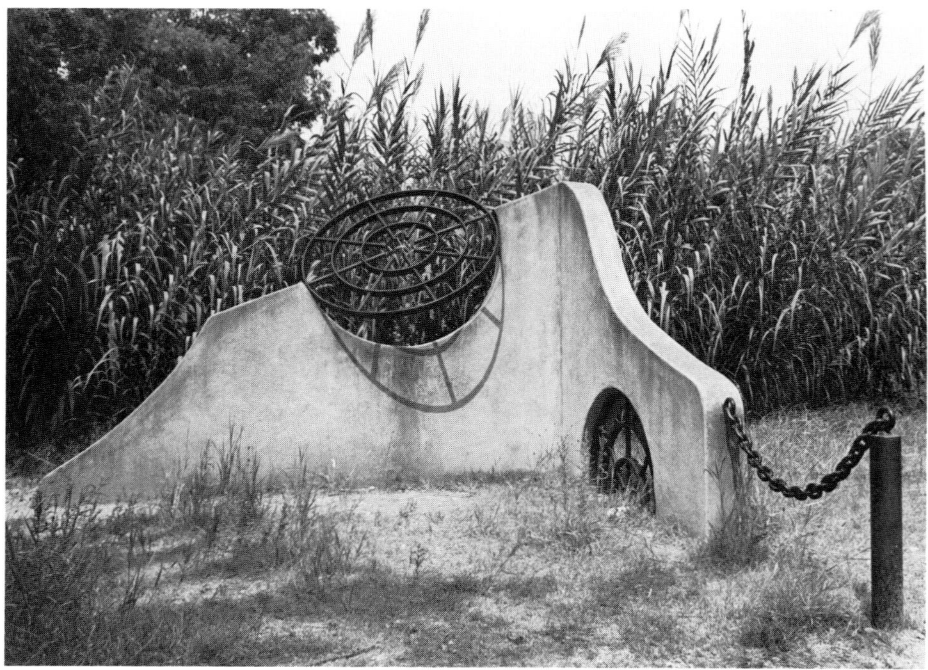

Nancy Holt, **Time Span**, *1981, Laguna Gloria Art Museum, Austin.*

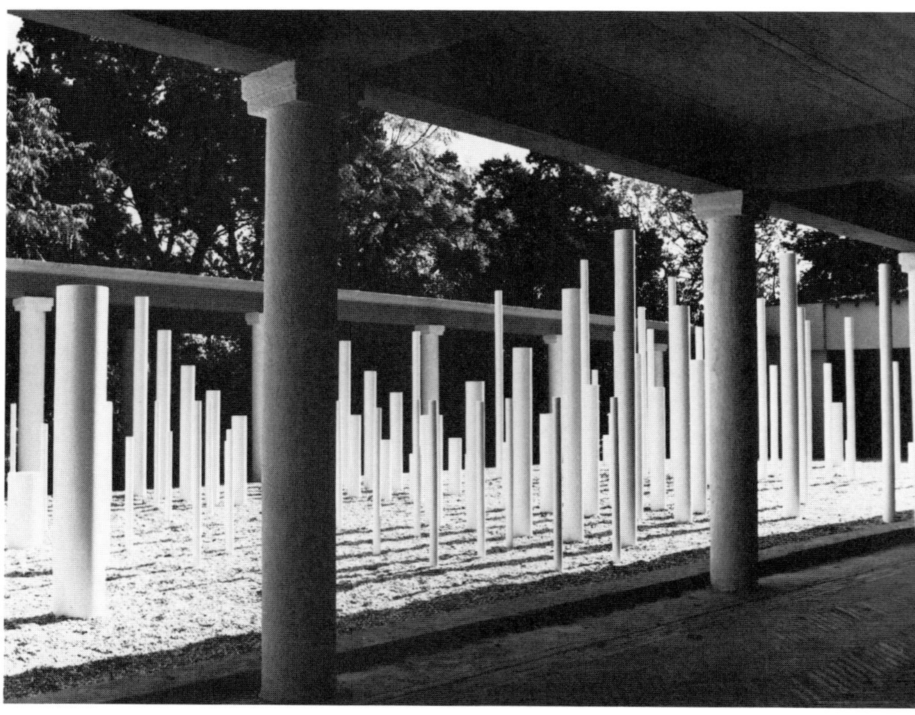

Herb Rogalla, **Huaco White**, *the Art Center Waco, 1977–1982, ll ft. × 31 ft. × 80 ft., white industrial PVC.*

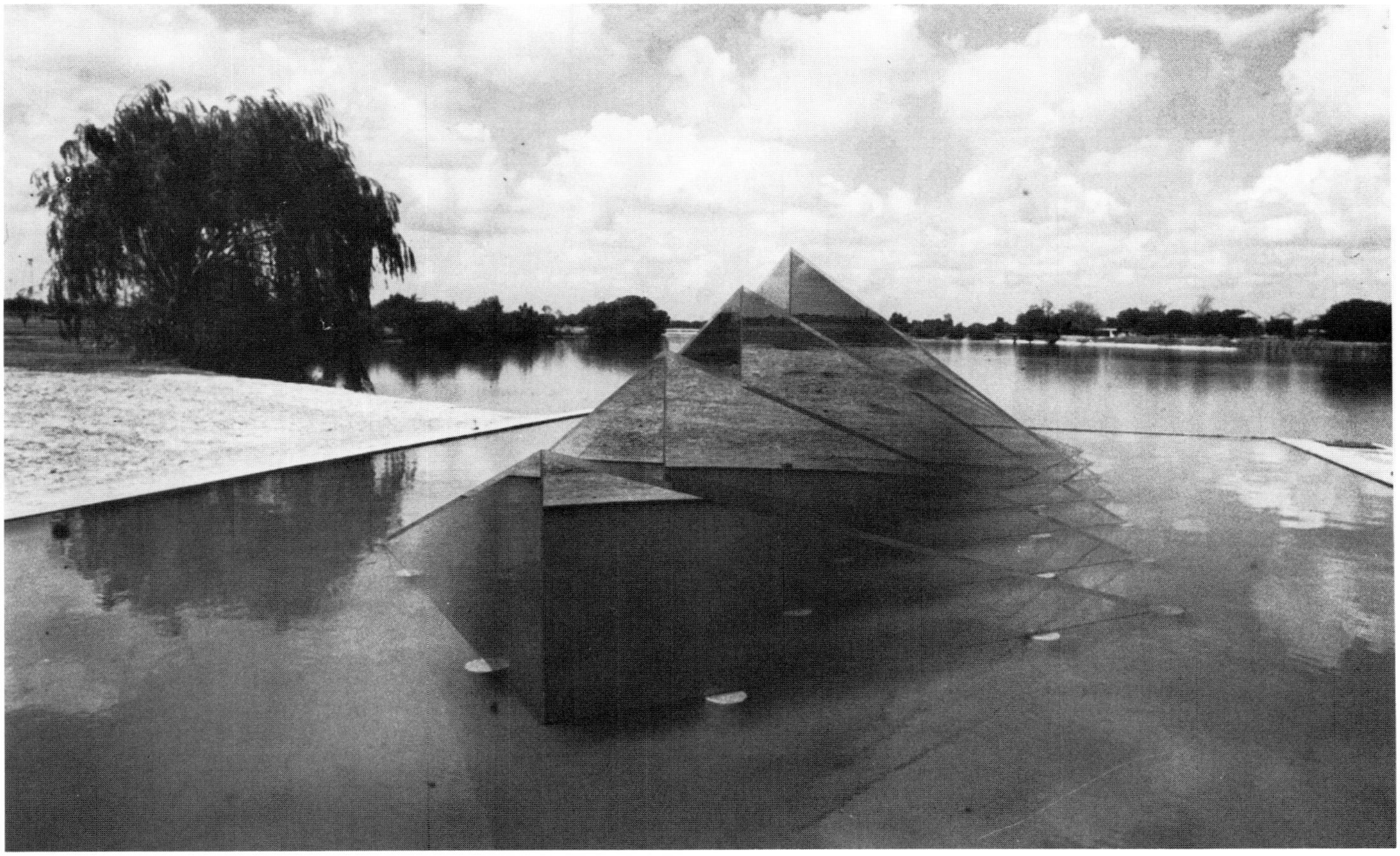

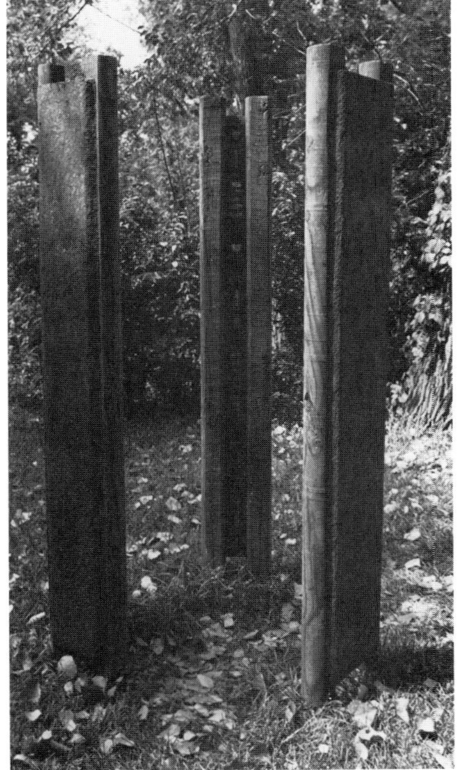

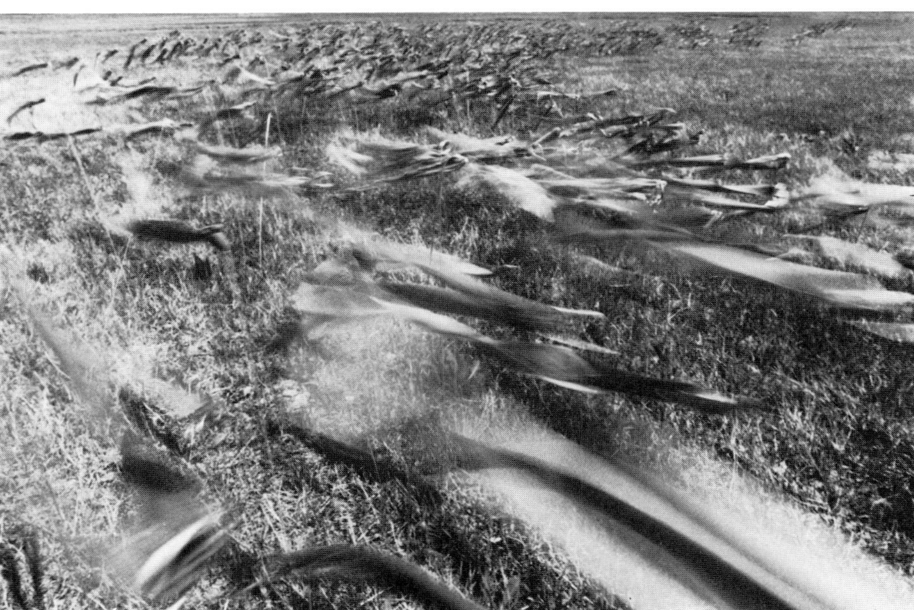

Larry Bell, **Wind Wedge,** 1982, plate glass,
Nelson Park Lake, Abilene.

Clyde Connell, **Interior/Exterior Place,** 1983,
Laguna Gloria Art Museum, Austin.

Frances Bagley, **Lost Sounds,** 1986, cloth, wind,
environmental sculpture.

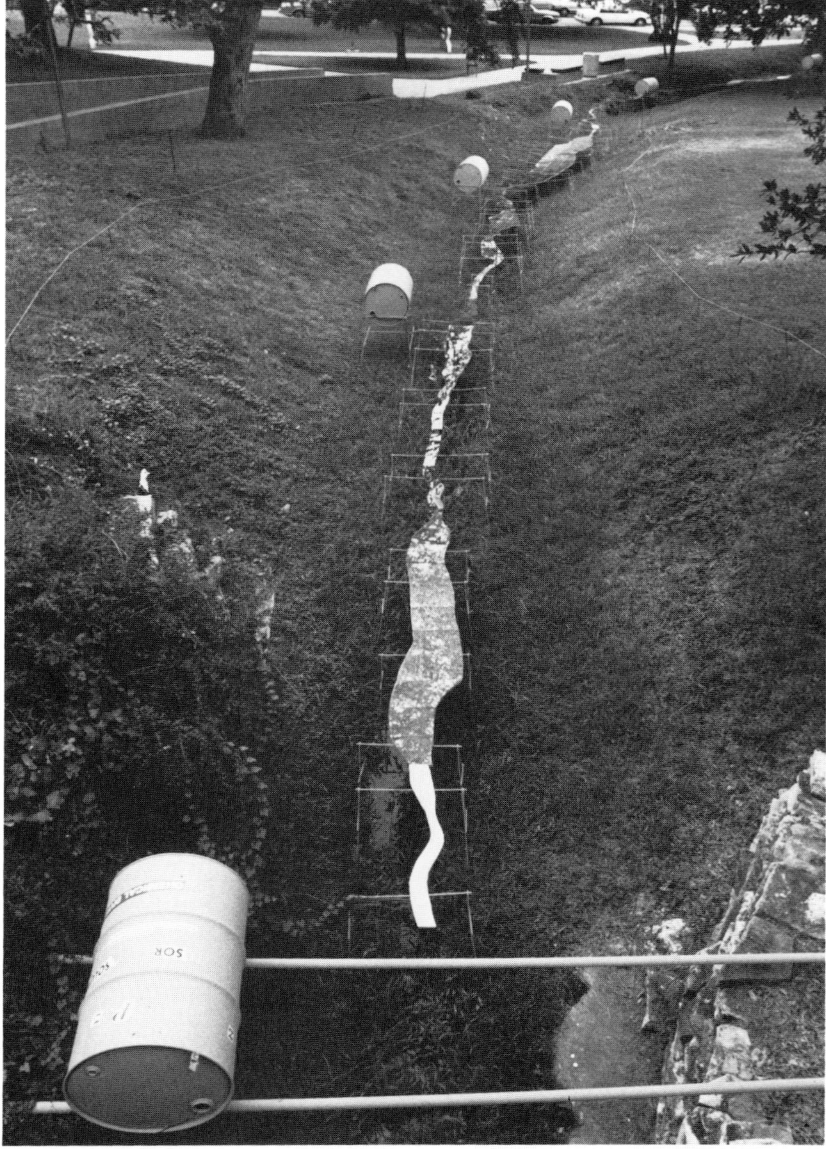

THANA LAUHAKAIKUL, Austin

A Song of Yellowcake
1989
mirrored tile, stereo equipment, pencil steel,
steel drums
36 in. × 24 in. × 7,200 in. (3 ft. × 2 ft.
× 600 ft.)
environmental sculpture
Courtesy of the artist

Thana Lauhakaikul in his *A Song of Yellowcake* incorporates the land in his deeply felt work of art which goes beyond site in its message. Lauhakaikul's art investigates people and their spiritual awareness. The works express "the poetry of a cosmic vision," and they attempt "a synthesis of eastern and western thought . . . they offer an emotional richness rarely communicated in recent art."[85] Of this piece, constructed of industrial steel barrels painted yellow; hundreds of mirrored glass tiles; synthesized and amplified sound ensconced in a small creek bed on the University of Texas at Austin campus Lauhakaikul said:

"It will be clear like crystal, cool like ice at the end of light beams, and dangerous like a calculating heart of murder. I predict that it will still itself when we stop walking but, when we move, the stream will flow and, on a sunny day, it may blind us."[86] Ultimately, Thana Lauhakaikul's *A Song of Yellowcake* resonates with elegistic meaning and ecological apprehension.

85. Annette Di Meo Carlozzi, *New Works, Summer 82*, exhibition catalog, Laguna Gloria Art Museum, Austin, 1982, p. 11.

86. Artist's statement, January 1989.

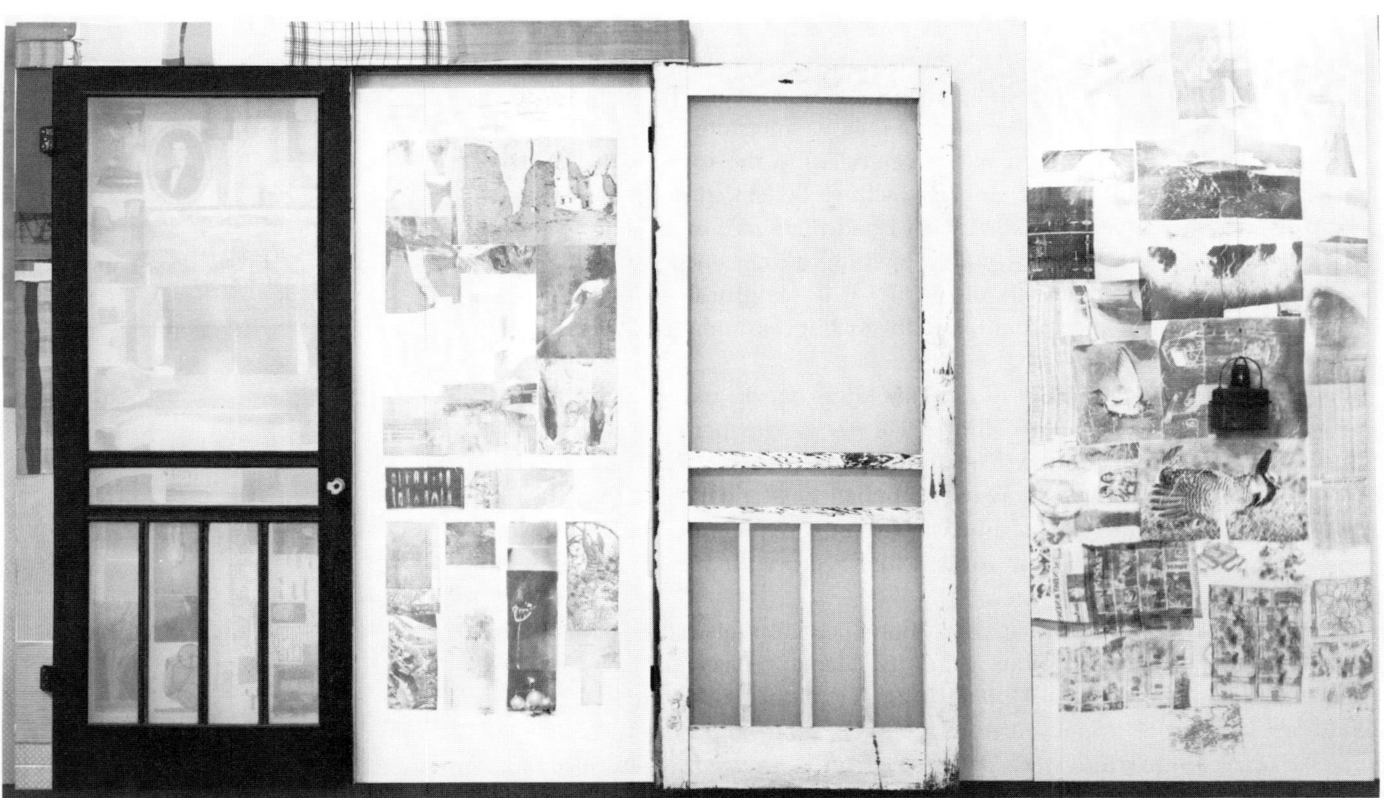

Robert Rauschenberg, **Whistle Stop (Spread),**
1977, combine painting, mixed media, five panels,
each 84 in. × 36 in. Collection of the Modern Art
Museum of Fort Worth, Museum Commission and
Purchase, the Benjamin J. Tillar Memorial Trust.

The art of Texas-born Robert Rausch-
enberg almost single-handedly redefined twentieth-century concepts of painting
and sculpture. His works, which he called "combines," go beyond traditional
definitions and offer inventions of a new form of art. Originating in the collages
and constructions of Kurt Schwitters and some of the Dadaists, Rauschenberg's
art includes references to specific topics and associations as it combines Abstract
Expressionist paint surfaces with actual objects. Rauschenberg's influence on the
art of our time has been monumental. In 1976 Richard Koshalek, then director
of the Fort Worth Art Museum, organized an exhibition entitled The Great
American Rodeo. Rauschenberg — along with Red and Mimi Grooms, John Al-
berty, Terry Allen, Ed Blackburn, George Green, Joe Ferrell Hobbs, Andy Mann,
Garry Winogrand, and Joe Zucker — was included in the exhibition. Within a
year Rauschenberg created *Whistle Stop (Spread)* which was subsequently purchased by the Modern Art Museum of Fort Worth. A mammoth piece, *Whistle
Stop (Spread)* included two doors which open to reveal art reproductions, newspaper collage, and other disparate elements. Rauschenberg's art had, of course,
influenced artists in the state before his inclusion in this exhibition, but The
Great American Rodeo brought Rauschenberg's art up-close and back to Texas
subjects.

Artist Vernon Fisher, like Rauschen-
berg, defies definition as either a painter or a sculptor. Fisher's art encompasses
both traditions in his work, which characteristically incorporates sculptural and
painterly elements. In his narrative canvases or in his installations painted directly on gallery or museum walls with added three-dimensional elements, Fish-

er's work goes beyond categorization. In *Fountain of Sorrow,* he transforms a raw object into a witty comment on art and the "inside" art world. Fisher takes a urinal like Duchamp did in 1917 and presents it as a work of art. He goes further, however, by incorporating a reference to a famous anecdote about Jackson Pollock but written in Fisher's own narrative style. On the inside surface of the urinal he writes: "I told her the story of Jackson Pollock at a party, pissing in Peggy Guggenheim's fireplace. 'Gee I wish I had the nerve to do that,' she said. 'Well, you could,' I said, 'but it wouldn't look quite the same.'"[87] In this piece, Fisher unites various components of his art: it is sculptural, it is narrative, it plays with historic form and content, and through its assimilation it derives new meaning.

Joe Guy's work, too, challenges traditional concepts of painting and sculpture. He stretches paper over struts, which he then soaks and dries. He next covers the paper's surface with graphite and burnishes it until he captures an all-over monochromatic darkness. Guy, trained as an architect, melds the two disciplines of art and architecture in his stunningly simple, exquisitely contemplative works, which require the viewer to search quietly for their meaning.

Bob Tiemann also offers work that goes beyond established definitions. Recently, Tiemann has embraced new ideas due to direct association with Donald Judd. Tiemann works with the concept that all art is abstract — removed from reality as it is — and that, therefore, specific form is irrelevant. In *Sand Collection,* Tiemann works with conceptual ideas based on time and space. The form the work takes is a series of photographs, which, if one were to believe the captions, represent sand collected from the major beaches of the world. A bottle full of sand accompanies the series of framed, narrative photographs. Tiemann says the work also has to do with per-

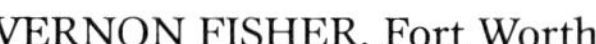

VERNON FISHER, Fort Worth

Fountain of Sorrow
1986
paint on porcelain
41 in. × 13½ in.
Courtesy of the artist and Hiram Butler Gallery, Houston

Joe Guy, **Volume: Book of Hours,** *1988,*
16 in. × 19 in. × 2¾ in.

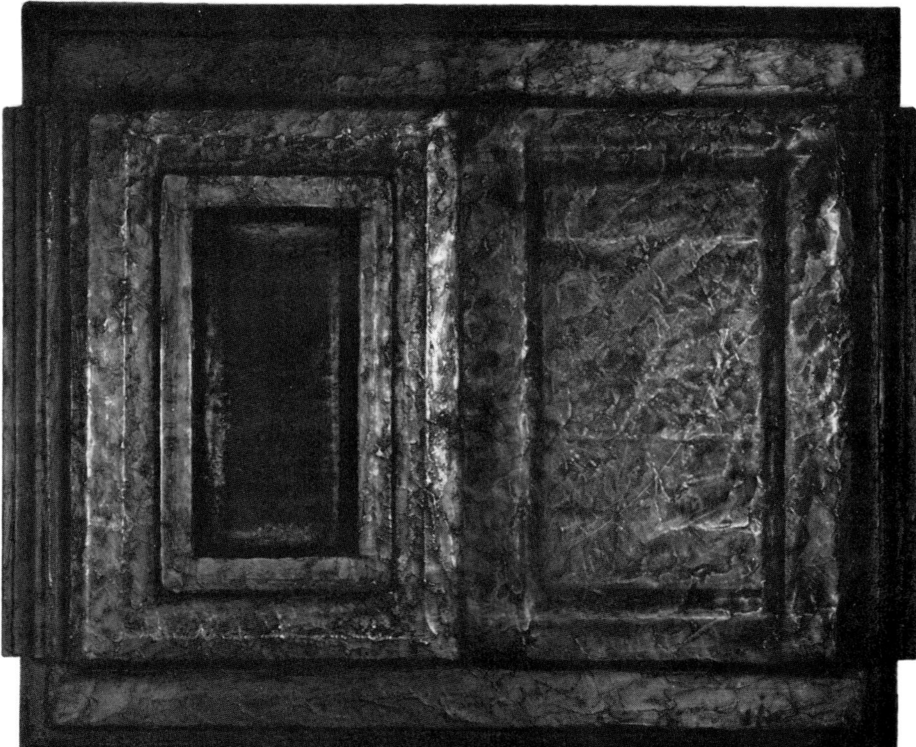

87. Vernon Fisher, *Navigating by the Stars: Writings by Vernon Fisher* (Chicago: Landfall Press, 1989), p. 22.

88. Bogdan Perzysnki, in exhibition catalog, *Bogdan Perzynski, Works, 1984–87,* essay by Robert McDonald, Shoshana Wayne Gallery, Santa Monica, 1987, unpaginated.

89. Ibid.

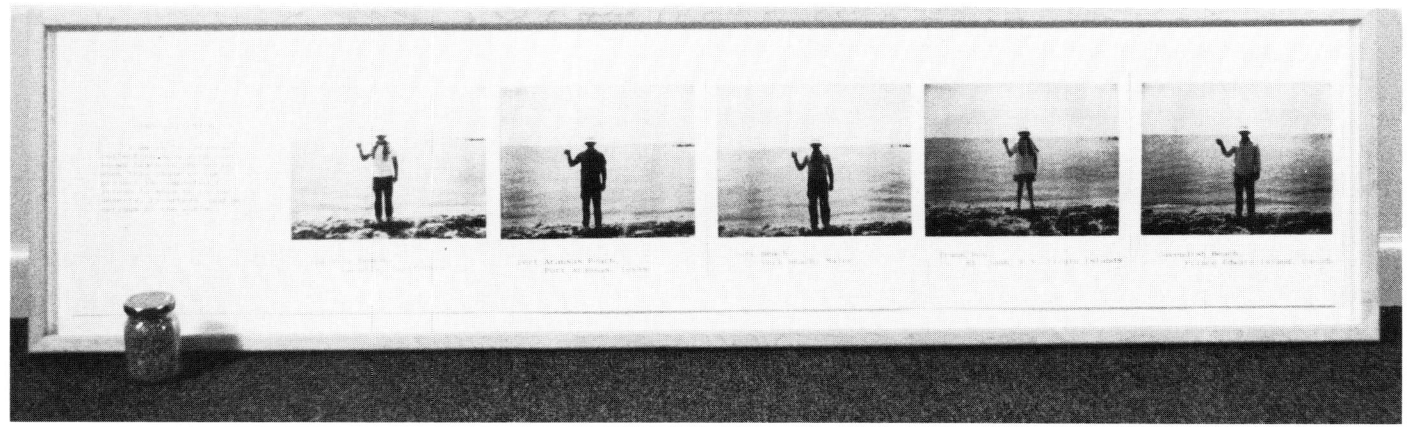

Bob Tiemann, **Sand Collection,** *1988, photo collage with jar of sand.*

ceptions, for if you look closely, you realize that what appear to be different beach locations are in reality the same site. Tiemann plays with the perceptions of both viewer and artist in this work, which is both conceptual and ostensibly site specific at the same time.

"As an artist, painting is no different to me than sculpture,"[88] observes Bogdan Perzynski. It is equally apparent that Perzynski's art is dense and multileveled in meaning while it is subtly evocative and elusive in form. Perzynski's works are self-defining and come directly from his personal life.[89] In *Ultimate,* sheets of burgundy-colored dyed canvas drape from covered supports; two steel and lead banners lean on the canvas; in a glass case is lint from an electric dryer; a canvas bag leans against the wall next to the banners; on the floor in front of the piece are lead letters that spell the word *ultimate.* The work derives, the artist says, from a domestic, everyday occurrence. His studio occupied the same space as the family washer and dryer. The comings and goings necessary in doing the laundry continually interrupted Perzynski's thought and work. Rather than struggle with his situation, Perzynski incorpo-

BOGDAN PERZYNSKI, Austin

Ultimate
1986–87
lint in glass box, dyed canvas, oil on canvas, lead, steel
64 in. × 108 in. × 43 in.
Courtesy of the artist and Shoshana Wayne Gallery, Santa Monica

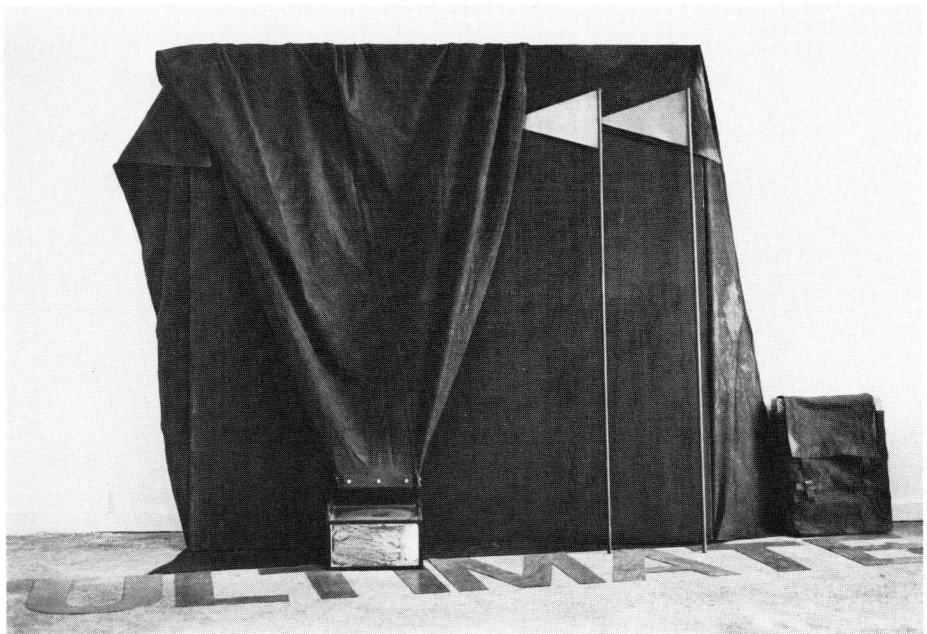

rated it into his art. The piece then could represent the "ultimate" conclusion of his circumstances. He could make a work of art about the laundry, about the continual interruptions, and *ultimately* about the basic and fundamental reality of his place at that moment and at that time. Perzynski's art more characteristically draws on his European and specifically Polish roots. There is a deep level of political examination in the work; it is based on existentialist philosophy, and it is demanding in its interpretation. Perzynski brings to the United States and to Texas his carefully constructed and deciphered observations on life, art, and politics.

Bill Lundberg has used film in his installations — which he has termed "film sculptures" — since the mid-1970s. The subject of Lundberg's work generally comes from examination of human relationships. He has said: "... I was compelled to elaborate this theme with a combination of symbolism, visual games, illusions and real documentation."[90] Lundberg's art, like Bogdan Perzynski's, exists on numerous levels. Lundberg's references include literature and psychotherapy, with lighter shades of Surrealism. His work examines the world around him; it questions assumptions and through the questioning offers solutions. In *Vacation Console*, Lundberg juxtaposes a two-hour video that depicts blowing sand on a beach within a plain pine box that also displays a bug lamp enclosed within Plexiglas. The piece examines the idea of expectations: a family vacation planned to be a happy occasion in reality evolves into a frustratingly irritating experience. In *Vacation Console* Lundberg makes deft statements on aspects of life often overlooked or repressed.

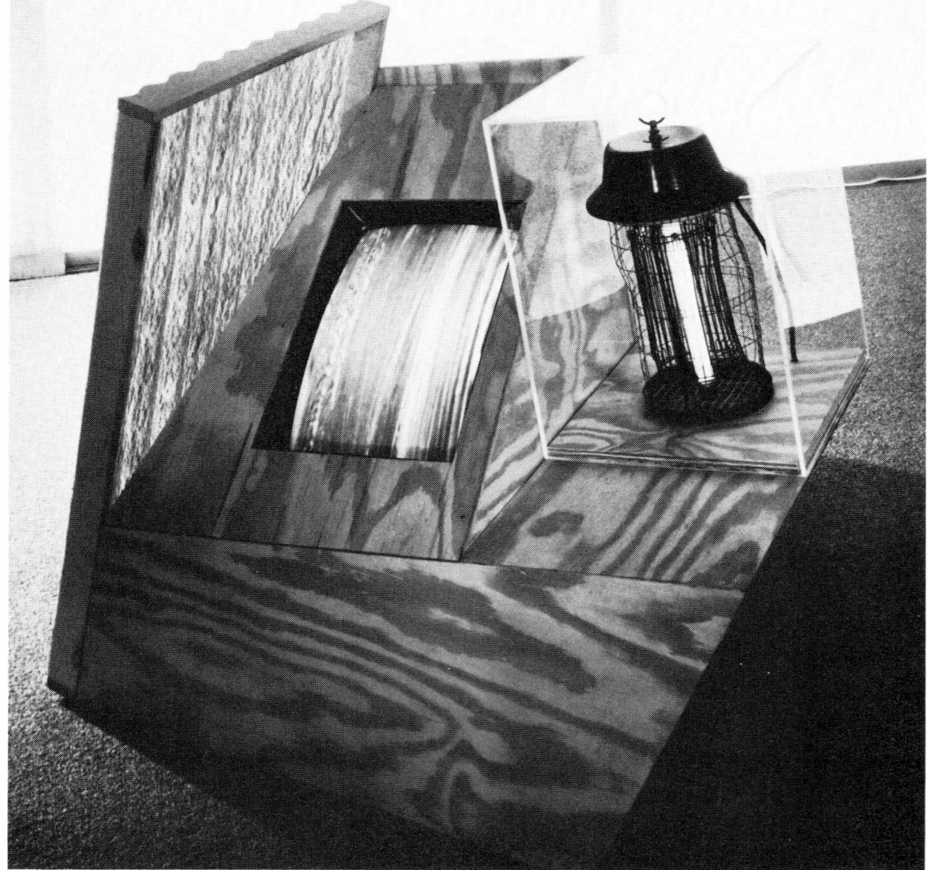

WILLIAM LUNDBERG, Austin
Vacation Console
1988
mixed media: wood, acrylic, video, bug lamp
40½ in. × 41½ in. × 26¾ in.
Courtesy of the artist

90. Bill Lundberg, in *Film Installations*, exhibition catalog, Emily Davis Gallery, University of Akron, Akron, Ohio, 1987, p. 36.

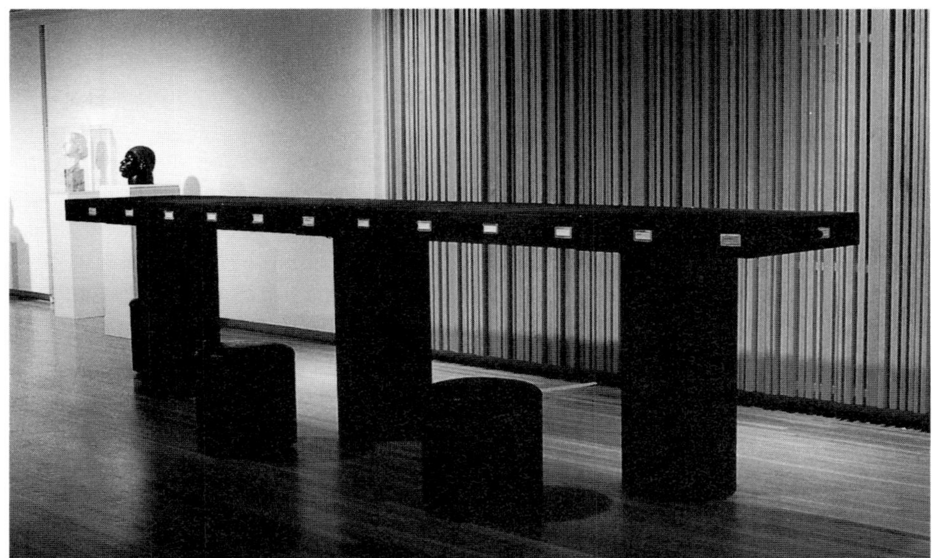

JIM POMEROY, Arlington

Reading Lessons and Eye Exercises
1985–1988
mixed media: 26 stereoscopic views installed
on wooden table w/stools
192 in. × 45 in. × 35 in.
Courtesy of the artist

Performance and installation artist Jim Pomeroy's *Reading Lessons and Eye Exercises* posits imaginary and impossible artworks placed within landscapes through the process of photomontage. Drawing upon old stereo archives, Pomeroy appropriates images and then bedecks them with wry labels[91] that derive from his interest in language and the pun. Long interested in adaptations of late-nineteenth and early-twentieth century photographic techniques, Pomeroy challenges both Mr. Wizard and the viewer in his optical inventions and reinterpretations.

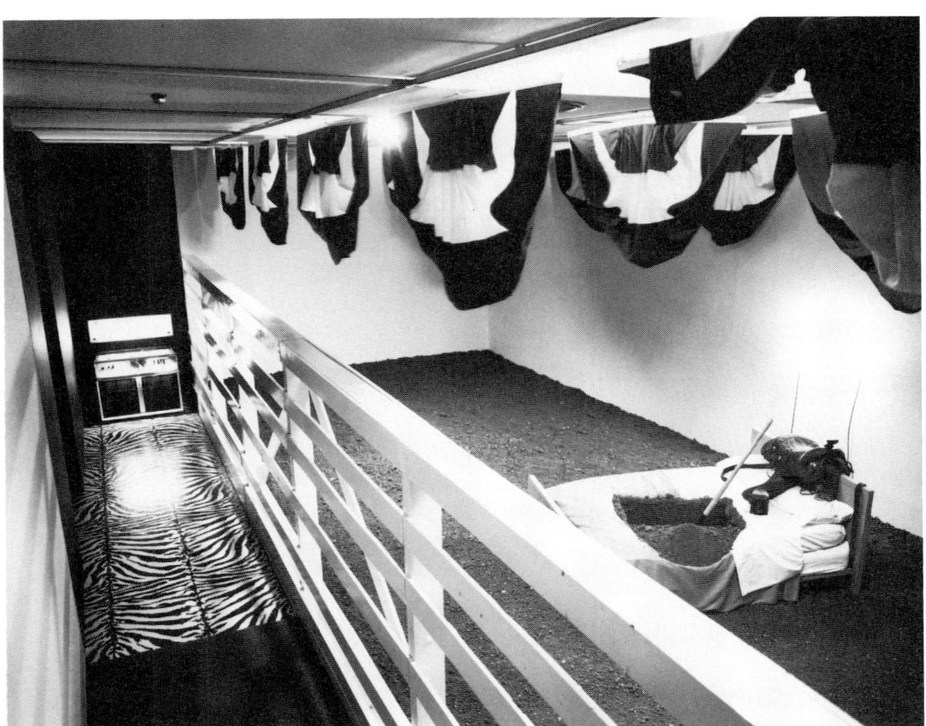

*Terry Allen's installation **The Paradise** was commissioned by the Modern Art Museum of Fort Worth for The Great American Rodeo exhibition of 1976. The work reproduced a sleazy lounge and motel room that metamorphosed into a rodeo arena.*

What can we hope to surmise from an exhibition as disparate and potentially unwieldy as A Century of Sculpture in Texas? Setting out to survey a large number of artists (often represented by only one work of art) assures diversity. By discussing artists within stylistic categories, however, we are better able to understand through juxtaposition divergent examinations of a shared theme. For example, artists as dissimilar as Patricia Tillman and Joseph Havel incorporate architectural themes within their work — yet each approaches the subject from totally differing points of view. Jill Sablosky and Jesús Bautista Moroles share an aesthetic sensibility toward stone, but each produces objects of distinct style. Grouping sculpture into unique categories can assist the viewer to comprehend an otherwise overwhelming body of visual information. There is not one distinct style of Texas sculpture. Artists in the state incorporate mythic imagery as much as they look to national and international trends in contemporary art. Styles of abstraction and figuration, Expressionism and Minimalism find outlets in the artistic creations produced in the state.

Texas artists are also creating sculpture that is of high caliber. There is an originality of artistic vision in the state that truly stands on its own. There is a strength of ideas and emotions conveyed in the works' intent and in the technical proficiency employed by the artists. In Texas, unlike other states without our shared mythology, attitudes linger that deal more with intangibles like a belief in self, optimistic approaches to everyday concerns, and the ability of the individual to triumph. The history of the state provides these inground belief systems, which at either a conscious or a subconscious level pervade our thought.

What can we surmise from A Century of Sculpture in Texas? We realize that it is possible to learn from our past and to value our history. We understand that artists of our day have unique and often compelling visions. And, we learn that by studying the art they present we are able to comprehend events with added insight. These sculptors are providing the ultimate gift of enlightenment. We surmise, then, that A Century of Sculpture in Texas enables us, the viewers, to enrich ourselves, on the one hand, and to foster the creative contributions that Texas artists have made, on the other.

PHOTO CREDITS

Abilene Cultural Affairs Council
Amarillo Art Center
Bruce Berman
Steve Denme
Tracy Hicks
George Holmes
John Hooper
Richard Krall
Ted Kuykendall
Frank Martin
Peter Mears
Connie Moberly
Linda Schlecht

compiled by Adele Thanheiser   **BIOGRAPHIES OF THE CONTEMPORARY ARTISTS**

RONALD BOLING

Born 1943, St. Joseph, Missouri

1966   B.F.A., Kansas City Art Institute and School of Design, Kansas City, Missouri

1968   M.F.A., Alfred University, Alfred, New York

Lives in New Braunfels, Texas

Selected Solo Exhibitions:

1988   Matrix Gallery, Austin, TX
1985   The University of Texas at San Antonio, San Antonio, TX
1984   Matrix Gallery, Austin, TX
1978   Tulane University, New Orleans, LA
1972   Bienville Gallery, New Orleans, LA
1970   Bienville Gallery, New Orleans, LA

Selected Group Exhibitions:

1986   Celebrating Texas Sculpture, Austin, TX
1985   New Works, Laguna Gloria Art Museum, Austin, TX
1980   Texas Sculpture and Sculptors, Lawndale Annex, University of Houston, Houston, TX
1979   Seven from Texas, Contemporary Arts Center, New Orleans, LA
1968   Rochester Art Festival, Rochester, NY
1967   The 15th Syracuse Regional, Syracuse, NY

ROBERT BOURDON

Born 1947, West Chester, Pennsylvania

1970   A.B., Dartmouth College, Hanover, New Hampshire
1972   M.A., University of California at Berkeley, Berkeley, California

Lives in Houston, Texas

Selected Solo Exhibitions:

1986   Moody Gallery, Houston, TX
1984   Allen Stone Gallery, New York, NY
1982   Museum of Art, Carnegie Institute, Pittsburgh, PA
1981   University of California Art Museum, Santa Barbara, CA

Selected Group Exhibitions:

1986   New Orleans Triennial: The Centennial Exhibition, New Orleans Museum of Art, New Orleans, LA
        The Medium Is the Illusion, California State University Art Gallery, Fullerton, CA
1984   Houston Profiles, Art League of Houston, Houston, TX
1983   Sculpture on the Wall, San Antonio Art Institute, San Antonio, TX
1982   Seize Artistes — Un Materiau, Abbaye de St. Andre, Meymac, France
        Wood into the 80's, Turman Gallery, Indiana State University, Terra Haute, IN
1981   Collage and Assemblage, Mississippi Museum of Art, Jackson, MS, traveling exhibition
1973   Wood Works, Dartmouth College, Hanover, NH, traveling exhibition

JULIE BOZZI

Born 1943, San Jose, California

1974   B.A., M.F.A., University of California at Davis, Davis, California

Lives in Fort Worth, Texas

Selected Solo Exhibition:

1978   Julie Bozzi — Agricultural Landscape, Candy Store Gallery, Folsom, CA

Selected Group Exhibitions:

1988   Six Artists/Six Idioms, Sarah Campbell Blaffer Gallery, University of Houston, Houston, TX
1987   Third Coast Review: A Look at Art in Texas, Aspen Art Museum, Aspen, CO, traveling exhibition
1986   Natural Settings, Corcoran Gallery of Art, Washington, DC
1985   At the Edge of Town, The Nave Museum, Victoria, TX, and Corpus Christi State University, Corpus Christi, TX
1984   New Work: New York/Outside New York, The New Museum, New York, NY
1983   Images of Texas, Archer M. Huntington Art Gallery, The University of Texas at Austin, Austin, TX
1980   The Tableau Show, Los Angeles Institute of Contemporary Art, Los Angeles, CA
1979   Various Directions, Ruth Schaffner Gallery, Los Angeles, CA

STEVE BRUDNIAK

Born 1961, Topeka, Kansas

Lives in Austin, Texas

Selected Solo Exhibition:

1987   The Science of Brudniak, Blue Collar Gallery, San Antonio, TX

Selected Group Exhibitions:

1988   The Functional Show, On Waugh Gallery, Houston, TX
1987   Realism Exhibition, Texas Fine Arts Association, Atrium Gallery, St. Edward's University, Austin, TX
        Museum of Neon Art, Los Angeles, CA
1986   Diverse Works, Houston, TX

JOHN CHRISTENSEN

Born 1954, New York, New York

1977   B.A., Harvard University, Cambridge, Massachusetts
1988   M.F.A., The University of Texas at Austin, Austin, Texas

Lives in Austin, Texas

Selected Group Exhibitions:

1988   Internal Order, Transco Tower, Houston, TX
        Collaborator in 64 Beds, an interdisciplinary performance, subsidized by the NEA and organized by Sally Jacques

50th Anniversary Faculty Show, Archer M. Huntington Art Gallery, The University of Texas at Austin, Austin, TX
M.F.A. Thesis Show, Archer M. Huntington Art Gallery, The University of Texas at Austin, Austin, TX
1987   Mexic-Arte Annual, Austin, TX
Blue Collar Gallery, San Antonio, TX
1986   San Antonio Museum of Art Open, San Antonio, TX
1981   Moviehous Studio, Millerton, NY
1980   Moviehous Studio, Millerton, NY
1976   Installation, Carpenter Center for the Visual Arts, Cambridge, MA

J. MICHAEL CISZEK

Born 1954, Chicago, Illinois
1982   B.A., University of St. Thomas, Houston, Texas
Lives in Houston, Texas

Selected Group Exhibitions:
1987   Introductions '87, Harris Gallery, Houston, TX
1985   Two-Man Show, O'Kane Gallery, University of Houston, Houston, TX
1984   Artist and Models Ball, Diverse Works, Houston, TX
1983   East End Show, Lawndale Annex, University of Houston, Houston, TX
1982   Works by Seven New Artists, Link-Lee House Gallery, University of St. Thomas, Houston, TX
1981   Festival of the Dead, University of St. Thomas, Houston, TX

THELMA COLES

Born 1952, Portsmouth, Virginia
1975   B.A., San Diego State University, San Diego, California
1978   M.A., San Diego State University, San Diego, California
Lives in New Braunfels, Texas

Selected Solo Exhibition:
1988   Visiting Artist Exhibition, Kent State University, Kent, OH

Selected Group Exhibitions:
1989   Texas Metal Invitational, San Antonio Museum of Art, San Antonio, TX
1987   Coles, Cook, and Brown, R. S. Levy Gallery, Austin, TX
Sculpture: Ideas Defined, Art Gallery, The University of Texas at San Antonio, San Antonio, TX
1986   Form beyond Function: Recent Sculpture, traveling exhibition
1985   Contemporary Metals U.S.A., Downey Museum of Art, Downey, CA
1984   Coles and Loyd, National Ornamental Metal Museum, Memphis, TN
1983   New Works by Austin Artists, Laguna Gloria Art Museum, Austin, TX
1982   Texas Fine Arts Association 71st Annual, Laguna Gloria Art Museum, Austin, TX
Contemporary Metals Invitational, Huntington Galleries, Huntington, WV
1981   30 Americans: An Invitational Exhibition, Galveston Arts Center, Galveston, TX
Two Decades of Metal, Art Museum, San Diego State University, San Diego, CA, traveling exhibition
1980   Young Americans: Metal, American Craft Museum, New York, NY, traveling exhibition
Crafts 14, Pennsylvania State Museum of Art, University Park, PA

1979   Texas: Silver, Mud, Paper, Contemporary Arts Center, New Orleans, LA
1978   Landscape: New Views, Herbert F. Johnson Museum of Art, Ithaca, NY
1977   Ornament and Object, Costa Mesa Junior College, Oceanside, CA

STEPHEN J. DALY

Born 1942, Governors Island, New York
1964   B.A., San Jose State University, San Jose, California
1967   M.F.A., Cranbrook Academy of Art, Bloomfield Hills, Michigan
Lives in Austin, Texas

Selected Solo Exhibitions:
1985   Corridor, installation, Atrium Gallery, Amarillo Art Center, Amarillo, TX
Brown-Lupton Gallery, Texas Christian University, Fort Worth, TX
1980   Main Gallery, San Antonio Art Institute, San Antonio, TX
1975   American Academy in Rome, Rome, Italy
1969   Galeria del Sol, Santa Barbara, CA

Selected Group Exhibitions:
1986   Texas Visions, Museum of Art of the American West, Houston, TX
New Sites/New Work, San Jose State Institute of Contemporary Art, San Jose, CA
The Blue Star Exhibition, Contemporary Art for San Antonio, San Antonio, TX
1985   Texas Currents, San Antonio Art Institute, San Antonio, TX
1983   Daly/Washmon, Art Gallery, The University of Texas at the Permian Basin, Odessa, TX
1982   Celebration of Texas Sculpture, Sam Houston State University, Huntsville, TX
The Lawndale Competition, Lawndale Annex, University of Houston, Houston, TX
1981   Corpus Christi Art Foundation Exhibition, Art Museum of South Texas, Corpus Christi, TX
1979   Sculpture Invitational, Visual Arts Center, Anchorage, AK
1976   Texas Fine Arts Association 65th Annual, Laguna Gloria Art Museum, Austin, TX
1973   The Plastic Earth, John Michael Kohler Arts Center, Sheboygan, WI
1971   Two Sculptors, with Manuel Neri, University of Nevada, Reno, NV
1969   Objects: USA, The Johnson Collection, Nordness Galleries and ACC, traveling exhibition
1964   Sculpture Invitational, Laguna Gloria Art Museum, Austin, TX

DAVID L. DEMING

Born 1943, Cleveland, Ohio
1967   B.F.A., Cleveland Institute of Art, Cleveland, Ohio
1970   M.F.A., Cranbrook Academy of Art, Bloomfield Hills, Michigan
Lives in Austin, Texas

Selected Solo Exhibitions:
1983   Patrick Gallery, Austin, TX
1982   Texas A&M University, College Station, TX
RGK Foundation, Austin, TX
1979   Longview Museum and Arts Center, Longview, TX
1977   Art Museum of South Texas, Corpus Christi, TX

Selected Group Exhibitions:

1986   Chicago International Art Exposition, Navy Pier,
       Chicago, IL
1985   Three Sculptors: Beverly Pepper, Xavier Corbero, David
       Deming, Adams-Middleton Gallery, Dallas, TX
1983   International Exhibition of Contemporary Metals, Florence,
       Italy
       Fall Exhibition, San Antonio Art Institute, San Antonio, TX
       Third Annual Abilene Outdoor Sculpture Exhibition,
       Abilene, TX
1982   Shidoni Annual Outdoor Exhibition, Tesuque, NM
       Invitational '82, Longview Museum and Arts Center,
       Longview, TX
1981   A Celebration of Texas Sculpture, Sam Houston State
       University, Huntsville, TX
1980   Deming/White, Archer M. Huntington Art Gallery, The
       University of Texas at Austin, Austin, TX
       Julius Schmidt Invitational, Cameron University, Lawton, OK
1979   Made in Texas, Archer M. Huntington Art Gallery, The
       University of Texas at Austin, Austin, TX
1978   Texas Society of Sculptors Exhibition, Austin, TX
       Texas Fine Arts Association 67th Annual, Laguna Gloria Art
       Museum, Austin, TX
1977   6th Annual Festival on the Strand Art Exhibition, Galveston
       Arts Center, Galveston, TX
1976   Corpus Christi Art Foundation Annual Exhibition, Art
       Museum of South Texas, Corpus Christi, TX
1975   Texas Fine Arts Association 64th Annual, Laguna Gloria Art
       Museum, Austin, TX
       Creative Collaboration '75, Sarah Campbell Blaffer Gallery,
       University of Houston, Houston, TX
1974   Southwest Fine Arts Biennial, Museum of New Mexico,
       Santa Fe, NM
1973   Invitational Beaux-Arts Exhibition, Laguna Gloria Art
       Museum, Austin, TX
1971   Texas Painting and Sculpture Exhibition, Dallas Museum of
       Fine Arts, Dallas, TX
       Southwest Art Association Conference Exhibition,
       El Paso, TX
1967   50th Annual Cleveland Museum of Art May Show,
       Cleveland, OH

JAMES DRAKE

Born 1946, Lubbock, Texas
1969   B.F.A., Art Center College of Design, Los Angeles, California
1970   M.F.A., Art Center College of Design, Los Angeles, California
Lives in El Paso, Texas

Selected Solo Exhibitions:

1988   Alternative Museum, New York, NY
       Barbara Fendrick Gallery, New York, NY
1987   Adair Margo Gallery, El Paso, TX
1986   Texas Gallery, Houston, TX
       Arthur Roger Gallery, New Orleans, LA
1983   Brown-Lupton Gallery, Texas Christian University, Fort
       Worth, TX
1982   Galveston Arts Center, Galveston, TX
       Robert Speaker Gallery, Los Angeles, CA
1981   Amarillo Art Center, Amarillo, TX, traveling exhibition
1976   Museo de arte y historia, Ciudad Juárez, Mexico

Selected Group Exhibitions:

1987   Third Coast Review: A Look at Art in Texas, Aspen Art
       Museum, Aspen, CO, traveling exhibition
       Texas Figurative Drawings, Art Museum of South Texas,
       Corpus Christi, TX

Recent Drawings, Main Gallery, The University of Texas at
El Paso, El Paso, TX
1986   Third Western States Biennial, The Brooklyn Museum, New
       York, NY, traveling exhibition
       Personal Environments, Museum of Fine Arts, Santa Fe, NM
       New Orleans Triennial: The Centennial Exhibition, New
       Orleans Museum of Art, New Orleans, LA
       Texas Visions, Transco Tower, Houston, TX
1985   Southwest '85, Museum of Fine Arts, Santa Fe, NM
1984   Texas on My Mind, Contemporary Visions of the Lone Star
       State, Artrain, traveling exhibition
1983   Southern Fictions, Contemporary Arts Museum,
       Houston, TX
       New Orleans Triennial, New Orleans Museum of Art,
       New Orleans, LA
1982   Invitational '82, Longview Museum and Arts Center,
       Longview, TX
       Fun and Games, The Art Center, Waco, TX
1980   Copper II, University of Arizona Museum of Art, Tucson, AZ
       University Art Gallery, San Diego State University, San
       Diego, CA
1979   Made in Texas, Archer M. Huntington Art Gallery,
       The University of Texas at Austin, Austin, TX
1976   Mid-Western Graphics 4th Annual Exhibition, Tulsa City
       County Library, Tulsa, OK
1975   International Biennial of Graphic Art, Ljubljana Moderna
       Galerija, Ljubljana, Yugoslavia

ROWENA C. ELKIN

Born 1917, Fort Worth, Texas
1938   B.S., Texas State College for Women, Denton, Texas
Lives in Dallas, Texas

Selected Group Exhibitions:

1988   50th Reunion Exhibition, Texas Woman's University,
       Denton, TX
       Peace Exhibition, Southern Methodist University Gallery,
       Dallas, TX
       Top Floor Gallery, Women's Caucus for Art, Dallas, TX
       ReView: Ten Years of Women and Their Work, One
       Congress Plaza, Austin, TX
1987   National Sculpture Conference for Women, Closson Gallery,
       Cincinnati, OH
1986   150 Artists, Women's Caucus for Art, City Hall, Dallas, TX
1985   Sculpture Exhibition, Ruth Wiseman Gallery, Dallas, TX
1983   Zoo Invitational, Clifford Gallery, Dallas, TX
1982   Susan H. Brown, Paper Pieces/Rowena C. Elkin, Sculpture,
       Ruth Wiseman Gallery, Dallas, TX
1981   American Association of University Women Centennial
       Exhibition, Boston University, Boston, MA
1979   Women-in-Sight: New Art in Texas, Women and Their
       Work, Dougherty Cultural Arts Center, Austin, TX, traveling
       exhibition
       Artist Equity Invitational, James K. Wilson Gallery,
       Dallas, TX
       Texas Fine Arts Association, Dallas, TX
1978   Texas Fine Arts Association, Dallas, TX
1977   First Texas Sculpture Symposium, Southern Methodist
       University, Dallas, TX
1976   Saenger National Jewelry and Small Sculpture Exhibition,
       University of Southern Mississippi, Hattiesburg, MS
1971   Regional Painting and Sculpture Exhibition, Richardson
       Civic Art Society, Richardson, TX
1968   Invitational Exhibition, Museum of the Southwest,
       Midland, TX
1951   Los Alamos Artists Invitational, Museum of Fine Arts,
       Santa Fe, NM

1950 New Mexico Alliance for the Arts, Museum of Fine Arts, Santa Fe, NM
1949 Canyon Gallery Artists, Santa Fe, NM
1948 Los Alamos Artists and Craftsmen, Los Alamos, NM
1947 Los Alamos Artists and Craftsmen, Los Alamos, NM

DAVID EVERETT

Born 1950, Beaumont, Texas
1972 B.F.A., The University of Texas at Austin, Austin, Texas
1975 M.F.A., The University of Texas at Austin, Austin, Texas
Lives in Austin, Texas

Selected Solo Exhibition:
1987 San Angelo Museum of Fine Arts, San Angelo, TX

Selected Group Exhibitions:
1988 Sensual Surfaces, Marilyn Butler Fine Art, Santa Fe, NM
1987 Handmade in Texas, presented by the Dallas Craft Guild, LTV Center, Dallas, TX
1985 Valley House Gallery, Dallas, TX
      R. S. Levy Gallery, Austin, TX
1982 Hoey, Barrow, Smith, Osborne, Everett, SOHO Gallery, Austin, TX
1979 Austin Contemporary Visual Arts Show, First Federal Bank, Austin, TX
1977 11th Annual National Drawings and Small Sculpture Show, Corpus Christi, TX
1976 Texas Fine Arts Association 65th Annual, Laguna Gloria Art Museum, Austin, TX

VERNON FISHER

Born 1943, Fort Worth, Texas
1967 B.A., Hardin-Simmons University, Abilene, Texas
1969 M.F.A., University of Illinois at Urbana-Champaign, Urbana, Illinois

Lives in Fort Worth, Texas

Selected Solo Exhibitions:
1988 Lost for Words, Dallas Museum of Art, Dallas, TX
1987 Perdido en el Mar, installation, Lannan Museum, Lake Worth, FL
1985 Polar Eclipse, Butler Gallery, Houston, TX
1984 Barbara Gladstone Gallery, New York, NY
1983 Installation, Madison Art Center, Madison, WI
1982 Galerie T'Venster, Rotterdam, The Netherlands
1981 Breaking the Code, Franklin Furnace, New York, NY
1980 Vernon Fisher: Story Paintings and Drawing, Contemporary Arts Museum, Houston, TX
      Denise Rene/Hans Mayer Gallery, Dusseldorf, West Germany

Selected Group Exhibitions:
1987 Comic Iconoclasm, Institute of Contemporary Arts, London, England, traveling exhibition
      Avant-Garde in the Eighties, Los Angeles County Museum of Art, Los Angeles, CA
      Past Imperfect: Eric Fischl/Vernon Fisher/Laurie Simmons, Walker Art Center, Minneapolis, MN, traveling exhibition
1986 Text & Image, The Wording of American Art, Holly Solomon Gallery, New York, NY
      Momento Mori, Centro Cultural Arte Contemporáneo, Mexico City, Mexico
      Public and Private: American Prints Today, 24th National Print Exhibition, The Brooklyn Museum, New York, NY, traveling exhibition

New Orleans Triennial: The Centennial Exhibition, New Orleans Museum of Art, New Orleans, LA
1984 Content: A Contemporary Focus, 1974–1984, Hirshhorn Museum and Sculpture Garden, Smithsonian Institution, Washington, DC
      Narrative Forms, Museo Rufino Tamayo, Mexico City, Mexico
1983 Language, Drama, Source and Vision, The New Museum, New York, NY
      Southern Fictions, Contemporary Arts Museum, Houston, TX
      The Comic Art Show, Whitney Museum of American Art, Downtown Branch, New York, NY
1982 Mediums of Language, installation, Hayden Gallery, Massachusetts Institute of Technology, Cambridge, MA
      Fifth India Triennial, New Delhi, India
1981 The Southern Voice: Terry Allen, Vernon Fisher, Ed McGowin, Fort Worth Art Museum, Fort Worth, TX
      Words as Images, The Renaissance Society at the University of Chicago, Bergman Gallery, Chicago, IL
      Directions 1981, Hirshhorn Museum and Sculpture Garden, Smithsonian Institution, Washington, DC
      Whitney Biennial, Whitney Museum of American Art, New York, NY
      19 Artists – Emergent Americans: 1981 Exxon National Exhibition, Solomon R. Guggenheim Museum, New York, NY
1980 Response, Tyler Museum of Art, Tyler, TX

ROY FRIDGE

Born 1927, Beeville, Texas
1950 B.A., Baylor University, Waco, Texas
Lives in Port Aransas, Texas

Selected Solo Exhibitions:
1978 Reflections of an Amateur Hermit, Art Museum of South Texas, Corpus Christi, TX
1966 David Gallery, Houston, TX
1959 Waco Museum of Art, Waco, TX

Selected Group Exhibitions:
1988 The Poetic Object, San Antonio Museum of Art, San Antonio, TX
      Texas Art, Richmond Hall, The Menil Collection, Houston, TX
      Visions of Fate, Minneapolis College of Art and Design, Minneapolis, MN
1987 Found, Diverse Works, Houston, TX
1986 Texas Landscape, 1900 – 1986, Museum of Fine Arts, Houston, TX
      Shrines and Altars: Tradition and Innovation, John Michael Kohler Arts Center, Sheboygan, WI
      Artist's Response to Architecture, The Nave Museum, Victoria, TX
1985 Boats: Artists and Artisans, Galveston Arts Center, Galveston, TX
      Texas Currents, San Antonio Art Institute, San Antonio, TX
1984 Texas on My Mind: Contemporary Visions of the Lone Star State, Artrain, traveling exhibition
      Return of the Narrative, Palm Springs Desert Museum, Palm Springs, CA
      Gateway Gallery Experience, Dallas Museum of Art, Dallas, TX

1983   Alternative Museum, New York, NY
Fact and Fiction: New Work by James Surls, Roy Fridge, Ed Blackburn, Vernon Fisher, Aspen Center for the Visual Arts, Aspen, CO
A Partial Look: Selected Works from the Corporate Art Collection of Atlantic Richfield Company, Dallas, Texas, Art Museum of South Texas, Corpus Christi, TX
Southern Fictions, Contemporary Arts Museum, Houston, TX
A Salute to Houston Artists, Midtown Art Center, Houston, TX
Regional Transformations, Victoria Museum, Victoria, TX
1982   Hearts and Flowers, The Art Center, Waco, TX
Celebration of Texas Sculpture, Sam Houston State University, Huntsville, TX
Houston Art in Norway, Stavanger Museum, Stavanger, Norway
The Americans: The Collage, Contemporary Arts Museum, Houston, TX
Conversations from the Woods, Moody Gallery, Houston, TX
Shrines/Altars, Objects Gallery, San Antonio, TX
1981   Inside/Out — Self beyond Likeness, Newport Harbor Art Museum, Newport Beach, CA, traveling exhibition
The Image of the House in Contemporary Art, Lawndale Annex, University of Houston, Houston, TX
1980   Response, Tyler Museum of Art, Tyler, TX
Souvenirs of the Voyage, Moody Gallery, Houston, TX
1979   18 Texans, Corpus Christi State University, Corpus Christi, TX
Fire, Contemporary Arts Museum, Houston, TX
Wood in Art, Museum of Fine Arts, Houston, TX
1977   Texas Thirty, The Nave Museum, Victoria, TX
Installation for Corner Spaces, Fort Worth Art Museum, Fort Worth, TX
1976   Altered Image, Texas A&I University, Kingsville, TX
Gulf Coast Invitational Sculpture Exhibition, San Antonio College, San Antonio, TX
1975   Artists Make Toys, Art Museum of South Texas, Corpus Christi, TX
1971   one i at a time, Pollock Galleries, Southern Methodist University, Dallas, TX
1968   Atelier Chapman Kelley, Dallas, TX
1967   University of Oklahoma Museum, Norman, OK
Six Sculptors, Jewish Center, Houston, TX
1966   Rice University, Houston, TX
Made of Iron, University of St. Thomas, Houston, TX
1963   Young Sculptors of the South and West, Arkansas Art Center, Little Rock, AR
1961   Three Sculptors of the Southwest, Dallas Museum for Contemporary Art, Dallas, TX
The Art That Broke the Looking Glass, Dallas Museum for Contemporary Art, Dallas, TX
1959   Baylor Theater, Baylor University, Waco, TX
1958   Humor in Art, Dallas Museum for Contemporary Art, Dallas, TX
Made in Texas by Texans, Dallas Museum for Contemporary Art, Dallas, TX

HARRY GEFFERT

Born 1934, Live Oak County, Texas

1957   B.F.A., Southwest Texas State University, San Marcos, Texas
1963   M.F.A., New Mexico Highlands University, Las Vegas, New Mexico

Lives in Crowley, Texas

Selected Solo Exhibitions:

1986   Fort Worth Gallery, Fort Worth, TX
1985   Artist's Eye Exhibition, Kimbell Museum, Fort Worth, TX
1972   Fort Worth Art Museum, Fort Worth, TX

Selected Group Exhibitions:

1987   Third Coast Review: A Look at Art in Texas, Aspen Art Museum, Aspen, CO, traveling exhibition
The Flower and Garden Show, D.W. Gallery, Dallas, TX
1986   Texas Invitational, Fort Worth, TX
1984   Art in the Metroplex, Texas Christian University, Fort Worth, TX
Delta Show, Little Rock, AR

LINNEA GLATT

Born 1949, Bismarck, North Dakota

1971   B.S., Moorhead State University, Moorhead, Minnesota
1972   M.A., University of Dallas, Irving, Texas

Lives in Dallas, Texas

Selected Solo Exhibition:

1985   Sculpture Invitational, Laguna Gloria Art Museum, Austin, TX

Selected Group Exhibitions:

1988   Texas Women, National Museum of Women in the Arts, Washington, DC
1987   Third Coast Review: A Look at Art in Texas, Aspen Art Museum, Aspen, CO, traveling exhibition
Sculpture: The Spectrum, Lawndale Annex, University of Houston, Houston, TX
1986   Artist's Response to Architecture, The Nave Museum, Victoria, TX
Women of the Big State: Current Art, Arts Warehouse, Austin, TX
3 Sculptors — Linnea Glatt, Frances Bagley, Joseph Havel, Austin College, Sherman, TX
1985   Tenth Anniversary Exhibition, D.W. Gallery, Dallas, TX
1984   Presenting Nine, D'Art, Dallas, TX
1983   Construction Site, D.W. Gallery, Dallas, TX
Showdown, The Sculpture Center, New York, NY, and Diverse Works, Houston, TX
1981   Invitational '81, Longview Museum and Arts Center, Longview, TX
1979   12, Dallas Museum of Fine Arts, Dallas, TX
Fire, Contemporary Arts Museum, Houston, TX
D.W. Gallery, Dallas, TX
1978   Cedar Valley College, Duncanville, TX
1976   Women in the Arts Festival, The University of Texas at Arlington, Arlington, TX

GEORGE GREEN

Born 1942, Paris, Texas

1964   B.A., Texas Tech University, Lubbock, Texas
1968   M.A., University of Dallas, Irving, Texas

Lives in Long Island, New York

Selected Solo Exhibitions:

1986   George Green: Recent Paintings, Tyler Museum of Art, Tyler, TX
1981   Landfall Gallery, Chicago, IL
1978   Hansen Gallery, New York, NY
1977   Rebecca Cooper Gallery, Washington, DC

1973   Smither Gallery, Dallas, TX
1970   A Clean Well-Lighted Place, Austin, TX
1969   Witte Museum, San Antonio, TX

Selected Group Exhibitions:

1988   Nocturne: Portraying the Night, Kemper Gallery, Kansas
        City Art Institute, Kansas City, MO
        In the Garden, Transco Tower, Houston, TX
1987   Line and Form: Contemporary Texas Figurative Drawing,
        Art Museum of South Texas, Corpus Christi, TX
        Tough Realism, Dimock Gallery, George Washington
        University, Washington, DC
1986   The Texas Landscape, 1900 – 1986, Museum of Fine Arts,
        Houston, TX
1985   Ten-Year Anniversary Exhibition, Moody Gallery,
        Houston, TX
1984   Venice Biennale, Paradise Lost/Paradise Regained: American
        Visions of the New Decade, United States Pavilion, organized
        by the New Museum, New York, NY
1983   Poetic Object, Washington Project for the Arts,
        Washington, DC
1979   America Now: Paintings of the Seventies, sponsored by the
        International Communication Agency, Washington, DC,
        organized by the New Museum, New York, NY, tour of
        Eastern Europe
        Fire, Contemporary Arts Museum, Houston, TX
        Made in Texas, Archer M. Huntington Art Gallery,
        The University of Texas at Austin, Austin, TX
1978   Painting and Sculpture Today, Indianapolis Museum of Art,
        Indianapolis, IN
1976   The Great American Rodeo, Fort Worth Art Museum, Fort
        Worth, TX, traveling exhibition
1975   Whitney Biennial, Whitney Museum of American Art,
        New York, NY
1973   Texas, Galerie Simonne Stern, New Orleans, LA
1972   Interchange, Walker Art Center, Minneapolis, MN, and
        Dallas Museum of Fine Arts, Dallas, TX
1971   Project South by Southwest, Fort Worth Art Center, Fort
        Worth, TX
1970   Six Sculptures by Six Artists, A Clean Well-Lighted Place,
        Austin, TX
1965   Amarillo Invitational, Amarillo Art Center, Amarillo, TX

ALLAN HACKLIN

Born 1943, New York, New York

1965   B.F.A., Pratt Institute, Brooklyn, New York

Lives in Houston, Texas

Selected Solo Exhibitions:

1987   Meadows Museum, Dallas, TX
1984   Meredith Long and Co., Houston, TX
1978   Truman Gallery, New York, NY
1975   Betty Parsons Gallery, New York, NY
1971   Forum Kunst, Rottweil, West Germany
        Betty Parsons Gallery, New York, NY
1970   Galerie Furneisen, Hamburg, West Germany
        Galerie Zwirner, Cologne, West Germany
1969   Betty Parsons Gallery, New York, NY
        Galerie Muller, Stuttgart, West Germany
1967   Allan Stone Gallery, New York, NY

Selected Group Exhibitions:

1988   Sewall Art Gallery, Rice University, Houston, TX
1987   Meredith Long and Co., Houston, TX
        Davis/McClain Gallery, Houston, TX
1984   50 Years of American Sculpture, Museum of Fine Arts,
        Houston, TX

1972   Painting and Sculpture Today, Indianapolis Museum of Art,
        Indianapolis, IN
        Recent Painting, Munson Williams Proctor Institute,
        Utica, NY
1971   Four Painters, Dallas Museum of Fine Arts, Dallas, TX
        Internationale Zeichnungen, Kunsthalle, Darmstadt, West
        Germany
        Kunstmarkt, Cologne, West Germany
1970   Color and Field, 1890 – 1970, Dayton Art Institute, Dayton,
        OH, traveling exhibition
        Recent Acquisitions, Whitney Museum of American Art,
        New York, NY
        Zeichnungen Amerikanischer Kunstler, Galerie Ricke,
        Cologne, West Germany
        Whitney Annual, Whitney Museum of American Art, New
        York, NY
        Kunstmarkt, Cologne, West Germany
        Carmen Lamanna Gallery, Toronto, Ontario, Canada
1969   A Tendency in Contemporary Painting, Kolnicsher
        Kunstverein, Cologne, West Germany
        Inaugural Exhibition, New School Art Center, New York, NY
        Concept, Vassar Collge, Poughkeepsie, NY
        Reductive Vision, Betty Parsons Gallery, New York, NY
        Selective Eye, Art Gallery of Ontario, Toronto, Ontario,
        Canada
        Kunstmarkt, Cologne, West Germany
1968   Carmen Lamanna Gallery, Toronto, Ontario, Canada
        Kunstmarkt, Cologne, West Germany

AL HARRIS

Born 1946, Cananea, Sonora, Mexico

1970   B.A., The University of Texas at El Paso, El Paso, Texas
1984   M.A., New Mexico State University, Las Cruces, New
        Mexico
1985   M.F.A., Stephen F. Austin State University, Nacogdoches,
        Texas

Lives in El Paso, Texas

Selected Solo Exhibition:

1985   Stephen F. Austin State University, Nacogdoches, TX

Selected Group Exhibitions:

1987   The House in Contemporary Art, California State University,
        Fullerton, CA
        Recent Work, The University of Texas at El Paso,
        El Paso, TX
        Adair Margo Gallery, El Paso, TX
        Graham Gallery, Houston, TX
1986   Texas Annual, Texas Fine Arts Association, Laguna Gloria
        Art Museum, Austin, TX
        New American Talent, Laguna Gloria Art Museum,
        Austin, TX
1985   Black and White, Foster Goldstrome Gallery, Dallas, TX
1984   New Mexico State University, Las Cruces, NM
1979   Governor's Gallery, Santa Fe, NM
1976   Adelle M. Fine Arts, Dallas, TX

JOSEPH G. HAVEL

Born 1954, Minneapolis, Minnesota

1975   B.F.A., University of Minnesota, Minneapolis, Minnesota
1979   M.F.A., Pennsylvania State University, University Park,
        Pennsylvania

Lives in Sherman, Texas

Selected Solo Exhibitions:
1987   D.W. Gallery, Dallas, TX
1985   Texas Woman's University, Denton, TX

Selected Group Exhibitions:
1986   3 Sculptors — Francis Bagley, Linnea Glatt, Joseph Havel,
       Austin College, Sherman, TX
       Art in the Metroplex, Texas Christian University, Fort
       Worth, TX
1985   Four Sculptors, College of the Mainland, Texas City, TX
1984   Nine Sculptors, Midtown Art Center, Houston, TX
1982   Texas Sculptors Invitational, Pensacola Community College,
       Pensacola, FL
1980   Tulane University, New Orleans, LA
1979   Penn State University, University Park, PA
1978   Central Pennsylvania Festival of the Arts, State College, PA

JOHN HERNANDEZ

Born 1952, San Antonio, Texas
1975   B. A., Our Lady of the Lake University, San Antonio, Texas
1980   M.F.A., North Texas State University, Denton, Texas
Lives in Dallas, Texas

Selected Solo Exhibition:
1985   D.W. Gallery, Dallas, TX

Selected Group Exhibitions:
1988   Hernandez/Twaddle, D.W. Gallery, Dallas, TX
       Contemporary Art from Texas, Groninger Museum,
       Groningen, The Netherlands
       The Chicano Experience: John Hernandez and Benito
       Huerta, Inter-American Art Gallery, Miami-Dade
       Community College, Miami, FL
1987   Third Coast Review: A Look at Art in Texas, Aspen Art
       Museum, Aspen, CO, traveling exhibition
       Emerging Faces, North Lake College, Irving, TX
1986   State of the Arts: Texas!, Contemporary Arts Center, New
       Orleans, LA
       Chulas Fronteras, Midtown Art Center, Houston, TX
       Dead Days, Blue Star Art Space, San Antonio, TX, and Bath
       House Cultural Center, Dallas, TX
1985   On View, The New Museum, New York, NY
       Texas Artist, Moody Gallery, Houston, TX
       Patrick Gallery, Austin, TX
       Post February, The University of Texas at Arlington,
       Arlington, TX
1984   Patterns, Laguna Gloria Art Museum, Austin, TX
       A Partial Look, Art Museum of South Texas, Corpus
       Christi, TX
       Singular Points of View, Art Museum of South Texas, Corpus
       Christi, TX
1982   The Lawndale Competition, Lawndale Annex, University of
       Houston, Houston, TX
1977   G WIZ, North Texas State University, Denton, TX

TEME PAUL HERNANDEZ

Born 1953, Winnsboro, Louisiana
1977   B.F.A., Louisiana State University, Baton Rouge, Louisiana
1980   M.F.A., The University of Texas at Austin, Austin, Texas
Lives in Austin, Texas

Selected Group Exhibitions:
1988   Black and White Exhibition, AIR Gallery, Austin, TX
       Flights of Fancy, Texas Fine Arts Association, Austin, TX

1987   New Works, Laguna Gloria Art Museum, Austin, TX
       Tribute to Texas Artists, Gubernatorial Inauguration Show,
       Performing Arts Center, The University of Texas at Austin,
       Austin, TX
       Austin Visual Arts Association 10th Anniversary Exhibition,
       301 Congress, Austin, TX
1986   San Antonio Museum of Art Open, San Antonio, TX
1985   Texas Annual, Texas Fine Arts Association, Laguna Gloria
       Art Museum, Austin, TX
1984   Austin Arms, LA Heights Alternate Gallery,
       San Antonio, TX
       The Next Wave, Diverse Works, Houston, TX
1980   On the Strand Gallery, Galveston, TX

EMILY JENNINGS

Born 1951, Abilene, Texas
1974   B.F.A., California College of Arts and Crafts, Oakland,
       California
1982   M.F.A., Rhode Island School of Design, Providence, Rhode
       Island
Lives in Abilene, Texas

Selected Solo Exhibitions:
1987   D.W. Gallery, Dallas, TX
1986   Edith Baker Gallery, Dallas, TX
1983   Sarah Doyle Gallery, Brown University, Providence, RI

Selected Group Exhibitions:
1988   Texas Women, National Museum of Women in the Arts,
       Washington, DC
       Top of the Triangle, University Art Gallery, North Texas
       University, Denton, TX
1987   Texas Annual, Texas Fine Arts Association, Laguna Gloria
       Art Museum, Austin, TX
       The Domesticity in Art, Hartwich College, Oneida, NY
1984   Images of Childhood: A Contemporary Iconography,
       Whitney Museum of American Art, New York, NY
       Artist's Toys, Vanderwoude-Tannenbaum Gallery,
       New York, NY

LUIS JIMENEZ

Born 1940, El Paso, Texas
1964   B.S., The University of Texas at Austin, Austin, Texas
Lives in Hondo, New Mexico

Selected Solo Exhibitions:
1987   Marilyn Butler Fine Art, Santa Fe, NM
       Moody Gallery, Houston, TX
1986   Luis Jimenez: Recent Work, Adair Margo Gallery,
       The University of Texas at El Paso, El Paso, TX
1985   Dallas Museum of Art, Dallas, TX
1984   Luis Jimenez: Sculpture and Graphics, Roswell Museum and
       Art Center, Roswell, NM
       Luis Jimenez: Sculpture and Works on Paper, Alternative
       Museum, New York, NY
       Phyllis Kind Gallery, New York, NY
1983   Laguna Gloria Art Museum, Austin, TX
       Rudy M. Fernandez, Elaine Horwitch Galleries, Santa Fe, NM
       Candy Store Gallery, Folsom, CA
1982   Plains Art Museum, Moorhead, MN
1981   Luis Jimenez: Cut-Outs and Drawings, Frumkin and Struve
       Gallery, Chicago, IL
       Luis Jimenez: Sculpture, Prints, Drawings, Pepperdine
       University Art Gallery, Malibu, CA

1979 Luis Jimenez: Sculpture, Drawings, and Prints, Museum of
Fine Arts, Santa Fe, NM
1977 Luis Jimenez: Sculpture, Drawing, Graphics, de Saisset
Gallery, University of Santa Clara, Santa Clara, CA
1976 Meredith Long and Co., Houston, TX
1975 O.K. Harris, New York, NY
Luis Jimenez: Sculpture, Hill's Gallery, Santa Fe, NM
1974 Luis Jimenez: Progress I, Contemporary Arts Museum,
Houston, TX
1972 O.K. Harris, New York, NY
1970 Graham Gallery, New York, NY
1969 Graham Gallery, New York, NY

Selected Group Exhibitions:

1988 Different Drummers, Hirshhorn Museum and Sculpture
Garden, Smithsonian Institution, Washington, DC
1987 Hispanic Art in the United States, Museum of Fine Arts,
Houston, TX, traveling exhibition
The Francis J. Greenburger Foundation Awards, Jack
Gallery, New York, NY, and Mira Godard Gallery, Toronto,
Ontario, Canada
1986 Honky Tonk Visions, The Museum, Texas Tech University,
Lubbock, TX, traveling exhibition
1985 Awards in the Visual Arts Four, Albright-Knox Art Gallery,
Buffalo, NY, traveling exhibition
Cowboys and Indians Common Ground, Loch Haven Art
Center, Orlando, FL, and Boca Rotan Museum of Art, Boca
Raton, FL
1984 Automobile and Culture, Museum of Contemporary Art, Los
Angeles, CA
1982 Recent Trends in Collecting, National Museum of American
Art, Smithsonian Institution, Washington, DC
1981 Alternative Realities in Contemporary American Painting,
Katherine Nash Gallery, University of Minnesota,
Minneapolis, MN
1979 Western States Biennial, Denver Art Museum, Denver, CO,
traveling exhibition
1977 Ancient Roots/New Visions, Tucson Museum of Art,
Tucson, AZ, traveling exhibition
1975 Richard Brown Baker Collects, Art Gallery, Yale University,
New Haven, CT
1973 Whitney Biennial, Whitney Museum of American Art,
New York, NY
1969 Human Concern/Personal Torment, Whitney Museum of
American Art, New York, NY, and University Art Museum,
University of California at Berkeley, Berkeley, CA

DONALD JUDD

Born 1928, Excelsior Springs, Missouri
1953 B.S., Columbia University, New York, New York
1962 M.F.A., Columbia University, New York, New York
Lives in Marfa, Texas

Selected Solo Exhibitions:

1988 Galerie Rolf Ricke, Cologne, West Germany
Whitney Museum of American Art, New York, NY
Galerie Aronowitsch, Stockholm, Sweden
1987 Adair Margo Gallery, El Paso, TX
Galerie Maeght Lelong, Paris, France
1986 Waddington Galleries, London, England
1985 Texas Gallery, Houston, TX
1984 Neueberger Museum, Purchase, NY
Donald Judd Furniture, Max Protech Gallery, New York, NY
1983 Donald Judd: Eight Works in Three Dimensions, Knight
Gallery, Spirit Square Art Center, Charlotte, NC
Carol Taylor Art, Dallas, TX

1981 Newport Harbor Art Museum, Newport Beach, CA
1980 Galerie Annemarie Verna, Zurich, Switzerland
1979 Galerie Annemarie Verna, Zurich, Switzerland
Donald Judd: Survey of Work 1963–1979, Leo Castelli
Gallery, New York, NY
1978 Kroller-Muller Museum, Otterlo, The Netherlands
Heiner Friedrich, Munich, West Germany
1977 Contemporary Arts Center, Cincinnati, OH
Art Museum of South Texas, Corpus Christi, TX
1976 Museum of Modern Art, Oxford, England
Janie C. Lee Gallery, Houston, TX
Kunsthalle Bern, Bern, Switzerland
Kunstmuseum Basel, Basel, Switzerland, traveling exhibition
1975 National Gallery of Canada, Ottawa, Ontario, Canada
1974 Portland Center for the Visual Arts, Portland, OR
1973 Galleria Gian Enzo Sperone, Turin, Italy
1971 Pasadena Art Museum, Pasadena, CA
1970 Konrad Fischer, Dusseldorf, West Germany
Stedelijk Van Abbemuseum, Eindhoven, The Netherlands
Whitechapel Art Gallery, London, England
1969 Galerie Rudolph Zwirner, Cologne, West Germany
Galerie Ileana Sonnabend, Paris, France
1968 Whitney Museum of American Art, New York, NY
1966 Leo Castelli Gallery, New York, NY
1963 Green Gallery, New York, NY

JANET ENGLE KASTNER

Born 1954, Mineola, New York
1977 B.F.A., Kansas City Art Institute, Kansas City, Missouri
1979 M.F.A., State College of Ceramics at Alfred University,
Alfred, New York
Lives in Austin, Texas

Selected Solo Exhibition:

1988 R. S. Levy Gallery, Austin, TX

Selected Group Exhibitions:

1988 Concepts in Clay, Abilene Fine Arts Museum, Abilene, TX
1987 Austin Visual Arts Association 10th Anniversary Exhibition,
301 Congress, Austin, TX
Third Coast Review: A Look at Art in Texas, Aspen Art
Museum, Aspen, CO, traveling exhibition
Texas, The Museum Gallery, San Francisco Museum of
Modern Art, San Francisco, CA
Sculpture: Ideas Defined, Art Gallery, The University of
Texas at San Antonio, San Antonio, TX
1985 New Works, Laguna Gloria Art Museum, Austin, TX
1983 RGK Invitational, RGK Foundation, Austin, TX
1982 10 Women/10 Artists, Diseno Studios Gallery, Austin, TX
1981 New Works V, Laguna Gloria Art Museum at First Federal,
Austin, TX
Invitational '81, Longview Museum and Arts Center,
Longview, TX
1980 New Talent, Delahunty Gallery, Dallas, TX
Texas Only, Laguna Gloria Art Museum, Austin, TX
1979 In Western New York 1979, Albright-Knox Gallery,
Buffalo, NY
1978 The Syracuse Show 1978, Everson Museum of Art,
Syracuse, NY

SHARON KOPRIVA

Born 1948, Houston, Texas
1970 B.S., University of Houston, Houston, Texas
1981 M.F.A., University of Houston, Houston, Texas
Lives in Houston, Texas

Selected Group Exhibitions:

1988   12 Texas Women, National Museum of Women in the Arts,
Washington, DC
1987   Sculpture: The Spectrum, Lawndale Annex, University of
Houston, Houston, TX
Sharon Kopriva/Amy Solomon, Cydney Payton, Artfolio,
Denver, CO
1986   Texas Art Celebration '86, Assistance League of Houston,
Houston, TX
1985   Fresh Paint: The Houston School, Museum of Fine Arts,
Houston, TX
Assistance League Show, Two Houston Center, Houston, TX
1982   Thirteen Artists: A Look at Houston, Georgia State
University, Atlanta, GA
1979   Texas Fine Arts Association 68th Annual, Laguna Gloria Art
Museum, Austin, TX

HAYDN LARSON

Born 1946, Houston, Texas
1970   B.F.A., The University of Texas at Austin, Austin, Texas
Lives in Houston, Texas

Selected Group Exhibitions:

1988   Internal Order, Transco Tower, Houston, TX
1987   Abstract Sensibilities Now, Lawndale Annex, University of
Houston, Houston, TX
Texas Annual, Texas Fine Arts Association, Laguna Gloria
Art Museum, Austin, TX
Visual Articulations '87, Texas A&M University, College
Station, TX
Discoveries in Sculpture '87, Museum of East Texas,
Lufkin, TX
1986   Sculpture '86, Houston, TX
Texas Annual, Texas Fine Arts Association, Laguna Gloria
Art Museum, Austin, TX
New American Talent, Texas Fine Arts Association, Laguna
Gloria Art Museum, Austin, TX
Texas Visions, Transco Tower, Houston, TX
1974   Two Sculptors: Larson and Walsh, Sarah Campbell Blaffer
Gallery, University of Houston, Houston, TX
1970   New Artists Exhibit, Whitney Museum of American Art,
New York, NY
1969   Two-Man Show, Union Gallery, The University of Texas at
Austin, Austin, TX
A Clean Well-Lighted Place, Austin, TX

THANA LAUHAKAIKUL

Born 1941, Bangkok, Thailand
1968   B.F.A., Silphakorn University, Bangkok, Thailand
1974   M.S., Massachusetts College of Art, Boston, Massachusetts
Lives in Austin, Texas

Selected Solo Exhibitions:

1987   Bird Cage, Installation-Sculpture, Danna Center Gallery,
Loyala University, New Orleans, LA
1986   Celebration, Installation-Sculpture, Gallery of Valencia
Community College, Orlando, FL
1985   Infinite Dimensions, Installation-Sculpture, Art Gallery, The
University of Texas at San Antonio, San Antonio, TX
1984   Installation-Sculpture, Charlotte Crosby Kampe Gallery,
Kansas City Art Institute, Kansas City, MO
1981   Installation-Sculpture, The Art Gallery, J. Paul Leonard
Library, San Francisco, CA
1979   Galveston Arts Center, Galveston, TX

Selected Group Exhibitions:

1987   12 Contemporary Thai Artists, MM Shinno Gallery,
Los Angeles, CA
1986   Collage Exhibition, The University of Texas at San Antonio,
San Antonio, TX
Diverse Idioms, Lawndale Annex, University of Houston,
Houston, TX
1982   New Works, Summer '82, Part II, Laguna Gloria Art
Museum, Austin, TX
1981   Sculpture Documentation, in conjunction with College Art
Association of America exhibition, sponsored by the San
Francisco State University School of Creative Art, San
Francisco, CA
1979   Memorial to Those Who Served and Died in the Vietnam
War Exhibition, Lyndon Baines Johnson Library, Austin, TX
1967   XVIII National Exhibition, Bangkok, Thailand

KEN D. LITTLE

Born 1947, Canyon, Texas
1970   B.F.A., Texas Tech University, Lubbock, Texas
1972   M.F.A., University of Utah, Salt Lake City, Utah
Lives in San Antonio, Texas

Selected Solo Exhibitions:

1988   Jennifer Pauls Gallery, Sacramento, CA
1986   Portland Center for the Visual Arts, Portland, OR
1984   Brown-Lupton Gallery, Texas Christian University, Fort
Worth, TX
San Antonio Art Institute, San Antonio, TX
1983   Ken Little: Shattered Portraits and Unlikely Heros, John
Michael Kohler Arts Center, Sheboygan, WI
Quay Gallery, San Francisco, CA, traveling exhibition
1973   Valencia Community College, Orlando, FL

Selected Group Exhibitions:

1988   3-D Animal Exhibition, Joan Robey Gallery, Denver, CO
Mary Warner-Ken Little, Art Gallery, The University of
Texas at San Antonio, San Antonio, TX
1987   Celebration: Fur, Feathers, and Scales, Bellevue Art
Museum, Bellevue, WA
The Eloquent Object, traveling exhibition
Sculpture: Looking into Three Dimensions, Anchorage
Museum of Art, Anchorage, AK
1985   Texas Fantasies, Tyler Museum of Art, Tyler, TX
Body and Soul: Recent Figurative Sculpture, Contemporary
Arts Center, Cincinnati, OH, traveling exhibition
1983   Fleming, Mariscol, Warashina, Little, Kansas City Art
Institute Gallery, Kansas City, MO
Southern Fictions, Contemporary Arts Museum,
Houston, TX
1982   1st Annual Wild West Show, Alberta College of Art, Calgary,
Alberta, Canada
Sculptors at U.C. Davis: Past and Present, Richard Nelson
Gallery of Art, University of California at Davis, Davis, CA
1981   The Image of the House in Contemporary Art, Lawndale
Annex, University of Houston, Houston, TX
Wind and Dust, Lawndale Annex, University of Houston,
Houston, TX
The Taft Menagerie, The Taft Museum, Cincinnati, OH
Animal Images, Renwick Gallery, Smithsonian Institution,
Washington, DC
1980   The Mask as Metaphor, Craft and Folk Art Museum, Los
Angeles, CA
1979   100 Years of American Ceramics, Everson Museum of Art,
Syracuse, NY
1978   Ken Little/Jack Earl, University of Akron, Akron, OH

1977 Reflections of Missoula: 30 Months, Boise Art Gallery, Boise, ID
1976 Land, John Michael Kohler Arts Center, Sheboygan, WI
1975 Rising Stars, Carborundum Museum, Niagara Falls, NY
Scripps Invitational Exhibition, Lang Art Galleries, Claremont, CA

CHARMAINE LOCKE

Born 1950, Waltham, Massachusetts
1973 B.S., Southern Methodist University, Dallas, Texas
Lives in Splendora, Texas

Selected Solo Exhibition:
1985 Graham Gallery, Houston, TX

Selected Group Exhibitions:
1984 Face to Face, Back to Back, California State University at Fullerton, Fullerton, CA
Showdown Houston, Center for Art and Performance, Houston, TX
1983 The House That Art Built, California State University at Fullerton, Fullerton, CA
Artists of the Southwest, The Sculpture Center, New York, NY
Connemara Outdoor Sculpture Exhibition, Connemara, Dallas, TX
1982 The Houston Festival, Commissioned Artist, Interfirst Plaza, Houston, TX
1981 The Image of the House in Contemporary Art, Lawndale Annex, University of Houston, Houston, TX
1980 Couples, Fendrick Gallery, Washington, DC
Two from Texas, Galerie Simonne Stern, New Orleans, LA
1979 Temples, Max Hutchison Gallery, Houston, TX
A Closer Look, Contemporary Arts Museum, Houston, TX
Fire, Contemporary Arts Museum, Houston, TX
1977 Max Hutchison Gallery, Houston, TX

BERT L. LONG, JR.

Born 1940, Houston, Texas
1966–72 Los Angeles Trade Technical College, Los Angeles, California
1972 University of California at Los Angeles, Los Angeles, California
Lives in Shepherd, Texas

Selected Solo Exhibitions:
1988 Concentrations 18, Dallas Museum of Art, Dallas, TX
1987 Art Museum of Southeast Texas, Beaumont, TX
L. A. Louver Gallery, Venice, CA
Butler Gallery, Houston, TX
College of the Mainland, Texas City, TX
1983 Art a Healing Force, Lawndale Annex, University of Houston, Houston, TX
1980 Gallery New Ice Era, Galveston Arts Center, Galveston, TX
1977 Brown & Shurlock Galleries, Beaumont Art League, Beaumont, TX

Selected Group Exhibitions:
1989 Now/Then/Again, Dallas Museum of Art, Dallas, TX
Four Artists Working in Texas, Frito-Lay, Inc., Plano, TX
1988 Art for the Museum: A Legacy, Art Museum of Southeast Texas, Beaumont, TX
Twentieth Century Art in the Museum Collection, Museum of Fine Arts, Houston, TX

Texas Art, Richmond Hall, The Menil Collection, Houston, TX
1987 Third Coast Review: A Look at Art in Texas, Aspen Art Museum, Aspen, CO, traveling exhibition
Small Wonders, Barry Whistler Gallery, Dallas, TX
Phoenix Museum Biennial, Phoenix Art Museum, Phoenix, AZ
Found, Diverse Works, Houston, TX
Expositions in Black, Contemporary Arts Center, New Orleans, LA
From the Object: Still Life Themes & Variations, Glassell School of Art, Museum of Fine Arts, Houston, TX
1986 Texas Invitational 1986, Fort Worth Arts Festival, Fort Worth, TX
Texas Time Machine, Cullen Center, Houston, TX
1985 Fresh Paint: The Houston School, Museum of Fine Arts, Houston, TX
1983 The Watermelon Show, Brazos Gallery, Austin, TX
1982 A Look at Houston, Georgia State University Gallery, University Plaza, Atlanta, GA
1981 Impression of Houston, University of Houston, Downtown College, Houston, TX
1980 The Texas Invitational, Contemporary Arts Center, New Orleans, LA
1979 20th Dixie Annual Works on Paper, Montgomery Museum of Fine Arts, Montgomery, AL
1977 Creative Art Society, Texas Southern University, Houston, TX
1976 American Painters in Paris, Exhibition Center International of Paris, Paris, France

JESSE LOTT

Born 1943, Simmesport, Louisiana
Lives in Houston, Texas

Selected Solo Exhibitions:
1987 Hiram Butler Gallery, Houston, TX
1978 Robinson Galleries, Houston, TX

Selected Group Exhibitions:
1989 Four Artists Working in Texas, Frito-Lay, Inc., Plano, TX
1988 The First Texas Triennial, Contemporary Arts Museum, Houston, TX
1987 Bert Long, James Surls, Jesse Lott, Barry Whistler Gallery, Dallas, TX
1986 Artists of the Southwest, Sarah Campbell Blaffer Gallery, University of Houston, Houston, TX
1984 Collision, Lawndale Annex, University of Houston, Houston, TX
1982 Showdown, Alternative Museum, New York, NY
Recreating the World, University of St. Thomas, Houston, TX
Sense of Spirit, Lawndale Annex, University of Houston, Houston, TX
1981 Sun Show, Pomona Fairgrounds, Pomona, CA

JIM LOVE

Born 1927, Amarillo, Texas
1952 Baylor University, Waco, Texas
Lives in Houston, Texas

Selected Group Exhibitions:
1988 The Poetic Object, San Antonio Museum of Art, San Antonio, TX
Houston '88, 1600 Smith in Cullen Center, Houston, TX
Texas Art, Richmond Hall, The Menil Collection, Houston, TX

One Plus One: Collaboration by Artists and Writers, Glassell School of Art, Museum of Fine Arts, Houston, TX
1987 Third Coast Review: A Look at Art in Texas, Aspen Art Museum, Aspen, CO, traveling exhibition
Found, Diverse Works, Houston, TX
1986 Adjustments Must Be Made Continually, The Nave Museum, Victoria, TX, traveling exhibition
Outdoor Sculpture by Texas Artists, Laguna Gloria Art Museum, Austin, TX, traveling exhibition
1985 Tenth Anniversary Exhibition, D.W. Gallery, Dallas, TX
Comic Relief, Barry Whistler Gallery, Dallas, TX
1984 Le Rime et la Raison, Galeries Nationales du Grand Palais, Paris, France
Contemporary Art in Public Places, Diverse Works, Houston, TX
1983 Inaugural Exhibition, Gateway Gallery, Dallas Museum of Art, Dallas, TX
1979 Fire, Contemporary Arts Museum, Houston, TX
Made in Texas, Archer M. Huntington Art Gallery, The University of Texas at Austin, Austin, TX
1971 one i at a time, Pollock Galleries, Southern Methodist University, Dallas, TX
1968 Whitney Museum of American Art, New York, NY
Industrial Sculpture Park, Great Southwest Corporation, Atlanta, GA
Atelier Chapman Kelley, Dallas, TX, and HemisFair, San Antonio, TX
1966 Exhibition for the Benefit of the Marcel Duchamp Chess Foundation, Cordier and Ekstrom Gallery, New York, NY
1962 Eight Sculptors, Haydor Calhoun Gallery, Dallas, TX
1961 The Art of Assemblage, Museum of Modern Art, New York, NY

KEN LUCE

Born 1950, Houston, Texas
1973 B.F.A., University of Houston, Houston, Texas
1978 M.F.A., University of Houston, Houston, Texas
Lives in Houston, Texas

Selected Solo Exhibitions:
1988 Davis/McClain Gallery, Houston, TX
1986 Eugene Binder Gallery, Dallas, TX
1983 Galveston Arts Center, Galveston, TX
Dubose Gallery, Houston, TX
1979 The Nave Museum, Victoria, TX
1978 Sarah Campbell Blaffer Gallery, University of Houston, Houston, TX

Selected Group Exhibitions:
1988 Texas Art, Richmond Hall, The Menil Collection, Houston, TX
1987 Sculpture: The Spectrum, Lawndale Annex, University of Houston, Houston, TX
Found, Diverse Works, Houston, TX
1986 New Orleans Triennial: The Centennial Exhibition, New Orleans Museum of Art, New Orleans, LA
Texas Time Machine, 1600 Smith in Cullen Center, Houston, TX
1985 New American Talent, Laguna Gloria Art Museum, Austin, TX
Then, Now and Then, 50 Years of University of Houston Art, Lawndale Annex, University of Houston, Houston, TX
1984 Sixtieth Shreveport Art Guild National, Meadows Museum of Art, Centenary College, Shreveport, LA
1980 Houston Area, Sarah Campbell Blaffer Gallery, University of Houston, Houston, TX

1979 Doors, Waco Arts Center, Waco, TX
Hook, Line, and Sinker, Houston, TX
1976 Houston Area, Sarah Campbell Blaffer Gallery, University of Houston, Houston, TX
1974 Houston Area, Sarah Campbell Blaffer Gallery, University of Houston, Houston, TX

WILLIAM LUNDBERG

Born 1942, Albany, California
1964 B.A., San Jose State University, San Jose, California
1966 M.A., University of California at Berkeley, Berkeley, California
Lives in Austin, Texas

Selected Solo Exhibitions:
1989 Langford Architecture Center Gallery, Texas A&M University, College Station, TX
1987 Espace Lyonnais d'Art Contemporain, Lyon, France
Emily Davis Gallery, University of Akron, Akron, OH
1984 Museum of Art, Carnegie Institute, Pittsburgh, PA
1982 Whitney Museum of American Art, New York, NY
1980 P.S. 1, The Institute for Art and Urban Resources, Long Island City, NY
1979 Otis-Parsons Gallery, Los Angeles, CA
1977 Ellen Sragow Gallery, New York, NY
1976 Museum of Art, University of Michigan, Ann Arbor, MI
Detroit Institute of Arts, Detroit, MI
1975 Institute of Contemporary Art, London, England
1974 The Photographers Gallery, London, England
Art Meeting Place, London, England
1972 Gallery House London, The Goethe Institute, London, England

Selected Group Exhibitions:
1988 The First Texas Triennial, Contemporary Arts Museum, Houston, TX
This Is Not a Photograph, Twenty Years of Large Scale Photography, Chrysler Museum of Art, Norfolk, VA
1987 Art That Moves, Laguna Gloria Art Museum, Austin, TX
Installations, Blue Star Art Space, San Antonio, TX
Phoenix Biennial, Phoenix Museum of Art, Phoenix, AZ
1986 Stopped Time, Rockland Art Center, Nyack, NY
1985 A Passage Repeated, Long Beach Museum of Art, Long Beach, CA
1984 Artpark at Manhattan Art, Manhattan Art Gallery, New York, NY
1983 Whitney Biennial, Whitney Museum of American Art, New York, NY
Film as Installation, The Clocktower, New York, NY
1982 Drawing Distinctions: American Drawings of the Seventies, Stadtisch Galerie Im Lenbachhaus, Munich, West Germany
1981 Installations: Film & Video, Thorpe Intermedia Gallery, Sparkhill, NY
1980 Concept, Narrative, Document, Museum of Contemporary Art, Chicago, IL, traveling exhibition
1979 Kunstmarkt, Kunsthalle, Basel, Switzerland
Structure II, John Gibson Gallery, New York, NY
1978 Avant-Garde Film in Great Britain, Centre Beaubourg, Paris, France
1977 Perspectives on Avant-Garde Film, Hayward Gallery, London, England
The Artist's Book, Mandeville Art Gallery, University of California at San Diego, La Jolla, CA
1975 Art Film Tour, Arts Council of Great Britain and the Welsh Arts Council
Progresssionen 1, Cologne, West Germany

1972 Art/Video Confrontation, Musee d'Art Moderne, Paris,
      France
      A Survey of the Avant-Garde in Great Britain: Part 1, Gallery
      House London, The Goethe Institute, London, England
      Grazer Kunstmarkt, Graz, Austria

HEATHER MARCUS

Born 1939, Kansas City, Missouri
1961 B.F.A., University of Kansas, Lawrence, Kansas
Lives in Dallas, Texas

Selected Solo Exhibitions:
1988 The University of Texas at Tyler, Tyler, TX
      Jan Weiner Gallery, Kansas City, MO
1987 Marvin Seline Gallery, Austin, TX
      The University of Texas at the Permian Basin, Odessa, TX
1986 D.W. Gallery, Dallas, TX
      Janet Steinberg Gallery, San Francisco, CA
1984 Nimbus Gallery, Dallas, TX

Selected Group Exhibitions:
1989 Elaine Horwitch Gallery, Palm Springs, CA
1988 12 Texas Women, National Museum of Women in the Arts,
      Washington, DC
      Critic's Choice, D-Art, Dallas, TX
1987 2D-3D, Frito-Lay, Inc., Plano, TX
1986 Austin Visual Arts Association Statewide Spring Exhibition,
      Austin, TX
      Art in the Metroplex, Texas Christian University, Fort
      Worth, TX
      Alexandria Museum, Alexandria, LA
      San Diego Art Institute 1986 National Juried Exhibition, San
      Diego Art Institute, San Diego, CA
      Women of the Big State: Current Art, Women and Their
      Work, Austin, TX
1985 Images '85: A Fine Art Exhibition, sponsored by the El Paso
      Festival, El Paso, TX
      Texas Annual, Texas Fine Arts Association, Laguna Gloria
      Art Museum, Austin, TX
      Texas Visions, Transco Tower, Houston, TX
1984 Art in the Metroplex, Texas Christian University, Fort
      Worth, TX

DALTON MARONEY

Born 1947, Greenville, Texas
1969 B.S., East Texas State University, Commerce, Texas
1972 M.F.A., University of Oklahoma, Norman, Oklahoma
Lives in Arlington, Texas

Selected Solo Exhibitions:
1986 Dalton Maroney/Sculptures, Graham Gallery, Houston, TX
1983 Concentration VIII, Dalton Maroney/Sculptures, Sculpture
      Garden, Dallas Museum of Art, Dallas, TX
1980 Dalton Maroney/New Sculpture, Texas Christian University,
      Fort Worth, TX
1977 University Gallery, East Texas State University, Commerce,
      TX
1976 Mt. Marty College, Yankton, SD
1971 School of Art, University of Oklahoma, Norman, OK

Selected Group Exhibitions:
1985 Tenth Anniversary Exhibition, D.W. Gallery, Dallas, TX
      Off the Wall, Cultural Activities Center, Temple, TX
      Laguna Gloria Art Museum, Austin, TX

1984 Dalton Maroney/Terry Steadman, D.W. Gallery, Dallas, TX
1983 Sculpture on the Wall, San Antonio Art Institute, San
      Antonio, TX
      A Partial Look, Art Museum of South Texas, Corpus Christi,
      TX
1980 Invitational Sculpture Exhibition, Texas Sculpture
      Symposium, Lawndale Annex, University of Houston,
      Houston, TX
1979 Annual Eight-State Exhibition, Oklahoma Art Center,
      Oklahoma City, OK
1977 Competitive Painting and Sculpture, Spiva Art Center,
      Joplin, MO
1975 Invitational Sculpture Show, Storm Lake Art Center, Storm
      Lake, IA
1971 Texas Painting and Sculpture '71, Dallas Museum of Fine
      Arts, Dallas, TX
1970 Annual Eight-State Exhibition, Oklahoma Art Center,
      Oklahoma City, OK

JACK K. MAXWELL

Born 1956, Houston, Texas
1978 B.F.A., Abilene Christian University, Abilene, Texas
1981 M.F.A., University of Tennessee, Knoxville, Tennessee
Lives in Abilene, Texas

Selected Solo Exhibitions:
1988 Contract Design Center, Dallas, TX
1987 Jack Maxwell/Recent Drawings, Painting, and Sculpture,
      Artists League of Texas Gallery, Abilene, TX
1985 Jack Maxwell/Recent Works, Brazosport Center for the Arts
      Gallery, Lake Jackson, TX
1981 Fine Arts Gallery, Maryville, TN

Selected Group Exhibitions:
1988 Campus Outdoor Sculpture Show, Walter State Community
      College, Morristown, TN
      Shore Gallery 10th Anniversary Exhibit, Virginia Shore
      Gallery, Abilene, TX
1987 Sculpture Tour 87/88, University of Tennessee Campus,
      Knoxville, TN
      IMMIX Gallery, Dallas, TX
      ACU Group Exhibition, West Texas Junior College, Snyder,
      TX
      Jack Maxwell and Mel Ristau, Melody Gallery, Santa Fe, NM
1986 Edith Baker Gallery, Dallas, TX
1984 International Art Exposition, International Trade Center,
      Dallas, TX
1983 Jack Maxwell/Don Lacalio, Wilhelm Gallery, Houston, TX
      New Dimensions, Texas Commerce Tower, Houston, TX
1981 Jack Maxwell and Randy Hurst, McClung Museum of Art,
      Knoxville, TN

DAVID MCMANAWAY

Born 1927, Chicago, Illinois
1953–58 University of Arkansas, Fayetteville, Arkansas
Lives in Dallas, Texas

Selected Solo Exhibitions:
1986 Eugene Binder Gallery, Dallas, TX
1980 David McManaway, Works – 20 Years, University Galleries,
      Southern Methodist University, Dallas, TX
1975 Projects I: David McManaway, Dallas Museum of Fine Arts,
      Dallas, TX
1973 Contemporary Arts Museum, Houston, TX
1967 Atelier Chapman Kelley, Dallas, TX
1965 Symbols in Art, Chandler Gallery, Dallas, TX

Selected Group Exhibitions:

1988　The Poetic Object, San Antonio Museum of Art, San Antonio, TX
　　　Texas Art, Richmond Hall, The Menil Collection, Houston, TX

1987　Found, Diverse Works, Houston, TX
　　　Narrative Images — Folk Art and Related Contemporary Art, Crescent Gallery, Dallas, TX, traveling exhibition
　　　2D-3D, Frito-Lay, Inc., Plano, TX

1986　The Texas Landscape, 1900 – 1986, Museum of Fine Arts, Houston, TX

1985　Comic Relief, Barry Whistler Gallery, Dallas, TX

1982　Things Artists Collect, Brown-Lupton Gallery, Texas Christian University, Lubbock, TX
　　　Hearts and Flowers,The Art Center, Waco, TX

1981　Connell, McManaway, Fisher, Mims, Delahunty Gallery, Dallas, TX

1980　Fifteen from Dallas, The Art Center, Waco, TX

1979　Fire, Contemporary Arts Museum, Houston, TX
　　　Made in Texas, Archer M. Huntington Art Gallery, The University of Texas at Austin, Austin, TX

1978　Bag Show, Delta Gallery, Houston, TX
　　　Cowboys, Indians, Settlers, The Art Center, Waco, TX

1977　Gummelt-Love-McManaway, D.W. Gallery, Dallas, TX

1976　Permanent Collection, Fort Worth Art Museum, Fort Worth, TX

1975　Artists Make Toys, Art Museum of South Texas, Corpus Christi, TX

1974　Janie C. Lee Gallery, Dallas, TX

1973　Whitney Biennial, Whitney Museum of American Art, New York, NY

1971　Texas Painting and Sculpture, Pollock Galleries, Southern Methodist University, Dallas, TX
　　　one i at a time, Pollock Galleries, Southern Methodist University, Dallas, TX

1970　Southwest Oklahoma Annual, Oklahoma Art Center, Oklahoma City, OK

1969　Human Concern/Personal Torment, Whitney Museum of American Art, New York, NY

1966　Three-Man Show: Love, Fridge, McManaway, Trinity University, San Antonio, TX

1965　Witte Museum, San Antonio, TX

1961　The Art That Broke the Looking Glass, Dallas Museum for Contemporary Art, Dallas, TX
　　　The Art of Assemblage, Dallas Museum for Contemporary Art, Dallas, TX
　　　South Coast Art Show, Ringling Museum, Sarasota, FL

1959　Texas Annual Exhibition of Painting and Sculpture, Dallas Museum of Fine Arts, Dallas, TX

MARK MONROE

Born 1959, Fort Worth, Texas

1981　B.A., Austin College, Sherman, Texas

1987　M.F.A., The University of Texas at Austin, Austin, Texas

Lives in Splendora, Texas

Selected Solo Exhibition:

1987　Recent Work, Ida Green Gallery, Sherman, TX

Selected Group Exhibitions:

1989　Texas Art Celebration '89, 1600 Smith in Cullen Center, Houston, TX

1988　Houston Area, Sarah Campbell Blaffer Gallery, University of Houston, Houston, TX
　　　Distinctive Vision III, Alternate Gallery, Dallas, TX
　　　Four East Texas Artists, Studios James Surls, Splendora, TX

1987　Guilt by Association, Theatre Gallery, Dallas, TX

1985　On Their Way III, Saulsbury Gallery, Cultural Activities Center, Temple, TX

JESÚS BAUTISTA MOROLES

Born 1950, Corpus Christi, Texas

1978　B.F.A., North Texas State University, Denton, Texas

Lives in Rockport, Texas

Selected Solo Exhibitions:

1988　Davis/McClain Gallery, Houston, TX

1986　Wright Gallery, Dallas, TX
　　　Marilyn Butler Gallery, Scottsdale, AZ
　　　Eve Mannes Gallery, Atlanta, GA

1985　Janus Gallery, Santa Fe, NM
　　　Phyllis Weil & Company, New York, NY
　　　Baumgartner Galleries, Washington, DC

Selected Group Exhibition:

1986　Chulas Fronteras: An Exhibition of Contemporary Texas Hispanic Art, Midtown Art Center, Houston, TX

WILLIE RAY PARISH

Born 1947, Tupelo, Mississippi

1970　B.F.A., University of Mississippi, Oxford, Mississippi

1978　M.F.A., Otis Art Institute of Los Angeles, Los Angeles, California

Lives in El Paso, Texas

Selected Solo Exhibitions:

1988　Installation, Bridge Center for Contemporary Art, El Paso, TX

1983　Sculptural Elements: Sand, Glass, and Light, Art Museum, Ball State University, Muncie, IN

1981　Elemental Works, Mississippi Museum of Art, Jackson, MS

1980　Installation, Memphis State University, Memphis, TN

Selected Group Exhibitions:

1988　North American Sculpture Exhibition, Golden, CO

1987　New American Talent, Laguna Gloria Art Museum, Austin, TX

1986　Excellence '86, Texas Sculpture Association, Dallas, TX
　　　Close to the Border, New Mexico State University, Las Cruces, NM

GERALD J. PATRICK

Born 1946, Dallas, Texas

1970　B.F.A., The University of Texas at Austin, Austin, Texas

1974　M.F.A., The University of Texas at Austin, Austin, Texas

Lives in Austin, Texas

Selected Solo Exhibitions:

1985　Sculpture, Prints, and Drawings, AIR Gallery, Austin, TX

1977　Sculpture, Prints, and Drawings, Amarillo Art Center, Amarillo, TX

Selected Group Exhibitions:

1987　James/Schubert Gallery, Houston, TX
　　　Republic Plaza Sculpture Invitational, Republic Square Plaza, Austin, TX

1985　Group Invitational Show, SOHO Gallery, Austin, TX

1983　AIR Gallery, Austin, TX

1980　Helmut Barnett, David Elliot, Gerald Patrick, Robinson Galleries, Houston, TX

1979   Made in Texas, Archer M. Huntington Art Gallery, The
       University of Texas at Austin, Austin, TX
       Texas: Silver, Mud, Paper, Contemporary Arts Center, New
       Orleans, LA
1976   Personal Objects, The University of Texas at Austin,
       Austin, TX
1969   A Clean Well-Lighted Place, Austin, TX

BOGDAN PERZYNSKI

Born 1954, Poznan, Poland

1979   M.F.A., The Academy of Fine Arts, Poznan, Poland

Lives in Austin, Texas

Selected Solo Exhibitions:

1987   Shoshana Wayne Gallery, Santa Monica, CA
1983   20/26 Piwna Gallery, Warsaw, Poland
1981   Foto-Video Gallery, Cracow, Poland
       20/26 Piwna Gallery, Warsaw, Poland
1980   P.I. Gallery, Cracow, Poland
       Akumulatory 2 Gallery, Poznan, Poland

Selected Group Exhibitions:

1988   Art League of Houston, Houston, TX
       Blue Star Art Space, San Antonio, TX
1987   Los Angeles Contemporary Exhibitions — LACE, Los
       Angeles, CA
       De Saisset Museum, Santa Clara, CA
       College of Creative Studies, Santa Barbara, CA
1985   University Art Museum, University of California at Santa
       Barbara, Santa Barbara, CA
1981   Goethe Institute, Amsterdam, The Netherlands
       Goethe Institute, Cologne, West Germany
1980   Zamek Ksiazecy, Lublin, Poland

JIM POMEROY

Born 1945, Reading, Pennsylvania

1968   B.F.A., The University of Texas at Austin, Austin, Texas
1971   M.A., University of California at Berkeley, Berkeley,
       California
1972   M.F.A., University of California at Berkeley, Berkeley,
       California

Lives in Arlington, Texas

Selected Solo Exhibitions:

1987   Clear Bulbs Cast Sharp Shadows, Pro Arts, Oakland, CA
1986   Reading Lessons and Eye Exercises, California Museum of
       Photography, University of California at Riverside, Riverside,
       CA
       It's Only a Baby Moon: An Anamorphic Seance, University
       Art Gallery, SUNY, Binghamton, NY
1980   ANAGLADE, installation, San Jose Museum of Art,
       San Jose, CA
       Posed Farmalism, collaborative residency with Yura Adams,
       The Farm, San Francisco, CA
1979   Hayden Gallery, Massachusetts Institute of Technology,
       Cambridge, MA
1978   Artists Space, New York, NY
1975   Hansen Fuller Gallery, San Francisco, CA

Selected Group Exhibitions:

1986   The Magic Lantern: Recent Slide Shows, SF Camerawork,
       San Francisco, CA
       El Día de los Muertos, Galeria de la Raza, San Francisco, CA
       Seeing is Believing: The History of 3-D in Art and Popular
       Culture, Fort Wayne Museum of Art, Fort Wayne, IN
       Installed, Humboldt State University, Arcata, CA

1984   A Museum of Fun Part II, organized by Itsuo Sakane for The
       Asahi Shimbun, traveling exhibition throughout Japan
       A Decade of New Art, Artists Space, New York, NY
       Artists Call, Mission Cultural Center, San Francisco, CA
1981   The Stereo Show, Photography at Open Space, Victoria,
       British Columbia, Canada
       Fashion Moda-West, Galeria de la Raza, San Francisco, CA
1979   Space/Time/Sound — 1970's, San Francisco Museum of Art,
       San Francisco, CA
       Bay Area — New Strengths, University Art Museum,
       University of California at Santa Barbara, Santa Barbara, CA
1977   Bookworks, Mills College, Oakland, CA
       Art Stories, Libra Gallery, Claremont Graduate School,
       Claremont, CA
1975   Exchange DFW/SFO, San Francisco Museum of Modern Art,
       San Francisco, CA, and Fort Worth Art Museum, Fort
       Worth, TX
1974   Contemporary American Painting and Sculpture, Krannert
       Museum, University of Illinois, Champaign, IL
1971   Young Bay Area Sculptors, San Francisco Art Institute, San
       Francisco, CA

CHRIS POWELL

Born 1957, DeQueen, Arkansas

1980   B.F.A., Abilene Christian University, Abilene, Texas
1983   M.F.A., Bradley University, Peoria, Illinois

Lives in Fort Worth, Texas

Selected Solo Exhibition:

1986   Fort Worth Gallery, Fort Worth, TX

Selected Group Exhibitions:

1987   Texas Annual, Texas Fine Arts Association, Laguna Gloria
       Art Museum, Austin, TX
       Excellence '87, Texas Sculpture Association, Dallas, TX
       Sculpture: Chris Powell and Ed Haddaway, Fort Worth
       Gallery, Fort Worth, TX
1986   Art in the Metroplex, Texas Christian University, Fort
       Worth, TX
1985   Three-Man Show, Fort Worth Gallery, Fort Worth, TX
       Art in the Metroplex, Texas Christian University, Fort
       Worth, TX
1984   Art in the Metroplex, Texas Christian University, Fort
       Worth, TX

DAMIAN PRIOUR

Born 1949, Corpus Christi, Texas

1972   B.A., The University of Texas at Austin, Austin, Texas

Lives in Austin, Texas

Selected Solo Exhibitions:

1988   Marilyn Butler Fine Art, Santa Fe, NM
       Habatat Galleries, Chicago, IL, and Bay Harbor Islands, FL
1987   Kurland/Summers Gallery, Los Angeles, CA
1986   Habatat Galleries, Bay Harbor Islands, FL
       Conduit, Dallas, TX
       Anne O'Brien Gallery, Washington, DC
1985   Primitive Pets and Monoliths, Matrix Gallery, Austin, TX

Selected Group Exhibitions:

1988   Florida State University Museum, Tallahassee, FL
       A Generation in Glass Sculpture, Florida State University
       Museum, Tallahassee, FL
1987   Bildwerke in Glas, Darmstadt Museum, Darmstadt, West
       Germany

Third Coast Review: A Look at Art in Texas, Aspen Art Museum, Aspen, CO, traveling exhibition
Comparisons and Contrasts, Brunnier Gallery and Museum, Iowa State University, Ames, IA
Glass America 1987, Heller Gallery, New York, NY

1986 Texas Annual, Texas Fine Arts Association, Laguna Gloria Art Museum, Austin, TX

1985 Glass '85, Elaine Potter Gallery, San Francisco, CA
Plate Glass: An Alternative to Blown Glass, Valdosta State College, Valdosta, GA

1984 Two Views from Austin, Perception Galleries, Houston, TX

1983 Touch with Your Eyes, Feel with Your Mind: Surfaces in Contemporary Art, Laguna Gloria Art Museum, Austin, TX

1982 New Works, Laguna Gloria Art Museum, Austin, TX

DONALD REDMAN

Born 1957, Houston, Texas

1978–79 University of St. Thomas, Houston, TX
1979–81 University of Houston, Houston, TX

Lives in Houston, Texas

Selected Solo Exhibitions:

1987 Parkerson Gallery, Houston, TX
1982 Midtown Art Center, Houston, TX
1979 University of St. Thomas, Houston, TX
Little Egypt Studios, Houston, TX

Selected Group Exhibitions:

1987 Toy Show, The Nave Museum, Victoria, TX
Sculpture: The Spectrum, Lawndale Annex, University of Houston, Houston, TX
Art That Moves, Laguna Gloria Art Museum, Austin, TX

1986 Collaborators, Glassell School of Art, Museum of Fine Arts, Houston, TX
New American Talent, Laguna Gloria Art Museum, Austin, TX

1984 Fourth Annual Connemara Exhibition, Connemara, Plano, TX

1983 Third Annual Abilene Outdoor Sculpture Exhibition, Abilene, TX

1982 Monumental Art, Lawndale Annex, University of Houston, Houston, TX

1979 The Door Show, Houston Festival, Houston, TX

1978 Inaugural Pow Wow Show, Lawndale Annex, University of Houston, Houston, TX

1977 Six on Six: Monumental Sculpture, University of Houston, Houston, TX

CLAUDIA REESE

Born 1949, Des Moines, Iowa

1970 B.A., Connecticut College, New London, Connecticut
1974 M.F.A., Indiana University, Bloomington, Indiana

Lives in Austin, Texas

Selected Solo Exhibitions:

1988 Claudia Reese, Recent Sculpture, Southwest Crafts Center, San Antonio, TX

1987 Claudia Reese, Recent Sculpture, R. S. Levy Gallery, Austin, TX

1984 Recent Sculpture, Willingheart Gallery, Austin, TX
1981 Work in Clay, Purdue University, West Lafayette, IN

Selected Group Exhibitions:

1988 Invitational '88, Longview Museum and Arts Center, Longview, TX

1987 Fictional Figure, Caroline Lee Gallery, Houston, TX
Third Coast Review: A Look at Art in Texas, Aspen Art Museum, Aspen, CO, traveling exhibition
Handmade in Texas, presented by the Dallas Craft Guild, LTV Center, Dallas, TX
Austin Visual Arts Association 10th Anniversary Exhibition, 301 Congress, Austin, TX

1986 Animation/Imagination, Frito-Lay Corporation, Dallas, TX
Ateliers D'Art, Paris, France
Chicago International Art Form Exhibition, Chicago, IL
Artist's Eye Exhibition, Kimbell Art Museum, Fort Worth, TX
State of the Arts: Texas!, Contemporary Arts Center, New Orleans, LA

1985 Everyday Plus Clay, John Michael Kohler Arts Center, Sheboygan, WI
Figure It Out, Laguna Gloria Art Museum, Austin, TX

1984 New Talent in Texas, Texas Christian University, Fort Worth, TX

1983 Sculpture: Five Texas Artists, Mattingly Baker Gallery, Dallas, TX

1981 Animal Imagery, Renwick Gallery, Smithsonian Institution, Washington, DC

JOSE LUIS RIVERA

Born 1946, Kingsville, Texas

1970 B.S., Texas A&I University, Kingsville, Texas

Lives in San Antonio, Texas

Selected Solo Exhibition:

1984 Artists Alliance Center, San Antonio, TX

Selected Group Exhibitions:

1988 Sculpture Annual '88, Multi-Cultural Works, Mexic-Arte, Austin, TX
Artists of Texas A&I University, Ben P. Bailey Art Building, Texas A&I University, Kingsville, TX
Art Forms: A Survey of Contemporary Three Dimensional Works, Galeria Sin Fronteras, Austin, TX

1987 Influence, San Antonio Museum of Art, San Antonio, TX

1986 Significant Contributions, Mexic-Arte at Arts Warehouse, Austin, TX

1985 North Meets South Exhibition — An Indigenous Perspective, Dougherty Cultural Arts Center, Austin, TX
Austin Annual, Mexic-Arte at Arts Warehouse, Austin, TX

1982 Un Camino de Muchas Veredas, Ben P. Bailey Fine Arts Gallery, Texas A&I University, Kingsville, TX
Polyforum Cultural David Alfaro Siqueiros, Mexico City, Mexico

1981 St. Mary's University Academic Library, St. Mary's University, San Antonio, TX

1979 Fire, Contemporary Arts Museum, Houston, TX

1977 Dalé Gas: An Exhibit of Contemporary Chicano Art, Contemporary Arts Museum, Houston, TX

1974 Los Quemados, Instituto Cultural Mexicano, HemisFair Plaza, San Antonio, TX

1973 Chicano Art Center, University of California at Berkeley, Berkeley, CA

1970 Latin American Library, Oakland, CA

JILL SABLOSKY

Born 1954, Philadelphia, Pennsylvania
1976   B.A., University of Maryland, College Park, Maryland
1979   M.F.A., University of Pennsylvania, Philadelphia,
       Pennsylvania
Lives in Fort Worth, Texas

Selected Group Exhibitions:
1988   Excellence '88, Texas Sculpture Association, Dallas, TX
1986   Sculpture Outdoors, Beaver College, Wyncote, PA
       Cadme Gallery, Philadelphia, PA
1985   Networking: Italian and American Artists, Port of History
       Museum, Philadelphia, PA
       C.A.N. Gallery, Creative Artist Network, Philadelphia, PA
1984   84 Sculptures for '84, Rodger La Pelle Gallery,
       Philadelphia, PA
1983   Women: Self-Image, Philadelphia Art Alliance, Women's
       Caucus for Art, Philadelphia, PA
1981   Foreign Sculptors in Italy, Commune di Forte dei Marmi,
       Italy
1979   Institute of Contemporary Art, University of Pennsylvania,
       Philadelphia, PA
1976   University of Maryland, College Park, MD

DANIEL SELLERS

Born 1948, Lawton, Oklahoma
1980   B.A., Cameron University, Lawton, Oklahoma
1982   M.F.A., Southern Methodist University, Dallas, Texas
Lives in Fort Worth, Texas

Selected Solo Exhibitions:
1985   Fort Worth Gallery, Fort Worth, TX
1984   Fort Worth Gallery, Fort Worth, TX
1983   Fort Worth Gallery, Fort Worth, TX
       Dean's Invitational, The University of Texas at Dallas,
       Richardson, TX

Selected Group Exhibitions:
1985   Dubose Gallery, Houston, TX
1984   16 Sculptors, Nimbus Gallery, Dallas, TX
       Fort Worth Gallery, Fort Worth, TX
       Critic's Choice, D-Art, Dallas, TX
1983   Art in the Metroplex, Dallas, TX
       Nimbus Gallery, Dallas, TX
       Cal-Tex Permanent Collection, Las Colinas, TX
       Fort Worth Gallery, Fort Worth, TX
1982   500 Exposition Gallery, Dallas, TX
1977   Armory Show, Lawton Armory, Lawton, OK
1976   19th Annual Delta Exhibition, Little Rock Museum of Art,
       Little Rock, AR
1975   18th Annual Delta Exhibition, Little Rock Museum of Art,
       Little Rock, AR

GEORGE SMITH

Born 1941, Buffalo, New York
1969   B.F.A., San Francisco Art Institute, San Francisco, California
1972   M.A., Hunter College, New York, New York
Lives in Houston, Texas

Selected Solo Exhibitions:
1983   George Smith, New Works, Sewall Art Gallery, Rice
       University, Houston, TX
1973   Everson Museum of Art, Syracuse, NY

Selected Group Exhibitions:
1987   Graham Gallery, Houston, TX
       Art in Public Places, Museum of African American Art and
       Culture, Los Angeles, CA
1986   A Sampler, 30 Sculptors, Longview Museum and Arts
       Center, Longview, TX
       Contemporary Sculpture, Selections from the Permanent
       Collection, Studio Museum in Harlem, New York, NY
       Artist at Hunter, Hunter College, New York, NY
       A Houston Dozen, Beaumont, TX
       Sculpture '86, site project, Houston, TX
       New Directions in Public Art, Dallas, TX
1984   Art in Public Places, sponsored by Diverse Works,
       Houston, TX
       Environmental Sculpture Project, Houston Art Festival,
       Houston, TX
1983   Conceptions, Galveston Arts Center, Galveston, TX
1982   A Celebration of Texas Sculpture, Sam Houston State
       College, Huntsville, TX
       Ritual and Myth, Studio Museum in Harlem, New York, NY
1980   Ten-Year Retrospective Exhibition, Studio Museum in
       Harlem, New York, NY
       11th International Sculpture Conference, Washington, DC,
       and Baltimore, MD
1979   Environmental Sculpture Installation, Herbert F. Johnson
       Museum of Art, Ithaca, NY
1978   Environmental Sculpture Project, Roosevelt Art Workshop
       and Museum, Long Island, NY
1976   Hallwalls, Buffalo, NY
1973   Nine Artists of Western New York, traveling exhibition
       Contemporary American Artists, Arnot Museum of Art,
       Elmira, NY
       Enviro Vision, New York Cultural Center, New York, NY
1971   Three Environmental Sculptors, Rutgers University, New
       Brunswick, NJ
1970   Contemporary Black American Artists, Hudson River
       Museum, Yonkers, NY
       Sculpture Biennial, Whitney Museum of American Art,
       New York, NY
1968   New Perspectives in Black Art, Oakland Museum of Art,
       Oakland, CA

HILLS SNYDER

Born 1950, Lubbock, Texas
1969–70   University of Kansas, Lawrence, Kansas
1970–73   Texas Tech University, Lubbock, Texas
Lives in Austin, Texas

Selected Solo Exhibitions:
1989   Yellowstone Art Center, Billings, MT
1987   June Rise Ramble, Custer County Art Center, Miles City, MT
       Garage Optimism, Patrick Gallery, Austin, TX
1985   Hills Snyder: Constructions and Drawings, Tyler Museum of
       Art, Tyler, TX
1974   Working as If the World Ended, Y.W.C.A. Community
       Center, Lubbock, TX

Selected Group Exhibitions:
1988   Small Sculpture, Robischon Gallery, Denver, CO
       Austin Art at Large, circulating billboard, Austin, TX
       West Texas Homecoming, Lubbock Fine Arts Center,
       Lubbock, TX
       Distinctive Vision 3, Alternate Gallery, Dallas, TX
       Beyond Sculpture: Constructions by Texas Artists, Abilene
       Fine Arts Museum, Abilene, TX

1987　Third Coast Review: A Look at Art in Texas, Aspen Art
　　　Museum, Aspen, CO, traveling exhibition
　　　Distinctive Vision 1, Alternate Gallery, Dallas, TX
　　　Handmade in Texas, presented by the Dallas Craft Guild,
　　　LTV Center, Dallas, TX
　　　Gardens — Reality and Myth, Patrick Gallery, Austin, TX
　　　Austin Visual Arts Association 10th Anniversary Exhibition,
　　　301 Congress, Austin, TX
1986　A Question of Scale, Missoula Museum of the Arts,
　　　Missoula, MT
　　　Texas Select, Art League of Houston, Houston, TX
　　　Sculpture Symposium '86, Transco Tower, Houston, TX
1985　John Hernandez/Hills Snyder/Randy Twaddle, Patrick
　　　Gallery, Austin, TX
　　　Off the Wall, Cultural Activities Center, Temple, TX
　　　Texas Visions, Transco Tower, Houston, TX
1984　New Works by Austin Artists, Laguna Gloria Art Museum,
　　　Austin, TX
　　　Texas on My Mind: Contemporary Visions of the Lone Star
　　　State, Artrain, traveling exhibition
　　　Four Texas Artists, Galveston, TX
　　　Patrick Cronin and Hills Snyder, Corvallis Arts Center,
　　　Corvallis, OR
　　　3 Dimensions, Main Gallery, Fox Fine Arts Center, The
　　　University of Texas at El Paso, El Paso, TX
1983　Visual Short Stories: Five from Austin, The Art Center,
　　　Waco, TX
　　　Touch with the Eyes, Feel with the Mind: Surfaces in
　　　Contemporary Art, Laguna Gloria Art Museum, Austin, TX
　　　Sculpture on the Wall, San Antonio Art Institute, San
　　　Antonio, TX
1982　New Visions, Patrick Gallery, Austin, TX
1981　Mythmakers and Storytellers, Patrick Gallery, Austin, TX
1980　Night Journeys, Lubbock Lights, Lubbock, TX
1979　Miniatures, Lawndale Annex, University of Houston,
　　　Houston, TX
1978　Why American Men Wear Veils, InterArtWorks, Austin, TX
1977　Three at Trinity, Trinity House Gallery, Austin, TX

C. M. STAGG

Born 1939, Beaumont, Texas

1971　B.F.A., Baylor University, Waco, Texas
1974　M.F.A., Tyler School of Art, Temple University, Elkins Park,
　　　Pennsylvania

Lives in Vidor, Texas

Selected Solo Exhibitions:

1986　Dishman Gallery, Lamar University, Beaumont, TX
1979　The Clocktower, New York, NY
　　　Anyart Gallery, Providence, RI
1974　Tyler School of Art, Elkins Park, PA
1971　McLennon Community College, Waco, TX
1970　Baylor University, Waco, TX

Selected Group Exhibitions:

1986　Exhibition at the Kyle, Beaumont, TX
1980　Points of View: The Eighties, Cheltenham Art Center,
　　　Cheltenham, England
1972　Artists Salon, Oklahoma Museum of Art, Oklahoma City, OK
　　　Southwest Fine Arts Biennial, Santa Fe, NM
　　　Jefferson County Arts Festival, Port Arthur, TX
1971　Artists Salon, Oklahoma Museum of Art, Oklahoma City, OK
　　　The Five-State Art Exhibition, Port Arthur, TX
1970　Oklahoma Art Center, Oklahoma City, OK
　　　Laguna Gloria Art Museum, Austin, TX
1969　El Paso Museum of Art, El Paso, TX

GISELA-HEIDI STRUNCK

Born 1945, Deggendorf, Germany

1962–66　Studied in Madrid, Florence, Athens, and Oslo
1970–72　University of Dallas, Irving, TX

Lives in Grapevine, Texas

Selected Solo Exhibitions:

1985　Recent Sculptures, Conduit Gallery, Dallas, TX
1981　Clifford Gallery, Dallas, TX
1980　The Art Center, Waco, TX
1977　University of Wisconsin at Stout, Stout, WI
　　　Sculptures 1976, D. W. Gallery, Dallas, TX
1976　Gisela-Heidi Strunck — Sculptures, Tyler Museum of Art,
　　　Tyler, TX

Selected Group Exhibitions:

1988　Texas Women, National Museum of Women in the Arts,
　　　Washington, DC
　　　ReView: Ten Years of Women and Their Work, One
　　　Congress Plaza, Austin, TX
　　　Beyond Sculpture: Constructions by Texas Artists, Abilene
　　　Fine Arts Museum, Abilene, TX
1987　Texas Annual, Texas Fine Arts Association, Laguna Gloria
　　　Art Museum, Austin, TX
　　　2D-3D, Frito-Lay, Inc., Plano, TX
　　　Gisela-Heidi Strunck — Sculpture, Kenneth
　　　Holden — Landscape Paintings, Conduit Gallery, Dallas, TX
1986　Women of the Big State, Current Art, Arts Warehouse,
　　　Austin, TX, traveling exhibition
　　　Texas German Art, Goethe Institute, Houston, TX
　　　150 Works by Texas Women Artists, Dallas City Hall, Dallas,
　　　TX
　　　Critic's Choice, D-Art, Dallas, TX
　　　Juergen Strunck — Prints, Gisela-Heidi Strunck — Sculptures,
　　　East Texas State University, Commerce, TX
1985　Texas Visions, Museum of Art of the American West,
　　　Houston, TX
　　　Diversity '85, D-Art, Dallas, TX
　　　Gisela-Heidi Strunck — Sculptures, Juergen Strunck — Prints,
　　　Corpus Christi State University, Corpus Christi, TX
　　　Juergen Strunck, Gisela-Heidi Strunck, Brazos Gallery,
　　　Richland College, Dallas, TX
1984　Line, Color, Form, and Texture, Gateway Gallery, Dallas
　　　Museum of Art, Dallas, TX
1983　7th Biennial Five-State Art Exhibition, Port Arthur, TX
1982　Texas Fine Arts Association 71st Annual, Laguna Gloria Art
　　　Museum, Austin, TX
1981　6th Biennial Five-State Art Exhibition, Port Arthur, TX
1979　Women-in-Sight: New Art in Texas, Women and Their
　　　Work, Dougherty Cultural Arts Center, Austin, TX, traveling
　　　exhibition
1978　1-2-3-4-5 Exhibition, Tyler Museum of Art, Tyler, TX
1976　D. W. Gallery, Dallas, TX
　　　Invitational '76, Longview Museum and Arts Center,
　　　Longview, TX
1975　Women Artists, Austin College, Sherman, TX
1974　Smither Gallery, Dallas, TX
1973　North Texas Painting and Sculpture Exhibition, Dallas
　　　Museum of Fine Arts, Dallas, TX

JAMES SURLS

Born 1943, Terrell, Texas

1966　B.S., Sam Houston State University, Huntsville, Texas
1969　M.F.A., Cranbrook Academy of Art, Bloomfield Hills,
　　　Michigan

Lives in Splendora, Texas

Selected Solo Exhibitions:

1984   Visions: James Surls, 1974–1984, Dallas Museum of Art,
          Dallas, TX, traveling exhibition
          Fuller Goldeen Gallery, San Francisco, CA
          Delahunty Gallery, New York, NY
          James Surls: New Sculpture, Delahunty Gallery, Dallas, TX
1982   Allan Frumkin Gallery, New York, NY
1981   Daniel Weinberg Gallery, San Francisco, CA
          Delahunty Gallery, Dallas, TX
1980   James Surls: New Sculpture, Allan Frumkin Gallery, New
          York, NY
1979   Robinson Galleries, Houston, TX
          Delahunty Gallery, Dallas, TX
1977   James Surls: Recent Drawings, Contemporary Arts Museum,
          Houston, TX
          James Surls: Sculpture, Delahunty Gallery, Dallas, TX
1975   James Surls: Recent Works, Austin College, Sherman, TX
          James Surls: Sculptor, Contemporary Arts Museum,
          Houston, TX
1974   Tyler Museum of Art, Tyler, TX

Selected Group Exhibitions:

1984   Contemporary Wood Sculpture, Crocker Art Museum,
          Sacramento, CA
          Painting, Drawing, and Sculpture, American and European,
          L. A. Louver Gallery, Venice, CA
          Visions of Paradise: Installations by Vito Acconci, David
          Ireland, and James Surls, Hayden Gallery and MIT campus,
          Massachusetts Institute of Technology, Cambridge, MA
          American Art Since 1970: Painting, Sculpture, and Drawings
          from the Collection of the Whitney Museum of American
          Art, New York, NY, traveling exhibition
1983   The House That Art Built, The Main Gallery, Visual Arts
          Center, California State University, Fullerton, CA
          Southern Fictions, Contemporary Arts Museum, Houston, TX
          New Art from a New City — Houston, Salzburger
          Kunstverein, Salzburg, Austria
          Minimalism to Expressionism: Painting and Sculpture since
          1965 from the Permanent Collection, Whitney Museum of
          American Art, New York, NY
          Fact and Fiction, Aspen Center for the Visual Arts,
          Aspen, CO
          A Century of Modern Sculpture: 1882 – 1982, Museum of
          Fine Arts, Houston, TX
1982   Houston Art in Norway, Stavanger Museum, Stavanger,
          Norway
          Lucero, Scanga, Surls, Texas Gallery, Houston, TX, and
          Delahunty Gallery, Dallas, TX
          American Artists: Sculpture 1982, San Francisco Museum of
          Modern Art, San Francisco, CA
          A Sense of Spirit, Lawndale Annex, University of Houston,
          Houston, TX
1981   The Image of the House in Contemporary Art, Lawndale
          Annex, University of Houston, Houston, TX
          First Annual Abilene Outdoor Sculpture Exhibition,
          Abilene, TX
1980   Across the Nation: Fine Art for Federal Buildings,
          1972 – 1979, National Collection of Fine Arts, Smithsonian
          Institution, Washington, DC
          Eleventh International Sculpture Conference, International
          Sculpture Center, Washington, DC
          The Texas Invitational, Contemporary Arts Center, New
          Orleans, LA
          Visions and Configurations, Fullerton Art Gallery, California
          State University, Fullerton, CA
          Inside Texas Borders, South Texas Artmobile, Corpus Christi
          State University, Corpus Christi, TX

Charmaine Locke and James Surls, Stephen F. Austin
University, Nacogdoches, TX
Response, Tyler Museum of Art, Tyler, TX
1979   18 Texans, Weil Gallery, Corpus Christi State University,
          Corpus Christi, TX
          Made in Texas, Archer M. Huntington Art Gallery, The
          University of Texas at Austin, Austin, TX
          Fire, Contemporary Arts Museum, Houston, TX
          Whitney Biennial, Whitney Museum of American Art, New
          York, NY
1978   Four Houston Artists, University Fine Arts Gallery, Florida
          State University, Tallahasse, FL
          Texas in Chicago, Marianne Deson Gallery, Chicago, IL
          Art in Texas, The Renaissance Society at the University of
          Chicago, Chicago, IL
          One Person Exhibitions: Janis Provisor, Jim Richard, James
          Surls, Casey Williams, New Orleans Museum of Art, New
          Orleans, LA
1977   New Orleans Biennial, New Orleans Museum of Art, New
          Orleans, LA
          Installations for Corner Spaces, Fort Worth Art Museum,
          Fort Worth, TX
          Nine Artists: Theodoron Awards, Solomon R. Guggenheim
          Museum, New York, NY
1976   The Philadelphia Houston Exchange, Institute of
          Contemporary Art, University of Pennsylvania, Philadelphia,
          PA, and Contemporary Arts Museum, Houston, TX
          Artpark 1976, The Program in Visual Arts, Artpark,
          Lewiston, NY
          Tex/Lax: Texas in L.A., Union Gallery, California State
          University, Los Angeles, CA
1975   The Dog Show, University Galleries, Southern Methodist
          University, Dallas, TX
          Artists Make Toys, Art Museum of South Texas, Corpus
          Christi, TX
          Texas Tough, Witte Museum, San Antonio, TX
1974   12 Texas, Contemporary Arts Museum, Houston, TX
          First Biennial Invitational Painting and Sculpture
          Exhibition, Beaumont Art Museum, Beaumont, TX
          Houston Designer Craftsmen '74, Sarah Campbell Blaffer
          Gallery, University of Houston, Houston, TX
1973   Tarrant County Annual, Fort Worth Art Museum, Fort
          Worth, TX

PATRICIA TILLMAN

Born 1954, Limestone, Maine
1976   B.F.A., The University of Texas at Austin, Austin, Texas
1978   M.F.A., University of Oklahoma, Norman, Oklahoma
Lives in Waco, Texas

Selected Solo Exhibitions:

1987   Fort Worth Gallery, Fort Worth, TX
1985   Fort Worth Gallery, Fort Worth, TX
1984   The Art Center, Waco, TX
          Brown-Lupton Gallery, Texas Christian University, Fort
          Worth, TX
1980   Koehler Cultural Center, San Antonio College, San
          Antonio, TX
          D.W. Gallery, Dallas, TX
1979   University Art Gallery, North Texas State University,
          Denton, TX
          About a House, Art Museum of South Texas, Corpus
          Christi, TX

Selected Group Exhibitions:

1988 12 Texas Women, National Museum for Women in the Arts, Washington, DC

1986 Artist's Response to Architecture, The Nave Museum, Victoria, TX
Small Sculpture Invitational Exhibition, University Gallery, The University of Texas at Arlington, Arlington, TX
Artists of the Western Stairstep, Patrick Gallery, Austin, TX
Texas Select, Art League of Houston, Houston, TX

1985 Tenth Anniversary Exhibition, D.W. Gallery, Dallas, TX
Texas Visions, Transco Tower, Houston, TX

1984 Line, Color, Form, and Texture, Gateway Gallery, Dallas Museum of Art, Dallas, TX

1983 Sculpture on the Wall, San Antonio Art Institute, San Antonio, TX
The Art Center 1983 Competition, The Art Center, Waco, TX

1981 Off the Wall: Installations and Environments, San Antonio Museum of Art, San Antonio, TX
The Image of the House in Contemporary Art, Lawndale Annex, University of Houston, Houston, TX

1980 Shreveport Art Guild National, Meadows Museum of Art, Shreveport, LA

1979 Women-in-Sight: New Art in Texas, Women and Their Work, Dougherty Cultural Arts Center, Austin, TX, traveling exhibition
Made in Texas, Archer M. Huntington Art Gallery, The University of Texas at Austin, Austin, TX

1978 Corpus Christi Art Foundation Exhibition, Art Museum of South Texas, Corpus Christi, TX

1977 Amarillo Art Competition, Amarillo Art Center, Amarillo, TX

MICHAEL TRACY

Born 1943, Bellevue, Ohio

1964 B.A., St. Edward's University, Austin, Texas
1969 M.F.A., The University of Texas at Austin, Austin, Texas

Lives in San Ygnacio, Texas

Selected Solo Exhibitions:

1987 Arthur Roger Gallery, New Orleans, LA
P.S.1, The Institute for Art and Urban Resources, Long Island City, NY

1986 Eloy Tarcisio, Mexico City, Mexico
Zolla/Lieberman Gallery, Chicago, IL
Vanguard Gallery, Philadelphia, PA
Adair Margo Gallery, El Paso, TX

1984 Hiram Butler Gallery, Houston, TX

1983 Delahunty Gallery, Dallas, TX
Contemporary Arts Museum, Houston, TX

1982 Hadler/Rodriguez Galleries, Houston, TX

1980 Mary Boone Gallery, New York, NY
Max Hutchison Gallery, Houston, TX

1979 Galeria Pecanins, Mexico City, Mexico

1977 Roberto Molina Gallery, Houston, TX

1974 Louisiana Gallery, Houston, TX

1972 Sarah Campbell Blaffer Gallery, University of Houston, Houston, TX
Art Museum of South Texas, Corpus Christi, TX

1971 Marion Koogler McNay Art Museum, San Antonio, TX

Selected Group Exhibitions:

1988 Contemporary Art from Texas, Groninger Museum, Groningen, The Netherlands

1987 Sacred Spaces, Everson Museum of Art, Syracuse, NY

1986 Texas Landscape, 1900 – 1986, Museum of Fine Arts, Houston, TX
Momento Mori, Centro Cultural Contemporáneo, Mexico City, Mexico
Collaborations/Transformations, San Antonio Art Institute, San Antonio, TX
Other Gods: Containers of Belief, Everson Museum of Art, Syracuse, NY
Personal Environment, Museum of Fine Arts, Santa Fe, NM

1985 Ripe Fruit, P.S.1, The Institute for Art and Urban Resources, Long Island City, NY

1984 Content, a Contemporary Focus, 1974 – 1984, Hirshhorn Museum and Sculpture Garden, Smithsonian Institution, Washington, DC

1983 New Art, Tate Gallery, London, England
New Art from a New City – Houston, Salzburger Kunstverein, Salzburg, Austria

1982 In Our Time, Contemporary Arts Museum, Houston, TX
Venice Biennale, Venice, Italy

1981 Mary Boone Gallery, New York, NY

1979 Made in Texas, Archer M. Huntington Art Gallery, The University of Texas at Austin, Austin, TX

ROBERT WADE

Born 1943, Austin, Texas

1965 B.F.A., The University of Texas at Austin, Austin, Texas
1966 M.A., University of California at Berkeley, Berkeley, California

Lives in Santa Fe, New Mexico

Selected Solo Exhibitions:

1987 Cowgirls' Cowboys, Atwell Gallery, Colorado Springs, CO

1985 Giant Eighteen Wheeler, Carl's Corner Truckstop, Hillsboro, TX

1983 Six Frogs over Tango, Tango, Dallas, TX

1982 Bronze Cowboy on Giant Armadillo, Pasadena Town Square, Federated Realty, Inc., Pasadena, TX

1980 Ghost Riders Installation, Florida School of the Arts, Palatka, FL

1979 Biggest Cowboy Boots in the World, Washington Art Site, Washington, DC
Art Museum of South Texas, Corpus Christi, TX

1978 Giant Iguana, Lone Star Cafe, New York, NY
Janus Gallery, Los Angeles, CA

1975 Map of the United States, Public Sculpture, National Endowment Bicentennial Project, Dallas, TX
Texas Formal Garden, Laguna Gloria Art Museum, Austin, TX
Mobile Home Installation, with photographs, Delahunty Gallery, Dallas, TX

1974 Kornblee Gallery, New York, NY

1973 University of California at San Diego, La Jolla, CA
Map of Texas, University of St. Thomas, Houston, TX
Waco Installation, Baylor University, Waco, TX
Kornblee Gallery, New York, NY

1972 Smither Gallery, Dallas, TX
Kornblee Gallery, New York, NY

1971 Kornblee Gallery, New York, NY

1967 Baylor University, Waco, TX

Selected Group Exhibitions:

1987 Myth Makers, William Campbell Contemporary Art, Fort Worth, TX
True Wit, Cullen Center, Houston, TX
Alcove Show, New Mexico Museum of Fine Art, Santa Fe, NM

1986   T-Shirts by Artists, Museum of Contemporary Art,
        Chicago, IL
        Artists' Books Exhibition, University Library of Oldenburg,
        Oldenburg, West Germany
        The Texas Landscape, 1900 – 1986, Museum of Fine Arts,
        Houston, TX
        Outdoor Sculpture by Texas Artists, Laguna Gloria Art
        Museum, Austin, TX, traveling exhibition
1985   Texas Visions, Museum of Art of the American West,
        Houston, TX
        The Big Car Show: Contemporary Visions of the Automobile,
        Herron Gallery, Indianapolis Center for Contemporary Art,
        Indianapolis, IN
1984   The Great Buffalo Art Show, Cameron University,
        Lawton, OK
        Line, Color, Form, and Texture, Gateway Gallery, Dallas
        Museum of Art, Dallas, TX
        Texas on My Mind: Contemporary Visions of the Lone Star
        State, Artrain, traveling exhibition
1983   2nd Annual Wild West Show, Alberta College of Art, Calgary,
        Alberta, Canada
1980   Longview Museum and Arts Center, Longview, TX
1979   The American Image, 1875 – 1978, Weil Gallery, Corpus
        Christi State University, Corpus Christi, TX
        Made in Texas, Archer M. Huntington Art Gallery, The
        University of Texas at Austin, Austin, TX
        Fire, Contemporary Arts Museum, Houston, TX
        Dollhouse Invitational, Princeton University, Princeton, NJ
1978   Dallas in Chicago: Fisher, Green, Surls, Wade, Marianne
        Deson Gallery, Chicago, IL
1977   American Artists in the Tenth Paris Biennale, Hudson River
        Museum, Yonkers, NY
        Tenth Paris Biennale, Musee d'Art Moderne, Paris, France
        Allen, Jimenez, Wade, American Cultural Center, Paris,
        France
        Photography and Painting in Dialogue, Kuntshaus, Zurich,
        Switzerland
        Artist's Maps, Museum of Modern Art, New York, NY
1976   Texas in Los Angeles, California State University, Los
        Angeles, CA
1975   Texas Tough, Witte Museum, San Antonio, TX
        Exchange DFW/SFO, San Francisco Museum of Modern Art,
        San Francisco, CA, and Fort Worth Art Museum, Fort
        Worth, TX
        New Orleans Biennial, New Orleans Museum of Art, New
        Orleans, LA
1974   10 Views of the West, Contemporary Arts Foundation,
        Oklahoma City, OK
        12 Texas, Contemporary Arts Museum, Houston, TX
1973   First Motorcycle Art, Phoenix Museum of Art, Phoenix, AZ
        Emerging Realism and Surrealism, Storm King Art Center,
        Mountainville, NY
        Green, Mims, Roche, Wade, Tyler Museum of Art, Tyler, TX
        Whitney Biennial, Whitney Museum of American Art, New
        York, NY
        New Orleans Biennial, New Orleans Museum of Art, New
        Orleans, LA
1972   Wade/Bladen, Temple University, Philadelphia, PA
1970   South/Southwest Young American Artists, Fort Worth Art
        Museum, Fort Worth, TX
        South Texas Sweet Funk, St. Edward's University, Austin, TX
1969   Whitney Biennial, Whitney Museum of American Art, New
        York, NY
        New Orleans Biennial, New Orleans Museum of Art, New
        Orleans, LA
1968   Sculpture Survey, HemisFair, San Antonio, TX

MAC WHITNEY

Born 1936, Manhattan, Kansas

1958   B.A., Kansas State Teachers College, Emporia, Kansas
1968   M.F.A., University of Kansas, Lawrence, Kansas

Lives in Midlothian, Texas

Selected Solo Exhibitions:

1986   LTV Center Pavilion, Dallas, TX
1979   Exhibition organized by Kristan Murchison on the estate of
        Mr. and Mrs. John Murchison, Dallas, TX
        Corcoran Gallery, Washington, DC
1978   Robinson Galleries, Houston, TX
1976   Robinson Galleries, Houston, TX
1971   DuBose Gallery, Houston, TX
1969   One Main Place Gallery, Dallas, TX

Selected Group Exhibitions:

1986   Two large-scale commissions for Cadillac Fairview, Park
        West, and I.B.M., Dallas, TX
        Outdoor Sculpture by Texas Artists, Laguna Gloria Art
        Museum, Austin, TX, traveling exhibition
1981   Great Plains Outdoor Sculpture Exhibition, Sheldon Art
        Gallery, Lincoln, NE
1977   Jewish Community Center, Houston, TX
        The Nave Museum, Victoria, TX
1976   Invitational Sculpture Exhibition, The University of Texas at
        Dallas, Richardson, TX

BEN WOITENA

Born 1942, San Antonio, Texas

B.F.A., The University of Texas at Austin, Austin, Texas
M.F.A., University of Southern California, Los Angeles, California

Lives in Houston, Texas

Selected Solo Exhibitions:

1986   The Houston Pioneer Artists Series, Midtown Art Center,
        Houston, TX
1983   Century Development — Allen Center Rotating Sculpture
        Program, Houston, TX
1975   Sol del Rio Gallery, San Antonio, TX

Selected Group Exhibitions:

1988   A Sense of Site Specific Sculpture, Sharon Arts Center,
        Sharon, NH
1987   Abstract Sensibilities Now, Lawndale Annex, University of
        Houston, Houston, TX
1986   A Houston Dozen: Twelve Sculptors, Beaumont, TX
        Collaborators: Artists Working Together in Houston,
        1971 – 1986, Houston, TX
        Excellence '86, Texas Sculpture Association, Dallas, TX
1985   Beverly Gordon Fine Art Gallery, Dallas, TX
1984   Two Houston Center: 1984 Show, Houston, TX
1983   Outdoor Sculpture, San Antonio Art Institute, San
        Antonio, TX
        Exhibition at Texas Commerce Bank Towers, Diverse Works,
        Houston, TX
1982   San Antonio Museum Association, San Antonio, TX
        Houston Art in Norway, Stavanger Museum, Stavanger,
        Norway
1981   Abilene Centennial Sculpture Exhibit, Abilene, TX

1980   Longview Museum and Arts Center, Longview, TX
1979   Made in Texas, Archer M. Huntington Art Gallery, The University of Texas at Austin, Austin, TX
      Robinson Galleries, Houston, TX
      Contemporary Arts Museum, Houston, TX
1978   Molina Gallery, Houston, TX
1977   Young Texas Artists Series, Amarillo Art Center, Amarillo, TX
1976   Beaumont Art Museum Invitational, Beaumont, TX
1975   Monumental Sculpture: Houston 1975, Houston, TX
      B. R. Kornblatt Gallery, Inc., Baltimore, MD
      Louisiana Gallery, Houston, TX
1974   Tibor de Nagy Gallery, Houston, TX
      Museum of Fine Arts, Houston, TX
      Beaumont Art Museum, Beaumont, TX
      University of Houston, Houston, TX
1972   Louisiana Gallery, Houston, TX
      Fort Worth Art Center, Fort Worth, TX
      Contemporary Arts Museum, Houston, TX
1970   San Francisco Art Institute, San Francisco, CA

1982   Sculpture — A Direction, Corpus Christi State University Art Gallery, Corpus Christi, TX
1980   Response, Tyler Museum of Art, Tyler, TX
      Art of the Spirit, Texas Christian University Art Gallery, Fort Worth, TX
      Fifteen from Dallas, The Art Center, Waco, TX
1979   Made in Texas, Archer M. Huntington Gallery, The University of Texas at Austin, Austin, TX
1978   Clayworks, Delahunty Gallery, Dallas, TX
      A Mano '78, Art Gallery, New Mexico State University, Las Cruces, NM
1977   Artist-in-Residence, Spring Residency, Artpark, Lewiston, NY

NICHOLAS W. WOOD

Born 1946, San Francisco, California

1972   B.A., San Francisco State University, San Francisco, California
1977   M.F.A., Alfred University, Alfred, New York

Lives in Arlington, Texas

Selected Solo Exhibitions:

1987   Sculptures, Drawings, Prints, Ida Green Gallery, Austin College, Sherman, TX
1986   Sculpture and Drawings, University of Houston at Clear Lake, Clear Lake, TX
1985   Sculpture and Drawings, East Texas State University Art Gallery, Commerce, TX
1984   Recent Works — Sculpture and Drawings, University Art Gallery, The University of Texas at Arlington, Arlington, TX
1981   Delahunty Gallery, Dallas, TX
1980   Recent Works — Sculpture, Midwestern State University Art Gallery, Wichita Falls, TX
1979   Focus — Nicholas Wood, Fort Worth Art Museum, Fort Worth, TX
1978   Texas Christian University Art Gallery, Fort Worth, TX

Selected Group Exhibitions:

1987   Wall Sculpture: Construction and Reliefs, Frito-Lay Corporation, Dallas, TX
      American Ceramics Now, Everson Museum of Art, Syracuse, NY, traveling exhibition
1986   Art in the Metroplex, Texas Christian University, Fort Worth, TX
      Texas Visions, Transco Tower, Houston, TX
1984   Nine Sighted, Midtown Art Center, Houston, TX
      Two Dimensions/New Dimensions in Clay, Brookfield Art Center, Brookfield, CT
      Line, Color, Form, and Texture, Gateway Gallery, Dallas Museum of Art, Dallas, TX
1983   Sculpture on the Wall, San Antonio Art Institute, San Antonio, TX
      Showdown — Perspective on the Southwest, Alternative Museum, New York, NY
      Houston Showdown, Center for Art and Performance, Houston, TX
      Texas Clay, Southwest Texas State University Art Gallery, San Marcos, TX, and Art Gallery, The University of Texas at San Antonio, San Antonio, TX
      Object as Metaphor, Patrick Gallery, Austin, TX

EXHIBITION CHECKLIST

Artists with dates following their names are found in Part 1.

Dimensions are given in inches: height by width by depth unless otherwise noted.

LOUIS AMATEIS (1855–1913)

The Confederate Flag
(Artist's Contest Submission for Confederate Heroes Monument), ca. 1899
Hand-colored photograph
14 × 20 in. sheet, including photograph and legend
Collection of the Rosenberg Library, Galveston, RL 71.041

Mother's Love, *1907*
Plaster bas-relief
17¼ × 11⁹⁄₁₆ in.
Collection of the Rosenberg Library, Galveston, RL 89.001

DOROTHY AUSTIN (b. 1911)

Cowboy, *1936*
White pine
71 × 24 × 17 in.
Collection of the City of Dallas Park and Recreation Department and the Dallas Historical Society, CD.1936.38

Male Torso, *1934*
Black walnut
23 in. high
Collection of the artist

Negro Head, *1932*
Bronze
17½ in. high with base
Collection of the artist

RONALD BOLING, New Braunfels

Crow Hunter's Trophy Case
1988–89
mixed media
100 in. × 48 in. × 48 in.
Courtesy of the artist and Read Stremmel Gallery, San Antonio

GUTZON BORGLUM (1867–1941)

Cowhand
(model for larger figure in uncompleted Trail Drivers Monument), ca. 1926
Initialed, top of base at r., "GB" within a circle
Plaster, painted
16 × 6 × 10 in.
Collection of The San Antonio Museum Association, gift of Mrs. Gutzon Borglum, 49–17–325G

Indians Pursue *(Apaches Pursued by U.S. Troops), ca. 1901*
Signedl l.l., "Gutzon Borglum"
Bronze with dark patina (cast by Roman Bronze Works, 1946)
17 × 9 × 23 in.
Collection of The San Antonio Museum Association, 46.111.163P

ROBERT BOURDON, Houston

Blue Velvet
1987
polychrome lindenwood
73 in. × 31 in. × 5 in.
Courtesy of the artist, Moody Gallery, Houston, and Shoshana Wayne Gallery, Santa Monica

JULIE BOZZI, Fort Worth

American Donuts ca. 1980
1985
mixed media
3⁵⁄₈ in. × 17 in. × 21 in.
Courtesy of the artist and Texas Gallery, Houston

STEVE BRUDNIAK, Austin

The Imogene Icon
1986
mixed media with electrical lightning
88 in. × 44 in. × 24 in.
Courtesy of the artist

ENRICO FILBERTO CERRACCHIO (1880[?]–1956)

First Woman Governor of Texas *(Miriam A. Ferguson), 1926*
White marble shoulder bust
21 × 20 × 10 in., attached marble base
48 × 24 × 15 in.
Collection of the State Preservation Board, Texas Capitol

JOHN CHRISTENSEN, Austin

Cuba 10, Pterodactyl
1986
folded steel
17 in. × 73 in. × 11 in.
Courtesy of the artist and R. S. Levy Gallery, Austin

J. MICHAEL CISZEK, Houston

Homage to the Egg:
The One That Got Away
1988
found-object assemblage
17½ in. × 16 in. × 13 in.
Courtesy of the artist and Harris
Gallery, Houston, and Eugene Binder
Gallery, Dallas

THELMA COLES, Austin

Provisional Subsistence
1984
mixed media
14½ in. × 34 in. × 59 in.
Courtesy of the artist and R. S. Levy
Gallery, Austin

POMPEO COPPINI (1870–1957)

The First Catch, *ca. 1933*
Bronze
32 in. high
Collection of the Coppini-Tauch Studio,
San Antonio

Colonel James Walker Fannin *(model for*
7 ft. figure), 1936
Signed, l. base, "P. Coppini"
Bronze
ca. 18 in. high, with self base ca. 1 in. high
Collection of the Coppini-Tauch Studio,
San Antonio

Love Awakening, *1927–1935*
Plaster, flesh-color paint
48 × 40 × 22 in. wide, including 1 in.
high base
Collection of the Coppini-Tauch Studio,
San Antonio

STEPHEN J. DALY, Austin

Looking
1983
pastel on paper/lacquer on steel
41 in. × 34 in. × 20 in.
Collection of Ms. Joanne Cassullo,
New York City

DAVID L. DEMING, Austin

Pivotal Concorde
1981
painted steel
180 in. × 540 in. × 180 in.
Courtesy of the artist and Adams Middleton
Gallery, Dallas

Walking Tall III
1988
polychromed steel
33½ in. × 9 in. × 7½ in.
Courtesy of the artist and Adams Middleton
Gallery, Dallas

JAMES DRAKE, El Paso

The Revolution (Orozco)
1988
steel, charcoal on paper
55 in. × 186 in. × 18 in.
Courtesy of the artist and Texas Gallery,
Houston

ROWENA C. ELKIN, Dallas

Ancient
1977
wood, rope, steel
50½ in. × 35 in. × 33 in.
Courtesy of the artist

DAVID EVERETT, Austin

Oranda Madonna
painted mahogany
57 in. × 35 in. × 18 in.
Collection of Mr. and Mrs. Marvin Seline,
Houston

VERNON FISHER, Fort Worth

Fountain of Sorrow
1986
paint on porcelain
41 in. × 13½ in.
Courtesy of the artist and Hiram Butler
Gallery, Houston

IONE RUTH FRANKLIN (1893–1976)

Young Mother, *1944*
Marble
23 × 15½ × 13 in.
Collection of Marcelle and David Orman

ROY FRIDGE, Port Aransas

Divine Sun Ship: Burial of the Dwarf Queen
1975–76
mixed media
33¾ in. × 5¾ in. × 16½ in.
Collection of Mr. and Mrs. Thomas
Marion O'Connor, Victoria

The Voyage of Initiation
1984
mixed media
43 in. × 10 in. × 118 in.
Collection of Mr. and Mrs. H. Irving
Schweppe, Houston

Figure
1959
mixed media
10 in. × 10 in. × 72 in.
Collection of Paul Rogers Harris, Dallas

HARRY GEFFERT, Fort Worth

Gardens of Invisible Snakes and God's
Little Buzzards
1987–88
bronze
288 in. × 288 in. × 84 in. (reduced for
exhibition)
Courtesy of the artist and Fort Worth
Gallery, Fort Worth

LINNEA GLATT, Dallas

Forum for a Family
1985
reinforced cement on polystyrene
16 in. × 60 in. × 60 in.
Courtesy of the artist

GEORGE GREEN, Long Island, New York

Fountain
1979
linoleum tiles on wood
54 in. × 17 in. × 35 in.
Collection of Laura Carpenter, Dallas

ALLAN HACKLIN, Houston

Dervish
1983
painted wood
60 in. × 30 in. × 30 in.
Courtesy of the artist and Meredith Long
Gallery, Houston

AL HARRIS, El Paso

Untitled
1987
steel/paint
25¼ in. × 21 in. × 9 in.
Courtesy of the artist and Graham Gallery,
Houston and Fort Worth Gallery, Fort Worth

JOSEPH G. HAVEL, Sherman

Marriage Is a Boat
1987
painted wood
84 in. × 114 in. × 42 in.
Courtesy of the artist and Barry Whistler
Gallery, Dallas

JOHN HERNANDEZ, Dallas

Breakfast Special
1987
mixed media
18 in. × 12 in. × 3 in.
Collection of Murray W. Camp, Austin

TEME PAUL HERNANDEZ, Austin

Spiritual Okra
1987
concrete
108 in. × 36 in. × 48 in.
Courtesy of the artist and AIR Gallery,
Austin

BESS BIGHAM HUBBARD (1896–1977)

Green Goddess *(Thinking Woman),*
1948–1949
Green marble
24 × 4½ × 5 in., base 3 × 7 in.
Collection of the Hubbard abc Estate,
Lubbock

NANNIE HUDDLE (1860–1951)

Marguerite Huddle, *August, 1903*
Signed and dated
Plaster shoulder bust
18½ × 14⅖ × 8⅖ in., including self base
Elisabet Ney Collection, Harry Ransom
Humanities Research Center, The University
of Texas at Austin, 67.78.18

Stephen F. Austin, *after 1893*
Plaster bas-relief
15⅘ × 15⅗ in.
Elisabet Ney Collection, Harry Ransom
Humanities Research Center, The University
of Texas at Austin, 67.78.19

EMILY JENNINGS, Abilene

Blindman's Bluff
1988
fiberglass/paint
5 pieces each 72 in. × 96 in.
Courtesy of the artist and Distinctive Vision,
Austin

LUIS JIMENEZ, Hondo, New Mexico

Old Woman with Cat
1969
acrylic on fiberglass
40 in. × 24 in. × 25 in.
Collection of Mr. and Mrs. T. Turner Pope III,
Houston

End of the Trail (with Electric Sunset)
1972–80
acrylic on fiberglass, with light bulbs
84 in. × 58 in. × 39 in.
Collection of The University of Texas at El
Paso: gift of the Frederick Weisman
Company

Vaquero
1981
acrylic on fiberglass
16½ ft. × 10½ ft. × 5½ ft.
Collection of Mr. Frank Ribelin, Dallas

Howl
1986
acrylic on fiberglass
60 in. × 30 in. × 30 in.
Courtesy of the artist and Moody Gallery,
Houston

DONALD JUDD, Marfa

Untitled
1967
stainless steel and Plexiglas
10 units, each measuring 9 in. × 40 in.
× 31 in.
Collection of Modern Art Museum of Fort
Worth, Museum Purchase and Commission,
the Benjamin J. Tillar Memorial Trust

MABEL FAIRFAX KARL (b. 1901)

Eurydice, *ca. 1934*
Signed l.l. rear, "KARL"
Wood
19½ × 4⅝ × 5⅛ in., base 8 × 8 × 8 in.
Collection of The Museum of Fine Arts,
Houston, Purchase Prize, 10th Annual
Houton Artists Exhibition, 34.2

Orpheus, *ca. 1934*
Signed l.r. rear, "KARL"
Wood
20⅛ × 4⅝ × 5⅛ in., base 8 × 8 × 8 in.
Collection of The Museum of Fine Arts,
Houston, Purchase Prize, 10th Annual
Houston Artists Exhibition, 34.1

JANET ENGLE KASTNER, Austin

Enchantress
1987
clay
75 in. × 26 in. × 20 in.
Courtesy of the artist and R. S. Levy Gallery,
Austin

SHARON KOPRIVA, Houston

Woman Marred by Tumors
1988
papier-mâché, bone, cloth
51 in. × 24 in. × 22 in.
Collection of Ed and Nancy Kienholz

HAYDN LARSON, Houston

Family Tree
1989
steel
91 in. high
Courtesy of the artist, Read Stremmel
Gallery, San Antonio and Sally K. Reynolds
Fine Arts, Houston

THANA LAUHAKAIKUL, Austin

A Song of Yellowcake
1989
mirrored tile, stereo equipment, pencil steel,
steel drums
36 in. × 24 in. × 7,200 in. (3 ft. × 2 ft.
× 600 ft.)
environmental sculpture
Courtesy of the artist

KEN D. LITTLE, San Antonio

Burn
1985
leather, paint, shoes (mixed media)
72 in. × 26 in. × 48 in.
Courtesy of the artist

CHARMAINE LOCKE, Splendora

The Natural World
1983
mixed media
32 in. × 13 in. × 7 in.
Collection of Toby Topek, Houston

BERT L. LONG, JR., Houston

Glass House
1983
mixed media with strobe light and recording
(6 minutes)
20¾ in. × 17¼ in. × 34 in.; base 81 in.
× 48 in.
Courtesy of the artist and Hiram Butler
Gallery, Houston

JESSE LOTT, Houston

Cowboy
1986
mixed media
26 in. × 13 in. × 8 in.
Courtesy of the artist, Hiram Butler Gallery,
Houston, and Barry Whistler Gallery, Dallas

JIM LOVE, Houston

The Pedestrian
1960
steel and cast iron
13¼ in. × 10¾ in. × 10¾ in.
The Menil Collection, Houston

The Honeymoon
ca. 1957
welded steel
12⅝ in. × 10 in. × 4⅝ in.
The Menil Collection, Houston

The Portable New You
1984
welded steel
11 in. × 4¾ in. × 6 in.
Courtesy of the artist and Janie C. Lee
Gallery, Houston

KEN LUCE, Houston

DBPB
1986
found-wood construction
114 in. × 38 in. × 16 in.
Courtesy of the artist and Davis/McClain
Gallery, Houston, and Eugene Binder
Gallery, Dallas

WILLIAM LUNDBERG, Austin

Vacation Console
1988
mixed media: wood, acrylic, video, bug lamp
40½ in. × 41½ in. × 26¾ in.
Courtesy of the artist

HEATHER MARCUS, Dallas

Tok
1988
oil/aluminum
57½ in. × 54½ in. × 15½ in.
Collection of Mr. and Mrs. Keith S. Wellin,
New York City

DALTON MARONEY, Arlington

Crecca
1987
wood/acrylic
69 in. × 22 in. × 10 in.
Courtesy of the artist and Graham Gallery,
Houston

JACK K. MAXWELL, Abilene

Untitled
1981
brass, aluminum, paint, ash, stainless steel,
fabric
40 in. × 50 in. × 50 in.
Courtesy of the artist

BONNIE MCLEARY (b. 1890–1971)

Aspiration, *1921*
Signed on l. self base, "Bonnie McLeary"
Bronze
30⅛ in. high
Collection of The Metropolitan Museum of
Art, gift of Jamie Nadal, 1924, 24.96

The Blessed Damozel, *1926*
Signed on base, below l. arm, "Bonnie
McLeary"
White marble shoulder bust
22 × 23 × 8 in.
Collection of The San Antonio Museum
Association, purchased from the artist,
43.4.191.P

DAVID MCMANAWAY, Dallas

Private Joko
1967
mixed media
25⅜ in. × 12⅜ in. × 14 in.; base 43 in. high
Collection of Paul Rogers Harris, Dallas

Jomo Board No. 6
1973–1975
mixed media
48¼ in. × 73 in.
Collection of Oz and Paul Srere, Dallas

OCTAVIO MEDELLIN (b. 1907)

Moses, *1955*
Black walnut
65 × 12 × 12 in.
Collection of the artist

The Spirit of the Revolution, *1932*
Texas limestone
32 × 16 × 20 in.
Collection of the artist

The Struggle, *1938*
Texas rose sandstone
28 × 12 × 13 in.
Collection of the artist

MARK MONROE, Splendora

Endless Appliance Column
1988
mixed media (stacked metal folding chairs,
lights)
120 in. × 16½ in. × 26 in.
Courtesy of the artist

JESÚS BAUTISTA MOROLES, Rockport

Bas Relief
1988
Georgia gray granite
114½ in. × 37 in. × 14½ in.
Courtesy of the artist and Davis/McClain
Gallery, Houston

Texas Stele
1986
Texas granite
44½ in. × 16½ in. × 11 in.
Courtesy of the artist and Davis/McClain
Gallery, Houston

ELISABET NEY (1833–1907)

Cherub, *1903*
Signed and dated
Plaster
15 × 17 × 19 in.
Elisabet Ney Collection, Harry Ransom
Humanities Research Center, The University
of Texas at Austin, 83.3

Lady Macbeth, *1903*
Plaster
73¾ × 25¾ × 29½ in.
Elisabet Ney Collection, Harry Ransom
Humanities Research Center, The University
of Texas at Austin, 67.78.23, in association
with the Elisabet Ney Museum, City of
Austin

Stephen F. Austin, *1893*
Plaster
Signed on base, r.: "Elisabet Ney, fec., 1893,
Austin, Tex."
76½ × 27 × 29 in. high, with base
Collection of the Eugene C. Barker Texas
History Center, The University of Texas at
Austin, in association with the Elisabet Ney
Museum, City of Austin

WILLIE RAY PARISH, El Paso

Vault
1986
wood, steel
60 in. × 72 in. × 48 in.
Courtesy of the artist

GERALD J. PATRICK, Austin

Slasher
1984
painted steel/aluminum
28⅛ in. × 28⅛ in. × 57⅛ in.
Courtesy of the artist and AIR Gallery,
Austin

BOGDAN PERZYNSKI, Austin

Ultimate
1986–87
lint in glass box, dyed canvas, oil on canvas,
lead, steel
64 in. × 108 in. × 43 in.
Courtesy of the artist and Shoshana Wayne
Gallery, Santa Monica

JIM POMEROY, Arlington

Reading Lessons and Eye Exercises
1985–1988
mixed media: 26 stereoscopic views installed
on wooden table w/stools
192 in. × 45 in. × 35 in.
Courtesy of the artist

CHRIS POWELL, Fort Worth

Until I Come to Meet with You
1988
stoneware
2 objects: 65 in. h, and 39 in. h
Courtesy of the artist and Fort Worth
Gallery, Fort Worth

DAMIAN PRIOUR, Austin

Stonelith #136
1987
Texas limestone/plate glass
79½ in. × 25 in. × 12½ in.
Collection of Mary M. Rollins, Houston, on
long-term loan to the Archer M. Huntington
Art Gallery, The University of Texas at
Austin

ALEXANDER PHIMISTER PROCTOR
(1862–1950)

***Seven Mustangs Maquette for Mustangs
Monument,*** *1939–1940*
Bronze
13 × 9 × 11 in.
Collection of the Texas Memorial Museum,
Austin, gift of Ralph R. and Ethel Ogden,
1948

DONALD D. REDMAN, Houston

Black Rogue
1987
stainless steel, aluminum, Dacron
132 in. × 84 in. × 84 in.
Courtesy of the artist

CLAUDIA REESE, Austin

Journey
1984
ceramic
15 in. × 65 in. × 22 in.
Courtesy of the artist and R. S. Levy
Gallery, Austin

JOHN MASSEY RHIND (1860–1936)

***Presentation Drawing "C" for Galveston
Foundation,*** *1897*
Watercolor on paper
12½ × 20 in., sight; 20 × 27 in., framed
Collection of the Rosenberg Library,
Galveston, RL 84.020

***Presentation Drawing "D" for Galveston
Fountain,*** *1897*
Watercolor on paper
12½ × 20 in. sight; 20 × 27 in., framed
Collection of the Rosenberg Library,
Galveston, RL 84.020

***Presentation Drawing "JKL" for Galveston
Fountain,*** *1897*
Watercolor on paper
9½ × 13¾ in., sight; 20 × 27 in., framed
Collection of the Rosenberg Library,
Galveston, RL 84.020

***Presentation Drawing "MNO" for
Galveston Fountain,*** *1897*
Watercolor on paper
9½ × 13¾ in., sight; 20 × 27 in., framed
Collection of the Rosenberg Library,
Galveston, RL 84.020

JOSE LUIS RIVERA, San Antonio

El Cucaracho
1981
mesquite
24 in. × 10½ in. × 5½ in.
Collection of Cesar A. Martinez, San Antonio

JILL SABLOSKY, Fort Worth

Guardian
1988
stone
34 in. × 28 in. × 26 in.
Collection of Dr. and Mrs. Blaine
McLaughlin, Fort Worth

DANIEL SELLERS, Fort Worth

Quixote V
1987
welded steel
68 in. × 18 in. × 20 in.
Courtesy of the artist and Fort Worth
Gallery, Fort Worth

EVALINE C. SELLORS (b. 1907)

Ode to a Cotton Picker, *1953*
Terra-cotta bust
20¼ × 7½ × 8½ in.
Collection of the Dallas Museum of Art, gift
of the Craft Guild of Dallas, 1953.3

Praying Mantis, *1954*
Bronze
27 in. high, Vermont marble base 11 in. high
Weiner Collection, Fort Worth

Winter *(Sleeping Fawn), 1947*
Limestone
6½ × 9½ × 7 in.
Collection of the Modern Art Museum of
Fort Worth, Museum Purchase

GEORGE SMITH, Houston

Buguturu
1983
steel
87 in. × 64 in. × 51 in.
Courtesy of the artist and Graham
Gallery, Houston

HILLS SNYDER, Austin

A Night in the Life of a Window
1973
mixed media
46 in. × 43 in. × 6 in.
Collection of David and Risa Sutton,
Big Sandy

URBICI SOLER (1890–1953)

Untitled *(Young Girl with Braids), 1933*
Initialed and dated; inscribed, "YSLA D
YUNUEN PATZCUARO"
Bronze shoulder bust
14¾ × 17 × 8 in.
Collection of the El Paso Public Library

ISHMAEL SOTO (b. 1932)

Standing Figure, *1960*
Bronze
22 × 9 in., base 7¼ × 6½ in.
Collection of The Museum of Fine Arts,
Houston, Purchase Prize, 23rd Annual Texas
Painting and Sculpture Exhibition, 62.14

C. M. STAGG, Houston

Untitled Number 11
1988
wood
36 in. × 8 in. × 8 in.
Courtesy of the artist and Graham
Gallery, Houston

GISELA-HEIDI STRUNCK, Grapevine

Summer Dream Stairs
1986
red cedar, maple, clay, cast paper, acrylic,
sisal rope, brass wire
77 in. × 42 in. × 17 in.
Courtesy of the artist and Conduit
Gallery, Dallas

JAMES SURLS, Splendora

Dancing Man
1977
oak, pine
96 in. × 60 in. × 60 in.
Courtesy of the artist and Hiram Butler
Gallery, Houston

She Brings Gifts to Me
1977
bois d'arc, elm, walnut, pecan, wool
77 in. × 8 in. × 8 in.
Collection of Mr. and Mrs. T. Turner Pope III,
Houston

WALDINE TAUCH (1892–1986)

After the Bath, *1946*
Bronze, with brown patina
53 in. high
Collection of the Coppini-Tauch Academy,
San Antonio

Gulf Breeze, *1929*
Signed, r. side of base, "W. A. Tauch-Sc."
Bronze with dark patina
18 × 4 × 4 in., marble base 1 × 5 × 4½ in.
Collection of The San Antonio Museum
Association, 44.15.311G

Surfboard, *ca. 1924*
Bronze with green patina
28 in. high
Collection of the Coppini-Tauch Studio,
San Antonio

ALLIE VICTORIA TENNANT (1898–1971)

Mrs. George K. Meyer, *ca. 1933*
Bronze shoulder bust
18½ × 17¾ × 13 in.
Collection of the Dallas Museum of Art,
Meyer Memorial Fund, 1933.23

Negro Head *(Negro), 1935*
Black Belgian marble
12 × 8 × 10 in.
Collection of the Dallas Museum of Art, Kiest
Memorial Fund Purchase Prize, Seventh
Annual Dallas Allied Arts Exhibition, 1935,
1935.57

PATRICIA TILLMAN, Waco

Untitled *(facades and crypts)*
1983
wood/latex paint
48½ in. × 62⅝ in. × 47⅛ in.
Courtesy of the artist and Fort Worth
Gallery, Fort Worth

MICHAEL TRACY, San Ygnacio

Epiphany
1982
acrylic on wood
34⅛ in. × 20¼ in. × 9 in.
Collection The Museum of Fine Arts
Houston, Museum purchase with funds
provided by Mr. and Mrs. Fayez Sarofim,
Mr. and Mrs. J. H. Kempner III, Joan
Fleming, and Ron Blakenship

CHARLES UMLAUF (b. 1911)

Standing Figure, *1947*
Rosewood
ca. 40 in. high
Collection of Jeannette and Irving
Goodfriend

Standing Horse, *ca. 1960*
Signed
Terra-cotta with white mat slip glaze
20⅜ in. high, including base (7 × 11 × 1⅞
in.)
Collection of the Amon Carter Museum of
Art, gift of Edward R. Hudson, Fort Worth

Pietà, *1944–1945*
Bronze (cast by Roman Bronze Works, 1947)
47 × 37 × 34 in.
Collection of the Umlauf Sculpture Garden,
Austin

ROBERT WADE, Santa Fe/Dallas

World's Longest Longhorns
1987
plaster on steel frame
276 in. long
Courtesy of the artist and Marvin Seline
Gallery, Houston

ELECTRA WAGGONER BIGGS (b. 1912)

Enigma, *date of original plaster, 1937*
Signed and dated, on back, l.l. shoulder
Bronze, with black patina (cast by
Castleberry Art Foundry, Weatherford, Tx.),
1988
15 in. high
Collection of the Red River Valley Museum,
Vernon

Self-Portrait, *1936*
Signed and dated, r. of self-base
Carrara marble with amethyst quartz base
21 in. high, base 5 × 7 in.
Collection of the Red River Valley Museum,
Vernon, 76.2

MAC WHITNEY, Midlothian

Cotulla
1979
welded steel
150 in. × 120 in. × 168 in.
Courtesy of the artist and Eugene Binder
Gallery, Dallas

Blanco III
1979
welded steel
86 in. × 62 in. × 48 in.
Courtesy of the artist and Eugene Binder
Gallery, Dallas

CHARLES TRUETT WILLIAMS
(1918–1966)

Torso, *1949*
Walnut
30 in. high
Collection of Anita Williams

THOMAS WILLOUGHBY (active Galveston
1884–1885, 1888–1891)

Young Galveston *(between 1884 and 1891)*
Pine bas-relief
23 × 14 × 7 in.
Collection of the Rosenberg Library,
Galveston

BEN WOITENA, Houston

Night Sea Passage
1985
welded/painted steel
120 in. × 240 in. × 72 in.
Courtesy of the artist

Crescent Blue
1988
welded steel, aluminum, and Plexiglas
12 in. × 20 in. × 9 in.
Courtesy of the artist

NICHOLAS W. WOOD, Arlington

Site II: Search for Home
1982
terra-cotta with slips, glaze
16 in. × 62 in. × 21½ in.
Private collection

ARCHER M. HUNTINGTON
ART GALLERY STAFF

Eric S. McCready, *Director*

Lynne Adele, *Administrative Assistant*
Henry (Pony) Allen, *Technical Staff Assistant*
Jonathan Bober, *Curator of Prints and Drawings*
Cecilia Carter, *Senior Office Assistant*
Virginia Fay, *Administrative Assistant*
Joann Goodman, *Administrative Assistant*
Patricia Hendricks, *Associate Curator of American Art*
Jessie Otto Hite, *Assistant Director, Public Affairs*
Clyde Holleman, *Carpenter*
George Holmes, *Photographer*
Sue Ellen Jeffers, *Registrar*
Bob Jones, *Technical Staff Supervisor*
Susan Mayer, *Education Coordinator*
Sara McElroy, *Conservator*
Cathy Nordstrom, *Assistant Curator of Prints and Drawings*
Fran Prudhomme, *Art Enrichment Coordinator*
Mari Ramirez, *Curator of Contemporary Latin American Art*
Becky Duval Reese, *Assistant Director, Public Programs*
Tim Reilly, *Technical Staff Assistant*
Amy Roberts, *Museum Shop Manager*
Jill Robertson, *Associate Registrar*
John Sager, *Technical Staff Assistant*
Jane Scroggs, *Friends Coordinator*
Susan Sternberg, *Tour Coordinator/Program Specialist*
Mark van Gelder, *Assistant Conservator*
Donna Vliet, *Art Teacher (Art Enrichment)*
Tanya Walker, *Administrative Associate*
George Weil, *Technical Staff Assistant*
David Willard, *Manager, Public Relations*